EARLY CHRISTIAN VOICES

BIBLICAL INTERPRETATION SERIES

Editors
R. ALAN CULPEPPER
ROLF RENDTORFF

Associate Editor
DAVID E. ORTON

Editorial Advisory Board
JANICE CAPEL ANDERSON • MIEKE BAL
PHYLLIS A. BIRD • ERHARD BLUM • WERNER H. KELBER
EKKEHARD STEGEMANN • VINCENT L. WIMBUSH • JEAN ZUMSTEIN

VOLUME 66

EARLY CHRISTIAN VOICES

In Texts, Traditions, and Symbols

Essays in Honor of François Bovon

EDITED BY

DAVID H. WARREN
ANN GRAHAM BROCK
DAVID W. PAO

BRILL ACADEMIC PUBLISHERS, INC.
BOSTON • LEIDEN
2003

Library of Congress Cataloging-in-Publication Data

Early Christian voices : in texts, traditions, and symbols / edited by David Warren,
  Ann Graham Brock, David W. Pao.
    p. cm — (Biblical interpretation series, ISSN 0928–0731 ; v. 66)
    Includes bibliographical references and index.
    ISBN 0–391–04147–9
      1. Bible—Criticism, interpretation, etc. 2. Christian literature, Early.
  I. Warren, David, 1956– II. Brock, Ann Graham, 1956– III. Pao, David W.
  IV. Series.

BS511.3.E25 2003
270.1—dc22

2003055690

ISBN 0928–0731
ISBN 0–391–04147–9

PRINTED IN THE UNITED STATES OF AMERICA

CONTENTS

PART THREE

EARLY CHRISTIAN VOICES IN ANCIENT MOVEMENTS

PART FOUR

EARLY CHRISTIAN VOICES AND ANCIENT INTERPRETATIONS

LIST OF ABBREVIATIONS

Abbreviations for the works of ancient authors are not listed below if the name of the author is cited along with the work. Rather, one can identify such works using the "Index of Ancient Sources," where the full title of each work is listed under its respective author.

A.D.	anno Domini ("in the year of our Lord")
AB	Anchor Bible
ABD	*Anchor Bible Dictionary*, ed. David Noel Freedman
abr.	abrégé en
Actes	Actes des Apôtres
AELAC	L'Association pour l'étude de la littérature des apocryphes chrétiens
AJT	*American Journal of Theology*
AnBoll	*Analecta Bollandiana*
ANF	*Ante-Nicene Fathers*
ANRW	*Aufstieg und Niedergang der römischen Welt: Geschichte und Kultur Roms im Spiegel der neueren Forschung*. Edited by H. Temporini and W. Haase. Berlin, 1972–.
ANT	J. K. Elliott, *The Apocryphal New Testament* (Oxford: Clarendon Press, 1993)
ANTC	Abingdon New Testament Commentaries
AOT	*Apocryphal Old Testament*, ed. H. F. D. Sparks (Oxford, 1984)
ap. J.-C.	après Jésus-Christ
Apoc	Apocalypse
Ascen. Isa.	*Ascension of Isaiah*
ASS	*Acta sanctae sedis*
Aug	*Augustinianum*
Augum.	Augmented/augmenté
av. J.-C.	avant Jésus-Christ
B. N.	Bibliothèque Nationale
Bar	Baruch
BAR	*Biblical Archaeology Review*
Barn.	*Epistle of Barnabas*
Barn.	*Barnabé*
B.C.E.	Before Common Era
BDAG	Bauer, W., F. W. Danker, W. F. Arndt, and F. W. Gingrich. *Greek-English Lexicon of the New Testament and Other Early Christian Literature*. 3d ed. Chicago 2000
beg.	beginning
BETL	Bibliotheca ephemeridum theologicarum lovaniensium

BEvT   Beiträge zur evangelischen Theologie
BGBE   Beiträge zur Geschichte der biblischen Exegese
BHG   *Bibliotheca hagiographica Graece*
Bib   *Biblica*
Bijdr   *Bijdragen: Tijdschrift voor filosofie en theologie*
BK   *Bibel und Kirche*
B. N.   Bibliothèque Nationale
BNTC   Black's New Testament Commentaries
BR   *Biblical Research*
BTB   *Biblical Theology Bulletin*
BTZ   *Berliner Theologische Zeitschrift*
ByzZ   *Byzantinische Zeitschrift*
BZ   *Biblische Zeitschrift*
BZNW   Beihefte zur Zeitschrift für die neutestamentliche Wissenschaft
c.   century
c.-à-d.   c'est-à-dire
C.E.   Common Era
ca.   circa ("about," "approximately")
Cant   Cantique des Cantiques
cap.   capitulum ("chapter")
cat.   catalog
CBET   Contributions to Biblical Exegesis and Theology
CBQ   *Catholic Biblical Quarterly*
CCCM   Corpus Christianorum: Continuatio mediaevalis
CCSA   Corpus Christianorum: Series apocrypha or apocryphorum
CCSG   Corpus Christanorum: Series graeca
CCSL   Corpus Christianorum: Series latina
cf.   *confer* ("compare"/"comparez")
ch(s).   chapter(s)/chapitre(s)
Chr   Chroniques
CJ   *Classical Journal*
CNRS   Centre National de la Recherche Scientifique
CNS   *Cristianesimo nella storia*
CNT²   Commentaire du Nouveau Testament
Col   Colossians/Colossiens
col(s).   column(s)/la colonne (les colonnes)
comm.   *commentarius* ("commentary")
compl.   complètement
cont.   continuing
Cor   Corinthians/Corinthiens
corr.   Corrected/corrigé
CQR   *Church Quarterly Review*
CSCO   Corpus scriptorum christianorum orientalium
CSEL   Corpus scriptorum ecclesiasticorum latinorum
CSHJ   Chicago Studies in the History of Judaism

CurTM	*Currents in Theology and Mission*
D	Codex Bezae (un manuscrit grec et latin du Nouveau Testament)
d.	died
Dan	Daniel
Deut	Deuteronomy/Deutéronome
Did.	*Didache*
diss.	dissertation
DRev	*Downside Review*
e.g.	*exempli gratia* ("for example")
EBib	*Études bibliques*
EBib²	*Études bibliques*, new series
ed(s).	edition(s) or editor(s) or edited by
éd.	éditeur ou édition ou édité par
EgT	*Église et théologie*
EHS	Europäische Hochschulschriften
EHS.T	Europäische Hochschulschriften Theologie
EKKNT	Evangelisch-katholischer Kommentar zum Neuen Testament
EKL	*Evangelisches Kirchenlexikon*, edited by Erwin Fahlbusch et al.
enarrat.	*enarratio* ("exposition")
enl.	enlarged
Ép Jér	Épître de Jérémie
ep.	*epistula* ("epistle")
Eph	Ephesians
Éph	Éphésiens
epist.	*epistula* ("epistle")
ÉPRO	Études préliminaires aux religions orientales dans l'empire romain
Ésa	Ésaïe
Esdr-Néh	Esdras-Néhémie
esp.	especially
EstBib	*Estudios bíblicos*
et al.	*et alii* ("and others")
ET	English translation
etc.	*et cetera* ("and the rest"/"et le reste")
ETL	*Ephemerides theologicae lovanienses*
ETR	*Etudes théologiques et religieuses*
ETS	Erfurter theologische Studien
Évang. héb.	*Évangile des hébreux*
EvT	*Evangelische Theologie*
EWNT	*Exegetisches Wörterbuch des Neuen Testaments*, ed. Horst Balz et Gerhard Schneider (3 vols.; Stuttgart: Kohlhammer, 1980–1983)
ExAud	*Ex auditu*
Exod	Exodus/Exode
exp.	*expositio* ("exposition")
ExpTim	*Expository Times*
Ézch	Ézéchiel

Ezek	Ezekiel
f(f).	and the following one(s)/et le(s) suivant(s)
fasc.	fascicle
FF	Foundations and Facets
fig.	figure
fol(s).	folio(s)
FRLANT	Forschungen zur Religion und Literatur des Alten und Neuen Testaments
FS	Festschrift
FTS	Frankfurter theologische Studien
FzB	Forschung zur Bibel
Gal	Galatians/Galates
GCS	Die griechische christliche Schriftsteller der ersten [drei] Jahrhunderte
Gen	Genesis/Genèse
GNS	Good News Studies
Gos. Nic.	Gospel of Nicodemus
Gos. Thom.	*Gospel of Thomas*
gr.	graecus (used in reference to a manuscript designation)
Heb	Hebrews
Héb	Hébreux
Hén	*Hénoch*
Herm.	*Pasteur d'Hermas*
HeyJ	*Heythrop Journal*
HO	Handbuch der Orientalistik
hom.	*homilia* ("homily," "sermon")
Hos	Hosea
Hs.	Handschrift ("manuscript")
HSCP	*Harvard Studies in Classical Philology*
HTKNT	Herders theologischer Kommentar zum Neuen Testament
HTR	*Harvard Theological Review*
HTS	Harvard Theological Studies
i.e.	*id est* ("that is")
IBC	Interpretation: A Bible Commentary for Teaching and Preaching
ibid.	*ibidem* ("in the same place"/"au même endroit")
ICC	International Critical Commentary
idem	"the same person"/"le même"
I. évg. 1 sz.	vol. 1, no. 1
infra	"below"/"ci-dessous"
intro.	introduction
inv.	inventory number
Isa	Isaiah
it	itala (= Old Latin version of the New Testament/l'ancienne version latine du Nouveau Testament)
JA²	*Journal asiatique*, new series

JAAR	*Journal of the American Academy of Religion*
Jac	Jacques
JAC	Jahrbuch für Antike und Christentum
JAC.E	Jahrbuch für Antike und Christentum Ergänzungsband
JBL	*Journal of Biblical Literature*
Jdt	Judith
JECS	*Journal of Early Christian Studies*
JEH	*Journal of Ecclesiastical History*
Jer	Jeremiah
Jér	Jérémie
JES	*Journal of Ecumenical Studies*
JHP	*Journal of the History of Philosophy*
JJS	*Journal of Jewish Studies*
Jos	Josué
JQR	*Jewish Quarterly Review*
JSNT	*Journal for the Study of the New Testament*
JSNTSup	Journal for the Study of the New Testament: Supplement Series
JSOT	*Journal for the Study of the Old Testament*
JSPSup	Journal for the Study of the Pseudepigrapha: Supplement Series
JTS	*Journal of Theological Studies*
JTS²	*Journal of Theological Studies*, new series
Jug	Juges
KEK	Kritisch-exegetischer Kommentar über das Neue Testament (Meyer-Kommentar)
Kgs	Kings
Lam	Lamentations de Jérémie
lat.	latinus (used in reference to a manuscript designation)
LCL	Loeb Classical Library
LD	Lectio divina
Lev	Leviticus
Lév	Lévitique
lib.	*liber* ("book")
lit.	literally
LumVie	*Lumière et vie*
LXX	Septuagint/Septante
m. Sanh.	*Mishnah*, tractate *Sanhedrin*
Mal	Malachi
Matt	Matthew/Matthieu
MBP	Mellen Biblical Press
MdB	Le Monde de la Bible
Mic	Micah
ms(s).	manuscript(s)/manuscrit(s)
MT	Masoretic Text
MTSR	*Method and Theory in the Study of Religion*
MThSt	Münchener theologische Studien

n(n).	note(s)
N.B.	Nota bene ("Note well")
n.d.	no date given in publication (date supplied in parentheses when known)
n.p.	no place or no publisher
Nah	Nahum
NDid	*Nuovo Didaskaleion*
NEchtB	Neue Echter Bibel
Neot	*Neotestamentica*
NHC	Nag Hammadi Codices
NHMS	Nag Hammadi and Manichaean Studies (sequel to NHS)
NHS	Nag Hammadi Studies
NIGTC	New International Greek Testament Commentary
Nmbr	Nombres
n$^{o(s)}$	numéro(s)
no(s).	number(s)
NovT	*Novum Testamentum*
NovTSup	Novum Testamentum Supplements
NPNF^1	*Nicene and Post-Nicene Fathers*, Series 1
NRSV	New Revised Standard Version
NRTh	*La nouvelle revue théologique*
n.s.	new series
ns.	new series (in periodical titles)
NT	le Nouveau Testament
NTD	Das Neue Testament Deutsch
NTS	*New Testament Studies*
NTTS	New Testament Tools and Studies
Num	Numbers
NumenSup	Numen: Supplement Series
Odes	les Odes ajoutées après les Psaumes dans la version des Septante
OFM	Ordo Fratrum Minorum
OLP	*Orientalia lovaniensia periodica*
OrChrAn	Orientalia christiana analecta
OCP	*Orientalia christiana periodica*
OTL	Old Testament Library
OTP	*Old Testament Pseudepigrapha*, ed. James H. Charlesworth (2 vols.; New York: Doubleday, 1983–1985)
OtSt	*Oudtestamentische Studiën*
p(p).	page(s)
p.ex.	par exemple
par.	parallel
ParOr	Parole de l'orient
PG	Patrologia graeca [= Patrologiae cursus completus: Series graeca]. Edited by J.-P. Migne. 162 vols. Paris, 1857–1886

Phil	Philippians/Philippiens
Phlm	Philémon
Pie	Pierre
PL	Patrologia latina [= Patrologiae cursus completus: Series latina]. Edited by J.-P. Migne. 217 vols. Paris, 1844–1864
pl(s).	plate(s)/planche(s)
PO	Patrologia orientalis
prol.	prologue
Prov	Proverbes
Ps(s)	Psalm(s)/Psaume(s)
Pss. Sol.	*Psalms of Solomon*
pt(s).	part(s)
PTMS	Pittsburgh Theological Monograph Series
Q	Qumran: Texts from the Dead Sea Scrolls/Quelle (source)
Q¹	Formative strata of Q (Quelle)
Q²	Redactional strata of Q (Quelle)
QD	Quaestiones disputatae
Qoh	Qohelet (Ecclésiaste)
Ques. Bart.	*Les Questions de Barthélemy*
r	recto (side of leaf from a manuscript)
RB	Revue biblique
REAug	*Revue des études augustiniennes*
réd.	rédigé
Reg.	Regula
réimpr.	réimpression
repr.	reprint edition
Rev	Revelation
rev.	revised by/revisé par
RGG	*Religion in Geschichte und Gegenwart.* Edited by K. Galling. 7 vols. 3d ed. Tübingen, 1957–1965
RGG³	Religion in Geschichte und Gegenwart, third edition
RevScRel	*Revue des sciences religieuses*
RHE	*Revue d'histoire ecclésiastique*
RHPR	*Revue d'histoire et de philosophie religieuses*
Rom	Romans/Romains
Royms	Royaumes
RSR	*Recherches de science religieuse*
RStB	Ricerche storico bibliche
RSV	Revised Standard Version
RTP	*Revue de théologie et de philosophie*
S.	Saint
sc.	scilicet
s.v.	*sub verbo* ("under the word"/"sous le mot")
SAC	Studies in Antiquity and Christianity

SAW	Studienhefte zur Altertumswissenschaft
Sag	Sagesse
SBAB	Stuttgarter biblische Aufsatzbände
SBB	Stuttgarter biblische Beiträge
SBLDS	Society of Biblical Literature Dissertation Series
SBLEJL	Society of Biblical Literature Early Judaism and Its Literature
SBLMS	Society of Biblical Literature Monograph Series
SBLSP	*Society of Biblical Literature Seminar Papers*
SBLSymS	Society of Biblical Literature Symposium Series
SBS	Stuttgarter Bibelstudien
SBT²	Studies in Biblical Theology, new series
SC	Sources chrétiennes
SCM	Student Christian Movement of Great Britain and Ireland
Scr	*Scripture*
SE	*Studia evangelica I, II, III* (= TU 73 [1959], 87 [1964], 88 [1964] etc.)
SecCent	*Second Century*
Sem	*Semitica*
Serm.	*Sermon*
SGKA.E	Studien zur Geschichte und Kulture des Altertums Ergän-zungsband
SHR	Studies in the History of Religions (supplement to *Numen*)
Sir	Siracide (L'Ecclésiastique ou la Sagesse de Jésus, fils de Sira)
SNTSMS	Society for New Testament Studies Monograph Series
SNTSU	Studien zum Neuen Testament und seiner Umwelt
Song or (Cant)	Song of Songs (Song of Solomon, or Canticles)
Soph	Sophonie
SP	Sacra pagina
SPCK	Society for the Promotion of Christian Knowledge
St(s).	Saint(s)
SThZ	*Schweizerische theologische Zeitschrift*
StPatr	Studia patristica
Str-B	Hermann L. Strack and Paul Billerbeck, *Kommentar zum Neuen Testament aus Talmud und Midrasch* (6 vols.; Munich: Beck, 1922–1961)
STRev	*Sewanee Theological Review*
Suppl Dan Bêl	Supplément à Daniel: Bêl et le dragon
SVTP	Studia in Veteris Testamenti pseudepigraphica
Syr.	Syriac
t.	tome
TD	*Theology Digest*
TDNT	*Theological Dictionary of the New Testament*, ed. Gerhard Kittel and Gerhard Friedrich (10 vols.; Grand Rapids, Mich.: Eerd-mans, 1964–1976)

TeSa	Teologia del Sacerdocio
Thess	Thessalonians/Thessaloniciens
ThH	Théologie historique
Tim	Timothée
TLZ	*Theologische Literaturzeitung*
tract.	*tractatus* ("tractate")
trad.	traduit par
trans.	translated by
TRE	*Theologische Realenzyklopädie*
TRSR	Testi e ricerche di scienze religiose
TSAJ	Texte und Studien zum antiken Judentum
TU	Texte und Untersuchungen
TUGAL	Texte und Untersuchungen zur Geschichte der altchristlichen Literatur
TWNT	*Theologisches Wörterbuch zum Neuen Testament*, ed. Gerhard Kittel and Gerhard Friedrich (10 vols.; Stuttgart: Kohlhammer, 1932–1979)
TZ	*Theologische Zeitschrift*
v	verso (side of leaf from a manuscript)
v(v).	verse(s)/verset(s)
VC	*Vigiliae christianae*
VCSup	Supplements to *Vigiliae christianae*
Vg.	Vulgate
vol(s).	volume(s)
Wis	Wisdom of Solomon
WMANT	Wissenschaftliche Monographien zum Alten und Neuen Testament
WUNT	Wissenschaftliche Untersuchungen zum Neuen Testament
WUNT²	Wissenschaftliche Untersuchungen zum Neuen Testament, second series
ZBKNT	Zürcher Bibelkommentare: Neues Testamentum
ZDMG	*Zeitschrift der deutschen morgenländischen Gesellschaft*
Zech	Zechariah
ZHT	*Zeitschrift für historische Theologie*
ZNW	*Zeitschrift für die neutestamentliche Wissenschaft und die Kunde der älteren Kirche*
ZTK	*Zeitschrift für Theologie und Kirche*
ZWT	*Zeitschrift für wissenschaftliche Theologie*
ℵ*	Codex Sinaiticus (un manuscrit grec du Nouveau Testament)
1QS	*Serek Hayahad* or *Rule of the Community*
4Q	Texts from Cave Four at Qumran

CONTRIBUTORS

Ellen B. Aitken
Assistant Professor of New Testament
Harvard University, The Divinity School
Cambridge, Massachusetts USA

Frédéric Amsler
Maître d'enseignement et de recherche
Faculté autonome de théologie protestante
Université de Genève
Genève, Suisse

Harold W. Attridge
Dean of Yale Divinity School and Lillian Claus Professor of New Testament
Yale University, The Divinity School
New Haven, Connecticut USA

Marianne Palmer Bonz
Boston, Massachusetts USA

Bertrand Bouvier
Professeur honoraire
Département de langues et littératures méditerranéennes, slaves et orientales
Faculté ès lettres
Université de Genève
Genève, Suisse

Monique Bovon
Morges, Suisse

Ann Graham Brock
Lecturer New Testament and Early Christianity
Iliff School of Theology
Denver, Colorado USA

Elizabeth R. Busky
Faculty Assistant for François Bovon
Harvard University, The Divinity School
Cambridge, Massachusetts USA

Ron Cameron
Professor of Religion
Department of Religion
Wesleyan University
Middletown, Connecticut USA

Alain Desreumaux
Directeur de recherche au Centre National de la Recherche Scientifique
Laboratoire des études sémitiques anciennes
Institut d'Études Sémitiques
Collège de France
Paris, France

Jean-Daniel Dubois
Directeur d'études
École pratique des hautes études
Section des sciences religieuses
Paris, France

John Duffy
Dumbarton Oaks Professor of Byzantine Philology and Literature
Department of the Classics
Harvard University
Cambridge, Massachusetts USA

J. Keith Elliott
Professor of New Testament Textual Criticism
Department of Theology
University of Leeds
Leeds, England

John J. Herrmann, Jr.
John F. Cogan, Jr. and Mary L. Cornille Curator of Classical Art
Museum of Fine Arts
Boston, Massachusetts USA

Annewies van den Hoek
Lecturer in Greek and Latin
Harvard University, The Divinity School
Cambridge, Massachusetts USA

F. Stanley Jones
Professor of New Testament and Ancient Christian History
Department of Religious Studies

California State University
Long Beach, California USA

Eric Junod
Professeur, Faculté de théologie
Université de Lausanne
Lausanne, Suisse

Jean-Daniel Kaestli
Professeur associé
Decanat Theologie
Institut romand des sciences bibliques
Université de Lausanne
Lausanne, Suisse

Beverly Mayne Kienzle
Professor of the Practice in Latin and Romance Languages, Director of Language
Studies, and Director of the Summer Language Program
Harvard University, The Divinity School
Cambridge, Massachusetts USA

Karen L. King
Professor of New Testament Studies and the History of Ancient Christianity
Harvard University, The Divinity School
Cambridge, Massachusetts USA

Helmut Koester
John H. Morison Research Professor of New Testament Studies and Winn
Research Professor of Ecclesiastical History
Harvard University, The Divinity School
Cambridge, Massachusetts USA

Dennis R. MacDonald
John Wesley Professor of New Testament
Claremont School of Theology
Co-Director of the Institute for Antiquity and Christianity at Claremont
Graduate University
Claremont, California USA

Daniel Marguerat
Professeur ordinaire de Nouveau Testament
Faculté de Theologie
Université de Lausanne
Lausanne, Suisse

Christopher R. Matthews
Co-Editor, *New Testament Abstracts*
Adjunct Associate Professor of New Testament
Weston Jesuit School of Theology
Cambridge, Massachusetts USA

Françoise Morard
Département de patristique et d'histoire de l'Église (retraitée)
Faculté de théologie
Université de Fribourg
Fribourg, Suisse

Enrico Norelli
Professeur adjoint de littérature apocryphe chrétienne
Faculté autonome de théologie protestante
Université de Genève
Genève, Suisse

David W. Pao
Assistant Professor of New Testament
Trinity Evangelical Divinity School
Deerfield, Illinois USA

Jean-Marc Prieur
Professeur d'histoire du christianisme ancien
Faculté de théologie protestante
Université Marc Bloch
Strasbourg, France

Yann Redalié
Professore di Nuovo Testamento
Facoltà Valdese di Teologia
Roma, Italia

James M. Robinson
Emeritus Professor of New Testament
Claremont Graduate University
Claremont, California USA

Willy Rordorf
Professeur honoraire
Faculté de théologie
Université de Neuchâtel
Neuchâtel, Suisse

Christine M. Thomas
Associate Professor of Christian Origins and the Archaeology of Religion
Department of Religious Studies
University of California
Santa Barbara, California USA

Yves Tissot
Pasteur de la Communauté romande
Nidau, Suisse

Peter Vogt
Assistant Pastor
Moravian Congregation of Niesky
Niesky, Germany

David H. Warren
Associate Professor of Biblical Literature
Heritage Christian University
Florence, Alabama USA

Jean Zumstein
Lehrstuhl für Neutestamentliche Theologie, Exegese und Hermeneutik
Institut für Hermeneutik und Religionsphilosophie
Theologische Facultät
Universität Zürich
Zürich, Schweiz

Photo of François Bovon courtesy of *The Harvard Divinity Bulletin*.

UNE BIOGRAPHIE DE FRANÇOIS BOVON:
SOUS LE VRAI JOUR D'UNE SŒUR

Monique Bovon

Le professeur David Warren m'a demandé d'écrire une biographie de François Bovon, puisque je suis sa soeur aînée. J'ai choisi de le faire de manière libre et un peu personnelle et d'y apporter quelques anecdotes qui peuvent montrer certains traits de François.

En ce samedi 12 mars 1938, Hélène Bovon attend d'un instant à l'autre la naissance de son troisième enfant. Son mari, André, est pasteur et aumônier dans l'armée suisse. Comme le lendemain il doit présider un culte militaire et qu'il souhaite assister à la naissance de son enfant, il prend sa femme par le bras et l'emmène faire une assez longue promenade dans un quartier des hauts de Lausanne, appelé "Plaines du Loup." Résultat: à cinq heures du matin, dimanche 13 mars naît le plus beau garçon du monde, François. Il a, paraît-il, de longs cheveux et est sage comme une image! Quelle obéissance à son père et quel sens des responsabilités ecclésiales montre ce petit poupon! Il fait la joie, non seulement de ses parents, mais aussi de ses deux soeurs: Monique pour qui ce petit frère est un magnifique cadeau d'anniversaire puisque, ce jour-là, elle fête ses cinq ans. Quant à Anne, trois ans et demi, elle se réjouit d'avoir un nouveau compagnon de jeux.

La famille Bovon habite un magnifique appartement à Lausanne, dans un quartier très tranquille. Reliant les sept pièces d'habitation, il y a un corridor, long de vingt mètres dans lequel les trois enfants font toutes sortes de bêtises, se déplacent en tricycle et jouent au football, quitte à faire sauter les ampoules électriques à l'étage d'en-dessous, chez la propriétaire. Heureusement, Madame Mermoud aime les enfants; ce qui fait que non seulement elle ne les gronde pas, mais parfois elle les gâte, et François se souvient encore des délicieuses tartes aux pommes que Madame Mermoud lui offrait. Nous avions aussi la jouissance du jardin dans lequel nous descendions en petit char en bois, faisions des parties de cache-cache ou de croquet et nous entraînions avec quelques engins de gymnastique.

Un magnifique cerisier offrait chaque année de très beaux fruits, et François aimait à y grimper pour les cueillir. Une année, il avale un noyau; quelques jours plus tard, il se met à tousser et à avoir de la fièvre. Le docteur fait une radiographie et constate une petite tache sur un poumon et pense que c'est le noyau de cerise que François a inhalé et non pas avalé. Il propose d'aller le chercher à l'aide d'un bronchoscope. Cette intervention était assez délicate à l'époque chez les petits enfants. Mais les parents, inquiets pour leur fils et confiants dans le médecin, acceptent. Il s'avère qu'il n'y a rien. François peut rentrer à la maison pour la plus grande joie de ses soeurs et le soulagement de ses parents; il se remet rapidement sur pied.

Comme tout enfant, à cinq ans, François commence l'école enfantine; celle-ci se trouve à quelques centaines de mètres de notre domicile. Le premier jour, Maman Bovon va chercher son fiston pour recueillir ses premières impressions. Elle l'entend faire des commentaires à un petit copain "qu'est-ce qu'on s'est em . . . cet après-midi!" Honte de la mère puisque ce mot n'était jamais prononcé à la maison. Les petits enfants cultivent un petit coin de jardin dans lequel poussent haricots, capucines et salades. Mais François n'y apprend pas le nom de toutes les plantes, ce qui fait que, quand il doit arracher des mauvaises herbes, il arrache également les bonnes!

Ce que j'ai toujours admiré chez François, c'est son organisation entre ses études et ses loisirs. En effet, à peine rentré à la maison, il mange son pain et son chocolat, et part faire ses devoirs pour le lendemain. Ensuite il sort jouer avec ses copains. Il n'a pas réussi à me montrer le bon exemple!

Mais ce sens du devoir et du sérieux a été interrompu à deux reprises, entre autres, avec un de ses bons amis qui habitait dans le quartier: ils montent un petit cirque en plein air; ils y font de l'acrobatie et de la prestidigitation à la grande admiration de leurs parents et de leurs amis. La deuxième fois, c'est avec un cousin qu'il se lance dans le cirque: même succès. L'argent récolté est allé à une bonne oeuvre. Comment se fait-il qu'il n'ait pas été engagé dans notre cirque national? un autre avenir lui était destiné.

Nous passions, en général, toutes les vacances d'été en famille; nous alternions les endroits de villégiature: une année à voyager, une année à la montagne. C'est ainsi que François a découvert Zermatt et le Cervin. Il a d'ailleurs fait un concours sur le thème de cette prestigieuse montagne. Non seulement il y décrit les différents itinéraires pour arriver au sommet, mais il interviewe de grands alpinistes et des guides qui ont escaladé plusieurs fois et selon différents itinéraires ce sommet de 4486 mètres environ. Il a reçu le premier prix pour son travail. Maintenant son amour pour la montagne s'est porté sur Saint-Luc (oh! ironie du sort!), dans une vallée parallèle à celle de Zermatt d'où l'on voit aussi le Cervin ainsi que de nombreux autres sommets de plus de 4000 mètres d'altitude. François n'a jamais fait de l'alpinisme car il souffre de vertige.

Une année, mon frère reçoit d'un de ses professeurs une lettre de recommandation pour un des jeunes qui a découvert fortuitement les grottes de Lascaux. Ainsi la famille Bovon se rend en Dordogne, dans le Sud-Ouest de la France où elle a le privilège d'admirer les fameuses peintures préhistoriques, datant d'environ 12000 ans avant Jésus-Christ; elles représentent des animaux et des chasseurs. Depuis lors, les grottes ont été fermées au public, car elles s'abîmaient trop rapidement. La Dordogne est célèbre pour ses églises romanes, ses cultures (vignes, céréales), ses truffes et son foie gras!

Après son baccalauréat, François décide de passer six mois à Vienne, en

Autriche, pour perfectionner son allemand. Il apprécie les charmes de cette ville, visite ses musées et assiste souvent à des représentations d'opéra, grâce à la secrétaire du célèbre chef d'orchestre, Herbert von Karajan, alors directeur de l'Opéra de Vienne.

A Échallens, où son père est pasteur, il participe aux activités du club de tennis et en devient le président ainsi que du club de football. Notre jeune homme entre alors à la Faculté de théologie de l'Université de Lausanne, en octobre 1956.

Pendant ses études universitaires, François fait partie de la société d'étudiants d'étudiants de Zofingues lorsqu'il en est le président, il distribuera un prix remis par la société tous les deux ans, à Robert Pinget, écrivain genevois pour son roman "Le Fiston."

Il devient également président de l'association d'entraide universitaire qui a comme mission d'aider des étudiants étrangers à trouver un logement bon marché et/ou un petit travail rémunéré. Il a ainsi l'occasion de rencontrer des jeunes de nombreux pays. Une année, François passe, avec sa famille, des vacances en Grèce. Arrivé dans la petite île de Cos, Monsieur Bovon, père, est arrêté par un jeune homme de l'île qui lui demande si des Suisses participent à la croisière. Notre père répond que oui et demande au jeune s'il connaît la Suisse. Oui, répond-il, j'ai étudié à l'Université de Lausanne où j'ai eu beaucoup de plaisir et où j'ai été bien aidé par le président de l'association de l'entraide, François Bovon! Aimeriez-vous le revoir, demande Monsieur Bovon. Oh! ça me ferait tellement plaisir. Et bien attendez un moment, il va arriver incessamment; comme le monde est petit!

Après sa demi-licence, François suit pendant quelque temps des cours à la Faculté de théologie de l'Université de Strasbourg, France, avant de continuer ses études à Bâle, Suisse, pendant une année. Après sa licence, obtenue à Lausanne, il part encore six mois à Göttingen, en Allemagne pour perfectionner son allemand. Il y rencontre celle qui deviendra sa femme, Annegreth Thurneysen, étudiante elle aussi en théologie à Bâle, où son père est pasteur et un de ses oncles professeur de théologie. Ils se marient en 1963, à Échallens, un gros bourg paysan, près de Lausanne où Monsieur Bovon est pasteur.

Comme François a l'intention de partir enseigner au Lesotho, en Afrique, ils partent une année à Édimbourg, Écosse, pour apprendre l'anglais. Mais il doit renoncer à son projet africain pour des raisons de santé. Il accomplit alors son stage d'une année à Cully, au Lavaux, pays des vins vaudois. Il est heureux de découvrir le rôle de pasteur de paroisse. Puis il part à Orbe, dans le Jura pour y faire deux ans d'auxiliariat, avec le pasteur Pierre-André Jaccard, devenu depuis un ami de François. Ils se retrouvent régulièrement en Suisse ou aux USA, ainsi François garde des contacts avec le pays et l'Église vaudoise. C'est en 1963 qu'il est consacré pasteur de l'Église Évangélique Réformée du Canton de Vaud.

En 1965, il soutient sa thèse avec le professeur Oscar Cullmann, à Bâle, sur

"De vocatione gentium: Histoire de l'interprétation d'Actes 10, 1–11, 18 dans les six premiers siècles."[1] En 1967, la Faculté autonome de théologie protestante de Genève offre à François le poste de professeur de Nouveau Testament, en remplacement du professeur Franz Leenhardt. Il devient, à vingt-neuf ans, le plus jeune professeur d'université.

D'autres que moi diront mieux tout ce qu'il a apporté aux étudiants de Genève au cours des vingt-cinq ans pendant lesquels il a enseigné. Ce que je ressens, c'est que François apprécie le contact avec les jeunes; il est toujours à leur disposition et aime à leur apporter tout ce qu'il sait. Ce qu'il entreprend, il le fait à fond; c'est un grand travailleur. Il reste modeste et discret quand il fait d'importantes découvertes en étudiant d'anciens manuscrits, soit au Mont Athos, avec son ami Bertrand Bouvier, professeur de grec moderne à l'Université de Genève ou à la Bibliothèque du Vatican, à Rome. En effet François passe six mois dans la cité romaine avec sa femme et leurs deux fils, Pierre sept ans et Martin, six ans. Ces mois, sans cours, lui permettent d'avancer dans ses écrits, tout en faisant des recherches théologiques et en découvrant la ville avec ses nombreuses églises et chapelles. François y retourne chaque année donner des cours aux étudiants de la faculté de théologie de l'Église des Vallées Vaudoises du Piémont.

En 1993, l'Université d'Uppsala lui décerne le titre de docteur honoris causa d'une des plus anciennes universités d'Europe. C'est en septembre 1993 que François commence son enseignement à la Divinity School of Harvard University.

N'était-ce pas courageux de commencer, si l'on peut dire, une vie nouvelle à cinquante-cinq ans ? quitter la Suisse, aller dans un pays dont il ne maîtrise pas complètement la langue, s'éloigner de sa famille, fils et petit fils, enseigner de manière différente de ce qu'il a fait jusqu'à présent. Mais François affronte toutes ces nouveautés avec courage et entrain. Il crée des séminaires pour les étudiants auxquels assistent parfois ses collègues. Il les invite pour discuter chez lui et leur offre à manger; il aime qu'on lui propose de nouvelles recettes culinaires. Il va visiter avec eux les musées de Boston ou de Cambridge en leur proposant un thème de découverte et d'étude. Il s'est senti rapidement bien accueilli par ses collègues, en particulier le professeur Helmut Koester qui est devenu depuis un ami. Ils font ensemble les croisières organisées en Grèce et en Turquie pour les Alumni, anciens étudiants de l'Université de Harvard et aussi en quelque sorte ses sponsors. François aime les contacts qu'il peut établir avec ces personnes de milieux différents et d'intérêts variés et des discussions qui en découlent.

Chaque année, François a la possibilité de revenir en Suisse au moment de Noël et aux vacances d'été. Il est heureux de retrouver son petit-fils, Antoine, onze ans, sa petite fille Camille, deux ans et leur famille. Cette année il fera

---

[1] Plus tard il a vu le jour comme François Bovon, *De vocatione gentium: Histoire de l'interprétation d'Act. 10, 1–11, 18 dans les six premiers siècles* (BGBE 8; Tübingen: Mohr/Siebeck, 1967).

la connaissance de sa nouvelle petite-fille Julie, née au mois de septembre. Il peut passer une journée entière avec Antoine à sillonner les rues de Genève ou à visiter des musées; c'est un garçon qui a l'esprit ouvert à plusieurs domaines: histoire, mythologie grecque, entre autres. Il est fier quand il voit Antoine jongler au cirque ou descendre à ski à toute vitesse des pentes déjà assez raides. Il aime aussi passer un après-midi avec Camille qui a très bien adopté son grand-père, même si elle ne le voit pas souvent.

Quand il revient en Suisse, François séjourne volontiers dans son chalet à la montagne, à Saint-Luc, au Valais d'où il a une vue imprenable sur plusieurs montagnes de plus de 4000 mètres d'altitude, dont le Cervin, la Dent Blanche, le Weisshorn ou le Rothorn de Zinal. Il aime travailler dans le calme et la tranquillité. Chaque jour il s'octroie une à deux heures de promenade ou de ski, mais pas plus car il doit avancer dans son commentaire de l'Évangile selon saint Luc, préparer une conférence ou revoir ses cours pour le semestre suivant. Il est reconnaissant à sa sœur, Monique, de monter avec lui en voiture pour lui apporter les nombreux livres dont il a besoin pour son travail.

François aime aussi naviguer sur le lac Léman avec son voilier ou y passer quelques nuits. C'est un moment de détente qui lui fait du bien: Il y invite souvent quelques membres de sa famille pour faire un petit bord ou se baigner; quel moment délicieux quand ça se termine autour d'une bonne bouteille de vin blanc du pays!

Lorsque le professeur Bovon séjourne à Genève, il est hébergé dans la famille du professeur Bertrand Bouvier. Cela leur permet de travailler ensemble et de mettre à jour les découvertes qu'ils ont faites ensemble. En 1974, ils ont découvert en particulier dans une bibliothèques des monastères du Mont Athos en Grèce un manuscrit, *Xenophontos 32*, qui contient des épisodes jusqu'alors inconnus des *Actes de Philippe*. Leur découverte a transformé notre compréhension de cette œuvre chrétienne ancienne importante. Ils espèrent pouvoir aller prochainement au monastère de Sainte-Catherine, en Égypte, qui possède une bibliothèque très riche, dans laquelle il est difficile de pénétrer. Ensemble ils font partie de l'association l'association pour l'étude de la littérature des apocryphes chrétiens. Ils ont eu le plaisir de voir leur travail récompensé par la parution du premier de leurs livres aux célèbres éditions de la Pléiade, à Paris.[2]

François Bovon a eu, en général, une existence heureuse. Enfant, la vie de famille était harmonieuse; nous étions entourés par des parents qui nous aimaient et qui, par leur culture et leur intelligence, nous ont initiés dans beaucoup de domaines, littéraires, esthétiques ou musicaux. Notre père a été pasteur dans deux paroisses, une de ville, Lausanne, et une de campagne, Échallens. Il a été membre des autorités de l'Église Évangélique Réformée du Canton de Vaud pendant de nombreuses années, ce qui lui a permis de rencontrer beaucoup de personnalités du pays. Souvent, celles-ci étaient invitées à la maison

---

[2] *Écrits apocryphes chrétiens I*, éd. François Bovon et Pierre Geoltrain, index établis par Sever J. Voicu (La Pléiade 442; Paris: Gallimard, 1997; deuxième et troisième tirage, 1998).

et nous pouvions participer au repas et aux discussions. Ainsi nous avons rencontré le général Henri Guisan qui fut commandant en chef de l'armée suisse pendant la guerre 1939–1945. Le pasteur Marc Boegner, président de l'Église Réformée de France et membre du Conseil Œcuménique des Églises, a séjourné plusieurs fois chez nous. Notre père aimait à inviter des conseillers fédéraux, des conseillers d'État, des juges fédéraux ou des écrivains pour des rencontres informelles où ils discutaient des problèmes touchant à la politique du moment ou de littérature. Nous avions l'habitude de participer aux différentes activités paroissiales et c'est avec plaisir que nous le faisions.

François a eu l'occasion d'être présenté au peintre Balthus qui est décédé au début de cette année, à Charlie Chaplin et à l'ex-reine d'Italie. Il le raconte avec la modestie qui le caractérise, comme un fait divers. Il en est de même pour tous les travaux qu'il entreprend; il faut bien le questionner pour savoir exactement ce qu'il fait, et de l'importance de ses écrits ou de ses découvertes.

Il y a eu dans la vie de François quelques événements douloureux. En 1964, notre sœur, Anne, meurt dans un accident de la circulation en Grèce où elle travaillait comme archéologue à l'École Française d'Archéologie. Ce fut un choc terrible pour toute la famille.

En 1971, notre père décède des suites d'une maladie et en 1975 c'est notre mère qui nous quitte. L'événement le plus douloureux fut certainement la mort, en 1996, de son fils Pierre, âgé de vingt-neuf ans. François est bon et doux de nature. Il n'aime pas blesser les gens, mais cherche au contraire à les entourer ou à les aider. Ainsi cette année, lors de la réunion à Montréal de la Studiorum Novi Testamenti Societas, il s'est démené en envoyant fax, email ou en téléphonant pour qu'une déléguée africaine puisse y participer et apporter sa contribution.

François a reçu peut-être l'honneur le plus grand lorsqu'il a été élu président de la Studiorum Novi Testamenti Societas par ses collègues. Il a prononcé l'adresse présidentielle devant la réunion de cette société savante à Tel-Aviv en Israël lundi le 31 juillet 2000 sur le thème des noms et nombres dans le christianisme primitif.[3]

Je remercie le professeur David Warren de m'avoir donné l'occasion de parler de mon frère. Je suis reconnaissante de l'affection qu'il me témoigne, des liens qui nous unissent à notre passé et au présent. J'espère avoir su relater quels furent les moments marquants de sa vie et ne pas en avoir oubliés. J'ai essayé de faire ressortir ce qui me paraissait anecdotique ou important. Qu'il puisse encore longtemps faire profiter ses étudiants et ses collègues de ses connaissances et de son savoir sur les enseignements du Christ et de ceux qui les ont suivis, des apôtres et des Pères de l'Église, montrer son affection à ses nombreux amis et témoigner son attachement et son amour à sa famille. Je suis fière de mon frère.

---

[3] François Bovon, "Names and Numbers in Early Christianity," *NTS* 47 (2001): 267–88.

BIBLIOGRAPHY OF FRANÇOIS BOVON

Elizabeth Busky

Articles and chapters of books are numbered in sequence of their publication. In the "Collections of Essays" section below, the order of the references (e.g., nos. 24, 44, 14, etc.) indicates the sequence of the articles as they appeared in the published volume.

Books

De Vocatione gentium: Histoire de l'interprétation d'Act. 10, 1–11, 18 dans les six premiers siècles. BGBE 8. Tübingen: Mohr/Siebeck, 1967.

Luc le théologien: Vingt-cinq ans de recherches (1950–1975). MdB 5. Neuchâtel: Delachaux et Niestlé, 1978. 2d ed., augm. Geneva: Labor et Fides, 1988. English translation of the 2d ed.: *Luke the Theologian: Thirty-Three Years of Research (1950–1983).* Trans. Ken McKinney. Princeton Theological Monograph Series 12. Allison Park, Pa., 1987.

Das Evangelium nach Lukas (Lk 1,1–9,50). EKKNT 3.1. Neukirchen-Vluyn: Neukirchener Verlag. Zurich: Benziger Verlag, 1989.
French translation: *L'Évangile selon saint Luc (1, 1–9, 50).* CNT² 3a. Geneva: Labor et Fides, 1991.
Spanish translation: *El Evangelio segun San Lucas, Lc 1–9.* Biblioteca de estudios bíblicos 85. Salamanca: Sigueme, 1995.
English translation: *Luke 1: A Commentary on the Gospel of Luke 1:1–9:50.* Translated by Christine M. Thomas. Hermeneia. Minneapolis: Fortress, 2002.

Das Evangelium nach Lukas (Lk 9,51–14,35). EKKNT 3.2. Neukirchen-Vluyn: Neukirchener Verlag. Zurich/Düsseldorf: Benziger Verlag, 1996.
French translation: *L'Évangile selon saint Luc (9, 51–14, 35).* CNT² 3b. Geneva: Labor et Fides, 1996.

Das Evangelium nach Lukas (Lk 15,1–19,27). EKKNT 3.3. Neukirchen-Vluyn: Neukirchener Verlag. Zurich/Düsseldorf: Benziger Verlag, 2001. French translation: *L'Évangile selon saint Luc (15, 1–19, 27).* CNT² 3c. Geneva: Labor et Fides, 2001.

Collections of Essays

Lukas in neuer Sicht: Gesammelte Aufsätze. Neukirchen-Vluyn: Neukirchener Verlag, 1985. German translations of nos. 24, 44, 14, 18, 37, 46, 20, 23, 32, and 39.

L'Œuvre de Luc: Études d'exégèse et de théologie. LD 130. Paris: Cerf, 1987. Nos. 36, 20, 23, 27, 5, 32, 49, 2, 14, 18, 35, 37 and 46. with nos. 46 and 49 translated into French for the first time.

Révélations et écritures: Nouveau Testament et littérature apocryphe chrétienne. Recueil d'articles. MdB 26. Genève: Labor et Fides 1993. Nos. 29, 43, 80, 92, 52, 4, 30, 13, 53, 40, 61, 65, 78, 47, 39, 81, and 79, with nos. 80, 81, and 92 translated into French for the first time.

New Testament Traditions and Apocryphal Narratives. Trans. Jane Haapiseva-Hunter. Princeton Theological Monograph Series 36. Allison Park, Pa.: Pickwick, 1995. English translations of nos. 29, 43, 32, 49, 18, 37, 46, 52, 61, 4, 53, 47, and 39.

Edited Books

Analyse structurale et exégèse biblique. Edited by Roland Barthes, François Bovon, Franz-J. Leenhardt, Robert Martin-Achard, Jean Starobinski. Bibliothèque théologique. Neuchâtel: Delachaux et Niestlé, 1971.
Spanish translation: *Análisis Estructural y Exégesis Bíblica.* Edited by Roland Barthes, François Bovon, Franz-J. Leenhardt, Robert Martin-Achard, Jean Starobinski, con una Introducción de François Bovon. Buenos Aires: Ediciones Megápolis, 1973.
Italian translation: *Analisi strutturale ed esegesi biblica.* Edited by R. Roland Barthes, François Bovon, Franz-J. Leenhardt, Robert Martin-Achard, Jean Starobinski. Universo Cristiano. Torino, Società Editrice Internazionale, 1973.
English translation: *Structural Analysis and Biblical Exegesis: Interpretational Essays.* Edited by Roland Barthes, François Bovon, Franz-J. Leenhardt, Robert Martin-Achard, Jean Starobinski. Trans. Alfred M. Johnson, Jr. PTMS 3. Pittsburgh: Pickwick, 1974.
Exegesis: Problèmes de méthode et exercices de lecture (Genèse 22 et Luc 15). Edited by François Bovon and Grégoire Rouiller. Bibliothèque théologique. Neuchâtel/Paris: Delachaux et Niestlé, 1975.
Spanish translation: *Exégesis: Problemas de método y ejercicios de lectura (Génesis 22 y Lucas 15).* Edited by François Bovon and Grégoire Rouiller. Trans. José Severino Croatto. Buenos Aires: La Aurora, 1978.
English translation: *Exegesis: Problems of Method and Exercises in Reading (Genesis 22 and Luke 15).* Edited by François Bovon and Grégoire Rouiller. Trans. Donald G. Miller. PTMS 21. Pittsburgh: Pickwick, 1978.
Les Actes apocryphes des apôtres: Christianisme et monde païen. Edited by François Bovon, Michel van Esbroeck, Richard Goulet, Éric Junod, Jean-Daniel Kaestli, Françoise Morard, Gérard Poupon, Jean-Marc Prieur, and Yves Tissot. Publications de La Faculté de théologie de l'Université de Genève 4. Geneva: Labor et Fides, 1981.
Écrits apocryphes chrétiens I. Edited by François Bovon and Pierre Geoltrain, with an index prepared by Sever J. Voicu. Bibliothèque de la Pléiade 442. Paris: Gallimard, 1997. 2d and 3d printings, 1998.
The Apocryphal Acts of the Apostles: Harvard Divinity School Studies. Edited by François Bovon, Ann Graham Brock, and Christopher R. Matthews. Religions of the World. Cambridge: Harvard University Press for the Harvard University Center for the Study of World Religions, 1999.

Coauthored Books

Traduction œcuménique de la Bible: Nouveau Testament. Édition intégrale. Paris: Cerf/Les Bergers et les Mages, 1972: with Jean Duplacy, Paul A. Harlé, Edgar Haulotte, and Michael Join-Lambert. "Les Actes des apôtres: Introduction, traduction et notes," 353–439. 2d ed. Paris: Cerf; Pierrefitte: Société biblique française, 1988. pp. 2607–90.
Évangiles synoptiques et Actes des apôtres. Edited with Joseph Auneau, Étienne Charpentier, Michel Gourgues, et al. Petite Bibliothèque des Sciences Bibliques. Nouveau Testament 4. Paris: Desclée, 1981.
Spanish translation: *Evangelios Sinópticos y Hechos de los Apóstoles.* Edited with Joseph Auneau, Étienne Charpentier, Michel Gourgues, et al. Trans. J. L. Sierra Cortés. Introducción a la lectura de la Biblia 9. Madrid: Cristiandad, 1983.
Genèse de l'écriture chrétienne with Helmut Koester. Mémoires premières. [Turnhout]: Brepols, 1991.
Actes de l'apôtre Philippe: Introduction, traduction et notes, with Frédéric Amsler, and Bertrand Bouvier. Apocryphes 8. Turnhout: Brepols, 1996.
Acta Philippi: Textus, with Bertrand Bouvier and Frédéric Amsler. Corpus Christianorum: Series apocryphorum 11. Turnhout: Brepols, 1999.

Popular Books

Les Derniers Jours de Jésus: Textes et événements. Flèches. Neuchâtel: Delachaux et Niestlé, 1974.
 Italian translation: *Gli ultimi giorni di Gesù: Testi e avvenimenti.* Trans. Guido Stella. Brescia: Morcelliana, 1976.
 Hungarian translation: *Jézus utolsó napjai.* Trans. Miss Zoltán. Budapest: Református Teológiai Akadémie, 1993.
Place de la liberté: Vivre libres selon le Nouveau Testament. Aubonne: Moulin, 1986. Expanded version of no. 9 below.
 Czech translation: *Místo svobody. Život ve svobodě podle Nového zákona.* Trans. Jan Sokol. Třebinice: Mlýn, 1993.
Nouvel Age et foi chrétienne: Un dialogue critique à partir des Nouveau Testament. Aubonne: Moulin, 1992.
L'Évangile et l'Apôtre: Le Christ inséparable de ses témoins. Aubonne: Moulin, 1993.

Articles and Chapters of Books

1. "L'*Histoire Ecclésiastique* d'Eusèbe de Césarée et l'histoire du salut." In *Oikonomia: Heilsgeschichte als Thema der Theologie: Oscar Cullmann zum 65. Geburtstag gewidmet*, edited by Felix Christ, 129–39. Hamburg: Reich, 1967.
2. "L'Origine des récits concernant les apôtres." *RTP*[3] 15 (1967): 345–50.
3. "L'Épître de saint Paul aux Romains dans la Traduction œcuménique de la Bible." *RTP*[3] 16 (1968): 34–46.
4. "Le Christ, la Foi et la Sagesse dans l'Épître aux Hébreux (Hébreux 11 et 1)." *RTP*[3] 16 (1968): 129–44.
5. "Tradition et rédaction en Actes 10, 1–11, 18." *TZ* 26 (1970): 22–45.
6. "Problèmes de méthode en sciences bibliques. Exégèse historico-critique et analyse structurale." In *Séance d'ouverture de l'année académique 1970–1971 (26 octobre 1970)*, 15–27. Geneva: Université de Genève, 1970.
7. "Strukturalismus und biblische Exegese." *Wissenschaft und Praxis in Kirche und Gesellschaft* 60 (1971): 16–26.
8. "Aimer Dieu (Luc 10, 38–42.)" *Les Échos de Saint-Maurice*, no. 1 (1971): 33–36.
9. "Vivre dans la liberté selon le Nouveau Testament." *Bulletin du Centre protestant d'études* 23, no. 1 (1971): 1–27.
10. "Liminaire." In *Analyse structurale et exégèse biblique*, edited by Roland Barthes, François Bovon, Franz-J. Leenhardt, Robert Martin-Achard, Jean Starobinski, 5–7. Bibliothèque théologique. Neuchâtel: Delachaux et Niestlé, 1971.
11. "Le structuralisme français et l'exégèse biblique." In ibid., 9–25. French translation of no. 7.
12. "Sciences bibliques et sciences humaines (à propos de deux ouvrages de James Barr et d'Erhardt Güttgemanns)." *Bulletin du Centre protestant d'études* 24, nos. 5–6 (1972): 17–26.
13. "Le Christ de l'Apocalypse." *RTP*[3] 22 (1972): 65–80.
14. "Le salut dans les écrits de Luc: Essai." *RTP*[3] 23 (1973): 296–307.
15. "Le baptême dans l'Église ancienne." *Les Cahiers protestants*, no. 5 (1973): 33–49.
16. "El Cristo del Apocalipsis." *Selecciones de teología* 49 (1974): 45–49. Spanish translation and adaptation of no. 13 by Tomás Admetlla.
17. "Communauté familiale et communauté ecclésiale dans le Nouveau Testament." *Les Cahiers protestants*, no. 6 (1974): 61–72.
18. "L'importance des médiations dans le project théologique de Luc." *NTS* 21 (1974–1975): 23–39.
19. "Introduction." In *Exegesis: Problèmes de méthode et exercices de lecture (Genèse 22 et Luc 15)*, edited by François Bovon and Grégoire Rouiller, 9–13. Bibliothèque théologique. Neuchâtel/Paris: Delachaux et Niestlé, 1975.

20. "La Parabole de l'enfant prodigue, Luc 15, 11–32, première lecture." In *Exegesis*, 36–54.
21. "L'Exegèse de Luc 15, 11–32, par Julius Wellhausen." In *Exegesis*, 82–85.
22. "Hermann Gunkel, historien de la religion et exégète des genres littéraires." In *Exegesis*, 86–97.
23. "La Parabole de l'enfant prodigue. seconde lecture." In *Exegesis*, 291–306.
24. "Orientations actuelles des études lucaniennes." *RTP*³ 26 (1976): 161–90.
25. "Premessa." In *Ermeneutica filosofica ed ermeneutica biblica*, edited by Paul Ricœur, 9–11. Studi Biblici 43. Brescia: Paideia, 1977.
26. "Recent Trends in Lucan Studies." *TD* 25 (1977): 217–24. English summary of no. 24.
27. "La Figure de Moïse dans l'œuvre de Luc." In *La Figure de Moïse: Écriture et relectures*, edited by Robert Martin-Achard, Esther Starobinski-Safran, François Bovon, Éric Junod, Yves Christe, F. Wüst, Pierre Crapon de Caprona, and Marc Faessler, 47–65. Publications de la Faculté de théologie de l'Université de Genève 1. Geneva: Labor et Fides, 1978.
28. "Nouveau Testament: De nouveaux outils sur l'établi de l'exégète." *RTP* 110 (1978): 65–72.
29. "Une formule prépaulinienne dans l'épître aux Galates (Ga 1, 4–5)." In *Paganisme, Judaïsme, Christianisme: Influences et affrontements dans le monde antique. Mélanges offerts à Marcel Simon*, edited by André Benoit, 91–107. Paris: Boccard, 1978.
30. "Foi chrétienne et religion populaire dans la première épître de Pierre." *ETR* 53 (1978): 25–41.
31. "Préface." In Bernard Gillièron, *Le Saint-Esprit, actualité du Christ*. Essais bibliques 1, 7–8. Geneva: Labor et Fides, 1978.
32. "Le Saint Esprit, l'Église et les relations humaines selon Actes 20, 36–21, 16." In *Les Actes des Apôtres: Traditions, rédaction, théologie*, edited by Jacob Kremer, 339–58. BETL 48. Gembloux: Duculot; Louvain: Leuven University Press, 1979.
33. "Le Point dans les études sur le Nouveau Testament." *Choisir* 231 (1979): 19–29.
34. "Évangiles canoniques et évangiles apocryphes: la naissance et l'enfance de Jésus." *Bulletin des Facultés catholiques de Lyon* 104, no. 58 (1980): 19–29.
35. "Évangélisation et unité de l'Église dans la perspective de Luc." In *Unterwegs zur Einheit: Festschrift für Heinrich Stirnimann*, edited by Johannes Brantschen and Pietro Selvatico, 189–99. Fribourg: Éditions Universitaires; Freiburg in Breisgau: Herder, 1980.
36. "Luc: Portrait et projet." *LumVie* 153/154 (1981): 9–18.
37. "Le Dieu de Luc." In *La Parole de grâce: Études lucaniennes à la mémoire d'Augustin George*, edited by Jean Delorme and Jean Duplacy, 279–300. Essays reprinted from *Recherches de science religieuse* 69 [1981]. Paris: Recherches de Science Religieuse, 1981.
38. "Évangile de Luc et Actes des apôtres." In *Évangiles synoptiques et Actes des apôtres*, edited by Joseph Auneau, Étienne Charpentier, Michel Gourgues et al., 195–283. Petite Bibliothèque des Sciences Bibliques, Nouveau Testament 4. Paris: Desclée, 1981.
39. "La vie des apôtres: Traditions bibliques et narrations apocryphes." In *Les Actes apocryphes des apôtres: Christianisme et monde païen*, edited by François Bovon, Michel van Esbroeck, Richard Goulet, Éric Junod, Jean-Daniel Kaestli, Françoise Morard, Gérard Poupon, Jean-Marc Prieur, and Yves Tissot, 141–58. Publications de La Faculté de théologie de l'Université de Genève 4. Geneva: Labor et Fides, 1981.
40. "Pratiques missionaires et communication de l'Évangile dans le christianisme primitif." *RTP* 114 (1982): 369–81.
41. "Non la pauvreté, mais le partage." *Foyers mixtes* 56 (July/September 1982): 24–27.
42. "Jésus-Christ, vie du monde." *Les Cahiers Protestants*, no. 5 (1983): 12–20.
43. "L'Homme nouveau et la loi chez l'apôtre Paul." In *Die Mitte des Neuen Testaments: Einheit und Vielfalt neutestamentlicher Theologie. Festschrift für Eduard Schweizer zum siebzigsten Geburtstag*, edited by Ulrich Luz and Hans Weder, 22–33. Göttingen: Vandenhoeck & Ruprecht, 1983.

44. "Du côté de chez Luc: Chronique." *RTP* 115 (1983): 175–89.
45. "Vers une nouvelle édition de la littérature apocryphe chrétienne: la *Series apocryphorum du Corpus christianorum.*" *Aug* 23 (1983): 373–78.
46. "Israel, die Kirche und die Völker im lukanischen Doppelwerk." *TLZ* 108 (1983): 403–14.
47. "Le Privilège pascal de Marie-Madeleine." *NTS* 30 (1984): 50–62.
48. "Heutige Schriftauslegung in der welschen Schweiz und im französischen Protestantismus." In *Schriftauslegung als theologische Aufklärung: Aspekte gegenwärtiger Fragestellungen in der neutestamentlichen Wissenschaft,* edited by Otto Merk, 28–33. Gütersloh: Gütersloher Verlagshaus/ Gerd Mohn, 1984.
49. "Schön hat der heilige Geist durch den Propheten Jesaja zu euren Vätern gesprochen (Act 28, 25)." *ZNW* 75 (1984): 226–32.
50. "Atmosphère apocalyptique et défaillance du sens." In *Conférences prononcées à l'occasion de l'Assemblée des délégués 1983 de la Société suisse des sciences humaines,* edited by André Benoit, Marc Philonenko, and Cyrille Vogel, 25–28. Berne: n.p., 1984.
51. "Le Dépassement de l'esprit historique." In *Le Christianisme est-il une religion du livre? Actes du Colloque organisé par la Faculté de théologie protestante de l'Université des sciences humaines de Strasbourg du 20 au 23 mai 1981,* 111–24. Études et travaux 5. Strasbourg: Association des publications de la Faculté de théologie protestante et Association pour l'étude de la civilisation romaine, 1984.
52. "Effet de réel et flou prophétique dans l'œuvre de Luc." In *A cause de l'Évangile: Études sur les Synoptiques et les Actes offertes au P. Jacques Dupont, O.S.B. a l'occasion de son 70ᵉ anniversaire,* 349–59. LD 123. Paris: Publications de Saint-André/Cerf, 1985.
53. "Possession ou enchantement: Les institutions romaines selon l'Apocalypse de Jean." *CNS* 7 (1986): 221–38.
54. "De Jésus de Nazareth au Christ Pantocrator." *Cahier Biblique de Foi et Vie* 25 (1986): 87–96.
55. With Éric Junod, "Reading the Apocryphal Acts of the Apostles." *Semeia* 38 (1986): 161–71.
56. "1 Corinthiens 2, 1–9. Prédication prononcée à l'Aula de l'Université, le 22 mai 1986, lors de l'office œcuménique du Dies academicus." In *Faculté de théologie de l'Université de Genève: 1536–1986. Contribution des professeurs aux cérémonies du 450ᵉ anniversaire de la Réformation,* 33–34. Geneva: Faculté de théologie de l'Université, 1986.
57. "Attendre: Un acte inutile et indispensable." *Approches* 26 (1987): 2–3.
58. "Paul comme document et Paul comme monument." In *Chrétiens en conflit: L'Épître de Paul aux Galates. Dossier pour l'animation biblique,* edited by Joel Allaz et al., 54–65. Essais bibliques 13. Geneva: Labor et Fides, 1987.
59. "Die Geburt und die Kindheit Jesu. Kanonische und apokryphe Evangelien." *BK* 42 (1987): 162–70. German translation of no. 34 by Elisabeth Hartmann.
60. With Pierre Reymond, "Une ténacité réformée. Écouter la Parole en lisant l'Écriture: Mt 16, 17–19 et Maurice Goguel." In *Actualité de la Réforme: Vingt-quatre leçons présentées par la Faculté de théologie de l'Université de Genève dans le cadre du 450ᵉ anniversaire de la Réformation, 1536–1986,* edited by Jean-Marc Chappuis, 93–105. Publications de la Faculté de théologie de l'Université de Genève 12. Geneva: Labor et Fides, 1987.
61. "Connaissance et expérience de Dieu selon le Nouveau Testament." In *La Mystique: [colloque de l'Academie internationale des sciences religieuses. Kolymbari, Crete, 12 au 18 septembre 1985],* edited by Jean-Marie van Cangh, 57–71. Relais-Études 4. Paris: Desclée, 1988.
62. "The Synoptic Gospels and the Noncanonical Acts of the Apostles." HTR 81 (1988): 19–36.
63. "Les Actes de Philippe." In *ANRW* 25.6:4432–4527.
64. "Himmelfahrt." *EKL* 2:522–23.
65. "Variété et autorité des premières éthiques chrétiennes." In "Hommage à Gabriel-Ph. Widmer." *Bulletin du Centre protestant d'études* 40, nos. 5–6 (1988): 6–20.

66. "Jean-Marc Chappuis et l'image du pasteur." *Les Cahiers Protestants*, no. 4 (1988): 5–8.
67. "L'Évangile de Jean, accès à Dieu aux origines obscures du christianisme." *Diogène* 146 (April/June 1989): 37–49.
68. "Lorsque l'humain et le divin se rencontrent: Les Actes des apôtres." In *En Actes. Textes et documents du Rassemblement catéchétique romand, Genève—1988*. Lausanne: Agence Romande d'éducation chrétienne, 1989. 69–73. This article first appeared in *Vie Protestante*, 2 September 1988.
69. "Parabel des Evangeliums—Parabel des Gottesreiches." In *Die Sprache der Bilder: Gleichnis und Metapher in Literatur und Theologie*, edited by Hans Weder, Zeitzeichen 4. Gütersloher Taschenbucher/Siebenstern 558. Gütersloh: Gütersloher Verlagshaus/Gerd Mohn, 1989. 11–21.
70. With Bertrand Bouvier, "Actes de Philippe, I, d'après un manuscrit inédit." In *Oecumenica et Patristica: Festschrift für Wilhelm Schneemelcher zum 75. Geburtstag*, edited by Damaskinos Papandreou, Wolfgang A. Bienert, and Knut Schäferdiek. Stuttgart: Kohlhammer, 1989. 367–94.
71. "Preface." In Harry W. Tajra, *The Trial of St. Paul: A Juridical Exegesis of the Second Half of the Acts of the Apostles*. WUNT[2] 35. Tübingen, Mohr/Siebeck, 1989. v–vi.
72. "Les Anciens dans l'œuvre de Luc." In *Servir au conseil de paroisse*. Lausanne: Église évangélique réformée du Canton de Vaud, 1989. 67–68.
73. "Lukasevangelium." *EKL* 3:188–91.
74. "Parabole d'Évangile, parabole du Royaume." *RTP* 122 (1990): 33–41. French translation of no. 69.
75. "The Gospel according to John, Access to God, at the Obscure Origins of Christianity." *Diogenes* 146 (1990): 37–50. English translation of no. 67.
76. "Luc: Une bonne nouvelle pour les Grecs." *Notre Histoire* 72 (1990): 37–41.
77. "Luka'cs—arckép és vázlat." In *Igehirdető. Az Erdélyi Református Egyház folvóirata*, I. évg. 1. sz. (1990. Reformáció hava): 4–8. Hungarian translation of no. 36 by Nagy László.
78. "L'Éthique des premiers chrétiens entre la mémoire et l'oubli." In *La Mémoire et le Temps: Mélanges offerts a Pierre Bonnard*, edited by Daniel Marguerat and Jean Zumstein. MdB 23. Geneva: Labor et Fides, 1991. 17–30.
79. "Les Paroles de vie dans les *Actes de l'apôtre André*." *Apocrypha* 2 (1991): 99–117.
80. "La funzione delle Scritture nella formazione dei racconti evangelici: Le tentazioni di Gesù (Lc 4, 1–13 e par.) e la moltiplicazione dei pani (Lc 9, 10–17 e par.)." In *Luca-Atti: Studi in onore di P. Emilio Rasco nel suo 70° compleanno*, edited by Gilberto Marconi and Gerald O'Collins. Commenti e studi biblici, nuova serie. Assisi: Cittadella, 1991. 38–45. Translated from French by Mirella Comba Corsani.
81. "The Suspension of Time in Chapter 18 of *Protevangelium Jacobi*." In *The Future of Early Christianity: Essays in Honor of Helmut Koester*, edited by Birger A. Pearson, 393–412. Minneapolis: Fortress, 1991.
82. "Gespenst." *Neues Bibel-Lexikon*, edited by Manfred Görg und Bernard Lang, 1:830. 3 vols. Zurich: Benziger, 1991.
83. "Évangiles synoptiques et *Actes apocryphes des apôtres*." In *Genèse de l'écriture chrétienne* with Helmut Koester, 107–38. Mémoires premières. [Turnhout]: Brepols, 1991. French translation of no. 62.
84. "Studies in Luke–Acts: Retrospect and Prospect." *HTR* 85 (1992): 175–96.
85. "Paul aux côtés d'Israël et des Nations." In *Racine et greffe: Juifs et chrétiens en chemin. Bulletin du Centre Protestant d'études* 44, nos. 7–8 (1992): 6–16.
86. "Editorial" and "Sciences religieuses, théologie et histoire du christianisme." *Bulletin I. Sciences humaines et socials. Fonds national suisse de la recherche scientifique* (9 Dec 1992): 1–4.
87. "Philip, Acts of." *ABD* 5:312.
88. "Conoscenza ed esperienza di dio nel Nuovo Testamento." In *La Mistica*, edited by Jean-Marie Van Cangh, 59–73. Cammini dello Spirito. Bologna: Dehoniane, 1992. Italian translation of no. 61.
89. "Le Discours missionnaire de Jésus: Réception patristique et narration apocryphe." *ETR* 68 (1993): 481–97.

90. "Études lucaniennes. Retrospective et prospective." *RTP* 125 (1993): 113–35. French translation of no. 84.
91. "Le Jésus historique à travers les recherches récentes." *Évangile et Liberté* 118 (April 1993): i–viii.
92. "Le Récit lucanien de la Passion de Jésus (Lc 22–23)." In *The Synoptic Gospels: Source Criticism and the New Literary Criticism*, edited by Camille Focant, 393–423. BETL 110. Louvain: Leuven University Press/Peeters, 1993.
93. "Wetterkundliches bei den Synoptikern (Lk 12:54–56)." *BTZ* 10 (1993): 175–86.
94. "The Role of the Scriptures in the Composition of the Gospel Accounts: The Temptations of Jesus (Lk 4:1–13 par.) and the Multiplication of the Loaves (Lk 9:10–17 par.)." In *Luke and Acts*, edited by Gerald O'Collins and Gilberto Marconi, 26–31, 215–16. New York/Mahwah, N.J.: Paulist Press, 1993. English translation of no. 80 by Matthew J. O'Connell.
95. "El evangelista Lucas. Retrato y projecto." In *Fuentes del cristianismo. Tradiciones primitivos sobré Jesús*, 203–20. Cordoba: Almendro; Madrid: Universidad Complutense, 1993. Augmented Spanish translation of no. 36.
96. "Pour l'amour de Dieu." *Campus* [Université de Genève] 20 (July/September 1993): 28–29.
97. "The Gospel and the Apostle." *Harvard Divinity Bulletin* 23, no. 2 (1994): 4–6. Abridged English translation by Beverly Kienzle with Kirsti Copeland from *L'Évangile et l'Apôtre. Le Christ inséparable de ses témoins*, 7–32. Aubonne: Moulin, 1993.
98. Ὁ Ἀπόστολος Παύλος ὡς μαρτιρία καὶ ὡς ἀνάμνηση, *Δελτίο Βιβλικῶν Μελετῶν* 13 (1994): 56–68. Modern Greek translation of no. 58 by Maria Campagnolo-Pothetou.
99. "Préface." In Samuel Ngayihembako, *Les Temps de la fin. Approche exégétique de l'eschatologie du Nouveau Testament*, 7–8. MdB 29. Geneva: Labor et Fides, 1994.
100. "The Words of Life in the *Acts of the Apostle Andrew*." *HTR* 87. 1994): 139–54. English translation of no. 79 by Jane Haapiseva-Hunter.
101. "Préface." In Yann Redalié, *Paul après Paul: Le Temps, le salut, la morale selon les épîtres à Timothée et à Tite*, 7–8. MdB 31. Geneva: Labor et Fides, 1994.
102. "Chronique du Nouveau Testament." *LumVie* 43.2, no. 217 (April 1994): 99–102.
103. "Une nouvelle citation des *Actes de Paul* chez Origène." *Apocrypha* 5 (1994): 113–17.
104. With Enrico Norelli, "Dal Kerygma al canone: Lo statuto degli scritti neotestamentari nel secondo secolo." *CNS* 15 (1994): 525–40.
105. "La Structure canonique de l'Évangile et de l'Apôtre." *CNS* 15 (1994): 559–76.
106. "The Church in the New Testament." *ExAud* 10 (1994): 45–54.
107. "Herberge." *Neues Bibel-Lexikon*, edited by Manfred Görg und Bernard Lang, 2:119–20. 3 vols. Zurich: Benziger, 1995.
108. "Magnificat." ibid., 2:686–87.
109. "Jesus' Missionary Speech as Interpreted in the Patristic Commentaries and the Apocryphal Narratives." In *Texts and Contents: Biblical Texts in Their Textual and Situational Contexts: Essays in Honor of Lars Hartmann*, edited by Tord Fornberg and David Hellholm, 871–86. Oslo: Scandinavian University Press, 1995. English translation of no. 88 by Jane Haapiseva-Hunter.
110. "De saint Luc à saint Thomas en passant par saint Cyrille." In *BOYKOΛEIA MÉLANGES: Mélanges offerts à Bertrand Bouvier*, edited by Anastasia Danaé Lazaridis, Vincent Barras, and Terpsichore Birchler, 93–102. Geneva: Les Belles Lettres, 1995.
111. "Miracles, magie et guérison dans les Actes apocryphes des apôtres." *JECS* 3 (1995): 245–59.
112. "Luc, une bonne nouvelle pour les Grecs." In *Les Évangiles*, 67–75. Notre Histoire. Paris: Desclée de Brouwer, 1995.
113. "Apocalypse 1, 4–6: Prédication." In Νικόλαος Αγγ. Νησιώτης· Θρησκεία, Φιλοσοφία, καὶ Αθλητισμός σε Διάλογο. Αναμνηστικός Τόμος = *Nikos A. Nissiotis: Religion, Philosophy, and Sport in Dialogue. In Memoriam*, edited by Marina N. Nissiotis, 179–82. Athens: Grigoris, 1994.
114. "Promenade universitaire américaine." *Bulletin I. Sciences humaines et sociales, Fonds national suisse de la recherche scientifique* (16 Jul 1996): 24–27.

115. "Ces chrétiens qui rêvent: L'Autorité du rêve dans les premiers siècles du christianisme." In *Geschichte-Tradition-Reflexion: Festschrift für Martin Hengel zum 70. Geburtstag*, edited by Hubert Cancik, Hermann Lichtenberger, and Peter Schäfer, 3:631–53. 3 vols. Tübingen: Mohr/Siebeck, 1996.
116. "Notes and Observations: After 'Paul after Paul,'" *HTR* 90 (1997): 105–8.
117. "Israël dans le théologie de l'apôtre Paul." In *Le Christianisme vis-à-vis des religions*, edited by Joseph Doré, 153–68. Publications de l'Académie internationale des Sciences religieuses. Namur: Artel, 1997. Summary of the article on p. 169.
118. "Réception apocryphe de l'Évangile de Luc et lecture orthodoxe des Actes apocryphes des apôtres." *Apocrypha* 8 (1997): 137–46.
119. "Apocalyptic Traditions in the Lukan Special Material: Reading Luke 18:1–8." *HTR* 90 (1997): 383–91.
120. "La Loi dans l'œuvre de Luc." In *La Loi dans l'un et l'autre Testament*, edited by Camille Focant, 206–25. LD 168. Paris: Cerf, 1997.
121. With Pierre Geoltrain. "Avant-propos." In *Écrits apocryphes chrétiens I*, edited by François Bovon and Pierre Geoltrain, with an index prepared by Sever J. Voicu, xi–xvi. La Pléiade. Paris: Gallimard, 1997.
122. With Pierre Geoltrain. "Introduction générale." In *Écrits apocryphes chrétiens I*, xvii–lx.
123. "The Child and the Beast: Fighting Violence in Ancient Christianity." *Harvard Divinity Bulletin* 27, no. 4 (1998): 16–21.
124. "The Canonical Structure of the New Testament: The Gospel and the Apostle." In *The International Bible Commentary*, edited by William R. Farmer, 212–14. Collegeville, Minn.: Liturgical Press, 1998.
125. "Luke: Portrait and Project." In *The International Bible Commentary*, edited by William R. Farmer, 1503–5. Collegeville, Minn.: Liturgical Press, 1998. English translation of no. 36.
126. "Preface." In *The Apocryphal Acts of the Apostles: Harvard Divinity School Studies*, edited by François Bovon, Ann Graham Brock, and Christopher R. Matthews, xv–xx. Religions of the World. Cambridge: Harvard University Press for the Harvard University Center for the Study of World Religions, 1999.
127. "Editing the Apocryphal Acts of the Apostles." In ibid., 1–35.
128. "Byzantine Witnesses for the Apocryphal Acts of the Apostles." In ibid., 87–98.
129. With Evie Zachariades-Holmberg, "The Martyrdom of the Holy Apostle Ananias." *BHG* 75y." In ibid., 309–31.
130. With Yuko Taniguchi and Athanasios Antonopoulos, "The Memorial of Saint John the Theologian." *BHG* 919fb. In ibid., 333–53.
131. "Jean se présente (Apocalypse 1, 9 en particulier)." In *1900th Aniversary* [sic] *of St. John's Apocalypse: Proceedings of the International and Interdisciplinary Symposium (Athens–Patmos, 17–26 September 1995)*, edited by the Holy Monastery of Saint John the Theologian in Patmos, 373–82. Athens: n.p., 1999.
132. "The Child and the Beast: Fighting Violence in Ancient Christianity." *HTR* 92 (1999): 369–92. Scholarly version of no. 122.
133. "Baptism in the Ancient Church." *STRev* 42 (1999): 429–38. English translation of no. 15 by Waring McCrady.
134. "The Words of Life in the Acts of Andrew." In *The Apocryphal Acts of Andrew*, edited by Jan N. Bremmer, 81–95. Studies in the Apocryphal Acts of the Apostles 5. Louvain: Peeters, 2000. Reprint of no. 99.
135. "Tracing the Trajectory of Luke 13, 22–30 Back to Q: A Study in Lukan Redaction." In *From Quest to Q: Festschrift James M. Robinson*, edited by Jon Ma. Asgeirsson, Kristin de Troyer, and Marvin W. Meyer, 285–94. BETL 146. Louvain: Leuven University Press/Peeters, 2000.
136. "Israel in der Theologie des Apostels Paulus." In *Israel als Gegenüber: Vom Alten Orient bis in die Gegenwart. Studien zur Geschichte eines wechselvollen Zusammenlebens*, edited by Folker Siegert, 125–39. Schriften des Institutum Judaicum Delitzschianum 5. Göttingen: Vandenhoeck & Ruprecht, 2000. German translation of no. 116.

137. *"Fragment Oxyrhynchus 840*, Fragment of a Lost Gospel, Witness of an Early Christian Controversy over Purity." *JBL* 119 (2000): 705–28.
138. "In Honor of Hans Dieter Betz." *Criterion* 39, no. 2 (2000): 7–11.
139. "John's Self-presentation in Revelation 1:9–10." *CBQ* 62 (2000): 693–700. English translation of no. 131.
140. "Facing the Scriptures: Mimesis and Intertextuality in the *Acts of Philip*." In *Mimesis and Intertextuality in Antiquity and Christianity*, edited by Dennis R. MacDonald, 138–53. SAC. Harrisburg, Pa.: Trinity Press International, 2001.
141. "Milagro, magia y curación en los hechos apócrifos de los apóstoles." In *En la frontera de lo imposible: Magos, médicos y taumaturgos en el Mediterráneo antiguo en tiempos del Nuevo Testamento*, edited by Antonio Piñero, 265–87. Cordoba: El Amendro; Madrid: Universidad Complutense, 2001. Spanish translation of no. 110.
142. "Names and Numbers in Early Christianity." *NTS* 47 (2001): 267–88.
143. "A Review of John Dominic Crossan's *The Birth of Christianity*." *HTR* 94 (2001): 369–74.
144. "Family and Community in the New Testament." *STRev* 45 (2002): 127–34.
145. "Mary Magdalene in the Acts of Philip." In *Which Mary?: The Marys of Early Christian Tradition*, edited by F. Stanley Jones, 75–89. SBLSymS 19. Atlanta: Society of Biblical Literature, 2002.
146. The Dossier on Stephen, the First Martyr." *HTR* 96 (2003): 279–315.
147. "Canonical and Apocryphal Acts of Apostles." *JECS* 11 (2003): 165–94.

INTRODUCTION

David H. Warren

Scripture says "Give honor to whom honor is due" (Rom 13:7) and "Acknowledge those who have worked hard among you" (1 Thess 5:12). It is for this purpose that we present this volume in honor of François Bovon. To some of us he has been a mentor; to others a cherished colleague of many years. To all of us he has proved himself a trusted and dear friend. His dedication and service to Christian scholarship has only been surpassed by his devotion to his students, to his colleagues, and to his friends. His contributions to scholarship have been many, and they are enumerated in the preceding bibliography prepared by Elizabeth Busky (his assistant at Harvard). It is with our own contributions herein contained that we now honor him.

For him, every voice deserves a hearing! For François Bovon, there are no early Christian writings that are "out." In his many publications he has excelled in showing the importance of *all* ancient Christian literature for our understanding of early Christianity. In his writings he has refused to relegate any literary evidence into oblivion. He has not allowed the label of "apocrypha" or the stigma of "heresy" to erect barriers that blind us to the variety of early Christian expression. Whether his focus has been on Christian writings "inside" the New Testament (especially those of Luke, as in his great commentary on the third gospel)[1] or on those that are "out" (e.g., his commentary with Bouvier and Amsler on the *Acts of Philip*,[2] or his collection of studies on *New Testament Traditions and Apocryphal Narratives*),[3] his method and purpose have always remained the same. Unafraid to cross boundaries or to transcend barriers, he has striven to explore new frontiers in his investigation of early Christianity.

His writings have also crossed the boundaries and barriers of language, nationality and religion. He has written several books and articles not only in

---

[1] Published in German as *Das Evangelium nach Lukas* (4 vols.; EKKNT 3.1–4; Neukirchen-Vluyn: Neukirchener Verlag; Zurich: Benziger Verlag, 1989–), and in French as *L'Évangile selon saint Luc* (4 vols.; CNT[2] 3a–d; Geneva: Labor et Fides, 1991–), in Spanish as *El Evangelio segun San Lucas* (4 vols.; Biblioteca de estudios biblicos 85; Salamanca: Sigueme, 1995–), and in English as *A Commentary on the Gospel of Luke* (3 vols.; Hermeneia—A Critical and Historical Commentary on the Bible; Minneapolis: Fortress, 2002–).

[2] *Acta Philippi* (with Bertrand Bouvier and Frédéric Amsler; CCSA 11–12; Turnhout: Brepols, 1999).

[3] *New Testament Traditions and Apocryphal Narratives* (trans. Jane Haapiseva-Hunter; Princeton Theological Monograph Series 36; Allison Park, Pa.: Pickwick, 1995); cf. his earlier work, *Révélations et écritures: Nouveau Testament et littérature apocryphe chrétienne. Recueil d'articles* (MdB 26; Genève: Labor et Fides 1993).

his native French but also in German, Italian, Spanish, Greek, and English. His commentary on Luke, originally written in German for the Evangelisch-katholischer Kommentar zum Neuen Testament (an ecumenical effort by Protestant and Catholic scholars), has now been translated into French, Spanish, and English. He and Pierre Geoltrain brought together several noted scholars from different languages, nationalities, and backgrounds to produce the impressive *Écrits apocryphes chrétiens*,[4] which will be the most exhaustive collection of Christian apocrypha yet assembled when it is complete. He even stepped over boundaries to bring the perspectives of two different religions together in his *Nouvel âge et foi chrétienne: Un dialogue critique à partir du Nouveau Testament* (Aubonne: Éditions du Moulin, 1992).

Before coming to Harvard University, François Bovon spent twenty-six years as a professor in the Divinity School at the famous University of Geneva, founded by John Calvin in 1559. From 1976 to 1979 he served as its dean, and he still holds the rank of honorary professor there. He became Frothingham Professor of the History of Religion at the Divinity School of Harvard University in 1993. His willingness to cross the ocean and to come to Harvard—to work through the barrier of teaching students in another language—has enabled him not only to interact with other scholars on a much broader scale internationally but also to share the riches of his knowledge of European biblical scholarship with those on this side of the Atlantic, thereby further building bridges and bonds toward the common goal of understanding and explaining early Christianity.

In appreciation of his work, we—his colleagues and students from both sides of the Atlantic—have reached across the ocean to join together in producing a variegated work highlighting not only the diversity in early Christianity itself but also the diversity in François Bovon's own talents and scholarship. Like him, we have emphasized in these contributions the need for scholars to cross the boundaries of religious expression and to remove the barriers that still impede the study of early Christianity.

This volume naturally falls into six parts, each one emphasizing an important aspect of François Bovon's own scholarship. In the first section (Early Christian Voices in Jesus Traditions), James M. Robinson, the unquestioned leader in the quest for Q, explores the earliest theology of Jesus as it is exemplified in this gospel and how this theology was later altered in the gospel's subsequent redaction. He is followed by his colleague of many years, Helmut Koester, who takes us on a different trajectory and provides us with another treasure from his storehouse of knowledge of ancient gospel narratives. Next Ron Cameron critiques the views of John Dominic Crossan and presents his own understanding of the relationship between the sayings in Q and those in the *Gospel of Thomas*. Harold Attridge, the Dean of Yale Divinity School, offers

---

[4] *Écrits apocryphes chrétiens* (ed. Francois Bovon and Pierre Geoltrain; Bibliothèque de la Pléiade 442; Paris: Gallimard, 1997).

an insightful essay on the evocative nature of the intentional and ironical anonymity of the Fourth Gospel.

Ann Graham Brock opens the second part of this volume (Early Christian Voices in Lukan Traditions) with a valuable contribution on how the game of politics played an important role in the development of early Christian literature. She is followed by Christopher Matthews, who traces the occurrences of the "Hellenists" in Acts as Luke's effort to link his own community to the "mother church" in Jerusalem. David Pao examines themes of concord and discord in the book of Acts, while Daniel Marguerat shows how Acts 8 can be viewed as a thematic paradigm for the entire work of Luke–Acts, and David Warren demonstrates how even the apparent inconsistencies in the outpouring of the Spirit within the narratives of Acts harmonize into a coherent argument intended by the author. Marianne Bonz concludes this section with her proposal that the Book of Acts is a deliberate revision of Paul's theology.

In part three, we turn to consider the impact that early Christian movements had on the development of Christianity and its literature in various locales. Christine Thomas argues that we should view Montanism not so much as "the tombstone of the prophetic spirit . . . as the first in a series of conflicts" over how the New Testament should be interpreted. Using the healing of the blind man in John 9, Jean Zumstein shows how the Johannine School attempted to achieve unity amidst the conflicting diversity of early Christian groups. Ellen Aitken considers how Christianity from a single, rigorous perspective—asceticism—influenced one understanding of Jesus. Alain Desreumaux illustrates how Christianity and its literature developed in one specific locale: northern Syria and upper Mesopotamia. And Éric Junod shows how some Christians—in particular, Athanasius—tried to marginalize other segments of Christianity through the relegation of their writings.

The fourth section concerns the ancient interpretation—or perhaps better, reinterpretation or rereading—of early Christian writings. Like an intrepid explorer, François Bovon has spent his life in the pursuit of new discoveries and of new perspectives to further our understanding of the early Christians and their literature. Following his lead, Yves Tissot offers a new explanation of how the early Christian understanding of Christ's resurrection developed. While he deals with Christian interpretation in the first century, Beverly Kienzle moves forward a millennium and finds important similarities in the "new and unheard-of" exegesis of Hildegard of Bingen. Yann Redalié returns to the first century in his research on the relationship between 1 and 2 Thessalonians. His essay considers whether the second letter can be understood as a "rereading" or reinterpretation of the first. We then turn to the second century, where Willy Rordorf discusses the symbolic interpretation of the *Acts of Paul*; Enrico Norelli does the same for the *Ascension of Isaiah* (and in doing so, critiques the conclusions of Jonathan Knight).

The largest section in the book, Part Five, is devoted to depictions, both rhetorical and iconical, of various motifs found in early Christian writings, and especially those found in the Christian apocrypha. This is a topic very dear to François Bovon's heart, as seen in his own essay, "The Child and the Beast."[5] As an aperitif for his larger work with David Cartlidge,[6] Keith Elliott opens this section with a discussion of how various motifs in the Christian apocrypha have influenced early Christian art, and vice-versa. Also concerned with Christian art, John Herrmann and Annewies van den Hoek explain the significance of "two men in white" along with other iconical motifs found on early medieval Ascension lamps from North Africa. In the next essay, Karen King turns to rhetorical motifs and shows how conceptual differences among Christians living in the second century regarding their relationship with God are still being replicated today by Christians living in the twenty-first century. Dennis R. MacDonald traces the simile of the Holy Spirit as "a dove" back to Homer, while similarly Jean-Daniel Kaestli seeks the origin of "the Fall of Satan" myth. Stanley Jones treats the theme of the Christian teacher in the *Pseudo-Clementines*, while Jean-Marc Prieur tracks the theme of the Cross throughout the second century. Peter Vogt traces the symbolic interpretation of another Christian motif, the allegory of "one bread from many grains," from its first appearance in the *Didache* early in the second century until the time of Luther and Calvin in the Reformation.

The last section of the book, Early Christian Voices and Ancient Manuscripts, emphasizes the importance of making accessible to scholars today those early Christian writings still locked away in ancient manuscripts. For François Bovon, this has been and still remains his greatest passion ever since he, along with Bertrand Bouvier and Éric Junod, experienced the joy of discovering together the Xenophontos manuscript of the *Acts of Philip* (*Xenophontos 32*) on Mt. Athos and published it for the first time so that scholars could read now for themselves portions of this ancient work that have been lost for centuries. With this very same purpose in mind, Frédéric Amsler and Bertrand Bouvier open this section with a French translation of a hagiographical text, "The Miracle of Michael the Archangel at Chonai," and so provide modern scholars with their look at this important ancient text. Next John Duffy plays detective in trying to track down the curious history of an ancient and forgotten manuscript at Harvard University. And then Françoise Morard presents the text of an early Christian writing that has never been published before. In her *editio princeps*, Morard provides us with the Coptic text, along with her French translation and notes, of a sermon on the Apostles and the Final Judgment. Finally, Jean-Daniel Dubois demonstrates how much information can be gleaned from a single letter, and through it we hear early Christian voices speak that have been silent for centuries due to the religious prejudice and intolerance of their own time.

---

[5] François Bovon, "The Child and the Beast: Fighting Violence in Ancient Christianity," *Harvard Divinity Bulletin* 27, no. 4 (1998): 16–21.

[6] David R. Cartlidge and J. Keith Elliott, *Art and the Christian Apocrypha* (London/New York: Routledge, 2001).

In closing, the editors of this volume wish to express our deepest gratitude to Annewies van den Hoek (Lecturer in Greek and Latin at Harvard University, The Divinity School) and Éric Junod (Professor of Theology at the University of Lausanne) for their support and help in getting this project off the ground. Without them, this volume may never have seen the light of day. We also wish to thank Bertrand Bouvier (Honorary Professor in the Department of Mediterranean, Slavic, and Oriental Languages and Literature at the University of Geneva) and Frédéric Amsler (Maître d'enseignement et de recherche at the University of Geneva) for proofreading all of the French and Greek in our volume. Their unstinting eye and meticulous concern for detail have spared us all from many embarrassments, while their sacrificial and unselfish service bespeaks of their great love and affection for their colleague and friend of many years. I am also grateful to the faculty and staff at Heritage Christian University (Florence, Alabama)—especially to Cyndi White, Phyllis Underwood, and Larry Murdock—for their assistance in helping me to complete the indexes found at the end of this volume. Finally, on behalf of my fellow editors, I wish to thank Patrick H. Alexander (Publishing Director for Brill Academic Publishers in Boston) for his personal interest in this project. Without him and his efficient staff—especially Renee Ricker, the Production Editor—this volume would never have been completed on time.

PART ONE

EARLY CHRISTIAN VOICES IN JESUS TRADITIONS

CHAPTER ONE

JESUS' THEOLOGY IN THE SAYINGS GOSPEL Q

JAMES M. ROBINSON

The publication of *The Critical Edition of Q*[1] makes it possible not only to use individual Q sayings to talk about Jesus, as has been the custom in previous scholarship, but also, perhaps even more importantly, one can now see this Sayings Gospel in its own right. Especially, one can distinguish between the redaction of Q,[2] which is now generally recognized to have superimposed a deuteronomistic, apocalyptic, judgmental slant on Q, and, on the other hand, the archaic collections imbedded in Q, much of which goes back to Jesus himself, and which are prophetic-sapiential in nature. And lest it seem that "prophetic" and "sapiential" should be set over against each other,[3] one should

---

[1] James M. Robinson, Paul Hoffmann, and John S. Kloppenborg, eds., *The Critical Edition of Q: Synopsis including the Gospels of Matthew and Luke, Mark and Thomas with English, German, and French Translations of Q and Thomas* (Minneapolis: Fortress, and Leuven: Peeters, 2000). An abbreviated edition, with only Greek and English on facing pages, has been published as well: *The Sayings Gospel Q in Greek and English with Parallels from the Gospels of Mark and Thomas* (CBET 30; Leuven: Peeters, 2001, and Minneapolis: Fortress, 2002). There is also an even more abbreviated edition, with only the English translation of Q: *The Sayings of Jesus: The Sayings Gospel Q in English* (Facet books; Minneapolis: Fortress, 2001).

[2] Dieter Lührmann, *Die Redaktion der Logienquelle* (WMANT 33; Neukirchen-Fluyn: Neukirchner Verlag, 1969).

[3] The prophetic and the sapiential have all too often been put over against each other as alternatives between which one must choose, e.g. Richard Horsley, "*Logoi Prophētōn?* Reflections on the Genre of Q," in *The Future of Early Christianity: Essays in Honor of Helmut Koester* (ed. Birger A. Pearson; Minneapolis: Fortress, 1991), 195–209. But see Walter Grundmann, "Weisheit im Horizont des Reiches Gottes: Eine Studie zur Verkündigung Jesu nach der Spruchüberlieferung Q," in *Die Kirche des Anfangs: Festschrift für Heinz Schürmann zum 65. Geburtstag* (ed. R. Schnackenburg, J. Ernst, and J. Wanke; ETS 38; Leipzig: St. Benno, 1977), 175–99: 175–76:

> Auch darin besteht in der Forschung eine weitgehende Übereinstimmung, daß die Ankündigung der genahten Himmelsherrschaft prophetische Art zeigt; darum erscheint Jesus den Leuten als Prophet und wird von ihnen als solcher beurteilt. Er gilt als der endzeitliche Prophet (nach Dtn 18,15.18f.). Aber die Eigenart dieses Jesus besteht darin, daß er zugleich wie ein Lehrer spricht, als solcher angeredet und von Freunden und Gegnern so betrachtet wird. Der Inhalt der Lehre dieses Lehrers ist Weisheit; die Leute seiner Heimatstadt fragen nach ihrem Woher (Mk 6,2). Er ist also prophetischer Weisheitslehrer und vertritt einen Typus, zu dem sich in der späteren nachexilischen Zeit, etwa vom dritten vorchristlichen Jahrhundert ab die Durchdringung von [176] Prophetie und Weisheit entwickelt hat. . . .
>
> Wenn Jesus die Nähe der Gottesherrschaft als prophetisch-eschatologischer Weisheitslehrer verkündet, dann wäre es wohl möglich, einen wesentlichen Zug seiner Verkündigung und seiner Lehre als Weisheit im Horizont des Reiches Gottes

note that it is Sophia herself who has sent both "prophets and sages" (Q 11:49). In Q, the sage Solomon and the prophet Jonah stand side by side as equal foretastes of what Jesus brings (Q 11:31–32).

Jesus' Sayings about God Reigning

There are in Q really only two formulations that could be designated as distinctive theological terminology: Kingdom of God and Son of Man.[4] With regard to the term Son of Man, a major shift has taken place over the past generation, namely the "dissolution" of the "one-time consensus" that "the title had eschatological content," as Dale Allison put it, admitting that he "has changed his mind on this issue several times and now lacks all confidence about it." He goes on: "With the faltering of the apocalyptic interpretation, the idiomatic or nontitular understanding of 'the Son of Man' has come into its own."[5]

This changing position regarding the Son-of-Man sayings in Q can best be exemplified by Paul Hoffmann: ". . . we should take final leave from the often too 'self-evident' assumption that in the SM [Son of Man] sayings we are dealing with the oldest Christian or even dominical tradition. In this respect I wish expressly to correct my own position."[6] His new position is: "that the SM concept gained special significance for Christian circles during this late phase in the transmission of Q, i.e. in the period around 70 C.E."[7]

---

zu bezeichnen. Unter bewußter Beschränkung auf die Traditionen der Jesus-verkündigung, wie sie in der sogenannten Spruchquelle (= Q) zusammengefaßt sind, soll an dieser Stelle dieser eben gestellten Frage nachgegangen werden.

[4] The preeminence of these two terms in seeking to understand Jesus' theology was given classical expression by Rudolf Otto, *Reich Gottes und Menschensohn: Ein religionsgeschichtlicher Versuch* (Munich: Beck, 1933, 1954³). ET: *The Kingdom of God and the Son of Man: A Study in the History of Religions* (Grand Rapids: Zondervan, 1938; London: Lutterworth, 1943, 1951).

[5] Dale C. Allison, Jr., in his review of Delbert Burkett, *The Son of Man Debate: A History and Evaluation* (SNTSMS 107; Cambridge: Cambridge University Press, 1999), in *JBL* 119 (2000): 766–68: 767. This would seem to be a significant shift from Allison's position in his monograph *Jesus of Nazareth: Millenarian Prophet* (Minneapolis: Fortress, 1998), "The Son of man," 115–20, where he speaks, 119, of "accept[ing] (as I do) the authenticity of one or more of the 'apocalyptic Son of man sayings.'" Burkett himself (p. 122) concludes: "I find it most plausible that the expression 'Son of Man' functions as a messianic title for Jesus throughout the tradition." But for him this alternative leaves open Jesus' own usage: "it originated as a messianic title applied to Jesus either by himself or by the early church." He thus himself remains uncertain (p. 124). See also James M. Robinson, "The Son of Man in the Sayings Gospel Q," in *Tradition und Translation: Zum Problem der interkulturellen Übersetzbarkeit religiöser Phänomene—Festschrift für Carsten Colpe zum 65. Geburtstag* (ed. Christoph Elsas et al.; Berlin and New York: Walter de Gruyter, 1994), 315–35.

[6] Paul Hoffmann, "The Redaction of Q and the Son of Man: A Preliminary Sketch," in *The Gospel Behind the Gospels: Current Studies on Q* (ed. Ronald A. Piper; NovTSup 75; Leiden: Brill, 1995), 159–98: 193 n. 56.

[7] Hoffmann, "The Redaction of Q and the Son of Man," 193:

The "faltering" of the apocalyptic, titular meaning of Son of Man in Jesus' usage only illustrates the truism that Jesus' focus was not on himself. If he spoke of himself as a son of man, a human, he used the expression as an idiom, not a title. It was not part of his "theology." This then suggests we should shift the focus to the other theological formulation, the kingdom of God. Though *we* want to talk about Jesus, *he* talked about the kingdom of God. Yet let us try to do justice to him at least for a moment, by investigating what *he* meant by the kingdom, not what *we* mean by Jesus.

Jesus was baptized by John.[8] Presumably he would not have undergone that rite of immersion, if he had not been immersed in John's message, which is normally thought to have been apocalyptic.[9] The problem is that Jesus' own message does not seem to have been apocalyptic.[10] Ernst Käsemann already put it pointedly: "Jesus obviously speaks of the coming of the *basileia* in a different sense from the Baptist and contemporary Judaism, namely, not exclusively, or

---

The Palestinian tradition from the time of the Jewish-Roman war, preserved in Mk 13, which—apart from Q—represents the earliest evidence of the Christian reception of the SM expectation of Dan 7 (though already transformed in its own way), now also sheds light on the appearance of the SM sayings in Q. . . . the parallel appearance of this expectation in Mk 13 and in QR [Q Redaction] could indicate that the SM concept gained special significance for Christian circles during this late phase in the transmission of Q, i.e. in the period around 70 c.e., and that it was then that its reception and theological integration into the traditional Q material that was not previously characterized by it came about.

[8] Morton S. Enslin, "John and Jesus," *ZNW* 66 (1975): 1–18: 7 argued conversely that they were completely unrelated: "their paths did not cross." Similarly Burton Mack, *The Lost Gospel: The Book of Q and Christian Origins* (San Francisco: Harper SanFrancisco, 1993), 153, 155.

[9] This standard assumption has been challenged by William Arnal, "Redactional Fabrication and Group Legitimation: The Baptist's Preaching in Q 3:7–9, 16–17," in *Conflict and Invention: Literary, Rhetorical, and Social Studies on the Sayings Gospel Q* (ed. John S. Kloppenborg; Valley Forge, Pa.: Trinity Press International, 1995), 165–80. His argument is that the sayings ascribed to John reflect the deuteronomistic, judgmental apocalypticism of the redaction of Q, from which they hence derive. But there is no significant shared vocabulary to document this hypothesis. John's reference to "the One to Come" (Q 3:16; 7:19) is not a creation of the Q redaction (Arnal, "Redactional Fabrication and Group Legitimation," 171: "coheres in substance with the Son of Man figure," 173: "a redactional creation," "unique to Q"), since it recurs in John 1:27 (ibid., 179 n. 18: "coincidental"), as well as in the familiar quotation of Ps 117:26 LXX found in Q 13:35 and Mark 11:9 par. The Deuteronomistic focus on God sending prophets who are put to death by the Israelites, leading God to let the temple be destroyed, is completely absent from Q sayings of John. The judgmental designation for the opponents of John is "snakes' litter" (Q 3:7), but for the Q redaction "this generation" (Q 7:31; 11:29, 30, 31, 32, 50, 51), "Pharisees" (Q 11:42, 49b, 41, 44), "exegetes of the Law" (Q 11:46b, 52). Arnal's evidence does not get beyond the fact that both the preaching of John and the redaction of Q are apocalyptic.

[10] For this claim see Risto Uro, "John the Baptist and the Jesus Movement: What Does Q Tell Us?" in *The Gospel behind the Gospels* (Leiden: Brill, 1995), 231–57. See also my critique of Uro, "Building Blocks in the Social History of Q," in *Reimagining Christian Origins: A Colloquium Honoring Burton L. Mack* (ed. Elizabeth A. Castelli and Hal Taussig; Valley Forge, Pa.: Trinity Press International, 1996), 87–112: 95.

even only primarily, in relation to a chronologically datable end of the world."[11]

The only overlap in language between John and Jesus in Q is the metaphor of the fruit trees, and precisely there one can see the basic difference: In the presentation of John, it is clearly apocalyptic (Q 3:9):

> And the ax already lies at the root of the trees. So every tree not bearing healthy fruit is to be chopped down and thrown on the fire.

But in Jesus' use of that same metaphor, there is no apocalypticism at all. Instead, he scored the ethical point of human integrity (Q 6:43–44a):

> No healthy tree bears rotten fruit, nor on the other hand does a decayed tree bear healthy fruit. For from the fruit the tree is known.

This striking divergence between the apocalypticism in the saying ascribed to John and the absence of apocalypticism in the saying ascribed to Jesus should warn against simply applying whatever one ascribes to John directly to Jesus.[12]

This caution is also appropriate in view of the striking divergences in their lifestyles and practice. I have argued elsewhere: "The pervasive distinction between the lifestyles and practice of the followers of Jesus and those of John . . . provides a strong working hypothesis that in the verbalization of their messages . . . there would also have emerged a constitutive divergence."[13]

---

[11] Ernst Käsemann, "Zum Thema der urchristlichen Apokalyptik," *ZTK* 59 (1962): 257–84: 260–61. ET: "On the Topic of Primitive Christian Apocalyptic," in *Apocalypticism: Journal for Theology and the Church* 6 (New York: Herder and Herder, 1969), 99–133: 103–4:

> Undisputed remain only the *basileia* sayings that go back to Jesus himself. That they mostly regard God's sovereignty as still outstanding cannot well be denied. It is characteristic, however, that in the reasonably certain instances this is not done in such a way that apocalyptic comes strongly to the fore, and it is precisely here that we have the constitutive difference from the preaching of the Baptist. We would do well not to forget that the baptism of Jesus by John belongs to the indubitable events of the historical life of Jesus. For this surely means that Jesus began with the glowing near expectation of the Baptist and for that reason suffered himself to be "sealed" against the threatening judgment of wrath and engrafted into the sacred remnant of the people of God. It is difficult not to feel that the path Jesus took in word and deed is a contradiction of this beginning. It is therefore no accident that the gospels draw an antithesis to the Baptist and his sect and portray Jesus as healing in the power of the Spirit, casting out demons, not practicing asceticism. . . . All this leads perforce to the [104] result that the Baptist's message of the distant God who is coming as judge recedes strangely into the background, . . . Jesus obviously speaks of the coming of the *basileia* in a different sense from the Baptist and contemporary Judaism, namely, not exclusively, or even only primarily, in relation to a chronologically datable end of the world. This means, however, that the alternative so useful elsewhere between present and futurist eschatology ultimately becomes as inapplicable to the message of Jesus as the question of the messianic consciousness does if it is not permissible to lay the title "Son of man" on Jesus' lips.

[12] Arnal, "Redactional Fabrication and Group Legitimation," 174, presents the converse alternative, that the Q redaction composed Q 3:17: ". . . has recast it in an apocalyptic fashion," "*literarily dependent upon the earlier recension of Q*" (italics his).

[13] Robinson, "Building Blocks in the Social History of Q," 90.

The apocalyptic Jesus, as Albert Schweitzer portrayed him, has long since been rejected by scholarship. To quote Käsemann again:

> Hardly any New Testament scholar still shares A. Schweitzer's answer, namely, that Jesus, animated by a glowing near expectation of the end, sent his disciples out on a lightning mission through Palestine and himself proclaimed an interim ethic, and that finally, when his hopes proved illusory, he tried to compel the divine intervention by moving to Jerusalem, and perished in the attempt.[14]

Of course it is usual to ascribe to Jesus the more euphemistic term "eschatology." But one carefully avoids getting tangled up *à la* Schweitzer in what that may have meant for Jesus in terms of his lifestyle. And one hardly even mentions the problem that what John predicted, and Jesus presumably believed enough to launch his "public ministry," did not happen. Even Käsemann, who in a sense relaunched apocalypticism by designating it the mother of Christian theology,[15] argued that Jesus himself was not an apocalypticist. Instead, he gave Easter credit for triggering Christian apocalypticism.

But Jesus himself *was* engrossed with "the kingdom of God," God reigning, itself a rare idiom that nonetheless dominates the sayings of Jesus. So what are we to make of that?

For Paul, the kingdom of God is something purely future, itself apocalyptic, as his apocalyptic chapter made clear: "Then comes the end, when he [Jesus] delivers the kingdom to God the Father" (1 Cor 15:24). Paul's idea was that God's reigning cannot take place in a literal sense so long as the hostile forces of evil continue, or, even more concretely: Only when death itself, the last enemy, is gone, will God really reign (1 Cor 15:26).

Jesus too must have realized that God is not literally and fully reigning everywhere and always now, since so much evil still prevails. Up to this point one may speak of Jesus' eschatology and know what one means. But the kingdom of God was not for Jesus just a cosmic revolution, whose imminent expectation was hence invalidated by the passage of time, indeed rendered unintelligible to us by the Enlightenment. For God reigning was something real in his world of experience,[16] about which he did in fact talk, and it is that on which we need to focus our attention.

---

[14] Käsemann, "Zum Thema der urchristlichen Apokalyptik," 260. ET: "On the Topic of Primitive Christian Apocalyptic," 102.

[15] Käsemann, "Zum Thema der urchristlichen Apokalyptik," 284. ET: "On the Topic of Primitive Christian Apocalyptic," 133: "I hope I have made clear why I call apocalyptic the mother of Christian theology."

[16] Helmut Koester, "The Sayings of Q and Their Image of Jesus," in *Sayings of Jesus: Canonical and Non-Canonical: Essays in Honour of Tjitze Baarda* (ed. William L. Petersen, Johan S. Vos, and Henk J. de Jonge; NovTSup 89; Leiden: Brill, 1997), 137–54: 154: "The earliest stage of Q's eschatology is not necessarily a direct reflection of Jesus' preaching. . . . The Jesus of the earliest formation of the Sayings Gospel Q proclaims the arrival of God's kingdom as a challenge to the disciples, who are asked to realize that their own existence belongs to a new eschatological moment."

One may go through each of the references to the kingdom of God in Q (made easily accessible by John S. Kloppenborg's "Concordance of Q" at the conclusion of *The Critical Edition of Q* and *The Sayings Gospel Q*). Though not all, yet an unusually high proportion of the Q sayings about the kingdom of God are usually ascribed to Jesus.[17]

One may begin with the best-known text in Q, the Lord's Prayer: Matthew has glossed the prayer several times to embellish it according to the more liturgical usage of his own congregation. One of these Matthean additions is the petition: "Thy will be done on earth as it is in heaven."[18] It was apparently not in Jesus' own prayer. It is not that Jesus would have had anything against this idea. It is just that, according to the Lukan form of the prayer, which is considered to be nearer the older form of the prayer in Q, this petition was absent. Apparently the petitions originally ran as follows (Q 11:2–4):

> Let your reign come: Our day's bread give us today; and cancel our debts for us, as we too have cancelled for those in debt to us; and do not put us to the test!

This is clearly not a prayer about the afterlife or another world, but about the here and now. Indeed, the interpretation of the Lord's Prayer, which follows directly in Q, makes this abundantly clear: Ask, search, knock, receive, find, be opened, for a human parent will not give a stone, but bread, not a snake, but fish, so "how much more will the Father from heaven give good things to those who ask him!" (Q 11:9–13). This hardly means that as surely as a human parent gives bread and fish in the here and now, the heavenly Father will give pie in the sky by-and-by. No, God will see to it that you have something to eat in the here and now.

Nor does the Beatitude on the poor mean that only in the eschatological future will they prosper: "Blessed are you poor, for God's reign is for you" (Q 6:20). Surely this does not mean that the poor will get into the kingdom of God at the end of time, imminent as it is, but that between now and then the poor should be happy to continue to be hungry and cold beggars. What consolation, blessedness, is there in knowing you will be fed at the eschato-

---

[17] Helmut Merklein, *Jesu Botschaft von der Gottesherrschaft: Eine Skizze* (SBS 111; Stuttgart: Katholisches Bibelwerk, 1989³), 23:

> Zur traditionsgeschichtlich ältesten (und damit am ehesten authentischen) Sprechweise dürften die Logien beziehungsweise Texte gehören, in denen die "'basileia' Gottes" als eine *aktiv-dynamische Größe* erscheint. Dazu ist neben den Gleichnissen (Mk 4,26–29.30–32 par; Lk 13,18f.20f par Mt 13,31f.33) und der ersten Seligpreisung (Lk 6,20b par Mt 5,3) der vor allem in Q belegte Satztyp zu rechnen, der die 'basileia' als Subjekt mit einem Verbum der Bewegung verbindet (Lk 10,9 par Mt 10,7; Lk 11,2 par Mt 6,10; Lk 11,20 par Mt 12,28; Lk 16,16ba par Mt 11,12a; vgl. Mk 1,15; 9,1).

He refers, p. 23, n. 36, to H. Schürmann coming "zu einem ähnlichen Ergebnis bezüglich der ipsissima verba in der Q-Tradition."

[18] *Q 11:2b–4* (James M. Robinson, Paul Hoffmann, and John S. Kloppenborg, eds., *Documenta Q: Reconstructions of Q Through Two Centuries of Gospel Research Excerpted, Sorted, and Evaluated* [Leuven: Peeters, 1996], 106–27).

logical banquet (Q 13:29, 28), even if meanwhile you starve to death! No, the Beatitudes are not so cynical and cold-blooded, but give good news (Q 7:22) for the here and now.

Perhaps this present reality of the kingdom is made most clear in the case of exorcism: "But if it is by the finger of God that I cast out demons, then there has come upon you God's reign" (Q 11:20). The abnormal symptoms of a disease, which led it to be called demon possession, are in the here and now, and the exorcism, as the coming of God's reign, is also in the here and now, as the abnormal symptoms fade away. The extent to which a day's bread, and healings, are already God reigning, is made clear in the Workers' Instructions: "And whatever town you enter and they take you in, eat what is set before you, and cure the sick there, and say to them: 'The kingdom of God has reached unto you'" (Q 10:8–9). Actually, the Q people thought they were already "in" the kingdom: "There has not arisen among women's offspring anyone who surpasses John. Yet the least significant in God's kingdom is more than he" (Q 7:28).

So the Woe pronounced against exegetes of the Law, who shut people out of the kingdom, does not just refer to closing access to the kingdom in the afterlife, when one might otherwise have hoped to enter it, but refers to these scribes as themselves not having entered the kingdom already now: ". . . for you shut the kingdom of God from people; you did not go in, nor let in those trying to get in" (Q 11:52). Q pinpointed rather precisely the point in time when the kingdom is present in history, namely just after the law and the prophets and John, since the kingdom is now violated and plundered: "From then on the kingdom of God is violated and the violent plunder it" (Q 16:16).

The parables of the Mustard Seed (Q 13:18–19) and the Yeast (Q 13:20–21) present the kingdom of God as having begun already, even if not yet fully developed. Perhaps earlier scholarship was wrong, to call them "parables of growth," with simply an evolutionary implication (belief in "progress"). The transition from seed to tree, from yeast to fermented dough, was for antiquity not really a natural process, but was more nearly imagined as a supernatural miracle. And yet they are not just "contrast parables,"[19] as others maintained, to play up the grandiose future by playing down the meager present.[20] For the parables do not limit the kingdom to the eschatological future,

---

[19] Absent from Q, but present in the Markan doublet (Mark 4:30–32), is the contrast between the mustard seed as "the smallest of all the seeds on earth" and the full-grown mustard bush as "the greatest of all shrubs." *The Gospel of Thomas* also makes the contrast explicit, Saying 20: "the smallest of all seeds," "a large branch," and Saying 96: "a little bit of yeast," "huge loaves of bread."

[20] Heinz Schürmann, "Das Zeugnis der Redenquelle für die Basileia-Verkündigung Jesu: Eine traditionsgeschichtliche Untersuchung," *Logia: Les Paroles de Jésus—The Sayings of Jesus* (ed. Joël Delobel; BETL 59; Leuven: Peeters and Leuven University Press, 1982 [1983]), 121–200: 185 n. 265:

H. Merklein, *Handlungsprinzip** (*Die Gottesherrschaft als Handlungsprinzip: Untersuchung zur Ethik Jesu* [FzB 34; Würzburg: Echter, 1978[1], 1981[2], 1984[3]]), 166, redet von

but describe it as something thrown now into the garden, hid now in three measures of flour. Thus the parables of the kingdom present the miracle of God, God reigning, as beginning already now. To be sure, this is not intended as a given status, like the "established church," extending over time and space, but rather as something that happens from time to time on given occasions.[21]

Jesus rejected the idea of locating any given place where the kingdom can be expected to come, since in fact it comes already "within" people (Q 17:20–21). Again, this saying should not be misunderstood, as if it had in view just a mystic inwardness. Though the rare preposition used here does seem to mean inside in contrast to outside,[22] the meaning would not seem to be far from the other alternate translation, "among you" or "in your midst," since it does stand over against some apocalyptic never-never land. The point of the saying is that the kingdom is not something that will take place somewhere sometime, but is a reality in the present experience of people in the world of today.

Jesus called on people to "seek" the kingdom (Q 12:31). But this is anything but hunting for some future cosmic event, be it here, or there, which Jesus had explicitly rejected (Q 17:21). Rather this seeking is set over against the other kind of seeking (Q 12:29–30), which anxiety-laden Gentiles do, when they ask: "What are we to eat? Or: What are we to drink? Or: What are we to wear?" Hence "seeking" for the kingdom returns full circle to the petition for the kingdom to come in the Lord's Prayer: One does not need to be anxiety-laden about scrounging for such physical necessities as something to eat, because one can trust in God reigning, that is to say, answering the petitions for God's reign to come, in the form of one day's bread: "Let your reign come," specifically: "Our day's bread give us today."

"Aus-Stand" und "Ein-Stand" der Basileia "in Jesus" und setzt sich mit Recht ab von denen, die den "Einstand" derselben nicht leugnen, aber als gegenwärtig doch nur "Zeichen" des kommenden Reiches sehen wollen. . . .

[21] Peter Kristin, "Nachfolge Leben: Drei Modelle von Kreuzesnachfolge in Q und Markus," in *Text und Geschichte: Facetten theologischen Arbeitens aus dem Freundes- und Schülerkreis. Dieter Lührmann zum 60. Geburtstag* (ed. Stefan Maser and Egbert Schlarb; MThSt 50; Marburg: N. G. Elwert, 1999), 89–106: 92, 95, speaks of what is present in the sense of taking place at individual points of time:

Sie praktizierten diese Worte und verstanden sich, aufgrund dieser performativ wirkenden Worte und der Beauftragung durch Jesus, als Boten des in ihrer Begegnung mit den "Kindern des Friedens" und in den diese Begegnung begleitenden Heilungen punktuell gegenwärtigen Gottesreiches. . . . [95]

Die charakteristische Vorstellung des punktuell schon präsenten Gottesreiches als einer alternativen Lebensform ist das Movens der Boten, die Sendung durch Jesus ihre Legitimation für ein Leben nach seinen Worten.

[22] T. Holmén, "The Alternatives of the Kingdom: Encountering the semantic restrictions of Luke 17,20–21 (ἐντὸς ὑμῖν)," *ZNW* 87 (1996): 214–29. In the formulation of this saying in Saying 3.3 of the *Gospel of Thomas* in P. Oxy. 654, the preposition cannot be understood and translated any other way, since it stands over against the converse preposition, "outside": "And the kingdom [of God] is within you, [and outside]." Though the decisive word is here in a lacuna, the restoration is certain, since the Coptic text in Nag Hammadi Codex 2 is here fully extant.

Thus the kingdom of God, the one clearly recognizable theological category of Jesus' message, in a sense elevated to theological relevance much of everyday living, such as sickness, the need for food and clothing, the evil with which people are always struggling. It was in the very real, everyday world that God reigning is very good news (Q 7:22).[23] For it was countercultural[24] and hence gave hope to the hopeless.

Jesus' Conduct and Action

Those who believe that the kingdom refers only to the apocalyptic can in a sense be excused for not going into specific details. A "new heavens and a new earth" is so completely new that one can hardly be expected to describe it. But to talk about God reigning in the here and now does suggest it should be possible to say something about what that means in concrete reality, since we know a very great deal about present reality from our own experience. We have language, our everyday language, for talking about everyday experience, and so if God is reigning here, one ought to be able to talk about where, when, how Jesus thought God to be reigning, and how, in concrete reality, he thought one is to relate to that reigning.

To this extent Albert Schweitzer was correct in proposing to go beyond Johannes Weiß' focus only on Jesus' sayings about the kingdom, by insisting that God reigning must have been decisive also in Jesus' "conduct and action."[25] But Schweitzer was basically misled in assuming that the Mission Instructions of Matt 10 were an eyewitness report of what exactly Jesus said, on a specific occasion, namely when he sent his disciples out to trigger the end of the world

---

[23] Kristin, "Nachfolge Leben," 93:
     Die Boten verstehen sich als legitime Nachfolgerinnen und Nachfolger Jesu und bringen denen, die sie aufgrund ihres Friedensgrußes aufnehmen, die Gegenwart des Gottesreiches (10,9), indem sie das verkündigen und tun, was Jesus (selbst getan und) ihnen aufgetragen hat. Das Gottesreich ist in ihrem Wirken angebahnt und in den ihnen aufgetragenen Heilungen und der Sphäre des Heils präsent und erfahrbar. Dieses Heil entwickelt sich als Folge der gastlichen Aufnahme in ein Haus. In ihrem ganzen Leben stellen sie die Prinzipien des Gottesreiches dar, wie sie in QJ erkennbar werden. Gewalt- und besitzlos (10,4) leben sie die Realität der Gottesherrschaft paradigmatisch, wie es in Q 12,31 ausgedrückt ist, im Vertrauen auf die *Fürsorge* des Vaters.

[24] Stephen J. Patterson, "Wisdom in Q and Thomas," in *In Search of Wisdom: Essays in Memory of John G. Gammie* (ed. L. G. Perdue, B. B. Scott, and W. J. Wisemann; Louisville, Ky.: Westminster/John Knox, 1993), 187–221; "Counter-cultural Wisdom," 205–7.

[25] Albert Schweitzer, *Die Geschichte der Leben-Jesu-Forschung* (Tübingen: Mohr Siebeck, 1913[2]), "Vorrede zur sechsten Auflage," (1951[6]), viii, and (München: Siebenstern-Taschenbuch 77/78, 1966), 32. This preface, and hence this comment, is first available in *The Quest of the Historical Jesus* (First Complete Edition; ed. John Bowden; London: SCM, 2000, and Minneapolis: Fortress, 2001), xxxiii–xliii: xxxvi (SCM) and xxxv–xlv: xxxviii (Fortress). The expression is translated by Bowden less literally and more colloquially as "life and work."

and bring in the millennium. But Schweitzer's basic question is nonetheless valid: What conduct and action would necessarily result from the message of the kingdom of God?

Even in our day, one has commonly used modern parables to speak of the kingdom in relation to the present. The standard instance: The kingdom is in the present only like the first drops of rain, before the clouds burst and the downpour, the kingdom itself, comes. Soon after World War II, Oscar Cullmann put it this way: It is like the Normandy landing was for us—a foothold on the Continent, assuring the final victory, even before that final victory actually came.

But such talk also just uses metaphors, modern equivalents to the parables of the Mustard Seed and the Yeast. What was Jesus actually talking about in terms of his and his followers' own life experience?

That which made one as carefree as the ravens and lilies was trust in the kingdom of God, God reigning, as a caring Father (Q 12:22b–28). This in turn is what explains the radical Workers' Instructions: "Carry no purse, nor knapsack, nor shoes, nor stick, and greet no one on the road" (Q 10:4). This then is what Jesus himself actually did during his "public ministry" in Galilee. It was not an instance of the asceticism that was commonly part and parcel of the religious lifestyle at the time. For Jesus' lifestyle moved more nearly in the opposite direction, as the caricature of him as a carouser makes clear: "The son of humanity came, eating and drinking, and you say: Look! A person who is a glutton and drunkard, a chum of tax collectors and sinners!" (Q 7:34).[26]

Indeed the Workers' Instructions go on to urge Jesus' followers, the "workers," to eat what is set before them, in the house of the "son of peace" who takes them in:

> And at that house remain, eating and drinking whatever they provide, for the worker is worthy of one's reward.[27] Do not move around from house to house. And whatever town you enter and they take you in, eat what is set before you . . . (Q 10:7–8)

---

[26] The attempt of Vaage, Leif E. Vaage. (*Galilean Upstarts: Jesus' First Followers according to Q* [Valley Forge, Pa.: Trinity Press International, 1994], 87–96), to present this not as a caricature but as historically accurate is based on his earlier presentations, "Q¹ and the Historical Jesus: Some Peculiar Sayings (7:33–34; 9:57–58, 59–60; 14:26–27)," *Forum* 5,2 (1989): 159–76, and, as he reports (p. 159), on an unpublished "Paper presented in the 1988 Spring meeting of the Jesus Seminar, Sonoma, CA," entitled: "An Archeological Approach to the Work of the Jesus Seminar." His portrayal there of Jesus as an alcoholic is dismantled in my essay, "*Galilean Upstarts*: A Sot's Cynical Disciples?" in *Sayings of Jesus: Canonical and Non-Canonical*, 223–49: "2. The alcoholic Jesus," 228–43.

[27] The absence of the purse means that one neither carries nor earns money, which would provide a security less visible than food and clothing. Matt 10:9 makes this explicit: "Take no gold, nor silver, nor copper in your belts." Apparently cash payment for services rendered became a temptation, leading Matt 10:10 to revise the text of Q to read: "the worker is worthy of one's food."

It is just here that one catches sight of the theological explanation that was intended to make sense of all this unusual conduct. For the Workers' Instructions go on: ". . . and cure the sick there, and say to them: The kingdom of God has reached unto you" (Q 10:9). The bestowal of "Peace" on the house with the opening "Shalom" (Q 10:5) and this retrospect of God having reigned among them, provides the theological framework for what takes place in the household: Not only is the cure of the sick, like the exorcism of Q 11:20, ascribed here to God reigning, but the provision of food is also God's kingdom coming, in the concrete sense of answering the petitions of the Lord's Prayer: "Let your reign come: Our day's bread give us today." One does not go looking for food and drink, any more than do the ravens (Q 12:24), but one seeks instead God's reign (Q 12:31), trusting that food and drink will be granted in the home of the "son of peace," where God's reigning will happen as the answer to the Lord's Prayer.

What one does not do is store up funds in a purse, or bread and clothing in a knapsack, as if one may have lucked out with God today, but tomorrow is another day, and one never knows, so be prepared for the worst! No, tomorrow, start out just as one started out today, praying: "Our day's bread give us today," and trusting that God will reign each day, just as he reigns today.

The absence of shoes would involve such debilitating deprivation, according to many exegetes, that they have hesitated to take it literally. But it must have been meant literally, just as everything else in the Workers' Instructions seems to be describing actual practice. Barefootedness is a standard symbol of penance (e.g., the Franciscans), and may have been characteristic of those baptized by John. For John is described as not worthy to take off Jesus' shoes,[28] as a metaphor for not being worthy to baptize him.

The injunction not to carry a stick is clearly intended to prevent self-defense against humans and even wild animals. For it hardly refers to a walking stick (NRSV Matt 10:10: "stave"), but rather a club, the poor man's weapon.[29] One

---

[28] The injunction not to wear sandals fits poorly with Q 3:16 and Mark 1:7, if they are understood as John being unworthy to perform a servant's task of taking off and putting on a master's sandals. For, if applied to Jesus, this would indicate Jesus continued to wear sandals and continued in association with John. But, more probably, it referred to removing Jesus' sandals permanently prior to immersion. John's unworthiness to do this would be a stage in the subordination of John to Jesus picked up and amplified by Matt 3:14–15. Norbert Krieger, "Barfuß Busse Tun," *NovT* 1 (1956): 227–28, referred to John 12:6; 20:13–15. He is cited with approval by Walter Bauer in Frederick William Danker, *A Greek-English Lexicon of the New Testament and Other Early Christian Literature* (3d ed.; Chicago and London: University of Chicago Press, 2000), based on Walter Bauer's *Griechisch-deutsches Wörterbuch zu den Schriften des Neuen Testaments und der frühchristlichen Literatur* (6th ed.; ed. Kurt Aland and Barbara Aland, with Viktor Reichmann), s.v. βαστάζω, i.e. "remove," citing also *Papyri Graecae Magicae: Die griechischen Zauberpapyri* (ed. K. Preisendanz et al.; Sammlung wissenschaftlicher Commentare 4; Stuttgart: Tübner, 1928), 1058: βαστάξας τὸ στεφάνιον ἀπὸ τῆς κεφαλῆς.

[29] The termination of Q's rigorous Workers' Instructions in Luke 22:36 indicates that one had in fact been forbidden to take what was understood as a weapon, though

is not to defend oneself against attack, but to turn the other cheek (Q 6:29).

One may well wonder how Jesus, much less anyone else he might talk into it, could sustain a life of such radical deprivation. He may indeed have chosen a site for his public ministry where such literal rigors as barefootedness, giving one's shirt off one's back, taking no provisions for the trip, having no form of self-defense, were not utterly impossible. He did center his public ministry on the Sea of Galilee, perhaps a relatively mild winter climate some 700 feet below sea level, indeed the lowest point in Galilee, which hence may have been more tolerant than the hill country of such an exposed existence as that which Jesus advocated and practiced. The proximity of his base camp at Capernaum to the frontier of the territory of the less threatening Philip, with a grateful centurion stationed nearby (Q 7:1–10), and a harvest at dawn each day as the fishermen returned to shore, may all have rendered the rigorous lifestyle Jesus practiced at least possible.[30]

God Reigning in Jesus' Public Ministry

How then is one to explain Jesus' so abnormal lifestyle? The radical list of what not to take along on the way is hard to explain in terms of the history of religions. Neither the Cynics, nor the Essenes, nor John the Baptist (Q 7:33; Mark 1:6), provides a precedent.

In recent research, one has drawn the comparison especially to the Cynics, with their minimalistic, indeed intentionally offensive, lifestyle.[31] Leif E. Vaage

---

it is here expressed in more middle-class terms: "And let him who has no sword sell his mantle and buy one." (The requirement of a sword is here necessitated by the following Markan story of the cutting off of an ear in Gethsemane.) The implication of the stick as a defensive weapon was first drawn to my attention by a student from Kenya, for whom this was so obvious as to need no further explanation. I then recalled having experienced such a weapon: At el-Kasr near Nag Hammadi, I have seen a very formidable weapon, long, heavy, solid, smooth, in the hands of a peasant, in a situation in which he felt he might be called upon to defend himself. The *Los Angeles Times* of 17 Dec. 92, reporting on the new sense of security provided by the arrival of U. S. military forces in the famine-ridden town of Baidoa in Somalia, provided the anecdote: "Wednesday, the feeding center was filled with optimism and a new sense of security, commodities as rare as grain in this parched land. 'Where's your gun?' Rice teased Abduhakim, 19, one of the center's security guards. Only a day before, he had been carrying an automatic weapon. Wednesday, he was carrying a walking stick." The stick was obviously not due to sudden lameness, but rather a return to the traditional local weapon to replace the automatic gun the American troops had just forbidden. The *Los Angeles Times* of 11 March 93 published a picture with the caption: "Two Somali men walk through the ruins of what was once the Hotel Aruba in the capital, Mogadishu. They carry sticks for protection."

[30] James M. Robinson, "Foreword: A Down-to-Earth Jesus," in Jean J. Rousseau and Rami Arav, *Jesus and His World: An Archaeological and Cultural Dictionary* (Minneapolis: Fortress, 1995), xiii–xviii: xiv.

[31] See my review article of Vaage, *Galilean Upstarts: Jesus' First Followers According to Q*: "*Galilean Upstarts*: A Sot's Cynical Disciples?" in *Sayings of Jesus: Canonical and Non-Canonical*, 223–49.

has renewed Gerd Theissen's Cynic interpretation of the specific instances in the Q Sermon, to turn the other cheek, give the shirt off one's back, go the second mile, and lend without asking for anything back (Q 6:29–30). The Cynic explanation of this core of the Sermon's ethics, as advocated by Gerd Theissen, is summarized by Vaage: "To turn the other cheek and give up both cloak and tunic were hardly expressions of 'universal love,' but just 'smart moves' under the circumstances."[32]

It was as a summary of these injunctions that the redactor created the over-arching generalization to love one's enemies (Q 6:27), which hence, according to Vaage, does not go back to Jesus at all.[33] This remarkable love command is just "a strategy for handling unfriendly opposition. 'Love your enemies,' in other words, and in this way take care of the 'jerks.'"[34] Vaage thus interprets the "itinerant radicalism" of the Q people as a shrewd strategy to evade hard-ship for themselves:

> The best enemies to love are those you meet only once. The best way to assure such a situation is not to stay too long in any one place.[35]

---

[32] Vaage (*Galilean Upstarts*, 50) writes:
   . . . every material means of manipulating and imposing oneself on the ancient Cynic and first follower of Jesus in Galilee had been taken out of their enemies' hands. . . .
   . . . at stake is the procurement of the maximum avail-able good for those who otherwise stand in danger of personal assault and battery as well as uninvited theft. The imperatives in 6:29—and 6:30 . . .—were originally prudential considerations provided for persons whose lives must wend their way through contexts of diverse insecurity. To turn the other cheek and give up both cloak and tunic were hardly expressions of "universal love," but just "smart moves" under the circumstances.

[33] Ibid., 159 n. 16.

[34] Ibid., 47.

[35] Ibid., 44. He translates in this connection Theissen, "Gewaltverzicht und Feindesliebe (Mt 5,38–48; Lc 6,27–36) und deren sozialgeschichtlicher Hintergrund," *Studien zur Soziologie des Urchristentums* (Tübingen: Mohr Siebeck, 1977), 191:
   Der seßhafte Christ geriete durch Nachgeben gegenüber seinem Feind in immer größere Abhängigkeit. Er muß ja damit rechnen, ihm immer wieder neu zu begegnen. Nachgeben bedeutet hier oft: zur Fortsetzung von Übervorteilung und Zurücksetzung aufzufordern. Der Verzicht auf Widerstand erhöht die Wahrscheinlichkeit, daß sich Übergriffe wiederholen. Dennoch steht auch vor ihm die große Forderung, seinen Feind zu lieben. Sie kann der wandernde Charismatiker viel überzeugender verwirk-lichen. Er ist wirklich frei. Er kann den Ort seiner Niederlage und Demütigung ver-lassen. Er darf damit rechnen, daß er seinem Gegner nicht mehr begegnet. Indem er weiterzieht, kann er seine Unabhängigkeit und Freiheit wahren. Der Preis für diese Freiheit ist eine rigorose Askese: ein Leben am Rande des Existenzminimums.
Vaage's translation:
   The sedentary Christian falls into ever greater dependence by giving way to his enemy. Indeed, he must reckon with the fact that he will meet him repeatedly again and again. Giving way often means in this case inviting continuation of the fact that one is taken advantage of and degraded. Non-resistance heightens the prob-ability that infringements will repeat themselves. Nevertheless, the great command to love his enemy exists for him as well. The *Wandercharismatiker* can realize the command much more convincingly. He is truly free. He can abandon the site of his defeat and humiliation. He may reckon with the fact that he will not meet his enemy again. As long as he keeps moving on, he can maintain his independence

The purpose of mentioning here the Cynic interpretation of Jesus is not to criticize it, which I have done elsewhere,[36] in a way that Frans Neirynck characterized as "devastating,"[37] but to point out how the Cynic interpretation was given an opening in our times due to a deficiency in the rest of scholarship, namely the failure to identify the real center of thought behind Jesus' conduct.

The dominant effort to place eschatology at the center of Jesus' thought has in fact not succeeded, as already Hans Conzelmann recognized: "At first glance his [Jesus'] teaching about God and his eschatology, his eschatology and ethics appear to stand alongside one another in a relatively disconnected way. . . . [58]"

> Over against a "consistent eschatological" interpretation of the teaching of Jesus it must be emphasized that where God's governance as such is developed, the prospect of the imminent end of the world is lacking. The world appears simply as creation, the sphere of the rule and care of God.[38]

But though there would seem to be no clear correlation of Jesus' ethic and teaching about God to his eschatology, there is indeed an explicit correlation between the latter two: Jesus' teaching about God and Jesus' ethic are indeed correlated to each other. For example (Q 6:36): "Be full of pity, just as your Father is full of pity." Here Jesus explicitly appeals to God's pity, as the model to be followed by God's people. This he does again and again: He petitioned a caring heavenly Father to "cancel our debts for us, as we too have cancelled for those in debt to us" (Q 11:4). For Jesus called upon his followers to forgive daily, just as they expect from God daily forgiveness: "If seven times a day [your brother] sins against you, also seven times shall you forgive him" (Q 17:4). And the central appeal of Jesus to love one's enemies is based on God's conduct: "Love your enemies, and pray for those persecuting you, so that you may become sons of your Father, for he raises his sun on bad and good and rains on the just and unjust" (Q 6:35).

---

and freedom. The price of this freedom is a rigorous asceticism: a life on the edge of the bare minimum for existence. But the profit is great.

[36] James M. Robinson, "The History-of-Religions Taxonomy of Q: The Cynic Hypothesis," in *Gnosisforschung und Religionsgeschichte: Festschrift für Kurt Rudolph zum 65. Geburtstag* (ed. Holger Preißler and Hubert Seiwert; Marburg: Diagonal-Verlag, 1994 [1995]), 247–65, "4. The Cynic Getup," 257–59. See also Robinson, "Building Blocks in the Social History of Q," on "The Cynics' and the Q People's Getups," 87–90.

[37] Frans Neirynck, in his review of *Sayings of Jesus: Canonical and Non-Canonical* in *ETL* 73 (1997): 456–58: 457.

[38] Hans Conzelmann, "Jesus Christus," in *RGG*³ (vol. 3; Tübingen: Mohr Siebeck, 1959), 634, 637:

> J. entwirft kein System einer Lehre. Es fällt im Gegenteil auf, daß Gotteslehre und Eschatologie, Eschatologie und Ethik auf den ersten Blick relativ unverbunden nebeneinander zu stehen scheinen. . . . [637]
>
> Gegenüber einer "konsequent eschatologischen" Deutung der Lehre Jesu ist zu betonen: Wo Gottes Walten als solches entfaltet wird, da fehlt der Ausblick auf das nahe Weltende. Die Welt erscheint einfach als Schöpfung, Bereich des Regierens und der Fürsorge Gottes.

ET: *Jesus* (Philadelphia: Fortress, 1973), 51, 58.

Thus, at the core of the archaic collections behind the redaction of Q, there is a striking correlation between the actual conduct that Jesus exemplified and advocated in his sayings and the way that he conceived of God as a forgiving Father. It is almost as if he invented Voltaire's shockingly flippant witticism of the French Enlightenment: Forgiving, that's what God is there for, it's his job! It is not surprising that Jesus' shocking view of God has been largely ignored, as has his corresponding ethic.

It took a distinguished classics scholar, Albrecht Dihle, to lay out in detail the dramatic extent to which this new ethic Jesus derived from his new understanding of God transcends the common-sense justice of reward and punishment that pervaded antiquity: "... the proclamation of Jesus of Nazareth and the early Christian theology connecting to it have eliminated that concept of retaliation as the basis for, or ingredient in, an ethical order."[39]

The love of enemies, as the highest ethic of Jesus and the Q people, was indeed very unusual. And it was rooted in an equally unusual vision of a God who gives sunshine and showers to the bad as well as to the good.

It is striking that Jesus, at this most central point, did not derive his unusual vision of God, and his highest ethic, from the Hebrew scriptures, or indeed from anywhere in the culture of the Ancient Near East. For in that case it could hardly have centered in God's impartiality to foe as well as friend, as the Matthean antithesis makes clear: "You have heard that it was said, You shall love your neighbor and hate your enemy. But I say to you, Love your enemies . . ." (Matt 5:43–44a).

Love of enemies does indeed fly in the face of the common-sense everyday judgment that the punishment should fit the crime. It is surprising indeed that Jesus' rare view of God, and its resultant radical ethic, is derived from his experience of the world of nature around him. Presumably, in Nazareth, the climate on the wrong side of the tracks was the same as the climate on the right side of the tracks. What was unusual was for someone, namely Jesus, to draw such a radical ethic from this simple observation of nature. God is in charge of nature, and on all sides is showing you how he is, and how his sons should be in imitation of him—kind to all, to the bad as well as to the good.

From Jesus forward to the Redaction of Q

To the Q people, nothing was as important as Jesus' revelation of God. It was to score this point that they portray Jesus making use of the solemn

---

[39] Albrecht Dihle, *Die Goldene Regel: Eine Einführung in die Geschichte der antiken und frühchristlichen Vulgärethik* (SAW 7; Göttingen: Vandenhoeck & Ruprecht, 1962), "Prinzipielle Überwindung des Vergeltungsdenkens, b) Christentum," 72–79: 72: "Unter gänzlich anderen Voraussetzungen hat die Predigt Jesu von Nazareth und die an sie anknüpfende frühchristliche Theologie den Vergeltungsgedanken als Grundlage oder Bestandteil einer sittlichen Ordnung ausgeschieden." See my review, *JHP* 4 (1966): 84–87.

Thanksgiving formula of Qumran,[40] to praise God most explicitly that Jesus had finally revealed him in such a way that, for the first time, one could truly know him: "I praise you, Father, Lord of heaven and earth, for you hid these things from sages and the learned, and disclosed them to children; . . . nor does anyone know the Father except the Son, and to whomever the Son chooses to reveal him" (Q 10:21a, 22b).

This Thanksgiving in Q thanks the Father for only one thing: A vision of God higher than what had been understood before, presumably God's amazingly impartial love for the bad as well as the good.

But what happened to this shocking revelation of God? Something did change in the outlook of the Q community, as reflected in the redactional level of the text of Q. For the ethic of loving one's enemies, though based on Jesus' vision of God, was replaced by quite a different ethic. It is odd that this is not generally recognized as a major problem, deserving more attention from New Testament scholarship.

Yet it has long since been sensed to be a problem, indeed it was so sensed by Walter Bauer almost a century ago.[41] He did find Jesus' ideal of love of

---

[40] James M. Robinson, "Die Hodajot-Formel in Gebet und Hymnus des Frühchristentums," in *Apophoreta: Festschrift für Ernst Haenchen* (BZNW 30; Berlin: Töpelmann, 1964), 194–235.

[41] Walter Bauer, "Das Gebot der Feindesliebe und die alten Christen," *ZTK* 27 (1917): 37–54: 39–40:

Vielmehr verlangt er [Paulus] Liebesgesinnung gegen sie [die Feinde] in einer Form, die beinahe die Vermutung zuläßt, daß ihn nicht nur der Geist seines Herrn berührt hat, sondern ihm dessen Forderung im Ohre klingt (Röm 12 $_{14-21}$, I. Thess 5 $_{15}$, vgl. I. Kor 4 $_{12}$). Wenn Paulus daneben gelegentlich scharfe Worte für die Verfolger der Gemeinde Gottes findet (I. Thess. 2 $_{14-16}$), so kann das in keinem höheren Grade befremden, als wenn in der Redenquelle außer dem Gebote der Feindesliebe auch Sprüche stehen wie Mt 23 $_{34}$ f. $_{37}$ f. = Luk 11 $_{49}$ f., 13 $_{34}$ f. [Q 11:49–51; 13:34–35]. . . . [40]

Auch in der, zu Lebzeiten des Heidenapostels komponierten Redenquelle hat die Feindesliebe die ihr gebührende Wertung erfahren. Da war sie nicht als eine Tugend neben anderen erschienen, sondern als das Höchste, was man überhaupt von einem Menschen erwarten kann, als etwas, was die Jünger Jesu hoch hinaushebt über die Sphäre des allgemein Menschlichen und sie Gott selber gleich macht (Mt 5 $_{45-48}$ = Luk 6 $_{32-36}$) [Q 6:32,34,35c–36]. Demgemäß hatte in der Urgestalt der Bergpredigt die Forderung der Feindesliebe die beherrschende Stellung eingenommen und war nach dem Auftakt der Seligpreisungen an die Spitze der ganzen Ermahnungsreihe getreten. Bei Matthäus, der jener Urform eine umfassende Bearbeitung hat zuteil werden lassen, ist das verwischt. In seinem Evangelium bleibt es auch gewissermaßen bei der einmaligen Mitteilung, daß Jesus so Großes von den Seinen gefordert habe. Und die Art, wie dort, wo der ἐθνικός und der τελώτης aus Mt 5 $_{46,47}$ wiederkehren, diese die Schar der Ungetauften repräsentierenden Menschen mit gleichgültiger Kälte zur Seite geschoben werden (18 $_{17}$), die Genugtuung mit der Mt berichtet, wie der König den Tod seiner Sendboten an den widerwilligen Geladenen rächt (22 $_{6,7}$), lassen nicht gerade erwarten, daß er auf Aeußerungen der Feindschaft von nichtchristlicher Seite mit Liebeserweisen zu reagieren geneigt gewesen wäre.

ET (unpublished):

Rather he [Paul] calls for a loving attitude toward them [one's enemies] in a form that almost permits the conjecture that not only the spirit of his Lord has

enemies both in Paul and Q. But he sensed the substantive tension between the emphasis on the love of enemies in Q's archaic collection, the Inaugural Sermon, and the condemnation of enemies in Q 11:49–51; 13:34–35, which was then continued in the redaction of the Gospel of Matthew itself.

This drastic change has recently been highlighted very forcefully in a dissertation by a pupil of Graham Stanton at King's College, London, David C. Sim, in an analysis of Matthew's apocalyptic eschatology. Yet his devastating analysis of Matthew's vengefulness is based largely on redactional material from Q, which was then incorporated into Matthew. Hence his analysis applies not just to Matthew, but also to the redaction of Q:

> Like most apocalyptic-eschatological schemes, Matthew's version does not merely treat the eschatological fate of the righteous; he also deals with the ultimate fate of the wicked. The evangelist depicts the fate of this group in the harshest of terms. One important function of this motif is to satisfy the desire for vengeance on the part of himself and his readers. . . . [234]
>
> In this section we have noted one of the evangelist's important uses of apocalyptic eschatology, particularly the abundant material relating to the horrific punishments awaiting the wicked. Matthew emphasizes this particular element and uses it to satisfy his apocalyptic community's psychological need for vengeance on those who are responsible for their suffering.[42]

---

touched him, but also his requirement echoes in his ear (Rom 12:14–21; 1 Thess 5:15; cf. 1 Cor 4:12). If in addition Paul at times finds sharp words for the persecutors of the congregation of God (1 Thess 2:14–16), that can surprise in no higher degree than when in the sayings source, in addition to the command of love of enemy, also sayings occur such as Matt 23:34–35, 37–38 = Luke 11:49–50; 13:34–35 [Q 11:49–51; 13:34–35]. . . . [40]

Also in the discourse source, composed during the lifetime of the apostle to the Gentiles, love of the enemy has received the evaluation it deserves. There it did not make its appearance as a virtue among others, but rather as the highest that one can ever expect from a person, as something that elevates the disciples of Jesus high above the sphere of the generally human, and makes them like God himself (Matt 5:45–48 = Luke 6:32–36 [Q 6:32,34,35c–36]). Accordingly, in the archaic form of the Sermon on the Mount the requirement of love of enemies had assumed the dominant position and, after the prelude of the Beatitudes, had come to stand at the head of the whole series of exhortations.

In Matthew, who subjected that archaic form to an all-encompassing revision, that has vanished. In his Gospel, it is also limited, so to speak, to just a single communication, that Jesus has required something so great of those who were his. And the way in which, where the ἐθνικός and the τελώτης are repeated from Matt 5:46–47, these people, representing the mass of the unbaptized, are pushed to one side with indifferent coldness (18:17), the satisfaction with which Matthew reports how the king avenges, on the invited who are unwilling to come, the death of his messengers (22:6–7), do not permit one to expect such a thing as that he would have been inclined to react to expressions of hostility from non-Christians with displays of love.

[42] David C. Sim, "Vengeance and consolation," in idem, *Apocalyptic Eschatology in the Gospel of Matthew* (SNTSMS 88; Cambridge: Cambridge University Press, 1996), 227–35: 227, 234.

Love your enemies? Sim continues: "The righteous can take heart that God (or Jesus Son of Man) will balance the ledger at the eschaton and exact vengeance on their behalf."[43] He raises his sun on bad and good and rains on the just and unjust? Jesus' amazing vision of God seems to have been completely lost from sight by the redaction of Q, and hence in the Gospel of Matthew!

What is it that caused Jesus' vision of God to be replaced by its reverse? Sim himself suggests:

> Owing to the high ethical demands of Jesus' interpretation of the Torah, the *ekklesia* was prohibited from taking its own revenge upon its enemies, even if it were in a position to do so. . . . These demands must have posed some problems for Matthew's community and raised doubts in their minds about the justice of God. How can God be just when he allows the righteous to suffer and the wicked to prosper and does not allow the former to take revenge on the latter?[44]

But what seems to be lacking in Sim's reflection has to do with the understanding of God. If "they were expected to be as perfect as their heavenly father," as Sim emphasizes,[45] should they not love their enemies, as God exemplified with his sun and showers? How is it that "doubt in their minds about the justice of God" replaced having as much pity as God had, forgiving as often as God forgives, loving enemies the way God helps the bad and unjust? The Q people seem to have reversed their ethics! But how could they reverse their ethics and leave Jesus' doctrine of God in place? That sublime doctrine of God must itself have given way. But how?

It may be no coincidence that the Q text cited by Bauer to document the replacement of love of enemies with vengeance (Q 11:49–51; 13:34–35) is precisely the text that Bultmann considered a quotation from an unknown sapiential text (since Q presents it as quoting Sophia),[46] which is today the main evidence for Q's deuteronomistic redaction and the late dating of the redaction of Q. For the destruction of the temple in 70 C.E. seems to be envisaged there,[47] when the text speaks of the temple, "your House," being "forsaken" by God (Q 13:35). His abandonment of the temple was thought to be theologically necessary before the temple could be destroyed again in 70 C.E., as it had been in 586 B.C.E., since God could be otherwise expected to pro-

---

[43] Ibid., 235.

[44] Ibid.

[45] Ibid.

[46] Rudolf Bultmann, *Die Geschichte der synoptischen Tradition* (Göttingen: Vandenhoeck und Ruprecht, 1931²), 119–21. ET: *The History of the Synoptic Tradition* (trans. John Marsh; New York and Evanston: 1968), 114–15. The English translation here (as elsewhere even in this revised edition) presupposes a lack of understanding of the German text, which hence has to be consulted in order to understand Bultmann's meaning.

[47] Hoffmann, "The Redaction of Q and the Son of Man," section 5: "The Son of Man and the Fall of Jerusalem," 190–98.

tect his temple. Thus God revealed himself as a vengeful God, by punishing Israel again with this second destruction of the temple. Thus the destruction of the temple in 70 c.e., experienced as a new devastating punishment by God, in effect replaced Jesus' revelation of God for the Q community. Accordingly, in the redaction of Q, God no longer shines his sun and rains his showers also on the bad and unjust, but throws them "out into the outer darkness, where there will be wailing and grinding of teeth" (Q 13:28), as victims of the "impending rage," who will "burn on a fire that can never be put out" (Q 3:7, 17).

From all of this, one can only conclude that it was what was left of the largely rejected Q community who produced a vision of God that replaced that of Jesus, together with an ethic of vengeance to replace his of the love of enemies, after having envisaged the destruction of the temple in 70 c.e. as an act of God. They seem to have paid only lip-service to love of enemies, knowing full well that the enemies will get it in the end from a just God of vengeance: "Vengeance is mine, I will repay."[48]

If nothing else, the critical text of Q, on the basis of Lührmann's distinction between the redaction of Q and the archaic collections imbedded in it, should make it possible to catch sight again of Jesus' vision of God. And, I submit to you, that would not be an unimportant achievement.

---

[48] Sim (*Apocalyptic Eschatology in the Gospel of Matthew*, 235) comments:

It is obvious from our discussion that Matthew responds to this problem in the same manner as other apocalyptic-eschatological thinkers. He provides an eschatological solution. Since the opponents of the *ekklesia* will be punished without mercy at the judgement, the members of the community can rest assured that God is just. While Matthew does not appeal to Deuteronomy 32:35, 'Vengeance is mine, I will repay,' as do Paul in Romans 12:19 and the author of Hebrews (10:30), he is firmly in agreement with this sentiment (cf. 16:27).

CHAPTER TWO

THE SYNOPTIC SAYINGS GOSPEL Q IN THE EARLY COMMUNITIES OF JESUS' FOLLOWERS

HELMUT KOESTER

Among the numerous questions that are discussed regarding the Synoptic Sayings Gospel Q I shall consider three issues in this essay:[1] (1) The geographical location of the community, which preserved the sayings tradition that resulted in the composition of Q, (2) the stratification of the document Q, and (3) the problem of the life situation (*Sitz im Leben*) of the materials in Q and related traditions. Arguments against the assumption of a relatively isolated community in Galilee that produced the Synoptic Sayings Gospel are formidable.[2] I myself have been critical of the "Galilee only" hypothesis for the origin of Q. But there are substantial problems not only with locating Q in Jerusalem but also with the attempt to understand Q within the context of mainline early-Christian developments. Arguments against a literary stratification of Q, which was proposed in an eminently persuasive way by John Kloppenborg,[3] have been brought forth a number of times,[4] most recently by Paul Hoffmann,[5] who is also one of the editors of the recently published critical edition of Q.[6]

---

[1] This paper has been developed on the basis of a response that I was asked to give to Birger Pearson's critique of recent hypotheses about the Synoptic Sayings Gospel Q. His paper and my response were presented at the annual meeting of the Society of Biblical Literature in Denver in November 2001. Birger Pearson affirms the validity of the Q hypothesis, but he wants to assign the document to Jerusalem as a kind of supplemental handbook. I do not pretend to be able to address all related issues of the debate—indeed I am not acquainted well enough with all the relevant literature. But I will try to elaborate my position as it reflects my more recent thinking on some of the issues.

[2] This was one of the arguments in the paper presented by Birger Pearson. He argued instead for Jerusalem as the place of origin; see also Marco Frenschkowski, "Galilee or Jerusalem: Die topographischen und politischen Hintergründe der Logienquelle," in *The Sayings Source Q and the Historical Jesus* (ed. A. Lindemann; BETL 158; Leuven: Leuven University Press, 2001), 535–59.

[3] John S. Kloppenborg, *The Formation of Q: Trajectories in Ancient Wisdom Collections* (SAC; Philadelphia: Fortress, 1987).

[4] See the review by John S. Kloppenborg, "The Sayings Gospel Q: Literary and Stratigraphic Problems," in *Symbols and Strata: Essays on the Sayings Gospel Q* (ed. Risto Uri; Göttingen: Vandenhoeck & Ruprecht, 1996), 1–66.

[5] "Mutmassungen über Q: Zum Problem der literarischen Gattung von Q," in Lindemann, *The Sayings Source Q*, 255–88.

[6] James M. Robinson, Paul Hoffmann, and John S. Kloppenborg, *The Critical Edition of Q: Synopsis Including the Gospels of Matthew and Luke, Mark, and Thomas* (Hermeneia Supplements; Minneapolis, Minn.: Fortress, 2000).

Finally, if more weight is shifted to the oral tradition, the life situation must be more rigorously defined as situation in the life of the community, for which the materials preserved in the *Didache* might serve as a helpful guide.

The Question of Geographical Isolation

More than thirty years ago, James Robinson and I proposed that the development of diverse early responses to the ministry, preaching, suffering, and death of Jesus presupposes formations of different traditions from and about Jesus in groups that existed in relative geographical isolation from each other.[7] Eventually, such groups committed their traditions, at the beginning preserved orally, to writing. Moreover, these older traditions and sources represent in each instance different answers to the question of Jesus' significance as a lasting source for salvation. Literature from the last third of the first century, that is, from the third generation after Jesus, demonstrates an effort to bring those different writings together, as is especially evident in the Gospels of Matthew and Luke, but must also be presupposed for the composition of the Gospel of John—efforts that still witness to the conflicting christological agendas of the older literatures and traditions. The most fundamental differences can be observed in the comparison of two major early developments: There is, on the one hand, the proclamation of Jesus' death and resurrection as the turning point of the ages and the subsequent development of the passion narrative and, on the other hand, the cultivation of the memory of Jesus' sayings together with their further enrichment and interpretation. These two traditions cannot have been wrought and cultivated in one and the same circle of the communities of the first and second generation. Each of them is self-sufficient. They were, to be sure, combined at a later stage; but these later combinations show that it was problematic to reconcile the different inherent theological biases of these two different answers to the significance of Jesus.

It is comparatively simple to delineate the development of the proclamation of the suffering, death, and resurrection of Jesus and of the passion narrative, because the letters of Paul and the traditions, upon which Paul relies, are accessible as direct sources that give evidence even for the very beginnings of this proclamation. An investigation of these traditions demonstrates that a formulation of "the gospel" of Jesus' death, burial, resurrection, and epiphanies existed before Paul's call, that is, in the very first years after the death of Jesus. Similarly, together with this "gospel," a tradition that interpreted the Eucharist in view of the death was simultaneously established in these very first years. Moreover, the two traditional formulae in 1 Cor 11:23–25 and 15:1–7 reveal that this interpretation of Jesus' suffering and death used the

---

[7] James M. Robinson and Helmut Koester, *Trajectories through Early Christianity* (Philadelphia: Fortress, 1971).

story of the suffering servant as the key to an understanding of the significance of Jesus for the understanding of salvation. Both the introduction to the words of institution, "in the night in which he was handed over," and the gospel formula, "he died for our sins according to the Scriptures," point to Isa 53.[8] Sayings of Jesus and stories about his miracles, although they were known in the context of these developments, did not play any role whatsoever in the interpretation of Jesus' significance for salvation.

The location of the development of the gospel/Eucharist tradition is evident. Most likely, this appeared in the Greek-speaking church, probably in Antioch; the allusions to Isa 53 presuppose the Greek rather than the Hebrew text. The missionary efforts of Paul and his associates carried this "gospel" to the major cities of the Aegean—Thessalonike, Corinth, and Ephesus. Also the deutero-Pauline letters were written in this geographical area, and the collection of the Pauline corpus was most likely brought together in Ephesus. How this tradition is related to Jerusalem is not clear. But the Jerusalem agreement between Paul, Barnabas, and Titus on the one hand, and James, Peter, and John, on the other hand, would suggest that the authorities in Jerusalem at least did not object to this understanding of the saving significance of the death and resurrection of Jesus. Indeed, the list of people to whom Jesus appeared after his death includes the names of the Jerusalem authorities Peter and James.

It is much more difficult to reconstruct the process in which the tradition of the sayings of Jesus was developed as a continuing instrument for the understanding of salvation. While the genuine Pauline letters were written in the fifties of the first century, there is no direct written documentation for the sayings tradition that can be dated to the time before the year 70 C.E. The Synoptic Sayings Gospel, in the form in which Matthew and Luke knew it, was hardly composed before the end of the Jewish War.[9] This late date is further confirmed by Egon Brandenburger's investigation of Mark 13. He establishes a close connection between the Son-of-Man sayings and the Jewish War or at least the unrest immediately before the war.[10] The *Gospel of Thomas* is certainly based upon earlier collections of sayings. In its extant versions (the Greek fragments and the Coptic translation), however, it must be assigned to some time in the second century. The Gospel of John and the *Dialogue of the Savior* presuppose an interpretation of the sayings of Jesus in which the meaning of these sayings was further explored in the form of dialogues between Jesus and his disciples. But the extant written documents cannot be dated any earlier than to the very end of the first century.

---

[8] Helmut Koester, "The Memory of Jesus' Death and the Worship of the Risen Lord," *HTR* 91 (1998): 335–50.

[9] On the dating of Q see Robinson, Hoffmann, and Kloppenborg, *Critical Edition of Q*, xlviii–lviii. The close relationship of some of the Q material to the events of the Jewish War makes it impossible to uphold a dating around or before 50 C.E.

[10] Egon Brandenburger, *Markus 13 und die Apokalyptik* (FRLANT 134; Göttingen: Vandenhoeck & Ruprecht, 1984).

On the other hand, the understanding of the sayings of Jesus as instruments of salvation must have begun very early after the death of Jesus. But in order to understand this process, it is necessary to investigate the possibility of written sources and oral traditions that were used by the authors of the extant documents. With respect to the second common source for the Gospels of Matthew and Luke, this task has been successfully completed in the publication of the reconstructed document Q. Did this document as it is now reconstructed depend on an earlier written version? In my earlier essay that was published in 1965[11] and then republished in *Trajectories through Early Christianity*,[12] I indicated that there must have been an earlier layer of the sayings tradition. I then followed Kloppenborg's thesis in my later work.[13] But like Kloppenborg, I am fully aware of the hypothetical character of reconstructing an earlier version of a document that is itself the result of a reconstruction, however carefully that reconstruction was done. As far as the *Gospel of Thomas* is concerned, a good many of its sayings can be dated to the first century, perhaps even to a time corresponding to an earlier stage of Q. The judgment here is, however, to a large degree dependent upon finding parallel sayings in the canonical Gospels. Furthermore, it is not certain whether they already expressed a gnosticizing interpretation at the time of their incorporation into the earliest version of the *Gospel of Thomas*. We may be on safer ground with respect to the sayings traditions used in the Gospel of John. These sayings traditions presuppose developments that must have occurred before the writing of the Fourth Gospel: their meaning was explored in the form of dialogues and discourses, and these dialogues interpreted the sayings in a gnosticizing manner.[14]

What geographical locale can be assigned to the development of the sayings tradition as the saving words of Jesus? The Gospel of John contains a number of place names that reveal familiarity with Palestine, especially Samaria, Galilee, and the area of the Jordan Valley. The Samaritans appear as the first converts of Jesus' ministry (John 4). The use of the Son-of-Man title also points to the area of Palestine and Syria outside of Antioch. Even after the acceptance of the passion narrative in the Johannine communities and the composition of the Gospel, the writing must have remained in a fairly isolated location. It was brought to Egypt early in the second century, as the find of Π^{52} demonstrates, but did not reach Asia Minor until the middle of the second century; Polycarp of Smyrna does not yet show any knowledge of the Gospel of John, although he was familiar with the Gospels of Matthew and Luke. Can we therefore locate the tradition of John in a specific area? It would be foolhardy

---

[11] Helmut Koester, "ΓΝΩΜΑΙ ΔΙΑΦΟΡΟΙ: The Origin and Nature of Diversification in the History of Early Christianity," *HTR* 58 (1965): 279–318.

[12] James M. Robinson and Helmut Koester, *Trajectories through Early Christianity* (Philadelphia: Fortress, 1971), 114–57.

[13] Helmut Koester, *Ancient Christian Gospels: Their History and Development* (Philadelphia: Trinity Press International, 1990), 128–71.

[14] Ibid., 173–87.

to suggest a specific place (e.g., Samaria, one of the cities of the Decapolis). On the other hand, some place or places in Greek-speaking Syria and Palestine are likely, while Jerusalem and Antioch and certainly Ephesus can be convincingly excluded.

The *Gospel of Thomas* should be located in some close proximity to the Gospel of John. The latter is the only Gospel in which the apostle Thomas occurs several times. Moreover, Thomas appears to be the one who expects a Gnostic answer from Jesus as, for example, in his quest for the way to the heavenly mansions in John 14. Furthermore, the Gospel of John knows and utilizes a number of sayings that have parallels only in the *Gospel of Thomas*. Even if later the authority of Thomas is primarily used in eastern Syria, these connections to the Fourth Gospel suggest that it originated in the area of southern Syria and Palestine. That is, of course, underlined by the many parallels to the sayings of the *Gospel of Thomas* in the Synoptic tradition (not only in Q, but also in the special materials of Matthew and Luke). Remarkable, however, is the total absence of the Son-of-Man sayings in spite of its close relationship with other Synoptic materials. Thus the tradition contained in the *Gospel of Thomas* was originally closely associated with that preserved in the Synoptic tradition but went a separate path at a fairly early time.

As far as the Synoptic Sayings Gospel Q is concerned, we have unfortunately no particular name that can be assigned as an authority for the tradition it preserves. Names are helpful because they can demonstrate the continuity of a tradition in spite of theological discontinuity. Consider the case of the Pastoral Epistles as part of the Pauline corpus. They certainly belong to the area of the Pauline mission in Western Asia Minor. It would be helpful if we were certain that Papias's remark about "Matthew who composed the sayings" indeed referred to some version of Q.[15] It would establish a link between Q and the Gospel of Matthew and the area of western Syria. This, however, is debated. But there are some telltale signs that point to one specific area rather than to another. It is well-known that names of places in Galilee appear frequently in the sayings of Q, especially in the second stage of Q. It still may be questioned whether this points to Galilee as the location of the sayings in the oral tradition or to the place of Q's final composition.

There is, however, one other indication for the location of the final composition, or at least for the final development of the sayings tradition preserved in Q: the designation of Jesus as the coming Son of Man, which is limited to Q, Mark, and the Gospel of John. Matthew and Luke do not count as independent witnesses because they draw that title, together with the respective

---

[15] On the discussion of the possible relationship of Papias' statement about "Matthew who composed the sayings (τὰ λόγια = "oracles") in the Hebrew language," see Dieter Lührmann, "Q: Sayings of Jesus or Logia?" in *The Gospel Behind the Gospels: Current Studies on Q* (ed. Ronald A. Piper; NovTSup 75; Leiden: Brill, 1995), 97–116. See also Robinson, Hoffmann, and Kloppenborg, *Critical Edition of Q*, xx–xxxiii.

materials, from Mark and Q. Even Mark is not necessarily a direct witness
for the location in which this title originated because the title may have come
to him via the tradition of sayings that are collected in the Synoptic Apocalypse
of Mark 13. This chapter is not an original Markan composition, and while
Mark was written somewhere in Phoenicia or Syria (not in Rome!), chapter 13
must belong to a different locale, namely to Palestine. The title Son of Man
cannot be assigned to the earliest traditions of sayings of Jesus. It is absent in
the *Gospel of Thomas* and never appears in Paul's writings, although Paul was
certainly familiar with some sayings of Jesus. Where and when did the Son-
of-Man sayings arise? I have been impressed by Egon Brandenburger's study
of Mark 13.[16] He argues persuasively that the announcements of the sudden
coming of the Son of Man were prophetic utterances that called the followers
of Jesus away from the growing messianic fervor that permeated the Jewish
society in Galilee and Judea during the years immediately before the Jewish
War. With the prophetic announcement of the expected sudden return of Jesus
as the Son of Man, the followers of Jesus distanced themselves from those
people in Palestine who believed that an uprising against Rome would bring
about the messianic age for Israel. These sayings pronounce that the followers of Jesus should not be engaged in messianically-inspired war and violence.
If Brandenburger's hypothesis is right, we would have to look for the community of Q as well as for the author of the Markan apocalypse somewhere
in Palestine.

There are several reasons, however, which argue against too narrow a local-
ization of Q in Lower Galilee. The Son-of-Man sayings that are at the basis
of the Markan apocalypse point to a wider area. Mark 13:14 says that those
in Judea must flee to the mountains. The final form of Q, on the other hand,
contained an oracle against Jerusalem (Q 13:34–35). The Gospel of John is
also dependent upon the identification of Jesus with the Son of Man, and its
tradition may not have originated in Lower Galilee. It is therefore necessary
to establish a wider geographical area in southern Syria/Palestine as the place
for the development of this sayings tradition and its eventual written form as
it is present in Q.

The essential weakness of the hypothesis that the community of Q with its
traditions of Jesus' sayings was located and remained in Galilee for many years
disregards an important fact about the early expansion of the movement deriv-
ing from Jesus, namely, that the expansion was explosive. Twenty years after
Jesus' death, Paul was already in Macedonia, and a few years later he wrote
to the Romans that from Jerusalem to Illyricum there was no longer any area
in which the gospel had not yet been proclaimed (Rom 15:19). To be sure,
this early expansion also implied a considerable diversity of traditions. But it
is unlikely that any part of this rapidly expanding movement should have got-
ten stuck in the small towns and villages of Lower Galilee for many decades.

---

[16] Brandenburger, *Markus 13 und die Apokalyptik*.

The development of the oral tradition in these circles of followers of Jesus did not take place in a community settled in the same place over more than one generation, but in a quickly moving missionary enterprise. Moreover, as Paul went to the major city centers of the Greek world, it is likely that those who preached salvation through the saving words of Jesus of Nazareth were also on the move. This is reinforced by the fact that the sayings tradition of Q from its very beginning reveals a clear eschatological urgency, driven by the expectation of the coming of the kingdom of God. I may add here in parenthesis that I am not at all impressed by the thesis that the Q people were some kind of wandering Cynic philosophers,[17] although they were certainly a community that was on the move from the rural milieu of Jesus' preaching to the cities of Syria and Palestine. It is interesting that even the *Gospel of Thomas* indicates a change from the rural milieu to the city.[18] It is necessary to draw a circle for the Q community and for its traditions that was much wider than the small town milieu of Lower Galilee.

Two features stand out: (1) this community was either bilingual or Greek-speaking, while the preaching of Jesus seems to have stayed within the rural and small-town Aramaic-speaking world of Galilee; (2) it must have preserved some ties to Jewish people in Palestine (be that Judea and/or Galilee). Evidence for an Aramaic substratum may exist, but it is not very strong. If the *Didache* preserves an Aramaic phrase like *Maranatha*, so does Paul.[19] Certainly there was never a written predecessor of Q in Aramaic, no matter how early one wants to date the earliest version of Q. There were a large number of Greek-speaking cities in Syria, like Damascus, and even in Palestine itself, like Caesarea Maritima and the cities of the Decapolis, which would have allowed for an expansion of the community without direct conflict with the missionary activity of Antioch. On the other hand, even though Gentile mission cannot be excluded,[20] there is an obvious Jewish constituency. There is no polemic against the observance of the Sabbath, although the Pharisees are criticized. (Note that one does not have to go to Jerusalem to find Pharisees. Paul, one of the best-known Pharisees of the time, came from a Greek city outside of Palestine, perhaps from Damascus rather than Tarsus.)

Finally, the Son-of-Man sayings point to a connection with Jewish communities of followers of Jesus in Palestine. The Synoptic Apocalypse (Mark 13) became known outside of Palestine very soon after the Jewish War. Similarly,

---

[17] For literature and a critical discussion of the Cynic hypothesis, see John S. Kloppenborg Verbin, "A Dog Among the Pigeons: The 'Cynic Hypothesis' as a Theological Problem," in *From Quest to Q: Festschrift for James M. Robinson* (ed. John A. Asgeirsson, Kristin de Troyer, and Marvin W. Meyer; Leuven: Leuven University Press, 2000), 73–117. For a recent defense, see Leif E. Vaage, "Jewish Scripture, Q and the Historical Jesus: A Cynic Way with the Word?" in Lindemann, *The Sayings Source Q*, 489–93.

[18] Cf. the Parable of the Banquet, saying #64.

[19] *Did.* 9.6; 1 Cor 16:22.

[20] See again Q 13:28–29.

the written "Gospel" of the community of Q became known in the areas of Antioch's mission at the latest during the seventies of the first century and was used by Matthew in the eighties; a decade later, the same document had been brought to Ephesus, if that was the place where Luke wrote his Gospel. But did Q originate in Jerusalem? Quite unlikely—and certainly not with the Hellenists of the time right after the death of Jesus! Barnabas and most likely also Peter were associated with the "gospel" of Paul, not with the preaching of either the coming kingdom of God or with the expectation of the Son of Man. On the other hand, if the final composition of Q took place only after the Jewish War, Jerusalem is the most unlikely place in the world.

The major writing that emerged from the tradition of Jesus' sayings, namely Q, arrived in the areas of the Pauline mission only after the Jewish War. But smaller collections of sayings that belong to this tradition were known in these areas much earlier. A clean geographical separation of the diverse traditions even in the earlier period of oral transmission is not possible in any case. Paul himself is not unfamiliar with smaller collections of the sayings of Jesus. In Rom 12 he alludes to two sayings that are paralleled in the inaugural sermon of Q.[21] First Corinthians 1–4 reveals that sayings related to the tradition of the *Gospel of Thomas* and to Q had made their way to the wisdom-hungry Corinthians.[22] The author of the Gospel of Mark, who was not familiar with Q, used a number of collections of sayings, apophthegmata, and parables as well as an apocalypse composed of sayings of Jesus. Matthew and Luke, in addition to their use of Q, had access to major collections of sayings and parables of Jesus. A small catechism of Jesus' sayings strayed as far as Rome, where it was used in *1 Clement* 13.[23] On the other hand, Q contained a miracle story of Jesus, and it is indeed the case that some of the Q sayings presuppose a knowledge of Jesus' death and allude to it. The question is not, whether such materials were known but whether they functioned in defining the central religious concern of the community, that is, whether they functioned christologically.[24]

---

[21] For Rom 12:14 and 17, cf. Q/Luke 6:27 and 29; see Koester, *Ancient Christian Gospels*, 53; Charles H. Talbert, "Tradition and Redaction in Romans XII," *NTS* 16 (1969/70): 87.

[22] Helmut Koester, "Gnostic Writings as Witnesses for the Development of the Sayings Tradition," in *The School of Valentinus* (vol. 1 of *The Rediscovery of Gnosticism*; ed. Bentley Layton; NumenSup 41; Leiden: Brill, 1980): 239–61; idem, *Ancient Christian Gospels*, 55–62.

[23] Helmut Koester, *Synoptische Überlieferung bei den apostolischen Vätern* (TU 65; Berlin: Akademie-Verlag, 1957), 12–19; idem, *Ancient Christian Gospels*, 66–68.

[24] On the implicit Christology of the Q tradition, see J. Schlosser, "Q et la christologie implicite," in Lindemann, *The Sayings Source Q*, 289–316.

Was there an Earlier Stage of the Composition of Q?

Birger Pearson, in his address at the 2001 meeting of the Society of Biblical Literature,[25] questioned the possibility of reconstructing an earlier stage of the composition of Q. In a major recent article Paul Hoffmann does the same.[26] I am, of course, partially responsible for the hypothesis of the existence of an earlier stage of the sayings tradition or even its composition in a written document.[27] I did this following the lead of Dieter Lührmann[28] and combining it with my own observation that the Son-of-Man sayings and the judgment sayings of Q left no trace in the sayings tradition that is preserved in the *Gospel of Thomas*. I therefore proposed that there must have been a stage of the development of the sayings tradition that did not contain the Son-of-Man sayings. Furthermore, if arguments for the literary and thematic consistency of Q are problematic,[29] why does the hypothesis of an older written version of Q remain so controversial? The most obvious problem with the reconstruction of Q1 is its bias towards rediscovering the historical Jesus, be he now a prophetic revolutionary or a mild-mannered Cynic philosopher. Moreover, if it is difficult to move from a hypothetical document written shortly after the year 70 (= Q2) to an earlier version of this document written perhaps ten or twenty years earlier, it is perilous to jump from that earlier version of the document over a distance of more than two decades to the historical Jesus.[30] That is especially the case if the reconstruction of that earlier version is dictated by a particular image of the historical Jesus—although John Kloppenborg Verbin cannot be accused of such a motivation. His reconstruction of Q1 is not dictated by an interest in the historical Jesus or by the isolation of theological motifs that distinguish the different layers of Q. Rather, his arguments are based on literary observations.[31]

It is essential that the question of the historical Jesus be excluded from the search for an earlier stage of Q. Just as the passion narrative, even in its earliest stages, cannot tell us anything about the way in which Jesus actually suffered and died, the earliest stage of the sayings tradition or the first written version of Q cannot be considered as a direct witness to the preaching of

---

[25] See above, note 1.

[26] Paul Hoffmann, "Mutmassungen über Q: Zum problem der literarischen Genese von Q," in Lindemann, *The Sayings Source Q*, 255–88.

[27] Koester, "ΓΝΩΜΑΙ ΔΙΑΦΟΡΟΙ," 114–57.

[28] Dieter Lührmann, *Die Redaktion der Logienquelle* (WMANT 33; Neukirchen-Vluyn: Neukirchener Verlag, 1969).

[29] In spite of the efforts of Paul Hoffmann ("Mutmassungen über Q," 255–88), I am not entirely convinced.

[30] See the cogent criticism of such attempts by Dieter Lührmann, "Die Logienquelle und die Leben-Jesus-Forschung," in Lindemann, *The Sayings Source Q*, 191–206.

[31] John S. Kloppenborg, "The Sayings Gospel Q and the Quest for the Historical Jesus," *HTR* 89 (1996): 307–44.

Jesus. On the other hand, those who deny the existence of an earlier written version of Q still face serious problems—*pace* all the difficulties of reconstructing an earlier version of a hypothetical document. The hypothesis of an earlier version of Q has one great advantage: it can explain the transition from a tradition in which the announcement of the coming kingdom of God was the guiding theological principle to a later version that emphasizes instead the coming of Jesus as the Son of Man on the clouds of heaven for the final judgment. I am aware of the fact that this is a history-of-religions rather than a literary argument. That is to say, the reconstruction of Q1 must proceed on the grounds of literary criteria. But the result can be instructive regarding a problem of the religious development within the history of the community of Q.

Philipp Vielhauer's elucidation of the fundamental difference between the proclamation of the kingdom of God and the expectation of the Son of Man, proposed about half a century ago, should not be forgotten.[32] These two different eschatological concepts are not easily reconcilable with each other. As the final version of Q as well as the Synoptic Gospels demonstrate, these two different eschatological expectations could later well be combined into one and the same literary document. The latest version of Q presents an uneasy and conflicting harmonization of the two—clearly a secondary development. It is a development that is not visible in the *Gospel of Thomas* or the letters of Paul. If one wants to throw out the hypothesis of an earlier version of Q, theologically dominated by the proclamation of the impending kingdom of God, it is necessary to explain why this expectation appears in combination with the secondary eschatological concept of the sudden appearance of the Son of Man in the final version of Q. In other words, denying the earlier version of Q does not get rid of the problem; it is simply passing the solution of the problem to the oral tradition.

The Situation of Q and its Traditions in the Life of the Community

Perhaps the challenge should be accepted and the functions of materials in the oral tradition should be explored further, rather than reconstructing an earlier written version of Q. But in more recent research this is burdened with a difficulty, because what form criticism had defined as the *Sitz im Leben* of the oral tradition has now been miraculously metamorphosed into the search for ideas held by individuals vis-à-vis social situations and, moreover, to the search for a social situation in a very small geographical area, such as Lower Galilee. It seems to have become a sacrilege even to speak of the political life situation of a community, not to mention communal religious identity and practices such as preaching, instruction for baptism, ritual, inter-community

---

[32] Philipp Vielhauer, "Reich Gottes und Menschensohn in der Verkündigung Jesu," in *Festschrift für Günther Dehn* (Neukirchen-Vluyn: Neukirchener Verlag, 1957), 51–79.

relationships and moral motivations. Unless future research is liberated from this stranglehold of social definitions as the *Sitz im Leben* and is willing to consider questions of theology, Christology, and religious experience, no progress can be made. Some recent scholarship has not always abided by the definitions of the *Sitz im Leben* as they were proposed in the beginnings of form criticism by Martin Dibelius,[33] Rudolf Bultmann,[34] and others.[35] It is necessary to relate oral traditions as well as any written versions of the sayings tradition to political and religious life situations of a community and to liberate them from their present captivity, as if these traditions were bearers of individuals' ideas regarding narrowly defined social circumstances. It is the great merit of Egon Brandenburger's[36] explanation of the origin of the Son-of-Man sayings that he tried to demonstrate, how political events could leave deep impressions in the understanding of the existence of a community and prompt a fundamental revaluation of previously held convictions. To disregard the momentous impact that the Jewish War must have had for those living in Palestine would be tantamount to saying that the September 11 attack upon the World Trade Center did not have any effects upon the American self-definition as a nation.

If the question of the *Sitz im Leben* is short-circuited to the situation of religious or philosophically concerned individuals in a secular social situation, it is easy to move back from the life situation of such individuals to an analogous situation in the life of another individual, such as Jesus. This, however, is not how *Sitz im Leben* should ever be understood, else we fall once more into the trap of Joachim Jeremias, who tried to find for the Synoptic traditions the *Sitz im Leben Jesu*.[37] Rather, *Sitz im Leben* refers to the situation and function of a tradition in the life of a religious community. What was the situation and function of the traditions incorporated in Q in the life of the religious community that formed and transmitted these traditions? It goes without saying that such an understanding of the situation of traditions in the life of a community cannot be used directly for an understanding of the historical Jesus. Whatever Jesus may have said has been transformed—Kloppenborg uses the term "inscribed"[38]—into tradition on the basis of the life situation of a community, just as the memory of Jesus' suffering and death has been transformed by the image and language of the suffering servant.

It has been repeatedly stated that the Synoptic Sayings Gospel Q does not present enough information about the organization and rituals of the community.

---

[33] Martin Dibelius, *From Tradition to Gospel* (2d ed.; New York: Scribner's, 1934).

[34] Rudolf Bultmann, *The History of the Synoptic Tradition* (2d ed.; New York: Harper, 1968).

[35] For a bibliography see Helmut Koester, "Formgeschichte/Formenkritik II: Neues Testament," *TRE* 11 (1983): 286–99.

[36] See above n. 10.

[37] Joachim Jeremias, "Kennzeichen der ipsissima vox Jesu," in *Synoptische Studien: Festschrift für A. Wikenhauser* (Munich: Zink, 1953), 86–93.

[38] Kloppenborg, "The Sayings Gospel Q," passim.

There may be hints; liturgical materials like the Lord's Prayer are present. Also instructions for the conduct of brothers and sisters in the community can be found. If Q sayings speak about the meal in the coming kingdom of God, does this imply that the community celebrated eschatological thanksgiving meals in anticipation of the coming meal in God's kingdom? Admittedly, Q itself offers only very limited information. There is, however, very ancient liturgical and instructional material preserved in another document, for which a meaningful life situation has not been found, namely the materials in the *Didache*. This book preserves eucharistic prayers about the cup and the bread that do not make explicit reference to the suffering and death of Jesus; it preserves instructions for wandering apostles and prophets; it knows other Synoptic materials that are not dependent upon the canonical Gospels; finally, it presents a form of the Lord's Prayer that is almost identical with, but not dependent upon, the form presented in the Gospel of Matthew.[39]

Most remarkable are the Eucharistic prayers of the *Didache*.[40] These prayers give witness to a community of followers of Jesus who celebrated a meal of the cup and the bread in the expectation of the coming kingdom of God and called for the coming of "the Lord," evident in the final words of the Eucharistic liturgy, *Maranatha*. Cup and bread here have a meaning that is analogous to the Eucharist, to which Paul provides evidence in 1 Cor 10 and 11. In both cases the cup is the symbol of the covenant; in both cases the bread is the symbol of the oneness of the community. But, unlike Paul's words of institution, the prayers of the *Didache* do not reflect on the significance of the death of Jesus. Rather, the prayer for the bread gives thanks "for the life and knowledge that you have revealed through Jesus, your servant."[41] The prayer after the meal gives thanks "for the knowledge, faith, and immortality that you have revealed to us through Jesus, your servant."[42]

Is it possible to relate these Eucharistic prayers to the community of Q? I am not the first to make this suggestion, but I agree that it is most likely that the Q community celebrated a common meal that must have been accompanied by prayers like the ones found in the *Didache*, namely Jewish meal prayers with an eschatological outlook.[43] There is a saying in Q about the coming meal in the kingdom of God (Q 13:28–29). The Lord's Prayer in Q connects the petitions for the coming kingdom and the will of God to be done on earth with the petition for the bread. Someone must have preserved the

---

[39] Koester, *Synoptische Überlieferung*, 203–9; Kurt Niederwimmer, *The Didache: A Commentary* (Hermeneia; Minneapolis: Fortress, 1998), 135–38.

[40] *Did.* 9–10.

[41] *Did.* 9.2.

[42] *Did.* 9.3.

[43] "The next chapters, [*Didache*] 9 and 10, offer an archaic liturgical formula without peer in the early Christian eucharistic liturgy. In *Didache* 9–10 we have the oldest formula for the Christian eucharistic liturgy" (Niederwimmer, *Didache*, 139). For a full discussion of these prayers, see ibid., 139–43.

Eucharistic prayers that belong to a practice of common meals with an eschatological outlook. If this were not the community of Q, we would have to invent a similar community of followers of Jesus. It is another question, whether this meal practice and these prayers derive from Jesus himself.[44] But these are typical Jewish meal prayers,[45] and if the members of the community of Q ever ate together (which is not unlikely), they would have spoken these prayers with an eschatological outlook to the coming kingdom of God. A community that preserved these prayers as part of its central religious ritual had no need to reflect on the death of Jesus, as long as not Jesus' death and resurrection but Jesus' words were the saving message.

As a final note on this question, it is evident that also the following instructions for the reception of apostles and prophets in *Did.* 11.4–12 belong into the context of the milieu of the Q communities.[46] While the instructions for missionaries in Q/Luke 10:2–12 are directed to the apostles regarding their behavior and rights, the instructions of the *Didache* address the communities' behavior with respect to wandering missionaries. The original situation in the life of the community can clearly be seen here. The materials in this section with parallels in Q show that they are analogous to a very early stage of the tradition of sayings of Jesus. This is especially evident in the command not to test any prophet who speaks in the spirit (*Did.* 11.7). In the form in which this command appears here, it predates the more elaborate form preserved in Q/Luke 12:10.[47]

Regarding the understanding of the traditions preserved in the Synoptic Sayings Gospel Q, the life situation of their development is the community. This is underlined by the parallels in the *Didache*. The *Didache* also demonstrates that some of these traditions, such as the exact wording of the Lord's Prayer, the Eucharistic prayers, and the instructions for the reception of missionaries, were committed to writing at an early date, that is, before the production of the Son-of-Man sayings and the crisis of the Jewish War.[48] It is all the more probable that also the final editor of Q relied on an earlier written compilation of relevant sayings of Jesus that communities outside of the circle of the mission of Antioch and the Pauline churches had developed, probably in the

---

[44] Koester, "The Memory of Jesus' Death," 335–50.

[45] Niederwimmer, *Didache*, 140 and special references to Jewish prayer parallels on the following pages in the commentary.

[46] With respect to the instructions for the reception of apostles, Niederwimmer (*Didache*, 173) writes: "The subject here is an archaic institution, preceded by the group of Jesus disciples and spreading thereafter within certain regions of the post-Easter church. . . . It should probably be located in the border region between Syria and Palestine."

[47] Niederwimmer, *Didache*, 179: "Our version of the Logion can scarcely be traced to Mark/Matthew or to Q (or Matthew/Luke), but probably presents a separate form of the tradition." See also Koester, *Synoptische Überlieferung*, 215–17; idem, *Ancient Christian Gospels*, 92–93.

[48] Note that a reference to the Son of Man is missing in the saying *Did.* 10.7 (cf. Q/Luke 12:10); see Niederwimmer, *Didache*, 179.

forties or fifties of the first century, in an area of Syria and Palestine outside of, but not unrelated to Galilee and Judea. Kloppenborg's reconstruction of Q^1 indeed has a lot of merit, especially since it is done on the basis of a literary analysis and not in the search for the historical Jesus, although I myself would be inclined to give a greater value to the external witness of the *Gospel of Thomas* in such a reconstruction. The final redaction of Q, however, cannot be dated until the end of the Jewish War. The further redaction of Q, the question of a Q-Matthew and a Q-Luke, and the question of the Sermon on the Mount as a dependent document are issues to be addressed at another time.[49]

---

[49] If the Sermon on the Mount, as reconstructed by Hans Dieter Betz (*The Sermon on the Mount: A Commentary on the Sermon of the Mount, including the Sermon on the Plain* [Hermeneia; Minneapolis: Fortress, 1995]), is dependent upon Q^2, it must also be dated to a time after the Jewish War.

CHAPTER THREE

ON COMPARING Q AND THE *GOSPEL OF THOMAS*

Ron Cameron

It has been nearly thirty years now since John Dominic Crossan undertook
"an archaeology of the parables of Jesus" using the *Gospel of Thomas*, together
with the synoptics, to propose "new ways of imagining" the "challenge of the
historical Jesus" proclaimed eschatologically *In Parables*.[1] Crossan would develop
his parable theory with a structural analysis of story types, ranging from myths
at one end of the spectrum to parables at the other, in *The Dark Interval*,[2] and
apply his literary methods to establish a "generative model" for a "transmis-
sional analysis" of the "aphorisms of Jesus" *In Fragments* found in Mark and
Q, and parallels.[3] Taking seriously Helmut Koester's "challenge [to] the scholarly world to write the literary history of the gospels in early Christianity [by]
considering all gospel materials which are available,"[4] Crossan has discussed
Four Other Gospels[5] and then, in the first of three substantial studies, taken up
the origins of the "passion and resurrection narrative" in *The Cross That Spoke*,[6]
which he revised and reissued in a popularizing account of *Who Killed Jesus?*[7]
Crossan's next major contribution addressed forthrightly the embarrassing
fact that, in his words, "historical Jesus research is becoming something of a
scholarly bad joke."[8] Accordingly, methodological issues were placed front and
center in his reconstruction of *The Historical Jesus: The Life of a Mediterranean
Jewish Peasant*. Invoking an archaeological model of research, Crossan proposed

---

[1] John Dominic Crossan, *In Parables: The Challenge of the Historical Jesus* (New York:
Harper & Row, 1973; repr., Sonoma, Calif.: Polebridge, 1992), 35, 33, 14, xiii.

[2] John Dominic Crossan, *The Dark Interval: Towards a Theology of Story* (Niles, Ill.:
Argus Communications, 1975; repr., Sonoma, Calif.: Polebridge, 1988), 9, 55, 59, 62.

[3] John Dominic Crossan, *In Fragments: The Aphorisms of Jesus* (San Francisco: Harper
& Row, 1983), 315, ix, viii.

[4] Cited in Bruce Corley, "Seminar Dialogue with Helmut Koester," in *Colloquy on
New Testament Studies: A Time for Reappraisal and Fresh Approaches* (ed. Bruce Corley; Macon,
Ga.: Mercer University Press, 1983), 62; cf. Helmut Koester, "History and Development
of Mark's Gospel (From Mark to *Secret Mark* and 'Canonical' Mark)," in *Colloquy on
New Testament Studies*, 35–57.

[5] John Dominic Crossan, *Four Other Gospels: Shadows on the Contours of Canon* (Minneapolis:
Winston, 1985), 183.

[6] John Dominic Crossan, *The Cross That Spoke: The Origins of the Passion Narrative* (San
Francisco: Harper & Row, 1988), 17.

[7] John Dominic Crossan, *Who Killed Jesus? Exposing the Roots of Anti-Semitism in the
Gospel Story of the Death of Jesus* (San Francisco: Harper San Francisco, 1995), 11.

[8] John Dominic Crossan, *The Historical Jesus: The Life of a Mediterranean Jewish Peasant*
(San Francisco: Harper San Francisco, 1991), xxvii.

a stratigraphic method of investigation, combining social anthropology, Greco-Roman history, and a literary analysis based on an inventory of all canonical and noncanonical texts, their stratification in proper chronological sequence, and their attestation in multiple, independent sources, privileging as "original" those sayings and stories that are found in his first stratum, which Crossan dates from 30 to 60 C.E.[9] This stratigraphic model has been extended in Crossan's latest book on *Excavating Jesus*, which seeks to integrate archaeology and exegesis by means of a "parallel layering," that is, by "excavat[ing] down or back to the archaeological layer of Jesus' world and the textual stratum of Jesus' life."[10]

The Birth of Christianity is one of the most recent of Crossan's considerable publications and the most important for comparing Q and the *Gospel of Thomas*. Presupposing his findings on parables and aphorisms, the *Gospel of Peter*, and the historical Jesus, Crossan turns here to "the lost years of earliest Christianity . . . the 30s and 40s of the first century . . . [to discover what happened in] those dark decades immediately after the execution of Jesus."[11] Although he both begins and ends his book with reference to the resurrection of Jesus, Crossan argues that a "vision, apparition, or resurrection . . . of a dead man . . . is not special enough of itself to explain anything." He therefore proposes the following thesis: "the birth of Christianity is the interaction between the historical Jesus and his first companions and the continuation of that relationship despite his execution."[12] Whereas, for Crossan, "Christianity's conception was the kingdom-of-God movement as Jesus and his first companions lived in radical but nonviolent resistance to Herod Antipas's urban development and Rome's rural commercialism in Lower Galilee of the late 20s," Christianity's "birth was in that movement's continuation as those same companions wrestled not only to imitate Jesus' life but also to understand Jesus' death." The focus of Crossan's work is thus on "*continuation*, on the linkage between the historical Jesus and earliest Christianity that is for [him] the birth of Christianity."[13]

The model that Crossan proposed for historical Jesus research has been refined and adopted here, in *The Birth of Christianity*, as an interdisciplinary

---

[9] Ibid., xxviii, xxxi, xxxii, 427–29, 434–43. For a critique of Crossan's method, see Christopher M. Tuckett, "The Historical Jesus, Crossan and Methodology," in *Text und Geschichte: Facetten theologischen Arbeitens aus dem Freundes- und Schülerkreis. Dieter Lührmann zum 60. Geburtstag* (ed. Stefan Maser and Egbert Schlarb; Marburger theologische Studien 50; Marburg: Elwert, 1999), 257–79.

[10] John Dominic Crossan and Jonathan L. Reed, *Excavating Jesus: Beneath the Stones, Behind the Texts* (San Francisco: HarperSanFrancisco, 2001), xvii, xviii; cf. 10–14, 36–39, 272–76.

[11] John Dominic Crossan, *The Birth of Christianity: Discovering What Happened in the Years Immediately After the Execution of Jesus* (San Francisco: HarperSanFrancisco, 1998), ix. See François Bovon, "A Review of John Dominic Crossan's *The Birth of Christianity*," *HTR* 94 (2001): 369–74.

[12] Crossan, *Birth of Christianity*, xviii, xxi.

[13] Ibid., x, 2 (emphasis his); cf. 15.

method for the study of Christian origins. It consists of three stages, to be taken up in the following order: (1) combining cross-cultural anthropology, Judeo-Roman history, and lower Galilean archaeology, to establish "the sharpest possible reconstruction of the context"; (2) stratifying the texts according to their literary contents, to determine "the earliest possible layer of the tradition"; and (3) seeking a conjunction of context and text, to construct "the tightest possible linkage" between that reconstructed "context and that earliest layer of text." If the "earliest layer [of a text] speak[s] from and to the situation of the 20s in Lower Galilee," then that, Crossan argues, is "the best reconstruction of [both] the historical Jesus and his [first] companions presently available."[14]

When he turns his analysis to the texts of the gospels, Crossan begins with a "comparison" of Q and the *Gospel of Thomas* in terms of the "formal structure" of the texts, their "common genre," and finally—and "most important"—the "stratification of [their] content." Since Q and *Thomas* share "about one-third of their content in common," their common corpus of sayings—what Crossan calls the "Common Sayings Tradition" that has been "absorbed into" Q and the *Gospel of Thomas*—is explained chiefly in terms of similarities. Moreover, since "stratification refers to evidence of successive layering of content within a text," a comparative stratigraphy is concerned not simply with "discerning where later material has been added to earlier material," but with "whether there are direct connections between discernible stratification processes" in Q and *Thomas*.[15] Accepting the arguments of William E. Arnal that, "on formal and thematic grounds," the *Gospel of Thomas* is "a stratified document," the product of "a social history" no less than Q,[16] and of Stephen J. Patterson that the tradition common to Q and *Thomas* may be inventoried according to the redactional tendencies of each gospel,[17] Crossan correlates the parallel content of these gospels with a corresponding stratification of the tradition, emphasizing how Q and *Thomas* "have divergently redacted their common content."[18] Note, however, that Crossan does not undertake a compositional stratigraphy of either Q or the *Gospel of Thomas*. Rather, he appeals to John S. Kloppenborg's observation that "tradition-history is not convertible with *literary history*,"[19] to argue that "some of the materials that an author used as the first layer of a composition could [have] be[en] created at that very moment, and some of the ones inserted as a second layer could have been

---

[14] Ibid., 147, 149; cf. 140, 247, 325, 330.

[15] Ibid., 239, 241, 245, 247, 238, 101, 247; cf. 587–89.

[16] William E. Arnal, "The Rhetoric of Marginality: Apocalypticism, Gnosticism, and Sayings Gospels," *HTR* 88 (1995): 476, 474.

[17] Stephen J. Patterson, "Wisdom in Q and *Thomas*," in *In Search of Wisdom: Essays in Memory of John G. Gammie* (ed. Leo G. Perdue, Bernard Brandon Scott, and William Johnston Wiseman; Louisville, Ky.: Westminster/John Knox, 1993), 194–97.

[18] Crossan, *Birth of Christianity*, 230, 249–55, 238; cf. 589–91.

[19] John S. Kloppenborg, *The Formation of Q: Trajectories in Ancient Wisdom Collections* (SAC; Philadelphia: Fortress, 1987; repr., Harrisburg, Pa.: Trinity Press International, 1999), 245 (emphasis his); cf. Crossan, *Birth of Christianity*, 250.

there from long before." A "compositional stratification" tells one "nothing . . . about the comparative dates of those layers," it is claimed, but "only about the successive moments when an author brought them together." And so, since Crossan is "concerned with the more fundamental question of traditional stratification," with "the sequence in which a tradition was created," his method is to "tak[e] elements out of their present contextual positions" in Q and the *Gospel of Thomas* and "relocate them" within the life of the historical Jesus and his first followers in Lower Galilee. Accordingly, Crossan's "comparative stratigraphy" amounts to establishing an inventory of the parallel contents of Q and *Thomas*—not a literary layering of the texts—and developing a "typology" of "the tradition's trajectory," based on whether that common corpus of sayings has been "redacted internally toward [asceticism and] Gnosticism in the *Gospel of Thomas* or toward apocalypticism" in Q.[20]

When Crossan begins to assess the trajectory of "this early tradition," the first text he considers is the unit about John and Jesus in Q 7:24–27, 28 and *Gos. Thom.* 46, 78. I cite the latter passage in *Thomas*, since Crossan starts with this saying, which he refers to by the title "*Into the Desert*":[21]

> Jesus said, "Why have you come out to the countryside? To see a reed shaken by the wind? And to see a [person] clothed in soft garments [like your] kings and your princes? They are clothed in soft [garments] and cannot recognize truth." (*Gos. Thom.* 78)

The "unredacted Common Sayings Tradition," Crossan argues, was "*original[ly]*" neither Gnostic nor apocalyptic but "eschatological" and "world negati[ng]."[22] The circular evidence that is offered for such a judgment is the following: "The primary indication that the Common Sayings Tradition was eschatological is that it, like [Q] and the *Gospel of Thomas* after it, speaks repeatedly of the kingdom of God. . . . Kingdom eschatology did not arise in either [Q] or the *Gospel of Thomas*. It was already there in the Common Sayings Tradition." Accordingly, Crossan maintains that "the Common Sayings Tradition knows about apocalyptic eschatology from the teaching of John the Baptist and . . . negates [it] in favor of [Jesus'] kingdom-of-God program." The "earliest *non*-apocalyptic eschatology" that can be found is, therefore, "already an *anti*-apocalyptic one. In the beginning was John the Baptist, not Jesus."[23]

Since John is not mentioned by name in *Gos. Thom.* 78, "the important question" for Crossan is whether "the Common Sayings Tradition . . . [originally]

---

[20] Crossan, *Birth of Christianity*, 250, 147, 148, 253, 255; cf. 265, 271, 273, 589.

[21] Ibid., 255, 273, 305, 306 (emphasis his), 307. The critical text of the *Gospel of Thomas* is published in Bentley Layton, ed., *Nag Hammadi Codex II,2–7 together with XIII,2*, Brit. Lib. Or.4926(1), and P. Oxy. 1, 654, 655*, vol. 1 (2 vols.; NHS 20; Leiden: Brill, 1989). All translations of the Coptic text are my own.

[22] Crossan, *Birth of Christianity*, 256, 255 (emphasis his), 258; cf. 257–60, 274–75, 282, 305.

[23] Ibid., 282–83, 305 (emphasis his); cf. 309, 311, 316, 603; Crossan, *Historical Jesus*, 236–38, 292.

applie[d] the saying to John the Baptist" (as Q 7:24–25, 26 does), and thus, whether *Thomas* "removed" that application, presenting instead a "truncated version of the common tradition" preserved in Q. Moreover, since *Thomas*'s version of this saying neither characterizes John as a "prophet" (as Q 7:26 does) nor, crucially, includes a quotation of Mal 3:1; cf. 4:5—influenced by the wording of Exod 23:20—(as Q 7:27 does), one must ask whether Q has elaborated the tradition, or whether the absence of such references in *Gos. Thom.* 78 means that *Thomas* has "reject[ed]," and thus "eliminate[d]," the "apocalyptic eschatology" attributed to "John the Baptist [and his movement]," offering instead a "general . . . admonition against power and luxury."[24] Accepting the thesis of Gerd Theissen, that "the very mention of 'reed' links the saying explicitly with Herod Antipas," on whose "coins, which he had minted for the founding of his capital city, Tiberias (ca. 19 C.E.) . . . the reed appears,"[25] Crossan's argument is that, "even if [t]his 'reed' argument is too specific, it is hard to imagine this saying except in some conjunction with the conflict between desert and palace, between John and Antipas, and most likely after the former's execution by the latter."[26]

The problem with Crossan's reading of these sayings is that Q 7:18–35—not simply Q 7:24–26, 27, 28—is not only composite, with shifts in characterization and focus from Jesus, to John, and the community of Q, but that the entire pericope has been composed rhetorically on purpose.[27] Indeed, as "the critical text for working out the shift in discourse and ideology that took place" between the formative (Q^1) and the redactional (Q^2) strata of Q, this pericope was constructed, according to the Greco-Roman pattern of elaboration of the chreia, as an argument. Its "purpose was mythmaking at a certain juncture in Q's social history," a juncture that "had to do with rationalizing rejection and justifying the use of the language of judgment. . . . Fundamental to the entire operation is the identification of a chreia . . . at the core of the pericope,"[28] whose position on Jesus' identity and activity provided the logic and rationale for the elaboration to follow. The characterization of John as a "prophet" and, especially, Q's quotation of authoritative scripture—a conflation from Mal 3:1 and Exod 23:20, marking the first attested instance in early Christianity in which either of these texts is cited—mean that God's chosen envoy (who is called Elijah, the prophet, in the appendix in Mal 4:5) is identified as John and linked to the covenant code. The Hebrew epic and prophetic

---

[24] Crossan, *Birth of Christianity*, 306, 307, 308; cf. 305–6, 310.

[25] Ibid., 307; citing Gerd Theissen, *The Gospels in Context: Social and Political History in the Synoptic Tradition* (trans. Linda M. Maloney; Minneapolis: Fortress, 1991), 28.

[26] Crossan, *Birth of Christianity*, 308; cf. 230–33.

[27] See Ron Cameron, " 'What Have You Come Out To See?' Characterizations of John and Jesus in the Gospels," in *The Apocryphal Jesus and Christian Origins* (ed. Ron Cameron; *Semeia* 49; Atlanta: Scholars Press, 1990), 35–69.

[28] Burton L. Mack, "All the Extra Jesuses: Christian Origins in the Light of the Extra-Canonical Gospels," in *Apocryphal Jesus and Christian Origins*, 174, 175.

traditions were thus united. Linking John and Jesus together, and identifying John as his predicted precursor, serve to merge Jesus' "wisdom" with John's "prophecy." The chreia and its elaboration were thus designed to establish Jesus along with John as a founder allied with the prevailing currents of their Jewish heritage. Jesus is positioned with respect to the prophetic tradition, as well as distinguished by his appearance at the beginning of that new movement which the Q community imagined itself to be. These sayings thus originated in a group situation in which deliberations were taking place in response to contrasting claims about the identity of Jesus and the legacy of a community. Apocalyptic language was entertained on that occasion to reflect upon the rationale of the group's character. Bringing John into the discussion presented the opportunity to meditate on Jesus' sagacity by using John's activity as a foil. Accordingly, these sayings are not "reports" about Jesus or John, but "highly crafted anecdotes in the interest of a very selective memory."[29] The rhetorical problem facing this stage of the redaction of Q was how to incorporate the apocalyptic imagery secondarily ascribed to its founders and members with the full consciousness that John and Jesus did not really appear apocalyptic. As such, the conceptual concerns sustaining this entire pericope are governed by a sapiential way of viewing the world, not an apocalyptic vision.[30]

The next text of "primary importance" in Crossan's argument is a saying that "*concerns and replaces* apocalyptic eschatology," which he refers to by the title "*When and Where.*" It is a "complex unit involving multiple independent sources," as well as "multiple versions within the *Gospel of Thomas* itself," found in Q 17:23–24; Mark 13:21–23 par.; (special) Luke 17:20–21; and *Gos. Thom.* 3, 18, 51, 113.[31] I cite the principal version of this saying in *Thomas*, which is found at the end of the gospel:

> His disciples said to him, "When is the kingdom going to come?"
> "It is not going to come by waiting for it. They will not say, 'Look, here!' or 'Look, there!' Rather, the kingdom of the father is spread out over the earth, and people don't see it." (*Gos. Thom.* 113)

Emphasizing the unit's "common structure," "common elements," and "common matrix," Crossan posits a single "core saying" underlying the various sources and versions of the tradition, which "points to an alternative eschatological program—one that is present rather than future."[32] Note, however, that Crossan's reconstructed "saying" is synthetic, is of doubtful inclusion in Q,[33] is securely

---

[29] Burton L. Mack, "Anecdotes and Arguments: The Chreia in Antiquity and Early Christianity" (The Institute for Antiquity and Christianity Occasional Papers 10; Claremont, Calif.: Institute for Antiquity and Christianity, 1987), 39.

[30] For a critique of Crossan's use of the category of eschatology, see Ron Cameron, "The Anatomy of a Discourse: On 'Eschatology' as a Category for Explaining Christian Origins," *MTSR* 8 (1996): 231–45.

[31] Crossan, *Birth of Christianity*, 318, 311 (emphasis his).

[32] Ibid., 312, 315, 316, 306; cf. Crossan, *Historical Jesus*, 282–83.

[33] See Kloppenborg, *Formation of Q*, 154–55; idem, *Q Parallels: Synopsis, Critical Notes,*

attested only in special Lukan material and the *Gospel of Thomas*—not the Common Sayings Tradition preserved in both Q and *Thomas*[34]—and has been reconstructed from a variety of texts which agree, literally, only in "say[ing], 'Look, here!' or 'There!' " For, though Crossan regards all of the texts which he groups together in this unit as independent variants or "versions" of a single saying preserved in "four mutually independent sources" (Q, Mark, Luke, and *Thomas*), it is important to note not only that "the common elements" of this "single . . . matrix saying can be seen most clearly" in (special) Luke 17:20–21 and *Gos. Thom.* 113,[35] but also—and especially—that these elements are found only in Luke and *Thomas*. What is specific about the version(s) of this saying in the *Gospel of Thomas* and the synoptics, what actually constitutes the putative "common matrix," is not unambiguously attested in Q at all. The relation of Luke 17:20–21 to its larger Q context and the question of the possible inclusion of these verses in Q are debated in scholarship, with some scholars regarding Luke 17:20–21 as a "variant" of Q 17:23–24;[36] others arguing that, despite the absence of a clear parallel in Matthew, the repetitive "Look, here!" in Luke 17:21, 23 suggests that both verses "reproduce what was originally *one* single saying" (as in *Gos. Thom.* 113), from which Luke 17:20 "is [also] derived";[37] others proposing that the "doublet" in Luke 17:21 (// Matt 24:26) and Q 17:23 (// Matt 24:23; cf. Mark 13:21) indicates that Luke took one version of the saying from Mark and the other, either from "oral tradition" or from Q, to which Luke 17:20–21 could then be assigned;[38] and others maintaining that the similarities between, and among, all these sayings are due chiefly to their being linked by an "allegedly common theme": the coming of the kingdom, the Son of man, or the Christ.[39] Nevertheless, Crossan has violated his own method here, of using "only units with secure attestation in both Matthew and Luke" to determine what is said to be present in the Common Sayings Tradition.[40]

---

and Concordance (Foundations and Facets: Reference Series; Sonoma, Calif.: Polebridge, 1988), 188–89; James M. Robinson, Paul Hoffmann, and John S. Kloppenborg, eds., *The Critical Edition of Q* (Hermeneia Supplements; Minneapolis: Fortress; Leuven: Peeters, 2000), 494–99.

[34] *Pace* Crossan, *Birth of Christianity*, 587; cf. 254, 311, 312, 315, 316.

[35] Ibid., 311, 315–16.

[36] So, e.g., Rudolf Bultmann, *Die Geschichte der synoptischen Tradition* (9th ed.; FRLANT 29; Göttingen: Vandenhoeck & Ruprecht, 1979), 128.

[37] So, e.g., Helmut Koester, "Q and Its Relatives," in *Gospel Origins and Christian Beginnings: In Honor of James M. Robinson* (ed. James E. Goehring et al.; Forum Fascicles; Sonoma, Calif.: Polebridge, 1990), 59 n. 45, 63 (emphasis his).

[38] So, e.g., James M. Robinson, "The Study of the Historical Jesus after Nag Hammadi," in *The Historical Jesus and the Rejected Gospels* (ed. Charles W. Hedrick; *Semeia* 44; Atlanta: Scholars Press, 1988), 50–53.

[39] So, e.g., Joseph A. Fitzmyer, *The Gospel According to Luke (X–XXIV)* (AB 28A; Garden City, N.Y.: Doubleday, 1985), 1158, 1159.

[40] Crossan, *Birth of Christianity*, 587. Similarly, in his discussion of *The Historical Jesus*, Crossan has even more explicitly violated his own methodological principles by interpreting

If "the kingdom of God is present upon the earth already . . . *how* is it present?" The primary text which answers that question and, in Crossan's view, "affirm[s]" that, for Jesus and his first followers, the kingdom was "marked" by an *"ethical eschatology,"* is a unit found in Q 10:4–11; Mark 6:7–13 par.; and *Gos. Thom.* 14, which Crossan refers to by the title *"Mission and Message."*[41] I cite the saying as it is presented in the *Gospel of Thomas*:

> Jesus said to them, "If you fast, you will bring sin upon yourselves; and if you pray, you will be condemned; and if you give alms, you will do harm to your spirits. And if you go into any land and walk through the country-side, if they receive you, eat whatever is set before you and attend to the sick among them. For what goes into your mouth will not defile you; rather, what comes out of your mouth—that will defile you." (*Gos. Thom.* 14)

For Crossan, this is "the most important unit for understanding the historical Jesus, the Common Sayings Tradition, and the continuity from one to another. It is where [he] see[s] the continuation from the historical Jesus to his first companions most clearly. . . . It is also, for [him], the clearest evidence that Jesus and his earliest companions had not just a vision but a program, not just an idea but a plan."[42] Since Crossan understands this unit to be "the heart of the Common Sayings Tradition," he regards "its presence [as] mak[ing] that corpus coherent and help[ing] all the other units fall into place." Accordingly, he "interpret[s] many ambiguous sayings and open aphorisms from the Common Sayings Tradition in light of this complex."[43] Most of all, "this is the unit where," Crossan states, *"text* moves into closest *conjunction* with *context,* and therefore where [his] method succeeds or fails most fully and absolutely."[44] As he indicated in his book on *The Historical Jesus,* his wager has been that this unit is "the heart of Jesus' program. . . . If that is incorrect, this book will have to be redone."[45]

Since, as Crossan puts it, "all now stands or falls on detailed readings of specific sayings," let me clear up, first, one important detail in translation, and

---

the "symbolic destruction" of the Temple as involving, "originally," "an *action*" (as in Mark 11:15–19 par.) accompanied by "a *saying*" (as in *Gos. Thom.* 71) that "led directly to Jesus' arrest and execution," despite the fact that there is "no plural [textual] attestation *linking*" that "destruction and Jesus' execution" (idem, *Historical Jesus,* 357, 358, 359, 360 [emphases his]). For a critique of this reading of *Gos. Thom.* 71, see Ron Cameron, "Ancient Myths and Modern Theories of the Gospel of Thomas and Christian Origins," *MTSR* 11 (1999): 236–57, esp. 239–44; repr. in *Redescribing Christian Origins* (ed. Ron Cameron and Merrill P. Miller; SBLSymS; Atlanta: Society of Biblical Literature, forthcoming).

[41] Crossan, *Birth of Christianity,* 316, 317, 325 (emphases his); cf. 258, 284, 318. Note that this is a "Type 3" saying, "redacted both toward asceticism in the *Gospel of Thomas* and toward apocalypticism in [Q]," which has been inadvertently listed as an unredacted "Type 4" saying in Crossan's Appendix IB (ibid., 325, 590).

[42] Ibid., 325–26.

[43] Ibid., 326, 325.

[44] Ibid., 326 (emphasis his); cf. 280, 330, 335.

[45] Crossan, *Historical Jesus,* 304; idem, *Birth of Christianity,* 325.

thus of the discussion, of this pericope: a simple matter of syntax. Whereas Crossan understands *Thomas*'s version of this saying to describe "a regular situation or a normal occurrence" of "radical itinerancy,"[46] a time "when" they would go out, walk about, and be received, the Coptic uses the conditional "if" without the Greek temporal particle (ὅταν, "when"). We are dealing here with a hypothetical situation, not a historical report. *Gos. Thom.* 14 is, in fact, marked by conditionals: "if you fast . . . if you pray . . . if you give alms . . . if you go into any land . . . if they receive you." The questions that are set up thematically in saying 6, about whether (according to the Coptic text) or how (according to the Greek) the disciples should fast, pray, give alms, and observe a certain diet, are revisited here in legal terms.[47] Underlying the reference to "eat[ing] whatever is set before you and attend[ing] to the sick . . . if they receive you" is a legal issue. The question being raised concerns the etiquette of host-guest relationships; the implication is that a superordinate principle of equity takes precedence over law. The practices itemized in sayings 6 and 14 are markers, the kind of discriminations that create social boundaries and group identity. For this reason, the setting in which such concerns were discussed has to be, not itinerancy, but the *didaskaleion*, the study group, the scribal school.

Crossan's method requires that there "be some validly established context in which [to] relocate" elements of the sayings that he "tak[es] . . . out of their present contextual positions" in Q and the *Gospel of Thomas*, lest they "become meaningless words and deeds."[48] Since what he identifies as the "basic," "key elements" of this unit—"itinerancy," "eating," and "healing"—are present "only . . . residually" in *Thomas*, Crossan says that they "must, therefore, be earlier tradition," an index of continuity in lifestyle adopted by the Jesus movement, which he describes as "a dialectic of itinerants and householders" that "goes back as early into the tradition as [he] can trace the evidence," indeed, into the "life of the historical Jesus" himself.[49] But as Philip Sellew has reminded us:

> Our ease in extracting a statement from its textual life into the never-never land of scholarly reconstruction is in and of itself no defense of the procedure. . . . We have no more license to treat *Thomas* as a quarry to be mined for Jesus talk, consciously or heedlessly oblivious to literary and compositional realities, than we should have in the case of other Christian texts, be they narrative gospels in their basic orientation or sayings gospels.[50]

---

[46] Crossan, *Birth of Christianity*, 292, 327–28.

[47] See Bultmann, *Geschichte der synoptischen Tradition*, 139.

[48] Crossan, *Birth of Christianity*, 147–48.

[49] Ibid., 327, 329, 353, 407; cf. 328, 330, 404. For a critique of the itinerancy hypothesis, see Arnal, "Rhetoric of Marginality," 480–92; idem, *Jesus and the Village Scribes: Galilean Conflicts and the Setting of Q* (Minneapolis: Fortress, 2001).

[50] Philip Sellew, "The *Gospel of Thomas*: Prospects for Future Research," in *The Nag Hammadi Library after Fifty Years: Proceedings of the 1995 Society of Biblical Literature Commemoration* (ed. John D. Turner and Anne McGuire; NHMS 44; Leiden: Brill, 1997), 334–35.

Moreover, as Sellew observed in an essay on the very texts under discussion:

> The lack of any interpretive narrative context makes the function of these
> sayings in Thomas quite clear. Their meaning . . . cannot be imagined to
> represent any sort of annalistic record of Jesus' supposed words and deeds
> at particular temporal and geographical moments, but rather to appro-
> priate his authority on questions of contemporary belief and practice.
> What is generally (though not universally [or consistently]) conceded to
> be happening in the New Testament gospels thus cannot be disputed
> when interpreting the Gospel of Thomas: the "living Jesus" is speaking
> to his followers in their own circumstances, through the literary device of
> conversation between the master and his students.[51]

Even though Crossan entitles his discussion of Q and the *Gospel of Thomas* "a
comparison of two early gospels,"[52] by emphasizing their similarities he priv-
ileges what he calls the common content, common corpus, common elements,
common genre, common matrix, and common structure of the Common
Sayings Tradition. Here we should recall that a "principled postulation of similarity . . . is the ground of the methical comparison of *difference* being interesting." Therefore, "what is required is the development of a [redescriptive]
discourse of 'difference,' a complex term which invites negotiation, classification
and comparison, and, at the same time, avoids too easy a discourse of the
'same.'"[53] As Jonathan Z. Smith has argued:

> It is axiomatic that comparison is never a matter of identity. Comparison
> requires the acceptance of difference as the grounds of its being interesting,
> and a methodical manipulation of that difference to achieve some stated cog-
> nitive end. The questions of comparison are questions of judgment with respect
> to difference: What differences are to be maintained in the interests of com-
> parative inquiry? What differences can be defensibly relaxed and relativized
> in light of the intellectual tasks at hand?[54]

Lacking an adequate theory of comparison, Crossan has consistently collapsed
the significance of difference and engaged, instead, in a discourse of the same.
This may be seen, for example, in the way he insists upon continuity and tradition history, as opposed to a literary layering, of Q or the *Gospel of Thomas*. To
argue that a "stratigraphic analysis of Q does not imply that materials incorporated at a secondary stage were unknown at the first"[55] permits us—whether

---

[51] Philip Sellew, "Pious Practice and Social Formation in the Gospel of Thomas:
Thomas 6, 14, 27, 53, 104," *Foundations and Facets Forum* 10 (1994): 49.

[52] Crossan, *Birth of Christianity*, 239.

[53] Jonathan Z. Smith, *Drudgery Divine: On the Comparison of Early Christianities and the
Religions of Late Antiquity* (Jordan Lectures in Comparative Religion 14; London: School
of Oriental and African Studies, University of London; Chicago: University of Chicago
Press, 1990), 53 (emphasis mine), 42.

[54] Jonathan Z. Smith, *To Take Place: Toward Theory in Ritual* (CSHJ; Chicago: University
of Chicago Press, 1987), 13–14; idem, *Drudgery Divine*, 47.

[55] John S. Kloppenborg, "The Sayings Gospel Q and the Quest of the Historical

consciously or not—to continue to imagine the beginnings of Christianity the same way as before. That won't do. Even if "tradition-history is not convertible with *literary history*,"[56] surely there must be a way "to situate" the sayings in Q and *Thomas* "within some plausible social-historical contexts, contexts in and for which those sayings were created. For without a correlation of literary history and social history, one lacks the means to clarify and control the placement of [those] sayings in such a way that renders them intelligible."[57]

Moreover, by conflating sayings from both the formative (Q[1]) and the redactional (Q[2]) strata of Q, together with their parallels in *Thomas*, into a single first stratum of tradition, and by beginning his discussion with John and Jesus (from Q[2]), Crossan simply reproduces the dominant (gospel) paradigm of Christian origins (cf. Mark 1:2–3 par.).[58] And so, despite all Crossan's emphasis on "the problem of methodology,"[59] his "frame of reference for the historical description of Christian origins continues to be the New Testament picture itself,"[60] which he paraphrases by following the narrative account of the events in the canonical gospels[61] and "correlate[s] with [an implicit] theor[y] of religion . . . focused on personal experience, transforming events, and dramatic breakthroughs."[62] Accordingly, what Crossan has given us is a theology of Christian origins, not a history of Christian beginnings.[63] For the latter, another kind of comparison will have to be undertaken, which does not start with the historical Jesus, end up at the resurrection, reinscribe origins, privilege continuity, paraphrase the canonical gospels, and equate theory with method.[64]

Jesus," *HTR* 89 (1996): 337; cf. idem, *Formation of Q*, 244–45; John S. Kloppenborg Verbin, *Excavating Q: The History and Setting of the Sayings Gospel* (Edinburgh: T&T Clark, 2000), 151.

[56] Kloppenborg, *Formation of Q*, 245 (emphasis his); cf. Crossan, *Birth of Christianity*, 250.

[57] Ron Cameron, "The Sayings Gospel Q and the Quest of the Historical Jesus: A Response to John S. Kloppenborg," *HTR* 89 (1996): 354.

[58] See Ron Cameron, "Alternate Beginnings—Different Ends: Eusebius, Thomas, and the Construction of Christian Origins," in *Religious Propaganda and Missionary Competition in the New Testament World: Essays Honoring Dieter Georgi* (ed. Lukas Bormann, Kelly Del Tredici, and Angela Standhartinger; NovTSup 74; Leiden: Brill, 1994), 501–25; idem, "Gospel of Thomas and Christian Origins," 236–57; repr. in *Redescribing Christian Origins*, forthcoming; Burton L. Mack, "On Redescribing Christian Origins," *MTSR* 8 (1996): 247–69; repr. in *The Christian Myth: Origins, Logic, and Legacy* (New York: Continuum, 2001), 59–80.

[59] Crossan, *Birth of Christianity*, 139.

[60] Merrill P. Miller, "Introduction to the Consultation on Christian Origins," *MTSR* 8 (1996): 229.

[61] Crossan, *Birth of Christianity*, 176, 231, 287, 305–11.

[62] Miller, "Consultation on Christian Origins," above n. 60.

[63] For a critique of the entire quest of the historical Jesus, see Burton L. Mack, "The Historical Jesus Hoopla," in *Christian Myth*, 25–40, esp. 34–39.

[64] An earlier draft of this paper was presented at the One Hundred Thirty-Fifth Annual Meeting of the Society of Biblical Literature, Boston, Mass., November 23, 1999. I am grateful to Willi Braun, Barry Crawford, Burton Mack, Merrill Miller, and Jonathan Z. Smith for providing me with helpful comments and critical suggestions.

CHAPTER FOUR

THE RESTLESS QUEST FOR THE BELOVED DISCIPLE

HAROLD W. ATTRIDGE

It is a pleasure to contribute this essay to honor François Bovon, who has contributed so much to illuminating the role of the apostolic figures in early Christian literature.

The Fourth Gospel's mysterious Beloved Disciple continues to fascinate. While some commentators are agnostic about his identity,[1] others continue to make new proposals. Among the many recent attempts to wrestle with his identity and function,[2] several merit special attention.

The basic data on the Beloved Disciple as well as the vast spectrum of speculation are ably summarized in recent studies by Allen Culpepper[3] and James Charlesworth.[4] The "one whom Jesus loved," appears explicitly four times: at the last supper (13:23–25), the crucifixion (19:26–27), the empty tomb (20:2–10), and at Jesus' final lakeside appearance in Galilee (21:7–20). Three other passages mention anonymous disciples, who are possibly the Beloved Disciple. The first chapter (1:35–42) reports the initial encounter of Jesus and two disciples of the Baptist, Andrew, and an anonymous companion. When Jesus, under arrest, goes to High Priest's house, Peter and an anonymous "other disciple" follow (18:15). The intriguing note that this anonymous figure was known to the High Priest (18:16) has generated hypotheses about the

---

[1] For three recent examples, see Francis J. Moloney, *The Gospel of John* (SP 4; Collegeville, Minn.: Liturgical Press, 1998), 6–9; R. Alan Culpepper, *The Gospel and Letters of John* (Interpreting Biblical Texts; Nashville: Abingdon, 1998), 29–37; and D. Moody Smith, *John* (ANTC; Nashville: Abingdon, 1999), 24–27.

[2] Among the more recent works in an ever expanding corpus, see Joachim Kügler, *Der Jünger, der Jesus liebte: Literarische, theologische und historische Untersuchungen zu einer Schlüsselgestalt johanneischer Theologie und Geschichte* (SBB 16; Stuttgart: Katholisches Bibelwerk, 1988); Kevin Quast, *Peter and the Beloved Disciple: Figures for a Community in Crisis* (JSNTSup 32; Sheffield: JSOT Press, 1989); Franz Neirynck, "The Anonymous Disciple in John 1," *ETL* 66 (1990): 5–37, repr. in *Evangelica II 1982–91: Collected Essays* (BETL 99; Leuven: Leuven University Press, 1991), 617–49; Eugen Biser, "Was ist mit diesem? Eine theologische Improvisation über das Thema des von Jesus geliebten Jüngers," in *Anfänge der Christologie: FS Ferdinand Hahn* (ed. Cilliers Breytenbach et al.; Göttingen: Vandenhoeck & Ruprecht, 1991), 323–26; Lutz Simon, *Petrus und der Lieblingsjünger im Johannesevangelium: Amt und Autorität* (EHS 23/498; Frankfurt: Peter Lang, 1994).

[3] R. Alan Culpepper, *John the Son of Zebedee: The Life of a Legend* (Studies on Personalities of the New Testament; Columbia: University of South Carolina Press, 1994; repr., Minneapolis: Fortress, 2000).

[4] James H. Charlesworth, *The Beloved Disciple: Whose Witness Validates the Gospel of John?* (Valley Forge, Pa.: Trinity Press International, 1995).

Beloved Disciple's connections and social status.[5] Finally, the report that Jesus' pierced side poured forth blood and water is attributed to an eyewitness (19:35), whose "witness is true," as is that of the Beloved Disciple in 21:24. Such verbal similarity, coupled with the reported presence of the Disciple at the cross (19:26–27), suggests that here lies another reference to the mystery man.[6]

The final reference (John 21:24) makes the claim that this figure is "the one who wrote these things." Most scholars construe the verse to claim that the Beloved Disciple authored the text, or at least chapters 1–20.[7] Some, however, have argued that the passage merely claims that the Beloved Disciple is the authoritative witness who *caused* the work to be written,[8] or who perhaps wrote an early account of Jesus on which the final gospel was based.[9] This distinction between evangelist and his authoritative source has most frequently bolstered speculation about the role in the gospel's composition of the "Elder or Presbyter" John, mentioned by Papias.[10] The most recent defender, Martin Hengel, has argued that John the elder is the author, whom later tradition mistook for John the Son of Zebedee.[11]

In all his appearances, both actual and possible, the Beloved Disciple remains anonymous. Anonymity, apparently abhorrent to readers of the gospel, has bred constant speculation, in both traditional and modern scholarship. The main stream of Christian tradition since the second century identified the

---

[5] E.g., François-Marie Braun, *Jean le Théologien: Les grandes traditions d'Israël et l'accord des Écritures selon le quatrième Évangile* (EBib; Paris: Gabalda, 1964), 93.

[6] Not all agree. Some (J. Ramsey Michaels, "The Centurion's Confession and the Spear Thrust," *CBQ* 29 [1967]: 102–9; Hartwig Thyen, "Johannes und die Synoptiker," in Adelbert Denaux, ed., *John and the Synoptics* [BETL 101; Leuven: Peeters, 1992], 101–4) have argued that it is the soldier who pierced the side of Jesus in v. 34 who testified to what he saw. The demonstrative "that one" (ἐκεῖνος) of 19:35 would then refer to someone else, perhaps the Beloved Disciple, who transmitted the soldier's testimony. So Paul S. Minear, "Diversity and Unity: A Johannine Case-Study," in *Die Mitte des Neuen Testaments: FS E. Schweizer* (ed. Ulrich Luz and H. Weder; Göttingen: Vandenhoeck & Ruprecht, 1983), 162–75. See also Maurits Sabbe, "The Johannine Account of the Death of Jesus and Its Synoptic Parallels (Jn 19,16b–42)," *ETL* 70 (1994): 49. One might also distinguish the one who saw (i.e., the Beloved Disciple) from "that one," who vouches for the truth of the Disciple's testimony, but understand this second figure as Jesus or the Spirit. So Howard M. Jackson, "Ancient Self-Referential Conventions and Their Implications for the Authorship and Integrity of the Gospel of John," *JTS* 50 (1999): 32, with other references.

[7] For a defense of the integrity of chapter 21 on this point, see Paul Minear, "The Original Functions of John 21," *JBL* 102 (1983): 85–98, and Jackson, "Self-Referential Conventions."

[8] Among many others, see C. K. Barrett, *The Gospel According to St. John* (2d ed.; Philadelphia: Westminster, 1978), 115; Charlesworth, *Disciple*, 21–28.

[9] N. E. Johnson, "The Beloved Disciple and the Fourth Gospel," *CQR* 167 (1966): 28–91.

[10] Papias apud Eusebius, *Hist. eccl.* 3.39.4. See Charlesworth, *Disciple*, 215–17, citing as early proponents: F. Uechtritz, *Studien eines Laien über den Ursprung, die Beschaffen-heit und Bedeutung des Evangeliums nach Johannes* (Gotha: Perthes, 1876), vi; and B. F. Streeter, *The Four Gospels: A Study of Origins* (London: Macmillan, 1924, 1851), 430–61.

[11] Martin Hengel, *The Johannine Question* (London: SCM Press, 1989). The German expands these lectures: *Die johanneische Frage: Ein Lösungsversuch mit einem Beitrag zur Apokalypse von Jörg Frey* (WUNT 67; Tübingen: Mohr Siebeck, 1993).

anonymous figure with John, the Son of Zebedee,[12] but some early church sources entertained other alternatives.[13] Although the identification still has defenders,[14] Johannine scholarship is littered with other possibilities: Lazarus, either as a Judaean disciple,[15] or as a literary fiction based on Luke 16:19–31,[16] John Mark,[17] Matthias,[18] the rich young ruler,[19] Paul,[20] Apollos,[21] Judas Iscariot,[22]

---

[12] Charlesworth, *Disciple*, 394–99, usefully compiles patristic testimonies including: Irenaeus, *Haer.* 2.22.5; 3.3.1; 3.3.4; Polycrates of Ephesus, apud Eusebius, *Hist. eccl.* 5.24.3–4; Origen, apud Eusebius, *Hist. eccl.* 6.25.9; Tertullian, *De praescriptione haereticorum* 22; Dionysius of Alexandria, apud Eusebius *Hist. eccl.* 7.25.12.

[13] See Charlesworth, *Disciple*, 399–413.

[14] For a history of the position, see Culpepper, *John*, 73–76; Charlesworth, *Disciple*, 197–213. Indicative of a shift in sentiment are the changes of heart by Raymond Brown, *The Gospel According to John* (2 vols.; AB 29, 29a; Garden City, N.Y.: Doubleday, 1966–1970), 1.xcviii and c, revised in idem, *The Community of the Beloved Disciple* (Paramus, N.J.: Paulist/Newman, 1979), and Rudolf Schnackenburg, *The Gospel according to St. John* (3 vols.; trans. Kevin Smyth; London: Burns & Oates; New York: Crossroad, 1968–82), 1.97–104, revised in 3.383–87, see also idem, "Der Jünger, den Jesus liebte," in *Evangelisch-katholischer Kommentar zum Neuen Testament: Vorarbeiten* (Neukirchen-Vluyn: Neukirchener Verlag, 1970), 97–117.

[15] First proposed, apparently independently, by J. Kreyenbühl, "Der Verfasser des Evangeliums," in idem, *Das Evangelium der Wahrheit: Neue Lösung der Johanneischen Frage* (Berlin: Schwetschke, 1900), 146–39, K. Kickendraht, "Ist Lazarus der Lieblingsjünger im vierten Evangelium?" *SThZ* 31 (1914): 49–54; and, in English, B. Grey Griffith, "The Disciple Whom Jesus Loved," *ExpTim* 32 (1920–21): 379–81. More recently: Vernard Eller, *The Beloved Disciple, His Name, His Story, His Thought* (Grand Rapids: Eerdmans, 1987), esp. 53–73, and Mark W. G. Stibbe, *John as Storyteller: Narrative Criticism and the Fourth Gospel* (SNTSMS 73; Cambridge: Cambridge University Press, 1992), 154. See further Culpepper, *John*, 76–77, and Charlesworth, *Disciple*, 185–92, particularly thorough on early speculation.

[16] Hartwig Thyen, "Die Erzählung von den bethanischen Geschwistern (Joh 11,1–12,19) als 'Palimpsest' über synoptischen Texten," in *The Four Gospels: Festschrift Frans Neirynck* (ed. Frans Van Segbroeck et al.; BETL 100; Leuven: Peeters, 1992), 3.2021–50, esp. 2043.

[17] Culpepper, *John*, 77–79; Charlesworth, *Disciple*, 192–96. The suggestion appears first in D. Völter, *Die Offenbarung Johannis* (Strassburg: Heitz, 1904) and idem, *Mater Dolorosa und der Lieblingsjünger des Johannesevanelium* (Strassburg: Heitz, 1907). Julius Wellhausen (*Das Evangelium Johannes* [Berlin: Reimer, 1908], 87–88) championed it. It is clear that John the Son of Zebedee and John Mark were confused. See J. Edgar Bruns, "John Mark: A Riddle within the Johannine Enigma," *Scr* 15 (1963): 91; idem, "The Confusion between John and John Mark in Antiquity," *Scr* 17 (1965): 23–26. Such confusion generated the further suggestion that John Mark wrote the Fourth Gospel and John of Galilee wrote Mark. See Pierson Parker, "John and John Mark," *JBL* 79 (1960): 97–110; idem, "John the Son of Zebedee and the Fourth Gospel," *JBL* 81 (1962): 35–43. An even less plausible option, that Lazarus was the Beloved Disciple, but that John Mark wrote the gospel, is suggested by J. N. Sanders, "St. John on Patmos," *NTS* 9 (1962): 75–85.

[18] See Eric. L. Titus, "The Identity of the Beloved Disciple," *JBL* 69 (1950): 323–28, noted by both Culpepper, *John*, 79, and Charlesworth, *Disciple*, 154–56.

[19] Culpepper (*John*, 79–80) notes H. B. Swete, "The Disciple whom Jesus Loved," *JTS* 17 (1916): 371–74. Charlesworth (*Disciple*, 166–70) traces the suggestion to E. G. King, "The Disciple that Jesus Loved—A Suggestion," *The Interpreter* 5 (1909): 167–74.

[20] Culpepper, *John*, 80–81; Charlesworth, *Disciple*, 159–64. See Benjamin W. Bacon, "The Disciple Whom Jesus Loved and His Relation to the Author," *Expositor* 7,4 (1907): 324–39, repr. in idem, *The Fourth Gospel in Research and Debate* (London: Fisher Unwin, 1910; New York: Moffat, Yard, 1918), 301–31.

Judas, the brother of Jesus,[23] Andrew,[24] Philip,[25] Nathanael,[26] or a character based on a figure from the Old Testament, such as Benjamin[27] or Joseph.[28] Some scholars, though hesitant to identify the Beloved Disciple, yet confidently affirm that, as author of the gospel, he was a Sadducee[29] or Essene.[30] Charlesworth, after his thorough review of scholarship, makes the novel suggestion that the Beloved Disciple was Thomas.[31]

Charlesworth's bold suggestion merits consideration. He has certainly done an enormous service in surveying so comprehensively the whole Johannine problem and in assembling relevant data on John and Thomas in early Christian sources. His argument that there may have been a positive appreciation of the Fourth Gospel among "Thomasine" Christians offers a healthy challenge to those who see tension between Johannine and partisans of Thomas.[32] Nonetheless,

---

[21] Charlesworth, *Disciple*, 157–59. For early speculation see J. T. Tobler, "Über den Ursprung des vierten Evangeliums," *ZWT* 3 (1860): 169–203; later, Simone Pétrement, "Apollos and the Fourth Gospel," in idem, *A Separate God: The Christian Origins of Gnosticism* (trans. Carol Harrison; San Francisco: Harper, 1990, ET of *Le Dieu Séparé* [1984]), 276–97.

[22] Charlesworth, *Disciple*, 170–79. Implausibly suggested by L. Noack, *Die Geschichte Jesu auf Grund freier geschichtlicher Untersuchungen über das Evangelium und die Evangelien* (4 vols.; Mannheim: Schneider, 1876), but defended as a literary possibility by Frank Kermode, *The Genesis of Secrecy: On the Interpretation of Narrative* (Cambridge: Harvard University Press, 1979), 92.

[23] Charlesworth, *Disciple*, 196–97, citing J. J. Gunther, "The Relation of the Beloved Disciple to the Twelve," *TZ* 37 (1981): 129–48.

[24] Charlesworth, *Disciple*, 179–80, noting E. C. J. Lützelberger, *Die kirchliche Tradition über den Apostel Johannes und seine Schriften in ihrer Grundlosigkeit* (Leipzig: Brockhaus, 1840).

[25] Charlesworth, *Disciple*, 180–81, noting M. É. Boismard, *Du Baptême à Cana (Jean 1.19–2.11)* (Paris: Cerf, 1956), 72–73.

[26] Charlesworth's quest (*Disciple*, 181–85) for the author of this suggestion uncovered H. Spaeth, "Nathanael: Ein Beitrag zum Verständniss der Composition der Logos-Evangeliums," *ZWT* 11 (1868): 309–43, M. A. N. Rovers, *Nieuw-testamentische Letterkunde* (Hertogenbosch: Muller, 1888), 172, and F. S. Gutjahr, *Der Glaubwürdigkeit des Irenäischen Zeugnisses über die Abfassung des Vierten Kanonischen Evangeliums* (Graz: Leuschner & Lubensky, 1904), 184.

[27] Culpepper, *John*, 81–82, citing Paul S. Minear, "The Beloved Disciple in the Gospel of John: Some Clues and Conjectures," *NovT* 19 (1977): 105–23. See also Charlesworth, *Disciple*, 164–66.

[28] Joseph Grassi, *The Secret Identity of the Beloved Disciple* (New York: Paulist, 1992), 47–55.

[29] D. E. H. Whiteley, "Was John Written by a Sadducee?" *ANRW* 2.25.3 (1985): 2481–2505.

[30] Eugen Ruckstuhl, "Der Jünger, den Jesus liebte," *SNTSU* 11 (1986): 131–67, reprinted in idem, *Jesus im Horizont der Evangelien* (SBAB; Stuttgart: Katholisches Bibelwerk, 1988), 355–95.

[31] Charlesworth, *Disciple*, 225–87, 415–21, followed Philippe de Suarez, *L'Évangile selon Thomas* (Marsanne: Metanoia, 1975), 260, and Hans-Martin Schenke, "The Function and Background of the Beloved Disciple in the Gospel of John," in *Nag Hammadi, Gnosticism, and Early Christianity* (ed. Charles W. Hedrick and Robert Hodgson, Jr.; Peabody, Mass.: Hendrickson, 1986), 111–25.

[32] Gregory J. Riley, *Resurrection Reconsidered* (Minneapolis: Fortress, 1995); April DeConick, *Seek to See Him: Ascent and Vision Mysticism in the Gospel of Thomas* (VCSup 33; Leiden: Brill, 1996) and idem, *Voices of the Mystics: Early Christian Discourse in the Gospels of John and Thomas and Other Ancient Christian Literature* (JSNTSup 157; Sheffield: Sheffield Academic Press, 2001).

his case has one fatal flaw, John 20:8, the report that the Beloved Disciple entered the tomb after Peter, saw the folded burial cloths and believed (εἶδεν καὶ ἐπίστευσεν). If the Beloved Disciple is Thomas, his belief is hard to reconcile with the skepticism that is quieted only when confronted with the evidence of Jesus' resurrected body (20:24–29).

Charlesworth confronts the problem squarely. He first reviews the extensive literature on 20:8, and illustrates a diversity of exegetical opinion about the Beloved Disciple's faith.[33] Yet he relies most heavily on the verse that follows the report of the Beloved Disciple's belief. John 20:9 reports "For they did not yet know the scripture that it was necessary for him to rise from the dead" (οὐδέπω γὰρ ᾔδεισαν τὴν γραφὴν ὅτι δεῖ αὐτὸν ἐκ νεκρῶν ἀναστῆναι). Charlesworth takes the verse to be a decisive qualification of the "belief" attributed to the Beloved Disciple in the previous verse. Without knowledge of the scriptures, the Disciple could not have had the full resurrection faith. Charlesworth then follows those interpreters who take ἐπίστευσεν as inceptive: "he began to believe."

Pace Charlesworth, John 20:9 does not deny the simple meaning of the preceding verse. It does not, that is, suggest that the Beloved Disciple could not have come to belief. Instead of saying something about the non-belief of the Beloved Disciple, the verse explains why Peter, so widely hailed as the first to come to resurrection faith, did not do so when confronted with the witness of the empty tomb. The narrator's comment, that is, makes sense of a differentiated reaction, with the Beloved Disciple coming to belief and Peter remaining confused. The latter could not yet have belief because he did not have the crutch of scriptural testimony. The Beloved Disciple saw for himself, understood, and needed nothing further. Perhaps his vision was aided by what he saw at the crucifixion (19:26–27, 35), a sight that the Gospel had long since promised would be salvific (3:14–15). Despite Charlesworth's ingenuity, the report of the Beloved Disciple's reaction to the empty tomb precludes his identification with Thomas.

Another analysis introduces new data to the quest. Howard M. Jackson brings to bear conventions of documentary papyri to analyze the crucial final reference to the Beloved Disciple and lay the groundwork for a renewed defense of the traditional identification of the figure with the Son of Zebedee.[34] Like Charlesworth's suggestion, Jackson's merits serious consideration, primarily because of the interesting use of non-literary texts as a point of comparison with the Fourth Gospel. Jackson argues that the convention of attesting the identity of the author of a document through a validating clause expressed in the third person is the closest parallel to the conclusion of chapter 21. The intriguing parallels undercut the widespread hypothesis that chapter 21 is an appendix to the gospel, written after the death of the Beloved Disciple. On that more generally accepted reading, the pericope would be taking pains to

---

[33] Charlesworth, *Disciple*, 68–118.
[34] Jackson, "Self-Referential Conventions," 1–34.

explain away a saying of Jesus, such as Mark 9:1, which had been applied to the Beloved Disciple. No, argues Jackson, the codicil is the Beloved Disciple's own authorial attempt to undercut the application of such a saying to him.

Although Jackson's analysis is intriguing, like Charlesworth's, it remains unconvincing. Its major problem lies precisely at the point of its originality, in the assumption that a non-literary form will have the same function when transferred to a literary environment. Jackson may well be correct that the Fourth Gospel has appropriated the kind of documentary device to which he points, but interpreters should be cautious when they find such generic parallels. Partial instantiations of various literary forms appear throughout the gospel, from miracle stories to passion narratives, from revealer dialogues to parables, yet the gospel's literary strategy constantly transforms those genres, sometimes by internal manipulation, sometimes by juxtaposition with other forms.[35] The gospel that so delights in irony[36] delights also in counter-conventional uses of traditional literary vessels, in its attempt to ponder how words are altered when the Word itself takes on flesh.

If a documentary device for authorial self-attestation concludes John 21, it remains problematic because the self-identity of the author is not, in fact, revealed. The authentication of an anonymous witness is systematically disappointing and constitutes an ironic, almost parodic use of a convention for self-authentication.

Irony may simply conceal the aim of making a pseudepigraphic claim to authorship, as Martin Rese suggests in his analysis of the Beloved Disciple passages generally.[37] Yet the conclusion that the mysterious disciple is to be identified with John the Son of Zebedee is hardly ineluctable. It requires the reader to know the Synoptics and make an elaborate series of inferences, that, for instance, the unnamed disciple of John 1:35–42 is the Beloved Disciple and is the son of Zebedee mentioned in Mark 1:19. This is a slender reed indeed on which to hang a pseudepigraphic claim. The Sons of Zebedee do,

---

[35] I have explored this feature of Johannine technique in "Genre Bending in the Fourth Gospel" *JBL* 121 (2002): 3–21.

[36] Johannine irony has been much discussed of late. See, e.g., George W. MacRae, "Theology and Irony in the Fourth Gospel," in *The Word in the World: Essays in Honour of F. L. Moriarty* (ed. Richard J. Clifford and George W. MacRae; Cambridge, Mass.: Weston College, 1973), 83–96, repr. in Mark W. G. Stibbe, *The Gospel of John as Literature: An Anthology of Twentieth-Century Perspectives* (NTTS 17; Leiden: Brill, 1993), 103–13; Paul D. Duke, *Irony in the Fourth Gospel* (Atlanta: John Knox Press, 1985); Gail O'Day, *Revelation in the Fourth Gospel: Narrative Mode and Theological Claim* (Philadelphia: Fortress, 1986); Eugene Botha, "The Case of Johannine Irony Reopened I: The Problematic Current Situation," *Neot* 25,2 (1991): 209–20; idem, "The Case of Johannine Irony Reopened II: Suggestions, Alternative Approaches," *Neot* 25,2 (1991): 221–32; R. Alan Culpepper, "Reading Johannine Irony," *Exploring the Gospel of John: In Honor of D. Moody Smith* (Louisville: Westminster/John Knox, 1996), 193–207.

[37] Martin Rese, "Das Selbstzeugnis des Johannesevangeliums über seinen Verfasser," *ETL* 72 (1996): 75–111.

of course, appear in John 21:2, *but alongside two other unnamed disciples.* The text may invite the reader to find the identity of the man of mystery in one of the named Galilean fisherman, but it immediately sows the seeds of doubt by placing two other anonymous disciples on the shore. Rather than deftly revealing its alleged author, the text solicits an identification, but works overtime to keep the reader doubtful of the reliability of that identification.

While scholars such as Charlesworth and Jackson continue the quest for the identity of the Beloved Disciple, others seek to explore his function. Complicating this analysis is the possibility that redactional activity may have changed the function of the figure.[38]

Some interpreters find that the Beloved Disciple works symbolically. He may be a paradigm of faithful discipleship, intimate with Jesus, faithful to him even in death, quick to believe, and eager to be an active disciple.[39] The figure may serve an ecclesiological purpose. As hero of the Johannine Christians, his virtues contrast with the obtuseness of Peter and thereby exalt the community of the Beloved Disciple over other communities of Christians, some of whom might revere other "eponymous heroes"[40]: Peter, the first witness of the resurrection,[41] or James, the brother of the Lord.[42] The strikingly repeated contrast with Peter has been variously interpreted, as a correction or rebuke to Petrine Christians,[43] or, more positively, at least in chapter 21,[44] as Peter's rehabilitation, recommending him and his followers to Johannine Christians.[45]

---

[38] For claims that redaction, particularly the added chapter 21, altered the function of the Beloved Disciple, see Schenke, "The Function and Background," 124–25, and Charlesworth, *Disciple,* 420, who attributes the references in chapters 13, 19 and 20 to the Evangelist, but chapter 21 to a redactor, whose work obscures the Disciple's identity.

[39] See Grassi, *Secret Identity,* 115–18 for a brief catalogue of the values frequently associated with the Beloved Disciple.

[40] Cf., perhaps, the situation that Paul ridicules in 1 Cor 1:12–13.

[41] Cf. 1 Cor 15:5.

[42] Cf. Gal 1:19; 2:12; cf. Acts 15:13. For the suggestion that the Fourth Gospel criticizes the kind of Jewish Christianity epitomized by James, see Christian Dietzfelbinger, "Der ungeliebte Bruder: Der Herrenbruder Jakobus im Johannesevangelium," *ZTK* 89 (1992): 377–403.

[43] B. W. Bacon, *The Fourth Gospel in Research and Debate* (New Haven: Yale University Press, 1918), 303–4; Graydon F. Snyder, "John 13.16 and the Anti-Petrinism of the Johannine Tradition," *BR* 16 (1971): 5–15; W. W. Watty, "The Significance of Anonymity in the Fourth Gospel," *ExpTim* 90 (1979): 209–12; J. J. Gunther, "The Relation of the Beloved Disciple to the Twelve," *TZ* 38 (1981): 129–48; Michael Theobald, "Der Jünger, den Jesus liebte: Beobachtungen zum narrativen Konzept der johanneischen Redaktion," in *Geschichte-Tradition-Reflexion: Festschrift für Martin Hengel zum 70. Geburtstag* (ed. Hubert Cancik, Hermann Lichtenberger, and Peter Schäfer; 3 vols.; Tübingen: Mohr Siebeck, 1996), 3.219–55.

[44] Raymond F. Collins, "Representative Figures of the Fourth Gospel–II," *DRev* 94 (1976): 118–32; A. H. Maynard, "The Role of Peter in the Fourth Gospel," *NTS* 30 (1984): 531–48. Such readings follow the common assumption that chapter 21 is an appendix.

[45] Quast, *Peter,* offers a fine overview.

Other symbolic readings of the Beloved Disciple take him to represent Gentile Christianity[46] or as an embodiment of a principle such as spiritual versus hierarchical authority.[47]

Such readings of the figure, particularly as he appears in tandem with Peter, have a certain plausibility. The gospel is indeed concerned with ecclesial realities and pointedly builds into its narrative about Jesus certain elements of the experience of his followers.[48] The Beloved Disciple, like so many other elements of the Fourth Gospel, no doubt performs more than one duty in the text. Yet the ecclesiastical-political reading of the function of the Beloved Disciple does not do justice to all features of the Beloved Disciple's portrait, particularly the studied anonymity.[49]

The plethora of suggestions about the identity and function of the Beloved Disciple should itself give us pause. Is their number a function of modern curiosity, of now quaint historical-critical exegesis gone awry? Or is their existence a testimony to an effective literary strategy? One might take the collection of solutions to the "problem" of the Beloved Disciple as evidence that the Fourth Evangelist, or at least that hand responsible for the Beloved Disciple passages, was a tease. The text elicits expectations of a reliable witness, especially in 19:35 and 21:24, but systematically defeats any attempt to identify who that witness was. What might be the function of such a game?

Crucial to unraveling the mystery is to recognize the *anonymity* of the Beloved Disciple. There is simply no sure identification of the figure, neither with the Son of Zebedee, nor with Thomas, nor with any of the other figures that have been proposed.[50] Whatever functions the figure exercises as model or polemical cipher, he does so anonymously.

Yet it is equally important to note that, in its final form, the text asserts that the anonymous disciple is a witness to the life and death of Jesus and to the truth being proclaimed throughout the gospel. These affirmations, which seem to be designed to assure, continue only to disturb. In order for the witness's testimony to be fully effective, the reader/hearer desperately wants to know

---

[46] Rudolf Bultmann, *The Gospel of John* (Philadelphia: Westminster; Oxford: Blackwell, 1971), 530; Margaret Pamment, "The Fourth Gospel's Beloved Disciple," *ExpTim* 94 (1983): 363–67.

[47] Alv Kragerud, *Der Lieblingsjünger im Johannesevangelium: Ein exegetischer Versuch* (Hamburg: Wegner, 1959); Raymond Brown, *Community of the Beloved Disciple* (New York: Paulist, 1979).

[48] This dimension of the Gospel has been noted since J. Louis Martyn, *The Gospel of John in Christian History: Essays for Interpreters* (New York: Paulist, 1978), and idem, *History and Theology in the Fourth Gospel* (rev. ed.; Nashville: Abingdon, 1979).

[49] Whatever they make of the Disciple's function, many contemporaries recognize his unavoidable anonymity. So, e.g., Quast, *Peter*, 12; Franz Neirynck, "John 21," *NTS* 36 (1990): 321–36, esp. 335 (= idem, *Evangelica II 1982–91: Collected Essays* [BETL 99; Leuven: Leuven University Press, 1991], 601–16); Patrick Chatelion Counet, *John, A Postmodern Gospel: Introduction to Deconstructive Exegesis Applied to the Fourth Gospel* (Biblical Interpretation Series 44; Leiden: Brill, 2000).

[50] Charlesworth's review offers apt criticism of alternative possibilities.

who this witness is. This is not an *a priori* judgment about implied readers. The lengthy history of intense speculation on the figure offers empirical evidence that the text has worked in this way. Jackson's form-critical observations here potentially illuminate this effect. If Jackson is correct that the style of the concluding remarks mimics the authenticating codicils of documentary papyri, they reinforce the expectation that the identity of the witness will be clear. But if there is anything that the history of investigation of the Johannine problem also shows, it is that such expectations are doomed to disappointment.

In the tension generated by the evanescent witness lies an answer to the problem of the Beloved Disciple. As the brief review of scholarship indicates, the mystery of this character's identity has constantly enticed readers back into the text that they have finished reading.[51] The Disciple stands as a witness, who "writes" much, but immediately fades into the background. Who is it, the reader asks, who bears such testimony? The only way to answer that question is to return to the text, to engage in a quest for the Disciple's identity. Every attempt to pursue that quest runs into a dead end. Such dead ends have not discouraged the pursuit but only whetted appetites for another try.

With every plunge back into the sea of the gospel, the quester finds a new bit of evidence, a new hint about the source of the quest, but if she is attentive to the process of re-engaging the text, she will notice another feature of the work. The search for a witness, a sure foundation for belief in the incarnate Word, keeps pointing beyond that witness to the One Witness whose testimony is compelling, the Word incarnate.

The motif of testimony runs through the Gospel,[52] although it is particularly prominent in certain key episodes, such as John 5. Jesus' lengthy discourse, which responds to charges stemming from his healing of the paralytic, finally poses a challenge that dominates the gospel as a whole. Other witnesses, John the Baptist, the scriptures, the Father,[53] may be brought to bear to support claims about Jesus. Nonetheless, in order to hear and accept those witnesses, the hearer/reader must accept the testimony of Jesus himself that the scriptures speak of him and that the Father testifies to him. The theme of witness in the Gospel is a vortex that draws its audience into a process that strips away ordinary presuppositions about intellectual warrants, and offers a confrontation with the stark challenge of the Word enfleshed, nailed to a cross. If one can see and understand that witness, then everything else will make sense. No other witness will count for ought.

---

[51] Or, as my colleague Allen Hilton suggests, "hearing," if their primary mode of encounter with the text was oral.

[52] As noted decades ago by Johannes Beutler, *Martyria: Traditionsgeschichtliche Untersuchungen zum Zeugnisthema bei Johannes* (Frankfurter theologische Studien 10; Frankfurt-am-Main: Joseph Knecht, 1972).

[53] John 5:36–39.

The Beloved Disciple's anonymity, *qua* witness, *qua* author of this story, performs primarily a *literary* role, re-engaging the reader, drawing her back time and again to a potential encounter with the one Witness sent by the Father.

Conclusion: Techniques of Reader-Engagement

The Fourth Gospel concludes with a tantalizing but ultimately self-defeating identification of its author. This conclusion parallels, in a curious way, the famously ambiguous ending of Mark 16:8. The stunned silence of the women at the tomb invites the reader to wonder how news of the resurrection spread. He is also invited to make a decision, to go with those women into fear-filled quiet, or to go forth and proclaim the news of the resurrection.

The ending of the Fourth Gospel engages the reader differently. It does not implicitly urge the reader to hopeful proclamation. Instead, it draws the reader back into the world of the story in a quest for evidentiary confirmation and certitude. The quest is doomed to failure if it is pursued on its own terms. Only if the quester learns to see beyond the presuppositions of the investigation to abandon external witnesses, and to confront directly the witness of the Word, the witness that speaks most forcefully from the Cross, will the quest have any hope of success. If the reader encounters and hears that Witness, then the identity of the Beloved Disciple will not matter.

That the figure of the Beloved Disciple works in such a fashion is not surprising, given other examples of Johannine characterization. Like Nicodemus or the Samaritan Woman, the Beloved Disciple has a first-order function to display some aspects of what it is to encounter Jesus. The Disciple models intimacy and fidelity, by displaying a faith that eschews empirical verification and by remaining faithful to Jesus through and beyond death. Yet, like Nicodemus and all the women who encounter Jesus, he fades into the background, disappearing behind the whispered claim that he is a witness. As each of the other witnesses made way for Jesus, so too does the Beloved Disciple, in his invitation to pursue the only One whose testimony is Truth.

PART TWO

EARLY CHRISTIAN VOICES IN LUKAN TRADITIONS

CHAPTER FIVE

LUKE THE POLITICIAN: PROMOTING THE GOSPEL BY POLISHING CHRISTIANITY'S ROUGH EDGES

ANN GRAHAM BROCK

Over the years scholars have attempted to discern the primary objectives of the author of Acts, but despite their learned examinations of basically the same text, they have often reached profoundly different conclusions, as evidenced in François Bovon's in-depth survey of scholarship on the topic.[1] This essay will show ways in which the deeply divided and often scholarly interpretations are due to characteristics inherent in the book of Acts itself. These internal characteristics provide the fuel for scholarly debate to the level that scholars now often repeat the well-known description of Luke–Acts as a "storm-center in contemporary scholarship."[2] An example of such an apparent contradiction reveals itself in the way the author so generously provides narratives of the Jewish people, including their leaders, history, and scripture, and yet at the same time often portrays them unfavorably and primarily culpable for the persecution of early Christians.[3] The text likewise appears to champion the role of Paul, devoting almost twenty of twenty-eight chapters to this figure, but nevertheless often contradicts Paul's theology, diminishes his independent status, and even defines the concept "apostle" in a way that excludes him. Furthermore, some scholars hail Luke–Acts for its rich variety of narratives that feature women in early Christianity, while others denounce the way it diminishes women's leadership and contributions. This essay examines these apparent inconsistencies and suggests ways in which the author's political emphases evoke such diametrically opposed points of view. Although the political and social exigencies affecting the author's perspectives are difficult—if not impossible—to uncover, the following analysis of emphases and tendencies provides some glimpses into the author's unique presentation of Christian history. It sets forth evidence that the author has shaped the narratives to present

---

[1] In acknowledgment of the scholarship that Professor François Bovon has fostered in the academic world, especially with respect to Luke–Acts and Christian apocryphal texts, I offer this essay to honor his research and scholarship. For insight into the range of scholarly interpretations of Luke–Acts, see his text, *Luke the Theologian: Thirty-Three Years of Research* (Allison Park, Pa.: Pickwick, 1987).

[2] W. C. van Unnik first introduced this description in his essay, "Luke–Acts, A Storm Center in Contemporary Scholarship," in *Studies in Luke–Acts* (ed. L. E. Keck and J. L. Martyn; Philadelphia: Fortress, 1980), 15–32.

[3] Eldon J. Epp, *The Theological Tendency of Codex Bezae Cantabrigiensis in Acts* (Cambridge: Cambridge University Press, 1966), 1–34.

a politically sedated and conventionalized portrayal of early Christianity—so much so that one could supplement the title "Luke the theologian" with an additional epithet "Luke the politician."

In at least five ways the author applies a certain political and theological tenor to the Christian message: (1) by reducing the text's political volatility in granting greater exoneration to the Romans in their dealings with the Christians; (2) by emphasizing the movement as divinely legitimized, especially in the confirmation that comes with its depictions of signs and wonders; (3) by emphasizing Christianity's religious stability in a close bond with Jewish ancestral roots; (4) by emphasizing an organized leadership structure in Jerusalem, especially by lifting up Peter as the primary spokesperson, healer, and guarantor of the tradition; and (5) by modeling women's contributions in terms of nurturing and financial support, thus depicting roles that may have been more acceptable to a wider audience or a patriarchal culture.

Exonerating the Romans and the Christians

The first characteristic mentioned above is especially easy to argue: the extent to which the author of Acts positively portrays the Roman authorities. Throughout Acts the author takes great care to show "how friendly and correct had been the behaviour of Roman officials towards Paul."[4] Hints of positive Roman portrayals arise frequently in the text, starting already with the first pagan convert being a Roman centurion named Cornelius (10:1–48), and continuing through to the centurion Julius who saves Paul from being killed (27:43). The text also describes the Roman proconsul Sergius Paulus as an "an intelligent man" who becomes a believer "for he was amazed at the teaching about the Lord" (13:7–12). This sympathetic portrayal of Roman authorities extends also to Gallio, proconsul of Achaia, who refuses to entertain complaints against Paul in Corinth and urges the Jews to settle their own matters (18:12–17).

The author diminishes Roman culpability in the persecutions of the Christians and repeatedly glosses over Roman deficiencies.[5] Luke–Acts more than other texts in the New Testament tends to shift the blame for the persecution of the first Christians away from the Romans and squarely into the laps of the Jewish leaders. Noteworthy, for example, are the details the author provides concerning the death of Stephen, martyred at the hands of the Sadducees, but by contrast the mere one verse reference to the death of James the son of Zebedee, who died at the hands of the government under King Agrippa I (Acts 12:2), not to mention the absence of any reference to the death of Jesus'

---

[4] Ernst Haenchen, *The Acts of the Apostles: A Commentary* (Philadelphia: Westminster, 1971), 106.

[5] Paul W. Walaskay, *'And so we came to Rome': The Political Perspective of St Luke* (Cambridge: Cambridge University Press, 1983), 12.

brother James.[6] An appreciation of such pro-Roman leanings may also help explain why Acts stops just short of recording the execution of Paul in Rome.

Positive descriptions of Paul's dealings with Roman authorities abound, as Cadbury aptly summarizes, "The proconsul in Cyprus and the Primus in Malta welcome him, the Asiarchs in Ephesus became his friends and sheltered him, Roman soldiers repeatedly defended him from violence, treated him with kindness and respect, and stood in awe of his Roman citizenship when they discovered it."[7] Such political leanings go hand-in-hand with an appreciation of Roman law, which often appears as a "savior" for Paul (22:22–30; 18:12–16; 21:31–32; 23:10). With examples such as these, "Luke brings to its final destination that endeavour which we have observed again and again . . . the effort to prove that the Roman government was favourably disposed to early Christianity and permitted its proclamation."[8]

The Romans, however, are not the only ones the author portrays in a more favorable light—so, too, are the Christians. The author of Acts portrays Paul saying, for example:

> My brothers, although I have done nothing against our people or against the customs of our ancestors, I was arrested in Jerusalem and handed over to the Romans. They examined me and wanted to release me, because I was not guilty of any crime deserving death. But when the Jews objected, I was compelled to appeal to Caesar. (Acts 28:17–19)

Haenchen points out that most readers of Acts "may scarcely have realized what great pains Luke took to make it understandable why the innocent Paul was not released from custody."[9]

Even the shift in Paul's speeches at the end of Acts illumines the author's political leanings. At the end of the volume, Paul's speeches deal not so much with his own impending trial, as one would have expected under the circumstances, but rather with the recurrent theme: "to prove Christianity itself innocent of all crimes against Roman law."[10] Haenchen explains, "Luke was most anxious to impress upon his readers that the Roman authorities treated the Christian missionaries with benevolence and acknowledged them to be politically harmless."[11]

---

[6] Haenchen, *Acts*, 732. Walaskay notes how the incident concerning John the Baptist's beheading had great potential as remarkable narrative and yet is downplayed in the text. See Walaskay, *And so we came to Rome*, 50.

[7] Henry J. Cadbury, *The Making of Luke–Acts* (London: SPCK, 1927; reprinted 1968), 302.

[8] Haenchen, *Acts*, 731.

[9] Ibid.

[10] Ibid., 104 n. 1.

[11] Ibid., 106. Such an emphasis began already in Luke and is most evident in the way the author makes a point of imperial innocence at the trial of Jesus.

Portraying Divine Support

In addition to portraying the Romans as generally favorably disposed toward the Christians, the author of Acts also portrays God's favorable support and powerful legitimation of the early Christian church. God unquestionably confirms the mission of the early church by means of divine intervention, especially in portrayals of visions, miracles, signs, and wonders. By such means, the author rarely misses an opportunity to reveal how events have occurred according to divine will: "Jesus of Nazareth was a man accredited by God to you by miracles, wonders, and signs" (Acts 2:22). The author not only repeatedly mentions revelatory instances, such as, "the apostles performed many miraculous signs and wonders among the people" (Acts 5:12), but also underscores the positive reactions towards them. Simon Magus, for example, "astonished by the great signs and miracles he saw," followed Philip everywhere (Acts 8:13). Apparently, for the author of Acts, "miracles did not challenge the structure of the universe; they displayed it."[12]

The author both implicitly and explicitly describes how these signs function to legitimate and demonstrate divine guidance: "So Paul and Barnabas spent considerable time there, speaking boldly for the Lord, who confirmed the message of his grace by enabling them to do miraculous signs and wonders" (Acts 14:3). The text provides extensive evidence of divine confirmation beginning with Peter (2:43; 3:4–8; 4:30; 6:8; 7:36; 8:6, 13; and 15:12), and continuing through Paul, who in the course of such miracles, healed the blind man Elymas (13:6–12) and the crippled man at Lystra (14:8–10), exorcized an evil spirit (19:12), and even brought Eutychus back to life (20:7–12). Through all these demonstrations the author emphasizes to the readers that God willed this and nothing else, thus "miracles and signs form the visible, demonstrable, reliable legitimation" for the Acts of the Apostles.[13]

The author of Acts brings together this divine legitimation with the pro-Roman perspective to show that the providence of God worked through and in tandem with the imperial army and with Roman law to insure the preservation and expansion of the gospel message.[14] By means of signs, the audience learns that God ordained the mission to be transferred to the Gentiles.

Portraying Political Stability through Ancestral Traditions

An argument for the author's pro-Roman sentiments logically requires an explanation for the seemingly contradictory and curiously abundant references

---

[12] Mikeal C. Parsons and Richard I. Pervo, *Rethinking the Unity of Luke and Acts* (Minneapolis: Fortress, 1993), 94–95.

[13] Haenchen, *Acts*, 113.

[14] Walaskay, *And so we came to Rome*, 60.

to Jewish historical events, to Jewish leaders, and especially to the plethora of Jewish scripture. Acts literally brims with excerpts from scripture (especially from the Psalms and the Prophets), frequently evoking the names of such Jewish greats as Abraham, Moses, and David, and even offering periodical summaries of Jewish history (Acts 7 and 13). All these aspects seem to indicate some intensive effort on the author's part to maintain close ties with a Jewish constituency, but, interestingly, at the same time the author seems to distance Christianity from Judaism.

Links to Jewish roots and heritage appear with numerous references to historical figures of Israel's past (3:13; 5:30; 15:10; 22:14; 26:6; 28:25). The primary characters in Acts often display close Jewish ties, especially in the first half of the book, where the emphasis is on Peter and those around him in Jerusalem who had interacted with Jesus. Luke, more than the other gospel writers, emphasizes the "twelve apostles" in presenting the first leaders as an exclusively-defined circle of twelve—a number that hearkens back to Israel's past with its twelve tribes. As the narrative continues in Acts, the author likewise portrays Paul as beginning at the synagogue whenever possible upon entering a new city. The emphasis on Paul's Jewishness also seems to be part of this strategy, as according to Acts, Paul even studied at the feet of the rabbi Gamaliel, was completely loyal to the Law, abided by the apostolic decree, circumcized Timothy, submitted to Jerusalem authorities, and observed Jewish festivals.[15]

Such appeals to Jewish roots have not escaped the notice of scholars of Acts, many of whom believe that they were meant to tap into the Roman respect for ancestral religion.[16] In this way scholars such as Conzelmann make a case for Acts as an *apologia pro ecclesia*—a defense of the church to the Roman administration.[17] These references to Jewish scripture and history are therefore part of an organized appeal to Roman leaders for whom the author presents Christianity's ancient roots. Again, however, a completely contradictory viewpoint emerges as P. W. Walaskay argues that Luke–Acts is not a defense of the Christians to the Romans, but a defense of the Romans to the Christians—an *apologia pro imperio* to counter anti-Roman sentiments in certain Christian circles.[18] Walaskay traces this theory back to scholars such as Matthias Schneckenburger, for instance, who long ago pointed out that it was Jewish Christians in Rome rather than Roman authorities to whom Luke was writing.[19]

---

[15] Philipp Vielhauer, "On the 'Paulinism' of Acts," in *Studies in Luke–Acts* (ed. Leander E. Keck and J. Louis Martyn; Philadelphia: Fortress, 1980), 38.

[16] Some scholars, such as Foakes-Jackson, Kirsopp Lake, B. S. Easton, and Henry J. Cadbury, have advanced the theory that Rome licensed some foreign relations, and these references are part of a *religio licita*. See Cadbury, *The Making of Luke–Acts*, 302.

[17] Hans Conzelmann, *The Theology of St. Luke* (trans. Geoffrey Buswell; London: Faber and Faber 1960) 144. He is in the company of others, such as Eduard Zeller, Johannes Weiss, and William Ramsay.

[18] Walaskay, *And so we came to Rome*, 50.

[19] Walaskay, *And so we came to Rome*, 3, 69 n. 6, citing Matthias Schneckenburger, *Über den Zweck der Apostelgeschichte* (Bern: Christian Fischer, 1841).

Philip Esler presents the range of evidence for both sides of the issue and compellingly argues that the primary concern of these Jewish references is an attempt to legitimize Christianity for the Romans in Luke's audience.[20] Evidence of the author's active reshaping of material to deepen Christianity's religious roots appears, for example, in Luke 4:36 when the author deletes the word καινή ("new") from the Markan phrase διδαχὴ καινή ("new teaching"; cf. Mark 1:27). The author's accentuation of these roots appears also with the addition of the phrase "the old is best" in Luke 5:39 (cf. Mark 2:22), or such descriptions as, "from the days of old" (Acts 15:7) and "ancestral law" (Acts 22:3).[21] The author of Acts, exhibiting disdain for the way the Athenians love new teachings (Acts 17:19, 21), emphasizes instead the impression of Christianity's ancestral traditions—an aspect the Romans were known to respect within certain religious movements.[22]

Portraying Religious Stability

Establishing a deep connection to Jewish roots ties in closely with the strong emphasis on the role of Jerusalem and the early Jewish Christian leadership group there. The importance of Jerusalem for Luke–Acts begins already in the gospel with the abundant references to this city, tallying almost as much as all three of the other canonical gospels combined (Mark has eleven; Matthew, twelve; John, thirteen; and Luke, thirty-one). When Jesus gives his final instructions before ascending, for example, only in Luke does he command them to stay in Jerusalem until the Holy Spirit comes upon them (Luke 24:49), rather than going to Galilee, as in the other gospels. It is no surprise, as well, that the great missionary event for early Christianity at the beginning of Acts occurs in Jerusalem. Fifty-eight more references to this holy city in the subsequent narrative effectively emphasize Christianity's beginnings with the Jewish focal point of Jerusalem.

As the author focuses upon the beginnings of the Christian movement in Jerusalem (thus tying the origins closely to Judaism), there occurs a simultaneous privileging of the early Jewish Christian leadership there, especially with regard to Peter. An examination of Acts reveals a continuation and even elaboration of Peter's prominence already evident in Luke. In Luke, for example, there are no references to Jesus addressing Peter as Satan (as there are in the other three gospels), or to Jesus specifically chiding Peter for sleeping in the Garden, or to Peter swearing and calling down oaths upon himself when he denies Jesus. Instead, Luke is the only canonical gospel to present a solitary resurrection appearance to Peter ("It is true: the Lord has risen; he has appeared

---

[20] Philip Francis Esler, *Community and Gospel in Luke–Acts: The Social and Political Motivations of Lucan Theology* (SNTSMS 57; Cambridge: Cambridge University Press, 1987), 217–19.
[21] Ibid., 216.
[22] Ibid.

to Simon"; Luke 24:34). It is likewise probably no accident then that Peter is the last of the Twelve to be mentioned by name in Luke and the first of the Twelve to be mentioned in Acts.[23] Thus by means of words and deeds, the author of Acts narrates examples of Peter's significance at the earliest stage of the religion.[24]

Peter's deeds in Acts display his special status as he not only makes converts, but also experiences visions and performs miracles (healing a lame man in 3:1–11, for example, and a paralytic bedridden for eight years in 9:33). These words encapsulate his extraordinary powers: "As a result, people brought the sick into the streets and laid them on beds and mats so that at least Peter's shadow might fall on some of them as he passed by" (Acts 9:33). In addition to healing miracles, Peter has the power to cause death merely by pronouncing the words (5:1–11), and even brings a young girl named Tabitha back to life (9:32–35) in a miracle that mirrors Jesus' actions when he raised Jairus's daughter, including the detail that the crowd in the room was told to leave (9:36–42). Peter's miracle in Lydda converts the entire Plain of Sharon (9:32–35); from Joppa he continues on to Caesarea "where he to all intents and purposes founds the first Gentile Christian community."[25] In Samaria it is he who brings the Spirit to Philip's converts.

With respect to Peter the author emphasizes again the principle of divine legitimation in describing God's ordination of Peter as spokesperson through the sending of the Holy Spirit (Acts 2:12). The next chapters subsequently present Peter functioning as the primary spokesperson for the group (e.g., Acts 1:15), followed by examples of his success (1:15–22; 2:14–36; 3:12–26; 10:34–44).[26] According to Acts, the extraordinary strength of Peter's words on Pentecost converts three thousand (2:41), while the next Petrine sermon increases the number of Jewish Christians to five thousand (4:2).[27] Peter, filled with the Holy Spirit, speaks again in Acts 4:8, then, in the next chapter, he is the one who conducts the questioning of Ananias and Sapphira (Acts 5:3), and finally in yet another powerful speech before the council in Jerusalem, it is he who spearheads the most important religion-changing precedent: "Brothers, you know that some time ago God made a choice among you that the Gentiles might hear *from my lips* the message of the gospel and believe" (15:7–11).[28]

---

[23] Raymond E. Brown, Karl P. Donfried, and John Reumann, eds., *Peter in the New Testament* (Minneapolis: Augsburg, 1973), 128.

[24] For more on the role of Peter, see Ann Graham Brock, *Mary Magdalene, The First Apostle: The Struggle for Authority* (HTS 51; Cambridge: Harvard University Press for Harvard Theological Studies, 2003).

[25] Haenchen, *Acts*, 461.

[26] Terence V. Smith, *Petrine Controversies in Early Christianity* (WUNT 2.15; Tübingen: Mohr [Siebeck], 1985), 160–62.

[27] Haenchen, *Acts*, 128.

[28] Only after Peter speaks to the council do Paul and Barnabas take a turn. Then so does James (who refers to Peter's declaration of God's will, not the more recently uttered words of Barnabas and Paul). When James stands up, he affirms the Gentile decision. It seems that the author "assumes that such a major change must begin with

The portion of Acts concentrating on Peter and climaxing with the Cornelius incident presents Peter as the pivotal figure in the extension of the gospel to the Gentiles. In fact, this incident is so significant that the author presents the entire event a second time in chapter eleven. At a critical point in early Christianity, Acts shows how, in accordance with divine approval, this incident with Peter turns the religious tide in Jerusalem: "When they heard this, they had no further objections and praised God, saying, 'So then, God has granted even the Gentiles repentance unto life'" (Acts 11:18). Thus in Acts, the author portrays Peter, as head of twelve Jewish men, quoting Hebrew scripture, divinely empowered to change the course of early Christian history.

Portraying Religious Organization and Political Cooperation

An essential component of this legitimizing process is therefore the presentation of Christianity's stability as an organized movement with a clear leadership structure. The author not only emphasizes Peter's role and Jerusalem's early centrality, but also, in the process, effectively places other early Christian missionary figures under such jurisdiction. As Scott Spencer points out, "Luke makes his point by magnifying the apostles' centralized, Jerusalem-based authority over the expanding church, including their unique prerogative to impart the Spirit to new believers."[29]

The extent of Peter's preeminence in Acts emerges even more clearly when one examines how other figures, such as John, Philip, and Paul fare by comparison to Peter. The figure of John illuminates the privileged position of Peter, as he clearly exists as a mere shadow in relation to Peter's portrayal. The book of Acts mentions John fourteen times, but always in conjunction with Peter and always in a secondary position to him (Acts 1:3; 3:1, 3, 4, 11; 4:1, 3, 7, 13, 19, 23; 8:14, 17, 25). In this entire book, the figure of John proclaims no independent words and performs no independent actions; John merely quietly accompanies Peter (in 4:3) and is consequently arrested with him (in 8:14). In all these references it is instead Peter who inevitably possesses the voice and the focus.

A similar technique of subsumation occurs with Philip, an independent evangelist whom the author subordinates to Peter in a number of ways. Even though, for example, Philip evangelizes Samaria, it is Peter (with John as his companion) who annexes it for Jerusalem (8:14–25). By making the converts

---

the Twelve and has interpreted the Cornelius episode as the key point even though Acts itself preserves evidence of different beginnings to the gentile mission." Pheme Perkins, *Peter: Apostle for the Whole Church* (Columbia, S.C.: University of South Carolina Press, 1994), 119. She cites Paul Achtemeier, *The Quest for Unity in the New Testament Church* (Philadelphia: Fortress, 1987), 36–43.

[29] F. Scott Spencer, *The Portrait of Philip in Acts: A Study of Roles and Relations* (JSNTSup 67; Sheffield, England: JSOT Press; Copyright Sheffield Academic Press, 1992), 216.

wait to receive the Spirit through official channels (such as Peter and the Twelve), the author of Luke effectively brings them under the "ecclesiastical umbrella."[30] Käsemann astutely provides further examples of how the author "has purposefully downgraded Philip's evangelistic achievements."[31] Spencer undergirds his insights, "Is it not an odd feature of the Acts narrative that a charismatic missionary like Philip, so evidently imbued with the Spirit (6:3; 8:29, 30), does not himself administer to those he evangelizes?"[32] In other words, Philip "fails to match" the prowess of Peter "at the point of imparting the Spirit to his converts."[33] Haenchen likewise maintains that Luke's account of the Spirit's outpouring in Acts 8:14–17 is designed to emphasize "the mission to the Samaritans was not completed by any subordinate outsider [= Philip], but was carried out in due form by the legal heads of the Church [= the Twelve]."[34]

This shaping of an organized power structure, focused upon Peter, the Twelve, and Jerusalem, in preference to John and Philip is relatively clear. Scholars do not always notice, however, the subtle shifting of authority with respect to Paul as well. In fact, despite all these textual nods to the authority of the Jerusalem group, scholars often describe Acts as a Pauline text, primarily because of the significant amount of material that focuses on Paul instead of Peter.[35] I disagree with such an assumption and contend instead that the amount of narrative devoted to particular subjects in Acts does not represent the author's devotion to them but instead the intensity of the author's efforts to portray them in a certain way. Although the author of Acts attributes significantly more narrative to Paul than to Peter, an analysis of their position relative to each other provides some important revelatory clues to the politics of the text.

The first and foremost indication of the author's preferences emerges as this text credits the first evangelism of the Gentiles to Peter rather than Paul—a role that Paul in his letters unquestionably attributes to himself.[36] Second, whereas Acts emphasizes not only Peter's role as an apostle, even chief among them, in this text the title of "apostle" for the most part eludes Paul. Indeed, of the twenty-eight occurrences of the word "apostle(s)" in Acts, only in one

---

[30] Ibid.

[31] Ernst Käsemann, *Essays on New Testament Themes* (London: SCM, 1964), 90, 136–48; and Spencer, *Philip in Acts*, 216. In numerous ways the author portrays the Seven as being under the jurisdiction of the Twelve. One example is Luke's use of the Greek word καταστήσομεν to portray the Twelve appointing a committee of Seven. "Elsewhere in Luke–Acts καθίστημι occasionally denotes a ruler's assignment of duty to one of his subjects—for example, a householder's charging his steward to manage the estate" (Luke 12:42, 44). See Spencer, *Philip in Acts*, 195–96.

[32] Spencer, *Philip in Acts*, 189.

[33] Ibid.

[34] Haenchen, *Acts*, 306. See also Spencer, *Philip in Acts*, 216.

[35] Barrett, for instance, claims, "The author of Acts was at least some kind of Paulinist." (C. K. Barrett, *The Signs of an Apostle* [London: Epworth Press, 1970] 50. Walaskay refers to Luke as the "faithful Paulinist." Walaskay, *And so we came to Rome*, 52.

[36] Gal 1:16; 2:7–9; Rom 1:5, 13–15; 11:13; 15:15–21.

section is this term applied to Barnabas and Paul (14:4,14) and in this case, it is used in the broader sense to refer to persons sent on a mission, not in the sense of the "twelve" used elsewhere in Acts (13:2–3).[37] In his own letters Paul is so conscientious about claiming this title for himself that he employs the term at least sixteen times and almost always begins his epistles with this term. Although Acts depicts Paul performing miracles, these miracles more often function to depict Paul's divine legitimation rather than uplifting his status in the text. Furthermore, Acts portrays Paul as needing to appeal to the authority of the apostles (Acts 13:31), a description that also directly contradicts Paul's self-attestation.[38] Indeed, the author of Acts contradicts many of Paul's self-descriptions in order to portray him as someone completely loyal to the Law, abiding by the apostolic decree, and submitting to Jerusalem authorities. Schmithals is among those scholars who are not led astray by the extensive amount of material on Paul. He points out "it is not to be doubted that in the book of Acts Paul clearly is 'downgraded.' "[39]

As further evidence of Paul's being downgraded it is important to note that this early Christian missionary so historically crucial to the spread of the religion as to have become known as "the apostle Paul" literally does not qualify to be called an apostle according to Acts. By focusing on the tightly-knit leadership in Jerusalem, the author of Acts explicates three exclusionary criteria in defining the requirements for being an apostle. The text reads, for example, "Therefore it is necessary to choose one of the men who have been with us from the beginning" (Acts 1:21). The exclusion comes not only with the phrase, "from the beginning," but also by limiting the length of time for Christ's appearance to forty days after Jesus' resurrection.[40] Scholars, such as Hans von Campenhausen, point out the author's exclusionary move in restricting the authority to that of "the first 'apostolic' generation."[41] It has "momen-

---

[37] Some scholars credit the term as usage of a source (Conzelmann, *Acts*, 108; Haenchen, *Acts*, 420 n. 10) and others as indicating a use of the term apostle in a more generalized, nontitular way (Eduard Lohse, "Ursprung und Prägung des christlichen Apostolates," *TZ* 9 [1953]: 273 n. 46).

[38] Vielhauer contends, "The author of Acts is in his Christology pre-Pauline, in his natural theology, concept of the law, and eschatology, post-Pauline. He presents no specifically Pauline idea." Vielhauer, "On the 'Paulinism' of Acts".

[39] Walter Schmithals, *The Office of Apostle in the Early Church* (trans. J. E. Steely; Nashville: Abingdon Press, 1969), 269; Günter Klein, *Die zwölf Apostel: Ursprung und Gehalt einer Idee* (FRLANT 77; Göttingen: Vandenhoeck & Ruprecht, 1961), 192–201.

[40] According to Philippe H. Menoud, it appears that Luke introduced the limitation of the symbolic "forty days" to undergird the institution of a special small group of witnesses with the task of preaching to the world. See his article, "Pendant Quarante Jours," *Jésus-Christ et la Foi: Recherches néotestamentaires*, Bibliothèque théologique (Neuchâtel/ Paris: Delachaux et Niestlé, 1975), 110–18; see also, Haenchen, *Apostelgeschichte*, 126.

[41] Hans von Campenhausen, *Ecclesiastical Authority and Spiritual Power in the Church of the First Three Centuries* (Peabody, Mass.: Hendrickson, 1997), 23. See also Elaine Pagels, "Visions, Appearances, and Apostolic Authority: Gnostic and Orthodox Traditions," in *Gnosis: Festschrift für Hans Jonas* (ed. Barbara Aland; Göttingen: Vandenhoeck and Ruprecht, 1978), 416.

tous consequences" that the appearances of Christ are limited to this group.[42] The issue revolves around whether direct access to Christ is available by means of special revelation "through visions long after the resurrection" and whether such revelations are granted only to certain persons and not to others.[43] Such a statement has profound implications for the independent evangelists (such as Paul, Philip, and others who spread the gospel), as it attempts to restrict the legitimizing authority of independent charismatic leaders who claimed their own place. Finally, the exclusionary move mandates that: δεῖ οὖν τῶν συνελθόντων ἡμῖν ἀνδρῶν ("It is necessary [to choose] one of the men"). This exclusionary requirement with respect to the gender of the apostles appears only here. As a result, among those whose roles are sacrificed for the "greater good" of the controlled and structured portrait are the early Christian female leaders.

Portraying Politically/Culturally Acceptable Female Leadership Roles

Both the Gospel of Luke and Acts present an impressive number of narratives about women, so much so that many scholars have argued that Luke had an especially high regard for women's roles in early Christianity.[44] A comparison of the four canonical gospels shows that the Gospel of Luke holds the distinction of presenting the greatest number of verses concerning women—a total of forty-two passages with twenty-three unique to Luke.[45] Although many scholars have explored this topic, this section can highlight only a few aspects concerning the shaping of women's roles.[46] One of the author's techniques for

---

[42] Karl Holl, "Der Kirchenbegriff des Paulus in seinem Verhältnis zu dem der Urgemeinde" in *Gesammelte Aufsätze zur Kirchengeschichte: Der Osten* (Tübingen: Mohr Siebeck, 1921), 2:50–51; see also Pagels, "Visions, Appearances, and Apostolic Authority," 417.

[43] Pagels, "Visions, Appearances, and Apostolic Authority," 424.

[44] Swidler, for example, states, "In sum it can be said that beyond the evidence that clearly points to the fact that Jesus himself was a vigorous feminist, Luke's Gospel reflects this feminism most intensely of all the Gospels." Leonard Swidler, *Biblical Affirmations of Women* (Philadelphia: Westminster, 1979), 280–81. Dornish likewise describes how Luke "puts these women and especially Mary at the center of the drama as it begins." Loretta Dornish, *A Woman Reads the Gospel of Luke* (Collegeville, Ind.: Liturgical Press, 1996), 36.

[45] Swidler, *Biblical Affirmations*, 255.

[46] Elisabeth Schüssler Fiorenza, *Jesus: Miriam's Child* (New York: Continuum, 1994); Luise Schottroff, Silvia Schroer, and Marie-Theres Wacker, *Feminist Interpretation: The Bible in Women's Perspective* (trans. Martin and Barbara Rumscheidt; Minneapolis: Fortress, 1998); Lilia Sebastiani, *Tra/Sfigurazione. Il personaggio evangelico di Maria di Magdala e il mito della peccatrice redenta nella tradizione occidentale* (Brescia: Queriniana, 1992); Martin Hengel, "Maria Magdalena und die Frauen als Zeugen," *Abraham unser Vater: Festschrift Otto Michel* (Leiden: Brill, 1963), 243–56; Carla Ricci, *Mary Magdalene and Many Others: Women Who Followed Jesus* (trans. Paul Burns; Minneapolis: Fortress, 1994), 51–110; Turid Karlsen Seim, *The Double Message: Patterns of Gender in Luke–Acts* (Edinburgh: T&T Clark, 1994). For those that perceive Luke's treatment of women more positively, see Swidler, *Biblical Affirmations of Women*, 280–81; Ben Witherington III, "On the Road

presenting women's roles involves a unique methodology of pairing narratives about men with those about women.[47] Examples begin already in the Gospel of Luke, with the pairing of the man with the mustard seed and the woman with the leaven (Luke 13:18–21); the man searching for his lost sheep and the woman searching for her lost coin (Luke 15:4–10); as well as the widow's only son and Jairus's only daughter (Luke 7:12; 8:42).

An examination of the role of women in Acts follows a similar pattern to that in Luke. The narratives of Ananias (Acts 5:1–6) and Sapphira (Acts 5:7–11) is a sample of the continuation of such pairing in Acts.[48] Such pairing suggests a certain egalitarianism in the presentation of men's and women's roles. A closer look, however, reveals that Luke's portrayals of pairs are not necessarily advantageous to the leadership status of women.[49] In fact, some scholars have discerned the subtle ways in which the author typically portrays women in the role of followers.[50] According to Jane Schaberg, "the Gospel attempts to meet various needs, such as instructing and edifying women converts, appeasing the detractors of Christianity, and controlling women who practice or aspire to practice a prophetic ministry in the church."[51]

Generally, speeches that authors place upon the lips of the apostles and their accompanying characters are one of the means by which authors subtly convey their messages. Martin Dibelius counted twenty-four speeches in Acts, with eight attributed to Peter and nine to Paul (300 of the book's 1000 verses).[52] Women are present in the text of Acts, but rarely speak. "The two individual women of Acts spoken to in direct speech are condemned and silenced (Sapphira in Acts 5, like her husband Ananias, is silenced effectively by death; the slave girl in Acts 17 who has been annoying Paul is silenced by means of an exorcism)."[53] The highest leadership role depicted is that of Prisca who

---

with Mary Magdalene, Joanna, Susanna, and Other Disciples—Luke 8:1–3," *ZNW* 70 (1979): 243–48; Susanne Heine, *Women and Early Christianity: Are the Feminist Scholars Right?* (London: SCM, 1987) who has "corrective" to the feminist angle; E. Jane Via, "Women in the Gospel of Luke," in *Women in the World's Religions: Past and Present* (ed. Ursula King; New York: Paragon House, 1987), 38–55. Via supports Swidler's hypothesis that the author of Luke could have been a woman (p. 50).

[47] Helmut Flender, *Heil und Geschichte in der Theologie des Lukas*; ET: *St. Luke, Theologian of Redemptive History* (Philadelphia: Fortress, 1967), 9–10; Jane Schaberg, "Luke," in *The Women's Bible Commentary*, 275–92 (ed. Carol A. Newsom and Sharon H. Ringe; Louisville, Ky.: Westminster/John Knox, 1992), 279; Joachim Jeremias, *The Parables of Jesus* (New York: Scribner, 1963), 90; Constance F. Parvey, "The Theology and Leadership of Women in the New Testament," in *Religion and Sexism*, (ed. Rosemary Radford Ruether; New York: Simon & Schuster, 1974), 139–49, esp. 149 n. 40.

[48] Gail O'Day, "Acts," *Women's Bible Commentary*, 308–9. She provides other examples as well.

[49] Schaberg, "Luke," 278.

[50] See Eugene H. Maly, "Women and the Gospel of Luke," *BTB* 10 (1980): 99–104 and the literature cited there.

[51] Schaberg, "Luke," 275.

[52] Martin Dibelius, *Studies in the Acts of the Apostles* (ed. H. Greeven; New York: Scribners, 1956), 150; Haenchen, *Acts*, 104.

[53] Schaberg, "Luke," 280.

along with her husband Aquila is referenced as a missionary (Acts 18:8) and teacher (Acts 18:26) but not as a minister or apostle. The text deftly presents women "as models of subordinate service, excluded from the power center of the movement and from significant responsibilities."[54] In such portrayals, "Luke restricts the roles of women to what is acceptable to the conventions of the imperial world."[55]

The numerous references to women as anonymous female characters are an important indication of their position within the text. One of the primary functions of women in the text is to act as receivers or beneficiaries of the preaching and healing powers of the men.[56] It appears that the primary female role in Acts is that of "mother" to the fledgling community, one who out of her wealth provides home, hospitality, and material aid to believers. Tabitha, for example, is an almsgiver (9:36–43).[57] Mary, identified as John Mark's mother, has a house in which many believers gather (Acts 12:12). Lydia, in Philippi, also provides her house (but again with no hint in the text of any active leadership role in it). This kind of status in Acts parallels the role of women in the gospel; thus, it is probably no coincidence that Luke is the only gospel that describes Mary Magdalene and the other women as helping to support Jesus and his followers financially out of their own resources (Luke 8:1–3).

One should, therefore, be cautious not to allow the numerous passages devoted to women in Luke and Acts to mislead one into thinking that the author is uplifting women's prominence in the early church. The way in which the text accords no apostolic role to women appears to be part of a programmatic presentation of the gospel message in a restrictive, structured, and nonthreatening format.[58] Perhaps the author's idea of legitimizing and supporting the

---

[54] Ibid., 275. A representative example of such pairing of characters: Simeon and Anna (Luke 2:25–38). Anna receives three verses as opposed to eleven for Simeon. With respect to Anna's role, what Luke stresses is her silent witness, as well as the great length of her widowhood and her continual presence, fasting, and praying in the Temple. Of the widow Anna, the text reads, "she spoke about him to all who were looking forward to the redemption of Jerusalem" (Luke 2:38). Anna, unlike Simeon, however, has no canticle and the Spirit is not said to be with her, although by contrast three times the text refers to the Spirit empowering Simeon (2:25, 26, 27) and attributes two canticles to him (p. 283). She is "presumably in the outer court, the only part of the precincts women were allowed to enter." This portrait of Anna may provide a trace of the important ministry of widows in the early church, but it does not elaborate on the nature of that ministry (p. 283). Luke's portrayal of Anna fits the strategy evident in the gospel as a whole of providing "female readers with female characters as role models: prayerful, quiet, grateful women, supportive of male leadership." See also Schüssler Fiorenza, *In Memory of Her*, 50.

[55] Schaberg, "Luke," 279.

[56] Ibid., 280.

[57] According to Reimer, Lydia's role may have been more comprehensive than almsgiving, "but includes charitable activity in the service of justice." Ivoni Richter Reimer, *Women in the Acts of the Apostles: A Feminist Liberation Perspective* (trans. Linda M. Maloney; Minneapolis: Fortress, 1995), 262.

[58] Turid Karlsen Seim explains, "When women in Acts are excluded from becoming

Christian mission meant minimizing the portrayal of women's active participation in evangelism in order to emphasize instead the importance of their financial contributions. Although financial support is significant—and this kind of portrayal in Acts serves the author's purpose—it does not accurately depict the full spectrum of leadership at such a crucial stage in early Christianity.

Conclusion

This examination has highlighted the paradoxical nature of the book of Acts in the way the author shapes and polishes the narratives to assert a revised form of Christianity, thereby removing possible grounds for its criticism. On the one hand it appears to champion the role of women by offering an immense amount of narratives that feature female subjects, and yet it tones down the diversity of their contributions evidenced by other early Christian texts.

It appears to champion the Jewish religion in its abundant references to Jewish narratives, Jewish figures, and Jewish scripture. Despite all the material pertaining to Judaism in the text, the author does not, however, place the needs of the Jewish people foremost. There appears to be no evidence of the author's lessening of Jewish culpability in the persecution of the first Christians (as the author does with the Romans); in fact, there is even more emphasis upon it. So the claim of common religious roots and common ancestry with the Jews is politically and religiously expedient in order to establish a link with this ancient religion. The emphasis on Christianity as an ancestral faith has "a vital political purpose—to attest that Christianity, unlike new and therefore revolutionary religions, was no threat to Rome, nor to the order and stability so prized by the Romans."[59] Once the author establishes this link, in part through an emphasis on Jerusalem, the geographical references to Jerusalem coexist with an ever-increasing number of references to Rome in the second half of Acts.

The author neutralizes the text politically with its sympathetic portrayals of Roman authorities: "Part of Luke's task was to present Christian history in such a way as to demonstrate that faith in Jesus Christ and allegiance to Rome were not mutually inconsistent."[60] The text also accentuates divine confirmation and approval through miraculous support for the first leaders of the movement. In accentuating the positive aspects, the author presents Christianity as an organized, structured movement, beginning with Jerusalem and its early leadership, especially Peter and the Twelve. The figure of Peter effectively functions in this text as guarantor of the tradition, especially with

---

apostles or from being leaders in other ways, this is a consequence of Luke's restricted and special concept of apostleship and acceptance of the public sphere as a man's world." Seim, *The Double Message*, 162.

[59] Esler, *Community and Gospel in Luke–Acts*, 218.

[60] Ibid., 210.

respect to significant changes in the tradition, such as the inclusion of the Gentiles. The independent evangelists such as Philip and Paul appear accountable to or confirmed in some way by the Jerusalem circle. The author pays homage to Paul and includes such an abundance of narratives because it would have been impossible to ignore his prominence. Indeed, Paul appears to receive a "lion's share of attention,"[61] but in retrospect one sees the shaping of the narrative such that Paul would never have become known by the popular epithet "the apostle Paul" had Acts been our only source.

By modeling women's roles in terms of nurturing and financial support, the author deemphasizes the active leadership roles that early Christian women historically held. In other words, although Luke and Acts present a number of stories involving women, no real counter-cultural role models emerge for them. In the process of such adjustments to the narratives, the text deemphasizes possible sources of criticism or politically sensitive material, especially for Gentile readers. By means of references to Peter, Jerusalem, and the host of Israel's historical contributions, the author shapes the narrative into a domesticated, legitimated portrayal of early Christianity. As Esler points out, "Legitimating Christianity to them inevitably involved providing a reassurance that faith in Jesus Christ was not incompatible with allegiance to Rome."[62] The author constructs the early history in accordance with his own vision by imposing his perspective of the church upon the historical situation. By so completely reshaping early Christian history of the first century, the author profoundly shapes the history of Christianity to come.

---

[61] O'Day, *Women's Bible Commentary*, 306.
[62] Esler, *Community and Gospel in Luke–Acts*, 217.

CHAPTER SIX

LUKE THE HELLENIST

Christopher R. Matthews

Who were the Hellenists? This question has always ranked high on the list of recurrent issues that face historians of early Christianity. In this short essay I want to suggest that Luke's treatment of the Hellenists in Acts makes sense, at least in part, as a way of tracing back the lineage of Luke's own community to the "mother church" in Jerusalem.[1] Space prohibits dealing with even a representative fraction of the scholarly output touching on the Hellenists. With apologies to many others from whose work I have learned much, I will focus here on the analysis of the Hellenists found in C. K. Barrett's extraordinary commentary on Acts.[2] Without wishing to imply that Barrett would agree with my reading of his work, I will interact with various of his assessments of Luke's compositional procedures to support the view that the Hellenists in Acts owe their strategic position in the early "Jerusalem community" in great part, if not completely, to Luke's imaginative "discourse on origins."[3]

At the outset I want to explore via several examples some tensions that I find in Barrett's treatment of Luke's presentation in the first part of Acts, especially as it bears on judgments about the historical credibility of various details.

---

[1] In my work on the Philip pericopes in Acts, I argue against Ernst Haenchen's view that Luke goes out of his way to suppress traditions associated with the Hellenists. François Bovon once made the comment while we were discussing my analysis that one factor in favor of my position was the fact that Luke himself was a "Hellenist." I have had that comment in mind while developing this piece in honor of François. For Haenchen's claim, see idem, *The Acts of the Apostles: A Commentary* (trans. R. McL. Wilson et al.; Philadelphia: Westminster, 1971), 315–16; idem, "Simon Magus in der Apostelgeschichte," in *Gnosis und Neues Testament: Studien aus Religionswissenschaft und Theologie* (ed. K.-W. Tröger; Gütersloh: Mohn, 1973), 278. My argument against Haenchen's understanding is developed especially in the second chapter of my *Philip: Apostle and Evangelist. Configurations of a Tradition* (NovTSup 105; Leiden: Brill, 2002). On the validity of presuming the existence of a Gospel writer's community, see David C. Sim, "The Gospels for All Christians? A Response to Richard Bauckham," *JSNT* 84 (2001): 3–27.

[2] C. K. Barrett, *A Critical and Exegetical Commentary on the Acts of the Apostles* (2 vols.; ICC; Edinburgh: T&T Clark, 1994–98).

[3] I wish to prescind here from debates over the actual composition of the "Jerusalem community" along the lines of Craig C. Hill's *Hellenists and Hebrews: Reappraising Division within the Earliest Church* (Minneapolis: Fortress, 1992), which challenges the "consensus" view that the Jerusalem church was divided into Hebrew and Hellenist factions. I suggest that it will be more fruitful to locate the Hellenists in Luke's "historical" program rather than in history itself.

First, Barrett is quite sanguine about Luke's summary reports concerning the great numbers (Acts 2:41: 3,000; 4:4: 5,000) added to the early Jerusalem community as a consequence of Peter's preaching.[4] Rather than suggest that a dramatic hyperbole attaches to these figures, he justifies them by reasoning that only in Jerusalem could one expect to find great numbers of people who were sympathetically aware of Jesus and his message and who "needed only such impetus as the events of Pentecost and a supernatural healing could give to bring them over the boundary into the company of believers" (1:222). In this fashion fantastic events, which are really beyond a historian's purview, are allowed to verify fantastic numbers.[5] That Barrett continues to take these numbers seriously emerges in his explanation of the availability of the "young men" who carry out the bodies of Ananias and Sapphira (5:6, 10). He notes that "among the thousands involved (4.4) some would be active and eager enough to perform unpleasant duties" (1:268). Of course it may be that the "problem" Barrett perceives to be in need of a solution here only arises as an outcome of this type of historicistic reading, which fortunately is not employed in a thoroughgoing manner throughout his commentary.

In the instances just reviewed we see the Lukan picture of Christian origins itself operative in Barrett's reconstruction. That he seems to allow for no other possibility appears to be the implication of his comments on Luke's summary statement at 2:42: "In this verse Luke gives an idealized picture of the earliest church. . . . There is no ground for doubting the outline of Luke's account; if he had not given it we should doubtless have conjectured something of the kind" (1:166). Yet Barrett himself in another connection provides evidence that belies the credibility of Luke's census-like reports on the exponential growth of the Jerusalem congregation. Thus when commenting on the setting of the scene in 4:23–31, he notes that "it is probably true that Luke thought of a church gathering such as he himself knew, of a size that could meet in a private house" (1:243). Although Barrett precedes this observation with the caveat that the text refers to "the community 'as a whole', but not necessarily the whole of it," there is no denying that it is the "house church" that is truly consistent with everything that we know about the principal social setting of Christian groups in their first centuries. Barrett operates under the assumption that in the period covered by the first part of Acts, the only church that exists is the one in Jerusalem (1:390). He holds to this presupposition even though he warns that the existence of Christians in Damascus (9:2) is

---

[4] Barrett, *Acts*, 1:159, 162, 222. Subsequent references to Barrett's commentary will be noted in the text. Unless specified otherwise, biblical references in the text are to Acts.

[5] Rodney Stark's study (*The Rise of Christianity: A Sociologist Reconsiders History* [Princeton: Princeton University Press, 1996], 4–13) of conversion and Christian growth estimates the total number of Christians by the year 40 at 1,000; by the year 50 at 1,400; and by the year 100 at only 7,530. See also Keith Hopkins, "Christian Number and Its Implications," *JECS* 6 (1998): 185–226, who provides a graphic representation (p. 193) of Stark's figures covering 40–350 C.E.

"a valuable reminder of the fact that Acts provides us not with a full record of everything that happened in the early years of Christianity but with a few selected events" (1:447). It is no doubt fair to say that Luke thought of the Jerusalem church as "the mother church of all Christendom" and that it "must have manifested every kind of true Christian life" (1:561). But the modern scholar must resist the temptation to allow Luke's narrative construction of the Jerusalem church to fill in the vacuum left by the dearth of our knowledge about the course of events in earliest Christianity.[6]

A second example of tensions in Barrett's analysis concerns the reports about the practice of community of goods in the early Jerusalem community (2:44–45; 4:32–35). Barrett observes when commenting on 2:44 that the existence of various experiments with communal ownership of possessions contemporary with the birth of the church makes it reasonable to suppose that Christians engaged in a similar pursuit (1:168). Later in his treatment of 4:32–35, after acknowledging the idealizing aspect and edificatory intention of Luke's depiction of the early community's life, he notes somewhat more modestly that "it is probable that some kind of sharing was practised in Jerusalem" (1:252). Finally he suggests that Luke's portrayals in this regard are probably based on traditions like the one about Barnabas in 4:36–37. This exemplary report about Barnabas highlights the ideal nature of Luke's report of universal sharing. Thus "wholesale community of goods must be regarded as Luke's idealizing generalization of what was done by some" (1:258). As far as we know "some" here includes no other cases apart from Barnabas. In this example as in the preceding, it is at least as reasonable to suppose that Luke's statements about community of goods are to be traced back to his rhetorical needs as it is to suppose that they have their basis in the transmission of historical facts. Such a conclusion by no means compromises their importance; rather, we come to see Luke's point. These images of the successful sharing of property illustrate for Luke's contemporaries how the early community heeded the numerous calls in Luke's Gospel (a significant number of which are found exclusively in special Lukan material) for the proper disposition of wealth and possessions.

At this point I want to shift my attention to several other characteristics of Barrett's analysis which are more prevalent, and I believe much more illuminating, than the "historicist" inclination sampled above. While Barrett regularly makes reference to the sources and traditions that he insists must be presupposed to underlie the various narratives and speeches in Acts, he also routinely and quite properly notes Luke's "idealizing" propensity along with his practice of retrojecting various details from the circumstances current in his own day into his characterization of the early church. Thus in lieu of a

---

[6] On the problematic posed by the well-ensconced scholarly habit of paraphrasing Luke's depiction of the centrality of the Jerusalem church in the spread of early Christianity in the absence of other evidence, see Merrill P. Miller, "'Beginning from Jerusalem . . .': Re-examining Canon and Consensus," *Journal of Higher Criticism* 2/1 (1995): 3–30.

historical source for the summary portrait of the Jerusalem community at 2:41–47, Barrett judges that Luke "simply transferred customs from his own time and place" (1:160). Again, at 2:46, "Luke is probably describing the Christian meals of his own day, idealizing them, and setting them back in his description of the first days of Christianity" (1:171). And again, at 4:23–31, "Luke probably used liturgical models . . . current in his own time . . . adapting them to suit his own purpose" (1:242). Thus the prayer in 4:24–30 probably belongs to a Christian liturgical setting toward the end of the first century, "not in the sense that it is simply borrowed from an existing liturgy . . . but in that Luke used the kind of words and phrases that were familiar to him from the church's worship" (1:243). In the same way the speeches that appear in Luke's narrative "represent what Luke himself believed. He was not the kind of critical historian who could say, 'This is what my research has shown that Peter said, or is likely to have said. . . .' Rather it was Luke's desire to believe and to speak as the apostles believed and spoke. . . . The speech then contains . . . the theology of the church as it was known to Luke" (1:132).

An important principle of Barrett's analysis emerges with his judgment that even in cases (such as Peter's Pentecost speech) where one may suspect that Luke is utilizing traditional material, "we have not answered the question of the date and origin of the information on which he drew, or of the channels by which it reached him, whether written or oral" (1:133). This leaves open the possibility that some "traditional materials" may in fact represent formulations that date closer to Luke's time than to the time of the earliest church. While Barrett finds it probable that Luke would have sought out "the oldest traditional material he could find," he also recognizes that it is "at least equally probable that he did not assess it as a critical historian" (1:133). To sum up, the previous paragraphs have sought to highlight the curious mix in Barrett's treatment of Acts consisting, on the one hand, of the acceptance of noteworthy historical detail in Luke's narrative of earliest Christianity, and, on the other, of the exposure of Luke's fondness for idealizing composition, which frequently establishes lines of connection between his own time and the paradigmatic period of Christian origins. In my view the latter disposition offers the more promising way to account for what Luke has done.

Accordingly, rather than focus on the identification of "real" historical detail along the lines of the examples documented above, we will do better to focus on the frequent and perceptive commentary that Barrett offers on the idealizing components of Luke's story of the Jerusalem church as well as Luke's fondness for rounding out his characterization of that church by reading into it elements of the situation of the church of his own day. The effectiveness of this analysis is bolstered by Barrett's keen discernment of the motivations that drive Luke's work. After observing that Luke faced serious problems in the composition of Acts 1–12 both with respect to the availability of material and criteria for arranging it, Barrett notes that Luke's "literary and historical work was controlled by two practical motives: he wished to paint a picture of the life and preaching of the earliest church that would provide instruction and inspiration for his contemporaries, and he wished to show how the Gospel had been taken beyond the Judaism in which it was cradled into the Gentile world" (1:56). One might quibble about the precision of the second concern, given Luke's clear preference to highlight in a variety of ways the proximity of Christianity to Judaism (as Barrett himself recognizes in many places, e.g., 1:493 on Luke's characterization of Cornelius). But it is particularly the first goal, which works in concert with the idealized representation of the Jerusalem church and the association of that paradigmatic community with the church of Luke's day through the incorporation of various details from the life of the latter into the description of the former, that holds explanatory power when seeking to account for the shape of Luke's narrative.

In light of Barrett's cautious analysis (especially with regard to sources and traditions) and sensitivity to Luke's programmatic objectives, his skepticism about the historical indebtedness of Luke's portrayal of the Hellenists takes on added significance. To be sure his initial comments on the implications of the use of the word Ἑλληνισταί at 6:1 run aground on historicistic concerns when he opines that "what must remain uncertain (so far as the word itself goes) is the extent to which these men had adopted along with Greek speech Greek ways of thinking and living. The answer is probably, only to a limited extent" (1:304). Barrett himself, however, renders this observation superfluous by his emphasis on the problem created by Luke's use of the word Ἑλληνιστής three times in Acts (6:1; 9:29; 11:20), each time with a different connotation. "This means that Luke had no precise understanding of a party of 'Hellenists' in the primitive church" (1:309). It is the third occurrence of the word "Hellenist" at 11:20, where it signals "Greek-speaking Gentiles," that leads Barrett to suggest that Luke does not rely on tradition for this verse, a judgment that carries with it "the conclusion that the Hellenists as a party are his invention" (1:550). The telltale word indicates to Barrett that Luke has modified a traditional Antiochene source, justifying the following verdict: "In any reconstruction of sources and of history it must always be borne in mind that Antioch is solid reality, a real place with real people, 'the Hellenists' a speculative idea to which Luke and modern historians have both contributed. Antioch has an assured place in history; whether 'the Hellenists' have is another question" (1:547–48).

At this point I must backtrack to clarify Barrett's position on the relation between the Hellenists and the Seven. The judgment that the Hellenists are a Lukan construction is not meant by him to carry over and cast doubt on the existence of the group of the Seven. Barrett states that Luke

> did not invent the fact that in the early years in Jerusalem there were Greek-speaking Jews who became Christians and had at their head a group of seven men, about two of whom he could hand on biographical details. . . . The Seven were somehow different from the Twelve, but the difference could be adequately stated in the fact that the one group was made up of Hellenists,

the other of Hebrews (v. 1). This was Luke's theory; the word Ἐβραῖος was traditional . . . and Ἑλληνιστής (Luke's use of this word is arbitrary . . .) served as a useful partner. (1:305)

Barrett himself, however, underlines Luke's lack of information about the men whose names are included in the list of the Seven. Further details are forthcoming only about Stephen and Philip, and even Barrett admits that we cannot assume that their stories reached Luke in connection with the list of the Seven in 6:5. Consequently, with respect to the Seven, "we can do little more than conjecture what their importance was and where their influence lay" (1:314). Barrett's analysis of 6:1–7 underlines the lack of concrete information at Luke's disposal in filling out the contours of this early leadership group. He proposes that the account of the choosing of the Seven probably "embodies the method of appointing ministers that was familiar to Luke himself" (1:304). Thus it serves as another example of how Luke can "translate back" procedures familiar from his own circumstances into his portrait of the exemplary past. Similarly, Barrett suggests that Luke's assumptions about relief for the poor (6:1) may rely on ecclesial practices of his own time (1:310). In sum, even if it is probable that Luke's knowledge of the existence of the Seven was based on traditional information, "their position is to some extent the artificial product of Luke's rationalization of old traditions" (1:316). Indeed, in summing up his introductory observations on 6:1–7, Barrett announces that

> it would not be proper at this point to attempt to dig much further into the history of which Luke has given a simple and edifying version. . . . Much of what is missing has in all probability simply dropped away with the passage of time. . . . Luke's intention is not to supply the curious with all the information they would like to have about the church of the first fathers, but to edify the church of his own day. (1:306)

Rather than add further configurations to the already abundant speculations about the "historical" Hellenists then, it is appropriate to examine more closely the situation that Luke wishes to establish in his narrative to see how it coordinates with his principal objectives in writing Acts in the first place.

It is my contention that the Hellenists tell us more about Luke and his community than they do about the early Jerusalem church, and that this was in line with Luke's intention from the beginning. As Barrett correctly observes, Luke writes above all to instruct and inspire his contemporaries, and he does so with certain convictions in mind. "One was that the early years of the church were exemplary." Another "was that the unity of the ideal church was rooted in the (twelve) apostles, who were not only its leaders but its link with Jesus himself (1.21f.)" (1:305). It is this latter emphasis in particular that suggests the motive for Luke's "invention" of the Hellenists.[7]

---

[7] Martin Bodinger ("Les 'Hébreux' et les 'Hellénistes' dans le livre des *Actes des Apôtres,*" *Henoch* 19 [1997]: 39–58) interprets the Hebrews and the Hellenists of Acts

I have already referred to Barrett's supposition that Luke inserted the Hellenists into an Antiochene tradition when he composed the important transitional verse at 11:20. Earlier Barrett attributed Luke's story of the Hebrew and Hellenist widows to "Luke's writing up of the Antiochene tradition in such a way as to relate it to the Twelve" (1:319). That Luke wants to relate the Hellenists to the Twelve makes perfect sense, but whether he needs or follows the guidance of an Antiochene tradition in making this move may be debated. Before we attribute the motive for Luke's narrative deployment of the Hellenists to a putative, otherwise nonextant source/tradition, we should consider the possibility that Luke's portrayal has emerged out of the exigencies that led him to tell the early church's story in the manner that he has. Barrett approaches Luke's account with the presupposition that "the earliest churches founded outside Jerusalem would wish to show that they had valid contacts with the original Jerusalem church" (1:52). But of course this is precisely the picture of Christian origins that has been rhetorically constructed by Luke in Acts.

Luke initially follows the story of the Hellenists in the wake of the persecution following Stephen's martyrdom by presenting two Philip stories (8:4–40).[8] He delays coverage of the momentous Hellenist innovation at Antioch (11:19–26) in order first to relate two other significant events for his narrative, namely, the conversions of Paul and Cornelius. We especially see his hand at work in the nearly identical phrasing shared by 8:1, 4, and 11:19, highlighted by the use of the word διασπείρειν, which occurs in these passages alone in the New Testament. Thus 8:4 serves to link together the elements of Luke's "genealogy" of the Hellenists as it connects the Philip stories that follow to the preceding narrative (8:1) and also looks ahead to 11:19–26. Barrett describes Luke's concerns in the latter passage as follows:

> It was important to Luke (and it may be that it was important also to the Jewish evangelists [i.e., the Hellenists]) that this development should not be and should not appear to be a new independent piece of religious enthusiasm. It must be, and be seen to be, a valid expression, result, and continuation of the work of Jesus. In historical terms this could be tested only by Jerusalem, which still housed the apostles who represented and maintained the link between the historical Jesus and the post-resurrection consequences of his work (1.21f). (1:545)

Barrett's parenthetical statement about the Jewish evangelists concedes that the analysis here is above all a good statement of Luke's own position. The import of his comment that the developments in Antioch could only be tested in "historical terms" by the apostles at Jerusalem is less clear. He notes that

---

as a construction that retrojects concerns of Luke's day into the past—the presence of the Hellenists is connected with the legitimizing of the Gentile mission. As will become clear in what follows, I find the point of Luke's "retrojection" to lie elsewhere.

[8] This persecution appears to owe much to the needs of Luke's narrative.

Luke had been "careful" to leave the apostles in Jerusalem at 8:1 (1:546), having earlier found the curious notice of the dispersal of the church from Jerusalem
"except for the apostles" attributable to Lukan composition (1:391). In noting
the overlap between the story of the missioners at Antioch and the account
about Cornelius in terms of the issue of acceptance of Gentiles, Barrett again
insists that

> it was important to Luke . . . to show that this new development (like that in
> Caesarea) was not an independent innovation but was based on the original
> Jerusalem Gospel and those who could guarantee its connection with Jesus. Since
> in the narrative as we have it this is done in two ways it is probable that
> the connection was already made in the Antiochene tradition on which Luke
> drew. (1:546)

The latter statement presents us with an important question: Has Luke inherited his Jerusalem-centric view from Antioch? Barrett thinks it probable that
the church at Antioch correctly believed that it was founded from Jerusalem.
Thus the story at 11:19–26 "may well represent Luke's own edited version of
a belief cherished in Antioch" (1:547). But we must inquire carefully whether
it was Antioch seeking or remembering a Jerusalem connection as Barrett
would have it, or whether it is Luke who makes this connection. The fact
that Luke has already employed the motif of "authorization visits" from
Jerusalem on two previous occasions (8:14–17; 11:1–18) suggests that it is Luke
who has arranged the material to highlight the role of Jerusalem and the apostles. Furthermore, this judgment is tellingly consistent with the well-known
redactional focus on Jerusalem in Luke's Gospel. There, in addition to the
compositionally engineered travel narrative that periodically emphasizes Jesus'
progress toward the holy city, culminating with his arrival in Jerusalem, we
may note among the more significant examples of Luke's Jerusalem emphasis the change in the order of the temptation scenes vis-à-vis Q (as preserved
by Matt 4:3–10) that leaves Jerusalem in the final position of emphasis; the
elimination of Mark's "passion week" in favor of the portrayal of Jesus' extended
teaching activity in Jerusalem (Luke 19:28–21:38; note especially 19:47–48;
20:1; 21:37–38); and the restriction of the resurrection appearances to Jerusalem
and its environs (Luke 24), and the consequent elimination of the Galilean
rendezvous predicted in Mark (Mark 14:28; 16:7).

I agree with François Bovon that Luke is an heir of the Pauline tradition,[9]
a circumstance which has its obvious influence on the second half of Acts in
which Paul emerges as the Christian hero par excellence. If we can suppose
along with Bovon that Luke received traditional information from Antioch
through the mediation of the Pauline churches, it becomes clear that the strategic connection of the Hellenists with both Antioch and Jerusalem allows Luke

---

[9] François Bovon, *Luke 1: A Commentary on the Gospel of Luke 1:1–9:50* (trans. C. M.
Thomas; ed. H. Koester; Hermeneia; Minneapolis: Fortress, 2002), 7.

to account for the origins of his church in a direct line of succession, as it were, back to the apostles in the "first church" in Jerusalem. Luke invents the Hellenists because he and his community are Hellenists, who reckon their lineage back through Paul, who is understood after his conversion to have emerged as the principal spokesman for the Hellenist position. As Barrett notes, immediately after the initial narration of the conversion of Paul, Luke wastes no time in portraying Paul's close association with the church in Jerusalem (1:461), taking pains in 9:26–30 to show that Paul was in harmony with the apostles. Barrett protests that he "is wrong in detail; and not only in detail" (1:462). But to complain about inaccuracies in Luke's account at this point does not take seriously all of the implications of "the fact that Luke is not following closely a clearly defined source but making his own composition on the basis of a rather sketchy general acquaintance not so much with the events themselves as with their outcome" (1:462). If Barrett is right in his judgment about Luke's focus on the "results" here, as I suspect he is, it follows that it is not at all necessary to describe Luke's acquaintance with the outcome of the "events" as sketchy. The mere existence of Acts shows that Luke has quite definite ideas about the contours of the birth and expansion of the Christian religion. We must acknowledge the influential significance of Luke's interpretative vantage point as a Christian believer looking back, two generations removed, toward the "founding events." In this light it is no surprise that Luke shows

> Paul as he wishes us to see him—no doubt as he himself saw him . . . as a converted Pharisee, exemplifying the truth that Luke commends in more ways than one, that Christianity is genuine, fulfilled Judaism. At the same time, as Stephen's successor, he is a Hellenist—a Hellenist Jew who has become a Christian and is not loved by Hellenist Jews who have not become Christians. (1:462–63)

Barrett is likely correct when he observes that Luke "probably wishes to suggest that Saul entered into the same conflict as Stephen." Consequently, "it was part of his understanding of events that Paul should early in his career be associated with Jerusalem." Thus "Paul was for Luke the new Stephen, a great Hellenist Christian leader" (1:470). Barrett is hesitant to assent to the supposition that in Luke's mind the acceptance of Paul by the apostles at 9:28 "constituted a bridge between Hebrews and Hellenists" (1:470), pointing out that Luke has nowhere suggested that there was a breach between them. But we may sidestep such scruples by recognizing that for Luke this bridge may be important not so much as an attempt to document a historical détente between rival factions in the early church, but as a way to connect his own Christian heritage and that of his "Hellenist" readers back through their most prominent representative to the original witnesses, the apostles, at the foundation of the church.

CHAPTER SEVEN

DISAGREEMENT AMONG THE JEWS IN ACTS 28

DAVID W. PAO

In his insightful treatment of Paul's final encounter with the Jews in Acts 28, François Bovon has pointed to the emphasis on the unity of voices behind the final pronouncement where one finds Paul, Isaiah, the Holy Spirit, and presumably the narrator were in agreement.[1] This focus in Acts on unity forces one to reevaluate the Lukan note on the disagreement among the Jews in Acts 28:24–25a: "Some were convinced by what he had said, while others refused to believe. So they disagreed with each other."[2]

In recent discussion on these two verses scholars have focused on the interpretation of Luke's note that some Jews "were convinced" (ἐπείθοντο). Some have argued that this should not be understood as a reference to the genuine conversion of those Jews. Ernst Haenchen, for example, has concluded, "in ἐπείθοντο there is no thought of a real conversion any more than in the similar scene at 23:9."[3] This conclusion is most often based on the negative tone of this final episode of Luke's narrative.[4] Others, however, point to the contrast expressed by the οἱ μέν . . . οἱ δέ construction and insist that ἐπείθοντο should be understood as the opposite of ἠπίστουν.[5]

---

[1] François Bovon, " 'Schon hat der heilige Geist durch den Propheten Jesaja zu euren Vätern gesprochen' (Acts 28:25)," *ZNW* 75 (1984): 227.

[2] In this study, all English biblical quotations are taken from the New Revised Standard Version (NRSV) unless otherwise noted.

[3] Ernst Haenchen, *The Acts of the Apostles* (trans. Bernard Noble and Gerald Shinn; Oxford: Basil Blackwell, 1971), 723. See also Hans Conzelmann, *Acts of the Apostles* (trans. James Limburg, Al Thomas Kraabel, and Donald H. Juel; Hermeneia; Philadelphia: Fortress, 1987), 227; and J. T. Sanders, *The Jews in Luke–Acts* (Philadelphia: Fortress, 1987), 296–99.

[4] See, for example, Robert C. Tannehill, *The Narrative Unity of Luke–Acts: A Literary Interpretation* (2 vols.; Minneapolis: Fortress, 1994), 2:347: "Paul's reaction makes clear that his intensive efforts ('from early morning until evening') have not been successful, so it is unlikely that the reference to some 'being persuaded' (ἐπείθοντο) means that they have committed themselves to the Christian way." Tannehill further appeals to the use of the imperfect as signifying the process of conversion that remains unconsummated.

[5] See, for example, Jacques Dupont, "La conclusion des Actes et son rapport à l'ensemble de l'ouvrage de Luc," in *Les Actes des Apôtres: Traditions, rédaction, théologie* (ed. J. Kremer; BETL 48; Leuven: Leuven University Press, 1979), 374–75; Jacob Jervell, *Luke and the People of God* (Minneapolis: Augsburg, 1972), 63; C. K. Barrett, *The Acts of the Apostles* (ICC; Edinburgh: T&T Clark, 1994–98), 1244.

While a consensus on the exact meaning of the word ἐπείθοντο is lacking, most would agree that the Jews remained divided in response to Paul's preaching. The contrast expressed by the οἱ μέν . . . οἱ δέ construction is explicitly stated in the phrase that follows: "So they disagreed with each other" (v. 25). The debate surrounding the word ἐπείθοντο has frequently drawn one's attention away from this Lukan emphasis on the disagreement of the Jews.

For those who have provided a sustained discussion of the division of the Jews in Luke–Acts, this Lukan theme is often understood as providing a way for Luke to leave open the possibility of the continuation of Jewish mission. This theme, therefore, is taken as a positive one. Jacob Jervell, in particular, notes:

> The picture is clear: Israel has not rejected the gospel, but has become divided over the issue. With the coming of the gospel to Rome the message is preached to the Jews of the whole world. And the last picture of the Jewish people in Acts is a picture of an Israel divided over the mission: some are convinced, others remain unbelieving (28:24f.).[6]

According to Jervell, the division of Israel shows that the portrayal of the Jews in Acts is not an entirely negative one:

> If it is really Luke's intention to describe the complete rejection of the gospel on the part of the Jews, then it is very strange that he seems to emphasize clearly the division among the Jews and appears to speak about the unbelief of only a portion of the Roman Jewish community.[7]

I see this reading as problematic, however, when the Lukan theme of discord among the Jews is read together with the emphasis on the unity of the Church.[8] In this article, I will attempt to locate the theme of the disagreement of the Jews within its wider narrative and literary framework. In examining this theme against the background of both the unity of the Church in Acts and the extensive discussion on unity and discord in Greco-Roman and early Christian literature, I will argue that the note of disagreement itself should be understood in a negative way given Luke's attempt to set up a contrast between the unified Church and the divided Israel. I will conclude by returning to the portrayal of the Jews in Acts 28.

---

[6] Jervell, *Luke and the People of God*, 49.

[7] Ibid., 63. In reading Acts 28 in light of the earlier chapters of Acts, Jervell (*The Theology of the Acts of the Apostles* [Cambridge: Cambridge University Press, 1996], 37) further maintains that the Jews "did not reject the gospel *en bloc*—not even an overwhelming majority of Jews oppose the message." See also Robert L. Brawley, *Luke–Acts and the Jews: Conflict, Apology, and Conciliation* (SBLMS 33; Atlanta, Ga.: Scholars Press, 1987), 142; and David Ravens, *Luke and the Restoration of Israel* (Sheffield: Sheffield Academic Press, 1995), 235.

[8] Other related readings can also be accused of failing to do justice to this contrast. Stephen G. Wilson (*The Gentiles and the Gentile Mission in Luke–Acts* [Cambridge: Cambridge University Press, 1973], 232), for example, sees the divisiveness of Jewish response as reflecting the tension between Luke's own theological position and the actual "historical facts." David P. Moessner ("Paul in Acts: Preacher of Eschatological Repentance to

Unity of the Church

The Lukan emphasis on the unity of the Church has long been recognized, but the focus is frequently placed on the Jerusalem council in Acts 15 where the divided church comes to a consensus regarding the inclusion of the Gentiles in the Church. This focus on Acts 15 can be explained by the influence of the work of F. C. Baur who argues that Acts, among other Christian documents, witnesses an attempt to present a unified picture of the Church where the various parties now appear to be reconciled as one movement.[9] Subsequent works on the Lukan emphasis on unity are frequently controlled by the agenda set by Baur; various readings of Acts 15 continue to aim at responding to and qualifying Baur's thesis in a number of ways.[10]

What is lacking is a treatment of the literary and theological theme of unity throughout Acts. Without going into a detailed discussion of this theme, a cursory survey of some of the relevant data would be sufficient. The first clear presentation of the unity of the believers can be found in the accounts of the sharing of possessions in Acts 2:43–47 and 4:32–35. These accounts reflect both the Hellenistic vision of ideal friendships and the biblical concept of divine blessings upon God's people.[11] Embedded within these passages is the description of the early Christian community as having "simplicity of heart" (lit.; ἀφελότητι, 2:46) and being of "one heart and one soul" (καρδία καὶ ψυχή μία, 4:32).

Beyond these explicit descriptions of the unity of the believers, the foundation of this unity also provides the glue that binds the narrative together. Among them is the focus on the Spirit as the unifying force behind the diverse early Christian movements. Not only is this Christian community characterized as the eschatological community of the Spirit (Acts 2),[12] the Spirit itself

---

Israel," *NTS* 34 [1988]: 96–104), on the other hand, considers the ambiguous response of the Jews as pointing to a prophetic call to Israel to respond to the gospel message. Others, such as Bart-Jan Koet ("Paul in Rome [Acts 28,16–31]: A Farewell to Judaism?" *Bijdr* 48 [1987]: 402), find hope in the Lukan vision concerning the future of the Jews since "although they are divided (28,24) there is no mention of aggressive opposition."

[9] For a helpful review of the influence of F. C. Baur in the study of Acts, see W. Ward Gasque, *A History of the Criticism of the Acts of the Apostles* (BGBE 17; Tübingen: Mohr Siebeck, 1975), 21–54.

[10] This is best represented by the works of Paul J. Achtemeier, "An Elusive Unity: Paul, Acts, and the Early Church," *CBQ* 48 (1986): 1–26; and *The Quest for Unity in the New Testament* (Philadelphia: Fortress, 1987).

[11] See, among others, Luke T. Johnson, *The Literary Function of Possessions in Luke–Acts* (SBLDS 39; Missoula: Scholars Press, 1977), 191–211. For a further location of this depiction of the early Christian community within the context of first-century Mediterranean kin groups, see also S. Scott Bartchy, "Community of Goods in Acts: Idealization or Social Reality," in *The Future of Early Christianity: Essays in Honor of Helmut Koester* (ed. Birger A. Pearson; Minneapolis: Fortress, 1991), 309–18.

[12] For a discussion of the early Christian community as an eschatological community of the Spirit, see my discussion in David W. Pao, *Acts and the Isaianic New Exodus* (WUNT 2.130; Tübingen: Mohr Siebeck, 2000), 131–35.

also functions as a sign of this unity. This is best reflected in Acts 8:17 when the gift of the Spirit symbolizes the inclusion of the believers in Samaria (cf. 10:44; 11:15; 15:8; 19:6).

Related to this is the unity provided by the apostolic witnesses. According to Luke, the apostles were faithful witnesses who provided continuity with Jesus' own preaching. This continuity is guaranteed by the Lukan emphasis on Jesus' instructing his apostles during the days before his public ascension (1:2). Luke in turn describes the early Christian community as building upon the teachings of the apostles: "They devoted themselves to the apostles' teaching and fellowship" (2:42). The unity of the teaching of the apostles is portrayed by the similar structure and content of the different speeches in Acts.[13] Moreover, Luke grounds the Pauline mission itself within this unity of the apostolic witness (cf. 9:26–30; 15:1–35).[14]

Throughout the narrative in Acts, Luke uses various terms and phrases to depict this unity. The most obvious of them is the use of πᾶς ("all") to characterize the Christian community. In 1:14, all the believers are portrayed as being devoted to prayer. In 2:1, 4, all the believers were filled with the Holy Spirit (cf. 4:31). After resolving the issue concerning the Hebrews and the Hellenists, all were pleased with the arrangement (6:5). The news of Gentiles converting "brought great joy to all the believers" (15:3), and they were all eager to listen to this report (15:12). Related to this is the emphasis on the continuity of this Christian community with the history of Israel, as the gospel that the apostles preach is the one to which "all the prophets" testified (10:43; cf. 15:15; Luke 24:44).

The use of ὁμοθυμαδόν can also be understood in the same way; the believers are portrayed as having one mind and voice (e.g., 1:14; 2:46; 4:24; 5:12; 8:6; 15:25). While the term may be used simply to mean "together,"[15] its frequent use in contexts where the unity of the believers is the dominating theme should at least alert us to this emphasis of the Lukan narrative. The phrase ἐπί τό αὐτό (e.g., 1:15; 2:1, 47) should likewise be understood as contributing to the Lukan theme of unity.[16]

---

[13] Marion L. Soards (*The Speeches in Acts: Their Content, Context, and Concerns* [Louisville, Ky.: Westminster/John Knox, 1994], 162–208), in particular, has shown how Luke "unifies the narrative through the phenomenon of repetition" (183). On a theological level, these speeches also convey the significance of unity in the Lukan understanding of early Christian teachings.

[14] See, for example, the treatment in Andrew C. Clark, "The Role of the Apostles," in *Witness to the Gospel: The Theology of Acts* (ed. I. Howard Marshall; Grand Rapids, Mich.: Eerdmans, 1998), 169–90, who further points to the Lukan emphasis of the unity of the missions of the Twelve and the Seventy in the third Gospel.

[15] See Barrett, *Acts of the Apostles*, 88–89.

[16] For this and other related phrases, see the helpful treatment in Jacques Dupont, "L'union entre les premiers chrétiens dans les Actes des Apôtres," *NRTh* 91 (1969): 905–8.

Disagreement Among the Jews

In contrast to the unity of the believers, Luke depicts the Jews as divided among themselves. This division characterizes the reaction of the Jews when confronted by the preaching of the gospel message (e.g., 2:12–13; 4:1–4; 5:12–18; 13:45–50; 14:1–7; 17:4–5, 12–14; 19:8–9). This division is explicitly noted in a number of passages. In 23:7, for example, it is noted that there was "dissension" (στάσις) between the Pharisees and the Sadducees, and that they were "divided" (ἐσχίσθη; cf. 14:4).

The way the disagreement among the Jews serves as a contrast to the unified Christian movement is best illustrated by the apparent discrepancy in 2:12–13: "All were amazed and perplexed, saying to one another, 'What does this mean?' But others sneered and said, 'They are filled with new wine.'" Many have pointed to the problem created by the juxtaposition of the "all" (πάντες) and the "others" (ἕτεροι) in these two verses. Most, however, have resorted to source-critical solutions to explain this combination of words. Hans Conzelmann, for example, represents many when he suggests that the relationship between the two words "cannot be determined in a quantitative way."[17] C. K. Barrett is even more explicit in arguing that "it is simply a matter of careless writing."[18] Without evaluating Luke's ability as a writer, one can at least point to Luke's emphasis upon maintaining the impact of the Pentecost event by noting the response of the entire people while at the same time insisting that the Jews disagreed among themselves.[19] This verse therefore also serves as an introduction to this theme of discord among the Jews in Acts.[20]

The care Luke has given to the issue of dissension is reflected in his treatment of the "dissension" (στάσις) among believers on the issue of the inclusion of the Gentiles in Acts 15:2. A detailed account indicates how this "dissension" was resolved and how the unity of the Church was maintained. This serves as a contrast to the disagreement of the Jews, one that remains unresolved and reappears throughout the narrative of Acts.

---

[17] Conzelmann, *Acts of the Apostles*, 154. See Haenchen, *Acts of the Apostles*, 171.

[18] Barrett, *Acts of the Apostles*, 125. It should be noted, however, that while Conzelmann considers this as a redactional issue, Barrett does not see any evidence of the use of a different source.

[19] When the Jews are presented as a unified people, it is almost always in contexts when the entire people fought against the ministers of the gospel (e.g., 7:57; 18:12).

[20] In the first volume of the Lukan corpus, one can point to the reference to "the falling and the rising of many in Israel" in Luke 2:34. A closer parallel to Acts 2 can be found in the Nazareth scene in Luke 4:16–30 where one also finds mixed responses to the preaching of the good news. See Donald R. Miesner, "The Circumferential Speeches of Luke–Acts: Patterns and Purpose," *SBLSP* 2 (1978): 235.

Concord and Discord in Context

When the contrast between the unified Church and the divided Jews is recognized, the portrayal of the Jews as disagreeing (ἀσύμφωνοι) among themselves in Acts 28:25 should also be examined within this contrastive framework.
Before examining Acts 28 in greater detail, it is necessary to situate this discussion within its proper context.

In ancient literature, discussion of unity and discord is not limited to the
Lukan corpus. In the most general sense, many recognize the significance of
the unity of a people. In pre-Socratic traditions, the search for unity signals
the beginning of Greek philosophy. The search for the primordial element
behind all substances sets out the search for the organizing principle through
which diversity could be understood. One could point to Thales, Anaximander, Parmenides, and others whose interest in teleology leads ultimately to the
question of cosmology.[21] When one comes to the classical philosophers, one
finds the continuation of the search for unity in the discussion of the life of
the *polis*. This is best represented by Plato's *Republic* in which his epistemological focus on the ideal form finds concrete expressions in his vision for the
political life of the community.[22] More specifically, his reference to the destructive power of discord is worth noting:

> In no other way is it possible for a city at strife (στασιάσασα) within itself to
> cease from evils, but strife and enmity and hatred and suspicion are wont to
> keep for ever recurring in cities when their inner state is of this kind. (*Epistle*
> VII.337 [LCL, Bury])

Discussions on concord and discord are not limited to the circle of philosophers. Polybius, in particular, has emphasized the importance of unity in the
survival of a state. In discussing internal disorder, he writes:

> As for plots and wars from outside, it is easy, if we are on the watch, to pre-
> pare to meet them and to find a remedy, but in the case of internal oppo-
> sition, sedition (στάσεις), and disturbance it is a difficult task to hit on a
> remedy, a task requiring great adroitness and exceptional sagacity. (*Hist.*
> 11.25.5 [LCL, Paton; slightly revised])

In a speech of Philip to his sons as recorded in Polybius, one again finds the
same emphasis on concord:

---

[21] See, for example, the discussion in Charles H. Kahn, *Anaximander and the Origins
of Greek Cosmology* (New York: Columbia University Press, 1960). For a general discussion of the theme of unity in early Greek philosophy, see also Stig Hanson, *The Unity
of the Church in the New Testament: Colossians and Ephesians* (Uppsala: Almqvist & Wiksells,
1946), 48–52; and Klaus Oehler, *Antike Philosophie und byzantinisches Mittelalter* (Munich:
C. G. Beck, 1969), 235–36.

[22] See, in particular, Arlene Saxonhouse, *Fear of Diversity: The Birth of Political Science
in Ancient Greek Thought* (Chicago: University of Chicago Press, 1992), 93–184. Saxonhouse
is also able to show how the issue of unity/diversity affects the development of Aristotle's
political vision.

And finally, I constantly as a cogent proof of this kept before your eyes these our contemporaries Eumenes and Attalus, telling you how, inheriting a small and insignificant kingdom, they increased it so much that it is now inferior to none, simply by their concord (ὁμόνοιαν) and agreement (συμφωνίαν) and their faculty of mutual respect. (*Hist.* 23.11.6–7 [LCL, Paton])

This emphasis on unity finds its fullest expression in a number of Hellenistic Jewish authors. Building on the Old Testament while reflecting the influence of the Hellenistic ideals, Philo points to creation as a perfect harmony (e.g., *Mos.* 2.48.8; *Opif.* 22.2; *Conf.* 150.8; *Spec.* 2.130.1).[23] While portraying the Egyptians as divided among themselves (*Flacc.* 17), Israel is pictured as a unified nation under one God:

> You see how unlimited is the number of the Hebrews, but their number is not so dangerous and menacing a weapon as their unanimity and mutual attachment (ἡ ὁμόνοια καὶ συμφωνία). And the highest and greatest source of this unanimity is their creed of a single God, through which, as from a fountain, they feel a love for each other, uniting them in an indissoluble bond. (*Virt.* 35 [LCL, Colson])

In Josephus, this emphasis on the unity of Israel becomes a distinct mark of Israel. In defending the God of Israel against the religions of the Greeks, Josephus criticized the gods of the Greeks as divided among themselves:

> Justly do these tales merit the severe censure which they receive from their intellectual leaders. Moreover, they ridicule the belief that some gods are beardless striplings, others old and bearded; that some are appointed to trades, this one being a smith, that goddess a weaver, a third a warrior who fights along with men, others lute-players or devoted to archery; and again they are divided into factions (στάσεις) and quarrel about men, in so much that they not only come to blows with each other, but actually lament over and suffer from wounds inflicted by mortals. (*C. Ap.* 2.242–43 [LCL, Thackeray])

In contrast to the pagans, the people of Israel are unified under one God and one creed:

> To this cause above all we owe our admirable harmony. Unity and identity of religious belief, perfect uniformity in habits and customs, produce a very beautiful concord (συμφωνίαν) in human character. Among us alone will be heard no contradictory statements about God, such as are common among other nations, not only on the lips of ordinary individuals under the impulse of some passing mood, but even boldly propounded by philosophers; some putting forward crushing arguments against the very existence of God, others

---

[23] With the (re)introduction of chaos, Philo maintains that perfect harmony can only be found in the heavenly realm (e.g., *Ios.* 145.5). In the Old Testament, the unity of creation is based on the affirmation of God as the one Lord of all (e.g., Exod 20:2; Deut 6:4). In a vision of the end of times, the restoration of this unity of creation is expected (e.g., Zech 14:9; Mic 4:1–4). Although the related set of vocabularies does not appear in the LXX, the significance of the theme of unity cannot be ignored.

depriving Him of His providential care for mankind. Among us alone will be seen no difference in the conduct of our lives. With us all act alike, all profess the same doctrines about God, one which is in harmony (συμφωνῶν) with our Law and affirms that all things are under His eye. Even our womenfolk and dependants would tell you that piety must be the motive of all our occupations in life. (*C. Ap.* 2.179–81 [LCL, Thackeray])

For Josephus, unity and concord become the distinguishing marks of Israel,[24] and it is this unity that guarantees the reliability of the ancient traditions of Israel.[25] In light of the affinities between Josephus and the Lukan writings, the common emphasis on the theme of unity should not be ignored.[26]

With the use of the συμφωνέω word group, the metaphor from the area of music is taken over to describe the unity of a state/people. While the use of the metaphor can be traced back to the works of the pre-Socratics, extensive use of this metaphor can be found from the time of Plato.[27] In Plato, the metaphor is often used to describe cosmic and metaphysical harmony:

And with reference to music we have to understand that *alpha* often signifies "together," and here it denotes moving together in the heavens about the poles, as we call them, and harmony in song, which is called concord; for, as the ingenious musicians and astronomers tell us, all these things move together by a kind of harmony. (*Crat.* 405 [LCL, Fowler])

This metaphor is extended to the social life of the community (*Symp.* 187), but this harmony is to find its roots in the inner soul of a person.[28] In the writ-

---

[24] In describing the virtues of the Jewish people, Josephus mentioned "justice, temperance, fortitude and mutual harmony (συμφωνίαν) in all things between the members of the community" (*C. Ap.* 2.170 [LCL, Thackeray]).

[25] A discussion of the lack of agreement in pagan historical writings can be found in *C. Ap.* 1.17–18 (LCL, Thackeray): "Even on Sicilian history Timaeus did not condescend to agree (συμφωνεῖν) with Antiochus, Philistus, or Callias; there is similar divergence on Attic affairs between the authors of the 'Atthides' and on Argive affairs between the historians of Argos. What need is there, however, to speak of the histories of individual states and matters of minor importance, when contradictory accounts of the Persian invasion and the events which accompanied it have been given by writers of the first rank? On many points even Thucydides is accused of error by some critics, notwithstanding his reputation for writing the most accurate history of his time" (cf. 1.293). For a further discussion of unity as a criterion of truth in Josephus, see Tessa Rajak, "The Sense of History in Jewish Intertestamental Writings," *OtSt* 24 (1986): 124–45; and Shaye Cohen, "History and Historiography in the *Against Apion* of Josephus," *History and Theory* 27 (1988): 1–11.

[26] I am here only speaking of affinity in the broadest sense. Regardless of the identity of Luke the author, his writings do betray influences of Hellenistic Jewish traditions. Furthermore, the two collections of writings can be understood within the general category of Hellenistic historiography. For a detailed comparison of the two, see Gregory E. Sterling, *Historiography and Self-Definition: Josephos, Luke–Acts and Apologetic Historiography* (Leiden: Brill, 1992).

[27] See Lillian B. Lawler, "The Dance in Metaphor," *CJ* 46 (1950/51): 383–91.

[28] See, for example, Plato's discussion of the virtues of friendship and "harmony" (ξυμφωνίαν) where he argues that "education in music is most sovereign, because more

ings of subsequent authors such as Philo and Josephus, this metaphor occurs extensively in polemical ways when the identity of the people is at issue.

Moving beyond the writings of Luke, the theme of unity resurfaces in the writings of a number of early Christian authors. In the epistles of Ignatius, for example, one finds extensive use of the metaphor in describing the unity of the Church. This is best represented by a passage in his epistle to the Ephesians:

> Now do each of you join in this choir, that being harmoniously in concord (σύμφωνοι ὄντες ἐν ὁμονοίᾳ) you may receive the key of God in unison, and sing with one voice through Jesus Christ to the Father, that he may both hear you and may recognise, through your good works, that you are members of his Son. It is therefore profitable for you to be in blameless unity, in order that you may always commune with God. (*Eph.* 4.2 [LCL, Lake])

In Ignatius, this unity is based ultimately on the unity of the Father and the Son;[29] this unity is then to be reflected in both the life and the structure of the community.[30] This focus on unity continues through the early Christian centuries, and it provides an instrument by which various theological assertions could be articulated.[31]

Concord and Discord in Acts 28

With Acts 28 situated within the wider discussion of concord and discord, the disagreement of the Jews in this final encounter takes on added significance. After describing the divided response of the Jews, Luke explicitly states that "they disagreed with each other" (ἀσύμφωνοι δὲ ὄντες πρὸς ἀλλήλους; 28:25).[32] The use of the term ἀσύμφωνοι evokes the power of the metaphor where the lack of harmony is expressed. In light of the emphasis on the unity of the Church, and in light of the ways the metaphor had previously been used, one can only conclude that this disagreement of the Jews becomes yet another

---

than anything else rhythm and harmony find their way to the inmost soul and take strongest hold upon it" (*Resp.* 401D [LCL, Shorey]).

[29] Throughout his writings, this unity is one that finds its source in God. As William R. Schoedel (*Ignatius of Antioch* [Hermeneia; Philadelphia: Fortress, 1985], 21) has noted, the focus in Ignatius is on "unity from God" and not "unity with God."

[30] The affirmation of the positions of the bishops and the elders is made within this same context of the discussion of unity (e.g., *Magn.* 7.1).

[31] The full-blown "doctrine" of unity in early Christian traditions can be found in Irenaeus where unity becomes the center of theological discourse. In his discussion on apostolic traditions, scriptural authority, episcopal succession, the work of the Spirit, and doctrinal purity, the theme of unity becomes a critical element. See Luis N. Rivera, "Unity and Truth: The Unity of God, Man, Jesus Christ, and the Church in Irenaeus" (Ph.D. diss., Yale University, 1970).

[32] In light of the emphasis on the divided response of the Jews in verse 24, the "disagreement" in verse 25 should only be understood as referring to the disagreement among the Jews themselves. See Bovon, " 'Schon hat der heilige Geist durch den Propheten Jesaja zu euren Vätern gesprochen' (Acts 28:25)," 227.

indictment of Israel. Instead of simply a historical note describing the reality of the Jewish response to Paul's preaching, this phrase contributes to Luke's portrayal of the Jewish rejection of the Gospel. Against competitive claims, this note further reflects Luke's understanding of the identity of the Church within which one finds the continuation of salvation history.

This reading is supported by other textual clues in Acts 28. The negative tone throughout this final encounter cannot be missed. Stephen Wilson is right in concluding, "the theme of Jewish obduracy (vv. 26–28) pervades the previous narrative, despite the fact that some Jews were converted."[33] The significance of the lengthy Isaianic quotation, especially considering its narrative location, should be noted.[34] Moreover, the move on the part of the Lukan Paul from his identification with the Jews in verse 17 to the introduction of the final quotation with the reference to "your ancestors" (τοὺς πατέρας ὑμῶν, v. 25) points to the distancing that separates the "us" and the "them." In this context, Luke portrays the Jewish audience as one entity.

Closer to the note of disagreement is the description of the entire audience leaving the scene. The portrayal that those who were "convinced" as well as those who "refused to believe" left signifies that the prophetic text that follows applies to both groups. Without focusing on the exact nature of the response of those who are said to have been "convinced," it is the description of the Jews as divided that carries significant weight.

The significance of the Jews' disagreement among themselves is apparently understood by some ancient readers of the text as reflected in the early insertions into the textual traditions: "when he had said these words, the Jews departed, arguing vigorously among themselves" (v. 29). While these words should not be considered as "authentic,"[35] they do reflect an early reading of the text that focuses on the element of disagreement.

The strongest support for this reading lies, however, in the emphasis of the unity of the Church in Acts. As noted at the beginning of this paper, the agreement between Luke, Paul, the Holy Spirit, and Isaiah (v. 25) characterizes Luke's portrayal of the early Christian movement throughout his work. The contrast is also captured by the first half of verse 25 where the note on the disagreement of the Jews is immediately followed by the "one word" (lit., ῥῆμα ἕν) uttered by Paul. In light of the discussions of concord and discord elsewhere in Greco-Roman literature, one should not be surprised by the use of this contrast in the writings of one who is not unaware of ancient *topoi*.

---

[33] Wilson, *Gentiles and the Gentile Mission*, 236.

[34] This narrative closure provided by yet another Isaianic quotation is significant especially when it recalls another quotation that introduces the Lukan narrative (Luke 3:4–6). See Pao, *Acts and the Isaianic New Exodus*, 101–9.

[35] The addition is present primarily in Western witnesses (383, 614, it^gig,p, vg^mss syr^h with *) and is not inconsistent with Western expansion elsewhere in the Lukan corpus.

CHAPTER EIGHT

ACTES 8: FAIRE TOMBER LE PUISSANT ET RELEVER L'HUMBLE

Daniel Marguerat

Au sein du livre des Actes, le chapitre 8 marque un premier et symbolique franchissement de limites. Dispersés par la persécution qui suit la mise à mort d'Étienne (6:8–7:60), les chrétiens de Jérusalem essaiment en Samarie, où ils répandent la parole (8:4). Cette diaspora d'un genre nouveau doit avoir été essentiellement composée de judéo-chrétiens hellénistes, issus du cercle d'Étienne, auxquels les juifs de Jérusalem reprochaient une attitude critique face à la Torah et au Temple (6:13). Le vecteur de la mission helléniste fut Philippe. Avec lui, la frontière du judaïsme jérusalémite est doublement franchie: d'une part en évangélisant la Samarie (8:5–25), d'autre part en baptisant l'eunuque d'Éthiopie (8:26–40). Cette percée missionnaire hors de Jérusalem marque un point de non-retour dans l'intrigue des Actes: elle correspond au scénario géographique tracé par le Ressuscité en 1:8 et prépare la rencontre décisive de Pierre et Corneille (10:1–11:18), où sera ouverte la mission aux non-juifs.[1] Fidèle à son habitude, l'auteur des Actes soigne les transitions. Entre le "printemps de Jérusalem" (Actes 1–7) et la mission païenne dont Dieu choisit paradoxalement le héros en la personne de Saul (Actes 9), le chapitre 8 marque le passage. De quels enjeux théologiques Luc a-t-il chargé cette traversée de frontières? Une cohérence est-elle perceptible dans cette étape de transition?

Qu'Actes 8:4–40 constitue une séquence narrative est un fait reconnu. Le verset 4 lie la dispersion des hellénistes à leur évangélisation; il fait inclusion avec le verset 40. Un riche vocabulaire kérygmatique traverse l'ensemble.[2] Philippe, agent de la mission helléniste, disparaît du récit après 8:40 pour réapparaître brièvement avec ses filles prophétesses en 21:8–9. En revanche, identifier la cohérence thématique de la séquence n'est pas aisé. Ni Philippe (absent en

---

[1] Je dédie affectueusement cet article à un homme qui cultive avec autant de talent la science exégétique que l'amitié: François Bovon. Mon essai sur Actes 8 rappelle ce que l'exégèse de Luc-Actes doit à ses travaux, à commencer par sa thèse de doctorat de Bâle sur Actes 10–11 (1965), publiée sous le titre: *De vocatione gentium: Histoire de l'interprétation d'Act. 10, 1–11, 18 dans les six premiers siècles* (BGBE 8; Tübingen: Mohr/Siebeck, 1967); Actes 8 précède et prépare ce texte où l'Évangile franchit définitivement les frontières du judaïsme.

[2] Récurrence du vocabulaire kérygmatique: εὐαγγίζεσθαι fait inclusion entre 4 et 40 et surgit aux vv. 11, 25, et 35; κηρύσσειν (v. 5); διαμαρτύρεσθαι (v. 25); λαλεῖν τὸν λόγον (v. 25). En outre, διέρχεσθαι (vv. 4 et 40) est le terme technique de l'itinérance missionnaire dans les Actes.

8:14–25) ni la Samarie ne constituent le motif unifiant. Les thèmes abordés au fil du récit sont variés: confrontation au syncrétisme magique, lien entre baptême et Esprit, dénonciation du pouvoir de l'argent à propos de Simon le mage, lecture de l'Écriture avec l'eunuque d'Éthiopie. Devant cette variété de thèmes, la critique des sources a postulé un assemblage de traditions disparates.[3]

Mon hypothèse de lecture est double. D'une part j'estime que Luc a traité ce premier franchissement de frontières en modèle de la mission chrétienne, pour exposer à la fois les chances et les risques qu'elle encourt. J'aimerais montrer d'autre part que la cohérence thématique de 8:4–40 se construit au fur et à mesure du récit, et qu'elle est à chercher sur le plan christologique; le cas de Simon le mage et la rencontre avec l'eunuque d'Éthiopie illustrent le renversement de valeurs qu'exprime Luc 1:52: "Il a jeté les puissants à bas de leurs trônes et il a élevé les humbles".

Je suivrai l'intrigue de la séquence au fil des trois scènes qui la composent: Philippe et Simon le mage (vv. 5–13), la venue de l'Esprit en Samarie (vv. 14–25), le baptême de l'eunuque d'Éthiopie (vv. 26–40).

Philippe et Simon le mage: la concurrence religieuse (8:5–13)

La ville de Samarie où se rend Philippe n'est pas nommée (v. 5); plutôt que la précision géographique, c'est la localisation samaritaine qui importe au narrateur. S'agit-il de la Samarie religieuse, qui fait schisme avec Jérusalem, ou de la Samarie ethnique à population cosmopolite, partiellement païenne? Luc ne mentionne pas les pratiques religieuses des habitants, sinon leur propension pour la magie; mais il écrit que Philippe leur prêche "le messie" (τὸν χριστόν), et le messianisme n'était pas absent de la foi samaritaine. Telle qu'elle est construite dans l'évangile, la figure des Samaritains est rattachée au monothéisme juif (Luc 17:15); mais ils sont taxés d'étrangers (ἀλλογενής, Luc 17:18) et entretiennent avec Jérusalem des rapports haineux (Luc 9:51–56). Flavius Josèphe les décrit ainsi: ni hors d'Israël, ni déjà païens.[4] Entre Jérusalem et le monde grec, la Samarie occupe une position d'entre-deux, qui se prête exactement à la fonction de transition que Luc lui accorde dans son récit. La succession d'Actes 7 à Actes 8 est également assurée: après la critique d'Étienne contre le Temple (7:44–50), l'évangélisation se tourne vers deux catégories exclues du sanctuaire de Jérusalem, les Samaritains et un eunuque.

Philippe s'avance cependant sur un terrain déjà occupé. Entre l'évangéliste et Simon le mage, le narrateur a artistement construit une situation de concurrence, qui se déroule en trois temps.

Un sommaire (vv. 6–8) commence par dépeindre la mission de Philippe en

---

[3] État de la question chez Axel von Dobbeler, *Der Evangelist Philippus in der Geschichte des Urchristentums: Eine prosopographische Skizze* (Texte und Arbeiten zum neutestamentlichen Zeitalter 30; Tübingen: Francke, 2000), 44–49.

[4] *Ant.* 9.291. Voir aussi le traité *Massèket Koutim* 1.

des couleurs très évangéliques: des paroles sont données à entendre; des signes sont donnés à voir: exorcismes bruyants et guérisons de paralysés et boiteux. L'action se solde par une grande joie, indice chez Luc de la réception du salut (Luc 2:10; 24:52; Actes 15:3). Le lecteur de Luc-Actes ne peut qu'en conclure: tout se passe comme avec Jésus![5]

Ensuite, par un habile procédé d'analepse ou *flashback* (vv. 9–11), le narrateur fait état du succès antérieur de Simon, dont la foule dit qu'il est "la Puissance de Dieu qu'on appelle la grande". Ce personnage au destin fascinant a généré un flot de littérature, à commencer par les Pères hérésiologues. Après Justin, Irénée (vers 180) a fait de Simon le père de toute hérésie et le prototype du gnostique (*Haer.* 1.23.2, 4).[6] Mais il serait anachronique de confondre Simon le gnostique, réclamé par la gnose du deuxième siècle, avec Simon le mage évoqué par l'auteur des Actes, même s'il s'agit originellement du même personnage; la recomposition de la figure fondatrice de Simon par la gnose simonienne est un phénomène postérieur à Luc. L'auteur des Actes ne fait pas de Simon un gnostique, mais un mage au moi hypertrophié, auquel la foule attribue un fluide divin qui le classe parmi les êtres pourvus d'attributs surnaturels (*theioi andres*). Deux notations précisent le portrait: l'étiquette de *magos*, qui lui est attribuée, est largement diffamatoire chez les écrivains gréco-romains; la fascination qu'il exerce sur les gens de Samarie est notifiée à l'aide du verbe ἐξιστάναι, qui a pour sens propre *placer hors de soi, déstabiliser*. Son succès englobe la totalité du peuple samaritain, "du petit au grand" (v. 10).

Troisième temps (vv. 12–13): la scène bascule avec le baptême des Samaritains, dont la conviction s'est inversée en faveur de Philippe, et par la conversion de Simon. L'adhésion des Samaritains est dite en termes surprenants: "ils ont cru à Philippe qui annonçait la bonne nouvelle du Règne de Dieu et du nom de Jésus Christ" (v. 12). Construire πιστεύειν (croire) avec le datif, ailleurs dans les Actes, sert à indiquer l'objet de la foi: croire à Dieu (16:34; 27:25), au Seigneur (5:14; 18:8), à la Loi (24:14), aux prophéties (26:27). Or ici, le prédicateur est l'objet du croire, mais avec cette précision: croire "à Philippe qui annonce." πιστεύειν ἐν a ici son sens hébraïque d'*avoir confiance*: les Samaritains ont fait confiance à Philippe à cause de la parole qu'il annonce. Le contenu de cette parole est spécifié dans une formule duelle: "la bonne nouvelle au sujet du Règne de Dieu et du nom de Jésus Christ". Cette formule condense,

---

[5] Comparer Luc 4:31–37, 40–41; 5:18; 6:18; 7:22. La conviction qui travaille la rédaction du texte, fréquemment exprimée dans les Actes, est que l'activité thérapeutique des disciples poursuit et perpétue celle de Jésus; mais pour la première fois dans Luc-Actes, le guérisseur n'a pas été compagnon du Nazaréen.

[6] Hippolyte au début du troisième siècle (*Haer.* 6.9–18) et Épiphane vers 375 (*Pan.* 21.1–4) suivent la ligne gnostique, tandis que les *Pseudoclémentines* voient en Simon un grand guérisseur concurrent des apôtres et disciple du Baptiste (*Ps.-Clem. Hom.* 2.22–25). Gerd Theissen tente de retracer la trajectoire historique de la figure de Simon, du charismatique dépeint par Luc au rédempteur gnostique des simoniens dans "Simon Magus—die Entwicklung seines Bildes vom Charismatiker zum gnostischen Erlöser" in *Religionsgeschichte des Neuen Testaments: Festschrift für Klaus Berger zum 60. Geburtstag* (éd. Axel von Dobbeler, Kurt Erlemann, et Roman Heiligenthal; Tübingen: Francke, 2000), 407–32.

conceptuellement, ce que la narration "évangélique" des versets 6–8 décrit narrativement: paroles et signes représentent la mise en œuvre du Règne et son actualisation au travers du Christ et de ses témoins. Après la mention rudimentaire de verset 5b (τὸν χριστόν), le "nom de Jésus Christ" fonctionne comme indicateur de la spécificité chrétienne du message. Ultime retournement au verset 13: Simon le mage accède lui aussi à la foi, reçoit le baptême et s'attache à Philippe. Le motif de ce revirement n'est pas caché: la vue des signes et des actes puissants réalisés par Philippe stupéfie Simon (ἐξιστάναι, v. 13b), comme il avait lui-même stupéfié auparavant les foules samaritaines (ἐξιστάναι, vv. 9b, 11). Cette dernière mention, aggravée par la rechute de Simon au verset 19, a conduit bien des commentateurs, Pères de l'Église en tête, à mettre en doute la sincérité du mage et de sa conversion.[7] Rien, dans le libellé du verset 13, ne nourrit ce soupçon. Un seul indice vient du thème de la stupéfaction, mentionné en finale du verset comme le motif de son revirement; il associe en effet la foi nouvelle de Simon à une surenchère sur le registre du merveilleux, qui aurait fait plier le mage.

Un regard porté sur l'ensemble de la scène montre que le narrateur a construit en miroir le portrait de Philippe et celui de Simon:[8] l'un et l'autre prêchent et font des merveilles; l'un et l'autre médiatisent un pouvoir surnaturel; l'un comme l'autre exerce une attraction sur la foule samaritaine, qui s'attache (προσέχειν) à eux. Ce mimétisme dénote, de la part de l'auteur, la conscience d'une ambiguïté fondamentale du phénomène miraculeux, et la nécessité de différencier la magie de l'Évangile.[9] Mais au sein du parallèle Philippe/Simon, un glissement subtil révèle que Luc s'attache à marquer, en

---

[7] Irénée: "Simon donc, feignit d'embrasser la foi (*fidem simulavit*). Il pensa que les apôtres eux aussi opéraient des guérisons par la magie, et non par la puissance de Dieu . . ." (*Haer.* 1.23.1). A la recherche d'une déficience chez les Samaritains qui expliquerait une privation de l'Esprit, James D. G. Dunn met en doute la foi que leur attribue Luc au v. 12 ("They Believed Philip Preaching [Acts 8:12]," in idem, *The Christ and the Spirit: Collected Essays of James D. G. Dunn* [2 vols; Edinburgh: Clark, 1998], 2:220); il pense qu'à la différence d'une construction avec εἰς, πιστεύειν + datif indiquerait un consentement intellectuel (*croire que*) et non une relation personnelle (*croire à*). L'examen de la construction au datif en Actes dément ce point de vue (cf. 5:14; 16:34; 18:8; 27:25).

[8] La symétrie Philippe/Simon tient en 7 points: (1) activité dans la même πόλις (Philippe au v. 5; Simon au v. 9a); (2) actions merveilleuses (Philippe fait des σημεῖα et des exorcismes, vv. 6b–7; Simon fait des μαγείαι, v. 11); (3) acte de parole (le κηρύσσειν de Philippe au v. 5, son λέγειν au v. 6a, et son εὐαγγελίζεσθαι au v. 12a; le λέγειν de Simon au v. 9b); (4) succès quantitatif (Philippe attire les ὄχλοι au v. 6a, et des πόλλοι au v. 7a; Simon attire des πάντες ἀπὸ μικροῦ ἕως μεγάλου au v. 10a); (5) grandeur (Philippe fait des δυνάμεις μεγάλας, v. 13b; Simon s'appelle la δύναμις μεγάλη, v. 10b); (6) effet d'attachement (προσέχειν à Philippe, v. 6a; à Simon, vv. 10a, 11); (7) effet de stupéfaction (ἐξιστάναι de Philippe au v. 13b; de Simon aux vv. 9a, 11). Voir F. Scott Spencer, *The Portrait of Philip in Acts* (JSNTSup 67; Sheffield: Sheffield Academic Press, 1992), 88–89.

[9] Avec Hans-Josef Klauck, *Magie und Heidentum in der Apostelgeschichte des Lukas* (SBS 167; Stuttgart: Verlag Katholisches Bibelwerk: 1996), 30. Pour Susan R. Garrett, la construction lucanienne de la symétrie Philippe/Simon vise précisément à récuser les valeurs du mage (*The Demise of the Devil* [Minneapolis: Fortress Press, 1989], 77).

l'état de concurrence, la spécificité du prédicateur chrétien: alors que le mage s'auto-proclame (v. 9b), Philippe prêche le Christ (v. 5); Simon personnalise le message et les Samaritains s'attachent à lui, tandis qu'ils s'attachent aux paroles de Philippe (v. 12a). D'un côté, Simon se dit, de l'autre Philippe annonce le Règne et le nom d'un Autre (v. 12a). La différence entre les deux ne tient pas à une technique, mais à une éthique. Faute d'avoir intégré le décentrement qu'implique l'acceptation de l'Évangile du Règne de Dieu, Simon fera une rechute dans son ancien fonctionnement (vv. 18–19).

I. *La venue de l'Esprit en Samarie (8:14–25)*

L'irruption en Samarie d'apôtres émissaires de Jérusalem, et l'imposition des mains aux nouveaux baptisés pour qu'ils reçoivent le Saint-Esprit, soulèvent de multiples questions: la foi des nouveaux convertis était-elle insuffisante? Leur baptême aurait-il été rituellement défectueux? La mission de Philippe nécessitait-elle un contrôle institutionnel de Jérusalem? Ces diverses hypothèses ont en commun de surcharger la lecture en affectant à la mission samaritaine un déficit dogmatique, rituel ou juridictionnel. Restons fixés au texte, tel qu'il se donne dans le cadre de l'intrigue des Actes. Car si le narrateur n'indique pas explicitement la raison de l'intrusion apostolique, plusieurs indices orientent l'interprétation du récit.

A quoi réagissent les apôtres à Jérusalem? Ils ont appris que "la Samarie a accueilli la parole de Dieu" (v. 14); on est passé d'une ville (vv. 5a et 8) à "la Samarie," ce qui montre que le succès de l'Évangile dans cette région pose une question de principe. Les apôtres réagissent en déléguant deux des leurs afin que les nouveaux croyants reçoivent l'Esprit saint: Pierre et Jean, représentants attitrés du collège des Douze (3:1–11; 4:1–19). Mais que signifie, dans les Actes, la venue de l'Esprit? Elle est la suite logique de l'accueil de la Parole. L'Esprit saint habilite les croyants au témoignage (1:8; 2:4; 4:31; 8:29) ou les oriente dans leur mission (8:29, 39; 10:19; 16:6–7). Que ce soit à la Pentecôte (2:38), dans la maison de Corneille (10:44) ou à Éphèse (19:2–6), le don de l'Esprit aux nouveaux croyants ratifie leur réception de la Parole. C'est le cas ici: la première expansion de l'Évangile hors de Jérusalem doit recevoir ce signe du consentement divin. Or, dans la construction lucanienne de l'histoire du salut, le collège des Douze représente une indispensable médiation: dépositaires du mandat missionnaire du Ressuscité (1:8), intouchés par la répression juive (8:1b), les Douze sont un pôle d'unité et de stabilité à la naissance du christianisme. Le même argument de continuité les conduira plus tard à déléguer Barnabé à Antioche (11:22).

C'est forcer le texte qu'interpréter leur intrusion comme l'émergence d'un pouvoir juridictionnel ou la volonté d'absorber une mission illicite.[10] Le droit

---

[10] Ernst Käsemann fait preuve d'anachronisme en attribuant à Luc un centralisme

ecclésiastique n'intéresse pas Luc. Pierre et Jean n'ont pas pour tâche d'inspecter la foi des nouveaux convertis, mais d'exercer une fonction médiatrice, soulignée à deux reprises: prier (v. 15) et imposer les mains (v. 17).[11] La prière préliminaire à l'imposition des mains est importante, car elle montre que Pierre et Jean ne jouissent pas d'un pouvoir à demeure. Prier les place en dépendance du pouvoir de Dieu, qu'ils sollicitent d'agir dans l'inviolable liberté de son Esprit. Je cite François Bovon: "Luc estime—que l'on appelle cela naïf ou *frühkatholisch*—que Dieu a confié à ceux qui lui appartiennent, donc qui ne vivent pas de façon autonome mais en serviteurs de la parole, une puissance dont ils savent qu'elle peut être transmise aux nouveaux convertis quand ces derniers auront été baptisés et qu'ils auront reçu, après une prière, l'imposition des mains."[12] Les deux apôtres sont ainsi les vecteurs d'une approbation divine à l'échappée samaritaine, coup d'envoi à la mission hors d'Israël.

La notation du verset 16 pourrait faire penser à une déficience du rituel baptismal,[13] mais il n'en est rien. Elle constitue un commentaire du narrateur, qui doit justifier auprès du lecteur l'écart face à la norme posée par Pierre en 2:38: le baptême devrait être suivi du don de l'Esprit. Si l'Esprit n'est pas encore "tombé" (du ciel), ce retard n'affecte en rien le baptême des Samaritains; il signale que l'approbation divine de cette nouvelle mission doit encore être manifestée. L'Esprit, signature de Dieu, vient sceller la communion entre la communauté originaire de Jérusalem et les nouveaux convertis. Une pareille dissociation du baptême et de l'Esprit surgira à nouveau avec la conversion du premier païen (10:44–48), mais à l'inverse: l'Esprit précède le baptême dans la maison de Corneille. Dans les deux cas, le lien baptême/Esprit est restauré après coup: la réception de l'Esprit est la condition normale du baptisé.[14]

Le récit rebondit par la réapparition de Simon, qui observant le lien entre l'imposition des mains et la venue de l'Esprit (v. 18), offre aux apôtres de leur

---

institutionnel de type protocatholique (*Exegetische Versuche und Besinnungen* [2 vols; Göttingen: Vandenhoeck & Ruprecht, 1960–1964], 1:131, 165–167).

[11] L'imposition des mains est un rite que l'Église a repris du judaïsme. Il est accompli lors du baptême (Actes 8:17; 19:6), à l'envoi en mission (13:3), à l'installation dans un ministère (6:6) ou avec la prière de guérison (5:12; 9:12, 17; 28:8). Le geste n'est pas réservé aux apôtres, mais peut être administré par un croyant (9:12, 17) ou la communauté entière (6:6; 13:3). Il implique, de la part de l'Église, la conscience d'être le canal d'une grâce reçue de Dieu (Joseph Coppens, "L'imposition des mains dans les Actes des Apôtres," in *Les Actes des Apôtres: Traditions, rédaction, théologie* [éd. Jacob Kremer; BETL 48; Gembloux: Duculot; Leuven: University Press, 1979], 405–38).

[12] François Bovon, *Luc le théologien* (2e éd.; MdB 5; Genève: Labor et Fides, 1988), 252.

[13] Michel Quesnel (*Baptisés dans l'Esprit* [LD 120; Paris: Cerf, 1985], 55–65, 74–78) croit déceler la présence de deux rituels baptismaux différents en Actes, l'un εἰς τὸ ὄνομα Ἰησοῦ Χριστοῦ (avec don de l'Esprit saint) et l'autre, comme ici, εἰς τὸ ὄνομα τοῦ κυρίου Ἰησοῦ (sans réception de l'Esprit). Or, ces variantes de formulation n'ont pas un statut doctrinal chez Luc.

[14] Avis contraire chez Michel Gourgues ("Esprit des commencements et Esprit des prolongements dans les *Actes*," *RB* 93 [1986]: 376–85), qui suggère de dissocier l'"Esprit tranquille," lié au baptême individuel, de l'Esprit glossolalique de Pentecôte, transmis par les apôtres à la communauté samaritaine; Luc ne connaît pas ce clivage.

acheter l'autorité de transmettre les charismes: "Donnez à moi aussi ce pouvoir (ἐξουσία)." Veut-il en faire une source de profit ou partager ce qui lui paraît être un pouvoir? Il était fréquent, dans les religions de l'Antiquité, que la charge de prêtre soit vendue à l'intéressé. Instrumentalisant les dons spirituels en moyens d'affirmation de soi, Simon est rattrapé par son passé.

La vivacité de la réplique de Pierre (vv. 20–23) est à la mesure du danger que discerne l'auteur des Actes: dans cette Samarie mi-juive mi-païenne, le syncrétisme favorise un amalgame entre pouvoir spirituel et pouvoir de l'argent. Sa première invective (v. 20b) voue à la perdition éternelle Simon et son argent; le langage, biblique, équivaut à: "Va au diable avec ton argent!" L'ancien mage a pensé pouvoir s'approprier par des biens ce qui est par définition un don de Dieu. Luc est seul, dans le Nouveau Testament, à parler de l'Esprit comme d'un don.[15] L'antithèse acquisition/don résume la rechute de Simon: sa logique d'acquisition et de pouvoir (vv. 9–10) n'a pas cédé face à la gratuité évangélique du don. La dénonciation très lucanienne du pouvoir corrupteur de l'argent trouve son apogée lorsqu'elle s'attaque, comme ici, à la marchandisation de la grâce. La deuxième invective de Pierre (v. 21) est une formule biblique d'excommunication. Plutôt que maudire, elle constate une exclusion: il n'y a pour le coupable "ni part ni héritage dans cette parole" (ἐν τῷ λόγῳ τούτῳ). Simon, par son initiative, est devenu étranger à ce λόγος: le terme ne doit pas être traduit par "affaire," mais conserve le sens de "parole," auquel Luc attache une extrême importance (cf. 8:4, 14, 25). En agissant comme il l'a fait, Simon prouve sa totale incompréhension de l'Évangile. En conséquence (vv. 22–23), Pierre l'appelle à la conversion—mais le succès de sa prière n'est pas garanti: Simon doit prier Dieu "si peut-être", "si éventuellement" (εἰ ἄρα)[16] le Seigneur lui accorde le pardon.

Comment réagit l'ancien mage (v. 24)? Il se fie plus à la prière des apôtres qu'à la sienne: "Suppliez vous-mêmes en ma faveur le Seigneur." La demande est ambiguë. Simon raisonne-t-il toujours en mage, captif de son système de pouvoir? Implorer l'intercession des apôtres trahit le recours à plus puissant que lui pour lever la malédiction qui pèse sur sa vie. Ou bien Simon fait pénitence, et en même temps révérence aux apôtres dont il confesse la supériorité. Solliciter leur prière dénote alors sa lucidité face à la gravité de sa faute.[17] Les commentateurs hésitent, mais la finale supporte les deux lectures. En contraste avec le dénouement tragique d'Actes 5:1–11, Luc a choisi de terminer sur cette demande pressante d'intercession, qui met en avant le

---

[15] Actes 2:38; 10:45; 11:17.

[16] εἰ ἄρα exprime l'attente face à une action future (Friedrich Blass et Albert Debrunner, *Grammatik des neutestamentlichen Griechisch* [rev. Friedrich Rehkopf; 17ᵉ éd.; Göttingen: Vandenhoeck & Ruprecht, 1990], §375).

[17] Le texte occidental va dans ce sens en composant l'image édifiante des pleurs de repentir de Simon: "Simon leur répondit: 'Je vous prie, suppliez vous-mêmes Dieu, pour que rien ne me survienne de ces maux que vous avez dit.' Il ne cessait de pleurer abondamment."

possible pardon divin et l'ambivalence d'un croyant repris par son passé. Terminer sur une finale ouverte, dont l'interrogation rejaillit sur le lecteur, ressortit à l'art narratif de Luc.

Le baptême de l'eunuque d'Éthiopie (8:26–40)

Changement d'atmosphère dans cette troisième scène, orchestrée par une impressionnante régie divine. Philippe est dirigé vers la route de Gaza par un ange du Seigneur, puis enjoint par l'Esprit de s'attacher de près au char de l'Éthiopien (v. 29). Tout aussi soudainement, l'Esprit le ravit en finale (v. 39). Si la mission en Samarie avait une couleur d'évangile, le présent épisode affiche une tonalité prophétique; il emprunte ses motifs à la tradition scolaire d'Élie/ Élisée.[18]

Après s'être fixée jusqu'en 1950 sur la dimension extatique de l'agir de Philippe, l'exégèse s'est interrogée depuis Haenchen sur la fonction du récit dans l'intrigue des Actes. Entre l'ouverture au judaïsme marginal de Samarie (8:4–25) et l'accueil du premier païen Corneille (Actes 10–11), quel rôle joue cette étape? La question tourne autour du statut religieux de l'eunuque éthiopien: juif de la diaspora? prosélyte? craignant-Dieu? Le mutisme du texte sur ce point est intrigant. Ce n'est pourtant pas faute d'une présentation détaillée du personnage de la part du narrateur (vv. 27–28).

Chaque détail compte dans ce portrait. (1) L'homme est Éthiopien: l'ancienne Éthiopie (en hébreu *Koush*) correspond à l'actuel nord du Soudan, la Nubie, entre Assouan et Karthoum. (2) Il est eunuque: εὐνοῦχος peut être dans la Septante le titre d'un haut fonctionnaire politique ou militaire, mais il s'applique le plus souvent à des hommes castrés;[19] les cours orientales, surtout celles des reines, recherchaient des dignitaires eunuques. (3) L'homme est un officiel de la cour (δυνάστης), responsable de la trésorerie de la Candace, la reine-mère d'Éthiopie.[20] (4) Il revient de Jérusalem où il est allé en pèlerinage (προσκυνεῖν = "adorer", "se prosterner"); sur le chemin du retour, il lit un rouleau du prophète Ésaïe. De ce luxe d'informations, on retient que l'extraordinaire de la rencontre tient à son identité. Mais ce portrait suscite deux étonnements.

Le premier étonnement tient au contraste eunuque/dignitaire, qui est un

---

[18] Issu de la tradition scolaire d'Élie/Élisée (1 Rois 18:12), le motif de l'enlèvement céleste avec transfert géographique est absent de la prophétie littéraire (sauf Ézch 3:14; 8:3; 11:1, 24; Suppl Dan Bêl 36); il revient en force dans l'apocalyptique et chez les hagiographes (Philostrate, *Vit. Apoll.* 4.10; 8.10; *Évang. héb.* frag. 2; Herm. *Vis.* 1.1.3; 2.1.1). Voir von Dobbeler, *Der Evangelist Philippus*, 131–44.

[19] εὐνοῦχος s'applique dans la Septante soit à des hommes castrés (Ésa 56:3–4; Sir 30:20), soit à des fonctionnaires comme Potiphar (Gen 39:1); le plus souvent, les deux usages se recoupent (cf. les nombreux usages dans le livre d'Esther). Si εὐνοῦχος n'était ici qu'un titre officiel, il ferait redondance avec δυνάστης.

[20] Pline l'Ancien, *Nat.* 6.35 (ligne 186).

contraste faiblesse/pouvoir. D'un côté, l'homme est puissant: il exerce une responsabilité considérable, et a les moyens financiers de s'offrir un char avec son équipage et un rouleau du livre d'Ésaïe. D'un autre côté, les eunuques sont des exclus: les auteurs grecs et latins ne cachent ni mépris, ni railleries à leur endroit.[21] Israël considère ces "arbres secs" (Ésa 56:3) comme des impurs et ne les admet pas dans les assemblées; dans l'enceinte du Temple, ils ne dépassent pas la cour des païens. Corporellement et socialement, les eunuques sont des êtres à part. "Il faut éviter les eunuques et fuir tout commerce avec ceux qui sont privés de leur virilité."[22] Le ministre éthiopien illustre le paradoxe de l'homme puissant et exclu, côtoyant dans l'œuvre de Luc des personnages pour lesquels le narrateur a une évidente sympathie: Zachée le riche détesté (Luc 19:1–10) ou le centurion de Capharnaüm implorant la guérison de son serviteur (Luc 7:1–10).

Second étonnement: explicite sur le plan ethnique et social, le portrait n'est pas clair sur le statut religieux de l'homme. Est-il juif, païen converti (prosélyte) ou païen sympathisant (craignant-Dieu)? La clef se trouve dans la formule qui énonce le but de son voyage: "il était venu pour adorer (προσκυνεῖν) à Jérusalem" (v. 27c). Or, προσκυνεῖν est l'un des verbes du pèlerinage eschatologique des nations à Jérusalem.[23] "L'Égypte a travaillé, et le commerce des Éthiopiens (Αἰθιόπων), les hommes de Séva, les hauts, te traverseront, et ils seront des serviteurs pour toi; ils te suivront, menottes aux poings, et ils se prosterneront devant toi (προσκυνήσουσιν)" (Ésa 45:14LXX). Une autre prophétie d'Ésaïe annonce l'intégration des étrangers et des eunuques dans le peuple saint:

> Que l'étranger (ἀλλογενής), celui qui est dévoué pour le Seigneur, ne dise pas: "Il me séparera certainement, le Seigneur, de son peuple." Et que l'eunuque (εὐνοῦχος) ne dise pas: "Moi, je suis un arbre sec." Voici ce que dit le Seigneur: "Aux eunuques, ceux qui gardent mes sabbats, qui choisissent [de faire] ce que moi je veux, et qui s'attachent à mon alliance, je leur donnerai dans ma maison et dans mon enceinte un endroit renommé, mieux que des fils et des filles, je leur donnerai un nom éternel, et il ne disparaîtra pas" (Ésa 56:3–5LXX).

Eunuque et étranger, l'Éthiopien remplit à un double titre les conditions de la prophétie; son statut est assimilable à ce que les Actes disent des craignant-

---

[21] Les eunuques appartiennent dans l'Antiquité "aux groupes humains les plus souvent méprisés et raillés" (Gerd Petzke, εὐνοῦχος, *EWNT* 2: 202). Lucien de Samosate (IIe siècle) ironise sur l'eunuque qui "n'est ni homme ni femme, mais je ne sais quel composé, un affreux mélange, un monstre étranger à la nature humaine" (*Eunuch.* 6).
[22] Flavius Josèphe, *Ant.* 4.290. L'anthropologie juive, qui lie la procréation à la bénédiction, ne peut que répudier la castration. Philon d'Alexandrie commente Deut 23:2: la Loi "refoule d'avance hors de la sainte congrégation tous les gens qui n'en sont pas dignes, à commencer par ces individus de sexe douteux. ... Elle exclut, en effet, les eunuques aux organes broyés ou mutilés" (*Spec.* 1.325).
[23] Ps 21:28; 65:4; 71:11; 85:9; Ésa 27:13; 66:23.

Dieu, païens admirateurs et sympathisants du judaïsme, associés à certains de ses rites.[24] Son intégration au peuple de Dieu prendra un tour imprévu.

L'origine géographique mérite attention: l'homme vient des antipodes et y retourne. Au premier siècle, l'Éthiopie et sa capitale Meroé font rêver l'Empire. Sénèque rapporte l'expédition lancée par Néron en 61–62 aux sources du Nil (*Nat.* 6.8). Le goût pour l'exotisme est à la mode. L'Éthiopie passe pour être l'extrême limite de l'Empire, et déjà Homère considérait les Éthiopiens comme les plus éloignés des hommes (*Od.* 1.23, ἔσχατοι ἀνδρῶν). L'origine de l'eunuque ne peut qu'exciter l'imaginaire du lecteur des Actes[25] et évoquer les "confins de la terre" (ἔσχατον τῆς γῆς) que doit atteindre le témoignage du Ressuscité (1:8).

L'échange verbal entre Philippe et le dignitaire africain (vv. 30–31)—un comble de raffinement langagier—aboutit à l'aveu d'incompréhension de l'eunuque. Cet homme en recherche a fait plus d'un millier de kilomètres pour approcher Dieu; il rentre chez lui en s'éloignant de Jérusalem et confesse le besoin de quelqu'un pour le guider (ὁδηγεῖν, v. 31). Le chemin qu'il suit (ὁδός, vv. 26, 36, 39) prend ainsi la connotation symbolique d'une quête spirituelle. Le texte d'Ésaïe 53 que lit l'eunuque a joué un rôle considérable dans la christologie des premiers chrétiens. L'extrait est choisi à dessein par le narrateur; il découpe deux versets dans le quatrième chant du serviteur de Yahveh (Ésa 52:13–53:12), qu'il cite dans la version des Septante: 53:7b–8c. La découpe est chirurgicale: elle évite deux allusions à la mort expiatoire du serviteur, qui précèdent (53:7a) et suivent (53:8d) immédiatement l'extrait; la lecture sacrificielle de la croix n'est pas du goût de Luc.

Le texte cité commence par exposer la détresse du serviteur acceptant sans protester la violence qui lui est faite (Actes 8:32); pour le lecteur de Luc-Actes, l'application à la croix est évidente. La compréhension de la seconde partie (v. 33) est par contre incertaine, déjà dans la Septante. A première vue, elle confirme la souffrance du serviteur: son droit (κρίσις) lui a été enlevé (ἤρθη), et personne ne pourra parler de sa descendance "car elle est enlevée (αἴρεται) loin de la terre, sa vie." Or, le verbe αἴρω signifie aussi bien "enlever," "ôter" que "lever," "élever." Si l'on adopte ce second sens, la dernière ligne de la citation sonne tout autrement: "car elle est élevée de la terre, sa vie." On lit

---

[24] Un eunuque ne peut devenir prosélyte selon Deut 23:1. Luc ne *définit* pas explicitement l'homme comme craignant-Dieu, à la différence de Corneille (Actes 10:2), mais il le *montre* à l'œuvre. Il faut cependant admettre que sa terminologie est fluide sur ce point; la figure la plus approchante est celle du centurion de Capharnaüm, un païen qui "aime notre peuple" (Luc 7:5).

[25] Les auteurs classiques idéalisent les Éthiopiens pour leur beauté et leur piété. Strabon situe l'Éthiopie aux "extrêmes limites" de l'Empire (*Geogr.* 17.2.1). De la lointaine *Koush*, l'Ancien Testament attend qu'elle apporte ses hommages au Seigneur (Soph 3:10; Ps 68:32). Sur l'image ancienne de l'Éthiopie, voir Erich Dinkler, "Philippus und der ΑΝΗΡ ΑΙΘΙΟΨ (Apg 8,26–40): Historische und geographische Bemerkungen zum Missionsablauf nach Lukas," in *Jesus und Paulus: Festschrift für Werner Georg Kümmel zum 70. Geburtstag* (éd. E. Earle Ellis et Erich Grasser; Göttingen: Vandenhoeck & Ruprecht, 1975), 85–95.

une référence à la résurrection du Christ, suivant un schéma christologique abaissement/exaltation que l'on rencontre en Phil 2:6–11. A cette lumière, le sens des lignes précédentes peut aussi être retourné: parce qu'il s'est abaissé, son jugement (autre sens possible de κρίσις) a été levé, c'est-à-dire suspendu par Dieu; et qui pourra raconter sa descendance spirituelle, tant elle est innombrable?[26] Quelle lecture Luc a-t-il retenue? Contrairement à sa pratique, il ne présente pas son exégèse de l'Écriture (cf. Actes 2:25–36; 4:25–28; 13:34–37). De deux choses l'une: ou il la suppose connue des lecteurs, ou il compte avec cette ambiguïté de la finale ésaïenne. La dernière solution s'inscrit dans ses habitudes: Luc cite un texte dont il préserve volontairement l'ambivalence, en vue de légitimer la question de sa compréhension. Du Christ seul, en effet, il est possible de dire que sa vie a été exaltée (Actes 2:34; 13:34–37).

L'intégralité de la citation permet aussi une application à la situation de l'eunuque: malgré sa haute position sociale, il a été victime de propos rabaissants face auxquels il ne pouvait protester; l'espoir d'une descendance terrestre lui est retiré; il peut cependant espérer que Dieu relèvera l'humilié et réhabilitera sa vie.[27]

La question herméneutique que pose l'eunuque—qui est le référent du texte?—n'est pas inconnue du judaïsme au premier siècle; elle est typique de l'interprétation chrétienne des Écritures et suit une règle que formulera plus tard Justin: "Quand vous entendez ainsi les prophètes s'exprimer comme en leur propre nom, ce ne sont pas ces hommes inspirés qui parlent, ne le croyez pas, mais le Logos divin qui les meut" (*1 Apol.* 36.1). La réponse de Philippe est un parcours scripturaire, dont seule la finalité est explicitée dans une formule synthétique: "il lui annonça la bonne nouvelle, Jésus" (Actes 8:35; cf. 5:42; 11:20; 17:18). Le texte éveille l'écho de l'histoire des pèlerins d'Emmaüs, à qui le Ressuscité expose la nécessité de la Passion "en commençant à partir de Moïse et de tous les prophètes" (Luc 24:27). Ce rapprochement prend place au sein d'un parallélisme appuyé des deux récits, mais de l'un à l'autre, le mouvement de la lecture christologique s'est inversé: en Luc 24, c'est la destinée de Jésus qui fait problème et l'Écriture qui vient l'éclairer; en Actes 8, la compréhension d'Ésaïe 53 fait difficulté, et la vie de Jésus en offre la clef. L'Écriture fait *anamnèse* de la vie de Jésus en Luc 24, alors que la vie de Jésus

---

[26] P. B. Decock défend la lecture résurrectionnelle d'Ésa 53:8 ici et déjà dans la LXX, l'exaltation du serviteur illustrant le renversement eschatologique des valeurs ("The Understanding of Isaiah 53,7–8 in Acts 8,32–33," *Neot* 14 [1981]: 111–33). Avis contraire chez von Dobbeler (*Der Evangelist Philippus*, 147–63), pour qui le passage porte au langage la radicalité de l'abaissement du serviteur.

[27] Joel B. Green voit avec raison dans ce renversement existentiel le corrélat sotériologique de la résurrection (" 'Witnesses of His Resurrection': Resurrection, Salvation, Discipleship, and Mission in the Acts of the Apostles," in *Life in the Face of Death* [éd. Richard N. Longenecker; McMaster New Testament Studies; Grand Rapids: Eerdmans, 1998], 222–46, surtout 233–37).

fait *exégèse* de l'Écriture en Actes 8.[28] Philippe a endossé le rôle du guide (v. 31) et fait passer du lire au comprendre; entre l'Écriture et l'eunuque, il a introduit une médiation christologique et ouvert un sens que le pèlerinage à Jérusalem avait maintenu fermé. Le baptême (v. 38) vient ratifier cet accès à l'Écriture.[29]

Comme en Luc 24:31–35, l'épilogue est rapide et poignant: l'Esprit escamote Philippe au retour du baptême et le délocalise à Azot où il poursuit sa mission jusqu'à Césarée (v. 40). De son côté, l'eunuque poursuit son cheminement, transformé. Irénée (*Haer.* 4.23.2) et Eusèbe de Césarée (*Hist. eccl.* 2.1.13) en disent trop lorsqu'ils font de ce dignitaire le premier missionnaire d'Afrique. Rencontre imprévisible aux causes surnaturelles, l'événement, déroulé sans témoin, reste exceptionnel à ce stade du livre des Actes; il anticipe prophétiquement la destinée universelle de l'Évangile, mais d'autres (Pierre, puis Paul) la mèneront à bien. Sans le dire, l'événement transgresse la Loi dans sa fonction de protéger la pureté du peuple élu; ce problème, avec ses conséquences ecclésiologiques, sera développé en Actes 10–11.

Conclusion

Actes 8 montre à quels succès et à quels chocs s'expose la mission chrétienne lorsqu'elle s'aventure hors de Jérusalem. La supériorité de l'Évangile lui est promise, mais une éthique du prédicateur est déployée, dont Simon est le contre-modèle: le porteur de l'Évangile doit être témoin, c'est-à-dire référence à un Autre que soi. Le paradigme de cette critique du pouvoir est christologique: Ésa 53:7–8 dresse le modèle d'un abaissement que Dieu relève par la résurrection. Dans le cas de l'eunuque d'Éthiopie, ce scénario a une relevance sotériologique: l'homme marginalisé est réhabilité par le baptême.

Actes 8 anticipe l'évangélisation des lointains et en affiche le programme: la résurrection de Jésus, cœur du kérygme, entraîne une dynamique de renversement des valeurs que le témoin est appelé à répercuter.

---

[28] Philippe Bossuyt et Jean Radermakers, *Témoins de la Parole de la Grâce: Actes des Apôtres* (2 vols; Collection de l'Institut d'Études Théologiques 16; Bruxelles: Institut d'Études Théologiques, 1995), 2:304.

[29] François Bovon a relevé l'importance du verbe κωλύω, qui surgit en Luc 9:50 juste après l'épisode de l'accueil de l'enfant et ici (Actes 8:36) dans la question de l'Ethiopien à Philippe: "Voici de l'eau; qu'est-ce qui empêche (τί κυλύει) que je sois baptisé?" Bovon conclut, "According to Luke, the kingdom of God is open to children and to those who comply with this metaphor, because his God opens the door to such people" ("The Child and the Beast: Fighting Violence in Ancient Christianity," *HTR* 92 [1999]: 383).

CHAPTER NINE

"CAN ANYONE WITHHOLD THE WATER?" (ACTS 10:47)
TOWARD AN UNDERSTANDING OF LUKE'S ARGUMENT
IN THE STORY OF CORNELIUS

David H. Warren

In his historical survey of how the early church understood the story of
Cornelius,[1] François Bovon deals with several themes and subthemes taken up
by the various patristic writers in the first six centuries of the church. Regarding
one of these subthemes, "Virtue and the Outpouring of the Holy Spirit,"
Bovon makes the following observation:

> Si les Pères s'étonnent moins que l'on aurait pu le penser de cette effusion
> anticipée du Saint-Esprit, c'est qu'il y a encore vivante en eux la conviction
> que l'Esprit ne se transmet pas uniquement par le canal du sacrement. Certains
> relient ainsi le Saint-Esprit à la vertu et le conçoivent comme une récom-
> pense. Son effusion sur Corneille sert alors à la parénèse: il faut imiter Corneille
> qui reçut l'Esprit avant d'être baptisé en récompense de ses bonnes œuvres.[2]

I find this situation quite surprising since I understand it to be the very *obverse*
of Luke's argument in this story. This patristic lack of astonishment at Cornelius'
receiving the Holy Spirit before his baptism in water stands in stark contrast
to the shock experienced by the Jewish Christians in Luke's story. In describing the reaction of the "circumcised believers" who accompanied Peter to
Cornelius' house, Luke emphasizes their utter astonishment:

> [44]While Peter was still speaking, the Holy Spirit fell upon all who heard the
> word. [45]The circumcised believers who had come with Peter were *astounded*
> that the gift of the Holy Spirit had been poured out even on the Gentiles, [46]for
> they heard them speaking in tongues and extolling God. Then Peter said,
> [47]"Can anyone withhold the water for baptizing these people who have received
> the Holy Spirit just as we have?" [Acts 10:44–47 with emphasis added].[3]

---

[1] François Bovon, *De vocatione gentium: Histoire de l'interprétation d'Act. 10,1–11,18 dans
les six premiers siècles* (BGBE 8; Tübingen: Mohr/Siebeck, 1967). This is the published
edition of Bovon's dissertation, completed under the direction of Oscar Cullmann at
the University of Basel in 1965. Words cannot express my heartfelt gratitude for his
help and guidance in the completion of my own dissertation. I offer this piece, the
first since my graduation, as an earnest effort to further the work that launched his
scholarly career.

[2] Ibid., 252.

[3] Unless otherwise stated, all quotations from the Bible are taken from the NRSV.

Luke states that the six Jewish Christians[4] present with Peter at Cornelius' house were astounded (ἐξέστησαν, v. 45).[5] They were amazed! We ask, what caused their astonishment? Why does Luke mention it in his story? And what does their reaction have to do with Peter's climactic question, "Can anyone withhold the water for baptizing these people?" (Acts 10:47)?

The Promise is for All

The inclusion of the Gentiles into the church is a major theme in the two-volume work of Luke.[6] "Die christliche Botschaft ist eine universale, nach Lukas frei von jeder partikularistischen Begrenzung."[7] But the cause of the surprise for the Jewish Christians—and for Peter himself—could not be merely the inclusion of the gentiles into the Christian faith. The earlier announcement of the risen Lord that "repentance and forgiveness of sins is to be proclaimed in his name to all nations"—that is, "to all the gentiles" (εἰς πάντα τὰ ἔθνη)—had occasioned no objection from the disciples (Luke 24:47). Luke depicts these Jewish Christians as knowing that the gospel needed to be proclaimed "to the ends of the earth" (Acts 1:8), that God would now fulfill the prophecy to pour out his Spirit "upon all flesh" (Acts 2:17), and that this promise was "for all who are far away, everyone whom the Lord our God calls to him" (Acts 2:39).

So if the Jewish Christians were supposed to have known from the beginning that the Gentiles were to be included into the church, why were they so surprised to see that Cornelius and his family and friends had received the Holy Spirit? And what did their reaction have to do with Peter's question, "Can anyone withhold the water for baptizing these people?" (Acts 10:47)?

---

[4] Later in the story we learn that the unnamed "brothers from Joppa" (Acts 10:23) or "the believers of the circumcision" (10:45) are actually six in number (11:12).

[5] Quite literally, to "stand out" of one's mind so as to be separated from one's senses (BDAG 350); cf. our English word *ecstatic*, a derivative. Luke reserves this word to describe the utter befuddlement and absolute consternation caused by an event so unexpected and so inexplicable as to leave a person completely dumbfounded: the utter amazement of the crowd on Pentecost at the glossolalia (with θαυμάζω in Acts 2:7 and with διαπορέω in 2:12); the bewitching of the Samaritans by Simon Magus (8:9, 11) and Simon's own bewilderment at the miracles wrought by Philip (v. 13); the unbelievable shock of seeing Saul the persecutor now the preacher (9:21; N.B. συνέχυννεν τοὺς Ἰουδαίους in the next verse) or of seeing Peter alive and unharmed, standing outside the door (12:16). See also Luke 2:47 (cf. ἐκπλήσσω—to *strike* one *out* of one's senses—in the next verse); 8:56; 24:22.

[6] On the scholarly debate over Luke's understanding of the church's relationship to Israel and its impact on the gentile mission, see the valuable surveys by François Bovon in his *Luke the Theologian: Thirty-Three Years of Research (1950–1983)* (Princeton Theological Monograph Series 12; Allison Park, Pa.: Pickwick, 1987), 323–43, and his "Studies in Luke–Acts: Retrospect and Prospect," *HTR* 85 (1992): 186–90.

[7] François Bovon, *Das Evangelium nach Lukas* (4 vols.; EKKNT 3; Zurich: Benziger Verlag, 1989–), 1:25.

The Gift of the Holy Spirit

As we have seen, Luke states that the Jewish Christians accompanying Peter were surprised to see Cornelius and the other Gentiles receive the Holy Spirit. More specifically, his text says that they were surprised to see them receive "the gift of the Holy Spirit" (ἡ δωρεὰ τοῦ ἁγίου πνεύματος, Acts 10:45). In order to appreciate Luke's mention of their astonishment, we must understand the connection that Luke intends his readers to make. The phrase "the gift of the Holy Spirit" occurs only twice in the New Testament, and both instances are found in the book of Acts. The other occurrence is found in Acts 2:38, and curiously it too comes from the lips of Peter. It is significant that the very same writer (Luke) in the very same book (Acts) has the very same speaker (Peter) use the very same phrase ("the gift of the Holy Spirit") on two separate occasions. It would seem that Luke intends his readers to make a connection here.

In Acts 2:38 Peter announces the conditions of salvation for the very first time following the death and resurrection of Jesus:

> [36]Therefore let the entire house of Israel know with certainty that God has made him both Lord and Messiah, this Jesus whom you crucified. [37]Now when they heard this, they were cut to the heart and said to Peter and to the other apostles, "Brothers, what should we do?" [38]Peter said to them, "Repent, and be baptized every one of you in the name of Jesus Christ so that your sins may be forgiven; and you will receive the gift of the Holy Spirit. [39]For the promise is for you, for your children, and for all who are far away, everyone whom the Lord our God calls to him." (Acts 2:36–39)

Luke intends "the promise" in verse 39 to refer primarily to "the gift of the Holy Spirit" in the previous verse. He makes the same connection earlier in verse 33: Having now been exalted at the right hand of the Father, Jesus has received *the promise* of the Holy Spirit, which he has just "poured out" in the manifestation here on Pentecost. The language of "pouring out" (ἐκχέω) the Spirit evokes the imagery of the prophecy from Joel cited earlier in verses 17–18. This is the origin of Peter's promise in verse 39. Through the prophet Joel, God promised to pour out his Spirit upon all people: "I will pour out my Spirit upon all flesh. . . . Even upon my slaves, both men and women, in those days I will pour out my Spirit" (Acts 2:17–18 = Joel 2:28–29^{ET}/ 3:1–2$^{MT/LXX}$).

But this promise is conditional. In Acts 2:38, the gift of the Holy Spirit is conditioned on two prerequisites: repentance and water baptism. By using the phrase "the gift of the Holy Spirit" in Acts 10:45 that he had used earlier in 2:38, Luke intends the reader to make a connection between these two passages. This connection explains the shock and surprise of the Jewish Christians present with Peter at the house of Cornelius. In Acts 2:38, Peter clearly makes the forgiveness of sins and the gift of the Holy Spirit dependent upon the conditions of repentance and water baptism. But the text in Acts 10:47–48 makes it clear that Cornelius and his family and friends had not been baptized in water when they received "the gift of the Holy Spirit" in verse 45. Luke intends the reader to surmise that their reception of the Spirit before their baptism in water accounts for the astonishment of the Jewish Christians in Acts 10:45. Cornelius and his household have not met the second requirement. If Peter's statement in Acts 2:38 lays down the general rule, then Cornelius and his family and friends are the exception.

Contradictions or Exceptions?

In their monumental work *The Beginnings of Christianity*, both F. J. Foakes Jackson and Kirsopp Lake recognized that Acts 2:38 laid down the general rule: "Baptism in water conferred the gift of the Spirit, but only if administered in the name of the Lord Jesus."[8] In commenting on Acts 2:38, they wrote, "The obvious meaning is—just as in Acts xix.1–7—that the gift of the Spirit is conditional on [water] baptism."[9] And not only did this premise underlie Peter's statement in Acts 2:38 and the story of the Ephesian twelve in 19:1–7, but they found the same teaching in the account of Paul's conversion in 9:17–18. Water baptism in the name of Jesus is a prerequisite for the reception of the Spirit.

But then they noted the exceptions to this pattern in the Pentecost experience of the apostles, the conversion story of the Samaritans, and the conversion story of Cornelius. On Pentecost, the apostles received the baptism in the Spirit apart from water baptism. In Acts 8, the Samaritans were baptized (v. 12), but their reception of the Spirit was delayed until the arrival of Peter and John (v. 17). And Cornelius and his household received the Holy Spirit without the benefit of water baptism (Acts 10:44–48). Foakes Jackson and Lake attributed these apparently contradictory elements to the various sources underlying the book of Acts. In redacting his narrative, Luke has failed to recognize some of these contradictory elements so that he did not fully remove them from his narrative. These contradictory elements betray the varying viewpoints of his sources.[10]

It is conceivable that Foakes Jackson and Lake are right in their estimation. These apparently contradictory elements may be vestiges of the varying viewpoints underlying Luke's text.[11] But I find it extraordinary that the three

---

[8] F. J. Foakes Jackson and Kirsopp Lake, *The Acts of the Apostles* (5 vols.; The Beginnings of Christianity 1; London: Macmillan, 1920–1933), 1:337–38. In fact, "Most readers of Luke–Acts have regarded Peter's instructions in Acts 2.38 . . . as paradigmatic for Luke's theology of baptism in the book of Acts" (Joel B. Green, "From 'John's Baptism' to 'Baptism in the Name of the Lord Jesus': The Significance of Baptism in Luke–Acts," in *Baptism, the New Testament and the Church: Historical and Contemporary Studies in Honour of R. E. O. White* [ed. Stanley E. Porter and Anthony R. Cross; JSNTSup 171; Sheffield: Sheffield Academic Press, 1999], 157).

[9] Foakes Jackson and Lake, *Acts of the Apostles*, 1:339.

[10] Ibid., 1:337–41.

[11] In the present essay, I am not concerned with the question of Luke's sources per

exceptions which they note actually coincide with three pivotal passages in Luke's narrative, the very transitions which he signals at the beginning of his book: "You will be my witnesses in Jerusalem, in all Judea and Samaria, and to the ends of the earth" (Acts 1:8).[12]

Jerusalem, Samaria, and the Ends of the Earth

On Pentecost, the apostles receive the Holy Sprit separate and apart from water baptism. Clearly this event seems to run counter to Peter's statement in Acts 2:38. But then Pentecost was an extraordinary event, as Peter himself noted before the Jerusalem church in Acts 11. When he described the Holy Spirit's coming upon Cornelius and his household, he had to reach back to Pentecost to find a parallel: "the Holy Spirit came on them as he had come on us at the beginning" (Acts 11:15), and he quoted the words of Jesus from Acts 1:5. Now if in the experience of the church the reception of the Holy Spirit commonly occurred separate and apart from water baptism, then why did Peter have to go back to "the beginning" in order to find a suitable comparison? If what happened to Cornelius and his company was ordinary and ubiquitous, then it should have been so familiar as to need no reference to what had happened at "the beginning." It would seem probable that the apostles, like their Lord, had already received water baptism.[13] But they still lacked the Spirit, since John's baptism did not involve the Spirit (Luke 3:16 and parallels).[14] And so on Pentecost, the apostles merely received the missing component. They had already complied with the condition of water baptism. Their case is an understandable exception to the general rule in Acts 2:38.

As for the Samaritans, we are told that the Holy Spirit had "not yet" (οὐδέπω) come upon any of them, even though they had been baptized in water (Acts 8:16). There seems to be some problem here, for the "not yet" would seem to imply—in accordance with Acts 2:38—that the Holy Spirit was expected to come. The trouble here lay perhaps with the strained relations between Samaritans and Jews. Though both peoples had descended from ancient Israel, there now existed a long-standing hostility between the two.

---

se. Rather, I purpose to show that these contradictory elements are actually intentional on Luke's part. On the possibility of sources underlying Acts 10, one should consult the epochal work of Martin Dibelius, "The Conversion of Cornelius," in *Studies in the Acts of the Apostles* (New York: Scribner, 1956), followed and revised by that of François Bovon, "Tradition et rédaction en Actes 10, 1–11, 18," *TZ* 26 (1970): 22–45.

[12] According to Hans Conzelmann, this statement "indicates the plan of the book" (*Acts of the Apostles: A Commentary* [Hermeneia—A Critical and Historical Commentary on the Bible; Philadelphia: Fortress, 1987], 7; see also xlii–iii).

[13] If we are to believe John 4:2, then it would seem unlikely that the apostles administered to others what they themselves had refused.

[14] The Fourth Gospel explains that John's baptism could not involve the Spirit since "Jesus was not yet glorified" (John 7:39).

Earlier Luke mentions how the Samaritans had rejected Jesus for the sole reason that he was on his way to Jerusalem (Luke 9:53). During his ministry, Jesus had endeavored to improve Jewish attitudes toward the Samaritans (Luke 9:55; 10:33–37; 17:16–17). But now the time had come for God to bring these two peoples together in the church. And God accomplished their union through an extraordinary event, a remarkable exception to the general rule in Acts 2:38. In order for the Samaritans to receive the Holy Spirit (and apparently salvation),[15] the Samaritans would now have to receive Jesus' apostles and not just Jesus' missionaries. In the same way, the Jerusalem church would also have to accept the Samaritans. By this remarkable exception to the general rule announced in Acts 2:38, God had finally brought Jew and Samaritan together. From now on they would enjoy healing and unity in the one church (Acts 9:31). The validity of their being accepted is confirmed by the laying on of hands.[16]

In the case of Cornelius, we find an even more astonishing exception, for Cornelius and his family and friends had never been baptized in water at the time that they received the Holy Spirit. *This single incident stands as the sole exception in Luke's entire work.* In the cases of both the apostles on Pentecost and the Samaritans, each had already received water baptism before they finally received the Holy Spirit. The delay in each case resulted from a special set of circumstances that required such an exception. The apostles had received an earlier baptism that had involved no promise of the Spirit. The Samaritans were kept from receiving the Spirit for the purpose of uniting them with the Jewish church. In either case, water baptism had preceded the reception of the Spirit. But now this order was suddenly reversed. Cornelius and his family had received the Holy Spirit without the condition of water baptism. This sudden reversal explains the astonishment of the Jewish Christians accompanying Peter to Cornelius' house. They were not astonished to learn that God had included the Gentiles into the church, for, as we have seen from Luke 24:47; Acts 1:8; 2:17, 39, they should have already known this. But they were astonished to see that Cornelius and his household had received "the gift of the Holy Spirit" (Acts 10:45) when up to this time God had always conditioned this blessing on the rite of water baptism (2:38).

"Who was I that I Could Hinder God?"

If the Jewish Christians in Acts considered water baptism as a prerequisite for the reception of the Holy Spirit, then one can understand their utter aston-

---

[15] In early Christianity, salvation and the indwelling of the Spirit are biconditional. The one implies the other, and vice-versa. A Christian cannot have the one without the other (e.g., Acts 5:32; Rom 8:9–12; 1 Cor 6:11, 17; 1 John 3:24; 4:13).

[16] For a discussion of the Holy Spirit and its link to baptism and the laying on of hands, see Bovon, *Luke the Theologian*, 229–38.

ishment at Cornelius and his household receiving "the gift of the Holy Spirit" before their baptism. But then why had not Peter baptized Cornelius and his family and friends beforehand? Cornelius and his company seemed receptive from the very beginning (Acts 10:33–34), and they already knew the basic facts of the gospel (ὑμεῖς οἴδατε, 10:37). So why was their baptism postponed until Peter asks his climatic question, "Can anyone withhold the water for baptizing these people?" (Acts 10:47)?

Apparently Luke wants to show that the Jewish Christians were withholding water baptism from these uncircumcised Gentiles.[17] In the previous chapter, Luke indicates only a little hesitation at the baptism of the eunuch. Though a gentile ("an Ethiopian"), he was nevertheless a proselyte who had been circumcised, for otherwise he could not have entered the temple in Jerusalem to worship (Acts 8:27). His baptism had occasioned no objection. But the baptisms of Cornelius and his household were objectionable. Why? They were not circumcised. With subtlety Luke argues in his narrative that the Jewish church had rationalized the divine plan for the inclusion of the Gentiles: Yes, God would accept the Gentiles into his church, but first they must become Jews. Before Gentiles can be baptized in water, they must undergo a circumcision of the flesh. But here in the story of Cornelius, God showed the Jewish Christians that their assumption was clearly wrong.

This connection between circumcision and water baptism may well point to an actual historical connection between Jewish proselyte baptism and John's baptism, and thus also to Christian baptism.[18] Though many modern scholars have cogently argued for the Jewish antecedent,[19] others remain unconvinced.[20] Perhaps future archaeological evidence will help solve this issue.[21]

---

[17] Even Irenaeus, the first writer that we know after Luke to comment on the Cornelius story, recognized that this problem was not just potential but real: Peter "was indicating that, unless the Holy Spirit had rested upon them, there was someone who would keep them from baptism" (. . . σημαίνων, ὅτι εἰ μὴ τὸ πνεῦμα τὸ ἅγιον ἐπ᾿ αὐτοὺς ἐπαναπέπαυτο, ἦν ὁ κωλύσων αὐτοὺς τοῦ βαπτίσματος, Haer. 3.12.15; the Greek text here is preserved in a catena: J. A. Cramer, ed., Catenae Graecorum patrum in Novum Testamentum [8 vols.; Oxford: Oxford University Press, 1838–1844], 3:183).

[18] Several scholars have suspected this connection as far back as John Lightfoot, A Commentary on the New Testament from the Talmud and Hebraica (4 vols.; Peabody, Mass.: Hendrickson, 1989), 2:54–67; repr. of Horae hebraicae et talmudicae (trans. Robert Grandell; Oxford: Oxford University Press, 1859; originally published in Latin, Cambridge: Field and Hayes, 1658–1678).

[19] The case is well argued by Emil Schürer in his History of the Jewish People in the Time of Jesus Christ (5 vols.; Clark's Foreign Theological Library² 23–25, 41, 43; Edinburgh: Clark, 1885–1890), 4:321–24.

[20] Among them is John J. Collins, "A Symbol of Otherness: Circumcision and Salvation in the First Century," in "To See Ourselves as Others See Us": Christians, Jews, "Others" in Late Antiquity (ed. Jacob Neusner and Ernest S. Frerichs; Scholars Press Studies in the Humanities 8; Chico, Calif.: Scholars Press, 1985), 171.

[21] William Sanford LaSor, "Discovering What Jewish Miqva'ot Can Tell Us about Christian Baptism," BAR 13, no. 1 (January/February 1987): 52–59; and Ronny Reich, "The Great Mikveh Debate," BAR 19, no. 2 (March/April 1993): 52–53.

The important aspect is to see such a connection for the time of Luke, and particularly in his narrative. If Peter and the six Jewish Christians regarded circumcision as a prerequisite for water baptism, then the reader can understand why they would have objected to Cornelius' baptism.[22] By giving Cornelius the Spirit before baptism—something that he should have never received without baptism—God was telling Peter and the Jewish Christians that they should have already baptized him even though he was still uncircumcised. To the chagrin of the Jewish Christians, God accepted the Gentiles in their *uncircumcision*.

This insight explains the significance of Luke's juxtaposition of Acts 11:18 with verse 19. In verse 18, we read that the Jewish church acknowledged that God has accepted the Gentiles. But then we learn in the very next verse that the Jewish Christians still refused to take the gospel to any of the Gentiles. They are still waiting for the Gentiles to come to them. They refuse to go to the uncircumcised. The matter comes to a head at the Jerusalem conference in Acts 15.

"Can anyone withhold the water for baptizing these people who have received the Holy Spirit just as we have?" (Acts 10:47). One cannot overemphasize the significance of this question for Luke, since it occurs at the climax of his story. The question is related to another issue raised by Peter in Acts 11:17 through the use of the same verb, κωλύω. Here Peter asks his fellow members of the Jewish church, "Who was I that I could hinder God?" (ἐγὼ τίς ἤμην δυνατὸς κωλῦσαι τὸν θεόν). God wanted the Gentiles to receive his Spirit even in their uncircumcision, a fact that in turn implies that God wanted them to be baptized in water even in their uncircumcision. Opposition to their baptism was thus opposition to God. By this clear exception to what Peter announced in Acts 2:38, God showed the Jewish Christians that physical circumcision was not a prerequisite to water baptism.

The Baptism with the Holy Spirit

We have seen where Luke connects "the gift of the Holy Spirit" (Acts 2:38) with "the promise from the Father" (Acts 2:33, 39) and "the outpouring of the Holy Spirit" (Acts 2:17–18, 33). Luke employs these three motifs to describe the same phenomenon. In Acts 1:4–5, he connects them with another important motif, "the baptism with the Holy Spirit."

> [4]While staying with them, he [i.e., Jesus] ordered them not to leave Jerusalem, but to wait there for the promise of the Father. "This," he said, "is what you have heard from me; [5]for John baptized with water, but you will be baptized with the Holy Spirit not many days from now." (Acts 1:4–5)

---

[22] This connection would explain why circumcision is often mentioned together with baptism in early Christian literature (e.g., Justin Martyr, *Dial.* 29.1), but it has become spiritualized (Col 2:11–12) so that it is no longer a circumcision of the flesh but "a circumcision of heart" (Rom 2:29): "*Repent* and be baptized" (Acts 2:38).

Here Luke equates "the promise of the Father" regarding the Holy Spirit's imminent coming on Pentecost (cf. Acts 2:33, 39) with the apostles' being "baptized with the Holy Spirit." In fact, Luke has Jesus here alluding to the earlier prophecy made by John the Baptist regarding this baptism with the Holy Spirit (Luke 3:16). John the Baptist states that he baptizes with water (ὕδατι βαπτίζω), but he predicts that there is someone coming "who is more powerful than" he and this one will "baptize you with the Holy Spirit and fire" (βαπτίσει ἐν πνεύματι ἁγίῳ καὶ πυρί).[23] One might conclude from the wording here that Jesus only baptizes with the Holy Spirit, just as John only baptized with water.[24] However, it is also possible that the phrase "baptize you with the Holy Spirit" does not exclude water. Rather, it merely states that which is in addition to the water. Since for Luke, baptism "in the name of Jesus Christ" clearly involves water (Acts 10:47–48; see also 8:26–39), Christian baptism must differ from John's only in the added element of the Spirit.

In Acts 11:15–17, Luke identifies the experience of Cornelius and his household as Spirit baptism. He compares it to that of Pentecost, "the beginning," when the apostles received the Holy Spirit (v. 15). Just like the apostles, Cornelius and the other Gentiles had received the very same, identical gift (τὴν ἴσην δωρεάν, v. 17). This gift was none other than the gift of the Holy Spirit (Acts 10:45), which was promised to everyone who would repent of his or her sins and be baptized in water (2:38). As with the apostles at Pentecost, the reception of the Spirit had occurred separate and apart from water baptism. In fact, this was the third and last exception in Luke's narrative. Normally for Luke, as for all early Christians, water and Spirit were always united in the same event.

---

[23] Contrary to the vast majority of expositors, I do not connect Luke's reference here to "fire" (πυρί) with that of his "divided tongues, as of fire" (διαμεριζόμεναι γλῶσσαι ὡσεὶ πυρός) associated with the baptism of the Holy Spirit on Pentecost (Acts 2:3). In context, the "fire" of Luke 3:16 must refer to the eschatological fire of judgment since this is clearly the use of "fire" in the following verse: "but the chaff he will burn with unquenchable fire" (τὸ δὲ ἄχυρον κατακαύσει πυρὶ ἀσβέστῳ; Luke 3:17; cf. Matt 3:10–12). We must allow Luke's obvious meaning of πυρί in verse 17 to illuminate his intended meaning of πυρί in the previous verse (see Tertullian, Bapt. 10.7). If we allow καί here to have the force of "or" (in the place of ἤ, see J. D. Denniston, The Greek Particles [2d ed.; rev. K. J. Dover; Oxford: Oxford University Press, 1950], 292), then we will see Luke's intended meaning. This reason explains why we find the "fire" only in Matthew's and Luke's accounts (= Q), for in them only we find present in the crowd two elements, the penitent sinners and the hypocritical, insincere "Brood of vipers" (Matt 3:7; Luke 3:7). In biting sarcasm, John the Baptist assures the former that someday they will be baptized in the Spirit, while he warns the latter that someday they will be immersed in (hell)fire. Since Mark does not identify any "Brood of vipers" among the crowd in his account, he does not have the term "fire" in his version of John's pronouncement (Mark 1:8). This rationale also explains why the term "fire" is missing from the similar phrase in John 1:33 and in Luke's own later repetitions of the phrase in Acts 1:5; 11:16.

[24] Foakes Jackson and Lake, Beginnings of Christianity, 1:341.

Water and Spirit

The early church tended to associate the reception of the Holy Spirit with water baptism. Contrary to the views of most Protestant theologians, baptism with the Holy Spirit and baptism with water are not two separate phenomena but one.[25] Their identity explains why early Christians can speak of having only "one baptism" (Eph 4:5) or of a new birth involving two elements, "of water and Spirit" (John 3:5; cf. 4:13–14; 7:37–39; Titus 3:5). It explains why Justin Martyr can say that he needs *no other* baptism than that "with the Holy Spirit" (*Dial.* 29.1).[26] Of course, Justin would not thereby dispense with water baptism, for he also believes that this rite is necessary for "the forgiveness of past sins" (*1 Apol.* 61.10). In making these two statements, Justin is not contradicting himself, since for him baptism with the Holy Spirit is the same phenomenon as baptism with water. And the same is true for Clement of Alexandria, who can refer to Christ's baptism, when the Spirit descended on him (*Paed.* 1.25.3 [= 1.6]), as the believer's "pattern" (ὑπογραφή) for receiving the Holy Spirit (*Paed.* 1.26.1). At our baptism in water, "from heaven above the Holy Spirit flows in upon us" (οὐρανόθεν ἐπεισρέοντος ἡμῖν τοῦ ἁγίου πνεύματος, *Paed.* 1.28.1). And for the same reason, Hippolytus can declare,

> Come from slavery to freedom, from tyranny to kingdom, from corruption to immortality. But someone says, "How shall we come?" How? By water and the Holy Spirit [δι' ὕδατος καὶ ἁγίου πνεύματος]. This is the water that participates with the Spirit [τοῦτο δέ ἐστιν τὸ ὕδωρ τὸ τῷ πνεύματι κοινωνοῦν] . . . in which also Christ was baptized, and in which the Spirit descended in the form of a dove. (Hippolytus, *Theoph.* 8)[27]

---

[25] Karl Barth is typical: "Baptism of the Spirit certainly calls for the baptism with water, . . . but it is not identical with this" (*Church Dogmatics* [trans. Geoffrey W. Bromiley; 5 vols. in 13; Edinburgh: Clark, 1956–1969], 4.4:32). James D. G. Dunn is even more extreme: "Water-baptism is clearly distinct from and even antithetical to Spirit-baptism" (*Baptism in the Holy Spirit: A Re-examination of the New Testament Teaching on the Gift of the Spirit in Relation to Pentecostalism Today* [SBT[2] 15; Naperville, Ill.: Alec R. Allenson, 1970], 5). Such a bifurcation among Protestants probably represents an overreaction to sacramentalism. Luke, of course, is no sacramentalist, for he sees baptism merely as the natural response of the penitent believer. Neither is his God, for the three exceptions show that his God can transcend the law stipulated in Acts 2:38. Nevertheless, Acts 2:38 still represents the general law for all believers.

[26] Observe that Justin's mention here of "that other baptism" (τίς ἐκείνου τοῦ βαπτίσματος χρεία ἁγίῳ πνεύματι βεβαπτισμένῳ;) is connected with Jewish circumcision and so refers to the rite of Jewish proselyte baptism. Note Justin's earlier retort in *Dial.* 28.2 that Trypho the Jew needs to become a "proselyte"—a proselyte to Christianity. Though uncircumcised, Justin does not need Trypho's fleshly circumcision and the Jewish rite of water. But in Justin's opinion, Trypho needs to circumcise his heart and submit to the Christian rite of water.

[27] While the authenticity of this work stands in question, it still nevertheless reflects the viewpoint of early Christians.

Finally, in his tract *On Baptism*, Tertullian makes the point with precision: "Not that in the water we obtain the Holy Spirit, but having been cleansed in the water . . . we are prepared for the Holy Spirit" (*Bapt.* 6.1). Later Origen will make the same argument: (*Comm. Jo.* 6.167 [= 6.33 or 6.17]). From this premise, Tertullian reasons that the reception of the Spirit is *subsequent* to immersion in water. After the believer emerges from the water, he or she receives the Holy Spirit through the imposition of hands (*Bapt.* 8.1, 4). Since the believer's sins are washed away in the waters of baptism, the reception of the Spirit must be subsequent to the immersion in water. The Holy Spirit cannot dwell in the presence of sin. Thus, the reception of the Spirit is conditioned on the rite of water. But the two are not to be regarded as separate events. As in the example of Jesus' baptism, the one naturally follows the other, and together they form "one baptism" (*Bapt.* 15.1).

Conclusion

For Luke, as for the Pauline tradition, there was only one baptism, and it involved both water and the Holy Spirit. For that reason, in the case of the twelve Ephesians who had not received the Holy Spirit, Paul immediately suspected a problem with their water baptism (Acts 19:2–3). Had they received the proper water baptism, then they should have already received the Holy Spirit. Paul could not be the agent of the Holy Spirit without their first submitting to the proper baptism.[28]

But the case of Cornelius was a different matter. It was an exception. Even though Cornelius and his family and friends received the Holy Spirit before their baptism, the Ephesians clearly could not. One can perhaps insist with Marshall that

> Luke had received several varying accounts of how the Spirit was received by men, but he has not tried to harmonize them and impose a pattern upon

---

[28] The ineffectual nature of John's baptism here in Acts 19:2–4 does not necessarily imply its invalidity per se. Luke (3:3, 16) and the other canonical gospels (Matt 3:6, 11, 13–17; Mark 1:4–5, 8–11; John 1:26, 31, 33; 3:23, 26; 4:1) seem to portray John's baptism as valid for its time. But after the inauguration of the Spirit on Pentecost, his spiritless baptism was no longer in force.

Luke does not say whether Apollos was rebaptized or not (Acts 18:26), even though, like the twelve (19:3), he too "knew only of the baptism of John" (18:25). Perhaps Luke intends that he did not have to be rebaptized, since he was obviously a veteran of many years (v. 24) so that his baptism, like that of the apostles, had occurred before Pentecost. The baptism of the twelve, on the other hand, was much more recent and took place after Pentecost, when John's spiritless baptism was no longer in effect. Since Apollos had just been in Ephesus (v. 24) where he had evangelized the synagogue (v. 26), perhaps the twelve at Ephesus were his own recent converts. While the text does not make it explicit, this insight would explain why Luke juxtaposes the two stories.

them. . . . If Luke was wishing to fit the work of the Spirit into a pattern, he had no need to record these anomalous experiences.[29]

I have tried to show, however, that indeed there is a pattern, and that the "anomalous experiences"—these exceptions to the pattern—are a part of the intentional argumentation of Luke's narrative.[30]

---

[29] I. Howard Marshall, *Luke: Historian and Theologian* (3d ed.; Exeter: Paternoster Press, 1988), 198–99.

[30] Bovon is one of the few expositors that see Acts 8 and 10 as "heilsgeschichtliche Ausnahmen" (*Lukas*, 1:177).

CHAPTER TEN

LUKE'S REVISION OF PAUL'S REFLECTIONS IN ROMANS 9–11

MARIANNE PALMER BONZ

Since François Bovon has repeatedly expressed to me his admiration for the short scholarly article, I dedicate the following brief essay to my esteemed former teacher, former employer, and former colleague.

Unbelieving Israel in Romans 9–11

Philipp Vielhauer's well-known essay[1] long ago outlined significant differences between the picture of Paul that one derives from reading his letters and the charismatic persona that Luke fashions in his narrative. So extensive is the disparity between the genuine Paul and the Lukan Paul that many New Testament scholars, both before and after Vielhauer, concluded that Luke either did not know the genuine letters of Paul or, more probably, deliberately suppressed this knowledge in creating a more colorful account of the Pauline mission.[2] Recent trends in Lukan studies have only served to highlight Luke's willingness to eschew historical fidelity in the service of more pressing creative or apologetic concerns.[3] Indeed, one might also argue that the distinctive depiction of Paul in Acts is not caused by Luke's ignorance of Paul's theology, but by his desire to make Paul the guarantor for a revised Pauline theology, more suitable to Luke's own time and historical situation.

---

[1] Philipp Vielhauer, "On the 'Paulinism' of Acts," in *Studies in Luke–Acts: Essays Presented in Honor of Paul Schubert* (ed. Leander E. Keck and J. Louis Martyn; 1966; reprinted Philadelphia: Fortress, 1980), 33–50.

[2] See, for example, John Knox, "Acts and the Pauline Corpus," in *Studies in Luke–Acts*, 279–87.

[3] With respect to Lukan literary creativity, see Richard I. Pervo, *Profit with Delight: The Literary Genre of the Acts of the Apostles* (Philadelphia: Fortress, 1987); Robert Tannehill, *The Narrative Unity of Luke–Acts: A Literary Interpretation* (2 vols.; Philadelphia: Fortress, 1986–1994); and Marianne Palmer Bonz, *The Past as Legacy: Luke–Acts and Ancient Epic* (Minneapolis: Fortress, 2000). Two studies emphasizing Luke's strong interest in apologetic at the expense of historical accuracy are Robert L. Brawley, "Paul in Acts: Lukan Apology and Conciliation," in *Luke–Acts: New Perspectives from the Society of Biblical Literature Seminar* (ed. Charles H. Talbert; New York: Crossroad, 1984), 129–47; and John T. Carroll, "Literary and Social Dimensions of Luke's Apology for Paul," in *The Society of Biblical Literature 1988 Seminar Papers* (ed. David J. Lull; Atlanta: Scholars Press, 1988), 106–18.

And although even today there is no clear consensus that Luke did in fact make use of any of the Pauline letters as sources for his own work, there is, I believe, a good argument to be made for Luke's conscious revision of Paul with respect to the latter's reflections on Jewish unbelief and the importance of its role in the divine economy. Although Paul's discussion of this issue was once routinely treated as a slightly extraneous excursus in his Letter to the Romans, within the last several decades interpreters have increasingly focused on Rom 9–11 as the climax of the letter, occasionally also noting the significance of these chapters for understanding Paul's own concerns regarding the unintended consequences of his mission to the Gentiles.[4]

The introduction to these chapters is contained within a few verses (Rom 9:1–5), in which Paul expresses a somewhat emotional and obviously sincere lament over what he regards as the failure of his kinsmen to take up God's final challenge, despite their long history as God's elect and despite the many divine gifts that Paul enumerates as having been bestowed upon Israel exclusively. Indeed, Paul writes, as kinsmen of the Messiah according to the flesh, Israel was even chosen as the bearer of God's ultimate gift of salvation (Rom 9:5).

Following these brief introductory remarks, Rom 9:6–29 launches the first of three main segments of Paul's reflections concerning the ultimate place of Israel according to the flesh in God's economy of salvation, the dominant theme of this first segment being God's sovereign freedom to elect or reject whomever he pleases. It is the next segment (Rom 9:30–10:21), however, that is most pertinent to the discussion at hand, namely, Paul's influence on Luke regarding the problem of Jewish unbelief. For in this central segment of his reflections on the fate of Israel, Paul questions the actions and motivations of his kinsmen in a manner analogous to that of Israel's ancient prophets, preaching a message of judgment and salvation to a people whose ears are closed and whose understanding is dulled. Apparently at a loss to explain Israel's refusal to abandon the Law as God's definitive word of salvation, in favor of the universally offered grace embodied in the gospel, Paul seeks answers in the scriptures.

In this central segment of his argument, Paul offers the harshest condemnation of Jewish unbelief found anywhere in his genuine letters. In Rom 9:32, Paul implies that his kinsmen are deluded; and in Rom 10:16–21, he accuses them of being incapable of hearing, of lacking understanding, and of being disobedient and contentious.

> [16]But not all have obeyed the gospel; for Isaiah says, "Lord, who has believed our message?" [17]So faith comes from what is heard, and what is heard comes from the word of Christ.

---

[4] See Krister Stendahl, "The Apostle Paul and the Introspective Conscience of the West," *HTR* 56 (1963): 199–215; J. Christian Becker, *Paul the Apostle: The Triumph of God in Life and Thought* (Philadelphia: Fortress, 1980), 87; and Stanley K. Stowers, *A Rereading of Romans: Justice, Jews, and Gentiles* (New Haven: Yale University Press, 1994), 285.

[18]But I ask, have they not heard? Indeed they have; for "Their voice has gone out to all the earth, and their words to the limits of the civilized world." [19]Again I ask, did Israel not understand? First Moses says, "I will make you jealous of those who are not a nation; with a nation lacking understanding I will make you angry." [20]Then Isaiah is so bold as to say, "I have been found by those who did not seek me; I have made myself manifest to those who did not ask for me."

[21]But of Israel he says, "All day long I have stretched out my hands to a disobedient and contentious people."

In these verses, Paul's own reflections on the failure of his kinsmen to receive the gospel favorably are intertwined with a mélange of scriptural quotations and reminiscences, most of which allude to previous instances in which Israel was deemed by its prophets to have been in error or unfaithful. Moreover, Ernst Käsemann is correct in noting that in v. 16 the quotation from Deutero-Isaiah[5] "takes on the character of a lament."[6] Paul regards Israel's unbelief as disobedience and rejection of the proclamation. And as the rejected bearer of God's new message of hope and salvation, Paul apparently finds consolation in the analogous experience of the Exilic prophet.

Next, Paul affirms both the integrity and the authenticity of the gospel message, which is in essence Christ's "self-revelation";[7] and he links the extraordinary reach of the apostolic mission to the near anticipation of the victorious end time, when, as the Psalmist declares, the glory of God will permeate all creation.[8] In fact, Paul's dismay at Israel's unbelief is heightened by his perception of a world virtually filled with the Christian proclamation.[9]

In v. 19, Paul asks himself: Why did Israel, so divinely gifted, fail to understand? And the bittersweet irony of his successful mission among the Gentiles calls to mind a passage from the concluding song of Moses' farewell address, words to be remembered when, after the prophet's death, Israel's transgressions provoke God to retaliation.[10] But even though v. 19 implies that it is God's grace that enables the Gentiles to receive the gospel, in v. 20 Paul slightly alters another quotation from Deutero-Isaiah,[11] so that the Gentiles are not merely depicted as instruments for the punishment of a guilty Israel. Rather, in contrast to Israel's willful unbelief, Paul asserts that Gentiles have actively embraced the salvation that God has extended to them. And Paul concludes this section with the judgmental pronouncement, again taken from

---

[5] Isa 53:1 (LXX).
[6] Ernst Käsemann, *Commentary on Romans* (ed. and trans. Geoffrey W. Bromiley; Grand Rapids, Mich.: William B. Eerdmans, 1980), 295.
[7] Ibid.
[8] Ps 19:4 (LXX).
[9] Käsemann, *Commentary on Romans*, 296.
[10] Deut 32:21b (LXX).
[11] Isa 65:1 (LXX).

deutero-Isaiah,[12] that despite God's steadfast faithfulness, Israel remains a disobedient and contentious people.

Thus, in Rom 10:16–21, Paul suggests that Jewish unbelief can neither be blamed on the inauthenticity of the message nor the ineffectiveness of the messengers. On the contrary, the proclamation is the word of Christ, and the message has been carried to the ends of the civilized world.[13] That this is truly the case is evident because so many Gentiles, by the grace of God, have received its message in faith. Thus, Israel's jealousy is divinely provoked, God's temporary retaliation against a people who are both disobedient and contentious.[14]

If Paul had ended his reflections in Romans with chapter 10, one might have been forced to conclude that, by the end of his mission, Paul no longer considered unbelieving Israel worthy of election or capable of attaining salvation. In Rom 11, however, Paul steps back from the brink regarding the fate of Israel. Already in the opening verses of this chapter, Paul retreats the first small step, affirming that God has rejected only unbelieving Israel (Rom 11:1–10), that he has indeed preserved those who are truly his people by selecting for salvation a faithful remnant.

Nor is Paul content to let the matter rest solely with the salvation of the small number of Israelites who have already accepted the gospel. Rather, in vv. 11–24 Paul calls forth the metaphor of Israel as an olive tree. Despite the breaking off of some of the tree's original branches and the engrafting of branches of wild stock, God intends the roots and trunk of Israel's proud tradition to support a healthy mixture of both wild and cultivated branches. Continuing to refine this powerful image, Paul appears to envision God as the patient gardener, who tirelessly cultivates his tree, pruning off any new branches that prove to be unfruitful and, at the same time, regrafting some previously discarded branches. Indeed, by the close of Rom 11, Paul appears to have completely reversed his earlier rhetoric regarding unbelieving Israel. For he now concludes that Israel's recalcitrance is only temporary, induced by God to facilitate the completion of the conversion of the Gentiles. Paul emphatically declares that all Israel will be saved (v. 26) and that the divine gifts (including Israel's status as God's chosen) once given cannot be rescinded, even by God (v. 29). Thus Paul's final word is that God's infinite mercy ultimately triumphs, even over his sovereign and arbitrary freedom.

---

[12] Isa 65:2 (LXX).

[13] Even though, at this point, it is only proleptically.

[14] I agree with Stowers (*Rereading of Romans*, 312) that Paul understands the phenomenon of massive Gentile conversion as divinely instigated, at least in part, to provoke Israel's jealousy. However, if the reference to Deut 32:21b is to be taken seriously, this jealousy is intended (at this point in Paul's reflections) as punishment for a faithless people.

Luke's Reconsideration of Romans 9-11

Even though Paul himself rethinks the harsh judgments he seems inclined to consider in Rom 10, this segment of Paul's reflections on Jewish unbelief, especially Rom 10:16–21, appears to have provided much fuel for at least one important follower of Paul. As a Gentile Christian of a later generation, Luke no longer feels Paul's ambivalence regarding the guilt of unbelieving Israel.

As Knox reiterated, there clearly is a lack of any distinctive verbal agreement between the genuine letters of Paul and Luke's narrative.[15] Nevertheless, at least with respect to Rom 10:16–21, there are several significant literary and theological motifs that this passage shares with Luke–Acts—and only with Luke–Acts. For example, in Rom 10:21 Paul ends his harsh reflections on Jewish unbelief by quoting the judgmental words of Deutero-Isaiah, which charge Israel with being a contentious (ἀντιλέγοντα) people.

The verb ἀντιλέγω is surprisingly rare in New Testament writings, and it is used to describe Israel only in this passage in Rom 10:21 and in Luke–Acts.[16] The first usage of this verb in Luke's narrative occurs in the context of Simeon's programmatic prophecies (Luke 2:28–35). Although the first of these oracles offers the hope of a universal salvation, the second oracle undercuts that hope with respect to Israel by introducing the specter of division. And the proof that this destructive division is part of God's plan is highlighted in the final segment of the second prophecy (v. 34d): Jesus will be a sign that will provoke *contention* or *opposition*. Then again, toward the close of the Gospel half of Luke–Acts, the Sadducees are identified with the nucleus of Jewish religious leaders opposing Jesus when they are described by Luke as the ones who *dispute* the resurrection (Luke 20:27).

More significantly for the concerns of this essay, the remaining three references to the verb ἀντιλέγω occur specifically within the context of the Pauline mission. The first of these references occurs in the reaction of the synagogue audience to Paul's Pisidian Antioch speech (Acts 13:26–47). Although the reaction of his audience is initially favorable, when the synagogue becomes overrun with enthusiastic Gentiles residing in the city, the synagogue members are described by Luke as filled with jealousy and as *disputing* or *opposing* what was preached by Paul (Acts 13:45).

The last two references to ἀντιλέγω occur in Acts 28, in the climactic scene in which the last reference to Israel also appears. First, in relating his arrest in Jerusalem to his audience in Rome (Acts 28:17–22), Paul remarks that, although the Romans had wanted to release him, the Jews *had opposed* him

---

[15] Knox, "Acts and the Pauline Letter Corpus," 282.

[16] The verb ἀντιλέγω does occur once in the Gospel of John, in which Jesus is accused by the crowds of *opposing* Caesar (John 19:12). It also appears twice in the Letter to Titus: in 1:9 with reference to those within the church who *dispute* or *oppose* sound doctrine, and again in 2:19 with reference to slaves who are commanded not to *dispute* or *oppose* their masters.

148   MARIANNE PALMER BONZ

(Acts 28:19). Moreover, with the final reference to ἀντιλέγω in Acts 28:22, Luke emphasizes that Jewish opposition extends to the entire Christian missionary effort: "for," say the Jews, "concerning this sect, we know that everywhere it is *opposed*."

From this brief survey it seems clear that Luke uses the verb ἀντιλέγω to depict an intransigent contentiousness on the part of unbelieving Israel, a contentiousness that was ordained by God, was evident in its hostile reception to Jesus, and was continued in its hostility to the early Christian mission, especially that of Paul. Furthermore, there is at least a good possibility that Luke received his inspiration for the development of this minor motif from his reading of Rom 10:16–21, in which Paul blames Israel's unbelief on the inherent disobedience and contentiousness of its people.

Indeed, even though Paul himself makes only occasional references to the opposition of unbelieving Jews to his missionary endeavors,[17] Luke makes Jewish opposition to Pauline preaching a dominant literary theme in his narrative of Paul's mission to the limits of the civilized world. This pattern of opposition (as does the first use of the verb ἀντιλέγω in the Pauline segment of Luke–Acts) begins with Paul's inaugural speech in Pisidian Antioch. Here the Jews become jealous that so many Gentiles from the town are flocking to Paul and Barnabas, jealousy and contentiousness being linked here (Acts 13:45) in the same way that they are linked in Paul's reflections in Rom 10:19–21. In Luke, however, this jealousy and contentiousness result in the persecution of the beleaguered apostles (Acts 13:50).[18]

Likewise in Iconium, Luke states that unbelieving Jews stirred up the Gentiles and poisoned their minds against Barnabas and Paul (Acts 14:2). And again in Lystra, where Paul and Barnabas were being favorably received by Gentiles, Luke writes that Jews, who had actually followed the apostles from their last two cities simply to keep harassing them, turned the crowds against Paul, stoning him and dragging him out of the city (Acts 14:19). And again in Thessalonica, jealous, unbelieving Jews form the nucleus of a mob, thereby forcing Paul to extend his missionary journey further west and ironically aiding in the fulfillment of the Spirit's directive that the gospel be proclaimed to the limits of the civilized world. Dixon Slingerland has documented Luke's use of this particular theme, which continues up to the very last scene in Acts.[19] Also well known is the ironic and paradoxical relationship in Luke's narrative between Jewish opposition and the consequent spread of the Christian proclamation.[20]

---

[17] As, for example, 2 Cor 11:24 suggests.
[18] I use the term "apostles" for Paul and Barnabas because this is the term that Luke uses (Acts 14:4, 14).
[19] Dixon Slingerland, "'The Jews' in the Pauline Portion of Acts," *JAAR* 54 (1988): 305–19.
[20] The most recent and lucid discussion of this paradoxical duality appears in Jerry Lynn Ray, *Narrative Irony in Luke–Acts: The Paradoxical Interaction of Prophetic Fulfillment and Jewish Rejection* (MBP 28; Lampeter, UK: Edwin Mellen, Ltd., 1996), 133, *passim*.

What is highly significant for the purposes of the present discussion, however, is that Luke has linked in dramatic fashion the theme of the opposition of unbelieving Israel with the themes of the mission to the limits of the civilized world and the embracing of the proclamation by ever-growing numbers of Gentiles. And although the divine charge to take the Christian proclamation to the ends of the earth may have been a common motif in early Christian writings of the late first century,[21] as was certainly the case regarding the conversion of Gentiles,[22] nowhere else in the New Testament, except for Rom 10:16–21, does one find the confluence of all three themes: (1) Jewish unbelief, jealousy, and contentiousness; (2) the spread of the proclamation throughout the civilized world; and (3) the divinely inspired acceptance of the gospel by large numbers of Gentiles.

In Rom 10, however, when read within the larger context of Rom 9–11, Paul's dismay and seemingly bitter disappointment at Israel's general reaction to the gospel—namely, that of jealousy, contentiousness, and disbelief—is tempered by his ultimately unwavering conviction that this state of affairs will eventually be reversed by God.[23] Whereas, in contrast to Paul's essentially irenic conclusion, Luke's reinterpretation of Jewish unbelief inspires no such hope in the mind of the attentive reader. Indeed, the condition of Jewish unbelief and contentiousness, which Paul regards as temporary, is reinterpreted by Luke as part of the divine plan from the beginning, a necessary reversal of fate that was heretofore hidden in Israel's scriptures and only fully revealed through Paul's ministry.

For Luke, as is also the case with the deutero-Pauline authors of Colossians and Ephesians, the mystery of the divine plan is extended to encompass the results of Paul's preaching: namely, that only a comparatively small number of Jews have embraced Christ as their Messiah, whereas in the Gentile world the gospel continues to win converts in ever greater numbers. Luke lays the groundwork for the unfolding of this mystery, which includes the eventual disinheritance of many Israelites, at the very beginning of his Gospel, by means of a series of ambiguous prophecies,[24] such as Simeon's oracles in Luke 2. As I noted previously, in these oracles the universality of salvation is at first affirmed and then undercut with respect to Israel alone.

Even within the Gospel narrative of Jesus' mission, in which traditional material abounds, Luke has found dramatic ways in which to advance his central theme. For example, Luke's version of Jesus' inaugural address (Luke 4:14–30), which is widely acknowledged to be programmatic, is unique in the

---

[21] See, for example, Matt 24:14.
[22] See, for example, Matt 28:19, Mark 13:10.
[23] Here I agree with Stowers, *Rereading of Romans*, 293.
[24] See François Bovon, "The Effect of Realism and Prophetic Ambiguity in the Works of Luke," in *New Testament Traditions and Apocryphal Narratives* (PTMS 36; trans. J. Haapiseva-Hunter; Allison Park, Pa.: Pickwick, 1995); and Charles H. Talbert, "Promises and Fulfillment in Lucan Theology," in *Luke–Acts: New Perspectives*, 91–103.

emphasis that it places on the precedent of Elisha's and Elijah's healings of outsiders and Gentiles. It is also unique in the way that Luke links this narrative allusion to the salvation of Gentiles with the rage that it arouses in Jesus' pious Jewish audience, who chase him to the edge of a nearby cliff. And although some interpreters have identified Luke's intention of creating a scene that foreshadows the passion,[25] it is equally true that the scene foreshadows the ultimate destruction of the unbelieving Jews, who, at the end of the scene, are left raging on the brink of a cliff as Jesus passes by unharmed (Luke 4:29–30).[26]

Gamaliel's warning (Acts 5:34–39) is another key Lukan speech signaling a pivotal turning point in the narrative with respect to the opposition of Israel; for, from this point on, the reader is made increasingly aware that Jewish opposition is God-driven. Indeed, the more the Jews oppose the gospel, the faster the mission spreads to new cities, and the more it gains both momentum and new converts. Furthermore, Luke actually has Paul articulate this ironic dynamic in his often-cited series of warnings that Jewish unbelief only facilitates the preaching of the gospel to the Gentiles.

Paul issues his first warning (Acts 13:46) after his preaching in the synagogue at Pisidian Antioch, when, as was noted earlier, Luke depicts the Jews as reacting with jealousy and contentiousness. Again, when Paul is preaching in the synagogue at Corinth, Jewish opposition and unbelief provoke a second warning from Paul (Acts 18:6). The reader should note, however, that these two warnings are delivered in either the present or future tense[27] and must therefore be considered provisional. Indeed, this element of contingency is reinforced by the narrative action, for even after these warnings Luke has Paul continue to preach to Jews, up to and including the final scene in Acts, which takes place in Rome.

Here, for the third and final time Paul issues what has now become a dismissal of unbelieving Israel. Significantly, this last and, I believe, definitive pronouncement on the consequences of Israel's unbelief is reinforced by a judgment oracle (Acts 28:26–27) taken from Isaiah,[28] which immediately precedes the pronouncement. These verses, which Luke probably took from an early Christian collection of scriptural sayings,[29] indict Israel for not seeing,

---

[25] Étienne Samain, "Le discours-programme de Jésus à la synagogue de Nazareth," *Foi et Vie* 70 (1971): 37; and Bovon, *L'Évangile 1–9*, 209–10.

[26] Bonz, *Past as Legacy*, 124.

[27] Acts 13:46: "... we are turning to the Gentiles" (στρεφόμεθα εἰς τὰ ἔθνη) and Acts 18:6: "... to the Gentiles I will go (εἰς τὰ ἔθνη πορεύομαι)."

[28] Isa 6:9–10 (LXX).

[29] It has often been suggested that Luke made use of such a collection. See Jacques Dupont, "Apologetic Use of the Old Testament," in *The Salvation of the Gentiles: Essays on the Acts of the Apostles* (New York: Paulist Press, 1979), 151–52. As for this particular quotation, its use in several other late first-century New Testament texts (e.g., Mark 4:12, John 12:39–40, and Matt 13:14–15) indicates its popularity in late first-century polemical writing.

not hearing, not understanding. And aside from the charge of spiritual blindness, a special Lukan motif,[30] these words of Isaiah in their Lukan context recall the themes of failure to hear and failure to understand that clearly characterize Paul's own reflections on Israel's unbelief in Rom 10:16–21. Therefore, the fact that Luke puts these particular words in Paul's mouth as he addresses the Jewish community of Rome may not be coincidental.

If, indeed, Paul's reflections on Jewish unbelief in Rom 10:16–21 did inspire Luke to rethink this problem from a considerably later and more wholly Gentile perspective, it is perhaps not surprising that he should place a sharpened version of Paul's original words in the apostle's mouth at the very close of Luke–Acts. Such a move not only recalls the genuine warnings and misgivings with which his hero struggled, it also serves as the effective climax to Luke's revision of Paul's reflections on the possible meaning of Jewish unbelief. For, whereas Paul's harsh words in Rom 10:16–21 are immediately followed by the more optimistic reflections of Rom 11, no such ameliorating counterpoint occurs in Luke–Acts.[31]

In Acts 28, Paul's harsh words of judgment taken from Isaiah 6 immediately precede a third and final warning to the Jews. Significantly, however, the use here of the past tense of the verb turns this last warning into a solemn pronouncement: "Let it be known to you then that this salvation of God *has been sent* (ἀπεστάλη) to the Gentiles; they will listen" (Acts 28:28). With this pronouncement, Luke's narrative essentially ends, making Paul's words of judgment against Jewish unbelief no longer an interim reflection but the final word—and not only Paul's final word, but God's final word as well.

---

[30] Although references to blindness are not nearly so numerous in Luke–Acts as they are in the Gospels of Mark and John, Simeon's prophecy that Jesus brings a light for revelation to the Gentiles (Luke 2:32) is programmatic for the entire work. As for the special significance of the sight/blindness motif in the call and mission of Paul, see Acts 9:8, 12, 18; 13:11; 22:11, 13; and 26:17, 23.

[31] *Contra* Brawley ("Paul in Acts," 133), Luke does not reverse the finality of his judgment against the Jews with the addition of verses 30–31. Here, Paul is depicted as having received favorably *all who came to him* (πάντας τοὺς εἰσπορευομένος πρὸς αὐτόν). After reading vv. 25–28, only the incurably naïve could believe that Luke intended the "all" of v. 30 to include unbelieving Jews.

PART THREE

EARLY CHRISTIAN VOICES
IN ANCIENT MOVEMENTS

CHAPTER ELEVEN

THE SCRIPTURES AND THE NEW PROPHECY: MONTANISM AS EXEGETICAL CRISIS

CHRISTINE M. THOMAS

Montanism is an unusual Christian heresy.[1] In all the writings of the heresiologists, no serious accusation of doctrinal heterodoxy managed to attach itself
to it. Hippolytus of Rome avers that the "Cataphrygians"[2] conceive of the
creator correctly, and that they receive the teachings of the gospels about
Christ (*Haer.* 8.19). In the fourth century, Epiphanius testifies that this is still
the case: the Montanists believe in the trinity and the resurrection of the dead
in the same way as the "holy catholic church," and accept both the Old and
New Testaments (*Pan.* 48.1).

Why did the rest of the church then battle so strenuously against Montanism?
Among the accusations are many causes of offense: the prominence of women
among their leaders, their excessive fasting, stringent regulation of marriage,
and eagerness for martyrdom. These are all essentially ethical issues. Moreover,
most of these criticisms entered the debate only later, as secondary issues. In
the earliest sources, the three second-century Asian sources preserved in Eusebius, and the Asian source in Epiphanius,[3] the main objection to Montanism—
or the "New Prophecy," as its adherents called it[4]—was precisely that it was
prophecy. Correspondingly, the standard characterization in modern scholarly
works is that Montanism was the last gasp of charismatic first-century Christianity.[5]

---

[1] This article is based on a lecture given at the Harvard Divinity School on 17
December 1996, at which the honorand was present. I thank him for his kind advice
and guidance, on this occasion and so many others.

[2] The typical name for the Montanists in the early anti-Montanist sources is
"Cataphrygians," or "those who have been named after the Phrygians" (οἵ τε κατὰ
Φρύγας ἐπικεκλημένοι), cf. Constantine's edict against sectarians in 324 C.E. (Eusebius,
Vit. Const. 3.64); Montanism first appeared in Phrygian towns such as Pepouza and
Tymion. "Montanist," i.e., a follower of the prophet Montanus, does not appear until
the mid-fourth century, in Cyril of Jerusalem (*Catech.* 16.8).

[3] Three sources in Eusebius: the "Anonymous," ca. 192–193 C.E. (*Hist. eccl.* 5.16–17);
Apollonius, ca. 210–212 C.E. (5.18); and Serapion, ca. 190–211 C.E. (5.19). The other
early source is Epiphanius, *Pan.* 48.1–13. On dating see Christine Trevett, *Montanism:
Gender, Authority, and the New Prophecy* (Cambridge: Cambridge University Press, 1996),
30–32, 47–49.

[4] Echoes of their self-designation appear in their opponents' works: "the so-called
New Prophecy" (Serapion, in Eusebius, *Hist. eccl.* 5.19.2; see also the Anonymous at
Hist. eccl. 5.16.4).

[5] See W. H. C. Frend, who characterizes the movement as the "continuance of a
non-institutional Christianity overlaid by the growth of episcopal church government,"

This leaves, however, a paradox. If the offense of the New Prophecy is the message of its prophets, then how is it that the heresiologists, one and all, cannot attribute to the New Prophecy any serious doctrinal innovation? Can there be prophecy without content?

I would argue that the contribution of the New Prophets was not new revelation as much as the conscious application of their prophecies as a hermeneutical key to passages in the Hebrew Scriptures and those early Christian writings that were already accepted as authoritative by both themselves and the orthodox. The conflict over the New Prophecy was thus a battle over proper exegesis. As such, the Montanist controversy marks not the end of the past, the past of primitive Christianity, but the beginning of the future, the future of Biblical interpretation.

The evaluation of Montanist prophecy differed according to geography and time.[6] Early sources from the western empire opposed the innovation inherent in Montanist prophecy, arguing that prophecy ceased with the apostles. This objection appears in nearly every source outside of Asia Minor after the middle of the third century.[7] The earliest sources, however, those located in late-second-century Asia Minor, nearest to the birthplace of the New Prophecy, do not question the existence of prophecy. The crux of the conflict was not whether prophecy should continue in the church into the present age, but whether the New Prophets were true or false prophets. The early Asian sources attributed to the New Prophets one of two stock characteristics of false prophets: they thought the Montanists were possessed by the devil (Eusebius, *Hist. eccl.* 5.16.9).[8]

An additional issue was whether true prophets ever prophesied "in ecstasy" (ἐν ἐκστάσει).[9] The earliest work against the New Prophecy, an unpreserved tractate by Miltiades, argued that a prophet should not.[10] The Anonymous

and as "a religion of prophecy and protest" against ecclesiastical authority ("Montanism: Research and Problems," *Rivista di storia e letteratura religiosa* 20.3 [1984]: 521–37, esp. 535). See also Kurt Aland ("Bemerkungen zum Montanismus und zur frühchristlichen Eschatologie," *Kirchengeschichtliche Entwürfe* [Gütersloh: Gütersloher Verlagshaus, 1960], 142–43): a hundred years earlier, the Montanists would have been accepted, but in the second century, "bedeutet er einen Versuch der Restauration, der auf keine Anerkennung rechnen konnte."

[6] See Ronald E. Heine, "The Role of the Gospel of John in the Montanist Controversy," *SecCent* 6 (1987): 1–19, and idem, "The Gospel of John and the Montanist Debate at Rome," *StPatr* 21 (1989): 95–100. Gregory Nazianzus already differentiates between a "new" and an "old" Montanism (*Or. Bas.* 22.12).

[7] Epiphanius is the exception, who preserves a long debate on ecstatic prophesy from an early Asian source; see above.

[8] Heine, "Role," 4; citing David Aune, *Prophecy in Early Christianity and the Ancient Mediterranean World* (Grand Rapids: Eerdmans, 1983), 222, 229. The second stock criticism is that a false prophet is a willful deceiver.

[9] See Trevett, *Montanism*, 87–89.

[10] Eusebius, *Hist. eccl.* 5.17.1. As Alistair Stewart-Sykes has pointed out ("The Original Condemnation of Asian Montanism," *JEH* 50 [1999]: 1–22, esp. 5), the definition of ecstasy is hard to determine, because it neither indicates the form of the prophecy or the means of inspiration. The Montanists seem to have practiced what Aune calls "possession trance" (*Prophecy*, 19–20).

criticized Montanus because he raved and babbled (*Hist. eccl.* 5.16.7). Something of the manner of prophecy can also be seen in one of the Montanist oracles attributed to Priscilla: "Purification produces harmony, and they see visions, and when they turn their faces downward they also hear salutary voices, as clear as they are secret" (Tertullian, *Exh. cast.* 10.5). Fasting and putting the head between one's knees are Elijah's visionary practices in 1 Kgs 18:42.

The Montanists claimed that Priscilla and Maximilla were heirs of a supramunicipal prophetic succession accepted by both sides of the debate in Asia Minor. It included Agabus, Judas, Silas, and the four daughters of Philip known from the Acts of the Apostles (11:28; 15:22; 15–18; 21:19); to these the Anonymous adds the otherwise unattested prophets Ammia of Philadelphia and Quadratus. He did not question this succession, but rather argued that Priscilla and Maximilla did not belong to it, since they had not transferred the prophetic gift to a successor.[11]

Outside Asia Minor, the later heresiologists reject prophecy and characterize it as an attempt to add to the holy scriptures. The Montanists were not, however, prolific authors of books. Hippolytus of Rome speaks of an infinite number of books by Priscilla, Maximilla, and Montanus (*Haer.* 8.19). Eusebius records Constantine's prescription that their books be burned (*Vit. Const.* 3.66). Yet the preserved testimonies indicate that these were not as numerous as Hippolytus would assume. In addition to the oracles of the New Prophecy, the literary sources attest the existence of some nine works by Montanists, excluding the Montanist works of Tertullian.

It is difficult to assess the criticism of the anti-Montanist writer Gaius who accuses them of composing καινὰς γραφάς (Eusebius, *Hist. eccl.* 6.20.3). The attested works are largely theological tractates, not "scriptures." The Anonymous excerpts a Montanist work that refutes the treatise of Miltiades against ecstatic prophecy (*Hist. eccl.* 5.17.1). Proclus wrote in favor of the New Prophecy at Rome at the beginning of the third century C.E.[12] The Asian source in Epiphanius seems to be an orthodox response to a Montanist work that defends the New Prophecy on the basis of the exegesis of the Hebrew Bible, the Gospels, and the letters of Paul. Although Themiso wrote a Catholic epistle in imitation of Paul (Eusebius, *Hist. eccl.* 5.18.5), one could make the same claim for Ignatius or Polycarp. Around 400 C.E., a Montanist sent Marcella, the friend of Jerome, a book of *testimonia* from the Gospel of John, desiring

---

[11] Eusebius, *Hist. eccl.* 5.17.3–4. See Aland, "Bemerkungen," 137–38, on the prophetic background of Asia Minor. Melito of Sardis, another Asian Christian, authored a prophetic work (λόγος προφητείας, Eusebius, *Hist. eccl.* 4.26.4); Stewart-Sykes suggests that this may be a collection of his own prophecies ("Condemnation," 8), since Melito had the reputation of being a prophet (Jerome, *Vir. ill.* 24).

[12] Eusebius, *Hist. eccl.* 2.25.5. Pacian of Barcelona (*Ep.* 1.2) cites numerous authorities (*auctoribus* can mean not only author but authority) on whom the Montanists rely including Proclus: Blastos, also mentioned in Eusebius, *Hist. eccl.* 5.15; Theodotus, Praxeas, Leukios. But it is not clear that these are written tractates, *pace* Nicola Denzey, "What Did the Montanists Read?," *HTR* 94 (2001): 427–48, esp. 427 n. 2.

to convert her to the New Prophecy (Jerome, *Epist.* 41.4). In contrast to these works of argumentation and exegesis, one could also mention a narrative work, the martyrdom of Perpetua and Felicitas, as potentially a Montanist product.[13] Thus with καινὰς γραφάς, it is likely that Gaius was criticizing the Montanists for making "new writings" rather than "new scriptures." In the second century, producing any new writings could be considered objectionable; the Anonymous expresses reservations about composing his own account lest he seem to write or command things in addition to "the word of the gospel of the new covenant" (*Hist. eccl.* 5.16.3).

Works that actually contained the Montanist prophecies, or Montanist literary works created on the analogy of the scriptures are few. The Montanists did not write gospels or acts of the apostles, nor letters in the name of Paul, in the manner of other Christian groups, whose products have been relegated to the Christian Apocrypha. The Anonymous knows of a work by Asterius Urbanus containing Montanist oracles, from which he cites (Eusebius, *Hist. eccl.* 5.16.17). The Muratorian fragment slates for rejection a book of psalms by Basilides the Asian, "leader of the Cataphrygians." Despite the circulation of the oracles attested in the citations by Tertullian and also by the Asian source in Epiphanius, only some twenty are known.[14] Of these, with the exception of six anonymous oracles, all are attributed to Priscilla, Maximilla, or Montanus, the original three prophets, which suggests that, true to the claims of their opponent,[15] the New Prophecy produced few—if any—authoritative prophets beyond the initial three. It seems that the New Prophets were neither prolific writers nor prolific prophets.[16]

Careful study of their opponents criticisms reveals that the accusation is not that the Montanists added texts to the canon, only that they *taught* things in addition to the Scriptures. With the exception of the oracles and the psalms of Basilides, the works they produced are largely the same sorts of texts that their opponents wrote against them, apologetic arguments. These if anything were more numerous than the works of the Montanists. The appearance of the New Prophecy unleashed a veritable paper war in the late-second and early-third centuries: Claudius Apollonaris, bishop of Hierapolis, wrote an anti-Montanist work. It was sent to Caricus and Pontius with the synodal letter of Serapion (Eusebius, *Hist. eccl.* 5.16.1). Abercius Marcellus was the recipient of

---

[13] Most recently Trevett, *Montanism*, 176–78, where one can find the older literature.

[14] Heine counts fourteen genuine and five spurious (*The Montanist Oracles and Testimonia* [Patristic Monograph Series 14; Macon, Ga.: Mercer University Press, 1989], 2–9); Aland numbers eighteen genuine and six spurious ("Bemerkungen," 143–48).

[15] The Anonymous in Eusebius, *Hist. eccl.* 5.17.4; see above.

[16] Contrast this with the various groups called Gnostic, even before the discovery of the Nag Hammadi Library. Von Harnack found within the patristic sources alone reference to fifty-five works claimed to be Gnostic, though indeed these works do not all emanate from a single identifiable group. On the study of Gnosticism in comparison with that of Montanism, see Denzey, "Montanists."

the three-volume work of the Anonymous.[17] Eusebius preserves a work of Apollonius (*Hist. eccl.* 5.18), who also wrote a lost tractate against prophecy in ecstasy.[18] Miltiades wrote on the same topic (*Hist. eccl.* 5.17.1). Gaius wrote against the Montanist Proclus in Rome (*Hist. eccl.* 2.25.5; 6.20.3). Clement of Alexandria addressed the issue in the lost work περὶ προφετείας (*Strom.* 4.13.93.1). Other possible early anti-Montanist writers include Rhodon, Soter, Dionysius of Corinth, and Melito of Sardis.[19] If one includes the writers of the later third centuries and beyond, the number is considerable.

Instead of imitating the Scriptures, the works of the New Prophets cited them heavily, as did their orthodox opponents. The opponents focused on the warnings in the Gospels about the false prophets. They must have used Matt 7:15, Jesus' warning to beware of false prophets who come in sheep's clothing. In one of the oracles, Maximilla alludes to it (Eusebius, *Hist. eccl.* 5.16.17): "I am pursued like a wolf among the sheep. I am not a wolf. I am word, and spirit, and power." The Montanists, for their part, called their orthodox opponents the slayers of the prophets, alluding to Matt 23:34 (*Hist. eccl.* 5.16.12).

The Asian source in Epiphanius is rife with prooftexts used by both sides. It refutes, point by point, the Montanist exegesis of Biblical passages. In support of their practices, the New Prophets cite any visionary or prophetic experience which comes to hand in the Scriptures: Peter, who saw the vision of the clean and unclean animals (Acts 10:10–12); and Paul, who ascended to heaven (2 Cor 12:2–4).[20] The example of Adam in the creation account (Gen 2:21) is particularly compelling, because the Septuagint text reads that God "threw ecstasy upon him" (ἔκστασιν ἐπέβαλεν). Adam is understood as a prophet here, because he said upon awakening and seeing the woman, "This is bone of my bone, flesh of my flesh," which was understood as a prophecy referring to Gen 2:24. Similarly, the *Dialexis* of the Montanist and Orthodox, an anonymous work usually dated to 384 C.E., is a concatenation of prooftexts used in different ways by both sides. The Montanist attempts to use the letters of Paul to demonstrate that prophecy is to continue, and the Orthodox the reverse. Such a process of argumentation is inconceivable without the acceptance by both Montanist and Orthodox of the normativity of the same sacred writings.

In addition to Paul, the Montanists seem to have depended on the Fourth Gospel and the Revelation of John.[21] Ronald Heine has attempted to demonstrate

---

[17] *Hist. eccl.* 5.16.3. W. M. Ramsay claims to have found his epitaph; see William Tabbernee, *Montanist Inscriptions and Testimonia* (Patristic Monograph Series 16; Macon, Ga.: Mercer, 1997), 53 n. 13 for discussion of this identification.

[18] Tertullian refutes Apollonius in a seventh book that he added to the six books of the lost work *de ecstasi* (Jerome, *Vir. ill.* 40, 53).

[19] For references, see Aland, "Bemerkungen," 106 n. 10.

[20] Other passages cited include Num 12:7; Isa 1:2; 6:1; and Ezek 4:8–12 cited above. See generally F. E. Vokes, "The Use of Scripture in the Montanist Controversy," *SE* V (= TU 103 [1968]): 317–20.

[21] Aland, "Bemerkungen," 127–32; Trevett, *Montanism*, 144.

that the Gospel of John was not used in early Montanist writings, but emerged as a point of argument only in the Western debate about the existence of prophecy after the apostles.[22] This can hold, however, only if one reinterprets the sources significantly. Irenaeus attests the centrality of both the Gospel of John and the Revelation to the New Prophets, and the attempts of the orthodox to undercut their arguments by discrediting the apostolicity of these books (*Haer.* 3.11.12). Irenaeus is an early source who had close ties to Asia Minor; although he also visited Rome, it is pressing the evidence to suggest that Rome is the main source of his information on the New Prophecy.[23] The same can be said for Tertullian, who employs the Fourth Gospel and Paraclete language extensively; though himself North African, he was clearly aware of developments in Asia Minor.[24] The Asian source in Epiphanius uses the Johannine Paraclete passages against the Montanists, but this is likely an echo of arguments used by the Montanists themselves. The opponent is attacking their claim to possess the Holy Spirit; his use of the Paraclete language shows that it was current as a designation of the Holy Spirit in Asia Minor, as indeed it was later in Montanist sources in North Africa and Rome.[25]

Among the writings of the Montanists, only the oracles became a focus of anti-Montanist rhetoric. They do not, however, introduce new doctrinal teachings. They are often examples of "charismatic exegesis," interpretive citations of the Christian sacred Scriptures that unlock their meaning with the help of the prophetic spirit.[26] Their content elevates the practice of prophecy itself and gives paraenesis on martyrdom and persecution, sin and righteousness, and the flesh.[27] What claims of authority did the oracles make? The two sides

---

[22] Heine, "Role" and "Gospel."

[23] Counting Irenaeus as a Roman source is the only way that Heine can claim that the earliest references to the Paraclete appear in the works of Tertullian, and that the term does not appear except in western and north African sources ("Role," 2–3; "Gospel," 95–96; see Trevett, *Montanism*, 140–41).

[24] As Trevett points out, Tertullian wrote a tractate refuting the work of the Asian Apollonius (Jerome, *Vir. ill.* 40), which was concerned with the quintessential Asian question of whether a prophet should prophesy in ecstasy (*Montanism*, 64). The similarities of Tertullian's exegetical positions to the Asian source in Epiphanius also speak for a close relationship between the two; see Pierre Labriolle, *Les sources de l'histoire du Montanisme* (Fribourg: Librairie de l'Université, 1913), lviii–lxiv; echoed in the later literature, Dennis Groh, "Utterance and Exegesis: Biblical Interpretation in the Montanist Crisis," in *The Living Text: Essays in Honor of Ernest W. Saunders* (ed. D. E. Groh and R. Jewett; Lanham, Md.: University Press of America, 1985), 82–83; Trevett, *Montanism*, 65, 72.

[25] For Heine, the very fact that the Paraclete passage is used against the Montanists is resounding proof that the Paraclete passages were *not* employed by Montanists in the early Asian debate (Heine, "Role," 9–10). This is disingenuous and overlooks the fragmentary nature of the source; see also Trevett, *Montanism*, 64.

[26] Groh, "Utterance," *passim*, esp. 90–95.

[27] Contra Denzey ("Montanists," 430), who avers that the oracles do not address issues such as martyrdom, marriage, fasting, and prophecy, and that these matters are "absent from the theological treatises either produced, or adopted, or circulated by Montanist communities." It is hard to see her point in the face of Tertullian's treatises *de fuga in persecutione, de monogamia, de exhortatione castitatis, de ieiunio,* and *de ecstasi* (the latter a lost tractate).

of the debate evaluate them differently. Hippolytus of Rome accused the Montanists of adding the oracles of Priscilla, Maximilla, and Montanus to the Law, Prophets, and Gospels (*Haer.* 8.19). This accusation initially seems to find implicit support in the writings of the Montanists. Tertullian typically cites the oracles alongside the Hebrew Bible and the Christian sacred writings. In his treatment of second marriage, he cites first the Old Testament injunctions to separateness and holiness before God; he then cites Paul on the preference of spiritual people for the things of the spirit. Last is a prophecy of Priscilla that promises visions from the spirit to the pure. Each of them is introduced by a citation formula. The Hebrew Bible is called *prophetica vox veteris testamenti*, the Pauline citation is referred to as *apostolus*, and the oracle as *sancta prophetis Prisca* (*Exh. cast.* 10). The chronological progression suggests a conception of progressive revelation. Significantly, only the Hebrew Bible is referred to as an abstract entity. The later two citations are attributed to their human authors.

Tertullian, however, views the New Prophecy not as a source of new doctrine, but primarily of new ethical teachings—ones more in line with the truth than previous Christian custom. The progressive revelation concerns practice, not the doctrines of salvation. As he writes:[28]

> Righteousness . . . was first in a crude state, fearing God by nature; hence it progressed through the law and the prophets to a state of infancy; from there through the gospel it knew the vigor of youth; now, through the Paraclete it is brought to maturity. . . . [The Paraclete] alone will be the teacher from Christ. . . . For he does not speak from himself, but speaks what he is commanded by Christ. . . . Those who have received him have preferred truth to custom.

According to Tertullian, it is the very role of the Paraclete to bring the church to maturity and to reveal the scriptures: "What then is the Paraclete's assistance if not this: to direct discipline, to reveal the Scriptures, to reform the understanding, to advance the understanding to better things?"[29] The Paraclete's work through the oracles of the New Prophecy is to interpret the Scriptures. They are "primitive instruments" that have been illumined by the outpouring of the Holy Spirit:[30]

---

[28] *Virg.* 1.10–11 (CSEL 76.81): *sic et iustitia . . . primo fuit in rudimentis, natura deum metuens, dehinc per legem et prophetas promovit in infantiam, dehinc per evangelium efferbuit in iuventutem, nunc per paraclitum componitur in maturitatem. hic erit solus a Christo magister. . . . non enim ab se loquitur, sed quae mandantur a Christo. . . . hunc qui receperunt, veritatem consuetudini anteponunt.* English translation from Heine (*Montanist Oracles*, 63–65), except that I have translated *a Christo* as "from Christ" rather than "after Christ."

[29] *Virg.* 1.8 (CSEL 76.80): *quae est ergo paracliti administratio, nisi haec, quod disciplina dirigitur, quod scripturae revelantur, quod intellectus reformatur, quod ad meliora proficitur?* English translation from Heine (*Montanist Oracles*, 63).

[30] *Res.* 63 (CSEL 47.124–125): *at enim deus omnipotens . . . effundens in novissimis diebus de suo spiritu in omnem carnem . . . et pristina instrumenta manifestis verborum et sensuum luminibus ab omni ambiguitatis obscuritate purgavit. nam quia haereses . . . sine aliquibus occasionibus scripturarum audere non poterant. . . . iam omnes retro ambiguitates et quas volunt parabolas aperta atque*

Almighty God . . . "by pouring out of his Spirit in the last days on all flesh" . . . has purged the primitive instruments from all their obscurity of ambiguity by the clear illuminations of their words and meanings. . . . The heresies . . . could not be bold without some occasions from the Scriptures. . . . But . . . he has now dispersed all the former ambiguities, even the parables which they like, with the plain and clear proclamation of the complete mystery through the New Prophecy, which is overflowing from the Paraclete.

For Tertullian, the oracles of the New Prophecy do not function as new scriptures, but as a hermeneutical key eradicating the difficulties in the Scriptures that may provide a basis for heresy. Tertullian and the New Prophecy already lived in a world in which heterodox and orthodox argued their positions on the basis of the same sacred writings. The arbitrariness of meaning that made it possible for the Scriptures to support both sides was an early recognition of serious exegetical quandaries in the Christian tradition. For Tertullian, the Paraclete through its oracles explained the meaning of the text and made it "heresy-proof." As Dennis Groh writes, for Tertullian, "Prophetic ecstasy insured a revelation uncorrupted by the frailties of either human transmission or exegetical dilemma."[31]

It has become a truism—which I accept—that the New Prophecy in Tertullian's North Africa was not necessarily representative of Montanism elsewhere. The other tractates of the Montanists, however, use the oracles in precisely the same way, as sources cited after and supplementally to the works of scripture accepted by both themselves and their opponents. Some of Tertullian's exegetical positions are so close to those reflected in the Asian Montanist work criticized in Epiphanius's source that it is likely that both Tertullian and the Montanist work had access to the same collection of oracles linked with scriptural prooftexts.[32] The anti-Montanist source preserved in Epiphanius does a "counter-exegesis" that is the mirror image of the Montanist hermeneutical pairing of oracles and scriptural prooftexts. He cites seven oracles and refutes them one by one on the basis of the scriptures. It is important to recognize that scriptural prooftexting was not the only way to make a theological argument in the second century;[33] both Tertullian and the source preserved in Epiphanius are among the earliest examples of the prooftexting of the Gospels and Epistles on both sides of the heterodox-orthodox debate.

The unwavering appeal to normative Christian scriptures in the arguments of the New Prophecy may have been its most serious problem, and may

---

perspicua totius sacramenti praedicatione discussit per novam prophetiam de paraclito inundatam. Translation from Heine, *Montanist Oracles,* 75.

[31] Groh, "Utterance," 90.

[32] Labriolle, *Sources,* lviii–lxiv; see also Douglas Powell, who argues that Montanism reached Africa from Phrygia, not Rome ("Tertullianists and Cataphrygians," *VC* 29 [1975]: 33–54).

[33] The Valentinians were careful exegetes, but often used philosophical argumentation rather than prooftexting to make their doctrinal points, as one can see, e.g., in the *Epistle to Flora.*

explain the surprising success and centuries-long tenacity of this so-called heresy. If the Montanists had genuinely appealed to alien revelations, it would have been much easier to ostracize them. On the contrary, their use of normative Christian writings occurred early, and they continued tenaciously to defend their views on that same basis for centuries, as did the acquaintance of Marcella who gave her a book of *testimonia* for Montanism from the Gospel of John. One of the attacks of the orthodox against them was precisely to reject both them and the early Christian writings they favored. The Revelation of John and the Fourth Gospel came under suspicion. Gaius, the Roman anti-Montanist writer, attributed them to the heretic Cerinthus (Hippolytus, *In evangelium Iœnnis apud Dionysius bar Salibi, Comm. Apoc.* 1), which should be viewed as an attempt to cut these texts out from under the feet of the Montanists as a basis of support. Irenaeus also mentions opponents of these works, whom he accuses of taking the prophetic gift from the church and making nothing of the promised spirit.[34]

Given the high scripturality of the Montanist debate, and the exegetical fashion in which the Montanists themselves used the oracles of the New Prophecy, it would seem that the conflict was essentially hermeneutical. What one side viewed as a valid hermeneutical procedure, a sort of "charismatic exegesis" as Dennis Groh has called it, the other side branded as "adding" to the scriptures. But all interpretation is "adding" to the text in some way. Issues of interpretation were just beginning to surface at this time. Papias of Hierapolis still could claim, around 130 C.E., to have listened to the students of the initial twelve disciples (Eusebius, *Hist. eccl.* 3.39.3–4). No one in the 160s, at the time of the Montanist crisis, could say the same. The voice of apostolic oral tradition was falling silent. The middle of the second century sees increasing attempts to construe apostolic tradition around written texts. The shift from oral to written authority raised the issue of the interpretation of written texts. Which authority was to decide hermeneutical issues? The New Prophets championed the tradition of prophecy; their opponents set out in a flurry of activity to convene councils of bishops to make rulings.[35] The Anonymous believed in prophecy, but complained that the New Prophets prophesied contrary to tradition. For him, the definitive word on the prophecies was not given by prophets, but by a political body: the councils in Asia examined the prophecies and rejected them (*Hist. eccl.* 5.16.10, 12). At issue was whether authority was vested in an apostolic succession of church office, or in prophetic succession.[36]

---

[34] *Haer.* 3.11.12. See Aland, "Bemerkungen," 139–41. This same position is ascribed to a group known as the Alogoi in Epiphanius (*Pan.* 51.3.34).

[35] As Frend notes, these anti-Montanist councils constitute the first evidence of concerted action on the part of church leaders since the Apostolic Council in Jerusalem during Peter's lifetime ("Montanism," 524).

[36] Trevett characterizes the debate over the New Prophecy and its teachings as being primarily about authority, with prophecy being a challenge to office-based apostolic authority (*Montanism*, 136; 146–50).

One of the most widely cited oracles of Montanus is also one of the most misunderstood in patristic sources. Its fate illustrates how the shift from prophetic exegesis of the scriptures, to a written text elucidated by councils of bishops, also signaled a change in the mode of communication. The sources preserve four versions of Montanus's oracle, "I am the father, and the son, and the Paraclete."[37] This led to one of the few doctrinal criticisms of Montanus in later sources, that he claimed to be the Paraclete; or the Father, Son, and Holy Spirit.[38] Some consider these oracles to be spurious.[39] They are, however, closely related to two oracles of Montanus that most consider to be genuine, "I am the Lord God, the Almighty dwelling in a man," and "Neither angel nor envoy, but I the Lord God the Father have come."[40]

Prophecy is an inherently oral form of communication, immediate, and bound to an audience. From a performative perspective Montanus was making no greater a claim than any prophet makes: to speak in the voice of God himself. It was an introductory formula, to signal those special moments in which he was God speaking.[41] That the statement or its related forms appears six times among the scanty number of preserved oracles shows its performative aspect: it was a statement often repeated. The multiforms are evidence of multiple performances of the same statement. The orthodox misunderstood the performative aspect of Montanus's utterance and took it to be a literal, propositional, and ontological statement, that Montanus was claiming to be God. His language was understood not as prophetic utterance bound to a specific moment in time, but as a general statement that could be ratified or rejected by a church council.

In conclusion, it was not the prophecy of the Montanists, but their exegesis that may have been the issue that precipitated a crisis. The difference was

[37] This statement appears in the *Dialexis* (Labriolle, *Sources*, 97) and Didymus the Blind (*Trin.* 3.41.1). The related statement, "I am the Father, the Son, and the Holy Spirit" appears twice in the *Dialexis* (Labriolle, *Sources*, 101, 103). Celsus also attests that it was common for Christian prophets to say, "I am God," or "a son of God," or "a divine spirit and I have come . . ." (Origen, *Cels.* 7.9).

[38] See Trevett, *Montanism*, 216–19.

[39] So Heine, *Montanist Oracles*, 6–9. He argues first that they appear only in late sources, which seems to assume that Montanist oracles cannot be older than the sources in which they appear. Second, he views them as being products of the trinitarian debate. Yet for the Montanists, one should look no further than the theology of the Fourth Gospel: the unity of Jesus and the Paraclete is stressed in 16:13–14; see also John 15:26 on the origin of the Paraclete in the Father. Aland accepts these oracles as genuine ("Bemerkungen," 143–44).

[40] Both in Epiphanius, *Pan.* 48.11. This is closely related to the characterization of Eusebius. In the introduction that he writes to his anti-Montanist sources, the primary claim of the Montanist movement is that Montanus was the Paraclete, and Priscilla and Maximilla, prophetesses (*Hist. eccl.* 5.14).

[41] Argued by Pierre Labriolle, *La crise montaniste* (Paris: E. Leroux, 1913), 40; similarly Aland, "Bemerkungen," 111–12; and Groh, "Utterance," 90, who calls this "a scandalous immediacy." So also Denzey, "Montanists," 437; and 434–38 on the similarities of Gnostic and Montanist "I am" statements generally.

in the mode of communication; the so-called "innovations" of the New Prophecy were content-free. It was the place of the Scriptures in a hermeneutical universe involving prophetic elucidation that was critical. All texts have "gaps," points requiring interpretation; at issue was the manner in which the New Prophets closed these gaps and made the bridge from the past of the text to the present of interpretation.

The New Prophecy thus takes its position in history, not as the tombstone of the prophetic spirit, but as the first in a series of conflicts over proper exegesis of the Christian scriptures. Although the terms of debate over the New Prophecy may seem strange and out of date, the Montanists show perspicuity in realizing that texts need a living interpretative tradition. The claim of the great church to be interpreting the text by apostolic tradition vested in office is rather less sophisticated than the procedures of the New Prophets. The Montanists stand out in Christian history for their centuries-long protest that an appeal to tradition alone does not solve the conundrums of textual interpretation.

CHAPTER TWELVE

CRISE DU SAVOIR ET CONFLIT DES INTERPRÉTATIONS SELON JEAN 9:[1] UN EXEMPLE DU TRAVAIL DE L'ÉCOLE JOHANNIQUE

JEAN ZUMSTEIN

1. *Introduction*

L'école johannique s'est non seulement attachée à mettre en récit les traditions sur Jésus dont elle était dépositaire, mais elle a encore développé une réflexion approfondie sur le problème du savoir. Elle a notamment concentré son attention sur la crise de la connaissance suscitée par la venue de celui dans lequel elle reconnaissait le Révélateur. L'épisode de Jean 9 est un exemple privilégié du travail théologique entrepris par cette école.[2] En s'appuyant sur un récit de guérison connu de la tradition, l'auteur implicite—et c'est sa prestation—expose le conflit des interprétations que peut déclencher un tel acte.

La mise en récit est particulièrement significative de ce fait. Après que le Christ johannique, entouré de ses disciples, a rendu la vue à un aveugle de

---

[1] Cet article est dédié à François Bovon en signe de reconnaissance à la fois pour sa riche production scientifique, sa capacité à réunir et à animer des équipes de recherche et, last but non least, pour sa fidèle amitié.

[2] Il est impossible dans les limites assignées à cet article de discuter de façon détaillée la littérature secondaire. Outre les commentaires classiques sur l'évangile selon Jean (Barrett, Becker, Brown, Bultmann, Schnackenburg, mais aussi Blank, Léon-Dufour. Moloney, Schnelle), les contributions suivantes ont retenu notre attention: Günther Bornkamm, "Die Heilung des Blindgeborenen," in idem, *Geschichte und Glaube II* (vol. 1 de *Gesammelte Aufsätze*; BEvT 53; München: Kaiser, 1971), 65–72; Michel Gourgues, *Pour que vous croyiez: Pistes d'exploration de l'Évangile de Jean* (Initiations; Paris: Cerf, 1982), 202–24; Michael Labahn, *Jesus als Lebensspender: Untersuchungen zu einer Geschichte der johanneischen Tradition anhand ihrer Wundergeschichten* (BZNW 98; Berlin/New York: de Gruyter, 1999), 305–77; Dorothy A. Lee, *The Symbolic Narratives of the Fourth Gospel: The Interplay of Form and Meaning* (JSNTSup 95; Sheffield: Sheffield Academic Press, 1994), 161–87; J. Louis Martyn, *History and Theology in the Fourth Gospel* (2e éd., rev. et agr.; Nashville: Abingdon, 1979); Rainer Metzner, *Das Verständnis der Sünde im Johannesevangelium* (WUNT 122; Tübingen: Mohr/Siebeck, 2000), 62–114; Gail R. O'Day, *The Word Disclosed: John's Story and Narrative Preaching* (St. Louis: CBP Press, 1987), 53–75; John Painter, *The Quest for the Messiah: The History, Literature and Theology of the Johannine Community* (Edinburgh: T&T Clark, 1991), 261–86; D. Moody Smith, *John* (2e éd.; Proclamation Commentaries; Philadelphia: Fortress, 1986), 44–51; Christian Welck, *Erzählte Zeichen: Die Wundergeschichten des Johannesevangeliums literarisch untersucht; mit einem Ausblick auf Joh 2* (WUNT² 69; Tübingen: Mohr/Siebeck, 1994), 175–202.

naissance, divers groupes de personnages occupent successivement le devant de la scène pour procéder à une évaluation de son geste. Ces différents regards portés sur le miracle entrent en conflit les uns avec les autres—et le conflit ainsi déclenché en l'absence du Christ est indépassable jusqu'à son retour en fin de récit, dans la position du juge eschatologique. A partir du verset 8, toute l'action se déroule au niveau cognitif; elle porte sur l'acquisition d'un savoir controversé à propos du miracle advenu et de la personne du thaumaturge.

L'analyse qui suit est consacrée à la découverte de ce conflit des interprétations, à cette crise de la connaissance[3] telle qu'elle est mise en récit en Jean 9. Elle est menée selon la méthode de l'analyse narrative.

2. *La problématique, le genre et la structure du récit*

Pour opérer une lecture fondée de Jean 9, il convient d'être attentif à trois points d'importance.

2.1   *L'intrigue* qui structure le récit johannique n'est pas de nature dramatique, mais thématique. L'auteur implicite ne met pas l'accent sur l'enchaînement des péripéties vécues par le héros de l'histoire—péripéties par lesquelles Jésus serait transformé et parviendrait au terme de sa quête. La question fondamentale qui sous-tend son récit est celle de *la foi*. Le programme narratif peut être formulé de la manière suivante: la mission de Jésus, le Logos incarné, est de révéler le Père. Le déroulement de la narration montre comment ce programme est accompli: l'identité de Jésus en tant que Fils pré-existant est contestée si bien que le coeur de l'intrigue johannique—ou, plus précisément, son thème—devient le conflit entre le croire et le non-croire.[4] Jean 9 s'inscrit dans cette problématique, il constitue un épisode dans cette dramaturgie de la foi.

De façon plus précise, l'épisode rapporté en Jean 9 expose *l'effet* de la révélation christologique.[5] Elle montre aussi bien le chemin qui conduit à la foi— le chemin qui permet de passer de l'obscurité à la lumière—que le chemin inverse—le chemin qui mène de la lumière à l'obscurité. La problématique est donc: comment la foi naît-elle? qu'est-ce qui lui permet ou l'empêche d'advenir?

---

[3] Le thème de la crise de la connaissance est un élément central de la théologie de la croix telle qu'elle est développé dans les lettres pauliniennes d'abord, puis dans l'évangile selon Marc ensuite (voir Ulrich Luz, "Theologia crucis als Mitte der Theologie im Neuen Testament," *EvT* 34 [1974]: 116–41; et Christophe Senft, *L'Évangile selon Marc* [Essais bibliques 19; Genève: Labor et Fides, 1991]). L'intérêt de l'évangile selon Jean est de lier la crise de la connaissance non pas en premier lieu à la croix, mais à l'incarnation.

[4] Sur ce point, voir l'analyse de R. Alan Culpepper, *Anatomy of the Fourth Gospel: A Study in Literary Design* (FF: New Testament; Philadelphia: Fortress, 1983), 79–98, et notre position dans Jean Zumstein, "L'Évangile johannique: Une stratégie du croire," dans idem, *Miettes exégétiques* (Publications de la Faculté de theologie de l'Universite de Neuchâtel [Suisse] 6 = MdB 25; Genève: Labor et Fides, 1991), 240.

[5] Jésus se présente de façon explicite comme lumière du monde au début du récit (Jean 9:5).

2.2 Le récit de Jean 9 met en oeuvre un *langage symbolique*. Or le propre d'un tel langage consiste dans l'articulation d'un sens second à un sens premier. Comme l'écrit Paul Ricoeur: "Il y a symbole lorsque le langage produit des signes de degré composé où le sens, non content de désigner quelque chose, désigne un autre sens qui ne saurait être atteint que dans et par sa visée."[6] Les symboles sont donc des expressions à double sens ou, si l'on préfère, des groupes de signes "dont la texture intentionnelle appelle une lecture d'un autre sens, dans le sens premier, littéral, immédiat."[7] Si le propre du symbole est de désigner un sens indirect dans et par un sens direct, quelle est alors la place du travail d'interprétation et comment doit-il être conduit? D'une part, même si certains termes utilisés dans le récit ont un sens métaphorique, il est insuffisant de limiter le travail d'interprétation au décryptage de quelques métaphores dispersées dans le texte. D'autre part, il est illicite de lire le récit comme une allégorie dont le sens premier ne serait qu'un habillage superficiel permettant d'accéder au sens second, seul important. Avec Ricoeur, il faut souligner, d'une part, que le sens second ne se lit que dans le sens premier, littéral, immédiat; il faut ajouter, d'autre part, que l'enquête ne concerne pas quelques concepts, mais l'ensemble du récit.[8]

2.3 *La structure* du chapitre 9 est claire.[9] Le récit se compose de trois parties principales, chacune d'entre elles comprenant à son tour plusieurs scènes.

La *première partie* tient dans les sept premiers versets (Jean 9:1–7) et se divise en deux scènes: a) les versets 1–5 retracent l'introduction et le dialogue entre Jésus et ses disciples, b) les versets 6–7 rapportent le miracle de guérison.

Cette première partie fait état de l'événement dont l'interprétation et les conséquences constituent la matière des parties deux et trois. Par ailleurs, les versets 3–5 introduisent les catégories théologiques qui ouvrent la voie à une interprétation symbolique du miracle; ils formulent l'horizon théologique sur le fond duquel l'ensemble du récit doit être lu.

La *deuxième partie* (Jean 9:8–34) se compose de quatre scènes: a) les versets 8–12 rapportent le dialogue des voisins et connaissances avec l'aveugle guéri; b) les versets 13–17 décrivent la première comparution de l'aveugle guéri devant les pharisiens; c) les versets 18–23 évoquent l'audition des parents de l'aveugle guéri; d) les versets 24–34 rendent compte de la seconde comparution de l'aveugle devant les pharisiens, comparution suivie de son exclusion.

Cette seconde partie déploie l'interprétation conflictuelle du miracle. Il est à noter que ce conflit des interprétations se déroule en l'absence de Jésus. Ce détail est d'importance: il s'agit probablement d'une allusion à l'époque post-pascale, marquée par le conflit entre les communautés johanniques et la

---

[6] Paul Ricoeur, *De l'interprétation: Essai sur Freud* (L'Ordre philosophique; Paris: Seuil, 1965), 25.

[7] Ibid., 21.

[8] Cet aspect est bien développé par Lee, *Symbolic Narratives*, 161–87.

[9] Voir les études détaillées chez Gourgues, *Pour que vous croyiez*, 203–9; Lee, *Symbolic Narratives*, 164–69; et Martyn, *History and Theology*, 30–36.

synagogue pharisienne.[10] Quoi qu'il en soit, cette deuxième partie prend la forme d'un procès. L'aveugle guéri est assimilé à un accusé qui est appelé et entendu par l'autorité judiciaire pour, en définitive, être condamné par elle. Fondamentalement, il y va du procès que le monde fait à la révélation.

La *troisième partie* (Jean 9:35–41) constitue la conclusion théologique du récit et tient dans deux scènes: la première scène (vv. 35–38) décrit la foi de l'aveugle guéri tandis que le seconde scène (vv. 39–41) dénonce l'aveuglement des pharisiens.

Cette conclusion théologique dévoile l'identité véritable de chaque personnage, de chaque groupe de personnages. *Jésus* est présenté comme le juge eschatologique qui ouvre l'accès à la foi et à la vie, mais qui, ce faisant, déclenche le jugement dernier. Le chemin que prend *l'aveugle* guéri est le chemin exemplaire de la foi, symboliquement figuré par le passage de l'obscurité à la lumière. En revanche, le chemin pris par les *Pharisiens* est le chemin inverse, celui de l'incrédulité, le passage de la lumière à l'obscurité.

3. *Parcours du récit*

Comment le récit construit-il l'interprétation du geste du Christ johannique?

3.1   *La guérison de l'aveugle de naissance (Jean 9:1–7)*

3.11   *Le point de départ de toute la séquence* est constitué par un récit de miracle, probablement fort ancien.[11] Jésus, de passage devant la porte du Temple (?), voit un aveugle de naissance et le guérit en recourant à la technique thaumaturgique d'alors. Dans ce récit du miracle, deux traits méritent mention. D'une part, le seul actant du récit est le Christ alors que l'aveugle semble être un simple figurant dont le seul rôle consiste à exécuter la volonté de Jésus. D'autre part, le fait que le miraculé soit un aveugle de naissance souligne la grandeur du miracle et en précise d'emblée l'enjeu symbolique: l'homme dont s'occupe Jésus, vit depuis toujours dans les ténèbres.

Comment cet acte de guérison qui va être au centre du conflit d'interprétation qui se déploie à travers le récit, doit-il être compris?

3.12   *L'entretien didactique* (Jean 9:2–5): *Les disciples* qui disparaîtront ensuite du récit sont les premiers à prendre position, avant même que le miracle n'ait eu lieu. Leur interprétation porte sur la cécité de l'aveugle (v. 2). Selon eux, cette infirmité doit être comprise comme l'expression de la justice rétributive de Dieu qui ne tolère pas le péché et le sanctionne en infligeant un châtiment terrible à ses auteurs ou à leurs proches.[12] Le Dieu des disciples assure

---

[10] Sur ce point, voir le travail fondateur de Martyn, ibid., en particulier 27–30.

[11] Voir l'état de la discussion chez Labahn, *Jesus als Lebensspender*, 317–41.

[12] Voir les parallèles juifs rassemblés par Hermann L. Strack et Paul Billerbeck dans Str-B 2:527–29, et l'analyse de Metzner dans *Verständnis der Sünde*, 74–76.

son autorité en pénalisant ses opposants. Il les enferme dans leur culpabilité qui les détruit. C'est la logique de la rétribution qui domine le jugement des disciples sur l'aveugle.

A cette première interprétation de la cécité de l'aveugle par les disciples s'oppose celle du Christ (vv. 3–5). Ce petit prologue herméneutique, fruit de la réflexion de l'école johannique, permet au lecteur de placer le miracle de guérison et le conflit qu'il suscite dans un cadre théologique et herméneutique adéquat. La position du Christ a la teneur suivante. Ce n'est pas la cécité de l'aveugle qui est de l'oeuvre de Dieu (τὰ ἔργα τοῦ θεοῦ), mais sa guérison. La misère humaine ne doit pas être comprise comme l'expression du châtiment de Dieu, mais comme le lieu de son intervention libératrice. Dans la personne du Christ, Dieu ne travaille pas à obscurcir et à enténébrer l'existence humaine, mais à la faire venir en pleine lumière et en pleine clarté (cf. v. 5). La note sotériologique est manifeste: là où règne la clarté advient le sens, la capacité d'orientation et de compréhension. Comme le souligne le ἡμᾶς ("nous") placé en tête du verset 4, les disciples sont non seulement les récipiendaires de l'action du Christ, ils sont également invités à la perpétuer.[13]

La dimension symbolique du récit est donnée d'emblée: c'est du péché et de l'oeuvre de Dieu telle qu'elle se révèle dans la personne du Christ, qu'il y va dans ce récit. Pourtant, le paradoxe de l'incarnation est maintenu: Jésus, la lumière du monde, vit dans la finitude. La mort imminente de l'envoyé du Père va mettre fin à la révélation (cf. v. 4).

Le lecteur est un privilégié. Il sait désormais ce que les personnages du récit ignorent. Il sait que le thaumaturge est l'envoyé de Dieu (v. 4, τοῦ πέμψαντός με)[14] et, à ce titre, la lumière du monde; il sait que l'oeuvre de Dieu consiste dans l'illumination de l'homme. Il sait que c'est dans ce cadre que doit être situé le miracle qui advient. Mais cela, les personnages du récit ne le savent pas. Comment vont-ils décrypter cet acte de guérison en l'absence du Christ?

3.2   *Les voisins et les proches (Jean 9:8–12)*

Les voisins et les proches du miraculé sont les premiers—en l'absence de Jésus—à débattre du miracle advenu. Dans le cadre de cette quête interprétative, trois questions sont posées: la question de la réalité du miracle (quoi?), la question de sa modalité (comment?), et la question de son auteur (qui?).[15] Pour répondre à ces trois questions, les voisins et les proches ne disposent que de l'expérience quotidienne et du système de valeur qui est en usage dans le

---

[13] Déjà Rudolf Bultmann, *Das Evangelium des Johannes* (19e éd.; KEK 2; Göttingen: Vandenhoeck & Ruprecht, 1968), 251 n. 9; ou Martyn, *History and Theology*, 28.

[14] La figure de l'envoyé est sans doute la catégorie centrale de la christologie johannique, cf. l'état de la discussion chez Jürgen Becker; *Das Evangelium nach Johannes* (2 vols.; Ökumenischer Taschenbuchkommentar zum Neuen Testament 4 = Gütersloher Taschenbücher Siebenstern 505–506; Gütersloh: Gerd Mohn; Würzburg: Echter Verlag, 1979–1981; 3e éd., 1991), 2:484–94 (la littérature).

[15] Point de vue bien mis en évidence par Gourgues, *Pour que vous croyiez*, 205–6.

monde. A ce titre, ils sont les représentants de "l'homme naturel." Or, le récit montre que l'homme naturel n'est pas en mesure d'interpréter ce qui advenu, à savoir l'irruption du divin dans la réalité. Comme l'illustre leur dispute (cf. v. 9), ils sont plongés dans la confusion et dans le désarroi. Leur capacité de compréhension est mise en échec. Leur système de conviction les empêche de s'ouvrir à la venue du divin. Ne pouvant s'accorder sur la réalité du miracle, ils sont bien incapables d'en saisir le caractère de signe. Ici surgit une thèse johannique qui mérite attention: l'irruption du divin, sous la forme d'un miracle, n'a aucun caractère d'immédiateté et d'univocité. Elle est perçue comme une perturbation et une énigme qui met en crise les évidences mondaines.

Le comportement de l'aveugle guéri mérite qu'on s'y arrête. Aussi bien le rapport qu'il fait de sa guérison (répondant ainsi à la question de la modalité, v. 11) que son aveu d'ignorance sur la question de l'auteur dénotent son attitude positive. L'honnêteté intellectuelle qui consiste dans une fidèle description des faits, alliée à une ignorance dépourvue de préjugés (cf. v. 7), con-point de départ de la foi.

3.3 *Première comparution devant les pharisiens*[16] *(Jean 9:13–17)*

La scène de la comparution devant les pharisiens est structurée de façon analogue à la scène précédente: ce sont toujours les trois questions sur la réalité du miracle, sur la question de sa modalité et sur son auteur qui sont en débat. La transition entre les deux scènes est provoquée par les voisins et les proches qui, constatant l'aporie dans laquelle ils se trouvent, décident de chercher une réponse à leur question auprès des autorités religieuses. La religion va-t-elle réussir là où le sens commun a échoué?

Les autorités religieuses se distinguent des voisins et des parents du fait que d'emblée elles reconnaissent la portée théologique de l'événement. La mention du sabbat (v. 14) signale l'irruption du religieux comme registre d'évaluation. Le phénomène de la guérison de l'aveugle doit être envisagé en relation avec l'agir de Dieu dans le monde. Non seulement les autorités religieuses placent la guérison dans son juste contexte, mais encore elles focalisent leur attention sur la question décisive, à savoir celle de la légitimité du guérisseur. Le rapport de l'aveugle les plonge cependant dans la plus profonde perplexité. Le dilemme dans lequel elles sont précipitées a la teneur suivante. Qu'est-ce qui est décisif dans la juste interprétation de la guérison de l'aveugle? La tradition établie avec ses normes reconnues, laquelle implique le respect du sabbat? Mesuré à ce système de références, Jésus ne révèle pas Dieu, mais s'oppose à sa volonté (v. 16a). Ou est-ce la guérison de l'aveugle qui est décisive parce

---

[16] Il va de soi que par "pharisiens" il faut entendre le personnage littéraire mis en scène par Jean et ne pas l'identifier d'emblée avec le mouvement des pharisiens au 1er siècle tel que la critique historique permet de le reconstituer (voir Culpepper, *Anatomy of the Fourth Gospel*, 130–31).

qu'elle actualiserait le pouvoir créateur de Dieu vivant? Dans ce cas de figure, Jésus serait l'envoyé de Dieu, nanti de son pouvoir (v. 16b).

De même que le geste révélateur et libérateur du Christ avait mis en crise le sens commun, il met en crise la tradition religieuse. La division (v. 16, σχίσμα) qui naît dans les rangs des pharisiens sanctionne l'échec du savoir théologique traditionnel. Elle montre que ces derniers ne sont pas prêts à renoncer à leur tradition séculaire pour s'ouvrir à la nouveauté du Dieu qui vient. La possession du savoir est devenu un obstacle à la rencontre du Dieu vivant.

En revanche, l'aveugle se signale à nouveau par son fidèle rapport des faits; il s'en tient à ce qui est advenu dans sa vie (v. 15). Néanmoins, la confrontation avec les pharisiens lui permet de progresser dans son interprétation de sa guérison. Sa comparution devant l'autorité établie lui fait percevoir la dimension religieuse de son aventure. Son honnêteté intellectuelle l'amène alors à franchir le pas auquel se refusent les pharisiens: celui qui actualise le pouvoir créateur de Dieu parmi les hommes est un prophète (v. 17b).

3.4   L'audition des parents (Jean 9:18–23)

L'audition des parents de l'aveugle guéri nous confronte à une dimension nouvelle du savoir, à savoir celle de sa perversion—et ceci sous deux formes incarnées successivement par l'autorité religieuse, puis par les parents.

La scène s'ouvre par un changement de terminologie dans la désignation des autorités juives. Les pharisiens se sont mués en "Juifs" (v. 18).[17] Dans le quatrième évangile, ce terme, dans la grande majorité de ses occurrences, désigne non pas une appartenance ethnique ou nationale, mais des personnes qui, confrontées au Christ, ont choisi le camp de l'incrédulité. Désormais, l'interprétation défendue par les pharisiens est une interprétation fermée et pervertie. Deux éléments du texte le montrent. D'une part, l'autorité religieuse refuse d'admettre la réalité de cette guérison (cf. vv. 18–19) du fait qu'elle ne peut l'intégrer dans son système de convictions. Ce déni de réalité disqualifie ses auteurs. D'autre part, pour rétablir son pouvoir ébranlé par la crise inhérente à la venue de la révélation, l'autorité fait acte de pouvoir. Elle instruit un procès destiné à condamner le savoir rebelle. Le verbe "convoquer" (φωνεῖν) appartient à la terminologie juridique et désigne l'ouverture d'une enquête.

L'autre face obscure du savoir est représentée par les parents. Bien que deux questions seulement leur aient ont été posées (celle de la réalité du miracle et celle de sa modalité), ils répondent à trois.[18] Ils confirment la réalité de la

---

[17] Sur le nouvel état de la discussion concernant le concept johannique des "Juifs" voir Reimund Bieringer et al., éds., *Anti-Judaism and the Fourth Gospel* (Assen: Royal van Gorcum, 2001).

[18] En déclarant: "Qui lui a ouvert les yeux, nous l'ignorons," ils répondent à la question de l'auteur qui n'a pas été posée; comparer les vv. 19 et 20–21.

guérison, mais refusent de se prononcer sur sa modalité et son auteur. Alors même qu'ils ont une parfaite connaissance des faits, ils refusent de témoigner (cf. v. 21). Le savoir est ici volontairement réduit au silence, car il pourrait menacer la sécurité de ceux qui l'attesteraient en public. La manifestation de la vérité s'avère ainsi être dangereuse et aboutit à une rupture des solidarités les plus étroites. Le règne de la double pensée a commencé et avec elle celui de l'hypocrisie sociale.

Le verset 22 fait allusion à l'exclusion des disciples de Jésus de la synagogue.[19] Cette indication anachronique (elle concerne la situation des églises johanniques et non celle des premiers disciples de Jésus) crée un effet de transparence.[20] A travers l'histoire racontée, les premiers lecteurs réels de l'évangile sont mis en mesure de comprendre la persécution et l'exclusion dont leur mémoire porte la trace douloureuse. Le récit leur permet de donner sens à leur expérience vécue et, ce faisant, de l'accepter et de la légitimer.

3.5 Deuxième comparution devant les pharisiens (Jean 9:24–34)

Le lecteur est invité à franchir un nouveau pas dans cette dernière scène de la partie centrale du récit. Ce qui est désormais au centre du conflit des interprétations, ce n'est plus la guérison de l'aveugle de naissance, mais la personne de Jésus. Le miracle est devenu signe aussi bien pour l'aveugle que pour les autorités religieuses, car, dorénavant, au-delà de lui-même, il renvoie à la personne de celui qui l'a accompli. La question décisive consiste dès lors à statuer sur la personne du thaumaturge, à savoir si Jésus est un pécheur (v. 24) ou un envoyé de Dieu (v. 33).

Ce dernier pas interprétatif revêt la forme d'une controverse christologique. Il ne s'agit pas d'une controverse d'école, mais d'une controverse qui a lieu dans le cadre d'un procès. Les pharisiens, figure du savoir théologique et détenteurs du pouvoir judiciaire, interviennent à titre d'adversaires de Jésus, ils soutiennent l'accusation. L'aveugle guéri, quant à lui, devient à la fois l'accusé et l'avocat de Jésus. Le procès en cours est cependant un procès factice. Le but des juges ne consiste pas à rechercher et à établir la vérité, mais à imposer leur propre savoir. L'accusé, parce qu'il refuse de faire acte de contrition,[21] se voit irrémédiablement condamné (v. 34b).

L'intérêt de la scène tient dans sa façon de trancher la question de l'iden-

---

[19] Il s'agit là d'une affirmation du monde du récit. La forme historique qu'a pu revêtir cette exclusion demeure controversée. Voir p. ex. Wolfgang Schrage, "ἀπο-συνάγωγος," *TWNT* 9:845–50, ou Klaus Wengst, *Bedrängte Gemeinde und verherrlichter Christus: Ein Versuch über das Johannesevangelium* (3ᵉ éd.; München: Kaiser, 1990), 75–104. Voir le résumé récent de la discussion chez Metzner, *Verständnis der Sünde*, 80–82.

[20] Cet effet de transparence a été mis en évidence par Martyn (*History and Theology*, 30), puis constamment repris dans la discussion.

[21] Le v. 24 a la forme classique d'une confession des péchés, voir Str-B 2:535, et Rudolf Schnackenburg, *Das Johannesevangelium* (4 vols.; HTKNT 4; Freiburg im Breisgau: Herder, 1971), 2:318.

tité de Jésus. Cette identité est établie et évaluée en recourant à un savoir de référence[22] commun à l'autorité religieuse et à l'aveugle voyant. Ce savoir qui s'appuie sur l'Écriture juive et, en particulier, sur l'autorité de Moïse, conduit les pharisiens à repousser Jésus. Leur savoir est en effet un savoir refermé sur lui-même, orienté vers le passé, légitimant une position de pouvoir, celle qui se manifeste en toute clarté dans le procès en cours. Ce même savoir traditionnel conduit, en revanche, l'aveugle guéri à prendre parti pour Jésus, parce que, dans son cas, son savoir est ouvert et opératoire. L'aveugle "voyant" fait mémoire d'une règle bien connue (v. 28) et l'applique à sa situation personnelle dans le plus total respect des faits. Par là-même, il lui devient possible de franchir un pas supplémentaire dans son approche de la personne de Jésus et de déclarer son origine divine (c.-à-d., παρὰ θεοῦ, v. 34).

La Torah de Moïse n'est ainsi pas un critère ultime. Utilisée pour stigmatiser le péché (v. 24: Jésus est déclaré pécheur; v. 34: l'aveugle guéri est stigmatisé comme pécheur), elle détourne l'homme de Jésus. En revanche, lue pour identifier la créativité divine et sa volonté de restauration de l'existence humaine, elle conduit à la découverte de l'envoyé de Dieu. La Bible juive est ainsi, elle aussi, emportée dans le conflit des interprétations. Elle peut aussi bien occulter le visage de Dieu qu'en indiquer la trace. La fin du procès culmine dans l'exclusion de l'aveugle de la synagogue (le v. 34c formule la sentence).[23] Alors même que, du point de vue de l'auteur implicite, l'aveugle a fidèlement rapporté les faits et correctement argumenté, son témoignage n'est pas reçu. Il est refusé, discrédité par le savoir officiel. Il n'a droit—et la vérité avec lui—à aucune reconnaissance sociale et religieuse.

3.6 La foi (Jean 9:35–38)

Les versets 35–38 ouvrent le troisième et dernier acte du récit. La première scène de cette ultime partie constitue le point culminant de l'histoire racontée. Elle met en scène la foi offerte et acceptée.

Dans les versets 35–38, l'itinéraire de foi de l'aveugle guéri atteint à la fois son but et son achèvement. En entrant en débat avec les autorités religieuses sur la signification du miracle advenu, le miraculé s'était engagé sur le chemin de la foi. C'est de son propre chef qu'il en avait parcouru les trois premières étapes. Le verset 12 s'achevait par un aveu d'ignorance; au verset 17, l'aveugle guéri discernait dans la personne du Christ un prophète, au verset 33 un homme venant de Dieu. Il n'avait cependant pas encore atteint la foi

---

[22] Le passage est dominé par le champ sémantique du savoir: noter bien le verbe οἶδα dans les vv. 24, 25, 29, 30, et 31.

[23] Le verbe ἐκβάλλω a un double sens: il signifie aussi bien "expulser de la salle de séance" au sens premier que "expulser de la synagogue" au sens figuré. Voir Walter Bauer, "ἐκβάλλω," *Griechisch-deutsches Wörterbuch zu den Schriften des Neuen Testaments und der frühchristlichen Literatur* (éd. Kurt Aland et Barbara Aland avec Viktor Reichmann; 6ᵉ éd., rev. compl.; Berlin/New York: de Gruyter, 1988), 478.

spécifiquement christologique. C'est précisément ce dernier pas qui constitue l'objet des versets 35–38.

A ce titre, cette scène mène à chef le processus d'interprétation du signe, mais pour ce faire, elle réintroduit la personne du Christ. Lui seul est, d'un point de vue johannique, l'herméneute qualifié de son oeuvre. Pour la première fois dans le récit, le miracle est compris de façon conséquente comme signe christologique. En effet, en posant la question "Crois-tu toi au Fils de l'homme?" (v. 35), le Christ indique sans ambiguïté que le miracle renvoie au-delà de lui-même pour désigner le Révélateur et son offre sotériologique. La portée symbolique du miracle est explicitée et présentée au lecteur comme possibilité existentielle. La guérison physique conduit à la découverte du Révélateur. Le voir véritable consiste dans la foi.

Comment cette foi véritable se constitue-t-elle? La relation qui s'établit entre le Christ et l'aveugle guéri permet de préciser cet aspect. *Jésus* est présenté comme l'actant principal: il trouve le miraculé (v. 35), il l'interpelle (v. 35), il se révèle à lui (v. 37). Par ses actes et ses paroles, il crée la condition de possibilité de la foi. La fin correspond au début. Dans les deux scènes (9:1–7 et 9:35–38), l'existence de l'aveugle exclu, puis guéri, est transformée par l'initiative du Christ.

Le miraculé, quant à lui, se tient en situation de réponse. D'un point de vue théologique, cela signifie que par ses propres moyens, il ne pouvait ni trouver le Christ, ni croire en lui. Élection et foi sont un don du Christ. Sa foi se concrétise dans une déclaration de foi (cf. le titre κύριος) et dans un geste (προσκυνεῖν comme signe d'adoration de Dieu).

3.7 *Le jugement (Jean 9:39–41)*

Les versets 39–41 constituent la deuxième scène du troisième acte et par là-même la dernière scène du récit. Si les versets 35–38 avaient illustré la découverte du Révélateur et l'accès à une foi achevée, les versets 39–41 décrivent le refus du Révélateur et le phénomène fatal de l'incrédulité.

Le verset 39 indique clairement que la révélation implique une crise de la connaissance. Il n'y pas de continuité simple, ni d'accès direct à la découverte de la présence de Dieu dans le monde. Seuls ceux qui se savent ou se découvrent aveugles peuvent être guéris; ceux qui croient voir ou savoir dans l'ordre du monde—fût-il religieux—sont condamnés à la cécité spirituelle. En ce sens, l'accès à la foi passe nécessairement par une crise de la connaissance.

Cette crise de la connaissance n'est pourtant pas un simple accident. Selon l'école johannique, elle a un enjeu eschatologique. Le Révélateur, qui prétend offrir la lumière au monde, n'est, en effet, personne d'autre que le juge eschatologique. Son jugement n'est pas associé à une apocalypse future et improbable, mais il advient dans le présent, dans la décision que chaque être humain prend face à l'agir du Christ dans le monde.[24] Il n'y a pas de révélation sans

---

[24] Bultmann: "Es ist die Paradoxie der Offenbarung, dass sie, um Gnade sein zu können, Ärgernis geben muss und so zum Gericht werden kann" (*Evangelium des Johannes*, 259).

scandale, il n'y a pas de scandale sans rupture. La séparation entre les aveugles clairvoyants et les voyants frappés de cécité est inévitable. Si le salut consiste dans le don de la lumière, plus précisément dans le don de la vie éternelle, le jugement se concrétise en ce que l'incroyant demeure définitivement dans les ténèbres (c'est-à-dire dans un monde séparé de Dieu).[25]

La question du péché qui avait été posée au début du récit (v. 2) est définitivement clarifiée dans cette dernière scène (inclusio!). Elle l'est à l'aide des concepts βλέπειν et τυφλός qui doivent être interprétés symboliquement. Ils connotent désormais de façon explicite la naissance de la foi, respectivement de l'incroyance.

Dans les versets 39–41, les aveugles sont ceux qui n'ont pas su interpréter les signes de Jésus, reconnaître son origine divine et qui, prisonniers des ténèbres du monde et de soit-disant préjugés légitimes, ne se sont pas laissé interpeller par la lumière du Révélateur.[26] En un mot, selon Jean 9, le péché consiste dans l'incroyance.[27] Bien que les pharisiens aient vu les actes de Jésus-Christ, ils n'ont pas voulu voir ce qu'ils auraient réellement dû voir, à savoir la présence de la Révélation. Le péché consiste précisément dans ce "ne-pas-vouloir-voir" dont la cause est à chercher dans leur prétendu savoir religieux. Ils prétendent, en effet, pouvoir statuer sur le divin, c'est-à-dire, en l'occurrence, ils s'arrogent le droit de censurer la Révélation. Mais quiconque prétend pouvoir statuer sur le divin a déjà cessé de laisser Dieu être Dieu.

4. Conclusion

La réflexion de l'école johannique sur la crise de la connaissance causée par la venue du Révélateur attire l'attention du lecteur sur les points suivants.

Comment faut-il lire l'histoire de Jésus en situation post-pascale? Qu'advient-t-il—c'est le propos de Jean 9—lorsqu'il s'agit d'interpréter les actes de guérison de Jésus en son absence? Le texte de Jean laisse entendre qu'une guérison par elle-même ne signifie rien. Elle constitue une énigme. Seul celui qui possède le code d'interprétation peut discerner dans telle guérison opérée par le Christ—à supposer qu'il en admette la réalité—un signe. Il n'y a donc pas d'immédiateté, ni d'univocité du signe. Parler d'un signe, c'est déjà disposer d'un registre herméneutique qui permet de l'identifier.

La deuxième réflexion qui s'impose à la lecture de ce récit, c'est que les codes d'interprétation sont multiples. Que ce soit l'homme naturel, l'autorité religieuse, l'honnête homme, les lectures s'entrecroisent et s'opposent. En l'absence du Christ, la lecture de l'histoire du Christ demeure irrémédiablement controversée.

---

[25] Voir sur ce point l'analyse de Josef Blank, *Krisis: Untersuchungen zur johanneischen Christologie und Eschatologie* (Freiburg im Breisgau: Lambertus, 1964), 262–63.

[26] Cf. Wolfgang Schrage, "τυφλός," *TWNT* 8:29.

[27] Voir, en dernier lieu, Metzner, *Verständnis der Sünde*, 91–102.

Mais—et c'est la troisième réflexion—ce conflit des interprétations n'est pourtant pas stérile, il permet à chaque acteur d'aller au bout de lui-même et de dévoiler les valeurs ultimes qui gouvernent son existence. L'interprétation de l'agir de Jésus n'est donc pas seulement une tâche cognitive, mais une entreprise qui met la totalité de l'existence en jeu.

Quatrièmement, le miracle—s'il est compris comme l'irruption du divin dans la vie des hommes—n'est, selon Jean 9, pas immédiatement lisible. Il se présente comme une déconstruction des certitudes, comme une perturbation, comme un élément que les systèmes de pensée existant peinent à intégrer. Il sème la confusion, il suscite des aveux d'ignorance, et, en définitive, il déclenche l'hostilité. En ce sens, l'agir du Christ johannique est à la fois grâce et jugement, et, de ce fait, crise de la connaissance.

Cinquièmement, quel est alors, d'un point de vue johannique, le chemin de la foi? L'aveugle "clairvoyant" progresse d'une double manière. D'une part, il s'en tient avec acharnement à une exacte relation de l'événement qui a transformé son existence, sans d'abord essayer de l'expliquer. Il sait son ignorance et c'est dans la confrontation avec les autres qu'il apprend à évaluer ce qui lui est arrivé. D'autre part, précisément parce qu'il est ouvert et vigilant, il sait découvrir le code là où il se trouve, c'est-à-dire dans la parole de Jésus.

Dans notre texte—et c'est le sixième point—c'est en effet le Christ et seulement lui qui est capable de présenter son acte comme un signe. C'est lui qui, du point de vue de l'auteur implicite, possède le véritable code. Par son enseignement du début (vv. 3–5) et par le dialogue de la fin (vv. 35–41), il donne au récit sa portée symbolique et permet par là-même au lecteur de découvrir un nouveau monde, susceptible de le questionner et de refaçonner son monde propre.

CHAPTER THIRTEEN

THE HERO IN THE EPISTLE TO THE HEBREWS:
JESUS AS AN ASCETIC MODEL*

Ellen Bradshaw Aitken

Narrative has the power not only to describe but also to create. It has the capacity not only to confirm and inform its audience's perception of the way things are, but also to create a subjectivity within its audience. In other words, narrative is capable of shaping an audience's understanding of themselves, their role in the world, and the behaviors that are proper to this understanding. When narrative is combined with explicit exhortations to certain stances and practices, as in a homily or in deliberative rhetoric, the exhortations or paraenesis are compelling insofar as they are consonant with the subjectivity created by the narrative.[1]

In this essay, I examine the first-century homiletic discourse known as the Epistle to the Hebrews in order to discern the relationship between narrative, particularly the construction of Jesus, and the ethical practices enjoined upon the inscribed audience.[2] I investigate how the particular way in which Jesus' actions are depicted in Hebrews provides the foundation for a distinctive ethical

* An earlier version of this article was presented in the Ascetic Impulse in Religious Life and Culture Group at the annual meeting of the Society of Biblical Literature (Boston, Mass., 21 November 1999). I thank the participants in this session, as well as my students at Harvard Divinity School in exegesis courses on Hebrews, for valuable comments and perspectives. I offer it here as a tribute to my colleague François Bovon, who, in keeping with the theme of this article, has been a model of traveling and "crossing boundaries" in transatlantic, ecumenical, and interdisciplinary scholarship.

[1] On the relationship between paraenesis and narrative in a homily, see, for example, Harold W. Attridge, "Paraenesis in a Homily (λόγος παρακλήσεως)," Semeia 50 (1990): 211–26.

[2] For the homiletic character of Hebrews, see Lawrence Wills, "The Form of the Sermon in Hellenistic Judaism and Early Christianity," HTR 77 (1984): 280–83; C. Clifton Black, "The Rhetorical Form of the Hellenistic Jewish and Early Christian Sermon: A Response to Lawrence Wills [77:277–299, 1984]," HTR 81 (1988): 1–18; and George W. MacRae, "Heavenly Temple and Eschatology in the Letter to the Hebrews," Semeia 12 (1978): 179–99. Hebrews characterizes itself as a λόγος παρακλήσεως ("word of exhortation") at 13:22; see Harold W. Attridge, The Epistle to the Hebrews (ed. Helmut Koester; Hermeneia; Philadelphia: Fortress, 1989), 14, 408, who points out that this designation is used in Acts 13:15 for Paul's synagogue address in Pisidian Antioch. More recently, David A. deSilva accepts the position that Hebrews is a sermon, but one that makes significant use of the conventions of Hellenistic epideictic rhetoric; see David A. deSilva, Perseverance in Gratitude: A Socio-Rhetorical Commentary on the Epistle "to the Hebrews" (Grand Rapids, Mich.: Eerdmans, 2000), 58, 514.

and practical orientation. I suggest that by attending to the heroic narratives underlying the portrayal of Jesus in Hebrews it is possible to discern the character of this orientation and to recognize the practices that embody it.

Near the close of the discourse, an explicit connection is made between Jesus' actions and the actions that are enjoined upon the audience, "Therefore, Jesus also suffered outside the gate, so that he might sanctify the people through his own blood. Let us, then, go out to him outside camp, bearing his reproach" (Heb 13:12–13).[3] I ask here about the practices entailed in "going to Jesus outside the camp and bearing his approach." Through what actions and attitudes is the audience able to carry out this exhortation? What self-understanding informs these practices? One way to answer these questions would be by simply collecting the few references in Hebrews to specific ethical behaviors (e.g., Heb 10:24–25, 32–34; 13:1–9). This method fails, however, to attend to the rhetorical strategies of the discourse and to the way in which a set of underlying narratives is employed to shape the ἦθος or character of the audience. I contend, accordingly, that it is possible to obtain a fuller understanding of the practices enjoined upon the audience if we attend to the narrative presentation of Jesus in this text. In particular, it is Jesus the traveler, who crosses cosmic and civic boundaries, who serves as a model for the inscribed audience of Hebrews. This construction of Jesus, as I shall show, is informed in part by stories of such Greek heroes as Odysseus and Herakles, whose journeys are marked by trials and contests. These stories function alongside of the available traditions of remembering Jesus' passion and death (e.g., Heb 5:7–8). The subjectivity created in the audience by such stories is characterized not only by undergoing trials, but also by crossing boundaries and shifting identity.

I propose further that an exploration of the interaction between the construction of Jesus and the practices enjoined upon the audience shows these practices to be distinctively "ascetic" and that in Hebrews Jesus is presented as an "ascetic" hero. In making this proposal, I follow the working definition of asceticism advanced by Richard Valantasis, namely, that "asceticism may be defined as performances designed to inaugurate an alternative culture, to enable different social relations, and to create a new identity" thus permitting the practitioner "to function within the re-envisioned or re-created world."[4] Central to this understanding of asceticism is the close connection among a

---

[3] On the various exegetical issues in this passage, see especially Helmut Koester, " 'Outside the Camp': Hebrews 13:9–14," *HTR* 55 (1962): 299–315.

[4] Richard Valantasis, "A Theory of the Social Function of Asceticism," in *Asceticism* (ed. Vincent L. Wimbush and Richard Valantasis; New York: Oxford University Press, 1995), 548, 550. This definition seeks to avoid conceiving of the ascetic as exotic, but draws instead upon the classical and Hellenistic Greek notion of ἄσκησις as exercise, practice, or training in a profession, set of skills (for example, in poetry, the gymnasium, or the military), or a mode of living. On the "asceticism," thus understood, of a variety of Greek heroes including Homer, see Philostratus *Heroikos* 25.2; 37.4; 49.3. The asceticism of the Hellenistic gymnasium aims at cultivating in the ephebes of the city the practices, relationships, and character appropriate to civic culture.

set of practices, the cultivation of character, and cultural identity. This definition, because of its emphasis on entering and functioning within a re-envisioned world, lends itself well to envisioning ascetic practices in terms of traveling.

This conceptual framework draws attention to the way in which some of the practices of asceticism more narrowly understood, such as the practices of withdrawal from the city to the wilderness, the movement into enclosure, or the practice of pilgrimage, may indeed entail an actual change of geographical location. Such an act of travel into a new location involves more than passage across borders; it may include speaking different languages, as well as naming objects and relations differently. In addition, the act of travel may require adopting the behaviors appropriate to new places and changing one's perspectives about the centers of power and authority.[5] It may include the frequent renegotiation of attitudes, relationships, and practices. Equally, however, "traveling" serves to describe the adoption of ascetic practices more broadly understood. It becomes an apt metaphor for the way in which those practices enable movement from one culture or world to another and cultivate behaviors and relationships appropriate to a new world.

In Hebrews the motif of "traveling" functions in a variety of related ways to portray both Jesus and the inscribed audience. Even though Hebrews does not advocate the physical relocation of the audience, it envisions the practices proper to the Christian life in terms of travel, of "going in" and "going out," metaphorical movement that is explicitly informed by the scriptures of Israel. When, moreover, we see how this travel is also informed by the heroic journeys such as those of Odysseus and Herakles, we are in a better position to understand both the culture of the world into which the audience is exhorted to travel and the characteristics that they require for living in this new world.

By attending to the language of "going in," we notice immediately that Hebrews depicts the inscribed audience as having the opportunity to enter (εἰσέρχομαι) God's "Rest" (κατάπαυσις).[6] This depiction depends upon the story of the Israelites' journey through the wilderness and the entry into the promised land and specifically upon the retelling in Psalm 95 of the disobedience of the wilderness generation, which names the promised land as God's Rest. In chapter 3, Hebrews takes the final verse of Psalm 95, "as I swore in my wrath, they shall not enter my Rest" (quoted in Heb 3:11; 4:3; 4:5) to set up the present situation of the audience. That is, by employing the story of the wilderness journey and the entry into the land—the cult legend of Israel—the author locates the inscribed audience of Hebrews as the generation that has the

---

[5] In feminist and post-colonial literary analysis and cultural theory, these aspects of movement into new or re-envisioned territory are developed in terms of theories of "deterritorialization" and nomadic consciousness. See, for example, Caren Kaplan, "Deterritorializations: The Rewriting of Home and Exile in Western Feminist Discourse," *Cultural Critique* 6 (1987): 187–98; and Rosi Braidotti, *Nomadic Subjects: Embodiment and Sexual Difference in Contemporary Feminist Theory* (New York: Columbia University Press, 1994).

[6] Heb 3:11, 18, 19; 4:1, 3, 5, 6, 10, 11.

opportunity to complete the journey and to enter the promised land. The disobedience of the wilderness generation, which resulted in their death and failure to enter the land, becomes a negative example for the audience. If they, the audience, do not likewise fall away but instead listen to God's word, they have a "window of opportunity" for entering into God's Rest. Thus, Hebrews stresses "today" as the time when the community addressed has the opportunity for entrance (Heb 4:7–11).

As Hebrews unfolds, the goal of the journey is named also as the heavenly sanctuary (Heb 10:19–20). Ernst Käsemann, however, has shown in the *Wandering People of God* that the underlying narrative is always that of the journey through the wilderness into the promised land.[7] George MacRae, moreover, has emphasized both the horizontal (through the land) and vertical (earth to heaven) dimensions of the journey that exist simultaneously in Hebrews' argument.[8] Thus, the existence of the inscribed audience is defined rhetorically by the simultaneous undertaking of these two journeys, which are intertwined through Hebrews' argument into a single journey.

It is crucial to recognize that Hebrews, unlike other early Christian texts, through the use of this narrative locates its audience as on the very verge of entering the promised land.[9] They stand, as it were, on Mount Pisgah (Deut 34:1) overlooking the Jordan. Their "window of opportunity" for going into the land is supplied by Jesus' death, which opens the way. As a homiletic or paraenetic discourse, Hebrews is thus above all concerned with warning its audience against falling away and thus losing the opportunity to enter the land (Heb 4:1; 10:36; 12:1–2). Its specific ethical exhortations can then be understood as toward those behaviors that uphold solidarity within the community that completes the journey. Moreover, because the way into the promised land is opened by Jesus, the forerunner (πρόδρομος; Heb 6:20) and leader (ἀρχηγός; Heb 2:10; 12:2), "not falling away," I contend, means staying close to Jesus in order to follow in his train. Thus the connection between the audience's journey and that of Jesus is integral to the argument and the success of the paraenesis. The practices and attitudes that the audience is enjoined to cultivate are accordingly those proper to Jesus' journey and to maintaining solidarity with Jesus.

---

[7] Ernst Käsemann, *The Wandering People of God: An Investigation of the Letter to the Hebrews* (trans. Roy A. Harrisville and Irving L. Sandberg; Minneapolis: Augsburg, 1984); trans. of *Das wandernde Gottesvolk: Eine Untersuchung zum Hebräerbrief* (2d ed.; FRLANT 55; Göttingen: Vandenhoeck & Ruprecht, 1957), 22–24.

[8] George W. MacRae, "Heavenly Temple," 190. See also Aelred Cody, *Heavenly Sanctuary and Liturgy in the Epistle to the Hebrews* (St. Meinrad, Ill.: Grail, 1960), 1–2.

[9] Hebrews' locating of the community thus stands in stark contrast to the *Epistle of Barnabas*, which locates the community in the land of promise as its heirs (*Barn.* 6:11–19). In 1 Cor 10, because of the scriptural events Paul utilizes to describe the community, it is envisioned as located closer to Mount Sinai or in the midst of the wilderness, rather than on the verge of entering the promised land. See Ellen B. Aitken, "The Morphology of the Passion Narrative" (Th.D. diss., Harvard University, 1997), 31–50, 125–26.

In order to understand the practices appropriate for a traveling existence, it is necessary to consider the two important journeys that Jesus undertakes, as these are constructed by Hebrews. Both of these journeys have been widely recognized in interpretations of Hebrews, but in neither case has the aspect of travel itself been emphasized. The first is simpler, namely, Jesus' entry into the heavenly sanctuary. In chapter 9, Hebrews relies on the typological interpretation of the actions of the high priest in the Jerusalem Temple on the Day of Atonement, as prescribed in Lev 16, in order to portray the atoning offering of Jesus. It is notable in this interpretation of the ritual actions that entering per se is emphasized: the high priest goes into the Holy of Holies with the blood of the animal sacrifices (Heb 9:6–7), Jesus goes into the heavenly sanctuary with the offering of himself (Heb 9:12, 24). This entering, the act of travel, is not incidental to the typological way in which Hebrews uses the rituals of the Day of Atonement; rather Jesus' entry into the heavenly sanctuary enables the community whom the text addresses to enter as well. They have "a hope that enters the inner shrine behind the curtain, where Jesus has entered as a forerunner for [them]" (Heb 6:19–20); they now have "confidence to enter the sanctuary by the blood of Jesus" because Jesus has "opened the way" for them (Heb 10:19–20). As Käsemann, among others, has pointed out, Jesus' journey is not only emblematic for the community; it makes possible the successful completion of their journey by opening the path for them.[10] When we focus our attention on the act of traveling, rather than on the goal alone, we notice that it is not only movement that is important to the construction of the actions of Jesus and the community. Hebrews emphasizes in addition the act of crossing boundaries—across the threshold of the temple sanctuary (Heb 6:19; 10:20), across the boundary of earth and heaven (Heb 2:7)—and affirms that it is Jesus who creates the passage across the boundary or threshold. It remains to explore the behaviors and practices appropriate to the journey up the threshold and across.

Before examining the characteristic ethic appropriate to the objective of the journey and its goal, however, it is necessary to consider how Hebrews constructs the second journey that Jesus makes. Jesus travels from the heavens to earth and back again, to sit down "on the right hand of the Majesty on high" (Heb 1:3). The story of divine Wisdom which underlies the exordium of the discourse in Heb 1:1–4 is here used to establish the journey of the Son, the radiance of God's glory, through whom God "created the universe," to a place lower than the angels (Heb 2:9) where he shares in the sufferings of humanity and makes purification for sins.[11] Thereupon he makes the journey of return

---

[10] Käsemann, *The Wandering People of God*, 227–28. That the heavenly sanctuary is the goal for the people of God is also apparent from the solidarity Jesus initiates with the community, claiming them as his "brothers and sisters" (Heb 2:12–18), whom he presents to God upon his return to the heavenly realm. Jesus is "forerunner" (πρόδρο-μος) and "leader" (ἀρχηγός) into the heavenly sanctuary for the people (Heb 10:19–20), as well as into God's Rest.

[11] On the role of a story about divine Wisdom (especially Wis 7:26) in informing

to the heavenly home, where he is now enthroned and crowned with glory and honor (2:9).[12] Attridge, among others, has pointed out that this sequence of preexistence, incarnation, descent, humiliation, and exaltation belongs to a classic early christological pattern,[13] which appropriates various ancient mythical soteriologies, including the plot of the Hellenistic hero such as Herakles or Orpheus who descends to the underworld.[14]

The descent of the hero to the underworld may comprise one part of a more extensive heroic story, and in particular a story of travel. By attending to the dimension of the journey in this pattern, we see also a correspondence between Hebrews' story of Jesus and the Greek νόστοι, the songs of the return of the hero to his or her homeland. Such songs or the plot of such songs include, for example, the accounts of Agamemnon's tragic return, blown off course, to Argos, and Menelaus's wanderings to Egypt after the Trojan War, before his return to Sparta. The preeminent example of a song of return, however, is the *Odyssey*, the song of Odysseus's homecoming. Such songs are concerned not simply with the hero's arrival home, but just as much with the trials and misfortunes encountered on the way home.[15] The journey is the occasion for suffering, loss and recovery of identity, endurance, and even a descent among the dead. In Book 11 of the *Odyssey* (the "Nekyia"), Odysseus indeed does enter the realm of the dead and converse with the dead heroes. This traveling and its travails require the full wiliness of Odysseus—his capacity for disguise, shape-shifting, deceit, and versatility. He is continually entering new worlds, adopting new identities, forming new relationships, until his arrival and showing of himself back home in Ithaca, where he is ultimately restored to his sovereignty and there receives the honor due the returning hero. I would suggest that such a "song of homecoming" provides a useful category for understanding Jesus' journey in Hebrews. With this suggestion, I

---

the exordium of Hebrews, see Attridge, *Hebrews*, 42–45; Craig R. Koester, *Hebrews: A New Translation with Introduction and Commentary* (AB 36; New York: Doubleday, 2001), 187–88.

[12] See Kenneth Schenck, "Keeping His Appointment: Creation and Enthronement in Hebrews," *JSNT* 66 (1997): 91–117.

[13] Attridge, *Hebrews*, 41.

[14] Attridge, *Hebrews*, 79, with particular reference to Heb 2:10–18. Attridge makes the point that the basic "plot" of this early Christian christological pattern is also found in the Greek stories of the descent of heroes, such as Orpheus or Herakles, in the underworld. See also Harold W. Attridge, "Liberating Death's Captives: Reconsideration of an Early Christian Myth," in *Gnosticism and the Early Christian World: In Honor of James M. Robinson* (ed. James E. Goehring et al.; Sonoma, Calif.: Polebridge, 1990), 103–15.

[15] On the "return" of Odysseus, see Douglas Frame, *The Myth of Return in Early Greek Epic* (New Haven and London: Yale University Press, 1978), 34–80. On νόστος as the song of return, see Gregory Nagy, *The Best of the Achaeans: Concepts of the Hero in Archaic Greek Poetry* (rev. ed.; Baltimore: Johns Hopkins University Press, 1999), 97–99. Note that inasmuch as νόστος designates not only the journey home per se, but also the song narrating this journey, it provides the hero a means of immortalization through the medium of song.

am not denying the contributions of other mythic, poetic, or scriptural patterns, but rather proposing that the story of the hero's homecoming also informs the presentation of Jesus in Hebrews.

It is apparent, moreover, that in Hebrews Jesus' two journeys can be merged, as though we were overlaying one map upon another. Jesus' journey into the heavenly sanctuary is also his successful journey homeward to his enthronement in heaven. Overlaying the maps in this manner helps us to recognize that Jesus' suffering and death belong not only to the soteriological scheme of atonement for sins, but also to the pattern of the hero's homecoming, the νόστος. Thus, what Hebrews has to say about Jesus' experience on earth, in "flesh and blood" (Heb 2:14) or in the "days of his flesh" (Heb 5:7), belongs to the story of his νόστος before his arrival home. This would include his being perfected through suffering (Heb 2:10), his being tested and his solidarity with those who are tested (Heb 2:18), the obedience that he learned from what he suffered (Heb 5:8), and his offering of his own blood.[16] In the heroic patterns of Greek epic, the hero's νόστος is a safe return from death and travail; the equilibrium that it brings comes only through enduring the greatest pain.[17] The νόστος is thus a vehicle of the hero's coming full circle, reaching completion (τέλος) or, in Hebrews' terms, perfection (τελειότης).[18]

The discussion of heroic models for the construction of Jesus in Hebrews has concentrated almost entirely upon Herakles. Attridge has argued compellingly, for example, that Hebrews is indebted to the myth of Herakles for the themes of perfection through suffering (Heb 2:10) and liberation of death's captives. In saying that Jesus "shared in the flesh and blood of the children of God so that through death he might destroy the one who has the power of death, that is, the devil, and free those who all their lives were held in slavery by the fear of death" (Heb 2:14–15), Hebrews is drawing upon the story of Herakles' descent to Hades to liberate those held captive there.[19] Herakles has also figured less successfully in discussions of the meaning of the term ἀρχηγός based on literary references to Herakles as the ἀρχηγός (or "founder") of certain cities.[20] David Aune has also suggested that Herakles' ascent to

---

[16] Aitken, "The Morphology of the Passion Narrative," 182–207. On the song or psalmic traditions in Heb 5:7–10, see Paul Andriessen, "Angoisse de la mort dans l'Épître aux Hébreux," *NRTh* 96 (1974): 2986–91; and August Strobel, "Die Psalmengrundlage der Gethsemane-Parallele: Hebr 5:7ff.," *ZNW* 45 (1954): 256.

[17] Nagy, *Best of the Achaeans*, 97–99. Frame (*Myth of Return*, 37) emphasizes that the "return" of the hero includes the hero's return from the realm of the dead.

[18] Gregory Nagy, *Greek Mythology and Poetics* (Ithaca: Cornell University Press, 1990), 202–22.

[19] Attridge, "Liberating Death's Captives," 110–15.

[20] See Ceslas Spicq, *L'Épître aux Hébreux* (2 vols.; Paris: Gabalda, 1952), 2:38; Attridge (*Hebrews*, 88 n. 104) lists the uses of ἀρχηγός as an epithet of Herakles. Note especially Dio Chrysostom *Or.* 33.47, on Herakles as the founder of the city of Tarsus. See also David E. Aune, "Heracles and Christ: Heracles Imagery in the Christology of Early Christianity," in *Greeks, Romans, and Christians: Essays in Honor of Abraham J. Malherbe* (ed.

Olympus after his immolation of Mount Oite informs Hebrews' Christology of Jesus' enthronement.[21] Moreover, because the audience's situation is depicted as an ἀγών ("contest, race"; Heb 12:1) and as struggle (ἀνταγωνίζομαι; Heb 12:4), parallel to Jesus' perfection through suffering, Aune and Attridge have pointed to a connection with the motifs of Herakles' labors (ἀγῶνες).[22] While I do not dispute these arguments, I would suggest that the motif of Herakles' travels during his labors is equally important in shaping the construction of Jesus and the community in Hebrews. That is, Herakles' ἀγῶνες take him not only all over the known world, but also beyond the Mediterranean, to the borders of Okeanos, and, as we have seen, to the realm of the dead and then to the heavenly Olympus. Herakles, like Odysseus, is a well-traveled hero; more importantly, for both heroes their travels and their sufferings bring them ultimately to equilibrium and completion. In Hebrews, Jesus' ἀγῶνες take place during his journey on earth and homeward to the heavenly sanctuary; as for Herakles and Odysseus, so for Jesus: the journey and the travails are inseparable. So too for the community addressed in Hebrews: their traveling is characterized by struggles, suffering, and travail, calling forth the development of practices particular to such a journey (see, e.g., Heb 10:32–36).

We receive an important clue to the nature of these practices at the very beginning of Hebrews, a clue that connects the entire discourse to the heroic songs of return. The exordium, marking the themes of the discourse, begins: πολυμερῶς καὶ πολυτρόπως πάλαι ὁ θεὸς λαλήσας τοῖς πατράσιν ἐν τοῖς προφήταις ("In many forms and many fashions God spoke of old to the ancestors in the prophets"; Heb 1:1). The clue lies in the word πολυτρόπως ("in many fashions"), the adverbial form of πολύτροπος ("of many forms"), the epithet distinctive to Odysseus in the ancient Greek epic tradition.[23] Odysseus is versatile, protean, multiform, the shape-shifter and trickster, and this motif is signaled in the first line of the Odyssey, ἄνδρα μοι ἔννεπε, Μοῦσα, πολύτροπον, ὃς μάλα πολλὰ πλάγχθη ("Sing to me, Muse, of the man of many forms who suffered much [on his return from Troy]," Homer Od. 1.12). The Odyssey announces in its proem that it is a song about the sufferings and travels of the πολύτροπος man, the man "of many forms"; similarly, I suggest that Hebrews announces in the exordium that it takes as its subject in part the πολύτροπος ("multiform") journey of the Word of God. Because Hebrews utilizes to such a great extent the ways in which "God spoke of old to the ancestors" to express who Jesus is and what the situation of the community is, the "type" or pattern by

David L. Balch, Everett Ferguson, and Wayne Meeks; Minneapolis: Fortress, 1990), 15–16. On ἀρχηγός more generally, see Paul-Gerhard Müller, ΧΡΙΣΤΟΣ ΑΡΧΗΓΟΣ: Der religionsgeschichtliche und theologische Hintergrund einer neutestamentlichen Christusprädikation (Europäische Hochschulschriften ser. 23; Theologie 28; Frankfurt/Bern: Lang, 1973).

[21] Aune, "Heracles and Christ," 19.

[22] Aune, "Heracles and Christ," 16–17; Attridge, Hebrews, 80; on Herakles' labors as ἀγῶνες, see Sophocles Trach. 159.

[23] On Odysseus as πολύτροπος, see Gregory Nagy, Pindar's Homer: The Lyric Possession of an Epic Past (Baltimore: John Hopkins University Press, 1990), 424–25. Nagy translates πολύτροπος here as "versatile in many ways."

which all understanding proceeds is πολύτροπος, multiform and versatile. This multiplicity is held in tension in Hebrews with the singularity with which God "has spoken" to the present community, that is, "in a Son" (Heb 1:2). This singularity makes sense, however, when we recognize that, from the perspective of Hebrews, the Son has completed his journey and travails; he has gone home and attained completion. The audience, however, has not: they are still journeying and have yet to cross the threshold. They are therefore to be πολύτροποι: versatile, protean, flexible, and capable of shifting their stances and attitudes. This is then a chief characteristic of the practices and attitudes appropriate to the journey and the crossing of boundaries. Moreover, to be "of many forms" enables Odysseus to survive the trials and suffering of the journey, including his journey to the underworld; his shape-shifting, his versatility and wiliness, his willingness to let go of his identity and to adopt new behaviors—all of these enable him to defeat or deceive his adversaries and to return home.

The requirement to be "of many forms" in order to complete the journey highlights the particular ethic Hebrews espouses. Of the few indications of ethical practice in this discourse, several are marked by the practice of solidarity with those who are suffering. In Heb 10:32–34, the audience is urged to recall

> those earlier days when, after you had been enlightened, you endured a hard struggle with sufferings, sometimes being publicly exposed to abuse and persecution, and sometimes being partners (κοινωνοί) with those so treated. For you had compassion for those who were in prison, and you cheerfully accepted the plundering of your possessions, knowing that you yourselves possessed something better and more lasting.

Similarly, in Heb 13.13, the audience is exhorted to

> let love within the community [φιλαδελφία] continue. Do not neglect to show hospitality to strangers, for by doing so some have entertained angels without knowing it. Remember those who are in prison, as though you were in prison with them; those who are being tortured as though you yourselves were in [their] body.

I would emphasize in these passages the ethic of adopting the situation of another as one's own. It is an ethic of crossing a boundary into the world of another and, in particular, into a situation of imprisonment, torture, abuse, and persecution. In this sense, we might characterize it more specifically as an ethic of crossing an important civic boundary from the world of perceived honor into the world of shame. As the audience makes this journey, they learn a new language: they learn to call what is shameful the vehicle of receiving honor, even as Jesus' shame enabled him to be crowned with honor (Heb 2:9).[24] It is, I suggest, an ethic of being πολύτροπος, multiform or protean,

---

[24] David A. deSilva's recent commentary on Hebrews, *Perseverance in Gratitude*, uses the cultural polarities of honor and shame as his primary interpretive framework for

capable of shifting into identity with the suffering and persecuted (as if you yourself were in their body), and sufficiently versatile to negotiate the crossing of civic boundaries.

In the concluding paraenesis, Hebrews urges its audience to "go out (ἐξέρχομαι) to Jesus outside the camp and bear the disgrace he bore" (Heb 13:13). This exhortation "to go out" stands in stark contrast to the language of "go in" which has marked the rest of Hebrews. Suddenly, it seems that the audience is not to go in, but to go out. But Jesus' suffering "outside the [city] gate" identifies his suffering as an act of crossing civic boundaries. In order to stay close to Jesus, so that they too might enter in the heavenly realm, the audience must also cross these civic boundaries. They do so by their practices of solidarity with those who are suffering and bearing abuse. In other words, they can "go in" only by "going out."[25]

In advocating these practices, Hebrews seeks to develop and encourage in its audience a certain way of being. By these practices of shape-shifting, boundary-crossing, traveling into solidarity with suffering, the audience may initiate an alternative culture, take on different social relations, and create a new identity for themselves—which is defined also as being in solidarity with Jesus whose journey was itself marked with suffering and struggle.[26] It is an asceticism suitable for travel and travail on the journey; it is an asceticism of being πολύτροπος, multiform, shape-shifting, and versatile.

---

the discourse as a whole. I do not adopt honor and shame as a thoroughgoing motif for reading Hebrews, but rather recognize these as one set of markers for the community's journey.

[25] Koester ("Outside the Camp," 301–3) argues that the exhortation to "go outside the camp" is a call "neither to lead an unworldly life as a member of a heavenly city, nor to escape from this world and life as soon as possible." Rather, according to Koester's reading, it is an appeal to a "radical openness to the challenges and sufferings that necessarily result from the existence 'outside the camp,'" that is, in "the acceptance of the secular reality." This is an anti-cultic interpretation, which contrasts cultic performances with acts of "thanksgiving and charity." My argument builds on Koester's emphasis on "outside the camp" as a place of profound engagement with the sufferings that come as a result of living in the world. I stress, however, that this ethic is one of movement into solidarity with the situation of the other who is suffering and "bearing reproach."

[26] On the ethic of solidarity within the community, as a stance of resistance to the imperial Flavian triumphal ideology and theology, see Ellen B. Aitken, "Portraying the Temple in Stone and Text: The Arch of Titus and the Epistle to the Hebrews," in *Religious Texts and Material Contexts* (Studies in Ancient Judaism; ed. Jacob Neusner and James F. Strange; Lanham, Md.: University Press of America, 2001), 73–88; repr. in *STRev* 45 (2002): 135–51.

CHAPTER FOURTEEN

LA COURONNE DE NEMROD:
QUELQUES RÉFLEXIONS SUR LE POUVOIR, L'HISTOIRE ET L'ÉCRITURE DANS LA CULTURE SYRIAQUE[1]

ALAIN DESREUMAUX

Si depuis quelques dizaines d'années déjà, ont paru plusieurs études dont certaines fort copieuses, sur le pouvoir de l'écrit dans l'histoire—pour reprendre de façon un peu détournée le titre d'un ouvrage d'Henri-Jean Martin,[2] il me paraît que ces études concernent surtout la naissance et les origines de l'écriture et les pouvoirs des scribes dans la haute antiquité orientale et les pouvoirs de l'écrit et l'apparition du livre dans le monde occidental.

Aucune étude d'ensemble ne s'est attachée à analyser ces questions dans la culture syriaque.[3] Cela tient sans doute au fait que, dans ce domaine, les études codicologiques et paléographiques sont encore peu avancées ou pas encore suffisamment rassemblées en synthèses disponibles, ce qui est paradoxal quand on considère que, depuis l'époque romaine impériale, inscriptions et manuscrits araméens puis syriaques se sont multipliés en Osroène, en Syrie, en Mésopotamie, jusqu'en Asie, en Chine et en Inde et qu'un grand nombre de ces documents sont une aubaine pour les historiens puisqu'ils indiquent dates et lieux de copie avec précision.

Je n'aurai certes pas la prétention d'essayer de faire pour la culture syriaque l'équivalent de ce que Marcel Detienne a su réaliser sur Les savoirs de

---

[1] Le présent texte a fait l'objet d'une communication orale lors de la table-ronde organisée par l'Institut d'études sémitiques, Écriture et pouvoir dans le Proche-Orient ancien, Paris, Collège de France, 20 novembre 1999.

[2] Henri-Jean Martin, *Histoire et pouvoirs de l'écrit* (avec la collaboration de Bruno Delmas, et une préface de Pierre Chaunu; Histoire et Décadence; Paris: Librairie académique Perrin, 1988).

[3] Araméen et syriaque tiennent bien sûr leur place dans les "histoires de l'écriture." Celle de James Germain Février (*Histoire de l'écriture, avec 135 figures dans le texte et 16 planches hors-texte* [Bibliothèque historique; Paris: Payot, 1948], 256) note bien que "l'évolution de l'écriture syriaque est liée étroitement aux événements religieux des débuts de l'église chrétienne. . . ." Peut-être des études seraient-elles à mener pour répondre dans le domaine syriaque aux questions posées par des ouvrages comme celui de Jack Goody, *La logique de l'écriture: Aux origines des societes humaines* (Paris: Armand Colin, 1986). Des perspectives prometteuses sont ouvertes par les recherches sur les textes historiques produits en syriaque, par exemple, récemment, la thèse de doctorat de Mme. Muriel Arruebo Debié, "L'écriture de l'histoire dans les siècles obscurs byzantins: Rupture ou continuité? L'exemple de l'historiographie syriaque" (Université de Paris 4; mars 1999).

l'écriture en Grèce ancienne.[4] Il me paraît en revanche approprié de rendre hommage à un savant tel que François Bovon en posant modestement sur une vaste interrogation quelques questions, afin de suggérer quelques hypothèses et d'esquisser une recherche que, pour ma part, je souhaite voir se poursuivre.

J'avance d'abord quelques points qui me semblent mériter réflexion, avant d'aborder une brève lecture de plusieurs textes peu connus.

Les deux premiers documents araméens édes-séniens datés sont l'inscription de Serrin, en Syrie du Nord, un peu au sud de l'actuelle frontière turco-syrienne[5] et une inscription du moyen-Euphrate, trouvée il y a un siècle dans la forteresse de Birtha, l'actuelle Birecik, sur la rive gauche de l'Euphrate, un peu au nord de la même frontière.[6] On date la première d'octobre 73 de notre ère et la seconde de mars 6; celle-ci, à mon avis, pose des problèmes de datation (une cassure affecte la date) et je ne verrais pas d'inconvénient à la dater de mars 106. En tout cas, les plus anciennes inscriptions édesséniennes datées apparaissent au premier siècle de notre ère. Les plus anciens manuscrits araméens édesséniens datés ont été trouvés aussi au bord de l'Euphrate en Syrie du Nord; ils sont datés autour de l'an 240.[7] On connaît actuellement une quinzaine de documents datés, s'échelonnant jusqu'au milieu du treizième siècle et l'on en compte de nombreux autres sans date mais très bien datables au cours de cette période. Ce groupe de documents, tous osroéniens et syriens du Nord, constitue l'ensemble des documents araméens édesséniens.[8] Leur écriture annonce les écritures syriaques, c'est-à-dire édesséniennes chrétiennes, dont les premières datées connues leur sont postérieures de cent cinquante ans, puisque le premier manuscrit estranghelo daté connu (contenant Ps.-Clément, Reconnaissances, Titus de Bostra, Contre les manichéens, Eusèbe, Théophanie et Martyrs de Palestine) a été achevé à Édesse en teshrin second 723 des Grecs (soit novembre 411 après J.-C.) et la première inscription chrétienne datée est de 482 de l'ère d'Antioche (soit 433 soit 434 de notre ère). A partir de là, manuscrits et inscriptions se multiplient, en se répartissant selon les diversités régionales et religieuses et ce jusqu'à la fin du dix-neuvième

---

[4] Marcel Detienne, *Les Savoirs de l'écriture: En Grèce ancienne* (avec la collaboration de Georgio Camassa, et al.; Cahiers de Philologie[3] 14: Série Apparat critique; [Villeneuve-d'Ascq, France]: Presses universitaires de Lille, 1988).

[5] Han J. W. Drijvers and John F. Healey, *The Old Syriac Inscriptions of Edessa and Osrhoene: Texts, Translations, and Commentary* (HO 1: Der nahe und mittlere Osten 24; Leiden: Brill, 1999), 193–97.

[6] Ibid., 140–44.

[7] Contrat de vente de Doura-Europos, écrit à Édesse en 243 ap. J.-C. (ibid., 232–36) et parchemins de l'Euphrate, écrits à Batnae en 240 et 242 ap. J.-C. publiés par Javier Teixidor, "Un document syriaque de fermage de 242 après J.-C.," *Semeia* 41–42 (1991–1992): 195–208.

[8] L'ouvrage de Drijvers et Healey offre une étude synthétique des inscriptions araméennes édesséniennes connues à ce jour, auxquelles il faudra ajouter plusieurs découvertes récentes; celles-ci confirment la cohérence du corpus.

siècle,[9] bien que la création littéraire proprement dite se fût arrêtée après Bar Hebraeus, à la fin du treizième siècle.

Ce très bref rappel sur les écrits araméens édesséniens et les écrits syriaques anciens suggère déjà quelques réflexions.

S'il est évident que l'écriture édessénienne est un développement de l'araméenne, on n'a encore trouvé aucun chaînon visible la reliant aux anciennes inscriptions connues. L'apparition de textes araméens édesséniens au début de notre ère est comme soudaine. Elle marque un phénomène nouveau que je trouve perceptible dans ces textes. Ceux-ci sont soit funéraires, votifs ou juridiques. Funéraires, ils appartiennent à des gens aisés, des notables, des princes, en premier lieu ceux de la famille dirigeante; avec les textes votifs, ils portent des références religieuses élémentaires fondées sur le besoin de protection, où les préoccupations familiales sont premières. Juridiques, ils sont les instruments d'une organisation sociale gérée avec soin selon des concepts complexes que J. Teixidor a mis en évidence dans les parchemins de l'Euphrate. Beaucoup de documents comportent des références historiques précises, dates et personnages. Enfin, tant les concepts juridiques notariaux que les décors funéraires—je pense surtout aux mosaïques—indiquent une adoption de pratiques romaines.

Ainsi, ces documents écrits semblent correspondre à la formation d'une société nouvelle, structurée autour d'un clan qui jouit tranquillement du pouvoir (et le conservera assez longtemps) à l'ombre de l'Empire romain. Ses textes gravés et écrits, explicitement ancrés dans une chronologie, manifestent clairement une conscience identitaire paisible. Je serais tenté d'ajouter que cette formation sociale comporte une dimension culturelle importante. En effet, outre les textes juridiques mentionnés, les deux plus anciennes œuvres édesséniennes, la *Lettre de Mara bar Serapion*[10] et le *Livre des lois des pays*[11] montrent que

---

[9] Pour une bibliographie synthétique sur les manuscrits, voir Alain Desreumaux, *Répertoire des bibliothèques et des catalogues de manuscrits syriaques* (avec la collaboration de Françoise Briquel-Chatonnet; Documents, études et répertoires publiés par l'Institut de recherche et d'histoire des textes; Paris: Éditions du Centre national de la recherche scientifique, 1991).

Pour une bibliographie sur les inscriptions syriaques, on utilisera le volume fait par Sebastian P. Brock, *Syriac Studies: A Classified Bibliography 1960–1990* (ParOr 1; Kaslik, Liban: Parole de l'Orient, 1996).

[10] Friedrich Schulthess, "Der Brief des Mara bar Sarapion (Spicilegium Syriacum ed. Cureton p. 43ff.): Ein Beitrag zur Geschichte der syrischen Litteratur," *ZDMG* 51 (1897): 365–91. L'Étude la plus récente est celle de Kathleen E. McVey, "A Fresh Look at the Letter of Mara bar Sarapion to His Son," dans René Lavenant, ed., *Quintum Symposium Syriacum 1988: Katholieke Universiteit, Leuven, 29–31 aout 1988* (OrChrAn 229; Rome: Pontificium Institutum Studiorum Orientalium, 1987), 257–72.

[11] Écrit par Philippe, disciple de Bardesane, l'édition est une traduction française par François Nau, *Bardesane l'astrologue: Le Livre des lois des pays. Texte syriaque et traduction française avec une introduction et de nombreuses notes* (2 vols.; Paris: Leroux, 1899; réimpr., Paris: Librairie Orientaliste Paul Geuthner, 1931).

cette société a un ancrage culturel dans la philosophie grecque. Il y a donc, lors de la formation de cette société, un parti-pris culturel s'exprimant vigoureusement par écrit. C'est sans doute cette mise par écrit qui en a fait l'efficacité. De fait, on constate que cette Édesse-là est à l'origine d'une histoire à long terme et à vaste rayonnement, celle de la culture syriaque. Réussite en effet quand on songe à la fragilité économique et militaire de l'ancienne cité hellénistique bien vite qualifiée de "bénie."[12] Combien plus durable que Palmyre, sa voisine syrienne (il est consolant de constater que, dans l'histoire humaine, le commerce n'est pas toujours plus puissant que la culture . . .)!

Si cette formidable puissance culturelle a ensuite perduré si longtemps, c'est bien grâce à l'écrit. Labubna, l'auteur de la *Doctrine d'Addaï*,[13] l'un des textes fondateurs de l'univers culturel syriaque, l'avait bien compris, qui insiste, au quatrième siècle, sur l'existence des archives royales, pratique héritée de la grande tradition mésopotamienne. Dès le début du cinquième siècle, la qualité des manuscrits réalisés dans cette écriture d'apparat qu'est l'estranghelo est saisissante et va de pair avec une richesse de contenus dont l'ampleur est d'autant plus remarquable que cette puissance culturelle ne repose sur aucune puissance politique et qu'elle ne vise à en servir aucune. Je suggère que l'absence de puissance politique est pour beaucoup dans l'incessante quête de repères historiques, qui occupe une telle place dans la culture syriaque.

Ailleurs, dans le monde romain, on voyait les choses autrement.

Il n'a évidemment pas échappé à Luciano Canfora, dans sa reconstitution de l'histoire de la bibliothèque d'Alexandrie, que la Lettre d'Aristée à Philocrate contenait une intéressante réflexion sur le rôle essentiel que jouent les écrits dans l'exercice du pouvoir royal. Le long questionnement des Sages juifs par Ptolémée Philadelphe révèle ce but utilitaire: "Comment conserver son royaume? . . . Comment transmettre le royaume intact à ses héritiers? Comment faire face aux imprévus sans en être troublé? . . . Tu dois lire, lui répondit l'un des vieillards, surtout les relations de voyage concernant les divers royaumes de la terre. Tu sauras ainsi mieux sauvegarder la sécurité de tes sujets; en faisant cela, tu acquerras la gloire et Dieu exaucera tes souhaits."[14]

On ne doit cependant pas oublier que l'auteur de la Lettre d'Aristée se préoccupe surtout de la place que tiennent ses Écritures saintes dont il veut faire la promotion, parmi les dizaines de milliers de rouleaux rassemblées dans le monde entier sur l'ordre du souverain. La question centrale n'est-elle pas alors de savoir s'il vaut la peine de consacrer de l'énergie à faire figurer les livres mosaïques dans la plus grande bibliothèque du monde et comment

---

[12] D'où le titre de l'ouvrage de Judah Benzion Segal, *Edessa, 'the Blessed City'* (Oxford: Clarendon, 1970).

[13] Alain Desreumaux, *Histoire du roi Abgar et de Jésus: Traduction, introduction et notes* (Apocryphes: Collection de poche de l'AELAC [3]; Turnhout: Brepols, 1993).

[14] Luciano Canfora, *La véritable histoire de la bibliothèque d'Alexandrie* (Paris: Desjonquères, 1988), 44–45.

assurer la lecture grecque correcte de la Loi hébraïque? Les nombreux commentateurs anciens de l'œuvre ne s'y sont pas trompés, depuis Philon jusqu'aux chroniqueurs byzantins en passant bien sûr par Jérôme. Les historiographes syriaques se contentèrent, eux, d'enregistrer l'événement, qui a permis de transmettre les Écritures aux païens. Seule, l'Écriture proprement dite les préoccupaient et non le pouvoir politique qu'ils ne possédaient pas.

En tout cas, je m'étonne que Canfora, qui a bien perçu le rôle de l'écrit pour la puissance royale de l'époque de la *Lettre d'Aristée*, n'ait pas été alerté pour interpréter un texte syriaque qui, bien que postérieur de plusieurs siècles, relève de cette problématique. Il lit en effet la *Lettre du patriarche Jean* au sujet de l'entretien qu'il eut avec l'émir des Agaréens[15] pour dresser un portrait psychologique de l'émir—en l'occurrence *ʿAmrou ibn al-ʿAs*—et montrer que celui-ci n'était pas un guerrier inculte, mais était capable de s'intéresser à "des questions subtiles sur les saintes écritures et la nature prétendument divine du Christ. Il avait même demandé à vérifier dans l'original hébraïque l'exactitude de la traduction en grec d'un passage de la Genèse." Or, le texte syriaque a pour moi une tout autre portée et beaucoup plus intéressante. Outre le fait qu'il nous indique indirectement qu'en 639, il n'y avait pas encore de traduction arabe de la Bible que l'émir puisse lire, il nous transmet sans équivoque une préoccupation politique de ce dernier. Le patriarche jacobite Jean I (635–648) respecte d'ailleurs cette fonction de l'émir et le texte syriaque prend soin de toujours lui donner son titre officiel de ܡܫܒܚܐ, (*Mshabho*), qui correspond exactement, dans la titulature byzantine, au titre nobiliaire d'ἰλλούστριος, "*illustris*."[16] En homme d'État, la préoccupation de l'émir qui a convoqué le patriarche, est de pouvoir se référer à un livre de lois. Il en a besoin pour gouverner: "Quelles sont les lois des chrétiens et comment sont-elles, sont-elles dans l'Évangile ou non?" Le patriarche, lui, refuse de répondre à la question sous cet angle juridique et politique. "L'évangile divin enseigne et impose les doctrines célestes et les préceptes vivifiants, dit-il; il maudit tous les péchés et tous les maux; il enseigne l'excellence et la justice. . . ." Dialogue de sourds, évidemment. L'émir n'en démord pas: "Ou vous me montrez que vos lois sont écrites dans l'Évangile et vous vous conduisez par elles, ou vous adhérez à la loi musulmane." Bref, choisissez une loi, celle que vous voulez, mais une loi identifiable. Le patriarche, de son côté, ne peut céder: "Nous avons des lois justes et droites, qui concordent avec l'enseignement de l'Évangile et les canons apostoliques." L'écriture est pour le patriarche une référence qui

---

[15] François Nau, "Un colloque du patriarche Jean avec l'émir des Agaréens et faits divers des années 712 à 716 d'après le ms. du British Museum Add. 17193 avec un appendice sur le patriarche Jean I, sur un colloque d'un patriarche avec le chef des mages et sur un diplôme qui aurait été donné par Omar à l'évêque du Tour ʿAbdin," *JA*[2] 6 (1915): 225–79.

[16] Je dois cette information précise à Frédéric Alpi qui a soigneusement rassemblé les preuves de cette équivalence à l'époque de Sévère d'Antioche.

n'a pas la même portée politique que pour l'émir; ce dernier y voit le code juridique qui lui permet de gouverner.

À la fin du douzième siècle, la réflexion avait progressé. Michel le Syrien élabore sa monumentale Chronique[17] en connaissance de cause. Rarement un historien exprime avec autant de franchise et de clarté les objectifs de son travail. On les trouve dans la finale du 2e appendice intitulé "Souvenir des empires qui ont été constitués dans l'Antiquité par notre race des Araméens. . . ."[18] Et de préciser que s'il a établi des chronologies et des computs, "avec autant de soin que possible par le témoignage de l'écrit," c'est parce qu'il voulait montrer que son peuple descend des anciens souverains mésopotamiens précédant le royaume perse et expliquer pourquoi leurs noms ont disparu de son histoire. Privé de rois pendant 550 ans par les conquêtes des Perses, d'Alexandre et des Séleucides, ce peuple adhéra avec empressement à l'Évangile au point "de brûler tous les livres dans lesquels étaient compilé le souvenir des anciens rois araméens, parce qu'y étaient entremêlés les histoires diaboliques de leur paganisme." On perçoit, dans cette argumentation désespérée, la profonde interrogation sur la destinée d'un peuple qui n'a plus de roi et se cherche des origines, resserrant son identité présente dans son orthodoxie.

L'astucieuse explication a eu deux fâcheuses conséquences. Elle a acrédité l'idée que toute une partie de la documentation syriaque avait été brûlée ne laissant subsister que les textes religieux et d'autre part, elle a fondé les anachroniques revendications nationalistes encore perceptibles aujourd'hui.

Néanmoins, ce n'est pas trop dire que l'œuvre historique du célèbre patriarche jacobite est un hommage exceptionnel à la puissance de l'écrit. Cet immense labeur mobilise toutes les capacités des sources écrites, en tant que documentation et dans les possibilités de la mise en pages, pour affirmer une identité à la fois ethnique et religieuse en unifiant un peuple dans son histoire: pour lui et les siens, les Syriens monophysites sont les descendants des Araméens, qui se sont attachés au Christ sans tomber dans les erreurs des Grecs.

Il y a fort peu de textes de la littérature syriaque où transparaisse ainsi une conception du pouvoir et une réflexion sur l'histoire. Sans doute parce qu'il n'y a pas, dans les théologies syriaques, de pouvoir qui soit indépendant du déroulement de l'histoire organisée selon la disposition divine. Tout a été dit, par Moïse, David, les Prophètes, l'Apôtre. L'Écriture est d'abord une Parole, et son commentaire écrit est tout entier consacré à expliquer sa réalisation dans l'histoire.

J'ai trouvé dans un recueil syro-oriental, un texte particulièrement significatif de cette conception.[19] Il est difficile à dater, mais on peut suggérer qu'il appar-

---

[17] Jean-Baptiste Chabot, *Chronique de Michel le Syrien Patriarche jacobite d'Antioche, 1166–1199, éditée pour la première fois et traduite en français* (4 vols. en 7; Paris: Leroux, 1899–1910). La Chronique de Michel a été achevée en 1195 ap. J.-C.

[18] Ibid., 3:442.

[19] Il se trouve dans deux manuscrits datés du début du dix-huitième siècle, l'un du Vatican, l'autre de British Library; une édition critique avec une traduction annotée est en préparation.

tient aux textes utilisés dans le cercle du grammairien mystique nestorien du début du treizième siècle Jean bar Zuʻbi.[20]

Il s'agit du *Livre des Témoignages sur l'Économie du Christ*, ouvrage encore inédit, qui a été transmis avec la *Caverne des Trésors*, le *Livre de l'Abeille*, le *Testament d'Adam*, et l'*Apocalypse de Paul*. Il rassemble une grande quantité de citations et de traditions recueillies dans la Bible et plusieurs livres apocryphes, en montrant que celles-ci annonçaient les divers événements christologiques et de l'histoire chrétienne. Cette Économie commence à la Création. Ses divers moments sont annoncés par les prophètes de l'Écriture. L'histoire de l'humanité, de l'unité primordiale des hommes, lorsque ceux-ci parlaient une seule langue, le syriaque bien entendu, jusqu'à la dispersion, contribue à mettre en place l'institution centrale du salut: Israël, dont les vrais fils sont les chrétiens syriens de la Jérusalem nouvelle. Les juifs ayant refusé d'accueillir le Messie annoncé par les prophètes, les chrétiens sont les héritiers d'Abraham, père des nations. Ainsi, l'Église est-elle la Jérusalem nouvelle, pierre et tête des douze fleuves irriguant la Création. Il n'y a jusque-là rien de bien nouveau. La deuxième partie de cette histoire est plus originale. Elle rassemble plusieurs traditions pour montrer comment les annonces prophétiques se sont réalisées. Conformément à celles-ci, la venue du Christ s'est effectuée au cours du sixième millénaire, en l'an 5500. Les offrandes dont la *Caverne des Trésors* raconte qu'elles ont été placées au tombeau d'Adam, ont été rapportées par les rois perses, qui sont au nombre de dix, à la grotte de la Nativité. Cela inaugure les derniers temps. Là, la synthèse devient saisissante. En deux folios et demi, on parcourt l'*Histoire depuis le premier royaume du monde*, celui du grand chasseur antédiluvien, jusqu'au règne de l'empereur chrétien, responsable de la couronne et de la croix, chargé de remettre à Dieu le royaume à la fin des temps.

Avec Alexandre de Macédoine, Nemrod, l'arrière-petit-fils de Noé et fils de Koush est un personnage-clé de cette fresque. Sans doute parce que le livre de la Genèse en fait le fondateur de Babel, d'Akkad, de Ninive.[21] La *Caverne des Trésors* l'appelle le premier roi et raconte qu'il fit tisser en diadème l'image d'une couronne qu'il vit dans le ciel.[22] Le *Livre des Témoignages* développe fort intelligemment cette tradition pour montrer que la couronne est d'origine céleste, mais que le premier roi et ses successeurs n'en portent que la copie. Dans la *Caverne des Trésors*, le personnage de Nemrod est complexe. Il se fait initier à la sagesse et à l'écriture des révélations, c'est-à-dire l'astrologie et la magie démoniaque. Il est à l'origine du culte du feu et des mariages consanguins, mais il est aussi le constructeur de toutes les grandes villes de

---

[20] Sur Jean bar Zuʻbi, moine du couvent Sabrisho de Bet Qoqa, disciple de Simon de Shanqlawa, qui vivait autour de 1200, voir Anton Baumstark, *Geschichte der syrischen Literatur: mit Ausschluß der christlich-palästinensischen Texte* (Bonn: A. Marcus & E. Webers, 1922), 310–11 §50e.

[21] Gen 10:8–12.

[22] Caverne des Trésors 24.25 (éd. Su-Min Ri; *La Caverne des trésors: Les deux Recensions syriaques*; 2 vols.; CSCO 486 et 487, Scriptores Syri 207 et 208; Louvain: Peeters, 1987), 194–95, et traduction pp. 74–75.

l'Orient jusqu'à Nisibe, Édesse et Haran. Si Adam est le premier prophète, la première figure du Messie, Nemrod est le premier moment de l'histoire, comme s'il était un symbole où se concentrent la puissance royale, la sagesse de la première écriture et le surgissement des premières cités.

Le récit se poursuit: la couronne royale de Nemrod, demeurée sur la tête des Persans jusqu'à Darius le Mède, leur a été arrachée par Alexandre. Le voyage du grand roi vierge, résumé d'après l'*Apocalypse du Pseudo-Méthode de Patara*, lui permet de construire les portes pour protéger la terre contre Gog et Magog avant la fin des temps. C'est Alexandre qui transmet la couronne au roi des Romains chez qui elle demeure pour l'honneur de la sainte Croix.

L'audace est grande. Car enfin cette lecture de l'histoire fait de l'empereur chrétien l'héritier de toute l'histoire du monde et son dépositaire, l'aboutissement de toutes les annonces prophétiques. L'audace est d'autant plus grande que l'écriture de l'histoire permet au peuple de langue syriaque de se penser à l'origine antédiluvienne. L'entreprise est au fond semblable à celle de Michel le Syrien. On aimerait connaître exactement son auteur, car on ne mobilise pas ainsi, sans de profondes motivations, tant de prophéties et de traditions. Une histoire mondiale capable de rendre compte de toutes les péripéties des empires à la lumière d'une Écriture unique, a quelque chose d'effrayant, presque totalitaire. Heureusement, que dans le même *Livre des Témoignages*, les Sages nus (les fameux gymnosophistes) répliquent à Alexandre qui ne peut leur offrir l'immortalité: "Alors ta royauté n'est bonne à rien, ni ta puissance."

CHAPTER FIFTEEN

QUAND L'ÉVÊQUE ATHANASE SE PREND POUR L'ÉVANGÉLISTE LUC (*LETTRE FESTALE* XXXIX SUR LE CANON DES ÉCRITURES)

Éric Junod

Quiconque a à faire avec affaire à l'histoire du canon des Écritures chré-tiennes connaît la *Lettre festale* 39 d'Athanase ou du moins sa liste des 22 livres de l'Ancien Testament et des 27 livres du Nouveau Testament, sa distinction entre livres "canoniques" et livres "à lire" suivie de la liste de ces derniers. L'ordre et le contenu de ces listes, leurs particularités par rapport à d'autres documents antérieurs et contemporains, leurs liens avec la tradition alexan-drine, leurs similitudes avec le contenu du *Vaticanus*, le jugement prononcé contre les apocryphes ont déjà retenu l'attention.[1] Sans revenir sur ces élé-ments, j'aborderai une question apparemment mineure: pourquoi l'évêque Athanase a-t-il jugé opportun de faire précéder sa liste d'une imitation du pro-logue de l'évangéliste Luc (Luc 1:1–3)?

Athanase constituera ainsi le point de rencontre de deux champs d'études dans lesquels François Bovon apporte inlassablement une contribution majeure: l'œuvre de Luc et sa réception d'une part, la relation entre écrits canoniques et apocryphes d'autre part.

I. *Remarques générales sur la* Lettre festale *39*

Sa transmission

A la fin de 366 ou au début de 367, l'évêque Athanase, âgé d'environ 70 ans, envoie, comme tous les ans ou presque, une lettre aux Églises d'Égypte

---

[1] Parmi les études réservant une large place à la lettre d'Athanase, voir Joseph Ruwet, "Le canon alexandrin des Écritures. Saint Athanase," *Bib* 33 (1952): 1–29; Éric Junod, "La formation et la composition de l'Ancien Testament dans l'Église grecque des quatre premiers siècles," in *Le canon de l'Ancien Testament, sa formation et son histoire* (éd. Jean-Daniel Kaestli et Otto Wermelinger; MdB 10; Genève: Labor et Fides, 1984), 124–34; Bart D. Ehrman, "The New Testament of Didymus the Blind," *VC* 37 (1983): 1–21. Consulter par ailleurs les ouvrages de référence sur la formation du canon et sur la LXX; en particulier Albert C. Sundberg, *The Old Testament of the Early Church* (HTS 20; Cambridge: Harvard University Press, 1964); Sidney Jellicoe, *The Septuagint and Modern Study* (Oxford: Clarendon, 1968); Bruce M. Metzger, *The Canon of the New Testament: Its Origin, Development, and Significance* (Oxford: Clarendon, 1987).

qui se conclut par l'indication de la date de la prochaine fête pascale. Cette pratique égyptienne de la lettre festale donne aussi à l'évêque d'Alexandrie l'occasion de traiter de problèmes d'actualité touchant l'ensemble des communautés chrétiennes de l'Égypte.[2]

La collection des *Lettres festales* d'Athanase n'est pas conservée en grec, mais seulement, et de façon partielle, en syriaque et en copte.[3] Il subsiste, par cette double voie, d'importants extraits (en copte surtout) de la lettre 39, auxquels s'ajoutent des témoins en grec, en syriaque et en copte du passage sur le canon des Écritures; cette partie a en effet été très tôt détachée de la lettre et s'est transmise indépendamment de la collection.[4]

En simplifiant considérablement le problème, l'état de la base documentaire pour la lettre 39 est le suivant:[5] [*début manquant*]—extrait copte 1 (= 40 lignes)—[*lacune de 2 pages*]—extrait copte 2 (= 150 lignes): texte partiellement transmis aussi en grec et en syriaque (passage sur le canon)—[*lacune*]—extrait copte 3 (= 30 lignes avec *deux lacunes internes, respectivement de 12 et 16 lignes*)—[*lacune*]—extrait copte 4 (= 35 lignes): fin de la lettre (*à l'exception des tout derniers mots*).

Les inconvénients résultant de cette transmission indirecte et incomplète n'empêchent pas de repérer une structure qui s'apparente à celle des autres lettres athanasiennes.[6] S'il manque l'introduction, on retrouve l'essentiel de l'ample partie centrale, une brève exhortation, l'annonce des différentes dates suivie de la doxologie et d'une formule de salutation, enfin le début d'un postscriptum.

---

[2] Sur les *Lettres festales* d'Athanase, voir l'étude de Alberto Camplani, *Le lettere festali di Atanasio di Alessandria: Studio storico-critico* (Corpus dei manoscritti copti letterari; Roma: C. I. M., 1989), et Annik Martin, *Athanase d'Alexandrie et l'Église d'Égypte au IVe siècle (328–373)* (Collection de l'École française de Rome 216; Rome: École française de Rome, 1996), 156–71, 690–707.

[3] Voir Camplani, *Lettere festali di Atanasio*, 31–86.

[4] Voir ibid., 50–53. Je n'ai pas pu consulter l'étude de St. Sakkos, "Ἡ ΛΘ΄ ἑορταστικὴ ἐπιστολὴ τοῦ Μ. Ἀθανασίου," in *Τόμος ἑόρτιος χιλιοστῆς ἑξακοσιοστῆς ἐπετείου Μεγάλου Ἀθανασίου (373–1973)* (éd. G. Mantzarides; Thessaloniki: Aristoteleion Panepistemion Thessalonikes, 1974), 129–96, qui contient notamment une traduction du copte et une nouvelle édition de l'extrait grec sur le canon.

[5] Cet état ne tient pas compte des fragments syriaques, mais les différences textuelles entre le grec, le syriaque et le copte sont mineures. Pour le texte copte, voir L.-Theophile Lefort, *S. Athanase: Lettres festales et pastorales en copte* (2 vols. en 1; CSCO 150 et 151, Scriptores coptici 19 et 20; Louvain: Durbecq, 1955), 1:15–22, 58–62 (texte copte) et 2:31–40 (traduction française); pour le texte grec (extrait sur le canon transmis dans la collection des lettres canoniques officiellement reconnue au concile In Trullo), voir Pericles-Pierre Joannou, *Les canons des Pères grecs*, t. 2 de *Discipline générale antique, IVe–IXe siècles* (3 vols. en 4; Fonti: Pontificia commissione per la redazione del codice di diritto canonico orientale 9; Roma: Tipografia Italo-Orientale "S. Nilo," 1962–1964), 71–76. Dans la suite, nous nous référerons pour les extraits en copte à la traduction de Lefort et pour le passage transmis en grec à l'édition de Joannou (en retouchant sa traduction française).

[6] Sur la structure des lettres festales d'Athanase, voir Camplani, *Lettere festali di Atanasio*, 23.

Le message d'Athanase[7]

Le mouvement de la pensée dans la partie centrale, tel qu'on peut le reconstituer, est le suivant.

1) Le Christ est l'unique docteur et les Écritures livrent son enseignement parfait

Le Christ s'est manifesté comme le docteur. L'enseignement du culte de Dieu n'est pas une fabrication humaine; il vient du Seigneur qui révèle son Père à ceux qu'il aime. Il l'a révélé en premier à ses disciples, et aux apôtres, auxquels il a ordonné de proclamer ce qu'ils avaient appris de lui.

Seul le Christ est docteur par nature. Le propre des hommes est d'être instruits; cependant ils sont appelés à être docteurs, après qu'ils auront été disciples car toute science vient du Seigneur.

A l'inverse des Ariens et Mélitiens qui célèbrent la Pâque de façon sournoise, il faut la fêter selon les traditions de nos pères et lire les saintes Écritures qui suffisent à notre parfaite instruction.

2) Rappel des livres "canoniques" de l'Écriture et mention des autres livres "à lire"

Il est à craindre que des membres de l'Église ne se laissent égarer loin des Écritures et ne se mettent à lire des apocryphes, en se laissant induire par leur homonymie avec les livres authentiques. Il faut donc rappeler quels sont les livres saints. Suit l'énumération des livres des deux Testaments,[8] définis comme la source intégrale du salut; il n'y rien à y ajouter ou à y retrancher.

Dans un souci de précision, Athanase juge nécessaire d'ajouter qu'il existe d'autres livres qui ne sont pas "canonisés" (κανονιζόμενα), mais qui, selon l'usage reçu des pères, sont prescrits comme "à lire" (ἀναγινωσκόμενα) par ceux, nouvellement venus, qui veulent recevoir l'enseignement de la doctrine de la piété; il en dresse la liste.[9]

3) Les apocryphes

Nul apocryphe ne se trouve rappelé parmi les κανονιζόμενα et ἀναγινωσκόμενα. Ils sont une invention des hérétiques qui les ont composés et leur ont attribué de l'âge pour leur donner une apparence de vérité qui trompe les simples. Comment croire qu'il existe des livres d'Énoch alors qu'il n'y a pas d'Écriture

---

[7] Pour une mise en situation historique et une analyse de cette lettre, voir ibid., 275–79, et Martin, *Athanase d'Alexandrie et l'Église d'Égypte*, 598–600, 692–98.

[8] Dans l'ordre pour l'Ancien Testament: Gen, Exod, Lév, Nmbr, Deut, Jos, Jug, Ruth, 1–4 Royms (comptant pour deux livres), 1–2 Chr, Esdr-Néh, Ps, Prov, Qoh, Cant, Job, les douze Prophètes, Ésa, Jér (avec Bar, Lam et Ép Jer), Ézch, Dan. Pour le Nouveau Testament: Matt, Marc, Luc, Jean, Actes, Jac, 1–2 Pier, 1–3 Jean, Jude, Rom, 1–2 Cor, Gal, Éph, Phil, Col, 1–2 Thess, Héb, 1–2 Tim, Tite, Phlm, Apoc.

[9] Sagesse, Siracide, Esther, Judith, Tobie, la Didachè et le Pasteur.

avant Moïse, des apocryphes d'Ésaïe, lui qui ne parlait pas en cachette, des apocryphes de Moïse, lui qui proclama le Deutéronome?

Paul a dûment prédit que viendrait un temps où les hommes détourneraient leurs oreilles de la vérité (cf. 2 Tim 4:3–4). Les apocryphes ne sont effectivement que des fables, nées d'un esprit de dispute chez des hommes. Ils sont à rejeter. Et même si l'on y trouve un passage profitable, il vaut mieux ne pas s'y fier. . . . *[La lacune entre les extraits 2 et 3 et les lacunes internes à l'extrait 3 empêchent de bien saisir la suite du développement. Apparemment Athanase cherche à établir que jamais l'Écriture ne cite des apocryphes, ce qui l'amène à mentionner le cas de Paul dans 1 Cor 2:9.]* . . . Quand Paul dit "comme il est écrit" sans plus de précision, nous savons où cela est écrit dans l'Écriture. Ainsi la parole "ce que l'œil n'a pas vu" (1 Cor 2:9) se trouve-t-elle dans l'Écriture (cf. Ésa 64:3). Si elle figure dans les apocryphes, c'est que les hérétiques ont volé les mots de Paul.

L'instruction doit être fondée sur les paroles de l'Écriture, sauf pour les catéchumènes débutants encore incapables d'en appréhender les mystères et auxquels il faut d'abord apprendre à haïr le péché et s'écarter de l'idolâtrie.

4) Conclusion

Je n'ai pas écrit pour vous faire la leçon, conclut l'évêque, mais parce que j'ai entendu que les hérétiques, surtout les Mélitiens, se glorifient des apocryphes. Je vous ai appris ce que j'ai entendu de la bouche de mon père. Tenons-nous-en à l'Écriture. C'est ainsi que nous célébrerons la fête comme il convient.

Objectifs et effet

La nature du message transmis par Athanase n'offre rien d'inattendu. L'injonction à s'en tenir exclusivement à l'Écriture, l'énumération des livres saints, la condamnation des apocryphes sont des thèmes d'actualité dans les Églises d'Orient dans les années 350 et suivantes.[10]

Athanase affirme qu'en Égypte des apocryphes sont utilisés et diffusés par les Ariens et les Mélitiens, soit le couple traditionnel de ses adversaires. Un accent particulier est mis sur les Mélitiens qui se glorifient de leurs lectures.[11] En 357–358, dans son *Histoire des Ariens*, Athanase avait déjà dénoncé leur ignorance des Écritures chrétiennes.[12]

Pour éviter que des membres de l'Église n'en viennent à lire des écrits non scripturaires en pensant qu'ils le sont, Athanase donnera la liste exhaustive des livres κανονιζόμενα. Au-delà des hérétiques, il s'adresse ainsi à ceux qui

---

[10] Voir le dossier textuel réuni dans Kaestli et Wermelinger, éds., *Canon de l'Ancien Testament*, 140–50.

[11] A. Martin (*Athanase d'Alexandrie et l'Église d'Égypte*, 694–96) rattache cette accusation à l'usage par les Mélitiens d'hymnes non scripturaires dans la liturgie, usage dénoncé ultérieurement dans les *Canons d'Athanase*.

[12] Voir *H. Ar.* 78.1.

subissent leur influence, c'est-à-dire à des communautés monastiques et villa-geoises de la chôra qui, sans y voir nécessairement malice, recourent dans leurs assemblées à des livres placés frauduleusement sous le nom de personnages saints. Sa lettre pastorale répond manifestement à une carence d'information au sein de l'Église égyptienne.

En dénonçant l'usage des apocryphes, à quels textes Athanase pense-t-il? Il n'en désigne aucun, mais le fait qu'il mentionne les personnages d'Hénoch, Moïse et Ésaïe suggère qu'il vise des textes portant leur nom. On songera en particulier à l'*Ascension d'Ésaïe*, et cela pour deux raisons: le développement sur la mystérieuse "citation" scripturaire de Paul en 1 Cor 2:9 ("ce que l'œil n'a pas vu") dont on trouve un écho dans l'*Ascen. Ésa.* 11.34,[13] l'existence de plusieurs manuscrits coptes de cet ouvrage au quatrième siècle.[14] Toute autre hypothèse sur les livres visés (par exemple écrits gnostiques ou manichéens)[15] reste pure spéculation.

La lettre d'Athanase produisit un effet immédiat. L'année même de sa pu-blication, Théodore, qui dirigeait alors les communautés pachômiennes, en fit l'objet d'un enseignement à ses frères.[16] Il ordonna même qu'elle fût traduite en copte et placée dans le monastère "comme une loi" pour les frères.

Ce précieux témoignage, outre qu'il atteste l'autorité et l'influence d'Athanase en Égypte, confirme que la lettre festale répondait à un réel besoin dans des cercles chrétiens de la chôra, notamment dans les monastères pachômiens qui comptaient parmi les milieux les plus instruits et s'étaient sans doute dotés de bibliothèques.[17]

---

[13] Sur les variantes textuelles de l'*Ascension d'Ésaïe* 11.34, ses rapport avec 1 Cor 2:9 et d'autres textes, voir Enrico Norelli, *Ascensio Isaiae: Commentarius* (CCSA 8; Turhout: Brepols, 1995), 590–92. Intrigué par la "citation" de 1 Cor 2:9 qu'on ne retrouve nulle part dans l'Écriture, Origène (*Comm. Matt.* 5.29 sur Matt 23:37) l'avait attribuée à un apocryphe d'Élie ("in secretis Eliae"); de façon générale, Origène admettait que les évangélistes et les apôtres avaient emprunté des citations à des apocryphes (*Comm. Cant.* prol. 4.34). Athanase, pour sa part, rejette toute piste de ce genre: Si la phrase se retrouve dans un apocryphe, c'est que ses auteurs hérétiques l'ont dérobée à l'Écriture.

[14] Sur ces témoins coptes de l'*Ascension d'Ésaïe*, voir Tito Orlandi, "Gli Apocrifi copti," *Aug* 23 (1983): 59–61; notons que l'un d'eux fait partie d'une collection contenant des ouvrages rattachés à la tradition pachômienne. Selon Orlandi, l'*Ascension d'Ésaïe* aurait été traduite en copte au troisième siècle. Dans son étude il signale d'autres ouvrages apocryphes dont il existe des textes ou fragments coptes anciens, en particulier Hénoch (mais pas avant le sixième siècle).

[15] Camplani (*Lettere festali di Atanasio*, 278) exclut qu'Athanase s'en prenne par exem-ple aux ouvrages retrouvés à Nag Hammadi. De fait, rien dans sa lettre ne suggère une allusion à des traités gnostiques ou hermétiques.

[16] Cf. *Vie (bohaïrique) de Pachôme* 189 in *La Vie de saint Pachôme selon la tradition copte* (trad. Armand Veilleux; Begrolles en Mauge: Abbaye de Bellefontaine, 1984), 224–26.

[17] Sur les bibliothèques monastiques, notamment dans les cercles pachômiens, voir Harry Y. Gamble, *Books and Readers in the Early Church: A History of Early Christian Texts* (New Haven: Yale University Press, 1995), 170–74.

II. L'imitation (μίμησις) du Prologue de l'Évangéliste Luc

Athanase en quête de protections

Le ton de la lettre festale de 367 est ferme, et l'évêque n'hésite pas à parler en "je." Toutefois, en même temps qu'il engage son autorité, il paraît quérir de hautes protections. La formule qui conclut son message le montre bien:

> En fait je n'ai pas écrit ceci comme vous faisant la leçon, car je n'en suis pas arrivé à pareil niveau; mais, comme j'ai entendu que les hérétiques et surtout ces malheureux Mélitiens, se glorifiaient des livres apocryphes, voilà pourquoi tout ce que j'ai entendu de la bouche de mon père je vous l'ai appris. . . .[18]

Athanase se défend d'être un donneur de leçons. Son enseignement au sujet du corpus des Écritures n'est pas le sien, mais celui qu'il a appris de son père.

Alexandre, son prédécesseur, n'est pas la seule caution invoquée par Athanase. Dans le corps de la lettre, juste avant de donner la liste des écrits canoniques, il s'entoure de protections plus élevées: celles de l'apôtre Paul et surtout de l'évangéliste Luc. Examinons ce développement avant de nous demander pourquoi Athanase use de tant de précautions.

L'invocation de Paul comme première protection

Toute l'introduction d'Athanase à la liste des écrits saints est placée sous le signe du "rappel," ce qui ne manque pas d'apparaître comme paradoxal: si la mention de cette liste n'est rien d'autre que le rappel de ce qui est bien connu, pourquoi prendre tant de gants avant d'en venir au fait?

Dans une première phrase, Athanase explique pourquoi il lui faut "rappeler" quels sont les livres vrais. De façon explicite, il reprend à son compte des expressions de l'apôtre Paul:

> Mais puisque nous avons fait rappel (ἐμνήσθημεν) des hérétiques comme de gens morts, et de nous-mêmes comme de ceux qui possèdent pour leur salut les Écritures divines, et que *j'ai peur*, comme l'écrit Paul aux Corinthiens,[19] qu'un petit nombre de gens simples ne s'égarent *loin de la simplicité et de la pureté* du fait de *l'astuce* des hommes et qu'ils ne se mettent désormais à lire d'autres livres, appelés les apocryphes, parce qu'induits en erreur par leur homonymie avec les livres vrais, *supportez* (ἀνέχεσθε), je vous en prie, si vous êtes au courant au sujet de ces derniers, que moi aussi j'en fasse le rappel (μνημονεύων) par écrit pour la nécessité et le profit de l'Église.[20]

Le renvoi au début de 2 Cor 11—passage dans lequel Paul dit sa peur de voir les Corinthiens s'égarer en écoutant le premier prédicateur venu—ne

---

[18] La traduction de Lefort, *S. Athanase: Lettres festales et pastorales en copte*, 2:39.
[19] Cf. 2 Cor 11:3; et aussi 11:1, 4, etc. pour ἀνέχεσθε.
[20] Joannou, *Discipline générale antique*, 71.10–72.7.

manque pas de pertinence. S'appuyant le ἀνέχεσθε de Paul, Athanase demande à ceux qui sauraient déjà ce qu'il va énoncer de bien vouloir supporter qu'il le leur répète par écrit. Cet emploi de ἀνέχεσθε n'indiquerait-il pas aussi que, à l'instar de Paul réclamant qu'on supporte sa folie, Athanase prie à son tour qu'on supporte son téméraire rappel que seul justifie le bien de l'Église? La phrase suivante vient clairement à l'appui de cette hypothèse. Au lieu du rappel annoncé, elle signale un risque qui impose un détour.

Un rappel audacieux qui requiert une seconde protection

> Sur le point de les rappeler [μνημονεύειν], je vais recourir, en guise de soutien à ma propre audace [πρὸς σύστασιν τῆς ἐμαυτοῦ τόλμης], à la formule [τύπῳ] de l'évangéliste Luc, en disant moi aussi....[21]

Les raisons impératives qui conduisent Athanase à reprendre la formule de l'évangéliste Luc sont l'audace (τόλμη) de son entreprise et le besoin de lui donner une indiscutable protection (σύστασις). Dans le langage religieux, les mots de la famille de τολμάω désignent une démarche qui joue avec les limites du permis et souvent les transgresse. Ainsi ce qu'Athanase présente avec insistance comme un rappel représente aussi à ses yeux une authentique audace. Il recherche donc une σύστασις (un "soutien," une "garantie") dans le τύπος de "l'évangéliste Luc"; sans doute faut-il traduire ici par "formule," mais en se rappelant que le mot signifie aussi l'exemple. Ce sont en effet tout à la fois la phrase et l'attitude de Luc qu'il imite. Comme l'évangéliste et avec les mêmes mots que lui, il annonce solennellement une entreprise qu'il lui a paru bon de mener.[22]

La μίμησις du prologue de Luc

> **Puisque** certains *ont entrepris de composer* pour eux-mêmes ce que l'on appelle les apocryphes et de les mêler à l'Écriture divinement inspirée, au sujet de laquelle—*conformément à ce qu'ont transmis* aux pères *ceux qui sont devenus dès le début témoins oculaires et serviteurs de la parole*—nous avons pleine certitude, *il m'a paru bon, à moi aussi*, qui ai été exhorté par de vrais frères et qui l'ai appris *dès le début*, d'exposer les livres canonisés, transmis par la tradition, et crus comme divins, *afin que* chacun, s'il a été trompé, condamne ceux qui (l')ont égaré, et que celui qui est resté pur se réjouisse en se le voyant à nouveau rappeler (ὑπομιμνησκόμενος).
>
> Il y a donc en tout vingt-deux livres de l'Ancien Testament . . . [suit la liste]

---

[22] Martin Tetz ("Athanasius und die Einheit der Kirche," in idem, *Athanasiana: Zu Leben und Lehre des Athanasius* [éd. Wilhelm Geerlings et Dietmar Wyrwa; BZNW 78; Berlin: de Gruyter, 1995], 198–99) voit dans ce procédé une reprise de la παρῳδία et il signale un parallèle intéressant: au début de son *Apologie à Constance* (1), Athanase déclare reprendre à son compte les mots du bienheureux Paul (allusion à Actes 24:10); une "parodie" d'un type particulier puisqu'elle est dépourvue d'une intention humoristique ou ironique. Dans l'esprit d'Athanase, l'Écriture représente pour la prédication et la prière de l'Église un modèle et se prête donc à la pure et simple répétition.

Sans redouter la lourdeur, Athanase reprend fidèlement la structure compliquée de la phrase de Luc[23] et, autant qu'il le peut, les mots mêmes de l'évangéliste:

Athanase	Luc
Ἐπειδή πέρ τινες	[1:1] Ἐπειδήπερ πολλοὶ
ἐπεχείρησαν ἀνατάξασθαι	ἐπεχείρησαν ἀνατάξασθαι
ἑαυτοῖς τὰ λεγόμενα	διήγησιν περὶ τῶν
ἀπόκρυφα καὶ μῖξαι ταῦτα	πεπληροφορημένων ἐν ἡμῖν
τῇ θεοπνεύστῳ γραφῇ,	πραγμάτων,
περὶ ἧς ἐπληροφορήθημεν,	
καθὼς παρέδοσαν τοῖς πατράσιν οἱ	[1:2] **καθὼς παρέδοσαν** ἡμῖν οἱ
ἀπ' ἀρχῆς αὐτόπται καὶ	ἀπ' ἀρχῆς αὐτόπται καὶ
ὑπηρέται γενόμενοι τοῦ	ὑπηρέται γενόμενοι τοῦ
λόγου,	λόγου,
ἔδοξε κἀμοί,	[1:3] ἔδοξε κἀμοί,
προτραπέντι παρὰ γνησίων	παρηκολουθηκότι
ἀδελφῶν καὶ μαθόντι	
ἄνωθεν ἑξῆς ἐκθέσθαι τὰ	**ἄνωθεν** πᾶσιν ἀκριβῶς **καθεξῆς**
κανονιζόμενα καὶ παραδοθέντα,	σοι γράψαι,
πιστευθέντα τε θεῖα εἶναι	κράτιστε Θεόφιλε,
βιβλία,	
ἵνα ἕκαστος, εἰ μὲν	[1:4] **ἵνα** ἐπιγνῷς περὶ
ἠπατήθη, καταγνῷ τῶν	ὧν κατηχήθης λόγων τὴν
πλανησάντων, ὁ δὲ καθαρὸς	ἀσφάλειαν.
διαμείνας χαίρῃ πάλιν	
ὑπομιμνησκόμενος.	
Ἔστι τοίνυν....[24]	

La circonstance négative qui fonde l'intervention d'Athanase est le double fait que certains ont composé pour eux-mêmes des apocryphes et qu'ils les ont mêlés à l'Écriture divine. Influencé par la phrase de Luc, Athanase est conduit à mettre ici en cause "ceux qui ont composé." Sa volonté de coller au texte de l'évangéliste rend ensuite quelque peu maladroite la subordonnée rattachée à la proposition causale. Faute de pouvoir suivre son modèle en la liant à ce qui a été composé—ce seraient les apocryphes!—Athanase la rattache à l'Écriture pour souligner que, puisqu'elle a été transmise par "les témoins dès le début," elle est reçue avec une complète assurance. La mention des "pères" est importante; ils constituent le chaînon de la tradition entre les témoins du début et l'Église d'aujourd'hui.

---

[23] Je reprends la description que donne François Bovon de Luc 1:1–3; voir *L'Évangile selon saint Luc 1–9* (Commentaire du Nouveau Testament 3a; Genève: Labor et Fides, 1991), 35: une subordonnée causale introduite par ἐπειδήπερ, une subordonnée de la subordonnée introduite par καθώς, la proposition principale—solennelle où l'auteur parle à la première personne du singulier—enfin une proposition finale débutant par ἵνα. Bovon relève que chez Luc la subordonnée est une "fausse" causale.

[24] Joannou, *Discipline générale antique*, 72.11–26.

Cela étant, "il m'a paru bon à moi aussi." Si le "moi aussi" s'explique chez Luc qui écrit après d'autres, il sonne étrangement sous la plume d'Athanase. Que fait-il donc "lui aussi" que d'autres, selon ce qu'il aurait dit plus haut, auraient déjà fait? Sans doute veut-il laisser entendre que, comme les pères, il transmet à son tour. Dès ce ἔδοξε κἀμοί, les liens avec le texte de Luc, autres que purement structurels, deviendront toujours plus distants, l'entreprise menée par l'un et l'autre étant de nature bien différente. N'en finissant pas d'invoquer des raisons, Athanase mentionnera encore la pression exercée sur lui par de vrais frères et le fait que "dès le début"—rapprochement artificiel avec le texte de Luc—il a été enseigné.

Vient enfin l'annonce de ce qu'il va faire: "exposer, énumérer les livres κανονιζόμενα, transmis par la tradition, et crus comme divins"; il s'agit bien d'un rappel. Le terme juridique κανονιζόμενα, qui sera repris plus loin à deux reprises dans le cadre de la distinction entre livres canoniques et livres à lire (ἀναγινωσκόμενα) par les catéchumènes débutants, désigne ici des livres qui font loi "dès le début" au sein de l'Église. Athanase l'utilise comme un terme technique reçu, qui ne demande pas à être explicité.[25] Toutefois, s'il se référait à un catalogue consistant en un document ecclésiastique dûment consigné et conservé à Alexandrie, il ne manquerait pas de l'indiquer.

Le dernier élément de la phrase indique l'effet bénéfique de l'exposition des livres saints tant pour les chrétiens abusé par les hérétiques et leurs apocryphes que pour ceux qui sont restés à l'abri de cette contamination. Dans ces deux cas, la communauté sera affermie autour de la seule Écriture, dont l'évêque finira par dire de quels livres elle est constituée.

III. La Signature de l'Évêque de la Communauté d'Alexandrie

Comme Luc, Athanase dit à sa façon ce qui lui a été transmis oralement

Athanase se livre à cette μίμησις du prologue de Luc—un texte programmatique s'il en est: le seul texte évangélique dans lequel un auteur parle à la première personne du singulier pour présenter et justifier son propre récit— parce qu'il est lui aussi amené à exposer quelque chose qui n'existe pas sous la forme sous laquelle il le transmettra. Mais pour autant, à l'instar de l'évangéliste, il n'innovera pas; il se bornera à rapporter ce qui a été fidèlement transmis. Il s'agit bien d'un rappel, toutefois ce qui est rappelé n'a jamais existé sous la forme du catalogue présenté. Athanase fixe la mémoire de ce qui comportait alors une part d'indéterminé.

---

[25] Il s'agit cependant de la première attestation de ce verbe en référence avec les livres scripturaires. Sur l'histoire des mots κανών, κανονικός et κανονίζειν, voir Metzger, *Canon of the New Testament*, 289–93.

La 39e lettre festale prescrit une règle pour toute l'Église d'Égypte. Elle trace sans appel, sans hésitation, sans nulle discussion savante sur le statut ou la réception de tel ou tel livre, la limite d'un corpus saint de l'Ancien Testament et du Nouveau Testament. En même temps, mais sans s'attarder sur ce point, elle définit en négatif le monde des apocryphes: tout écrit qui, bien que portant le nom d'écrivains et de héros de l'Écriture, est absent de la liste.

Un canon égyptien traditionnel, marqué par la signature de l'évêque d'Alexandrie

Évêque expérimenté, Athanase ne peut être pris au dépourvu face au sujet qu'il aborde dans la lettre festale de 367. Le κανών est une notion qui lui est familière.[26] Et l'on sait qu'antérieurement, durant son séjour en Occident, il a fourni, à la demande de l'empereur Constant, des πυκτία τῶν θείων γραφῶν,[27] ce qui l'a conduit à délimiter un corpus des Écritures. Du reste, parmi les livres mentionnés dans le canon de la lettre festale, il n'en est aucun dont la présence soit de nature à scandaliser les chrétiens d'Alexandrie et sans doute de la chôra. Jusque dans son inclusion de l'Apocalypse, le canon d'Athanase est respectueux d'une tradition propre à l'Égypte.

La hardiesse de son entreprise se limiterait-elle alors à tracer par écrit une délimitation déjà bien établie des Écritures? Non. Son instruction comporte quelque chose de tranchant qui, bien que traditionnel, porte la marque spécifique de l'évêque de la communauté alexandrine. Ce quelque chose consiste en deux éléments conjoints: la définition d'un canon "restreint" et l'énumération, après ce canon restreint, d'une seconde liste, elle aussi close et présentée comme traditionnelle, de livres "à lire" dans l'enseignement catéchétique.[28]

Les κανονιζόμενα d'Athanase constituent un canon restreint parce qu'ils n'incluent pas des livres dont les chrétiens d'Égypte, à commencer par Athanase lui-même, font usage en les présentant parfois comme scripturaires: par exemple la Sagesse de Salomon, le Siracide et Tobie.[29] En excluant du cercle défini et intangible des "sources du salut" certains livres jugés et utilisés comme scripturaires, Athanase crée inévitablement un trouble: s'agirait-il d'apocryphes?

Pour dissiper tout flou, il juge "nécessaire," sitôt après avoir traité des καν-

---

[26] Dans *Decr.* 18 (ouvrage écrit entre 351–355), Athanase signale que le Pasteur n'appartient pas au "canon" (μὴ ὂν ἐκ τοῦ κανόνος).

[27] Cf. *Apol. Const.* 4. Dans l'hypothèse indémontrable où il existerait un quelconque lien entre ces πυκτία et les codd. Vaticanus ou Sinaiticus, on relèvera que la collection scripturaire réunie dans chacun de ces codices dépasse le corpus des κανονιζόμενα de la lettre festale.

[28] Ces deux éléments, s'ils représentent l'originalité majeure de l'enseignement d'Athanase, ne sont pas les seuls à faire problème. La présence ou au contraire l'absence parmi les livres "à lire" de tels textes n'allait pas de soi; l'examen de ce point exigerait des développements qui ne trouvent pas leur place ici. A ce sujet voir Ruwet, "Le canon alexandrin des Écritures," 1–29, et Ehrman, "Didymus the Blind," 1–21.

[29] Cf. Ruwet, "Le canon alexandrin des Écritures," 9 n. 5; et Geoffrey Mark Hahneman, *The Muratorian Fragment and the Development of the Canon* (Oxford Theological Monographs; Oxford: Clarendon, 1992), 80 nn. 13 et 14.

ονιζόμενα, de fournir une explication à leur propos. Il en donne également une liste et il attribue à ce second groupe de livres un nom et un statut particuliers qui les intègrent à la vie et à l'enseignement de l'Église.

Mais pour plus d'exactitude il est nécessaire que j'ajoute aussi ceci par écrit, à savoir qu'il y a d'autres livres en dehors de ceux-là, qui ne sont pas canonisés, mais qui ont été définis par les pères comme à lire [τετυπωμένα δὲ παρὰ τῶν πατέρων ἀναγινώσκεσθαι] par ceux qui sont récemment entrés et qui veulent être catéchisés par l'enseignement de la piété: la Sagesse de Salomon et la Sagesse de Sirach et Esther et Judith et Tobie et la Didachè dite des apôtres et le Pasteur.[30]

L'existence de deux groupes distincts, les κανονιζόμενα et les ἀναγινωσκόμενα,[31] et la fonction spécifique attribuée au second constituent vraisemblablement des éléments traditionnels dans la communauté d'Alexandrie.[32] Dans leur substance sinon dans leur désignation et leur contenu exacts, elles sont déjà attestées chez Origène: celui-ci avait indiqué que certains des livres divins dispensent un enseignement moral, exotérique et simple, destiné aux débutants dans les études divines; ainsi Esther, Judith, Tobie et les préceptes de la Sagesse.[33]

On tiendra donc pour probable que dans l'instruction catéchétique pratiquée à Alexandrie les livres désignés par Athanase comme ἀναγινωσκόμενα constituaient l'armature de l'enseignement moral initial des catéchumènes.[34] Il est intéressant d'observer que sa liste n'inclut plus uniquement des ouvrages antérieurs à la venue du Christ, mais aussi la Didachè et le Pasteur.

En définissant un canon restreint, suivi d'un groupe clos de livres "à lire," Athanase cautionne et peut-être durcit une règle et une distinction sans doute reconnues à Alexandrie, et il l'impose à toute l'Égypte. Les groupes monastiques, les communautés urbaines et villageoises de la chôra ne pouvaient manquer d'être plus ou moins surpris d'apprendre que la Sagesse, par exemple,

---

[30] Joannou, *Discipline générale antique*, 75.14–25.

[31] Cf. les mots qui suivent immédiatement: "Cependant, bien-aimés, ni parmi les κανονιζόμενα, ni parmi ces ἀναγινωσκόμενα, il n'est fait mention de l'un des apocryphes" (ibid., 75.26–76.3).

[32] En revanche, cette distinction n'a pas cours en Palestine. Cyrille de Jérusalem, vers 350, avait énuméré une liste des livres des deux Testaments, de type elle aussi restreint, mais en qualifiant d'apocryphes ou de pseudépigraphes tous ceux qui n'y figuraient point (voir *Catech. illum.* 4.33–36). Rien ne prouve qu'Athanase ait connu la liste de Cyrille, et, de toutes façons, il parle en Égyptien à l'Église d'Égypte.

[33] Voir *Hom. Num.* 27.1. Cette distinction s'est sans doute imposée sous l'influence du judaïsme et de la différence existant entre le corpus de la Bible hébraïque et celui de la LXX: voir notamment Ruwet, "Le canon alexandrin des Écritures," 1–29; Sundberg, *Old Testament of the Early Church*, 138–42, 159; et Junod, "L'Ancien Testament dans l'Église grecque," 124–34.

[34] Athanase précise à la fin de sa lettre qu'il n'est pas question d'exposer aux catéchumènes débutants les paroles mystérieuses et voilées de l'Écriture, mais qu'il convient en revanche de leur apprendre à haïr le péché et à s'écarter de l'idolâtrie (voir la traduction de Lefort, *S. Athanase: Lettres festales et pastorales en copte*, 2:39); les ἀναγινωσκόμενα ont cette fonction propédeutique.

n'était pas un livre canonique, qu'il ne fallait pas utiliser de livres canoniques au début de la catéchèse, mais qu'il existait un groupe défini de textes "à lire" appropriés à cette première phase de l'instruction chrétienne, sans que les termes utilisés par l'évêque permettent de déterminer si l'on pouvait les utiliser comme des références dans un enseignement autre que catéchétique.[35]

Conclusion

Dans une situation de flottement au sein de l'Église d'Égypte sur l'appartenance de tels textes au nombre des livres saints—situation d'autant plus préoccupante que les Mélitiens font usage d'apocryphes et même les répandent— Athanase apporte une clarification sur les κανονιζόμενα, qui constituent à eux seuls et de façon parfaite les "sources du salut," et il met son Église en garde contre les apocryphes. Le bien-fondé de cette instruction est confirmé par l'écho immédiat que la lettre trouvera au sein du monachisme pachômien.

L'évêque d'Alexandrie, qui ne dispose pas de liste écrite des κανονιζόμενα, se réfère aux pères en général et en particulier à Alexandre. S'il se place résolument sous le signe de la mémoire et de la tradition, il ne peut ni ne veut dissimuler qu'il accomplit un acte audacieux, parce que sans précédent: la solennelle transmission par écrit des livres saints. Non sans habileté et aussi non sans raison, il tend à se prendre pour Luc dans le prologue de son évangile, puisque comme lui il expose la tradition sous une forme inédite.

Mais il va plus loin dans son audace, en définissant pour toute l'Église égyptienne un canon restreint et, hors de lui, mais à côté et sans le moindre rapport avec les apocryphes, un groupe de livres ἀναγινωσκόμενα appropriés aux catéchumènes débutants. Il fixe ainsi une distinction problématique, qui doit correspondre à une tradition alexandrine mais dont rien n'indique qu'ailleurs en Égypte elle était clairement établie dans les usages et les esprits.

---

[35] A Alexandrie même les deux listes d'Athanase ont peut-être été une source d'étonnement. Ehrman ("Didymus the Blind," 1–21) relève que Didyme n'utilise pas certains des textes rangés par Athanase dans les vingt-sept livres du *Nouveau Testament*, qu'il semble tenir pour canoniques Hermas, l'Épître de Barnabé, la Didachè et la première Épître de Clément, enfin qu'il ne fait pas état de la distinction entre écrits "canoniques" et "à lire."

PART FOUR

EARLY CHRISTIAN VOICES AND
ANCIENT INTERPRETATIONS

CHAPTER SIXTEEN

LE DÉVELOPPEMENT DES NARRATIONS PASCALES

Yves Tissot

μετὰ φόβου καὶ χαρᾶς μεγάλης
(Matt 28:8)

Si l'on m'avait demandé, il y a quelques années comment la tradition pascale
narrative s'était développée, j'aurais répondu qu'on a dû raconter d'abord les
christophanies en Galilée, que la découverte du tombeau vide est sans doute
une légende tardive, et que la réception de cette légende a permis à Luc de
situer sa christophanie à Jérusalem. Aujourd'hui, je dirais tout le contraire:
que la découverte du tombeau vide, avec la christophanie du soir qui en donne
le sens, représente la tradition la plus ancienne, tandis que la christophanie
en Galilée, annoncée par Marc et narrée par Matthieu, résulte d'un audacieux remaniement théologique de Marc.

A l'origine de ce revirement, une prédication sur Jean 20:1–10. En m'y préparant, j'ai été intrigué par une apparente maladresse du récit, car si le disciple bien-aimé ne devait *voir et croire* qu'au verset 8b, pourquoi lui avoir fait
entrevoir les linges au verset 5a déjà? En analysant de plus près les versets
3–8, il m'a semblé que le verset 5a avait pour fonction de disqualifier par
avance les linges en tant que signe pour la foi, si bien que *seul le suaire* (v. 7)
a dû frapper le disciple. Jean ne nous le décrit-il d'ailleurs pas *par opposition
aux linges* lorsqu'il nous dit qu'il n'était pas posé avec eux—ce qui explique
que le disciple n'ait pu le voir d'emblée, mais roulé à part—ce qui suggère
qu'on en avait pris un soin particulier? Avant ces précisions, il a tenu aussi
à relever que c'était là "le suaire *qui était sur sa tête.*" Qu'est-ce que cela pouvait donc bien signifier? Et voilà que soudain, je pensai au voile de Moïse,
ce voile que Moïse *ôtait* "lorsqu'il entrait devant Yahvé pour parler avec lui"
(Exod 34:34), si bien qu'à Pâques, j'expliquai hardiment à mes paroissiens
qu'à la vue du suaire laissé dans le tombeau, le disciple avait saisi que le
Seigneur était retourné définitivement auprès de Dieu.[1]

J'étais persuadé d'avoir touché juste. Cependant je m'étonnais de n'avoir
rien trouvé de pareil chez les auteurs que j'avais lus à la hâte. C'est pourquoi

---

[1] Y aurait-il une inclusion avec le prologue qui en 1:14, 16–18 paraît se référer à
Exode? Voir Anthony Tyrrell Hanson, "John 1.14–18 and Exodus 34," *NTS* 23 (1977):
90–101; H. Mowley, "John 1:14–18 in the Light of Exodus 33:7–34:35," *ExpTim* 95
(1983–1984): 135–37.

je décidai de lancer, deux mois plus tard, une série d'études bibliques sur les récits pascals. Je voulais notamment m'assurer que le verset 7 était rédactionnel. Or, en préparant ces études, j'ai été surpris de découvrir que les exégètes s'intéressaient au fond assez peu à ce verset, mais rassuré aussi de me découvrir deux précurseurs au moins.

En 1973, William E. Reiser a souligné que l'intrigue des versets 3–8 désigne le suaire seul comme signe ayant conduit le disciple bien-aimé à la foi.[2] Il estimait que Jean avait voulu établir ainsi un contraste avec le suaire qui recouvrait toujours le visage de Lazare à sa sortie du tombeau (cf. Jean 11:44). Mais B. Osborn lui a répondu non sans raison que son interprétation était insuffisante, car elle n'explique pas pourquoi le suaire seul est un signe, à l'exclusion des linges.[3]

Indépendamment de Reiser, Sandra M. Schneiders est revenue sur la question en 1983, dans un article remarquable, quoique assez peu remarqué. Elle observe à son tour que, d'après les versets 3–8, le suaire seul a valeur de signe, mais pour en saisir la symbolique, elle s'est référée de façon originale à Exod 34:33–35:

> Like Moses, who put aside the veil when he ascended to meet God in glory, Jesus, the New Moses, has put aside the veil of his flesh as he ascends into the presence of God to receive from him that glory which he had with the Father before the world was made (cf. Jn 17:5). But, unlike Moses who reassumed the veil each time he returned from God to the people, the New Moses has definitively laid aside the veil, for now he is no more in the world, but has gone to the Father (cf. Jn 17:11).[4]

Pour légitimer cette lecture, Schneiders relevait aussi que les targums d'Exode 34 désignent le voile de Moïse par le terme *sudara*—une remarque qui prend tout son poids si on la rapproche de cette autre, faite par Xavier Léon-Dufour: la terminologie de Jean est inhabituelle, puisqu'il est le premier à parler de σουδάριον en contexte funéraire![5]

Un point cependant me chicanait encore: la plupart des exégètes consultés

---

[2] William E. Reiser, "The Case of the Tidy Tomb: The Place of the Napkins of John 11:44 and 20:7," *HeyJ* 14 (1973): 47–57, esp. 51: "We can only assume that because he did not believe when he looked in and saw the cloths but came to believe only after getting inside and noting the cloths *and* the napkin in its place apart, the napkin was instrumental in his coming to faith."

[3] B. Osborn, "A Folded Napkin in an Empty Tomb: John 11:44 and 20:7 Again," *HeyJ* 14 (1973): 437–40: "An analysis of this kind cannot be completely satisfactory, however, for though it can show that the napkins function as signs in both narratives . . ., it can say nothing more about *why* a napkin should be able to function as a sign in these situations than that it is in some sense a 'natural' symbol" (437). Osborn lui-même propose d'interpréter Jean 20:7 par Ésa 25:7 (targ.).

[4] Sandra M. Schneiders, "The Face Veil: A Johannine Sign (John 20:1–10)," *BTB* 13 (1983): 94–97, esp. 96. La valeur symbolique du voile (cf. 2 Cor 3: 7–18) est aussi suggérée par Bruno Bonnet-Eymard (1986) et par Réné Robert (1988); voir Xavier Léon-Dufour, *Lecture de l'Évangile selon Jean* (4 vols.; Parole de Dieu; Paris: Seuil, 1988–1996), 4:210.

[5] Ibid., 4:209.

tenaient le verset 7 pour traditionnel. Certes, cela n'invalidait pas mon exégèse, mais pour l'étayer, il eût été évidemment préférable qu'il fût rédactionnel! Or sur cette question, Reiser et Schneiders étaient plutôt discrets. Le premier remarquait bien que si Luc 24:12, où il n'est question que des linges, provenait d'une tradition pré-johannique, le suaire ajouté en Jean 20:7 ne pouvait qu'avoir un sens spécifique—mais il y avait un *si*. Quant à Schneiders, elle récusait vertement le témoignage de Luc 24:12—une glose tardive! Il me fallait donc aller y voir de plus près, et c'est ainsi que j'ai senti peu à peu vaciller tout ce que je croyais savoir des traditions pascales.

La tradition lucano-johannique

A tout seigneur, tout honneur! Commençons par le cas de Luc 24:12. Ce verset a longtemps paru suspect, car

a) il est absent d'une partie de la tradition manuscrite (D it);
b) il semble mal venu dans son contexte actuel, puisque la visite des femmes au tombeau s'achève sur le refus des disciples de croire à leur témoignage (v. 11)—ce que dément la démarche même de Pierre;
c) il paraît contredit par Luc 24:24, où Cléophas évoque la visite de plusieurs disciples (τινὲς τῶν σὺν ἡμῖν) au tombeau;
d) il comporte un présent historique (βλέπει), forme que Luc évite d'ordinaire, et des termes non lucaniens qui apparaissent en revanche dans le récit parallèle de Jean: παρακύπτειν, ὀθόνια (et non σινδών comme en Luc 23:53).

Pour toutes ces raisons, on y voyait donc une glose tardive inspirée de Jean 20:3–10—sans trop se demander d'ailleurs comment le récit complexe de Jean avait pu être résumé à ce point! Cependant, l'authenticité de ce verset est aujourd'hui communément admise, car

a) il est attesté par des témoins de valeur et, très anciennement, par 𝔓[75];
b) son disparate avec le contexte vient de ce que Luc opère une transition délicate entre Marc qu'il a suivi jusque là et une autre source (cf. *infra*);
c) il est présupposé par le v. 24, qui n'est formulé au pluriel que par assimilation au v. 22 (γυναῖκές τινες ἐξ ἡμῶν);[6]
d) les termes non lucaniens ne sont pas davantage johanniques, car Jean n'y recourt lui-même qu'en 20:3–10 ou dans les abords immédiats de ce texte, soit en 20:11 pour παρακύπτειν et en 19:40 pour ὀθόνια; en revanche, on trouve en Luc 24:12 des traits typiquement lucaniens comme le participe auxiliaire ἀναστάς (2/6/**17**/0/**19**), θαυμάζειν (8/4/**13**/6/**5**; + acc: 0/0/**2**/1/**1**), τὸ γεγονός (0/1/**4**/0/**3**), ce qui donne à penser que Luc a remanié un texte qui avait primitivement la forme suivante:

---

[6] John Muddiman, "A Note on Reading Luke XXIV, 12," *ETL* 48 (1972): 542–48, esp. 547.

> Or Pierre . . . courut au tombeau
> et, s'étant penché, il voit les linges seuls,
> et il s'en revint chez lui. . . .

Ce texte, tiré d'un document que je désignerai par le sigle *P*, correspond à Jean 20:3, 5a, 10. Serait-il donc la source directe de Jean 20:3–10?

La plupart des exégètes conviennent que Jean a remanié ici un récit où il n'était d'abord question que de Pierre. Les indices relevés en ce sens sont les suivants:

a) le redoublement inhabituel de la préposition πρός au v. 2 suggère que les termes "et vers l'autre disciple, celui que Jésus aimait" sont secondaires;
b) la formulation du v. 3, avec un premier verbe au singulier et le second au pluriel, est certes possible en grec, mais elle surprend;
c) le v. 6b reprend le v. 5a, quoique avec un autre sujet;
d) la foi du disciple bien-aimé au v. 8 est sans effet sur la suite du récit, puisqu'il finit par s'en aller avec Pierre comme si de rien n'était.

On relève aussi souvent, mais à tort selon moi (cf. *infra*), une incohérence entre les versets 8 et 9, en faisant valoir que l'ignorance d'un certain texte annonçant la résurrection ne saurait expliquer (notez bien le γάρ!) la foi du disciple.

Pour retrouver le fonds traditionnel du récit de Jean, il ne suffit pourtant pas d'omettre tout ce qui concerne le disciple bien-aimé, car Luc 24:12 montre que Jean lui a attribué au verset 5a un trait qui à l'origine concernait Pierre. Aussi la plupart des exégètes préfèrent-ils s'en tenir au critère suivant: sont rédactionnels les passages qui évoquent d'une manière ou d'une autre la rivalité des deux disciples, soit les versets 4:5b–6:8a. Jean aurait donc connu une forme amplifiée de *P* (= Proto-Jean), comprenant déjà les versets 7, 8b* ("et il vit et il s'étonna"), et 9. Mais à mon avis, rien n'est moins sûr.

Pour soutenir le caractère traditionnel du verset 8b, on relève volontiers sa formulation au singulier, en faisant valoir que, confrontés aux mêmes indices dans le tombeau, les deux disciples ont dû croire selon Jean. Ainsi Hartmann: "Er muß jetzt beide Jünger meinen, denn die Konkurrenz zwischen Petrus und dem Lieblingsjünger ist in v. 4f. dargestellt, nicht mehr in v. 8."[7] Mais cette interprétation, qui présume que les linges ont gardé chez Jean la fonction apologétique qu'ils avaient sans doute en *P*, est évidemment erronée, car la finalité de la compétition entre les deux disciples n'apparaît qu'au verset 8 lorsque, à peine entré dans le tombeau, le bien-aimé croit, à la différence de Pierre. Ainsi donc, Jean n'a pas remanié l'épisode de l'inspection du tombeau en y insérant une petite digression sur la valeur respective des deux disciples, mais il a recouru à la thématique de leur rivalité pour mettre en relief le signe du suaire que seul le bien-aimé a su percevoir. Par ailleurs, il faut avouer que "et il vit" serait bien redondant après le verset 5a ("il voit les linges"); il ne

---

[7] G. Hartmann, "Die Vorlage des Osterberichte in Joh 20," *ZNW* 55 (1964): 202. Voir aussi Rudolf Bultmann, *Das Evangelium des Johannes* (10ᵉ éd.; Göttingen: Vandenhoek & Ruprecht, 1968), 530.

pourrait se justifier (et encore!) que comme une reprise après le long verset 7—pour autant bien sûr que ce verset ait déjà figuré dans la source! Quant à la conjecture selon laquelle le Proto-Jean aurait parlé de l'étonnement de Pierre au vu des linges, elle est bien improbable puisqu'elle s'inspire d'une retouche *lucanienne* de Luc 24:12. Je tiens donc pour ma part le verset 8 pour entièrement rédactionnel.

Qu'en est-il maintenant du verset 9? Ce verset est difficile à comprendre chez Jean, car on ne voit ni en quoi il explique (γάρ!) la foi du bien-aimé, ni pourquoi il est formulé au pluriel. Bien des exégètes y sentent comme un léger reproche à l'adresse du disciple, qui aurait dû croire sans même voir les linges, du moment qu'une certaine écriture annonçait la résurrection du Seigneur— à moins que ce ne soit une excuse rappelant que, pour croire, il lui avait bien fallu voir les linges, attendu que ni lui ni personne n'avait encore repéré ladite écriture. Persuadés que Jean avait cherché à nous décrire, tout au long du chapitre 20, "la genèse progressive de la foi pascale,"[8] d'autres pensent que la foi du disciple était encore imparfaite: ignorant l'écriture qui annonçait la résurrection, comment aurait-il pu songer en effet *à une résurrection?* Tout ce qu'il a pu croire au tombeau, c'est qu'il se trouvait "devant un mystère de l'action de Dieu."[9] La difficulté d'interpréter le verset 9 dans son contexte actuel a amené d'autres exégètes encore à y voir une glose tardive.[10] Ou au contraire un trait traditionnel, ce verset devant à l'origine excuser l'incompréhension de Pierre; mais c'est là reculer simplement le problème car, à moins d'opter avec Leaney pour la leçon ᾔδει (ℵ* it),[11] qui est manifestement secondaire, le pluriel ᾔδεισαν reste inexpliqué.

Pour ma part, j'estime que le verset 9 est rédactionnel. J'en veux pour preuve d'une part sa similitude avec les prolepses de 2:22 et 14:26 où l'on trouve le même vocabulaire "synoptique," mais surtout le fait que, tout en reformulant ensuite le verset 10 au pluriel, Jean a dû le retoucher sur deux autres points encore:

a) au simple δέ de *P* (cf. Luc 24:12), il a substitué un οὖν qui, n'ayant pas de fonction logique, semble indiquer comme souvent qu'il renoue avec sa source après y avoir inséré un passage de son cru;

b) il a surtout explicité le sujet en fin de phrase, en ajoutant termes οἱ μαθηταί; or cette précision n'aurait guère de sens si plus haut le verbe ᾔδεισαν concernait déjà Pierre et son compagnon; ce n'est donc pas d'eux particulièrement qu'il est question au v. 9: ᾔδεισαν est un pluriel impersonnel.

L'interprétation du verset 9 doit donc tenir compte des données suivantes: les versets 8 et 9 sont tous deux rédactionnels; la particule γάρ indique qu'ils sont en rapport étroit l'un avec l'autre, mais elle n'a évidemment pas ici de sens

---

[8] Ignace de la Potterie, "Genèse de la foi pascale d'après Jn 20," *NTS* 30 (1984): 27.
[9] Ibid., 31.
[10] Ainsi Bultmann, *Evangelium des Johannes*, 530–31.
[11] A. R. C. Leaney, "The Resurrection Narratives in Luke (xxiv.12–53)," *NTS* 2 (1955–1956): 113.

causal; le pluriel impersonnel du verset 9 montre enfin que Jean ne cherche ni à blâmer ni à excuser le disciple bien-aimé. En fait, il n'a pu que le louer d'avoir cru (v. 8b) *alors même que* personne ne connaissait encore ladite écriture (v. 9)! La seule difficulté du verset réside donc dans l'emploi de la particule γάρ, mais elle se résout, si la on rapporte à une réflexion implicite: "Il vit et il crut [ce qui était étonnant], *car* on ne savait pas encore l'écriture . . ." (Jean 20:8–9).[12] Quoi qu'il en soit du verset 7, le Proto-Jean avait donc un texte identique à celui de celui de *P*. Cela étant, je vois mal ce qui aurait pu l'inciter à mentionner le suaire en plus des linges, et à nous en donner une description si élaborée. Il faut beaucoup de naïveté pour imaginer que, même en disposant d'informations complémentaires, il ait pu gloser le texte de *P* pour lui donner la forme suivante: "Pierre courut au tombeau et, s'étant penché, il voit les linges *posés et le suaire qui était sur sa tête, non pas posé avec les linges, mais roulé à part dans un endroit*, et il s'en revint chez lui." En effet, cette description qui oppose le suaire aux linges n'a de sens que si cette opposition a une fonction narrative. Or cela n'apparaît que dans le récit de Jean, où l'énigme du tombeau apparemment violé (v. 2) trouve sa résolution dans la foi du disciple bien-aimé (v. 8) *grâce au signe du suaire*. Il est significatif en effet de voir que, sans raison contraignante, Jean a transféré le verset 5a de Pierre (cf. Luc 24:12) à l'autre disciple—alors qu'il aurait pu tout simplement écrire: "*L'autre disciple, plus rapide que Pierre, vint le premier au tombeau, mais il n'y entra pas. Pierre vint à son tour*, il entra dans le tombeau et il voit les linges *posés et le suaire*." Or, au lieu de cela, il a tenu

a) à nous préciser que, même si le bien-aimé a pu voir les linges de l'extérieur, il lui a fallu entrer dans le tombeau pour être à même, comme Pierre, d'y remarquer la présence du suaire "roulé à part";
b) à créer un contraste entre le v. 5 où le bien-aimé ne réagit pas à la vue des linges, et le v. 8 où ce qu'il voit, à peine entré dans le tombeau, le pousse à croire,

d'où il découle que seul le suaire a compté pour lui. Tous les incidents de la course des deux disciples convergeant vers cette conclusion, le verset 7 doit être tenu pour rédactionnel. Autrement dit, la source de Jean 20:3–10 n'était autre que le texte de *P*,[13] et la métamorphose[14] s'est faite en un seul coup.

---

[12] Cf. Walter Bauer, *Griechisch-deutsches Wörterbuch zu den Schriften des Neuen Testaments und der übrigen urchristlichen Literatur* (5ᵉ éd.; Berlin: Töpelmann, 1958), s.v. γάρ 1e: "Häufig ist d. zu begründende Gedanke nicht ausgesprochen, sondern aus d. Zshg. zu erg" (col. 301). Le γάρ de Marc 16:4b a la même valeur: "elles virent que la pierre avait été roulée de côté, (ce qui était surprenant) car elle était fort grande!"

[13] Frans Neirynck, "The Uncorrected Historic Present in Lk xxiv.12," *ETL* 48 (1972): 548–53, estime que la source de Jean n'était pas *P*, mais Luc 24:12 "as a redactional doublet of the traditional visit to the tomb of xxiv.1–9, par. Mk xvi.1–8" (550); voir aussi idem, "John and the Synoptics," in *L'Évangile de Jean: Sources, rédaction, théologie* (éd. M. de Jonge; BETL 44; Gembloux: Duculot; Louvain: Leuven University Press, 1977), 73–106, esp. 98–104. Cette hypothèse me paraît insoutenable, car Pierre appa-

Il est bien évident que le petit récit de *P* n'était pas une tradition isolée, et rien que sa forme le révèle: "Pierre *courut* au tombeau." Cette précipitation de Pierre n'a de sens en effet que s'il a été informé que quelque chose d'insolite y avait été remarqué.[15] Pour savoir comment *P* racontait l'événement qui l'a mis en émoi, on ne peut évidemment pas compter sur Luc, qui suit ici le récit de Marc 16:1–8. On notera cependant qu'en situant la préparation des aromates non plus à l'issue du sabbat (Marc 16:1), mais le vendredi soir déjà (Luc 23:56a), Luc a remanié Marc de telle sorte que le premier acte du jour pascal est chez lui, comme chez Jean, le départ des femmes pour le tombeau, et que leur introït pascal est le même: τῇ δὲ μιᾷ τῶν σαββάτων.[16] Est-ce un hasard?

Oui, répondront la plupart des exégètes, car Jean 20:1 est le début d'un autre récit, celui de la christophanie à Marie! C'est là en fait un préjugé tenace qui égare la recherche depuis qu'en 1908, Wellhausen a affirmé que l'épisode de la course des disciples au tombeau (= **T**) s'était surajouté au récit de l'apparition du Seigneur à Marie (= **M**), "denn in Vers 11 steht sie noch auf dem selben Fleck wie in 1."[17] Mais l'argumentation de Wellhausen est assez déconcertante: tout ce qu'il trouve à dire, c'est que cet épisode burlesque, qui cherche à déposséder Marie de son privilège pascal, n'a vraiment rien à faire ici, et qu'il suffit d'omettre les versets 2–10, ainsi d'ailleurs que les deux anges du verset 12, pour retrouver l'évangile dans sa splendeur première.

Tout a bien changé depuis. **M** nous apparaît comme un récit complexe, surchargé, et il semble même chimérique d'y vouloir isoler un noyau traditionnel, tant les versets 11a, 14–18 relatifs à la christophanie sont truffés de traits johanniques. Quant à **T**, la réhabilitation de Luc 24:12 nous a permis d'y voir un récit traditionnel, très sobre avant sa métamorphose johannique. Tout a donc changé, sauf le décret de Wellhausen: le verset 1 se poursuit au

---

raît en retrait sur deux points par rapport aux femmes: d'une part, il n'est pas dit clairement qu'il est entré dans le tombeau—même si Neirynck a montré que le participe παρακύψας n'exclut pas qu'il l'ait fait (voir idem, "ΠΑΡΑΚΥΨΑΣ ΒΛΕΠΕΙ. Lc 24,12 et Jn 20,5," *ETL* 53 [1977]: 133–52); d'autre part, faute d'angélophanie, il en repart penaud.

[14] Il va sans dire que je ne partage pas du tout l'avis d'Alfred Loisy, pour qui "cette course de Pierre et du disciple, avec ses petits détails et ses sous-entendus, est une invention subtile, aussi médiocre de conception que celle qui fait obtenir de Jésus par le disciple bien aimé la désignation du traître (XIII, 23–26)" (*Le Quatrième Évangile* [2ᵉ éd.; Paris: Nourry, 1921], 501).

[15] Gérard Claudel, *La confession de Pierre: Trajectoire d'une péricope évangélique* (EBib² 10; Paris: Gabalda, 1988), 80.

[16] Frans Neirynck (*Jean et les Synoptiques. Examen critique de l'exégèse de M. E. Boismard* [BETL 49; Louvain: Peeters, 1979], 73) cherche à minimiser cette rencontre en observant que le δέ est initial chez Jean, mais alternatif chez Luc (qui a μέν en 23:56b). C'est exact, mais ça n'empêche pas qu'après avoir déplacé Marc 16:1, Luc aborde le récit des événements du matin de Pâques de la même façon que Jean, alors que Marc 16:2 lui offrait une fort belle entrée: καὶ λίαν πρωῒ τῇ μιᾷ τῶν σαββάτων. . . .

[17] Julius Wellhausen, *Evangelienkommentare* (Berlin/New York: de Gruyter, 1987), 91 [691].

verset 11! On s'est en effet contenté d'adapter sa thèse, en présentant **T** non
plus comme une excroissance de **M**, mais comme un récit traditionnel *interpolé* en **M**, grâce à la suture du verset 2.

Le cas de cette "suture" est intéressant à suivre. Selon Wellhausen, son
auteur s'est inspiré de la plainte de Marie au verset 13 pour la composer,
sans prendre garde au fait que, pour se plaindre de la disparition du corps,
Marie aurait dû d'abord se pencher dans le tombeau (cf. vv. 11b, 12b)! Or
là aussi, la réhabilitation de Luc 24:12 a changé la donne, en montrant que
ce geste de Marie était en fait emprunté à **T** (cf. v. 5). Dès lors, pour porter
le coup de grâce à l'angélophanie (vv. 11b–13) que beaucoup trouvaient
gênante, on s'est mis à défendre l'originalité du verset 2, en soulignant que,
puisque Marie allait seule au tombeau dans le récit de base, jamais un rédacteur n'aurait changé en οὐκ οἴδαμεν le οὐκ οἶδα du verset 13b. Loin d'être une
suture, le verset 2 était donc constitutif de **T** et le pluriel employé par Marie
montrait que ce récit commençait, comme chez les synoptiques, par la visite
des femmes au tombeau. Et le plus souvent on s'est arrêté là, comme paralysé
par le décret de Wellhausen! Mais si le verset 2 n'est pas une suture, et si de
plus il présuppose la venue des femmes au tombeau, pourquoi vouloir obstiné-
ment que **T** ait été interpolé entre les versets 1 et 11–13 de **M**? Pourquoi ne
pas rattacher tout simplement le verset 1 à **T**?

La critique de Jean 20:1–2 donnerait alors ceci: au verset 2b, οὐκ οἴδαμεν
montre qu'à l'origine Marie n'était pas seule à venir au tombeau, et donc que
les versets 1–2a ont été secondairement focalisés sur elle quand **M** a été ajouté
à **T**. A l'inverse, le disciple bien-aimé est une addition de Jean. Sont par
ailleurs reconnus comme rédactionnels les termes σκοτίας ἔτι οὔσης (v. 1) le
nom Σίμωνα et la correction du pronom αὐτῷ en αὐτοῖς (v. 2). J'incline à
penser en outre que la présence de οὖν au début du verset 2 indique une
retouche, sans doute l'addition initiale du verbe τρέχει, emprunté à l'épisode
suivant de la course au tombeau.[18] D'où la reconstitution suivante du texte
de *P*:

> Or le premier jour de la semaine,
> Marie de Magdala <et *d'autres*>
> vont tôt . . . au tombeau
> et elles voient la pierre enlevée du tombeau.
> . . . elles viennent vers . . . Pierre . . .
> et lui disent: "Ils ont enlevé le Seigneur du tombeau
> et nous ne savons pas où ils l'ont mis."
> Or Pierre . . . courut au tombeau
> et, s'étant penché, il voit les linges seuls,
> et il s'en revint chez lui. . . .

---

[18] Antonio Ammassari, *La Risurrezione nell'insegnamento, nella profezia, nelle apparizioni di
Gesù* (2 vols.; Rome: Citta nuova, 1975–1976), 1:88, n'est pas du tout convaincant
lorsqu'il estime qu'au v. 2, "il redattore ha aggiunto 'al correre,' 'l'andare' per colle-
gare meglio questo verso al precedente, dove Maria Maddalena 'va' semplicemente."

"Récit sobre et sans merveilleux," commente Benoit qui en tirait la conclusion que le fait du tombeau vide a été "d'abord raconté pour lui-même,"[19] sans intention théologique. Son étude, remarquable à plus d'un titre, a été accueillie assez fraîchement, car comment "admettre l'existence d'une tradition qui se serait contentée de rapporter le fait brut de la découverte du tombeau vide"?[20] "Y a-t-il jamais eu de *récit* concernant le tombeau de Jésus sans qu'il ait été éclairé de quelque façon par la foi en la résurrection?"[21]

Pour répondre à ces critiques, Gérard Claudel a proposé de ranger Jean 20:3–10 parmi les récits d'enlèvement qui développent "le thème de la disparition et de la quête déceptive du héros disparu";[22] il estime en effet qu'en infirmant la thèse du vol, la présence des linges dans le tombeau ouvrait la voie à une telle interprétation, mais sa thèse se heurte au fait que tous les récits de ce genre mentionnent ou décrivent même l'enlèvement du héros. Or tout ce que nous trouvons en *P*, c'est le propos, certes *a posteriori* ambigu, de Marie: "On a enlevé le Seigneur du tombeau."

Mieux vaut convenir franchement qu'il n'y a jamais eu de récit pascal sans une affirmation claire de la résurrection, et conclure en conséquence que T n'est pas un *récit* pascal, mais le *prélude* d'un récit où l'inquiétude, née de la découverte du tombeau violé, devait trouver sa résolution dans une scène de christophanie.

Pour vérifier cette hypothèse, voyons comment Luc a dû s'y prendre avec Marc 16:7–8:

a) il remanie le v. 7 (= Luc 24:6b–7) en fonction de son récit de la christophanie aux disciples, qu'il situe le soir même, à Jérusalem (Luc 24:36–49); chez lui, les femmes ne sont donc plus chargées de leur annoncer qu'ils verront le Seigneur en Galilée, mais invitées à se rappeler elles-mêmes que Jésus, en Galilée, leur avait prédit sa résurrection—on a souvent dit de cette localisation de la christophanie à Jérusalem qu'elle convenait si bien aux vues de Luc qu'il fallait la lui imputer; mais cette conclusion est hâtive, car Jean a un récit parallèle (20:19–23);
b) il refond le v. 8 (= Luc 24:9.10b): au lieu de se taire, les femmes chez lui racontent tout aux Onze et aux autres (v. 9b), ainsi qu'aux apôtres (v. 10b). Luc aurait pu en rester là, et nous aurions alors pu croire que Pierre était allé vérifier l'état du tombeau pour s'assurer du sérieux des femmes qui avaient parlé de résurrection. Or au lieu de cela, il s'est senti obligé de

---

[19] Pierre Benoit, "Marie-Madeleine et les disciples au tombeau selon Joh 20:1–18," in *Judentum-Urchristentum-Kirche* (éd. Walter Eltester; BZNW 26; Berlin: Töpelmann, 1960), 148 et 150.

[20] Xavier Léon-Dufour, *Résurrection de Jésus et message pascal* (Parole de Dieu; Paris: Seuil, 1971), 224.

[21] Jean Delorme, "Résurrection et tombeau de Jésus: Marc 16, 1–8 dans la tradition évangélique," in Paul de Surgy et al., éd., *La Résurrection du Christ et l'exégèse moderne* (LD 50; Paris: Cerf, 1969), 138.

[22] Voir Claudel, *Confession de Pierre*, 84–85.

préciser au v. 11 que les disciples ne les avaient pas crues.[23] Pourquoi cela? On répond volontiers qu'il a voulu par là préparer les récits suivants où le Ressuscité rencontre des disciples déçus, sceptiques. Peut-être, mais je pense plutôt à ceci: la transition entre le récit de la découverte du tombeau vide (selon Marc) et l'épisode de l'inspection de Pierre (selon *P*) était délicate, car le récit de Marc comportait une proclamation pascale qui, dans la logique de *P*, était à tout le moins prématurée; en *P* en effet, les femmes annonçaient simplement que le tombeau avait été violé! En parlant du scepticisme des disciples à leur endroit, Luc recréait donc les conditions dans lesquelles Pierre s'était rendu au tombeau selon *P*, non pour valider le kérygme pascal, mais pour vérifier les allégations des femmes, ce qui signifie que **T** relevait d'un complexe narratif où le mystère du tombeau vide n'était levé que plus tard. En effet, si *P* avait "raconté pour lui-même" le récit de la visite des femmes au tombeau puis de l'inspection de Pierre, on comprendrait mal que Luc, qui a préféré au début suivre Marc, en ait retenu juste la fin qu'il a eu du mal à intégrer à son récit pascal; en revanche, on comprend parfaitement son choix si l'on admet que, ne pouvant plus s'appuyer sur Marc après l'épisode des femmes, il est passé à une autre source qui enchaînait avec l'inspection de Pierre *et le reste*.

Après **T** où ils dépendent de *P*, Luc et Jean divergent et leurs récits sur les disciples d'Emmaüs et Marie sont fortement marqués de leur empreinte respective. Puis ils convergent à nouveau pour la christophanie du soir (Luc 24:36–49; Jean 20:19–23); même si le texte occidental de Luc pose quelques problèmes, il est évident qu'ici, Luc et Jean ont une source commune qui, à mon sens, ne peut être que la fin de *P*.[24]

Du côté de chez Marc

Le récit pascal de Marc 16 est très différent de celui de *P*: pas de christophanie, tout se concentre sur une angélophanie dans le tombeau. Bien des exégètes estiment que les versets 1, 3, 4b, 7, et 8b sont rédactionnels. Pour ne pas allonger, je tiens ce point pour acquis, sauf à relever qu'au verset 1, la liste des femmes, qui ne recoupe pas celle de 15:47, doit être traditionnelle, et à rappeler les deux raisons généralement invoquées pour écarter le verset 7: il introduit dans le récit "une idée indépendante du v. 6,"[25] et reprend l'annonce, elle-même rédactionnelle, de 14:28: "Après ma résurrection, je vous

---

[23] Ce trait sera exploité par la finale de Marc dans 16:11, 13, et 14b; voir Joseph Hug, *La finale de l'Évangile de Marc (Mc 16, 9–20)* (EBib; Paris: Gabalda, 1978), 71–78.

[24] Avec Leaney, malgré les doutes de François Bovon, *Luc le théologien: Vingt-cinq ans de recherches (1950–1975)* (Neuchâtel: Delachaux et Niestlé, 1978), 181 n. 3.

[25] Ludger Schenke, *Le tombeau vide et l'annonce de la Résurrection (Mc 16, 1–8)* (LD 59; Paris: Cerf, 1970), 44.

précéderai en Galilée." Je pense cependant qu'il faut aller plus loin et mettre aussi en question les versets 5, 6, et 8a.

a) si Marc parle au v. 1 (réd.) de l'achat d'aromates pour en oindre le corps de Jésus, alors que rien ne suggérait en 15:41‑47 que l'ensevelissement avait été fait à la hâte, c'est pour donner aux femmes une raison d'*entrer* dans le tombeau—ce que visiblement sa source de disait pas; l'expression καὶ ἐξελθοῦσαι εἰς τὸ μνημεῖον est donc rédactionnelle au v. 5a, et il faut en dire autant de son pendant au v. 8a: καὶ εἰσελθοῦσαι . . . ἀπὸ τοῦ μνημείου;

b) le νεανίσκος du v. 5a est en rapport évident avec celui de 14:51s. Faute de pouvoir discuter ici les explications variées qui ont été proposées de ce dernier passage, j'avancerai simplement la mienne: avec son jeune homme qu'on saisit, mais qui s'enfuit nu en "laissant son drap" (σινδών, même terme qu'en 15:46!), 14:51s est une mise en abyme du récit de la Passion, dont il *annonce* mystérieusement l'issue—issue que le récit final *explicitera* en faisant intervenir le même jeune homme, vêtu cette fois-ci d'une robe blanche, pour proclamer le kérygme pascal. La corrélation de ces deux scènes indique à mon sens qu'elles sont l'une et l'autre rédactionnelles.

c) autres caractéristiques marciennes: le verbe ἐκθαμβεῖσθαι aux vv. 5b‑6a (0/**4**/0/0/0; verbe simple: 0/**3**/0/0/0); Ναζαρηνός dans le kérygme du v. 6b (0/**4**/2/0/0); le thème de la peur au v. 8a (ἔκστασις ne se retrouve qu'en Marc 5:42 et en Luc 5:26, mais le verbe ἐξίστασθαι est fréquent chez Marc: 1/**4**/3/0/8) . . .

Dans le récit pascal de Marc ne seraient donc traditionnels que les versets 2 et 4a, et encore faut-il les élaguer. La double indication horaire du verset 2 est en effet plutôt contradictoire, et puisque l'adverbe πρωΐ est bien attesté dans la tradition pascale par Jean 20:1, je tiens pour rédactionnelle l'expression ἀνατείλαντος τοῦ ἡλίου, qui a sans doute une signification symbolique; quant au verset 4a, Claudel a probablement raison d'en retrancher le participe ἀναβλέψασαι.[26] Le texte de la source de Marc (= *S*) devait donc être fort proche de celui de *P*:

P	*S*
Or le premier jour de la semaine,	Et très tôt, le premier jour de la semaine,
Marie de Magdala <et *d'autres*>	<Marie de Magdala, Marie de Jacques et Salomé>
vont tôt . . . au tombeau	vont à la tombe . . .
et elles voient la pierre enlevée du tombeau. . . .	et . . . elles voient que la pierre a été roulée. . . .

[26] Claudel, *Confession de Pierre*, 70‑71.

La suite du récit de Marc paraît s'égarer: un ange est là, dans le tombeau; il annonce aux femmes une prochaine christophanie en Galilée, mais au lieu d'en informer les disciples, celles-ci se taisent—tout comme Marc lui-même d'ailleurs, qui clôt brutalement son évangile à cet endroit-là, sans narrer la christophanie annoncée. Le texte paraît aussi surchargé: double propos de l'ange, qui proclame le kérygme (v. 6b) et annonce une christophanie (v. 7); doublet des versets 8a et 8b, qui soulignent l'un et l'autre la peur des femmes. On pourrait donc se demander s'il ne faut pas attribuer à un Proto-Marc les versets 5–6 et 8a, qui formeraient un récit d'angélophanie simple et cohérent, et à Marc lui-même les versets 7 et 8b; mais cela ne résoudrait rien, car il resterait à expliquer pourquoi Marc a défiguré cette belle angélophanie en un récit paradoxal, où les femmes *qui ne parleront pas* sont chargées d'annoncer une christophanie *qui ne serait pas narrée*.

Je tiens pour évident que ces deux apories, propres à Marc, sont corrélatives, et par conséquent j'écarte les explications qui tentent de rende compte de l'une sans impliquer l'autre. L'absence de la christophanie annoncée ne s'explique ni parce que Marc n'aurait pas senti le besoin de raconter ce que tout le monde savait déjà, ni parce que la tradition ne lui fournissait aucun récit de ce genre, ni parce qu'on aurait par la suite censuré sa christophanie jugée gênante, ni parce que son éditeur n'aurait eu à sa disposition qu'un exemplaire mutilé,[27] etc. De même, le silence des femmes n'est ni une justification de l'apparition tardive de la légende du tombeau vide, ni une inversion du secret messianique, ni un trait apologétique pour prouver que la foi des disciples était indépendante du témoignage des femmes, ni une pointe polémique pour disqualifier les disciples en tant que témoins de la résurrection, etc. Et il ne faut bien sûr pas le relativiser non plus en se disant que femmes, elles ont bien dû finir par parler!

Comparant le récit de Marc au récit prétendument "sobre et sans merveilleux" de la tradition pré-johannique, Benoit estimait que Marc a voulu achever son évangile par un récit centré

> sur l'expérience religieuse des femmes: le tombeau vide leur a révélé la résurrection du Christ, et cette perception est concrétisée, selon l'usage biblique, par les paroles d'un *angelus interpres*. . . . Littérairement, cette exploitation du tombeau vide dans la tradition de Marc pourrait venir de ce que Marc avait renoncé à raconter les apparitions du Christ et voulait cependant terminer son évangile sur un énoncé de la Résurrection.[28]

---

[27] Pierre Nautin conjugue cette explication de façon invraisemblable avec le silence des femmes, en attribuant le v. 8b à un éditeur de Marc dont l'exemplaire était mutilé après 16:8a et "comme [ce verset] parlait d'un message confié aux femmes et qu'il n'y avait plus rien après, il a pensé que les femmes n'avaient rien dit à personne et que c'était la fin de l'histoire"! (*L'Évangile retrouvé: Jésus et l'Évangile primitif* [Christianisme antique 5; Paris: Beauchesne, 1998], 272).

[28] Benoit, "Marie-Madeleine," 149–50.

Cette dernière observation est remarquable, mais les explications qui l'entourent ne satisfont guère, car si Marc avait renoncé à rapporter ces apparitions pour mettre le kérygme en relief, pourquoi en aurait-il gardé un vestige au verset 7?

Ce verset 7 est d'ailleurs étrange: les disciples ont à se rendre en Galilée pour y voir Jésus—comme si, ressuscité, celui-ci ne pouvait pas tout simplement se manifester à eux là où ils étaient! Pour expliquer cette anomalie, on a dit et répété que Marc avait ainsi voulu faire le lien entre la tradition récente de la découverte du tombeau et l'ancienne tradition qui situait les christophanies en Galilée—interprétation plutôt risquée quand on infère précisément de ce verset que les disciples avaient dû fuir en Galilée après l'arrestation de Jésus! Une bonne partie de nos difficultés ne vient-elle d'ailleurs pas de ce que très généralement on préjuge, en s'y référant, que "Marc connaissait donc une tradition qui situait en Galilée des apparitions du Ressuscité aux apôtres."[29] Or rien n'est moins sûr, et le fait même qu'il ne raconte pas la christophanie annoncée suggère bien plutôt le contraire.

Comme nous l'avons vu, le début de *S* ressemblait fort à celui de *P*. On peut en inférer que *P* et *S* étaient deux formes de la même tradition, si bien qu'après la visite des femmes au tombeau, *S* devait également narrer l'inspection de Pierre et la christophanie du soir à Jérusalem. Ce serait donc cette apparition-là que Marc a délibérément omise, non parce que parce que sa forme le gênait, mais parce qu'elle dérangeait son projet narratif qui était d'annoncer une *autre* christophanie.

Si l'on admet ces vues, son récit pascal devient parfaitement cohérent. Pour annoncer sa nouvelle christophanie, Marc crée une angélophanie qu'il place dramatiquement dans le tombeau même (vv. 5–7). En conséquence, il modifie le début du récit traditionnel où les femmes voyaient seulement le tombeau ouvert, et pour les y faire entrer il recourt au motif de l'onction (v. 1). Comme par ailleurs son choix narratif entraînait la disparition de tout ce qui suivait la visite des femmes au tombeau, il compense la perte de la christophanie primitive par la proclamation du kérygme: "Il est ressuscité!" (v. 6b), et celle de l'inspection du tombeau par Pierre, d'une part par la clause du verset 6c: "Il n'est pas ici: voici la place où ils l'avaient mis" (v. 6c),[30] et d'autre part par la mention particulière de Pierre au verset 7. Ceci fait, il introduit l'annonce de la christophanie par un vigoureux ἀλλά, pour bien marquer que la proclamation de la résurrection n'en était qu'un préalable; c'est maintenant seulement que vient le message essentiel: "Il vous précède en Galilée!" (v. 7a). Au verset 8 enfin, qu'il faut référer tout entier au verset 7, il prévoit (et prévient) l'effet que ne manquera pas de provoquer son récit pascal *new look*

---

[29] Charles Masson, "Le tombeau vide. Essai sur la formation d'une tradition," in *Vers les sources d'eau vive* (Lausanne: Payot, 1961), 115.

[30] Si Marc 14:51 est bien une anticipation pascale, le fait que le jeune homme s'enfuie καταλιπὼν τὴν σινδόνα montrerait indirectement que dans la tradition *S*, Pierre trouvait une σινδών dans le tombeau.

chez des auditeurs habitués au ronron du récit traditionnel: la stupeur!—et il leur explique aussi pourquoi rien n'a jamais filtré de cette nouvelle christophanie, pourtant prévue dès le premier jour: c'est que les femmes ont "fui" leur responsabilité! Elles avaient été chargées d'en informer les disciples, mais elles n'en ont rien dit à personne.

Que faut-il donc entendre par cette christophanie manquée en Galilée? Remarquons tout d'abord que la visée du verset 7 est d'ordre pragmatique, car s'il ne s'était agi que d'envoyer les disciples en Galilée, il eût suffi à Marc d'écrire que l'ange avait enjoint aux femmes d'aller leur dire ἵνα ἀπέλθωσιν εἰς τὴν Γαλιλαίαν (cf. Matt 28:10). Or au lieu de cela, elles doivent leur annoncer que Jésus "les y précède," si bien qu'on ne peut lire ce verset sans y percevoir l'écho du thème de la *suivance*: "Jésus les précédait, et ils étaient effrayés; ceux qui (le) suivaient avaient peur" (Marc 10:32)—cette même peur qui saisit les femme à l'annonce d'une nouvelle christophanie en Galilée.

Par ailleurs, Marc a parsemé son évangiles de notations qui prennent sens à la lueur de son récit final. Je pense en particulier au récit de la retraite de Jésus qui, s'étant "levé tôt, en pleine nuit (καὶ πρωῒ ἔννυχα λίαν ἀναστάς!)" pour prier à l'écart, avait répondu aux disciples qui le cherchaient: "Allons ailleurs, dans les bourgs voisins, afin que j'y *prêche* aussi, car c'est pour cela que je suis sorti!" (1:38). Ou encore au récit de la marche sur les eaux, avec le moment critique où Jésus, ayant rejoint les disciples qu'il avait envoyés vers l'autre rive, à Bethsaïda, "voulait les dépasser," même si la traversée s'était alors achevée à Gennésaret (cf. 6:45–52, 53), comme pour nous dire que si le passage *vers les païens* avait échoué cette fois-là, il était néanmoins voulu par Jésus. Bref, en faisant annoncer par l'ange sa nouvelle christophanie en Galilée, Marc ne voulait-il pas conforter sa communauté encore hésitante dans le choix qu'elle avait fait "d'annoncer aussi aux Grecs le Seigneur Jésus" (Actes 11:20)?[31]

Une intention que Matthieu comprendra parfaitement lorsque, plus tard, il invitera à son tour sa communauté à "partir pour la Galilée" (Matt 28:10)— et il ne lui suffira plus que cela soit dit par un ange: Jésus lui-même viendra confirmer ce tournant! Face au refus d'Israël, il lui fallait se rendre à l'évidence: elle s'était jusqu'alors conformée à la règle de ne s'occuper que des brebis perdues de la maison d'Israël (cf. 10:5b–6), mais maintenant, le Ressuscité l'envoyait solennellement auprès des païens: "Allez donc, enseignez πάντα τὰ ἔθνη . . ." (Matt 28:18–19).

---

[31] Ainsi Christopher F. Evans conclut: "Thus the promise uttered in Mk 14:28, which is already beginning to be fulfilled in 16:7, is a prophecy of the world-wide mission of the Church" (" 'I will go before you into Galilee,' " *JTS*[2] 5 [1954]: 13).

En guise de conclusion

Dans leur état présent, les récits pascals donnent l'impression d'un fouillis, et beaucoup d'exégètes semblent s'en accommoder, comme si c'était une preuve du bouleversement provoqué par la résurrection! D'autres l'expliquent en disant que la tradition ne savait des christophanies que ce qu'en disait le kérygme de 1 Cor 15:3–5, et que pour les décrire, les évangélistes y "sont allés, chacun de son côté, un tant soit peu à l'aventure"![32] Il me semble plutôt que cette impression de fouillis vient du fait que Marc a remanié profondément la tradition pascale primitive.

La *forme* de cette tradition narrative était celle d'un triptyque, narrant la découverte par les femmes du tombeau ouvert, puis l'inspection des lieux par Pierre, et enfin la christophanie du soir aux Onze, à Jérusalem. Ce qui signifie d'une part que cette tradition ne dérive pas de la tradition kérygmatique, plus riche en christophanies, et d'autre part qu'elle ne s'est pas formée par l'agrégation de petits récits à l'origine indépendants: les trois épisodes y formaient un tout. On estime souvent que l'épisode des femmes au tombeau s'est agrégé tardivement à la tradition pascale, mais le fait qu'il soit le seul élément commun à tous les évangiles montre bien plutôt qu'il en a toujours fait partie.

Le *développement* de cette tradition a dû être le suivant:

a) Marc a tout concentré sur l'épisode des femmes au tombeau, en y insérant une angélophanie dans laquelle il a glissé des allusions aux épisodes omis;

b) Matthieu a repris le récit de Marc, en y ajoutant deux christophanies de son cru: l'une aux femmes pour certifier le message de l'ange, et l'autre aux Onze en Galilée;

c) Luc a repris le récit de Marc, en le complétant d'après *P* pour l'inspection du tombeau et la christophanie du soir, épisodes entre lesquels il a inséré un récit particulier, celui des disciples d'Émmaüs, où il développe une catéchèse personnelle.

d) Jean a suivi la tradition primitive en développant l'épisode de l'inspection du tombeau et en dédoublant en 20:24–29 la christophanie du soir; entre deux, il a glissé, lui aussi, un épisode particulier, celui de la christophanie à Marie,[33] qui lui permet d'expliciter la foi du disciple bien-aimé: "Va vers mes frères et dis-leur: Je monte vers mon Père qui est votre Père, vers mon Dieu qui est votre Dieu" (20:18).

Le fait que Luc et Jean aient placé leur récit personnel avant la christophanie du soir tend à montrer que celle-ci, et elle seule, concluait la narration pascale traditionnelle.

---

[32] Loisy, *Quatrième Évangile*, 744.

[33] François Bovon, "Le privilège pascal de Marie-Madeleine," in *Révélations et Écritures: Nouveau Testament et littérature apocryphe chrétienne* (MdB 26; Genève: Labor et Fides, 1993), 216–20.

Cher François,

C'est avec crainte et grande joie que je t'offre ces réflexions qui demanderaient à être affinées.

Avec crainte, car je ne suis qu'un exégète amateur et, en osant m'aventurer dans le dédale des traditions pascales et la masse de réflexions qu'elles ont suscitées, j'en suis arrivé à une conclusion qui, tu le sens bien, ébranle le caractère archaïque du "privilège pascal de Marie-Madeleine."

Mais avec grande joie aussi, car depuis notre toute première rencontre, ton amitié et ta confiance ne se sont jamais démenties, et j'ai toujours pu apprécier la bienveillance avec laquelle tu acceptais d'envisager des idées qui ne sont pas forcément les tiennes.

CHAPTER SEVENTEEN

HILDEGARD OF BINGEN'S EXEGESIS OF LUKE

Beverly Mayne Kienzle

Hildegard of Bingen (1098–1179), the only medieval woman known to have authored works of exegesis, composed fifty-eight *Expositiones evangeliorum*, or homilies on the Gospels, expounding twenty-seven scriptural passages.[1] Of those twenty-seven pericopes, thirteen are from Luke's Gospel, and thirty, or just over half, of the fifty-eight homilies are devoted to Lukan texts.[2] Before proclaiming Hildegard as an *aficionada* of Luke, one must keep in mind that she followed the medieval lectionary in use at her monastery.[3] Yet she made choices, if not in the texts exegeted, then certainly in the interpretations she offered. This essay, inspired by and building on the work of François Bovon, examines Hildegard's exegesis of Luke, highlighting her departures from traditional exegesis and her distinctive method with its focus on salvation history and the individual sinner's struggles.

The Expositiones *and Hildegard's Exegetical Method*

Hildegard, author of numerous works including a visionary trilogy—*Scivias, Liber vitae meritorum*, and *Liber divinorum operum*—mentions *expositiones* in her

---

[1] *Expositiones evangeliorum*, in *Analecta Sanctae Hildegardis* (ed. Jean-Baptiste Pitra; vol. 8 of *Analecta Sacra*; Monte Cassino, 1882), 245–327. A new edition is being published from Wiesbaden, Hessische Landes-Bibliothek Hs 2 (Riesenkodex), fols. 434r–61v, and British Library MS Add. 15102, fols. 146–19 (a 1487 copy) for the *Corpus Christianorum Continuatio Mediaevalis* by Beverly Mayne Kienzle and Carolyn Muessig. On the Riesenkodex, see Albert Derolez, "Introduction," *Liber divinorum operum* (ed. A. Derolez and Peter Dronke; CCCM 92; Turnhout: Brepols, 1996), xcvii–ci, and L. Van Acker, "Einleitung," *Hildegardis Bingensis Epistolarium, Pars Prima I–XC* (ed. L. Van Acker; CCCM 91; Turnhout: Brepols, 1991), xxvii–xxix.

[2] Six pericopes are from Matthew: 1:18–21; 2:1–12; 2:13–18; 4:1–11; 8:1–13; 20:1–16; three from Mark: 7:31–37; 16:1–7; 16:14–20; five from John: 1:1–14; 2:1–11; 3:1–15; 6:1–14; 10:11–16.

[3] On the lectionary that would have been in use in Hildegard's community, inspired by the reforms of Hirsau, see Constant Mews, "Hildegard, visions and religious reform," in *"Im Angesicht Gottes suche der Mensch sich selbst": Hildegard von Bingen 1098–1998* (Berlin: Akademie Verlag, 2001), 333–42; Angela Carlevaris, "Ildegarda e la patristica," in *Hildegard of Bingen: The Context of her Thought and Art* (ed. Charles Burnett and Peter Dronke; Warburg Institute Colloquia 4; London: Warburg Institute, 1988), 72–73.

prologue to the *Liber vitae meritorum*.[4] She probably composed the *Expositiones* over a number of years, progressively adding to them and filling out her coverage of the liturgical year.[5] Hildegard also authored the first extant medieval morality play, the *Ordo virtutum*,[6] which dramatizes with words and music the struggle of a soul who falls into sin, experiences a battle between the devil and the rescuing virtues, and returns restored to her community. The dramatic vision that the *magistra* demonstrates in the *Ordo virtutum* manifests itself in the *Expositiones*, many of which represent the soul's conflict.[7]

Each *expositio* is structured as a progressive commentary on the biblical passage, phrase by phrase.[8] One may imagine the performance behind the texts; Hildegard would have spoken to the sisters of her community in accordance with Benedictine liturgical practice, the scriptural text either before her, read aloud to her, or recited from memory, section by section in sequential order. After each section, she added her explanations.[9] The monastic liturgy included commentary on the *Rule* and the Scriptures by the abbot or abbess, as well as listening to commentaries on the Scriptures read in the office. These daily practices must have influenced the form of the *Expositiones*.[10]

The method of Hildegard's exegesis, more difficult to characterize than its rhetorical form, relates to the visionary and prophetic grounding of her

---

[4] *Hildegardis Liber vite meritorum* (ed. Angela Carlevaris; CCCM 90; Turnhout: Brepols, 1995), 8.

[5] From the passage above in *Liber vite meritorum*, we can conclude that the *Expositiones* were composed at least in part by 1157. Intratextual references in two homilies probably place one during the schism of 1159–1177 and the other during the crisis over the Cathars burnt in Cologne in 1163. Homilies XXIV.2 and XXIV.3, "Erunt signa," Wiesbaden Hs 2, 459v–460v; *Expositiones evangeliorum*, 312–14.

[6] Scholars estimate that the *Ordo* had been written by 1151, when Hildegard was finishing the *Scivias*. A passage similar to the *Ordo virtutum* but shorter appears at the end of *Scivias*. Peter Dronke, "Problemata Hildegardiana," *Mittellateinisches Jahrbuch* 16 (1981): 100–101; *Liber divinorum operum*, lxxix.

[7] For fuller discussion of this, see Beverly Mayne Kienzle, "Hildegard of Bingen's Teaching in her *Expositiones evangeliorum* and *Ordo Virtutum*," in *Medieval Monastic Education* (ed. George P. Ferzoco and Carolyn A. Muessig; London: Leicester University Press, 2001), 72–86.

[8] See Beverly Mayne Kienzle, "Hildegard of Bingen's Gospel Homilies and Her Exegesis of the Parable of the Prodigal Son," in *"Im Angesicht Gottes suche der Mensch sich selbst,"* 299–324.

[9] Hildegard emphasizes the importance of committing the scriptures to memory in the *Explanation of the Rule of Benedict by Hildegard of Bingen* (trans. with intro. and commentary, Hugh Feiss; Peregrina Translations Series 15; Toronto: Peregrina, 1990), 24–25.

[10] A. Carlevaris calls attention to the importance of those readings in "Ildegarda e la patristica," 72–73. Moreover, the word *expositio* denotes the homiletic commentaries on Scripture read in the office; and the verb *exponere* is employed for the process by which the abbot or abbess expounds a passage (*sententia*) of the *Rule* in chapter. *Regula Benedicti. La Règle de Saint Benoît* (Texte latin selon le manuscrit S. Gall, Version française par Henri Rochais; Paris: Desclée de Brouwer, 1980), Cap. 9. 8. See also Christine Mohrmann, "*Praedicare-tractare-sermo*," *Études sur le latin des chrétiens* (vol. 2; Rome: Edizioni di storia e letteratura, 1961), 63–72.

authority to interpret Scripture. Hildegard's community recognized that her interpretations of Scripture were different from what they were accustomed to hear being preached or read from patristic homiliaries. A letter that Hildegard's first secretary Volmar drafted on behalf of the sisters expresses what the community valued most about Hildegard, including her "new interpretation of the Scriptures" and her "new and unheard-of sermons on the feast days of saints."[11] Hildegard's reputation as exegete is also evidenced by her *Solutiones triginta octo quaestionum*, a treatise she sent to Guibert of Gembloux for the monks at Villers.[12] She explained in a letter to the same Guibert, her secretary after Volmar, that the "shadow of the living light" illuminated her, with the result that the Scriptures, virtues, and other inspired writings shone forth with clarity for her. In her *vita*, Hildegard compares her inspiration to that of John the Baptist and describes the "soft raindrops" of God's inspiration that were sprinkled on her soul's knowledge.[13] Visionary gifts had been hailed in others in the monastic environment of the Rhineland since at least the late eleventh century; Hildegard was exceptional in the extensiveness of her *opera* and in her preaching tours to cathedrals and other religious houses.[14]

The *Expositiones* are constructed by allegory, what Peter Dronke has called "systematic allegorizing," where all the metaphors in a homily are interdependent.[15] The standard categories of historical-literal, allegorical, and moral interpretation are insufficient to describe Hildegard's exegesis. Dronke prefers the designations "psychological" or "microcosmic" versus "macrocosmic" or "cosmological."[16] While that differentiation is quite useful, one can also classify the

[11] *Hildegardis Bingensis Epistolarium, Pars Secunda XCI–CCLr* (ed. L. Van Acker; CCCM 91A; Turnhout: Brepols, 1993), Ep. CXCV, 443.

[12] I am grateful to Bernard McGinn for this insight. The *Solutiones* (PL 197:1037–54), are analyzed by A. C. Bartlett, "Commentary, Polemic, and Prophecy in Hildegard of Bingen's *Solutiones triginta octo quaestionum*," *Viator* 23 (1992): 153–65.

[13] On the Rhenish visionaries, see C. Mews, "Hildegard, Visions and Religious Reform," 326–42. See also Hildegard, *Letter to Guibert of Gembloux, Epistolarium* II, Ep. 103r, 261–62; Hildegard, *Vita* II, xvi, p. 43, ll. 1–10; the letter from Philip, dean of the cathedral at Cologne, in *Epistolarium* I, Ep. XV, 33; the comment from Robert of Val-Roi reported by Guibert of Gembloux, Ep. XVIII (ed. A. Derolez; CCCM 66A; Turnhout: Brepols, 1989), 229: and Constant Mews, "Hildegard and the Schools," in *Hildegard of Bingen: The Context of her Thought and Art*, 109 n. 96.

[14] On controversies around abbesses' preaching, see Alcuin Blamires, "Women and Preaching in Medieval Orthodoxy, Heresy and Saints' Lives," *Viator* 26 (1995): 135–52; Peter Biller, "Cathars and Material Women," in *Medieval Theology and the Natural Body* (ed. Peter Biller and A. J. Minnis; York Studies in Medieval Theology I; Woodbridge, UK: York Medieval Press/Boydell and Brewer, 1997), 68–69.

[15] Peter Dronke, "Platonic-Christian Allegories in the Homilies of Hildegard of Bingen," in *From Athens to Chartres: Neoplatonism and Medieval Thought. Studies in Honour of Edouard Jeauneau* (ed. Haijo Jan Westra; Leiden: Brill, 1992), 3–6. Dronke proposes categories of Hildegard's allegory: (1) Establishment of allegorical correspondence; (2–4) Self-revelation: gradual, direct, and allegory within allegory; (5) Allegoresis—allegorical reading of the sacred text.

[16] Hildegard demonstrates a command of the conventional modes of medieval exegesis when she explicates the first book of Genesis in the *Liber divinorum operum*, Book

Expositiones according to three thematic patterns: first and foremost, the unfolding of salvation history, and within that, the journey of the faithful soul,[17] and the moral life of the religious community. Salvation history generally shows three periods in the *Expositiones*: the first extends from the Creation to the Incarnation; the second from the Incarnation onward; and the third constitutes the period in which Hildegard was living. This scheme of history corresponds in part to that often found in her visionary works; she modifies the Augustinian notion of six ages while following Augustine in associating the history of humankind and the life of the individual.[18] Hence she divides the present into a distinct age, separate from the era that began with the Incarnation.

Hildegard's Lukan Texts

We shall now examine how the patterns of interpretation operate in some of the *Expositiones* that exegete Lukan passages. The table below presents the Lukan pericopes. Roughly half are parables and the others correspond to episodes in the life of Christ. Exegesis from several representative *expositiones* will be selected for analysis here. The exegetical works are selected as a sample, not an exhaustive survey, of the tradition preceding Hildegard.

Episodes from Life of Christ	Parables
Luke 1:57–68	Luke 14:16–24
Nativity of John the Baptist	The Great Supper
Luke 2:1–14	Luke 15:11–32
Christmas	The Prodigal Son

2, 32–33, as reflected in the manuscript rubrics: *Littera, Allegoria, Moralitas*. Bernard McGinn points out the originality of Hildegard's interpretation of Genesis in "Hildegard of Bingen as Visionary and Exegete" in *Hildegard von Bingen in ihrem historischen Umfeld* (ed. Alfred Haverkamp; Mainz: Philipp von Zabern, 2000), 344–49. See also Dronke, "Platonic-Christian Allegories," 386.

[17] Some of Hildegard's letters represent the struggle of the faithful soul, as does the sequence "O ignee Spiritus," *Symphonia: A Critical Edition of the "Symphonia armonie celestium revelationum"* (ed. and trans. Barbara Newman; 2d ed.; Ithaca: Cornell University Press, 1998), 142–47, 280–81. On Hildegard's moral thought and the notion of Christian life as an ongoing struggle, see Barbara Newman, "Poet," in *Voice of the Living Light: Hildegard of Bingen and Her World* (ed. B. Newman; Berkeley: University of California Press, 1998), 176–92; and *Sister of Wisdom. St. Hildegard's Theology of the Feminine*, with a new Preface, Bibliography, and Discography (Berkeley: University of California Press, 1998), 79–87, 188–90.

[18] See Kathryn Kerby-Fulton, *Reformist Apocalypticism and Piers Plowman* (Cambridge: Cambridge University Press, 1990), 8, on the Augustinian view of seven ages and 45–46 on Hildegard's modifications to that view. Another dimension of Hildegardian interpretation, not explored in this essay, takes a cosmic and eschatological perspective. See Pitra, *Expositiones*, 24.1–4, 311–15; Wiesbaden, Hs. 2, 459v–60v; and Beverly M. Kienzle, "Hildegard of Bingen's Teaching in her *Expositiones evangeliorum and Ordo Virtutum*," 79–81.

Luke 2:22–32
Purification
Luke 2:42–52
Jesus in the Temple
Luke 5:1–11
The Miraculous Catch
Luke 19:1–10
Zacchaeus
Luke 19:41–47
Jesus Expels the Moneychangers

Luke 16:1–9
The Dishonest Steward
Luke 16:19–31
Lazarus and the Rich Man
Luke 18:10–14
The Pharisee and the Publican
Luke 21:29–31 (included in 21:25–33)
The Fig Tree

While most of Hildegard's homilies offer a twofold interpretation of the scriptural text, the first grounded in salvation history and the second developing individual and/or collective moral lessons, three sets of the *Expositiones* consist of a threefold exegesis, that is three sets of three homilies. Two of those sets expound on Lukan texts: Luke 5:1–11, the miraculous catch; and Luke 19:41–47, the story of Jesus expelling the moneychangers. Both Lukan groups illustrate Hildegard's presentation of salvation history in what one could view as a three-act drama. The first two acts correspond to a historical allegory, with the first spanning the time from the Creation to the Incarnation and the second focusing on the impact of the Incarnation. The third act demonstrates moral allegory centering on the inner struggle, as it incorporates elements of the *psychomachia*.[19] Literature that dramatizes conflict between virtues and vices enjoyed great popularity throughout the Middle Ages, notably in the *Speculum virginum*, a text circulated in Rhenish religious communities during the twelfth century.[20] We begin with the two sets of three *expositiones* on Lukan pericopes, because they provide the broadest view of Hildegard's exegetical enterprise. Other homilies with a less expansive outlook will be analyzed later.

The first set of three homilies that we consider (20.1–3 for the Fourth Sunday after Pentecost) comments on Luke 5:1–11, the miraculous catch.[21]

---

[19] The third set of three homilies retains one interpretation devoted to the individual sinner, but the other two readings teach about the right understanding of creation. The three "acts" correspond roughly to Hildegard's three-level reading of the first book of Genesis (literal, allegorical, moral) set forth in the *Liber divinorum operum*.

[20] In spite of seeming similarities between the *Speculum virginum* and Hildegard's allegories of virtues and vice, significant differences are found. See Constant Mews, "Hildegard, the *Speculum virginum* and religious reform," in *Hildegard von Bingen in ihrem historischen Umfeld*, 237–67. On the virtues and vices, see Morton Bloomfield, *The Seven Deadly Sins* (East Lansing, Mich.: University of Michigan Press, 1952; repr. 1967); Adolf Katzenellenbogen, *Allegories of the Virtues and Vices in Medieval Art* (London: Warburg Institute, 1939; repr. Medieval Academy reprints for teaching 24; Toronto: University of Toronto Press, 1989); Richard Newhauser, *The Treatise on Vices and Virtues in Latin and the Vernacular* (Typologie des sources du moyen âge occidental, fasc. 68; Turnhout: Brepols, 1993).

[21] "Cum turbae irruerent," Wiesbaden Hs 2, 456r–57v; Pitra, 301–05.

The first homily in the set views salvation history briefly: beginning with Creation, it describes the human's endowment with the knowledge of good and evil, the fall, and Christ's coming to open the path to good works and the heavenly Jerusalem. The second starts from the Incarnation and treats the turning from the old law to the new in the Gospel, when humankind accepts belief in Christ's dual nature and subjects itself to God's commands. The third homily dramatizes the virtues' role in conversion and victory over the Devil.

Hildegard's consistent and terse interpretation of key elements in this narrative allows us to signal the successive readings of the text in series of threes. The crowds (Luke 5:1) in the three homilies represent respectively the substance of created beings, the Scriptures, and the virtues. Correspondingly the character of Jesus stands first for God the Creator, second for God incarnate, and third for the virtue of fortitude. The two boats (Luke 5:2) in the first homily designate the elements and other created things, in the second, the dual nature of Christ, and in the third, conversion and salvation. Simon Peter (Luke 5:3 et al.) denotes the human being at creation, the incarnated Son, and finally, the righteous. Lowering the nets (Luke 5:4–6) first indicates the human's transgression of divine commandments in Paradise, then Jesus' converting his disciples to the Gospel, and third, the righteous humans' recourse to the virtues for assistance. The nets (Luke 5:6) bring in vices and sorrow in the creation account; they reap heavenly desires in the second context; and when the righteous invoke the virtues, the nets haul in teachings about good works. In the first version, coming ashore and abandoning everything (Luke 5:11) represents remaining on earth and leaving the old law; in the second, those actions denote dismissing earthly things and relinquishing personal will; in the third *expositio*, drawing the boat to shore signifies conversion. Finally, following Jesus means following the Gospel; or in the second case, it indicates that believers subject themselves to God's commands; and in the third, sadness turns into joy for the righteous who persevere in fortitude with God.

Hildegard's readings of the miraculous catch depart from the interpretation observed in Ambrose, Gregory the Great, Bede, and others, where the boat represents the church and Peter its obedient leader. In that paradigm the fishermen stand for doctors of the Church or preachers; their nets signify the *apostolica instrumenta*, especially the subtleties of preaching that haul in sinners to Christ. An inward interpretation, such as Hildegard's third *expositio*, appears in the homilies of her near contemporary, Gottfried of Admont (+1165). He presents the two boats as the inner and outer human being. The boats' coming ashore signifies the sinners' conversion,[22] a theme also present in Hildegard.

---

[22] Ambrosius Mediolanensis, *Expositio Evangelii secundum Lucam* (ed. M. Adriaen; CCSL XIV; Turnhout: Brepols, 1957), IV, 68–72, 131–33. Gregorius Magnus, *Homiliae in evangelia* (ed. Raymond Etaix; CCSL 141; Turnhout: Brepols, 1999), Homilia XXIV, 198–99; Beda Venerabilis, *In Lucae evangelium expositio* (ed. D. Hurst; CCSL 120; Turnhout: Brepols, 1960), liber 2, cap. 5, 113–16; Heiricus Autissiodorensis, *Homiliae per circulum*

The three homilies on Luke 19:41–47 (Ninth Sunday after Pentecost), the story of Jesus expelling the moneychangers,[23] set forth a similar threefold interpretation of the Gospel text: salvation history before, then after the incarnation, and third, the inner drama of the sinner.

The first *expositio* extends from the moment of Creation to Christ's teaching. The creation and fall of humankind are highlighted as Hildegard gives a voice to the lamenting Creator who made the human in his own image and likeness. God weeps like Jesus (Luke 19:41) as he expresses foreknowledge of human death and transgression and cites Genesis 2:16–17: "From every tree of Paradise you may eat. . . ." The human, driven into exile and alienated from God, experiences night, death, and hardships "like a strong wind." Jesus' act of driving out the moneychangers (Luke 19:45) is interpreted as an event that alters the course of history, as God made the human being a temple and drove out unbelief and illicit desires. The "house of prayer" (Luke 19:46) signifies the chastity and holiness that should exist in the human, while the "den of robbers" (Luke 19:46) denotes the fraud and falsehood fabricated by the Devil.

The second homily has an incarnational focus, explaining Jesus' transformation of the law and of understanding the Scriptures. In addition, it contains Hildegard's views on exegesis. After commenting on Jesus' lament over those who do not recognize him and the new law, the *magistra* explains that Jesus and after him, the "doctors of the New Testament," that is, Gregory the Great, Ambrose, Augustine, and Jerome, have changed the old into the new, specifically into the spiritual meaning. They cleanse old ways of worship and lead carnal institutions to humility by means of spiritual understanding. They leave no written word and no worship without transformation; indeed, so profound is the change that not one word remains untransformed. Driving out the moneychangers (Luke 19:45) is read as the gospel's expulsion of avarice, idols, and other "filthy things." The "house of prayer" (Luke 19:46) denotes the house of truth and edifice of revelation, and the "den of robbers" (Luke 19:46) signifies the act of unbelief that exalts personal will and the "devil's filth in robberies." Hence Hildegard asserts a requirement for spiritual interpretation of Scripture and situates it in the broad context of the transformation of word, worship, and carnality.

Homily three focuses on the individual sinner and the drama of her conversion from sin to righteousness, from the thieves' den to the temple (Luke 19:47), where angels and saints openly and joyously praise the repentant sinner. Hildegard casts the Holy Spirit as the one weeping here, lamenting that the vice-filled human does not see dangers. The Spirit speaks with imagery that stems from the everyday world of the Rhineland: "If only you had recognized the dangers . . . ,"

---

anni, Pars estiva, Homilia 21, PL 124: 51–59; Godefridus (sive Irimbertus?) Admontensis, *Homiliae dominicales*, Homilia 66, PL 174: 463.

[23] "Cum appropinquaret Jesus," Wiesbaden Hs. 2, 457v–58r; Pitra, 305–7.

the Spirit exclaims to the human, "you would press yourself like a wine-press, and like a mill, you would turn yourself here and there." The "reddening light" of repentance will descend on the human and surround her with weeping and sighs, as repentance penetrates the soul and leaves no vice or filth. The Holy Spirit drives out the moneychangers when it chases pride from the human heart, represented by the "house of prayer." The Holy Spirit's active role here and elsewhere probably reflects the influence of Rupert of Deutz (ca. 1070–1129/30), a learned Benedictine exegete who described his own visionary experience and viewed the Holy Spirit as still working in the world.[24]

Looking at the exegetical tradition for this passage, we find that Ambrose uses it to criticize the selling of religious offices and to juxtapose the Church to the synagogue. Gregory, followed closely by Bede, echoes Ambrose's literal interpretation but includes a moral reading focused on the inner person, the errant soul besieged by evil spirits. The soul places "stone upon stone" by piling up errant thoughts. Gregory interprets verse 47, Jesus teaching in the temple, as Truth instructing the faithful, a notion similar to Hildegard's equating the "house of prayer" (verse 46) with the house of Truth in her second homily. Gottfried of Admont also focuses on the soul, borrowing some elements from Gregory, but stressing confession as the soul weeps over its sins. He compares the "house of prayer" to the heart, as does Hildegard in her third *expositio*. Gottfried, however, develops at length a conflict between four virtues (prudence, fortitude, temperance, and justice) and their opposing vices,[25] a path that Hildegard does not follow. None of these major exegetes relates the passage to the Creation or to the spiritual interpretation of Scripture.

We next consider two homilies for the Dedication of a church, where Hildegard relates the story of Zacchaeus (Luke 19:1–10) to salvation history and to the conversion of a wicked sinner. The close parallel structure of the two homilies allows for analyzing them simultaneously. Here Jesus (Luke 19:1) represents God in the first *expositio* and the Son of God in the other; while Zacchaeus (Luke 19:2) stands first for the human being, fallen and restored, and second, for the wicked person who transgresses commandments but later becomes righteous. In the context of salvation history, Hildegard interprets Jericho (Luke 19:1) as the fallen world, while in the microcosmic version the city designates those who are deficient in good works. Similarly Zacchaeus's small stature (Luke 19:3) points to humanity's smallness when compared to God, and then to the wickedness of individual thoughts. The tax collector's ascent of the sycamore tree (Luke 19:4) denotes humankind's boldness and self-deception in wanting to know good from evil, and on a smaller scale, the

[24] Rupert of Deutz, *De gloria et honore filii hominis super Mattheum* (ed. Rhaban Haacke, CCCM 29; Turnhout: Brepols, 1979), 366–85. See also C. Mews, "Hildegard, visions and religious reform," 337–42; John Van Engen, *Rupert of Deutz* (Berkeley: University of California Press, 1983), 50–54.

[25] Ambrosius, *Expo. evang. sec. Luc.*, IX.16, 337; Gregorius Magnus, *Homiliae in evangelia*, Homilia 39, 383–85; Beda, *In Lucae evang. expo.*, lib. 5, p. 349; Godefridus Admontensis, *Homiliae dominicales*, Hom. 76, PL 174: 542–49.

sinful human being's haste to follow her own desires and turn away from heavenly things. Jesus' reaching and calling Zacchaeus to come down (Luke 19:5) represent on the macro level God's decision to send his son and call humankind to descend from pride; on the micro level, Jesus' action stands for the Savior's seeing the sinner's evil way of life and humbling himself to call the sinner to repentance. Hildegard interprets the Savior's key words, *"in domo tua oportet me manere"* (Luke 19:5), first as the Incarnation with the house representing the flesh, and second as Jesus' entrance into the sinner's heart if she wants to be saved, with the house standing for the heart. Zacchaeus's climbing down from the tree (Luke 19:6) denotes penitence in the first homily and humility in the second, along with acts of repentance.

When Zacchaeus stands (Luke 19:8), Hildegard sees humankind beginning to do good works, and the sinner as stable in victory over sin. The tax collector's action of giving half his wealth to the poor (Luke 19:8) receives a similar interpretation in both texts: becoming poor in spirit and making oneself small and poor. Returning goods fourfold (Luke 19:8) denotes four virtues in the first homily: knowledge of the good, wisdom, humility, and charity; and four actions in the second: vanquishing the self, putting aside bad habits, doing good works, and persevering to the end—an echo of the *Rule of Benedict*. The house appears again (Luke 19:9), first as human beings in the body and second as the heart and soul. Lastly, becoming a son of Abraham (Luke 19:9) denotes being an inheritor of the kingdom in the first text and a victor over the Devil in the second, where Hildegard adds that one vanquishes the Devil with a dove's simplicity. The parallel exegesis of this passage emerges with clarity: the first homily of the set applies to humankind over history and the second to the individual sinner.

Ambrose expounds a moral interpretation of the Zacchaeus story, warning about the perils of wealth, then comparing Zacchaeus's small stature to wickedness or lack of faith. The crowds signify the many who cannot see the height of wisdom, whereas Zacchaeus's ascent of the tree points to the sublimity of faith among new fruits of new good works. Jerome interprets Zacchaeus's name as *justificatus*, or made righteous. Gregory the Great comments briefly on the Zacchaeus story, comparing his shortness to human limitations, which can be overcome by ascending the sycamore tree, that is, following God's commandments. Hildegard, in contrast, emphasizes the role of descent in repentance.[26]

---

[26] Ambrosius, *Expo. evang. sec. Luc.*, VIII.81–90, 329–31; Gregorius Magnus, *Moralia in Iob* (ed. Marc Adriaen; CCSL 143B; Turnhout: Brepols, 1979), lib. 27, par. 46, pp. 1392–93. Zacchaeus often appears in lists of the wealthy who give up their goods, but his story receives less attention than other Lukan passages studied here. Isidore of Seville cites Zacchaeus as representative of the Gentiles, small in the merits of grace, who are raised up by their efforts on earth to contemplate the mystery of the wood of the cross. Bede adduces the example of Zacchaeus in his exegesis of the Parable of the unjust steward. Isidorus, *Allegoria quaedam Sacrae Scripturae*, PL 83: 0127. Beda, *In Lucae evang. expo.*, lib. 5, p. 334. On this passage and the history of its reception, see François Bovon, *L'Évangile selon Luc (15,1–19,27), Commentaire du Nouveau Testament* IIIc (Geneva: Labor et Fides, 2001), 244–45.

One of Hildegard's *expositiones* on the Parable of the Great Supper (Luke 14:16–21) traces the story of salvation history,[27] but focuses on Adam, his children, and his relationship to creation. In the other homily on the same pericope, Hildegard stages one dimension of the *psychomachia*: the interaction between desire for pleasure and vanity.[28] Vanity serves as desire's messenger, searching for humans who will consent to desire. The individual soul plays only a small role here; and the virtues do not enter the conflict to usher in victory, as they do in some homilies and in the *Ordo virtutum*. Hildegard echoes some exegetical features from Origen, Augustine, and Gregory the Great, namely the interpretation of the five pair of oxen (one invitee's excuse for not attending) as the five senses; and the general emphasis on bodily versus spiritual pleasures. Other exegetes such as Ambrose and Augustine focus on the three excuses together as refusals made by heathens, Jews, and heretics.[29]

In contrast to Hildegard's emphasis on Adam above, her first homily on Luke 2:42–52 focuses on history after the Incarnation. The two *expositiones* for the Sunday within the Octave of Epiphany develop a christological focus from the story of Jesus teaching in the temple at age twelve (Luke 2:42–52).[30] The first homily's allegory begins with the Incarnation and opposes the old and the new law, with Joseph and Mary representing the Jewish people.[31] Mary designates the old law; Joseph stands for Abraham; and Jerusalem represents the peace of redemption. The number twelve refers to the prophets, and the three days stand for the revelation of the prophets, the sages, and the prudent. Jesus' going down to Nazareth and being subject to his parents Mary and Joseph designates coming into humanity through humility and obeying the law.

Knowledge of good and evil furnishes the point of departure for the second homily, a moral allegory where Jesus designates *rationalitas* and Jerusalem stands for faith. Mary designates wisdom and Joseph the admonition of the Holy Spirit. The number twelve refers to the age of reason and the three days to reason, faith, and will for doing good. Hildegard emphasizes here the human's alliance with the virtues: humility, fear of the Lord, wisdom, and obedience, in order to defeat pride, boastfulness, and vainglory. Again the Holy Spirit plays a decisive role. These two *expositiones* on Luke 2:42–52 correspond then *grosso modo* to acts two and three of the drama of salvation: history after the Incarnation, and the inner struggle.

Exegesis of this passage by Ambrose and Bede underscores the two parents of Christ and his two natures, divine from the Father and human from the mother. Jesus appears as both wise and humble, the latter for his listening

---

[27] "Homo quidam fecit coenam magnam," Wiesbaden Hs. 2, 454v–55r; Pitra, 296–98.

[28] "Homo quidam fecit coenam magnam," Wiesbaden Hs. 2, 455r–55v; Pitra, 298–99.

[29] On this passage and the history of its reception, see François Bovon, *L'Évangile selon Luc (9,51–14,35), Commentaire du Nouveau Testament* IIIb (Geneva: Labor et Fides, 1996), 456–57; Stephen Wailes, *Medieval Allegories of Jesus' Parables* (Berkeley: University of California Press, 1997), 161–66.

[30] "Cum factus esset," Wiesbaden Hs. 2, 441v–42r; Pitra, 259–60.

[31] "Cum factus esset," Wiesbaden Hs. 2, 441r–41v; Pitra, 258–59.

and questioning. Ambrose, with Bede following him, signals the heretical reading of verse 51, that Jesus was subordinate to the Father. Another strand of interpretation opposes Jews and Christians, with Joseph and Mary representing the Jews and the synagogue. Reaching the number twelve points to calling the disciples to preach Trinitarian faith everywhere, establishing the Church, represented by Jerusalem, and reaching spiritual understanding. One of Gottfried of Admont's two homilies on the passage illustrates this allegory of the Church, which influences Hildegard's first homily, but he also develops an allegory of the soul, where going up represents ascending to the heavenly city with the aid of virtues. Another reading in the same homily sees Jerusalem as the faithful soul and Jesus' human parents as body (Joseph) and soul (Mary). Hildegard's second homily shares this accent on the virtues but focuses distinctively on *rationalitas*.[32]

In conclusion, a survey of Hildegard of Bingen's exegesis of Lukan passages, both parables and episodes from the life of Christ, demonstrates her method of spiritual exegesis. While her approach is allegorical overall, she follows a pattern that connects the Gospel texts to the whole or part of salvation history, usually divided into two periods—before and after the Incarnation. A third approach focuses on another aspect of *psychomachia*, the soul's inner struggle as it lives out the promise of the Word with the aid of the Holy Spirit. Two sets of three homilies on the same pericopes (Luke 5:1–11; 19:41–47) include two *expositiones* that encompass the span of salvation history and a third that illustrates the human inner struggle. A pair of homilies on Luke 19:1–10, the story of Zacchaeus, exemplifies interpretations that dramatize salvation history either before or after the Incarnation and guards a microcosmic perspective for the second *expositio*. A final pair (Luke 2:42–52; 14:16–21), again selective and not exhaustive, illustrates Hildegard's decision to accentuate one aspect of salvation history before or after the Incarnation in one of the homilies, still retaining the inner allegory for the other. Recalling that Hildegard authored the first extant medieval morality play, one may view her exegetical narrative in terms of three acts in salvation history.

The distinctiveness of Hildegard's exegesis, called "new and unheard-of" by her contemporaries, stands out in comparison to the interpretations of other patristic and medieval exegetes. She weaves her own vision, incorporating elements of the exegetical tradition to develop an often new perspective. Furthermore, Hildegard's often "unheard-of" exegesis illustrates the lasting richness of the Lukan texts and the merit of exploring the full history of their reception.

---

[32] Ambrosius, *Expo. evang. sec. Lucam*, II, 63–66, 57–59; Beda, *In Lucae evang. expo.*, lib. 1, pp. 71–73; Anselmus Cantuariensis, *Homiliae*, Hom 7, PL 157, 628–30; Godefridus Admontensis, *Homiliae dominicales*, Hom 14, 15, PL 174: 95–101, 102–8.

CHAPTER EIGHTEEN

RELECTURE ET DROITS D'AUTEUR:
À PROPOS DE L'INTERPRÉTATION DE LA DEUXIÈME
ÉPÎTRE AUX THESSALONICIENS

Yann Redalié

1. *La leçon du passeur et la question de l'auteur*

Les pages de ce volume dédiées à François Bovon rendent hommage au passeur qui nous invite et nous enseigne à sortir des champs balisés de l'étude du Nouveau Testament, non seulement pour découvrir de nouveaux horizons au premier christianisme, mais aussi pour explorer à partir de territoires extérieurs des perspectives inattendues sur les contrées plus apprivoisées de l'enquête. Si pour le passeur la frontière n'est pas niée, toutefois elle n'est pas étanche. C'est un moment particulier de la communication. A l'écoute de cette leçon je me propose de réfléchir à nouveau sur les lignes de démarcation que dessine à l'intérieur du corpus paulinien la question de l'auteur et que signalent les termes "deutéropauliniennes," "pseudépigraphie," "authenticité." Plus particulièrement c'est de la deuxième épître aux Thessaloniciens qu'il s'agit. La question de l'auteur trace-t-elle pour l'interprétation de la lettre une frontière imperméable et commande-t-elle tout le sens du texte? Comment une interprétation qui considère 2 Thessaloniciens comme relecture de 1 Thessaloniciens contribue-t-elle à ce débat? C'est à ces deux questions que je tenterai de répondre en examinant de plus près l'action de grâce de 2 Thess 1:3–12.

En 1980 Wolfgang Trilling en appelait à une frontière mieux marquée à propos de l'interprétation de 2 Thessaloniciens. Certes depuis le début du dix-neuvième siècle le débat sur l'authenticité de l'épître avait une longue histoire et la critique, relancée de manière décisive par le travail de William Wrede (1903), disposait d'une série d'arguments devenus classiques.[1] Mais l'hypothèse de la pseudépigraphie de 2 Thessaloniciens restait encore le plus souvent

---

[1] William Wrede, *Die Echtheit des zweiten Thessalonischerbriefs untersucht* (TUGAL 24.2; Leipzig: Henrichs, 1903). Pour une histoire de la recherche voir Wilhelm Bornemann, *Die Thessalonischerbriefe* (Göttingen: Vandenhoeck & Ruprecht, 1894), 498–537; Béda Rigaux, *Saint Paul: Les épîtres aux Thessaloniciens* (EBib; Paris: Gabalda; Gembloux: Duculot, 1956), 124–52; Wolfgang Trilling, *Untersuchungen zum zweiten Thessalonicherbrief* (ETS 27; Leipzig: St Benno Verlag, 1972), 11–45; John W. Bailey, "Who Wrote II Thessalonians?," *NTS* 25 (1978–1979); 131–45; Robert Jewett, *The Thessalonian Correspondence: Pauline Rhetoric and Millenarian Piety* (FF: New Testament; Philadelphia: Fortress, 1986), 3–46.

cantonnée dans les questions d'introduction.[2] En fait, dit Trilling, 2 Thessaloniciens manque d'une interprétation qui en rende compte comme d'un écrit pseudo-nymique dans le détail de l'exégèse du texte.[3] C'est à combler cette lacune que s'attache son commentaire de 2 Thessaloniciens sur les traces duquel s'engagent de nombreux exégètes.[4] L'interprétation portera une attention particulière à la comparaison avec les autres épîtres de Paul et surtout avec 1 Thessaloniciens, pour souligner les distances, ou les continuités selon le côté de la frontière herméneutique où le commentateur se situe. Dans le même mouvement les différences relevées donnent son sens au texte et deviennent autant d'indices de sa pseudépigraphie.

Toutefois, dans ces dix dernières s'est exprimée également la nécessité de rééquilibrer une interprétation déterminée pour une large part par les pré-suppositions quant à l'auteur. C'est le sens, par exemple, de la confrontation présentée dans un des volumes de la Society of Biblical Literature consacrés à la théologie de Paul.[5] Tout d'abord, à partir de deux points de vue diver-gents quant à l'auteur, deux articles mettent en évidence, chacun dans sa per-spective, un trait constitutif de la communication théologique de 2 Thessaloniciens. Edgar Krentz dégage l'aspect profilé du message, ce qui le différencie des autres épîtres de Paul. Pour lui l'auteur pseudépigraphe réutilise des motifs de la tradition apocalyptique pour en faire le foyer unique qui met en per-spective toute la communication exclusivement orientée vers le salut futur. En

---

[2] Cf. Ernest Best, *The First and the Second Epistles to the Thessalonians* (BNTC; London: Black, 1972; 2ᵉ éd., 1979), 52: "It is curious how the vast majority of the commenta-tors accept the letter as genuine while its rejectors are found among those who approach the letter from the aspect of 'introduction.'"

[3] Wolfgang Trilling, *Der zweite Brief an die Thessalonicher* (EKKNT 14; Zürich: Benziger; Neukirchen-Vluyn: Neukirchener Verlag, 1980), 29–30.

[4] Gerard Krodel, "2 Thessalonians," in *Ephesians, Colossians, 2 Thessalonians, The Pas-toral Epistles* (éd. J. Paul Sampley et al.; Proclamation Commentaries; Philadelphia: Fortress, 1978), 73–96; Willi Marxsen, *Der zweite Thessalonischerbrief* (ZBKNT 11.2; Zürich: Theologischer Verlag, 1982); Franz Laub, *1 und 2 Thessalonicherbriefe* (NEchtB 13: Würzburg: Echter, 1985); Maarten J. J. Menken, *2 Thessalonians* (New Testament Readings; London/New York: Routeledge, 1994); Earl J. Richard, *First and Second Thessalonians* (SP 11; Collegeville, Minn.: Liturgical Press, 1995); Beverly Roberts Gaventa, *First and Second Thessalonians* (IBC; Louisville: John Knox, 1998); Eckart Reinmuth, "Der zweite Brief an die Thessalonicher," in *Die Briefe an die Philipper, Thessalonicher und an Philemon* (éd. Nikolaus Walter et al.; NTD 8.2; Tübingen: Vandenhoeck & Ruprecht, 1998), 159–202; Simon Légasse, *Les épîtres de Paul aux Thessaloniciens* (LD: Commentaires 7; Paris: Cerf, 1999).

[5] Voir dans Jouette M. Bassler, ed., *Pauline Theology 1: Thessalonians, Philippians, Galatians, Philemon* (Minneapolis: Fortress, 1991), les textes de Edgar Krentz, "Through a Lens: Theology and Fidelity in 2 Thessalonians," 52–62, de Robert Jewett, "A Matrix of Grace: The Theology of 2 Thessalonians as a Pauline Letter," 63–70, et de Jouette M. Bassler, "Peace in All Ways: Theology in the Thessalonian Letters: A Response to R. Jewett, E. Krentz, and E. Richard," 71–85; présentation critique de l'expérience dans Richard, *Thessalonians*, 24–25.

revanche, Robert Jewett, que sa compréhension de la lettre comme authentique rend attentif aux continuités, en valorise, dans les parties plus formelles (salutations, actions de grâce, prières) qu'elle partage avec 1 Thessaloniciens, les motifs non apocalyptiques. Ainsi le thème central de la lettre est la grâce qui donne à la communauté la force de supporter l'affliction et d'attendre le retour final du Seigneur.

D'autre part, en réponse aux contributions de ses deux collègues, Jouette M. Bassler s'efforce d'interpréter la lettre du seul point de vue littéraire, en laissant en suspens la question de l'auteur. Partant de l'inclusion "grâce et paix" du début et de la fin de la lettre (2 Thess 1:2; 3:16, 18), elle identifie dans ce don et cet appel à la paix la nervure et le motif principal qui réapparaît dans chacun des passages de l'épître comme invitation au calme et à la tranquillité.

Ce débat sur la frontière herméneutique quant à l'auteur met en évidence des aspects différents du message de la lettre et permet des rééquilibrages de l'interprétation qui rendent mieux compte de tout le texte. Dans cette direction on peut citer en outre les travaux de Maarten J. J. Menken, en particulier son étude sur la christologie de 2 Thessaloniciens,[6] et le commentaire de Earl J. Richard,[7] qui, tous deux, interprètent la lettre dans une perspective deutéropaulinienne. Au terme de son étude, Menken relève que si le message spécifique de 2 Thessaloniciens concerne l'eschatologie apocalyptique et ses conséquences pratiques, les parties les plus formelles de la lettre présentent Jésus comme le Seigneur qui assiste la communauté dans le présent, que l'on peut prier, qui donne la grâce et la paix. Or ces passages conventionnels, faits de formules qui dérivent le plus souvent de 1 Thessaloniciens, doivent être considérés comme porteurs d'une conception partagée entre auteur et destinataires et donc comme une présupposition permanente dans la communication. Dans une direction analogue Richard adresse sa critique aux tenants de la pseudépigraphie de la lettre qui, attentifs à relever les différences d'avec la christologie de Paul, interprètent trop unilatéralement la visée de l'auteur comme uniquement orientée vers le futur.[8] Selon lui il faut distinguer l'obsession apoca-lyptique présente chez les destinataires de l'intention de l'auteur de les en détourner en réaffirmant une approche traditionnelle à la pensée chrétienne et au comportement.

Dans cette recherche d'une interprétation moins marquée unilatéralement par la question de l'auteur, quelle peut être la contribution d'une approche qui considère 2 Thessaloniciens comme relecture de 1 Thessaloniciens?

---

[6] Maarten J. J. Menken, "Christology in 2 Thessalonians: A Transformation of Pauline Tradition," *EstBib* 54 (1996): 501–22; voir aussi son commentaire (plus haut n. 4).

[7] Richard, *Thessalonians*.

[8] Ibid., 27–28.

2. Si la seconde épître aux Thessaloniciens relit la première

Depuis Wrede la relation entre 1 et 2 Thessaloniciens est au centre de la discussion relative à l'auteur de 2 Thessaloniciens et l'argument principal en faveur de la pseudépigraphie.[9] Or dans les travaux récents que Jean Zumstein et Andreas Dettwiler consacrent aux phénomènes de "relecture" caractéristiques de la rédaction de l'évangile de Jean, le rapport entre les deux épîtres aux Thessaloniciens est plusieurs fois cité comme exemple de la diffusion de cette relation de relecture dans certaines traditions bibliques.[10] Certes, dire que 2 Thessaloniciens relit 1 Thessaloniciens n'est pas nouveau. Déjà Wrede représente le procédé littéraire de l'auteur de 2 Thessaloniciens comme une relecture de 1 Thessaloniciens. L'auteur écrit sa lettre en suivant des yeux son modèle (voir *Echtheit* 78, "Sein Blick blieb.... Dabei kehrte sein Auge zugleich zur Danksagung ... zurück....."). De même lorsque Trilling parle d'imitation quant à la forme et d'enseignement complémentaire quant au contenu.[11]

Ce qui distingue pourtant les nouvelles réflexions sur la relecture, c'est que la question n'est pas abordée dans la perspective de formuler des hypothèses sur l'auteur et sur la formation du texte dérivé. Ces interrogations sont secondaires et l'attention se porte en priorité sur l'ensemble de la relation entre les textes. De manière générale, la relecture désigne dans cette optique "une relation entre deux textes qui s'interprètent mutuellement. Un premier texte provoque la constitution d'un deuxième texte, qui n'est pleinement compréhensible que par rapport à son texte de base."[12] La relecture n'est pas seulement un phénomène interne comme dans le quatrième évangile, elle peut aussi s'effectuer comme reprise d'un écrit par un autre. Ainsi Matthieu relit Marc et 1 Jean le quatrième évangile. C'est également le type de relation que Daniel Marguerat reconnaît entre les Actes apocryphes de Paul et les Actes

---

[9] Wrede, *Echtheit*; Raymond F. Collins, *Letters that Paul Did Not Write: The Letter to the Hebrews and the Pauline Pseudepigrapha* (GNS 28; Wilmington, Del.: Glazier, 1988), 215–23; Trilling, *Untersuchungen*; Marxsen, *Der zweite Thessalonischerbrief*, 15–28; Menken, *2 Thessalonians*, 36–39; Richard, *Thessalonians*, 20–25; Andreas Dettwiler, "La Deuxième Épître aux Thessaloniciens," in *Introduction au Nouveau Testament: Son histoire, son écriture, sa théologie* (éd. Daniel Marguerat; Genève: Labor et Fides, 2000), 296–98.

[10] Andreas Dettwiler, *Die Gegenwart des Erhöhten* (FRLANT 169; Göttingen: Vandenhoeck & Ruprecht, 1995), §2.3, "Das Relecture-Modell," 44–52; idem, "Le phénomène de la relecture dans la tradition johannique: Une proposition de typologie," in *Intertextualités. La Bible en échos* (éd. Daniel Marguerat et al.; Genève: Labor et Fides, 2000), 197; Jean Zumstein, "Le processus de relecture dans la littérature johannique," *ETR* 73 (1998): 164.

[11] Trilling, *Der zweite Brief*, 25; idem, "Literarische Paulusimitation im 2. Thessalonischerbriefe," in *Paulus in den neutestamentlichen Spätschriften: Zur Paulusrezeption im Neuen Testament* (éd. Karl Kertelge; QD 89; Freiburg: Herder; 1981). Voir aussi Margaret M. Mitchell, "A Tale of Two Apocalypses," *CurTM* 25 (1998): 200–209, en particulier le paragraphe "2 Thessalonians, a revision of 1 Thessalonians."

[12] Dettwiler, "Le phénomène de la relecture," 188; sur le concept de relecture Zumstein et Dettwiler renvoient à Gérard Genette, *Palimpseste: La littérature au second degré* (Paris: Seuil, 1982), particulièrement 7–14, tout en relevant que Genette parle de transtextualité et non pas de relecture.

canoniques.[13] Cette relecture externe a lieu "lorsque la réception d'une oeuvre soulève des problèmes tels qu'elle appelle la naissance d'une nouvelle oeuvre disant comment l'oeuvre première peut être droitement comprise."[14] Dans notre cas, comment comprendre dans une situation nouvelle des enseignements, déjà donnés en 1 Thessaloniciens, sur la rencontre finale avec le Christ.

On précise en outre que le texte second "évoque plus ou moins manifestement [le texte qu'il relit] sans nécessairement parler de lui ou le citer."[15] On retrouve ici la complexité de la relation entre les deux lettres aux Thessaloniciens. La similitude formelle—les formules analogues semblent situées stratégiquement en 2 Thessaloniciens pour obtenir l'effet de parallélisme sur la structure d'ensemble de l'épître—fait penser à une imitation de la première de la part de la seconde, alors qu'on souligne leur différence quant au contenu du message. De plus en 2 Thess 2:2, 15 la lettre dont il est question peut-elle être identifiée à 1 Thessaloniciens? En 2 Thess 2:2, à une interprétation tendancieuse de ses énoncés eschatologiques objet d'une correction nécessaire, et en 2 Thess 2:15, à sa juste compréhension en harmonie avec le complément eschatologique à peine donné en 2 Thess 2:1–12? L'énoncé de ces interrogations indiquent que la relecture proposée par 2 Thessaloniciens s'inscrit dans un conflit d'interprétations.

A partir des thèses de Dettwiler, Marguerat résume en trois axiomes la relation de relecture.[16] J'en inverse l'ordre pour une meilleure discussion de la situation de 2 Thessaloniciens: (A) "la relecture n'abroge pas la validité du texte relu, mais la présuppose au contraire"; (B) "la motivation à relire tient à l'évolution interne de la tradition et aux changements de situation historique"; (C) "le texte relisant se distingue du texte relu par un jeu dialectique d'amplification explicitante et de déplacement d'accent." Qu'en est-il de 2 Thessaloniciens?

(A) Le premier axiome correspond à l'hypothèse à peine rappelée que la correction voulue par 2 Thessaloniciens porte sur l'interprétation donnée à l'enseignement eschatologique de 1 Thessaloniciens et non sur cet enseignement lui-même. Le texte relu, 1 Thessaloniciens, demeure le cadre de compréhension dans lequel la réflexion théologique se poursuit.[17] Cette hypothèse est d'ailleurs commune à un grand nombre de ceux qui interprètent la lettre comme venant de Paul[18] et de ceux qui aujourd'hui la considèrent comme pseudépigraphique. A cela l'hypothèse pseudépigraphique ajoute une fonction

---

[13] Daniel Marguerat, *La première histoire du christianisme: Les Actes des Apôtres* (LD 180; Paris: Cerf, 1999); voir ch. 13, "Les 'Actes de Paul', une relecture," ibid., 369–91.

[14] Zumstein, "Processus," 164.

[15] Genette, *Palimpseste*, 13, cité dans Marguerat, *Première histoire*, 377.

[16] Marguerat, *Première histoire*, 377–78; Dettwiler, "Le phénomène de la relecture," 188–98.

[17] Dettwiler, "Le phénomène de la relecture," 190, thèse 2.

[18] Jewett, *Correspondence*, 183; Abraham J. Malherbe, *The Letters to the Thessalonians: A New Translation with Introduction and Commentary* (AB 32b; New York: Doubleday, 2000), 373.

pragmatique à la reprise formelle de la structure d'ensemble de 1 Thessaloniciens: donner une autorité apostolique au nouveau texte.[19]

(B) Les réponses de Paul en 1 Thess 4:13–5:11—sur le sort de ceux qui seront décédés avant la venue du Seigneur et sur les temps de cette venue—se présentent déjà comme un complément d'enseignement requis par des questions précises nées elles-mêmes de la première prédication sur le rassemblement final avec le Seigneur. La tradition sur les temps derniers se développe, corrige éventuellement certains de ses propres effets, exige de nouvelles précisions sur le calendrier de la fin et sur le sort des adversaires.

Outre cette dynamique interne à la tradition,[20] la seconde motivation à la relecture est à chercher dans une situation historique détériorée par rapport à celle que présuppose 1 Thessaloniciens. Les rares traits concrets de la lettre indiquent une pression plus forte de l'extérieur due à des persécutions plus présentes et plus aiguës (2 Thess 1:4–6). A l'intérieur, le risque de déstabilisation s'est accru par la radicalisation des comportements désordonnés relatifs au travail (2 Thess 3:6–15) et par des troubles dus à un enseignement extrême quant à l'actualité du Jour du Seigneur (2 Thess 2:1–2). Encore une fois, que la perspective soit celle d'une épître authentique ou non, ce sont ces trois motifs qui servent à reconstituer une situation des destinataires nécessitant une seconde intervention. Marxsen relève d'ailleurs que "déplacer par l'hypothèse pseudépigraphique la date de la lettre de vingt ans ne changerait pas grand-chose dans l'identification de la situation des destinataires."[21]

(C) Les ressemblances et différences présentes dans le texte second sont l'expression d'un double mouvement de reprise et de développement de motifs du premier texte d'une part, et de l'autre, d'un déplacement d'accent et de reformulations suscitées par la nouvelle situation communicative.[22] Ce qu'il est important de souligner à propos de ce troisième axiome c'est que la dépendance littéraire ne se décide pas tant sur le langage commun aux deux textes que sur l'ensemble des relations de ressemblance et de dissemblance qui font partie de la signification. De même et inversement, le message du texte second ne s'obtient pas par extraction de l'apport original de l'auteur qui se

---

[19] Ce type de relation exclut les hypothèses substitutives. Si 2 Thessaloniciens imite formellement 1 Thessaloniciens, son auteur semble éviter de s'y référer explicitement pour son contenu. L'hypothèse substitutive répond à cette tension: 2 Thessaloniciens se présente comme la vraie lettre aux Thessaloniciens (imitation) traitant 1 Thessaloniciens de faux (la lettre de 2 Thess 2:2 est 1 Thessaloniciens présentée comme un faux) pour pouvoir substituer sa propre vision eschatologique à celle de 1 Thessaloniciens devenue problématique. Voir Andreas Lindemann, "Zum Abfassungszweck des Zweiten Thessalonicherbriefes," *ZNW* 68 (1977): 35–47; Franz Laub, "Paulinische Autorität in nachpaulinischer Zeit," in *The Thessalonian Correspondence* (éd. R. F. Collins; BETL 87; Leuven: Leuven University Press, 1990), 403–17, voir aussi 408 n. 11; Marxsen, *Der zweite Thessalonischerbrief*, 111–12.

[20] Dettwiler, "Le phénomène de la relecture," 192–93, thèse 5.

[21] Marxsen, *Einleitung*, 44, cité dans Trilling, *Untersuchungen*, 158, n. 83.

[22] Dettwiler, "Le phénomène de la relecture," 190–91, thèse 3; Zumstein, "Processus," 166.

détache sur le fond des éléments rapportés de ses sources; ici encore, c'est l'ensemble des relations qui est pris en compte.

Outre les nombreuses analogies formelles entre les deux lettres, relevons que les trois thèmes spécifiques de 2 Thessaloniciens—persécutions, comportement désordonné et eschatologie—sont déjà présents en 1 Thessaloniciens (1:6; 3:3–4; 4:11–12; 5:14; 1:10; 4:15–5:11). Nous verrons en 2 Thessaloniciens 1 comment le thème des souffrances et de la persévérance trouve son expansion et devient un motif clé de l'action de grâce.

A propos du comportement, 2 Thess 3:8b ("mais, dans la peine et la fatigue, de nuit et de jour, nous avons travaillé pour n'être à la charge d'aucun de vous") reprend presque mot pour mot 1 Thess 2:9 ("Vous vous rappelez, frères, nos peines et nos fatigues: c'est en travaillant nuit et jour, pour n'être à la charge d'aucun de vous. . . ."). Le déplacement s'opère sur le sens du savoir imiter introduit en 2 Thess 3:7. En 1 Thess 2:8 c'était l'amour et le dévouement total à la communauté, le partage de l'évangile et de la vie qui amenaient l'apôtre à la libre décision de travailler de ses mains. Le passage de 1 Thess 2:9 à 2 Thess 3:8 est conçu par Malherbe, pour qui 2 Thessaloniciens est authentique, comme un passage de l'implicite à l'explicite.[23] Ce serait le sens de la relecture faite par Paul lui-même. Paul, dont l'autoprésentation en 1 Thess 2:1–12 avait valeur parénétique d'exemple et préparait les exhortations de 1 Thessaloniciens 4 et 5, s'attend maintenant en 2 Thessaloniciens à être imité et indique comment cela doit être fait, jetant ainsi les bases d'une discipline ecclésiastique.

Cette même évolution est interprétée par le tenants de la pseudépigraphie comme une insistance sur l'autorité de la tradition paulinienne. La motivation donnée pour le comportement de l'apôtre n'est plus comme en 1 Thess 2:1–12 le lien intime entre prédication et don de soi, mais la constitution, l'institution d'un exemple apostolique qu'il "faut savoir imiter."[24]

Enfin, à propos de l'eschatologie, 2 Thess 2:1–2 reprend dans le même ordre trois motifs essentiels de 1 Thess 4:13–5:11: la parousie du Seigneur (1 Thess 4:15; 2 Thess 2:1), notre rassemblement auprès de Lui (1 Thess 4:17; 2 Thess 2:1) et le Jour du Seigneur (1 Thess 5:1, 2, 4; 2 Thess 2:2). Plus particulièrement c'est une fausse interprétation de ce dernier motif (1 Thess 5:1–11) qui trouble les destinataires et qui nécessite un recadrage.[25] Sur la base de cet enseignement certains auront prétendu avoir échappé au jugement du jour du Seigneur et vivre déjà dans la lumière du Jour (cf. 1 Thess 5:4–5). Il s'agit donc de compléter l'enseignement déjà donné.

Dans une telle optique de relecture, la comparaison des deux lettres ne se solde pas par une distinction entre éléments d'imitation formelle d'une part, et enseignements spécifiques, entre autres et surtout sur l'eschatologie, de l'autre.

---

[23] Malherbe, *Thessalonians*, 450–51.
[24] Laub, "Paulinische Autorität," 416.
[25] Malherbe, *Thessalonians*, 428–29.

Il y a une réelle reprise de thèmes et de motifs qui sont approfondis et réorientés. C'est dans cette perspective que nous considérerons l'action de grâce de 2 Thess 1:3–12.

3. *L'action de grâce de 2 Thessaloniciens 1, le sens d'une relecture*

La similitude quasi littérale du début des deux lettres aux Thessaloniciens porte à considérer l'action de grâce de la seconde comme une réélaboration de celle de la première.[26] Tout se passe en effet comme si le début de l'action de grâce de 1 Thessaloniciens avait été scindée et distribuée dans les deux parties— action de grâce proprement dite (1:3–4) et prière d'intercession (1:11–12)— qui, en 2 Thessaloniciens 1, forment l'inclusion où s'insère le rappel sur le jugement final (1:5–10). En ce sens l'action de grâce illustre et annonce en médaillon ce qui se produit sur toute l'épître, l'enseignement eschatologique de 1:5–10 est au premier chapitre ce que 2:1–12 est à l'épître: la contribution propre du texte qui se détache sur le fond des fortes analogies du cadre épistolaire des deux lettres. Du point de vue de la relecture pourtant, on l'a dit, ce n'est pas l'extraction de ce qui lui est propre mais c'est l'ensemble des relations, des reprises et des déplacements par rapport au texte d'origine qui donnent son sens au texte second.

Rappelons d'abord les points de contact de 2 Thessaloniciens 1 avec l'action de grâce de 1 Thessaloniciens 1:[27] les paroles d'action de grâce elles-mêmes (2 Thess 1:3 et 1 Thess 1:2), l'introduction de l'intercession (2 Thess 1:11 et 1 Thess 1:2), les trois termes "foi," "amour," et "persévérance" dans le même ordre (2 Thess 1:3, 4 et 1 Thess 1:3), la référence à la persécution et à l'affliction (2 Thess 1:4, 6–7 et 1 Thess 1:6; 2:15), l'expression "l'oeuvre de (la) foi" (2 Thess 1:11 et 1 Thess 1:3), "tous ceux qui croient" (2 Thess 1:10 et 1 Thess 1:7), venir "du ciel/des cieux" (2 Thess 1:7 et 1 Thess 1:10). A cela s'ajoutent des motifs analogues: la vocation des destinataires (2 Thess 1:11) et leur élection (1 Thess 1:4), la fierté des apôtres à leur sujet (2 Thess 1:4) et leur renommée qui se répand (1 Thess 1:7–9; 2:19), le jugement final (2 Thess 1:5–10) et la colère qui vient (1 Thess 1:10).[28]

La relation entre les deux actions de grâce est souvent décrite selon trois types de relation: l'*imitation du cadre formel* de 1 Thess 1:3–5, l'*élimination des élé-*

---

[26] Richard, *Thessalonians*, 314.

[27] Bornemann, *Die Thessalonischerbriefe*, 327–28. Cf. les synopses de W. Wrede, *Echtheit*, 3–7; Richard, *Thessalonians*, 314; Dettwiler, "Deuxième Épître," 296; Reinmuth, "Der zweite Brief," 168.

[28] Relations entre 2 Thess 1:3–12 et le reste de 1 Thessaloniciens: la croissance de l'amour (2 Thess 1:3 et 1 Thess 3:12), être dignes du Royaume de Dieu (2 Thess 1:5 et 1 Thess 2:12), la révélation du Seigneur (2 Thess 1:7 et 1 Thess 3:13), entouré de ses anges (2 Thess 1:7 et 1 Thess 4:16), ceux qui ignorent Dieu (2 Thess 1:8 et 1 Thess 4:5), ses saints (2 Thess 1:10 et 1 Thess 3:13).

ments d'anamnèse et l'*ajout du matériau apocalytique*.[29] Or justement la perspective de relecture, qui valorise l'ensemble des relations de ressemblances et dissemblances, nuance ces trois relations.

Ce qui nous intéresse dans la *reprise du cadre formel*, qui ne se réduit pas à l'imitation, c'est d'abord la triade paulinienne présente en 1 Thess 1:3 reformulée ici sous forme de deux parallélismes (foi et amour v. 3; foi et persévérance v. 4). Outre la différence de forme, on relève le remplacement de l'espérance par la persévérance (cf. 1 Thess 1:3, "la persévérance de l'espérance") que sa troisième position dans la triade met en évidence. L'effet d'emphase est en outre souligné par l'emploi de l'article défini et du pronom personnel au génitif (ὑπὲρ τῆς ὑπομονῆς ὑμῶν). Ensuite, étroitement liée à la persévérance, la terminologie de l'affliction empruntée à 1 Thess 1:6 (et 3:3) s'amplifie notablement (quatre emplois: θλίψεσιν dans le v. 4, τοῖς θλίβουσιν . . . θλῖψιν dans le v. 6, τοῖς θλιβομένοις dans le v. 7; auxquels on peut ajouter les deux verbes "supporter" dans le v. 4 [ἀνέχεσθε], et "souffrir" dans le v. 5 [πάσχετε]).[30] On notera également que le passage de la partie plus formelle (action de grâce proprement dite, vv. 3–4) à la partie apocalyptique (vv. 5–10) s'opère à l'intérieur de cette terminologie. Ainsi, couplée à la foi[31] la persévérance face aux afflictions et aux persécutions devient le pivot du passage, autour duquel les autres thèmes se développent. D'ailleurs, lorsque le motif est établi (vv. 4–5), le texte suit son propre cours (vv. 5–10).

Les *éléments d'anamnèse* ou de rétrospection[32] qu'on ne retrouve pas en 2 Thessaloniciens 1 racontent, en 1 Thess 1:5–10, la foi des destinataires— déclinée d'abord selon la double triade de 1 Thess 1:3—comme un récit qui se propage partout, en Macédoine, en Achaïe et au-delà. Ils ont accueilli les apôtres et la parole dans sa puissance, ils les ont imités eux et le Seigneur, ils ont affronté l'affliction avec joie et sont ainsi devenus à leur tour des modèles. Pourtant, en 2 Thessaloniciens 1, si la foi des Thessaloniciens n'est plus racontée comme cette joyeuse relation d'accueil des apôtres, elle n'en est pas moins présente et son expansion s'y exprime également, mais d'une autre manière. Articulée dans le double parallélisme de 2 Thess 1:3–4 elle est d'abord le sujet de verbes de croissance ("surabonder," ὑπεραυξάνει; "se multiplier,"

[29] Légasse, *Thessaloniciens*, 360; Raymond F. Collins, "'The Gospel of our Lord Jesus' (2 Thess 1:8): A Symbolic Shift of Paradigm," in *Thessalonian Correspondence* (éd. idem), 426–40.

[30] Sur la présence d'une théologie de la souffrance dans ces versets voir Jouette M. Bassler, "The Enigmatic Sign: 2 Thessalonians 1:5," *CBQ* 46 (1984): 496–510, discuté par Richard, *Thessalonians*, 316; Charles A. Wanamaker, *The Epistles to the Thessalonians: A Commentary on the Greek Text* (NIGTC; Grand Rapids: Eerdmans; Exeter: Paternoster Press, 1990), 222; Gaventa, *Thessalonians*, 102–3; Menken, *2 Thessalonians*, 85–86; et Malherbe, *Thessalonians*, 408.

[31] En raison du couplage avec la persévérance et du contexte en général, certains préfèrent le sens de fidélité à celui de foi. D'un avis différent Wanamaker, *Thessalonians*, 218.

[32] Collins, "Symbolic Shift of Paradigm."

"croître," πλεονάζει dans le v. 3) auxquels répond l'accomplissement demandé dans l'intercession (mener à terme, accomplir, πληρώσῃ dans le v. 11).

En 1 Thess 1:9–10, on raconte comment les destinataires s'étaient détournés des idoles pour servir le Dieu vivant. Le récit rapporté (1 Thess 1:9, "on raconte," ἀπαγγέλλουσιν) s'achève en fait sur une formule réélaborée par Paul à partir d'emprunts à des traditions (1 Thess 1:9–10)[33] et se conclut sur l'attente du retour de Jésus: "... pour attendre des cieux son Fils qu'il a ressuscité des morts, Jésus, qui nous arrache à la colère qui vient" (1 Thess 1:10). Plus que d'ajout *d'éléments apocalyptiques*—troisième relation—il s'agira donc en 2 Thess 1:5–10 d'expansion d'un motif présent en 1 Thessaloniciens dès l'action de grâce. En effet, ce passage apocalyptique, qui décrit le jugement final, prolonge le récit de 1 Thess 1:5–10 à partir de là où il se concluait (1 Thess 1:10). Que se passera-t-il quand le Seigneur Jésus viendra du ciel (cf. 2 Thess 1:7), pour nous arracher (cf. 2 Thess 1:7, 10) à la colère qui vient sous forme de jugement (cf. 2 Thess 1:5, 6, 8, 9)?

La non reprise du motif de la résurrection de Jésus est significative d'un déplacement d'accent quant au temps.[34] C'est de la relation entre le présent et le futur que traite avant tout 2 Thessaloniciens. Ainsi le second motif repris et développé en 2 Thessaloniciens 1 est celui de l'attente. En effet, en 1 Thess 1:10 "attendre" (ἀναμένειν)[35] la venue du Fils est le dernier verbe du récit qui exprime l'agir des destinataires. C'est aussi le moment où le récit cesse et où, à travers la reprise de traditions, il s'ouvre sur la durée présente. Or c'est bien cette étape-là, le temps de l'attente comme présent orienté vers le futur, qui trouve son développement dans les deux parties plus conventionnelles de 2 Thess 1:3–4 et 11–12.

Ainsi, du point de vue de la relecture 2 Thessaloniciens 1 poursuit et développe l'exhortation et la représentation de l'action de grâce à partir de là où 1 Thess 1:10 concluait, et cela sur les deux plans déjà présents dans la tradition reprise alors par Paul. D'une part, le texte de 2 Thessaloniciens 1 développe le contenu de l'événement attendu de la venue du Seigneur et du jugement final (2 Thess 1:5–10), et de l'autre, il explicite les conditions de cette attente (2 Thess 1:3–4, 11–12). Dans cette perspective, le couplage foi et persévérance face à l'affliction et aux persécutions propose cette durée de

---

[33] Raymond F. Collins, *Studies on the First Letter to the Thessalonians* (BETL 46; Leuven: Leuven University Press, 1984), 254, 339–41; Malherbe, *Thessalonians*, 118–22.

[34] Richard, *Thessalonians*, 51, 53–58, 73–76; Malherbe, *Thessalonians*, 131–32; 1 Thess 1:9–10 se présente comme un discours rapporté par Paul, un rapport oral ou écrit sur lequel Paul serait intervenu (passage de la 3ème à la deuxième personne). Une tradition sur les Thessaloniciens en train de se former. Ces versets sont donc considérés comme une composition paulinienne à partir d'éléments rapportés et traditionnels. Ainsi par exemple, en 1:10 Paul pourrait avoir ajouté la mention de la résurrection pour mettre le discours en ligne avec sa christologie (Richard, *Thessalonians*, 75).

[35] Unique dans le NT, on trouve le verbe dans la LXX en contexte eschatologique Ésa 59:11; Jdt 8:17; Jér 13:16.

l'attente du Fils qui vient des cieux comme occasion de croissance et d'accomplissement.[36]

4. Un horizon pour le présent

Or l'annonce, centrale dans cette action de grâce, du Seigneur Jésus qui vient comme juge eschatologique pour tirer vengeance des ennemis de la communauté, est considérée comme caractéristique d'un message deutéropaulinien. Le motif est double, d'une part une "christologie du Seigneur" orientée exclusivement vers le futur du jugement, de l'autre, l'insistance sur le sort final des adversaires alors que Paul ne s'arrête qu'à celui des croyants. Dans la perspective que nous avons présentée, cette interprétation demande à être rééquilibrée.

Tout d'abord, l'ensemble des relations de relecture de 1 Thessaloniciens 1 amène à valoriser la structure inclusive de l'action de grâce de 2 Thessaloniciens 1 et à interpréter le passage central dans et par son contexte. 2 Thess 1:5–10 se comprend comme la motivation eschatologique à l'attente fidèle sur la qualité de laquelle insiste 2 Thess 1:3–4, 11–12.

Ensuite, ce passage au Seigneur Jésus marque un déplacement de la perspective temporelle de 1 Thessaloniciens à 2 Thessaloniciens.[37] Il ne s'agit pas exclusivement d'une orientation vers le futur; l'attente vit également son présent. L'action de grâce part du présent des souffrances (2 Thess 1:3–4) pour retourner à celui d'une pratique chrétienne digne de la vocation qui a pour but la glorification du Seigneur et des croyants (1:11–12). Si l'on tient compte des différences et des ressemblances, les énoncés christologiques indiquent deux pôles: le Seigneur à venir du jugement final et le Christ élevé à qui appartient la communauté (v. 1), de qui vient la grâce et la paix de la salutation et de l'intercession (vv. 2, 12), dont le nom est glorifié par la qualité de l'existence des chrétiens et l'accomplissement des oeuvres de bien (v. 12). Le Seigneur est à la fois le Seigneur cosmique (v. 10) et celui qui est glorifié et reconnu dans la communauté (vv. 11–12). Cette double accentuation des temps, sur le futur et le présent, se fait jour à plus d'un endroit. Être digne trouve sa référence par rapport au Royaume (v. 5) mais aussi dans l'accomplissement quotidien du bien (v. 11). La glorification du Seigneur aura lieu "quand il viendra" (v. 10) mais aussi "en vous" dans ce temps d'attente objet de l'intercession (v. 12).[38]

Enfin, le jugement se répète trois fois. Au verset 5, en ouverture, seuls les croyants ("vous") seront récompensés pour leurs souffrances. Au versets 6–7, persécuteurs et persécutés trouvent leur juste compte, alors qu'en 1:8–9, effectivement, le passage le plus long est dédié à la seule punition des sans Dieu ni

---

[36] Luke Timothy Johnson, *The Writings of the New Testament: An Interpretation* (rev.; Minneapolis: Fortress, 1999), 289.

[37] Collins, "Symbolic Shift of Paradigm."

[38] Richard, *Thessalonians*, 320–21.

évangile. Le passage se conclut sur l'assemblée glorifiante et finale, accessible par la relation des destinataires aux apôtres (v. 10, "vous avez cru en notre témoignage"). Prolongeant l'attente exprimée en 1 Thess 1:10, la situation et le sort des destinataires de la lettre restent au coeur de l'attention. Ce qui est "nouveau" c'est sans doute cet équilibre, ce dualisme, où le sort final des réprouvés est également évoqué, alors qu'en 1 Thessaloniciens il n'était question que des croyants.[39] Est-ce dû à la détérioration de la situation, à l'accroissement de la pression extérieure, à un développement des traditions?

En outre, quoi qu'il en soit du rééquilibrage nécessaire, l'absence de référence explicite au passé est nette. Le centre de gravité se déplace sur la relation futur-présent, sur l'attente justement qui concluait l'action de grâce de 1 Thessaloniciens. Pourtant si par sa fonction épistolaire l'action de grâce est le lieu des "déjà" pour lesquels exprimer sa reconnaissance, ce lien futur-présent est lui aussi un "déjà" de l'attente confiante pour lequel rendre grâce et qui s'oppose au "déjà" qui nie l'attente et jette le trouble en 2 Thess 2:2.

5. Pour conclure

A la question de l'auteur il faudra certainement répondre. Pourtant je ne pense pas qu'elle commande tous les moments de l'interprétation de 2 Thessaloniciens. Au fil de ces remarques, qui se basent sur des constatations bien souvent partagées des deux côtés de la frontière herméneutique relative à l'auteur, il se confirme comment, pour une approche en terme de relecture, la question de l'auteur du texte second reste secondaire.[40] En outre la perspective de la relecture invite à dépasser une interprétation qui inscrirait les ressemblances de 2 Thessaloniciens au seul compte de l'imitation formelle de 1 Thessaloniciens, et cela, dans le but principal d'obtenir ainsi un surplus d'autorité apostolique pour transmettre un enseignement différent, avant tout dans le domaine eschatologique. D'ailleurs en 2 Thess 1:5–7 cet enseignement n'est pas tant un ajout repérable par différence, qu'une expansion de 1 Thess 1:10. Il s'agit de répondre aux nouvelles questions que le développement même de ces traditions suscite dans la confrontation à des situations qui se transforment. C'est l'ensemble des relations de continuité et de discontinuité qui est valorisé et rend mieux compte de tout le texte, même des passages qui, bien qu'ils semblent ne rien dire de nouveau, font partie intégrante du message.

---

[39] Cf. 1 Pier 4:16–19; Luc 16:25.
[40] Dettwiler, "Le phénomène de la relecture," 193–94, thèse 6.

CHAPTER NINETEEN

QUELQUES JALONS POUR UNE INTERPRÉTATION SYMBOLIQUE DES *ACTES DE PAUL*

WILLY RORDORF

Dans un très bel article: "The Child and the Beast: Fighting Violence in Ancient Christianity,"[1] François Bovon a montré, entre autres à l'aide de la littérature apocryphe chrétienne, l'importance de l'idée d'une réconciliation possible entre les animaux sauvages et les hommes sous l'effet de l'annonce de l'Évangile; il a montré, par la même occasion, qu'à la suite d'Ésaïe 11:6, la métaphore de l'enfant, appliquée à Jésus, joue dans ce contexte un grand rôle.

Bien qu'il ait cité dans son article les *Actes de Paul*[2] et qu'il se soit référé à une étude de Christopher R. Matthews consacrée au même problème,[3] j'aimerais reprendre le pinceau et essayer de compléter le tableau, espérant faire plaisir à notre ami à l'occasion de ses soixante-cinq ans.

Je me pencherai donc sur les parties des *Actes de Paul* où des animaux sauvages interviennent, d'une part sur les *Actes de Paul et de Thècle*, d'autre part sur l'Acte 9 des *Actes de Paul*, c'est-à-dire l'épisode d'Éphèse.

Thècle

Il ne faut pas trop s'étonner que les *Actes de Paul et de Thècle*—pourtant très appréciés dans les traditions hagiographique et iconographique—provoquent généralement un sourire amusé de la part du lecteur et de la lectrice modernes: tant les traits miraculeux y abondent et se cumulent; on trouve que c'est un exemple typique de cette littérature populaire, naïve, crédule qui se gave d'histoires invraisemblables et sans valeur pour un esprit quelque peu critique.

Et il ne faut pas non plus s'étonner que des chercheurs comme Margaret P. Aymer: "Hail-storms and Fireballs: Redaction, World Creation, and Resistance

---

[1] François Bovon, "The Child and the Beast: Fighting Violence in Ancient Christianity," *HTR* 92 (1999): 369–92.

[2] Ibid., 372–73 n. 11; 387–88.

[3] Christopher R. Matthews, "Articulate Animals: A Multivalent Motif in the Apocryphal Acts of the Apostles," in *The Apocryphal Acts of the Apostles: Harvard Divinity School Studies* (éd. François Bovon, Ann Graham Brock, and Christopher R. Matthews; Religions of the World; Cambridge: Harvard University Press for the Harvard University Center for the Study of World Religions, 1999), 205–32.

in the *Acts of Paul and Thecla*"[4] essaient, non sans succès, de démontrer que ce texte n'est pas fait d'une seule pièce, mais se compose de deux récits populaires réunis par un rédacteur ultérieur.[5]

Malgré ces observations judicieuses, la question reste ouverte: Pourquoi le rédacteur final a-t-il jugé bon de réunir ces deux récits et de les incorporer dans son roman sur l'apôtre Paul? N'est-il qu'un conteur d'histoires qui n'a d'autre but que d'en collectionner le maximum et de les présenter à son public friand de merveilles divertissantes sans sens profond, ou y a-t-il un concept dans ce qu'il fait, une logique interne, un sens symbolique que ses contemporains comprenaient sans peine, mais que nous autres, enfants d'un peine temps et d'une peine mentalité, devons nous efforcer de découvrir?

C'est ma thèse, dans ce qui suit, qu'il faut répondre par oui au deuxième terme de l'alternative. En effet, le presbytre qui, aux dires de Tertullien (*Bapt.* 17.5), a rédigé les *Actes de Paul*, a eu un projet en tête: il a voulu écrire un texte *initiatique*.

Au début des *Actes de Paul et de Thècle*, l'apôtre Paul prononce un discours, dans la maison d'Onésiphore, qui a valeur programmatique (3.5–6). Il s'agit d'une suite de macarismes qui tournent autour des thèmes ἐγκράτεια et ἀνάστασις et de leur relation;[6] on pourrait le formuler ainsi: la continence (sexuelle) est une force qui s'apparente à celle de la résurrection, une personne continente anticipe en quelque sorte l'état de la résurrection, elle personnifie le paradis retrouvé. Le baptême est le "sceau" de cette régénération qu'il faut garder intacte. Toute l'histoire de Thècle qui se convertit à la suite de cette prédication de l'apôtre, sert de démonstration à la vérité de cette thèse.

Dans un premier temps—il s'agit ici de l'épisode d'Iconium (*Actes de Paul* 3)—Thècle doit surmonter la passion amoureuse qui la lie à son fiancé Thamyris, pour se vouer corps et âme au Christ qui s'incarne pour elle sous les traits de l'apôtre. C'est un processus douloureux qui, extérieurement, lui attire l'incompréhension et ensuite la haine de ses proches et de toute la ville, mais qui, intérieurement, la mène au "martyre" du bûcher (qu'elle ne subit pas extérieurement!) où sa passion sexuelle est brûlée, extirpée jusqu'à la racine. Par la providence divine, une pluie abondante se déverse sur elle, de sorte que "le feu fut éteint et que Thècle fut sauvée" (*Actes Paul* 3.22). Elle demande à Paul de recevoir le "sceau" du baptême, mais l'apôtre lui dit: "Tu es belle, et je crains qu'une autre épreuve ne t'emporte, pire que la première, et que tu ne puisses la supporter, mais qu'en elle tu ne faiblisses. . . . Sois patiente, et tu recevras l'eau" (3.25).

---

[4] In *Semeia* 79 (1997): 45–61.

[5] Cf. Anne Jensen, *Thekla—die Apostolin: Ein apokrypher Text neu entdeckt* (Frauen, Kultur, Geschichte 3; Freiburg im Breisgau: Herder, 1995; réimpr., München: Kaiser, 1999), 71–116.

[6] Wilhelm Schneemelcher, *Neutestamentliche Apokryphen* [2 vols.; 5ᵉ éd. de la collection fondée par Edgar Hennecke; Tübingen: Mohr/Siebeck, 1987–1989], 2:213) a raison de mettre ces termes au centre de l'intérêt théologique des *Actes de Paul*.

Cette promesse se réalise à Antioche, l'étape suivante (*Actes de Paul* 4). L'aggression sexuelle qui se présente à elle en la personne d'Alexandre, n'a plus de prise sur Thècle. Elle est maintenant devenue "servante de Dieu" (δούλη θεοῦ, 4.1 [26]).[7] Le gouverneur la condamne aux jeux des bêtes sauvages dans l'arène. Or, à l'étonnement de tous les spectateurs, aucune des bêtes lâchées contre elle ne lui fait du mal. Lors du défilé des bêtes déjà, une lionne féroce lèche les pieds de Thècle (4.3 [28]). Dans l'arène, la même lionne prend sa défense et tue une ourse et un lion qui veulent s'attaquer à elle (4.8 [33]). Thècle se jette alors dans une grande fosse pleine d'eau, en disant: "C'est maintenant le moment de recevoir le bain." Le baptême a un effet foudroyant: les phoques qui se trouvent dans la fosse voient l'éclat flamboyant d'un éclair et en meurent. Quant à Thècle, un nuage de feu l'entoure, de sorte que les bêtes ne la touchent pas et que sa nudité échappe aux regards (4.9 [34]). Même des taureaux qu'on excite aux parties génitales et auxquels on l'attache ne peuvent pas lui faire de mal (4.10 [35]).

Thècle prononce à ce moment-là un discours; c'est son seul discours dans tout le récit, il doit donc avoir une certaine importance! Citons ce texte (4.12–13 [37–38]):

> 4.12 [37]Alors, le gouverneur fit amener Thècle du milieu des bêtes et lui dit: "Qui es-tu? Et quelle protection t'entoure[8] pour que pas une seule des bêtes ne t'ait touchée?" Thècle répondit: "Je suis la servante du Dieu vivant; la protection qui m'entoure, c'est d'avoir cru en celui en qui Dieu a mis son bon plaisir, en son Fils; c'est par lui que pas une seule des bêtes ne m'a touchée. Lui seul en effet est la pierre de touche[9] du salut, le fondement de la vie immortelle; car il devient le refuge de ceux qui sont agités par la tempête, le repos des affligés, l'abri des désespérés; en un mot, celui qui n'aura pas cru en lui ne vivra pas, mais mourra pour l'éternité." 4.13 [38]A ces paroles, le gouverneur ordonna qu'on apporte des vêtements et dit: "Revêts ces habits, Thècle!" Mais elle dit: "Celui qui m'a revêtue quand j'étais nue au milieu des bêtes fauves, celui-là, au jour du jugement, me[10] revêtira du salut."

Lors de son baptême dans la fosse aux phoques,[11] Thècle reçoit un "vêtement" qui la protège et qui cache sa nudité: il s'agit d'un nuage de feu.

---

[7] Cette expression qui marque l'appartenance de Thècle à son nouveau maître, revient plus loin dans le discours qu'elle prononce devant le gouverneur (voir plus bas). Le gouverneur la reprend dans son acte d'acquittement, ce qui contraste singulièrement avec l'accusation qu'on avait portée contre Thècle: ἱερόσυλος.

[8] La suite montre qu'il faut rendre ainsi l'expression grecque τίνα τὰ περὶ σέ.

[9] Les meilleurs manuscrits lisent ὅρος, au lieu de ὁδός. "Pierre de touche" est une manière de rendre intelligible le terme de "borne" ou de "limite." On pourrait peut-être aussi dire: "enclos" ou "lieu protégé."

[10] Tous les manuscrits grecs lisent σε au lieu de με; mais les éditeurs ont sans doute raison de corriger le texte. Dans une étude inédite, le Prof. Robert Doran (Amherst, Mass., États-Unis) a défendu la leçon des manuscrits grecs, mais il ne m'a pas encore convaincu.

[11] Il s'agit d'un baptême extraordinaire, certes, mais non pas d'un autobaptême, car

Apparemment, les animaux sauvages sentent la force surnaturelle qui se dégage d'elle, dès avant son baptême, et la laissent tranquille; les phoques sont même comme électrocutés par l'effet de l'éclair qui s'abat sur l'eau.

Tout cela n'est pas sans rappeler quelques traits dans certains récits qui racontent le baptême de Jésus. Dans l'Évangile de Marc (1:13), on nous dit que les bêtes sauvages servent Jésus dans le désert, après son baptême. La mention du feu, symbolisant le Saint-Esprit, n'est pas absente des Évangiles synoptiques (Matt 3:11; Luc 3:16), et est même très présente dans les récits judéo-chrétiens du baptême de Jésus: dans l'*Évangile des Ébionites* (Épiphane, *Haer.* 30.13.7–8), et chez Justin Martyr (*Dial.* 88.3).[12] Dans sa réponse au gouverneur, Thècle fait d'ailleurs elle-même le lien entre son baptême de feu et le baptême de Jésus, en disant: "La protection qui m'entoure, c'est d'avoir cru en celui en qui Dieu a mis son bon plaisir, en son Fils," ce qui est une allusion aux paroles divines qui se font entendre au moment du baptême de Jésus (Marc 1:11 par.). Rappelons que les mêmes paroles divines sont prononcées au moment de la Transfiguration de Jésus où le nuage de feu reparaît (Marc 9:7 par.).[13]

Il m'importe de souligner encore un autre détail. Le baptême inaugure pour le baptisé l'état de la résurrection, le paradis retrouvé. Thècle dit que Jésus en qui elle croit est "le fondement de la vie éternelle," et elle assure que "Celui qui m'a revêtue quand j'étais nue au milieu des bêtes fauves, celui-là, au jour du jugement me revêtira du salut."[14]

L'effet que le baptême de Thècle produit sur la reine Tryphaine confirme ce que je viens de dire. A l'annonce de la bonne nouvelle, elle s'exclame: "Maintenant, je crois que les morts ressuscitent; maintenant, je crois que ma fille vit" (4.14 [39]). En effet, Thècle avait intercédé auparavant pour la fille décédée de Tryphaine, Phalconille, pour qu'elle vive en éternité (4.4 [29]).[15] Le spectacle du baptême de Thècle donne maintenant à Tryphaine la démonstration que la force de la résurrection est à l'oeuvre en Thècle et que son intercession est par conséquent exaucée.

Ayant appris ce qui s'est passé, l'apôtre Paul n'hésite plus à lui reconnaître la dignité apostolique; il lui dit: "Va, et enseigne la parole de Dieu" (4.16 [41]), ce qu'elle fera sans tarder, à Séleucie (4.18 [43]).

Thècle dit plus tard à son propos: "J'ai reçu le baptême, Paul. En effet, celui qui a oeuvré avec toi pour la bonne nouvelle a aussi oeuvré avec moi pour que je sois baptisée" (*Actes Paul* 4.15 [40]). Je remercie Peter W. Dunn de m'avoir ouvert les yeux pour cette nuance.

[12] Cf. Daniel A. Bertrand, *Le Baptême de Jésus* (BGBE 14; Tübingen: Mohr/Siebeck, 1973), 45–46.

[13] L'iconographie du baptême de Jésus montre souvent la fuite des démons dans l'eau sous l'effet du Saint-Esprit qui descend, ce qui n'est pas sans rappeler le sort des phoques au moment du baptême de Thècle.

[14] Peter W. Dunn me rend attentif au fait que cette idée trouve son parallèle en *3 Cor* 10.5.26–27.

[15] Voir mon article dans *Liturgie, foi et vie des premiers chrétiens* (2ᵉ éd.; Paris: Beauchesne, 1988), 445–55.

L'ajout ultérieur au récit de Thècle, dans certains manuscrits grecs[16] et arméniens,[17] se situe tout à fait dans la ligne des *Actes de Paul et de Thècle*: Thècle, restée vierge, à l'âge de quatre-vingt-dix ans, ayant accompli beaucoup de miracles, reçoit la visite de jeunes gens dépravés qui veulent partager la couche de cette Artémis chrétienne;[18] en vain, car la nature elle-même protège la servante de Dieu: un rocher se fend et la reçoit vivante, lui servant d'abri.[19]

L'un des premiers témoins indirects des *Actes de Paul et de Thècle*, le traité anonyme du *Physiologue* qui semble dater de la fin du deuxième siècle,[20] mentionne les épreuves de Thècle sur le bûcher, en face des bêtes sauvages et des phoques, en disant qu'il faut étendre ses mains et faire le signe de la croix "pour traverser la mer des passions." Ce traité anonyme comprend donc la valeur symbolique des épreuves de Thècle exactement comme nous l'avons fait!

On pourrait avoir l'impression que les *Actes de Paul et de Thècle* seuls soutiennent le concept symbolique que nous venons d'esquisser; mais il n'en est rien. Un récit tout à fait parallèle se trouve dans un autre épisode incorporé dans les *Actes de Paul*, dans l'Acte 9 qui se situe à Éphèse. Cette fois-ci, c'est l'apôtre Paul lui-même et un lion qui sont au centre du récit.

Paul

Avant la découverte du papyrus grec de Hambourg, en 1927,[21] et surtout du papyrus copte Bodmer 41, en 1959,[22] on ne connaissait que l'existence de la

---

[16] Voir, en attendant mon édition critique nouvelle de ces textes, Léon Vouaux, éd., *Les Actes de Paul et ses lettres apocryphes* (Les Apocryphes du Nouveau Testament; Paris: Letouzey et Ané, 1913), 232–38; Gilbert Dagron avec Marie Dupré La Tour, *Vie et miracles de sainte Thècle* (Subsidia hagiographica 62; Bruxelles: Société des Bollandistes, 1978), 47–54, et 413–21.

[17] Pour ces derniers, voir Valentina Calzolari Bouvier, *La Leggenda di Santa Tecla nella letteratura armena antica* (diss., Milan, 1995), 44–55, et 195–210.

[18] Il est intéressant de faire le rapprochement entre Artémis, reine des animaux, et Thècle, celle qui a vaincu les animaux sauvages! Un texte compare même les jeunes gens dépravés à des lions! Cf. la représentation iconographique de cette scène sur un relief dans Claudia Nauerth et Rudiger Warns, *Thekla: Ihre Bilder in der frühchristlichen Kunst* (Göttinger Orientforschungen, Veröffentlichungen des Sonderforschungsbereiches Orientalistik an der Georg-August-Universität Göttingen², Studien zur spätantiken und frühchristlichen Kunst 3; Wiesbaden: Otto Harrassowitz, 1981), 63–81, et planche XIII.

[19] Dans un texte pseudo-chrysostomien, édité par P. Aubineau (*AnBoll* 93 [1975]: 351–50), un prétendant persécute Thècle et est comparé par elle à un lion!

[20] Cf. Rudolf Riedinger, "Der Physiologus und Klemens von Alexandrien," *ByzZ* 66 (1973): 304–5; Ursula Früchtel, *Physiologus: Frühchristliche Tiersymbolik* (Zürich: Ex libris, 1982), 113–14.

[21] L'édition est de Carl Schmidt, *ΠΡΑΞΕΙΣ ΠΑΥΛΟΥ: Acta Pauli nach dem Papyrus der Hamburger Staats- und Universitäts-Bibliothek* (avec Wilhelm Schubart; Glückstadt/Hamburg: Augustin, 1936). Pour une traduction française, voir *Écrits apocryphes chrétiens I* (éd. François Bovon and Pierre Geoltrain; avec index établis par Sever J. Voicu; Bibliothèque de la Pléiade 442; Paris: Gallimard 1997), 1159–60.

[22] Voir Rodolphe Kasser, "Acta Pauli 1959," *RHPR* 40 (1960): 45–57, et la traduction

"fable du lion baptisé," comme l'appelle avec dédain saint Jérôme dans son *De uiris illustribus* 7. Maintenant, grâce à ces deux papyrus, nous avons tout l'épisode d'Éphèse où l'histoire du baptême du lion par Paul et leur rencontre dans le stade est racontée. Je pense que ce récit est assez intéressant pour qu'il soit rendu ici textuellement. L'apôtre, venant de Smyrne, se trouve à Éphèse parmi les frères et raconte ce qui lui est arrivé après sa conversion à Damas:

> [9.7]Cependant, lorsque vint le soir, je quittai l'agape que donnaient Lemma la veuve et sa fille Ammia. Tandis que je marchais de nuit, voulant aller à Jéricho en Phénicie,[23] nous parcourûmes de longues étapes. Lorsque l'aube arriva, voici que Lemma et Ammia me suivaient, celles qui avaient donné l'agape, car elles m'avaient en très grande affection, si bien qu'elles ne s'éloignaient jamais de moi. Alors survint un énorme lion, affamé,[24] sortant de la vallée du champ des ossements [Ézéchiel 37?]. Cependant, nous restions en prière, tellement que, par l'intensité de la <prière>, Lemma et Ammia [tombèrent?] sur la bête. Toutefois, lorsque j'eus fini de prier, voici que la bête était couchée à mes pieds. Alors, je fus rempli de l'Esprit, je la regardai et lui dis: "Lion, que veux-tu?" Lui me répondit: "Je veux être baptisé!" [9.8]Alors, je rendis gloire à Dieu, qui avait, à la fois, donné une voix à la bête et leur salut à ses serviteurs. Cependant, il y avait un grand fleuve en ce lieu-là. J'y descendis, suivi par la bête. Comme des <colombes> terrorisées par des aigles, se réfugiant en quelque maison pour y être en sécurité, ainsi Lemma et Ammia [. . .];[25] elles ne [. . .] jusqu'à ce que j'aie béni Dieu et que je lui aie rendu gloire. J'étais, moi-même, rempli de crainte et d'étonnement, tandis que je conduisais le lion comme s'il était un boeuf, pour l'immerger dans l'eau. Alors, mes frères, debout au-dessus du fleuve, je m'écriai: "Toi qui habites dans les lieux très hauts, toi qui jettes tes regards sur les humbles, toi qui as fermé la gueule des lions par Daniel, toi qui m'as envoyé mon Seigneur Jésus-Christ, donne-nous d'échapper à la bête! Et, ainsi, le plan fixé (οἰκονομία), accomplis-le!" [9.9]Après avoir terminé cette prière, je conduisis la bête par sa crinière, puis, au nom de Jésus-Christ, je l'immergeai par trois fois. Lorsqu'elle sortit de l'eau, la bête secoua sa crinière en disant: "Que la grâce demeure avec toi!" Et je lui répondis: "Qu'il en soit de même pour toi!" Le lion, là-dessus, remonta en courant vers le champ des ossements, tout joyeux—ce qui me fut en effet révélé en mon coeur. Cependant, une lionne vint à sa rencontre. Mais lui ne se dirigea pas vers elle; au contraire, il s'en détourna et partit en courant vers les bois.

Plus tard, Paul rencontre le même lion dans le stade:[26]

> [9.23]C'est ainsi que Jérôme (le gouverneur) s'en alla siéger au stade. Il donna l'ordre de lâcher un lion féroce, dressé pour cette besogne, tant et si bien

---

française fournie par lui dans Bovon et Geoltrain, éds., *Écrits apocryphes chrétiens I*, 1151–55.

[23] Kasser (ibid., 1152) dit en note: "confusion entre 'Phénicie' et quelque dérivé de φοῖνιξ ('palmier')."

[24] Kasser (ibid., 1153) en note: "ou 'terrifiant.'"

[25] Brève lacune de deux mots, vraisemblablement.

[26] Bovon et Geoltrain, éds., *Écrits apocryphes chrétiens I*, 1159–60.

que toute la foule s'écria: "Lancez à l'attaque le lion sauvage, pour qu'il dévore l'homme qui possède Dieu!" Toutefois, quand on ouvrit la cage et quand le lion en sortit, Paul marcha encore, adressant ses supplications et prières au Seigneur Jésus-Christ. Lorsque les chasseurs envoyèrent le lion à l'attaque, ils restèrent stupéfaits de le voir si énorme, si effrayant. Paul, cependant, ne se retourna pas, <mais acheva> l'oeuvre de la prière qui lui incombait [. . .] le témoignage. <Le lion>, après avoir regardé autour de lui [. . .] et s'être fait voir tout entier, vint en courant <et se coucha> contre les jambes de Paul comme une brebis docile [. . .]. Lorsque <Paul> eut achevé sa prière, <le lion> se remit sur ses pattes et dit à Paul d'une <voix> humaine: <"Que la grâce soit avec> toi!" Or Paul ne s'effraya pas, mais <dit à son tour: "Que la grâce soit avec> toi, lion!" Il <lui> imposa la main, <et toute la foule> s'écria: "Enlève le magicien, enlève le sorcier!" [9.24]<Le lion regardait> Paul, et Paul <regardait le lion. Et> Paul <comprit> que c'était là le lion qui était venu à lui et avait été baptisé. Alors, porté par la foi, Paul dit: "Lion, serais-tu celui que j'ai baptisé?" Et le lion répondit à Paul: "Oui." Alors, Paul reprit la parole et lui dit: "Comment as-tu été capturé?" Le lion dit d'une voix divine: "Comme toi-même, Paul" [9.25]Lorsque Jérôme fit lancer un grand nombre de bêtes contre Paul pour le faire périr, ainsi que des archers contre le lion pour le faire périr lui aussi, alors, bien que l'air fût serein, une grêle compacte et très violente s'abattit du ciel, au point que nombreux furent ceux qui moururent et que tous les autres prirent la fuite. Elle ne toucha ni Paul ni le lion, mais les autres bêtes moururent du fait de l'abondance de la grêle, qui fut telle que Jérôme aussi en eut l'oreille frappée et arrachée, et que la foule s'écria en s'enfuyant: "Sauve-nous, ô Dieu, sauve-nous, ô Dieu de l'homme qui a lutté contre les bêtes!" [9.26]Paul, après avoir salué le lion, qui désormais ne parlait plus, sortit du stade, descendit vers le port et embarqua sur le bateau qui partait pour la Macédoine. Il y avait beaucoup de gens qui voulaient prendre la mer, pensant que la ville allait périr. Paul se joignit donc à eux, comme s'il faisait partie de ceux qui fuyaient. Quant au lion, il gagna les montagnes, comme cela était naturel pour lui.

Il y a plusieurs études récentes qui ont été consacrées au récit du lion baptisé des *Actes de Paul*.[27] Je ne veux pas les passer en revue en détail, pour ne pas allonger; le lecteur et la lectrice averti(e) verront où je m'en inspire et où je m'en éloigne.

---

[27] Wilhelm Schneemelcher, "Der getaufte Löwe in den Acta Pauli," in idem, *Gesammelte Aufsätze zum Neuen Testament und zur Patristik* (éd. Wolfgang Bienert und Knut Schäferdiek; Analekta Vlatadon 22; Thessaloniki: Patriarchal Institute for Patristic Studies, 1974), 223–39; Han J. W. Drijvers, "Der getaufte Löwe und die Theologie der Acta Pauli," in *Carl-Schmidt-Kolloquium an der Martin-Luther Universität 1988* (éd. Peter Nagel; Kongress- und Tagungsberichte der Martin-Luther-Universität Halle-Wittenberg; Wissenschaftliche Beiträge: Martin-Luther-Universitat Halle-Wittenberg 1990, no. 23; Halle [Saale]: Wissenschaftspublizistik der Martin-Luther Universität Halle-Wittenberg, 1990), 181–89; Tamas Adamik, "The Baptized Lion in the Acts of Paul," in *The Apocryphal Acts of Paul and Thecla* (éd. Jan N. Bremmer; Studies on the Apocryphal Acts of the Apostles 2; Kampen: Kok Pharos, 1996), 60–74; Matthews, "Articulate Animals," 205–32 (cité dans notre note 2 plus haut); Robert M. Grant, "Lions in Early Christian Literature," in *The Early Church in Its Context: Essays in Honor of Everett Ferguson* (éd. Abraham J. Malherbe, Frederick W. Norris, et James W. Thompson; NovTSup 90; Leiden: Brill, 1998), 147–54.

Il faut peut-être dire une chose pour commencer: je crois que c'est à tort qu'on cite souvent le récit de l'esclave Androclès comme "parallèle" de ce qui arrive à Paul.[28] Les arguments évoqués sont les suivants:[29]

- les deux fois, le récit se compose de deux volets: une première fois, l'homme et la bête se rencontrent dans la nature, la deuxième fois, ils se retrouvent captivés dans l'arène;
- les deux fois, le lion demande de l'aide à l'homme et est reconnaissant de la recevoir;
- les deux fois, le récit se termine en happy end, l'homme et le lion retrouvent la liberté;[30]
- les deux fois, le lion est décrit comme étant très grand.

Mais raisonner comme cela est méconnaître la différence fondamentale qui existe entre les deux récits. Dans les *Actes de Paul*, en effet, le lion n'est pas seulement guéri d'une plaie, mais demande, avec voix humaine, à être baptisé par l'apôtre. Et dans l'arène, il reprend la parole pour s'entretenir avec Paul. Et à la fin, au lieu de les laisser s'en aller libres, on veut tuer et l'apôtre et le lion.

S'il y a réminiscence du récit païen dans le récit chrétien, la transformation en est tellement radicale qu'on ne peut plus parler de "parallèle." Aussi les autres récits juifs ou païens où des animaux parlent,[31] n'éclairent pas vraiment le problème.[32]

La question cruciale qui se pose est la suivante: pourquoi le lion est-il *baptisé?*[33] Ma réponse est la suivante: le lion est une personnification de la tentation sexuelle qui guette Paul, mais qu'il surmonte à Jéricho déjà, et définitivement à Éphèse.[34] Je m'explique.

C'est quand même étonnant que l'histoire du lion baptisé s'ouvre par cette confession très personnelle de Paul:

> Lorsque vint le soir, je quittai l'agape que donnaient Lemma la veuve et sa fille Ammia. Tandis que je marchais de nuit, voulant aller à Jéricho en

---

[28] Aulus Gellius, *Noctes Atticae* 5.14. Pour la documentation, voir Gerard J. M. Bartelink, "Androclus en de leeuw. De geschiedenis van een literair motief," *Hermeneus* 51 (1979): 2–13.

[29] Voir p.ex. Adamik, "Baptized Lion," 70–72.

[30] Ce qui n'est pas tout à fait juste, puisque dans les *Actes de Paul*, on veut tuer les deux, l'apôtre et le lion, et c'est seulement par miracle qu'ils s'en échappent.

[31] Matthews, "Articulate Animals," 211–13.

[32] A part l'Acte 12 (cf. Actes 8–9) des *Actes de Philippe*, découvert par François Bovon et Bertrand Bouvier; voir leur édition, *Acta Philippi: Textus* (avec Frédéric Amsler; CCSA 11; Turnhout: Brepols, 1999), 300–309; mais ce récit est plus tardif que les *Actes de Paul* et ne peut donc pas être considéré comme un parallèle, et encore moins comme un modèle à ces derniers.

[33] Ainsi déjà, avec raison, Schneemelcher, "Der getaufte Löwe," 235–37.

[34] Puisque le rédacteur des *Actes de Paul* raconte ingénieusement l'événement qui s'est passé près de Jéricho comme préambule à l'épisode d'Éphèse, le lecteur les "téléscope" automatiquement comme une unité.

Phénicie, nous parcourûmes de longues étapes. Lorsque l'aube arriva, voici que Lemma et Ammia me suivaient, celles qui avaient donné l'agape, car elles m'avaient en très grande affection, si bien qu'elles ne s'éloignaient jamais de moi [*Actes Paul* 9.7].

Supposons un moment que l'apôtre avait à lutter lui-même contre un sentiment compréhensible d'amour humain, en face de cette veuve et de sa fille, et que le lion qui surgit tout d'un coup symbolise matériellement cette passion. Beaucoup de choses s'expliqueraient alors mieux.[35]

On comprendrait mieux par exemple les réactions divergentes des femmes et de Paul à l'apparition du lion. Paul et les deux femmes se mettent "intensément" à prier à l'approche du danger. Mais tandis que les femmes "tombent" (si c'est la bonne leçon!) sur le lion, et un peu plus tard, effrayées, restent dans l'attente, "comme des <colombes>," dit le texte, "terrorisées par des aigles, se réfugiant en quelque maison pour y être en sécurité," jusqu'au moment où Paul finit par bénir Dieu et lui rendre gloire, Paul fait l'expérience que le lion, grâce à sa prière, se met à ses pieds, ce qui donne le courage à l'apôtre, maintenant rempli de l'Esprit, de lui poser la question de savoir ce qu'il veut? Suite à la réponse de celui-ci qu'il veut être baptisé, l'apôtre rend gloire à Dieu "qui avait, à la fois, donné une voix à la bête et leur salut à ses serviteurs." Cette exclamation prend tout son sens si le "salut" ici signifie la libération du danger de succomber à la passion sexuelle.

Quoi qu'il en soit, Paul conduit en tremblant le lion au fleuve pour l'immerger. Il s'exclame: "Toi qui as fermé la gueule des lions par Daniel, toi qui m'as envoyé mon Seigneur Jésus-Christ, donne-nous d'échapper à la bête! Et, ainsi, le plan fixé (οἰκονομία), accomplis-le!" Par Jésus-Christ, l'apôtre peut échapper à sa propre sexualité, et ainsi, l'économie du salut peut être accomplie.

Fort de cette certitude, Paul attrape le lion par sa crinière—qui est justement le symbole de sa force sexuelle[36]—et l'immerge dans l'eau. La conséquence immédiate du baptême du lion est le fait que la bête souhaite à Paul: "Que la grâce demeure avec toi!" et que l'apôtre exprime le même voeu pour le lion, voeu qui s'accomplit sur le champ, puisque le lion se détourne de la lionne qui le rencontre et s'enfuit d'elle en courant.[37]

Essayons de résumer ce que nous avons vu jusqu'à présent: Paul, converti à Damas à la foi en Jésus-Christ, par une révélation directe (*Actes Paul* 9.5–6),

---

[35] Remarquons tout de suite que Drijvers ("Der getaufte Löwe," 186–88) a déjà pensé que le lion représente la sexualité, mais il met ce symbole à mon avis trop en rapport avec l'allusion à Ézéchiel 37 et donc avec l'idée de la mort, ce qui le mène à la supposition que les *Actes de Paul* sont encratites; Schneemelcher (*Neutestamentliche Apokryphen* 2:213) l'a déjà critiqué pour cette thèse. J'y reviendrai plus tard.

[36] Cf. Pline l'Ancien, *Nat.* 8.42, cité par Adamik, "Baptized Lion," 67.

[37] La suite du texte: "En sorte que vous aussi, Aquilas et Priscille, ayant cru au Dieu vivant et ayant été enseignés dans sa parole, proclamez-la!" (*Actes Paul* 9.10), est très curieuse. Dans mon commentaire (*Écrits apocryphes chrétiens* I, 1154 n.), je disais "l'enchaînement des idées n'est pas très clair. Aquilas et Priscille, auditeurs du discours précédent de Paul, doivent-ils proclamer la parole à la manière du lion, c'est-à-dire en vivant dans la continence?"

est maintenant converti à la continence sexuelle, par un événement qui le bouleverse et le guérit: sa propre force sexuelle lui apparaît sous la forme d'un lion, mais il arrive à dompter cette force et à la baptiser, au nom de Jésus-Christ. Dans un article,[38] j'ai déjà souligné la parenté entre cette "tentation dans le désert" de Paul et la tentation dans le désert de Jésus.

Ce n'est pas le lieu ici de décrire tout le parcours de l'apôtre vers la continence parfaite tel qu'il se dégage des *Actes de Paul*; il faudrait, pour cela, étudier chaque relation que Paul a avec une femme au cours de ses voyages.

Thècle y tient évidemment une place de choix. Mais elle peut justement servir d'exemple à quel point l'apôtre sait déjà maîtriser les tentations amoureuses. Il est encore homme, mais parfois il a déjà "un visage d'ange" (3.3). Lorsqu'il se trouve seul en face de Thècle, pendant la nuit,[39] dans la prison, il annonce les merveilles de Dieu à la jeune fille, et on nous dit très discrètement: "Paul n'avait peur de rien,[40] mais se conduisait avec l'assurance (παρρησία) de Dieu; sa foi à elle grandissait, et elle baisait ses chaînes" (3.18). Thècle se tient aux pieds de l'apôtre comme le lion! Plus tard, après avoir été flagellé et chassé de la ville à cause de Thècle (3.21), Paul se réfugie dans un tombeau, jeûne et prie pendant six jours pour Thècle, en disant: "Assiste-la, car elle est tienne" (3.23–24); mais il n'ose pas encore lui donner le baptême, devinant qu'une autre épreuve amoureuse l'attend, pire que la première. Or, comme nous le savons, Thècle surmonte aussi victorieusement son épreuve à Antioche, à la suite de quoi l'apôtre la considère comme égale à lui et l'envoie en mission apostolique.

Il faut maintenant que je mentionne encore un autre passage de l'épisode d'Éphèse que j'ai laissé de côté jusqu'à présent. En effet, Paul a, pendant son incarcération à Éphèse, deux autres femmes comme disciples: Artémylla, la femme du gouverneur Jérôme, et Euboula, la femme de Diophantos, affranchi de Jérôme. C'est d'ailleurs ce fait qui provoque la jalousie des deux hommes et les pousse à faire tuer Paul tout de suite. Puisque le combat de l'apôtre contre le lion doit se situer le lendemain—il n'est pas un hasard que Paul l'entend déjà rugir "sauvagement et violemment" et s'effraye (la sexualité se réveille de nouveau!)[41]—les deux femmes demandent à l'apôtre de les baptiser pendant la nuit!

Artémylla s'est d'ailleurs parée de beaux vêtements pour sa rencontre avec l'apôtre, ce qui lui vaut un blâme sévère de la part de celui-ci: "Femme, dominatrice de ce monde, maîtresse de l'or abondant, citoyenne au luxe débordant, orgueilleuse de tes vêtements, assieds-toi par terre (comme le lion!) et oublie ta richesse, ta beauté et tes vantardises mondaines. Car cela ne te servira de

---

[38] "Paul's Conversion in the Canonical Acts and in the *Acts of Paul*," *Semeia* 80 (1997): 142.

[39] Comme à Jéricho, le moment critique est de nouveau la nuit!

[40] Ou, selon une autre forme du texte, peut-être mieux: "Comme Paul ne semblait rien souffrir."

[41] *Actes Paul* 9.15.

rien si tu ne pries pas Dieu, lui qui considère comme des ordures les choses extraordinaires d'ici-bas, mais qui donne gracieusement les merveilles de l'au-delà. L'or périt, la richesse se perd, les vêtements s'usent, la beauté vieillit."[42] Plus loin, le récit devient si énigmatique que je dois le citer textuellement:[43]

> [9.18]Quant aux femmes, elles dirent à Paul: "Veux-tu que nous amenions un forgeron pour que, libéré par ses soins, tu puisses nous baptiser dans la mer?" Paul répondit: "Non, je ne veux pas, car moi, j'ai mis ma confiance en un Dieu qui a délivré de ses chaînes le monde entier." [9.19]Paul cria vers Dieu pendant le sabbat—car le dimanche s'approchait, jour où il devait lutter contre les bêtes—et il dit: "Ô mon Dieu, Christ Jésus, toi qui m'as délivré de tant de maux, accorde qu'en présence d'Artémylla et d'Euboula, qui sont tiennes, se brisent les chaînes de mes mains!" Et, pendant que Paul adressait cette instante prière, un enfant entra, extraordinairement beau et plein de grâce; lorsque l'enfant sourit, les chaînes de Paul se détachèrent, et l'enfant se retira aussitôt. A cause de l'apparition qui s'était produite pour Paul et du signe puissant des chaînes brisées, la tristesse de Paul d'avoir à lutter contre les bêtes s'envola, et il bondit d'allégresse comme s'il était au paradis. [9.20]Puis, prenant Artémylla, il sortit de ce <lieu> exigu et <sombre où sont> gardés les prisonniers. Quand [. . .] gardiens et en sécurité [. . .] <Paul pria> son Dieu en disant: "Que les <portes s'ouvrent> [. . .] ton oeuvre salutaire [. . .] afin qu'Artémylla reçoive l'initiation du sceau dans le Seigneur"; et [. . .] les portes s'ouvrirent au nom de Dieu [. . .] Les gardes étaient sous l'empire d'un profond sommeil. La matrone sortit <la première>, ainsi que le bienheureux Paul, <avec Euboula, dans> l'obscurité <épaisse>. Un jeune homme, alors, ressemblant [. . .] <corps> de Paul, éclairant non avec une lanterne, mais par le <rayonnement> de son corps, les précédait jusqu'à ce qu'ils parvinssent <à la mer>. [9.21]Et le <jeune homme> rayonnant prit place en face d'eux [. . .] <Paul> imposa la <main> à Artémylla; et <elle reçut> l'eau au nom du Christ Jésus, de sorte que la mer [. . .] s'agita et qu'<Artémylla>, saisie d'un grand effroi, était au bord de l'évanouissement [. . .] Paul dit alors; "Toi, le rayonnant et le lumineux, <viens à notre secours de peur que> les païens disent que le prisonnier Paul s'est échappé et a tué Artémylla." Au moment où le jeune homme sourit à nouveau, la matrone reprit haleine, et elle se mit en route pour regagner sa maison alors que le jour se levait déjà. Lorsque Paul pénétra à l'intérieur, les gardes dormaient; il rompit alors le pain, offrit l'eau et abreuva Artémylla de la parole; puis il la renvoya auprès de son mari Jérôme. Quant à lui, il priait.

Essayons d'interpréter ce récit[44] qui me semble être le combat décisif de Paul contre le lion, avant même qu'il l'affronte dans l'arène!

---

[42] Bovon et Geoltrain, éds., *Écrits apocryphes chrétiens I*, 1156–57.
[43] Ibid., 1157–58.
[44] Cf. le commentaire fouillé de ce passage par Gérard Poupon, "Le baptême d'Artémilla," in François Bovon et al., *Les Actes apocryphes des apôtres: Christianisme et monde païen* (Publications de La Faculté de théologie de l'Université de Genève 4; Genève: Labor et Fides, 1981), 86–93.

Remarquons d'abord que l'événement se joue dans la nuit qui est la veille de la Pentecôte (cf. le début des *Actes Paul* 9.19 en comparaison avec 9.3). Selon la tradition biblique, c'est le moment de l'effusion du Saint-Esprit; et dans la tradition liturgique de l'Église ancienne, c'est le point culminant de la période pascale où l'on attend l'accomplissement des promesses eschatologiques! C'est aussi un moment privilégié pour l'administration du baptême.

Est-ce que je lis trop dans le texte, si je pense que la rencontre avec Artémylla est de nouveau un moment délicat pour l'apôtre, un moment de tentation personnelle? Vu dans cette lumière, l'épisode de la délivrance des chaînes prend un sens fort. Paul ne veut en aucun cas sortir "naturellement" et dans le secret de la prison, il faut que Dieu lui-même donne son approbation par un miracle. La prison devient d'ailleurs à ce moment-là comme un symbole de la condition humaine, enchaînée, entre autres, par les forces de la passion: "Jai mis ma confiance en un Dieu qui a délivré de ses chaînes le monde entier."

Et le miracle se produit: un enfant extraordinairement beau et plein de grâce intervient, sourit, et les chaînes de Paul se détachent. Le commentaire qui suit cet événement, me semble donner tout son sens à cet épisode: "A cause de l'apparition qui s'était produite pour Paul et du signe puissant des chaînes brisées, la tristesse de Paul d'avoir à lutter contre les bêtes s'envola, et il bondit d'allégresse comme s'il était au paradis." Une nouvelle fois—et cette fois-ci, elle sera définitive—Paul a remporté la victoire sur le lion, sur la force de la sexualité. Il est dans l'allégresse, se sent transporté au paradis. On pourrait presque ajouter: il est devenu lui-même cet enfant beau et plein de grâce qui lui apparaît, il est devenu Adam innocent avant la chute, ou cet enfant d'Ésaïe 11 qui joue avec les bêtes sauvages sans que celles-ci lui fassent aucun mal.[45]

Dans la suite, l'apôtre et le jeune homme lumineux se confondent presque dans leur action; ils donnent à Artémylla (et à Euboula) le "sceau" du baptême, les guérissent de leur peur existentielle (symbolisée par la mer agitée) et les abreuvent à l'aide de l'eucharistie et de la parole.

En conséquence, le combat de l'apôtre contre le lion le lendemain matin n'est plus un véritable combat; la victoire est déjà remportée. Le lion se couche contre les jambes de Paul comme une brebis docile; ils n'ont plus qu'à se reconnaître comme de vieux amis et qu'à échanger la paix. Ils sont maintenant des frères solidaires dans leur sort: ils ont été capturés les deux, on veut les tuer les deux (*sic!*), mais le ciel répond souverainement de quel côté il se place: une grêle compacte et très violente s'abat sur le stade, si bien que les autres bêtes et de nombreux spectateurs meurent, tandis que l'apôtre Paul et le lion peuvent s'en aller dans la liberté sans que quiconque les en empêche, Paul sur le bateau qui l'amènera via Philippes et Corinthe à Rome où il subira le

---

[45] François Bovon, dans son article mentionné au début de cette contribution ("Child and the Beast," 388), cite le passage des *Actes de Paul* dont nous parlons dans ce sens; je le remercie de m'avoir ouvert les yeux pour cette interprétation qui me semble correcte.

martyre, couronnement de sa carrière d'apôtre, et le lion dans les montagnes, "comme cela était naturel pour lui."

Mais le plus extraordinaire suit encore: Quand on décapite Paul, du lait au lieu du sang jaillit sur les vêtements du soldat! (*Actes Paul* 14.5). Là, vraiment, le presbytre, auteur des *Actes de Paul*, déraperait carrément dans un mauvais goût du merveilleux, s'il ne donnait pas une valeur symbolique précise à ce détail. Dans le contexte de notre interprétation de l'ensemble, le sens de ce détail saute aux yeux: Paul est arrivé à la perfection, à son sang de chair et d'os s'est substitué le lait innocent de l'Évangile, le lait qui coule dans le paradis.

Ce n'est pas un hasard si la *Tradition apostolique*, qui date du début du troisième siècle, connaît la présentation du lait et du miel mélangés au moment de l'eucharistie des baptisés, en ces termes: "Alors l'oblation sera présentée par les diacres à l'évêque et il rendra grâces (sc. d'abord sur le pain et sur le vin, ensuite) sur le lait et le miel mélangés, pour (indiquer) l'accomplissement de la promesse faite à (nos) pères, dans laquelle il a parlé de la terre où coulent le lait et le miel, dans laquelle aussi le Christ a donné sa chair, dont, comme de petits enfants, se nourrissent les croyants, lui qui, par la douceur de la parole, rend douce l'amertume du coeur."[46]

Comme le Christ (dont, d'après cette conception, le corps contient aussi du lait?), son apôtre ressuscite par conséquent et apparaît à l'empereur Néron et à Tite et Luc au tombeau (*Actes de Paul* 14.6–7).

Puisque Drijvers[47] m'a inspiré en partie pour mon interprétation du baptême du lion dans les *Actes de Paul*, je dois encore, pour terminer, préciser en quoi je m'écarte de lui. Je crois qu'il a tort de dire, en les rapprochant des *Actes de Thomas*, que les *Actes de Paul* sont encratites. L'encratisme se définit comme une *exigence stricte* pour tous les chrétiens baptisés de vivre dans la continence sexuelle.[48] Or, les *Actes de Paul recommandent*, il est vrai, la continence sexuelle, comme le chemin royal à suivre, mais ne l'*imposent pas*. Ils vantent la force spirituelle de celui qui est baptisé et continent, car il anticipe en quelque sorte la résurrection; mais la continence sexuelle n'est pas une *condition* pour être sauvé et pour participer à la résurrection future. Peter W. Dunn s'est efforcé, avec bonheur, de démontrer cette évidence, dans sa thèse de doctorat, intitulée "The Acts of Paul and the Pauline Legacy," soutenue à Cambridge en 1994, mais malheureusement pas encore publiée.[49]

Une dernière chose: l'un ou l'autre lecteur ou lectrice se demanderont si je ne vais pas trop loin dans mon interprétation symbolique de l'épisode d'Éphèse?

---

[46] Bernard Botte, *La Tradition apostolique de saint Hippolyte: Essai de reconstitution* (2ᵉ éd.; Liturgiewissenschaftliche Quellen und Forschungen 39; Münster en Westfalie: Aschendorff, 1963), 55 et 57.

[47] Dans son article "Der getaufte Löwe," 181–89.

[48] Cf. encore maintenant l'étude clarifiante d'Yves Tissot, "Encratisme et Actes apocryphes," in Bovon et al., *Actes apocryphes des apôtres*, 109–19.

[49] Pp. 48–67.

A cette critique, je répondrai premièrement que je ne prétends pas qu'une lecture littérale de cet épisode ne soit pas possible; je trouve seulement qu'on a le droit de chercher plus loin si une interprétation purement littérale n'a pas assez de charme pour nous séduire.[50]

Et je répondrai deuxièmement que j'ai quand même un argument fort pour dire que le presbytre ayant composé les *Actes de Paul* "par amour de Paul" (selon Tertullien, *Bapt.* 17.5) a eu une idée claire de son entreprise.

Tous les chercheurs sont en effet d'accord pour constater qu'il a tiré profit des lettres pauliniennes, en particulier de la Première Épître aux Corinthiens,[51] pour rédiger son *opus*. L'épisode d'Éphèse, quant à lui, s'inspire du passage de 1 Cor 15:32:[52] "Si à Éphèse j'avais lutté contre les bêtes selon l'homme, à quoi cela me servirait-il?"

Il faut convenir que le presbytre a procédé avec raffinement pour en tisser son récit. Non seulement, il en a fait une jolie composition qui commence avec la rencontre de Paul avec le lion au désert et se sert ensuite de la tradition sur le séjour de l'apôtre à Éphèse qui nous est conservée également en Actes 19, mais il fait très attention à ce que Paul dit dans tout le passage y relatif dans 1 Corinthiens.

Un premier point: Qu'en est-il de la θηρομαχία? Tous les exégètes modernes tombent d'accord pour dire que ce "combat contre les bêtes" mentionné en 1 Cor 15:32 est une métaphore.[53] Le presbytre, quant à lui, n'ose pas mettre en question la réalité du combat, mais il en déduit un message spirituel. Avec cette procédure, n'est-il pas en accord avec Paul qui précise bien qu'il ne faut pas prendre sa lutte contre les bêtes uniquement comme un événement κατὰ ἄνθρωπον, mais comme un événement qui a une importance en tant qu'indice de la réalité de la résurrection?[54]

Et voilà le deuxième point: sa victoire sur les bêtes est pour l'apôtre un avertissement sérieux à l'adresse de ceux et de celles qui vivent comme s'il n'y avait pas de résurrection, à savoir dans le péché, dans la mauvaise compagnie (vv. 33–34)! Comment en arrive-t-il à cet avertissement? N'est-ce pas parce que les "bêtes" contre lesquelles il faut lutter sont justement la mauvaise compagnie qui se trouve peut-être dans notre propre coeur? Je n'ai qu'à rappeler que cette interprétation symbolique des animaux est fréquente dans la littérature antique, dans la tradition platonicienne, orphique, biblique et patristique. Je renonce à en donner des exemples, connus de tout le monde.

---

[50] Les notes 18 et 19 plus haut nous montrent clairement que dans l'Antiquité déjà, il y avait des gens qui comparaient les persécuteurs charnels de Thècle à des lions!

[51] Voir à ce propos en dernier lieu la thèse mentionné de Dunn.

[52] Cf. Dennis R. MacDonald, "A Conjectural Emendation of 1 Cor 15:31–32; or the Case of the Misplaced Lion Fight," *HTR* 73 (1980): 265–76.

[53] Cf. R. E. Osborne, "Paul and the Wild Beasts," *JBL* 85 (1966): 225–30; Abraham J. Malherbe, "The Beasts at Ephesus," *JBL* 87 (1968): 71–80; et l'état de la question par Anthony C. Thiselton, *The First Epistle to the Corinthians: A Commentary on the Greek Text* (NIGTC; Grand Rapids: Eerdmans, 2000), 1251–52.

[54] Cf. aussi 2 Cor 1:8–10.

Je ne prétends pas que le message spirituel que le presbytre tire de l'épisode d'Éphèse soit exactement le même que Paul entend en tirer; mais au moins, il suit l'apôtre dans l'*intention* de ne pas rester à une interprétation purement littérale. Et cela est son mérite à mes yeux que j'apprécie, moi, lecteur moderne des *Actes de Paul*.

Dans un certain sens, l'iconographie paléochrétienne me donne raison. A vrai dire, je ne connais aucune représentation de l'apôtre Paul face au lion, mais il se compare lui-même à Daniel au milieu des lions (*Actes Paul* 9.5) et Hippolyte, dans son *Commentaire sur Daniel* (3.29), fait de même. Or, il est connu que Daniel dans la fosse aux lions est un des sujets les plus fréquemment évoqués dans les catacombes et sur les sarcophages paléochrétiens. Comment expliquer ce succès? La raison n'en est certainement pas la peur des premiers chrétiens d'être jetés aux lions, mais ce succès est dû à la valeur *symbolique* de cette scène. Elle est presque une illustration de la demande du Notre-Père: "Ne nous soumets pas à la tentation, mais délivre-nous du mal," du mal qui nous opprime de l'extérieur et de l'intérieur; on est tenté de mettre à côté 1 Pier 5:8: "Soyez sobres, veillez! Votre adversaire, le diable, comme un lion rugissant, rôde, cherchant qui dévorer."

Thècle est le pendant féminin de Daniel. Sur beaucoup d'objets, en particulier des ampoules de pèlerins, elle est représentée en orante, au milieu des lions, parfois aussi des ours et des taureaux; toujours, ces animaux sont couchés à ses pieds, pour bien montrer qu'elle sort victorieuse de l'épreuve, par sa prière.[55] Ainsi, elle devient un symbole de l'espérance pour tous les chrétiens qui se trouvent encore au milieu des épreuves, mais en chemin vers le paradis.

---

[55] Cf. Claudia Nauerth et Rudiger Warns, *Thekla: Ihre Bilder in der frühchristlichen Kunst* (Göttinger Orientforschungen[2]: Studien zur spätantiken und frühchristlichen Kunst 3; Wiesbaden: Harrassowitz, 1981), photos nos. 8, 10, 14, 15, et 16; Claudia Nauerth, "Nachlese von Thekla-Darstellungen," in *Studien zur frühchristlichen Kunst* (éd. Guntram Koch; 3 vols.; Göttinger Orientforschungen[2]: Studien zur spätantiken und frühchristlichen Kunst 6, 8, et 9; Wiesbaden: Harrassowitz, 1982), vol. 1, photos nos. 1, 2, 3, 4, 6; et Rudiger Warns, "Weitere Darstellungen der heiligen Thekla," in ibid., vol. 2, planches 20, 21.1, 26.1, 32, 33, et 34.1–2.

CHAPTER TWENTY

THE POLITICAL ISSUE OF THE *ASCENSION OF ISAIAH*: SOME REMARKS ON JONATHAN KNIGHT'S THESIS, AND SOME METHODOLOGICAL PROBLEMS[1]

Enrico Norelli

Jonathan Knight's *Disciples of the Beloved One: The Christology, Social Setting and Theological Context of the Ascension of Isaiah*,[2] published in 1996, aims at a global interpretation of the *Ascension of Isaiah*. This book has been the only volume-size monograph in English on this apocryphon for many years—indeed, as far as I know, since Robert Henry Charles' influential edition with introduction and commentary[3]—except for a booklet issued by the same Jonathan Knight in 1995 under the title *The Ascension of Isaiah*, which was merely a synthesis of his monograph in the following year.[4] Since we may expect Knight's book to influence English-speaking scholars for some years to come, and since my own studies on the *Ascension* were published before Knight's two books, I think it might be interesting here to check one of Knight's main theses and, above all, to discuss some methodological problems raised by his procedure.

In opposition to most previous scholars, Knight gives up the thesis of a Jewish *Martyrdom of Isaiah* as forming the bulk of the first part of this apocryphon, which narrates the persecution and death of the prophet. In so doing, he relies mainly on an essay by professor Mauro Pesce, published in 1983 in a volume containing the proceedings of a meeting on the *Ascension of Isaiah* held in Rome in 1981,[5] and on a monograph on the *Ascension* published in

---

[1] It was François Bovon who, by calling me to the University of Geneva, allowed me to complete and to publish my research on the *Ascension of Isaiah*. This topic reminds me of all that I learned from him during the years of our collaboration in Geneva.

[2] Jonathan Knight, *Disciples of the Beloved One: The Christology, Social Setting and Theological Context of the Ascension of Isaiah* (JSPSup 18; Sheffield: Sheffield Academic Press, 1996).

[3] Robert Henry Charles, *The Ascension of Isaiah: Translated from the Ethiopic Version, Which, Together with the New Greek Fragment, the Latin Versions, and the Latin Translation of the Slavonic, Is Here Published in Full; Edited with Introduction, Notes, and Indices* (London: Adam & Charles Black, 1900).

[4] Jonathan Knight, *The Ascension of Isaiah* (Guides to Apocrypha and Pseudepigrapha; Sheffield: Sheffield Academic Press, 1995).

[5] Mauro Pesce, "Presupposti per l'utilizzazione storica dell'Ascensione di Isaia: Formazione e tradizione del testo; genere letterario; cosmologia angelica," in idem, ed., *Isaia, il Diletto e la chiesa: Visione ed esegesi profetica cristiano-primitiva nell'Ascensione di Isaia. Atti del convegno di Roma, 9–10 aprile 1981* (TRSR 20; Brescia: Paideia, 1983), 211–76.

1989 by professor Antonio Acerbi.[6] Now while I agree with his rejection of the Jewish source, I should add that in my opinion it is scarcely possible to work out a satisfying theory of the place of the *Ascension of Isaiah* in early Christianity without a satisfying theory of its literary composition. When I wrote my paper for the Rome meeting, as well as some other older articles quoted by Knight, I was persuaded that the *Martyrdom* had never existed. But I had not yet developed an adequate theory of the literary composition of the *Ascension* that might account for some problems arising when the *Ascension* is taken as a unitary work. In the following years I developed such a theory and published several accounts of it.[7] But apparently Knight never saw any of my work except for my critical edition and commentary, which he received between the submission of his manuscript and the correction of his proofs.[8] While understandably he could not take my commentary into account, one regrets his failure to consider my earlier work.

In Knight's opinion, there is a very important dimension to the *Ascension* (I would describe it as "political") that is crucial for dating this work. Since I did not take this dimension into consideration in my previous work, I would like to comment on it in the present contribution. Knight finds[9] that what he calls the First Vision—that is to say, the vision of Isaiah narrated in 3.13–4.22 concerning the descent of the Beloved (= the Christ), his activity, death, resurrection and ascension to heaven, followed by the events of church history leading up to the end of the world—reflects in fact what the author has to

---

[6] Antonio Acerbi, *L'Ascensione di Isaia: Cristologia e profetismo in Siria nei primi decenni del II secolo* (Studia patristica Mediolanensia 17; Milan: Vita e pensiero, 1989).

[7] "Interprétations nouvelles de l'Ascension d'Isaïe," *REAug* 37 (1991): 9–20; "L'Ascensione di Isaia nel quadro del profetismo cristiano," in *Il profetismo da Gesù di Nazaret al montanismo: Atti del IV Convegno di studi neotestamentari (Perugia, 12–14 settembre 1991)* (ed. Romano Penna; RStB 1993, no. 2; Bologna: Dehoniane, 1993), 123–48; *Ascension du prophète Isaïe* (Apocryphes: Collection de poche de l'AELAC [2]; Turnhout: Brepols 1993); *L'Ascensione di Isaia: Studi su un apocrifo al crocevia dei cristianesimi* (Origini² 1; Bologna: Dehoniane 1994); *Ascensio Isaiae: Textus* (critical edition and synopsis, in collaboration with several scholars; CCSA 7; Turnhout: Brepols, 1995); and *Ascensio Isaiae: Commentarius* (CCSA 8; Turnhout: Brepols, 1995). After Knight's books I published "Ascension d'Isaïe," in *Écrits apocryphes chrétiens I* (ed. François Bovon and Pierre Geoltrain; with an index prepared by Sever J. Voicu; Bibliothèque de la Pléiade 442; Paris: Gallimard, 1997), 499–545. I should mention here the very important contribution by Richard J. Bauckham, "The Ascension of Isaiah: Genre, Unity and Date," in idem, *The Fate of the Dead: Studies on the Jewish and Christian Apocalypses* (NovTSup 93; Leiden: Brill, 1998), 363–90. Unlike most scholars outside Italy, Bauckham knows well and discusses in a balanced and fair way my own contributions and those of the other members of the Italian research group that prepared the new critical edition of the *Ascension* published in 1995. Against my own view, he tries to show that the *Ascension* is a unitary work and that it dates from the years 70–80 (I had proposed the beginning of the second century). I cannot agree with his first thesis, but I think that the second is worth consideration. I discuss Bauckham's proposals in my forthcoming translation and commentary of the *Ascension* in the Hermeneia series.

[8] Knight states this in his preface, *Disciples of the Beloved One*, 7.

[9] Ibid., 44–53, 186–214; idem, *Ascension of Isaiah*, 28–45.

say concerning the situation in his own times, and consequently the very message that he wants to communicate.[10] Now in this section there are two parts, the first one embracing 3.13–31 and the second embracing chapter 4, and each part is concerned with something rather different from the other. In chapter three, the main topic is the decline of the church as the Second Coming of Christ approaches. Prophecy, a distinctive mark of the Christian church in its Golden Age, will become scarce. Shepherds and presbyters will become more and more corrupt and will despise and nullify the former prophecies. This rejection will include, as Isaiah says, "these visions of mine" (*Ascen. Isa.* 3.31), that is to say apparently the *Ascension of Isaiah* itself. So the problem in chapter three is an internal problem of the church concerning the hostile relation between authority and prophecy and the fact that the Christian prophets—who claim to be the legitimate heirs to Isaiah and to the whole succession of Old Testament prophets—become more and more marginalized and powerless. Instead, in chapter four what is prominent is the coming of the devil himself, Beliar, as the Antichrist in the form of *Nero redivivus*, and his activity in leading believers astray until Christ comes to destroy him.

Knight thinks that both parts of this vision are important for enabling us to understand the author's situation and message. But what is really decisive in Knight's eyes is the section about Beliar, in that it allows us not only to date the work but also to understand the connection between the first and the second part of the *Ascension*. First, I will address the problem of dating of the work.

Knight finds a direct polemic against Rome in what is said about Beliar in chapter four. Since the text states that Beliar will come down from his own see, the firmament, in the form of Nero, Knight believes the reader should infer from this that Beliar inspires the Romans, and that the author wants "to ward off harassment from the Roman government."[11] So the author must cope with two kinds of conflict at the same time. Or, as Knight would say, he "uses existing mythology about Nero to express dissatisfaction with the Roman administration in what appears to have been a critical situation for the author's circle."[12] According to Knight, there is a specific historical situation that can help us locate the *Ascension of Isaiah*. It is the context provided by the well-known letter of Pliny the Younger to the Emperor Trajan and the latter's answer in 112 C.E. When Pliny was *legatus pro praetore* in Bithynia, some people were accused before him of being Christians. He punished those who confessed thrice, because, as he puts it, "whatever it was that they confessed, I had no doubt that they had to be punished for their stubbornness and their

---

[10] I speak of the author as a man not only to simplify my language, but also because I positively fear that the author must have been a man, for a prophetess probably would not have mentioned only male prophets throughout the whole work.

[11] Knight, *Disciples of the Beloved One*, 14.

[12] Ibid., 48.

obstinacy."[13] Later he received an unsigned paper containing the names of many Christians. Pliny questioned them and, whenever they denied to be or to have been Christians, he ordered them (1) to invoke the gods, (2) to sacrifice to the statue of the emperor, that had been brought into the court together with the images of the gods, (3) to curse Christ, because he had heard that true Christians would never do such things. If they accomplished these acts, he acquitted them. Now one can read in *Ascension of Isaiah* 4.6–9:

> And he [= Beliar as Nero] will do everything he wishes in the world; he will act and speak like the Beloved, and will say, "I am the Lord, and before me there was no one." And all men in the world will believe in him. They will sacrifice to him and will serve him, saying, "This is the Lord, and besides him there is no other." And the majority of those who have associated together to receive the Beloved he will turn aside after him.[14]

Since we hear about this "sacrifice test" being used against Christians for the first time in the *cognitio* by Pliny, Knight thinks that this portion of the *Ascension* refers to that event. In Knight's words:

> Beliar's demand for worship (*Ascen. Isa.* 4.6–7) reflects the demand for obeisance to the statues produced in court, as do the references to "sacrifice" in 4.8 and to the erection of the imperial statue in 4.11. The reference in 4.6 (see 10.12–13) to Beliar calling himself "Lord" might reflect the epithet *dominus* which had earlier been attributed to Domitian. It is difficult to find a better setting for *Ascension of Isaiah* 4 in the known history of early Christianity, but this situation suits the chapter very well.[15]

Thus Knight is persuaded that the *Ascension of Isaiah*

> was written to address the fear of persecution among Christians in Syria who had heard about the events in Bithynia. . . . [T]hey feared . . . that their refusal to offer sacrifice would provoke a similar reaction from the Romans. Trajan's reply had established the sacrifice test as the norm for Roman governors who were confronted by the problem of the Christians. The author and his friends would have heard about it on the Christian grapevine. The *Ascension of Isaiah* was written to deal with this problem.[16]

A few remarks may be in place here. Some of them pertain to the structure of the narrative. First, Knight uses the two parts of what he calls the First

---

[13] "Neque enim dubitabam, qualecumque esset quod faterentur, pertinaciam certe et inflexibilem obstinationem debere puniri" (Pliny, *Ep.* 10.96.3). I am translating here from Marcel Durry, ed., *Pline le Jeune*; Tome IV, *Lettres, livre X: Panégyrique de Trajan* (Collection d'études anciennes; Paris: Les Belles Lettres, 1938; repr., 1972), 73 (Pliny's letter and Trajan's answer are on pp. 73–75).

[14] I am quoting here the English translation of the *Ascension* by Michael A. Knibb, "Martyrdom and Ascension of Isaiah," in *OTP* 2:161–62. I give an Italian translation of the Ethiopic text of the *Ascension* in *Ascensio Isaiae: Textus*, 45–129.

[15] Knight, *Disciples of the Beloved One*, 36.

[16] Ibid., 36–37.

Vision in order to grasp the perception of the present situation by the author. But this author by no means envisages the events described in these two parts as taking place at the same time. In fact, the vision is divided into two sections by 4.1: "Now, therefore, Hezekiah and Josab my son, these are the days of the completion of the world.[17] And after it has been brought to completion, Beliar will descend. . . ."[18] What is the subject of "has been brought to completion"? The Greek fragment is lacunary here, so we must rely on the Ethiopic version. Most translators think the subject to be the world, but the end of this world takes place after the defeat of Beliar, not before (4.18). For that reason, I think the subject is "the days of the completion of the world" ("the days" may have a verb in the singular in Ethiopic).[19] So the days of the completion of the world would be those of the decline of the church just described. Decline and corruption mark the last times of the world in traditional Jewish eschatological expectations.[20] These motifs have been taken up by our author, who identifies them as the decline of the church with its internal corruption and rejection of prophecy. As a matter of fact, this First Vision consists of a sort of prologue (3.13–20, the Golden Age with the life of the Beloved and the flourishing church), followed by a diptych: the corruption of the church (3.21–31) and then the activity of the Antichrist (4.2–13). Finally comes an epilogue with Christ's Second Coming and the defeat of evil. In Jewish and Christian traditions, descriptions of the evil last times usually have the function of describing and evaluating the author's time. This is a period dominated by the forces of evil, but at the same time it immediately precedes God's final intervention with the defeat of God's enemies and the triumph of the true believers. So I agree with Knight that this prophecy depicts the author's times.

But we have seen that there are two stages, and that they follow each other, so the question must arise: In which of these two stages does the author think that he is living? I cannot repeat here the analysis of the first stage that I developed in my commentary,[21] but I consider it quite obvious that this picture of the decline of the church reflects the author's judgment on the situation of the prophetic group to which he himself belongs. Moreover, such a demonstration is unnecessary here, because Knight is of the same opinion when he writes (even without any detailed analysis of the passage): "Asc. Isa. 3.21–31 has no precise parallels in other Christian literature and in my view it represents the author's own understanding of the church in his day."[22] And

---

[17] So the Greek fragment; the Ethiopic has "of the calling of the world," which very likely represents a corrupted text, though perhaps it could mean the same as the Greek.

[18] Knibb, "Martyrdom and Ascension of Isaiah," 2:161.

[19] See Norelli, *Ascensio Isaiae: Commentarius*, 241.

[20] The ancient literature on this theme is immense; see David Syme Russell, *The Method and Message of Jewish Apocalyptic 200 B.C.–A.D. 100* (OTL; London: SCM Press 1964), 263–84.

[21] Norelli, *Ascensio Isaiae: Commentarius*, 169–78, 237–40.

[22] Knight, *Disciples of the Beloved One*, 46.

further: "Where 3.21–31 is the author's own creation, 4.1–13 reworks a variety of imagery to address a new situation of conflict with the Romans in the early second century."[23] What I find rather inaccurate here is the notion that there are no parallels for 3.21–31. As I show in my commentary, it is true that our author takes up several traditional topics here too, but his reworking of such materials really offers a new product, where what is at stake is the fate of prophecy in his own church.

But what about the following section on the Antichrist? First of all, if the author wanted to hint at two different aspects of the situation at his time, it would be odd that he referred to them as pertaining to two subsequent stages in the course of time. Second, what allows us to say that in this second half of the prophecy the author is referring to his own time? In other words, is there in this section even one element that could compel us to recognize here a hint at contemporary events? I confess that I do not see any such item. According to Knight, the sentence "he will do everything he wishes in the world; he will act and speak like the Beloved, and will say, I am the Lord, and before me there was no one" (4.6) "reflects what was seen as Roman blasphemy in the demand for obeisance and also perhaps the title *dominus*, which had been attributed to earlier emperors."[24] I must disagree. Of course, the source here is Dan 11:36 concerning Antiochus Epiphanes: "And the king will act according to his will, and he will exalt himself and declare himself great above every god and he will speak enormities and he will prosper, until the wrath [of God] is fulfilled" (so Theodotion's Greek translation). Such a portrait had already been adopted by the author of the *Psalms of Solomon* to refer to Pompey who had profaned the Jerusalem Temple in 63 B.C. (*Pss. Sol.* 2.25–29; 17.11–14). And the author of *2 Thessalonians* drew on it for his description of the eschatological enemy who puts himself in God's place. To be sure, the *Sibylline Oracles* 5:33–34, 138 say that Nero wanted to be equal to God, but this is not enough to state that every text about a more or less diabolic king extolling himself above God reflects a living anti-Roman polemic. Knight emphasizes the statements about there being imperial statues erected "in every city" (*Ascen. Isa.* 4.11), the power of Beliar's miracles in every city and district (4.10), and the offering of sacrifice mentioned in 4.8. The first two items he takes as being possibly "an early indication of the widespread use of the sacrifice test against the Christians."[25]

Now concerning the statue of the Antichrist, one has just to remember Rev 13:14–15 with the connection between the statue, the miracles, and the veneration of the statue—the adoration of the beast by the inhabitants of the whole earth being mentioned in the same context (13:8). I am not suggesting that the author of the *Ascension* draws on Revelation—I do not believe that

---

[23] Ibid., 48.
[24] Ibid., 50.
[25] Ibid.

he does—but only that such imagery was spread quite independently apart from Pliny's "sacrifice test." Christians had inherited this imagery from the Jews, who had encountered many problems in Alexandria and elsewhere because of statues of the imperial cult being erected in their synagogues or even in Jerusalem (Philo, *Flacc.* 41–52; *Legat.* 134–36; 197–372; Josephus, *Ant.* 18.257–309). In general, one may say with Fergus Millar: "Statues of the Emperor were everywhere, and were the focus of a wide variety of religious, ceremonial and even legal functions. . . . [A]t least a large proportion of the cult acts directed towards the pagan gods were addressed also to the Emperor. Prayers and sacrifices were offered. . . ."[26] To be sure, the case of Pliny is the first one in which the use of the "sacrifice test" against the Christians is attested. But in the first place, can we really believe that it was its first application? I think that Pliny's letter shows precisely that the contrary is true. In fact, he writes that he asked those claiming that they neither were nor ever had been Christians to perform three acts: to recite a prayer to the gods; to make a supplication with incense and wine to the emperor's statue; and to curse Christ. He states he acted this way because these are "things which (so it is said) those who are really Christians cannot be made to do" (*Ep.* 10.96.5). Now if somebody suggested to him that a true Christian would never perform such acts, this must mean that Christians had already been requested to do so. At any rate, what we can say is that there was no custom of asking Christians in courts to sacrifice to the emperor's statue: Pliny had to have the statue brought into the court. Moreover, Pliny did not use the "sacrifice test" to detect Christians but only to be sure that those who denied being or having been Christians told the truth. Strictly speaking, his test concerned only apostates and not true believers. Finally, being very scrupulous, Pliny resorted to a triple test, whereas a magistrate might very well limit himself to just a sacrifice to the gods *in behalf of* the emperor rather than a sacrifice *to* the emperor. As a matter of fact, except for Caligula and Domitian, we have no explicit witnesses to any emperor positively claiming to be a god. But it is also true that "the fact of the Imperial cult in its very varied forms was accepted by all Emperors."[27] At any rate, in the case of Pliny, what is at stake is obviously not the Imperial cult as such but a practical problem: What should the governor do when somebody is accused of being a Christian? The "sacrifice test" is just one of several ways of settling at least some cases by ensuring that

---

[26] Fergus Millar, "The Imperial Cult and the Persecutions," in Elias Bickerman et al., *Le culte des souverains dans l'Empire Romain: Sept exposés suivis de discussions . . . 28 août–2 septembre 1972* (Entretiens sur l'antiquité classique 19; Vandœuvres/Geneva: Fondation Hardt, 1973), 147. See also Lucien Cerfaux and Julien Tondriau, *Un concurrent du Christianisme: Le culte des souverains dans la civilisation gréco-romaine* (Bibliothèque de théologie[3] 5; Tournai: Desclée, 1957), esp. 394–96; W. H. C. Frend, *Martyrdom and Persecution in the Early Church: A Study of a Conflict from the Maccabees to Donatus* (Oxford: Basil Blackwell, 1965), 217–22 (on Pliny).
[27] Millar, "Imperial Cult and the Persecutions," 157.

a person is not really a Christian. Admittedly, in a local hostile environment, some Christians might fear to be subjected to the request of sacrificing to the genius of the emperor. But to think that Pliny's letter to Trajan and Trajan's answer represent a crucial turning-point is—in my opinion—an over-simplified view. One might still object that, while Revelation and other texts mention the worship of statues, the *Ascension of Isaiah* mentions the act of sacrifice, which would conform exactly with Pliny's procedure. But one should not insist on this distinction. Pliny himself speaks first of "making supplication with incense and wine to your statue" ("imagini tuae . . . ture ac vino supplicarent," *Ep.* 10.96.5; he does not actually speak of sacrificing). Then he says that they "worshipped your statue and the images of the gods" ("imaginem tuam deo-rumque simulacra venerati sunt," *Ep.* 10.96.6). So both terms have the same meaning in this context.

Coming back to *Ascension of Isaiah* 4, one should notice that Beliar as the Antichrist is here a mythological figure, not a real Roman emperor. I have shown elsewhere that his activity is quite different from Nero's historical career.[28] Moreover, the mythical features of his rule (as the inversion of heavenly bod-ies) place him in a mythical future. Third, the mention of worshipping the Antichrist and of sacrificing to him has nothing to do with a test for Christians. The text simply states that most people in the world will accept the Antichrist's claim to be God, which is a quite general and widely spread notion. Fourth, if one were to adopt Knight's hypothesis, one would have to explain the mean-ing of the idea that the Antichrist will rule three years and seven months and twenty-seven days (4.12) or (one thousand) three hundred and thirty-two days (4.14). If the author were speaking of an entity of his own time, we should conclude that this entity has been existing for less than three and a half years at the time of his writing. Knight notes this figure,[29] but he does not explain how it fits into his interpretation. For all these reasons, I think that our author depicts his own times and their problems in *Ascen. Isa.* 3.21–31 when the shepherds and presbyters in the church have become corrupt and reject prophecy. But in his opinion, the time of Beliar/the Antichrist has not yet come. In his picture of these times, he makes use of traditions going back to a gloomy experience with political power, perhaps mainly with Roman impe-rial power. But his main topic in this work is *not* the church's relationship with the Roman authorities, much less the specific circumstances of Pliny's investigation of Christians.

Why, then, did he dwell upon this subject? He probably shared with his community a pattern of the last times embracing three stages: first, an increase in lawlessness (*anomia*), false prophecy, corruption, and mutual hate; then the coming and the domination of the Antichrist with an extreme reduction in the number of believers; and finally, the coming of the Lord. Such a struc-

---

[28] Norelli, *L'Ascensione di Isaia*, 183–86.
[29] Knight, *Disciples of the Beloved One*, 50–51.

ture is perfectly clear in *Didache* 16. A comparison between the *Didache* and the *Ascension of Isaiah* shows that both of them go back to the same apocalyptic pattern.[30] The *Didache*, or its source, connects the present time with the first stage, and it is quite probable that such a pattern was worked out precisely to frame a difficult situation in an overall structure that could explain it as a moment of God's plan. So it was quite natural to locate the present age in the period preceding the apparition of the Antichrist. As for the latter, his identification with Beliar on the one side, and with Nero on the other, might be traditional, but it suits the main features of the first part of the *Ascension*. In fact, this first part depicts Beliar as constantly acting in history against the prophets and the believers in the true God. He carries on this activity through false prophets and evil kings like Manasseh, who persecutes the prophets and kills Isaiah, or like Nero, who persecutes the church and kills the apostle Peter (*Ascen. Isa.* 4.3). So it is understandable that his supreme and final effort takes place through the immediate intervention of Beliar in the form of an earthly king. More precisely, this is a king whose activity—especially in the murder of Peter—had marked the beginning of the last times.[31]

One can now see how the features of the Antichrist's activity have been selected from the main subject in the first part of the *Ascension*: namely, the opposition between true and false prophecy in Isaiah's time and in the present. And so, just as in Isaiah's time, Sammael/Beliar lived in Manasseh and acted through him (*Ascen. Isa.* 2.1), in the end time Beliar will make his appearance as the Antichrist in the form of an earthly king, Nero. And just as Sammael imposed his worship in Jerusalem through Manasseh (2.3–4), in the same way in end the time the Antichrist's miracles must confirm his pretention to be God. And just as Sammael had caused apostasy in all of Manasseh's kingdom, save for the handful of prophets around Isaiah, so in the end time the Antichrist will lead astray nearly the whole of mankind, save a little remnant. For this reason, the severe reduction in the number of believers occurs three times: once under Manasseh, once again in the time of the decline of the church, and finally once more in the age of the Antichrist. In the first two instances, the remnant consists of prophets, and the same may also hold true for the third, if the mention of "those who have seen him for whom they were hoping, who was crucified, Jesus, the Lord Christ, after that I, Isaiah, had seen him who was crucified and ascended" (4.13) refers to the ecstatic vision of the Christ by Christian prophets, as I tried to establish in my commentary on this passage.[32]

---

[30] See the synopsis in Norelli, *Ascensio Isaiae: Commentarius*, 173–74.

[31] This is a theological notion worked out in Petrine communities and stated in the *Apocalypse of Peter* (Rainer fragment); in a previous contribution I tried to show that the *Ascension* belongs to the same theological milieu: Enrico Norelli, "Situation des apocryphes pétriniens," *Apocrypha* 2 (1991): 31–83, on this topic esp. 34–41.

[32] Norelli, *Ascensio Isaiae: Commentarius*, 259–62. It is fair to say, however, that Bauckham ("Ascension of Isaiah," 387–88) challenges my argument and sees this passage as

So we can now see that the passage about Beliar/the Antichrist, far from bringing in a second theme, viz. the criticism of the Roman Empire and its politics against Christians, is quite consistent with the theme of the destiny of prophecy. It functions to reassure the author's prophetic group that, although they are opposed by church leaders, they are on the side of right like Isaiah, who was persecuted and killed by the king of Israel and his false prophets. And it comforts them with the promise that they will be avenged by the Christ, who is to come soon because their very persecution proves that they live in the last times, just before the coming of the Antichrist and the final crisis. But Knight claims that it is precisely his interpretation that allows one to see the consistency between chapters four and five of the *Ascension*, as well as between the first and the second part of the book. Chapter five relates the story of the prophet's martyrdom and, according to Knight, it

> offers evidence that the apocalypse was written under the influence of the events of 112 C.E. It tells the story of how a Christian prophet refused to honour pagan demands for worship in a context where Beliar (whom the author says inspired the Romans) is a prominent figure. Isaiah's trial before the representative of Beliar shows the injustice of the punishment which has been imposed on the Christians by the Romans.[33]

Now I do not insist on the fact that nothing in this chapter connects Beliar with the Romans. What is rather unfortunate for the thesis of the *Ascension* as an exhortation to stand up bravely in trial is that in the *Ascension* there is no trial at all. In mentioning "Isaiah's trial before the representative of Beliar," Knight is thinking of Jewish stories about the prophet's death, not of the *Ascension*. Moreover, there is no "pagan demands for worship" here. What Beliar/Malkira asks Isaiah to do is to say the following: "I have lied in everything I have spoken; the ways of Manasseh are good and right, and also the ways of Balkira and those who are with him are good" (*Ascen. Isa.* 5.4). Obviously this has nothing to do with whatever might be exacted of Christians by a pagan court. Instead, the devil is trying to make Isaiah into a false prophet. According to the Mishnah, "he that suppresses his prophecy . . . or the prophet that transgresses his own words, his death is at the hands of

---

referring to those who have seen the "earthly" Jesus, since several of them are thought of as still living at the time of the Parousia (Bauckham dates the *Ascension* not later than A.D. 80). His argument deserves further consideration, and I will deal with it in my Hermeneia commentary.

[33] Knight, *Disciples of the Beloved One*, 54–55. Such a reading of this chapter resembles that of Acerbi, *L'Ascensione di Isaia*, esp. 89–93, 265–66, who also thought that the first part of the *Ascension* was intended to give courage to the Christian martyrs by proposing the example of Isaiah. Acerbi thought, however, that the first part of the vision (3.13–31) had been added later in order to bring in the theme of the distress of prophecy (ibid., 256–59), while Knight thinks that both themes, prophecy and martyrdom by the Romans, were there from the beginning.

Heaven" (*m. Sanh.* 11:5).[34] This is an action of the worst kind of false prophet, and it is precisely what Beliar is asking Isaiah to do. Moreover, one finds in the first part of the *Ascension* a tradition that only a false prophet approves and supports an apostate king.[35] And so we are brought back to the dominant theme of the first section of the *Ascension*: the conflict between true and false prophecy. Knight illustrates the dangers of prejudice in a footnote referring to Isaiah's answer to the devil Beliar, who is also called Malkira in this context: "If it is within my power, be an anathema, that is to say, you and all your hosts and all your house! For there is nothing further that you can take except the skin of my body."[36] According to Knight, "The reference to Isaiah 'cursing' his opponents in 5.9 perhaps counters the demand for Christians to 'curse Christ' which is mentioned by Pliny *Ep.* 10.96."[37] Without resorting to this rather over-elaborate hypothesis, one should recognize the affinity here with a curse found in Qumran and directed in one version against the men of the lot of Belial (1QS II, 4–18 and 4Q257 1a II, 1–7), in another against Belial, the spirits of his lot and all his followers (4Q286 7 II, 1–6 and 4Q287 6), and in still another (4Q280–282) against Malkî-reshaʿ, who is the same as Malkira in the *Ascension of Isaiah*. Now, in another Qumran text, Malkî-reshaʿ is the name of one of the three evil spirits who come to struggle with Melkizedek in order to take the soul of Amram, Moses' father, at his death.[38] So this fifth chapter of the *Ascension* can be explained as the death of the prophet, who, until his last hour, withstands the temptation of becoming a false prophet. The function of this episode was probably to be an example for Christian prophets confronted by church leaders described here as false prophets.

It is impossible here to consider the other claim of Knight, namely his thesis that the conflict with Rome is the main theme of the *Ascension of Isaiah* and that it establishes a consistency between the first and second parts of the work. I must limit myself to stating that—in my opinion—he tends to assimilate the second part to the first by simply sponging out the differences between them, which makes it extremely difficult to assign them to one and the same writer. I will give just one example. Throughout his study of this second part, Knight constantly identifies the demonic powers as Beliar. Now one should be aware

---

[34] I am quoting here from Herbert Danby, *The Mishnah: Translated from the Hebrew with Introduction and Brief Explanatory Notes* (Oxford: Clarendon, 1933), 400.

[35] As shown in Norelli, *L'Ascensione di Isaia*, 93–109.

[36] *Ascension* 5.9–10. I have slightly modified Knibb's translation here (OTP 2:164) in order to make it more literal.

[37] Knight, *Disciples of the Beloved One*, 54 n. 158.

[38] See a translation of the relevant texts and a discussion in Norelli, *L'Ascensione di Isaia*, 221–27 (with bibliography). The last text mentioned above was usually called *4Q Visions of Amram^b* when I wrote that book; it is now numbered as 4Q544 (in three fragments). For a convenient edition with an English translation, see Florentino García Martínez and Eibert J. C. Tigchelaar, eds., *The Dead Sea Scrolls: Study Edition* (1 vol. in 2; Leiden: Brill, 1997–1998), 1086–89.

that Beliar is nowhere mentioned in *Ascen. Isa.* 6–11. The other satanic name
that is common in the first part, Sammael, appears only twice in the second.
Of these two occurrences, *Ascen. Isa.* 11.41 should not count since it belongs
to the last three verses of the work (11.41–43), which bear a remarkable affinity
with the first part and thus most certainly belong to its author. This difference
between the two parts as to satanic names is not a formal one since it corresponds to a very different representation of the evil powers. The only other
mention of Sammael in the second part is in the form Sammael/Satan (7.9).
Here he is mentioned along with his angels, and elsewhere in chapters 6–11
one always finds the mention of this group of powers *without* any reference to
an individual as its leader. In the cosmological perspective of the seven heavens, these powers dwell on the firmament that is located under the lowest
heaven, so that they are extremely low and weak in comparison with God
and his Beloved, who live in the highest heaven. The subduing of the rebelled
powers does not take place through a war but through a deception. The
Beloved descends into the world first in the form of an angel and then of a
man. At first no resistance is possible or even envisaged. In the first part, on
the contrary, the principle of evil is extremely individualized as Beliar or
Sammael or Malkira or Mekenbekus.[39] What is central is the power he exercises in this world. The conflict between him and the Lord is very real in the
lives and troubles of the believers. In Knight's opinion, the two perspectives
are complementary, for the second part shows how Beliar, who seems so strong
in the first part, that is to say from a human perspective, is weak in comparison to God. In fact, God has already defeated him. But if Knight's interpretation were true, then the identity of Beliar should have been stressed in
both parts of the work. But this is not the case.

I am persuaded that we should beware of dissecting the *Ascension of Isaiah*—
as well as the other apocrypha—into parts corresponding to hypothetical sources.
We should also beware of searching at all costs for a consistency where a
sound hypothesis about the history of the composition of a work may help us
in locating the work and its development in the history of ancient Christianity.
But in doing so, we should remember that the consistency of a work is not
always apparent. As the case that I have discussed shows, inferring an historical or sociological situation directly from some textual elements may be
dangerous and lead one to false conclusions. Every individual element usually
belongs to a pattern that comes to the author through a tradition and conveys one or more possible meanings. An author may, of course, modify this
pattern in order to communicate a new message. The information that he
transmits often consists in the difference between the tradition that he takes
up and his own deviation from it. So, in order to discover the historical situation of communication in which a text was intended to function, we need

---

[39] On the satanic names and their respective roles in the *Ascension*, see Norelli,
L'Ascensione di Isaia, 79–92.

to take into account not only the individual elements, but also every pattern as a whole. For it is the pattern that conveys the meaning. In our case, for example, it was necessary to discover the tripartite eschatological pattern and its realization in the *Ascension of Isaiah* in order to understand the function of the Antichrist section and to escape the danger of selecting only some elements and of working out an interpretation of the text that cannot explain—in my opinion—the work as a whole.

PART FIVE

EARLY CHRISTIAN VOICES
AND ANCIENT MOTIFS

CHAPTER TWENTY-ONE

CHRISTIAN APOCRYPHA IN ART AND TEXTS

J. K. ELLIOTT

My contacts with François Bovon go back to the late 1960s when we were both relative newcomers to Studiorum Novi Testamenti Societas, the professional association of which he has been a recent distinguished President, and we have met most years at its annual conference. We have as well shared platforms in many locations, including the 1900th anniversary celebrations to mark the writing of the Book of Revelation held in Athens and Patmos in 1995.

Bovon is justifiably well known for encouraging biblical scholars and church historians to take seriously evidence found in those early Christian texts marginalized by the ecclesiastical establishment and which modern scholarship labels New Testament apocrypha or (better) early Christian apocrypha. The barrier formerly separating canonical and non-canonical texts is one he has successfully dismantled.

However, those Christian apocrypha are known not only in textual (rhetorical) form but also in their iconic versions in paintings, frescoes, mosaics, carvings, and other artistic forms. The inclusion of these iconic representations reveals a further boundary that needs to be crossed; it is another bridge in Christianity's expressing itself theologically with respect to its founders and its beliefs. The iconic forms can supplement details absent from the written apocrypha and even elucidate details in these rhetorical versions; more importantly, they are in their own right a valuable resource for our establishment of the history of the early church.

There have been calls for our recognizing the importance of the iconic productions of the church as both theological and historical statements. The requests have come from art historians and scholars of early church historiography.[1] Such calls must apply to the tremendous amount of Christian art that is the iconic version of Christian apocrypha as well as to that art that parallels canonical writings.[2]

---

[1] Such as G. F. Snyder, *Ante Pacem: Archaeological Evidence of Church Life before Constantine* (Macon, Ga.: Mercer Press, 1985); T. F. Mathews, *The Clash of Gods: A Representation of Early Christian Art* (Princeton, N.J.: Princeton University Press, 1993).

[2] Some pioneering work in German is to be seen in J. Weis-Liebersdorf, *Christus- und Apostelbilder: Einfluß der Apokryphen auf die ältesten Kunsttypen* (Freiburg: Herder, 1902) and U. Fabricius, *Die Legende im Bild des ersten Jahrtausends der Kirche* (Kassel: Oncken, 1956).

Filling in gaps in the Jesus story is often considered to have been a motive behind many apocryphal writings and illustrations (whatever we may wish to say about the influence of the rhetorical on the iconic or vice versa). The two main areas where gaps in the canonical Jesus' story were perceived to exist are his Nativity and his Passion. The birth and childhood of Jesus have given rise to apocryphal stories (in the *Protevangelium Jacobi*, *Pseudo-Matthew*, *Arundel 404*, *The Arabic Infancy Gospel* and others) as well as iconic parallels to those which illustrate the birth in a cave, the presence of divine light in that cave, the inclusion of two redundant midwives and of the ox and the ass, and also the Holy Family's travels in Egypt. Stories and pictures of the Passion include the involuntary lowering of the banners held by the ensigns when Jesus enters Pilate's presence, and the *Descensus ad Inferos* when Jesus raises the faithful dead immediately after his own death. (That scene is also known in dramatic art in the York cycle of medieval Mystery Plays, when the saddlers performed it). A filling-in of the biography of Mary also relates the beginning and end of her story. The birth gospels are in effect stories of Jesus' immediate antecedents, especially Mary, her parents, her birth and upbringing, and these traditions spawned many artistic representations too. At the end of Mary's life there are many tales of her death and Assumption, an event also beloved of artists. Gaps in the life stories of the earliest apostles were also filled by written tales and by cycles of paintings.[3]

Whenever we meet illustrated cycles of the lives of a Saint or of the Virgin Mary we may be encouraged to argue that these are based on and follow a written cycle. The many cycles of the life of Mary such as Giotto's famous illustrations for the Cappella degli Scrovegni (the Arena Chapel) in Padua seem to be based on the canonical Gospels and a version of an infancy gospel derived ultimately from the *Protevangelium of James*.

The illuminated manuscript of the Apocalypse in Trinity College, Cambridge (ms. R.16.2) contains a gloss on the Book of Revelation and, at its beginning and end, illustrations of scenes from the life of its supposed author, St. John the Theologian. The inspiration for this life of John appears to be the apocryphal *Acts of John*, but a closer inspection reveals that other apocryphal tales seem to have been used, for example, Pseudo-Abdias, *Virtutes Iohannis* and the *Acts of John in Rome*.

This implies that the artist was not merely working through one particular written form of the *Acts of John*, illustrating the scenes he read only there. Rather, the parallels between the iconic and rhetorical forms may well be due to earlier oral and written sources. In other words, the cycle in the Trinity Apocalypse and the various written forms of the John legends may have had

---

[3] Places where iconic representations of apocryphal scenes may be studied are G. Schiller, *Ikonographie der christlichen Kunst* (5 vols.; Gütersloh: Mohn, 1966–91); J. Lafontaine-Dosogne, *Iconographie de l'enfance de la vierge dans l'Empire byzantin et en Occident* (Brussels: Académie royale, 1992), and more recently in David R. Cartlidge and J. Keith Elliott, *Art and the Christian Apocrypha* (London and New York: Routledge, 2001).

independent histories and origins. Certainly, some of the pictures in the Trinity manuscript seem to be combinations of scenes that the illustrator may have known originally as independent iconic scenes—folio 1 verso includes within one frame John's being taken to a ship and his being on board, the two having originally been discrete scenes. Another frame (also fol. 1 verso) combines John's entering the vat of boiling oil and his stepping from it; fol. 28 verso has another double scene combining John's preaching to Craton and his baptizing him (cf. *Virtutes Iohannis* V). These double scenes certainly suggest that the Trinity Apocalypse of the mid-thirteenth century was based on earlier sources, possibly a fully illustrated form of the *Acts of John*. Illustrated early manuscripts of the biblical text are comparatively rare; surviving illustrated early manuscripts of the apocryphal texts are virtually nonexistent. That is not surprising, given their lack of ecclesiastical approbation.[4]

The *Acts of John* 113[5] includes a prayer by John in which he gives thanks for having been prevented from marrying no less than three times (!). The prayer suggests there may well have been an episode earlier in the story of John's life where such a scene occurred.[6] But that story is not to be found in our fragmentary *Acts of John* as presently reconstructed. However an iconic reference exists which implies that a fuller version of those acts was known. In an article in *Semeia*[7] David R. Cartlidge draws attention to an illustration in the Benedictine library at Admont (Stiftsbibliothek 289 fol. 56 recto) in which John in one scene leaves a woeful woman, possibly his betrothed, and in the second scene rests his head on Jesus' breast (a characteristic pose for the man identified as the beloved disciple). [The Imperial Library in St. Petersburg also has an illustration of a comparable scene in the manuscript published in facsimile as the *Louanges de Monseigneur St. Jean Evangeliste* vol. I plate XI,[8] although its iconography is quite different.]

The fragmentary nature of the surviving texts of the *Acts of John* has also meant that some elements in the story of Drusiana are absent, for example her conversion. In the Trinity Apocalypse (fol. 1 recto) is an illustration of such an episode. The famous story of John's being boiled in oil, also illustrated there, may have once stood in the second-century *Acts of John* although now it survives in written form only in the later *Acts of John in Rome* and in the *Virtutes Iohannis*.

---

[4] K. Weitzmann, "The Selection of Texts of Cyclic Illustrations in Byzantine Manuscripts," in *Byzantine Books and Bookmen* (Washington, D.C.: Dumbarton Oaks, 1975).

[5] In J. K. Elliott, *The Apocryphal New Testament* (Oxford: Clarendon Press, 1993), 336. [Hereafter *ANT*.]

[6] See Éric Junod and Jean-Daniel Kaestli, *Acta Iohannis* (CCSA 1–2; Turnhout: Brepols, 1983), 1:311–12.

[7] "An Illustration in the Admont 'Anselm' and its Relevance to a Reconstruction of the *Acts of John*," *Semeia* 80 (1997): 277–90.

[8] Edited by Alexandre de la Borde, *Les principaux manuscrits à peintures conservés dans l'ancienne bibliothèque publique de Saint-Petersbourg* (Paris: Bulletin de la société française de reproduction de mss à peintures, 1936).

John and the Robber Youth, similarly illustrated in the Trinity Apocalypse (fol. 30 recto), is a story not found in the written Acts although in this case Clement of Alexandria, *Quis dives salvetur?* 42 knows and uses this story of John's recapturing and baptizing a recidivist lad.

There are other cycles, notably of Thecla, Peter, Paul, Andrew, Thomas and Philip. Thecla cycles are well known. Tarragona cathedral has a particularly fine sequence of representations of the Thecla story paralleling the *Acts of Paul.*

In two of the best-known second-century apocrypha, the *Acts of Peter* and the *Acts of Paul,* the eponymous characters are kept separate—each has his own story to be told. The *Acts of Peter* actually begins with *Paul* in Rome but Paul leaves the city prior to Peter's arrival in chapter 4. Peter then confronts Simon Magus solus. On most iconographic representations of the apostles in Rome, however, Peter and Paul appear together. Monreale cathedral in Palermo has a picture in its Peter Chapel of both Peter and Paul witnessing the fall of Simon Magus. Kessler lists many such images.[9] The aim of these images is to show the two prime apostles as colleagues; the church is united—the old rivalry between the Jerusalem and Gentile churches personified by the antagonism of Peter and Paul in the New Testament has evaporated. Only in later written apocrypha such as Pseudo-Marcellus, *Passio sanctorum apostolorum Petri et Pauli* and the Greek *Acta Petri et Pauli* are the two apostles combined.[10]

In the case of Andrew, cycles of his life exist in, among other places, a Vatican Passional, in the fifteenth-century frescoes at Palma Cathedral and in Chartres Cathedral, all of which follow, but are not identical to, the various written forms of the *Acts of Andrew.* In the Vatican Passional (Vatican lat. 8541 pp. 16–20) the life of Andrew contains a story absent from the second-century *Acts of Andrew.* In an apparently posthumous miracle Andrew is seen (on its p. 20) rescuing a bishop from a demon in the form of a seductive female. This typical apocryphal tale, encouraging celibacy and chastity, is also known from a fresco in the crypt of St. Lorenzo in Doliolo at Sanseverino, at Palma and in a thirteenth-century painting in the Musée des arts décoratifs in Paris. But we must question whether a written form has just not survived or was never there in the first place—we turn to that problem below.

A Thomas cycle in Chartres keeps close to a form of the *Acts of Thomas* as that work was known in the Middle Ages. Even Philip's exploits are recorded, although surviving examples are sparse and medieval: in Bovon's volume on the *Acts of Philip,* coauthored with Frédéric Amsler and Bertrand Bouvier,[11]

---

[9] H. Kessler, "The Meeting of Peter and Paul in Rome: An Emblematic Narrative of Spiritual Brotherhood," *Studies in Art and Archeology (in Honor of Ernst Kitzinger on his Seventy-Fifth Birthday* [ed. W. Tronzo and I. Lavan]) 41 (1987): 265–75, see also Snyder, *Ante Pacem.*

[10] The combining of apostles in written apocryphal Acts is often taken to be a sign of their late composition. Examples include the *Acts of Andrew and Matthias,* the *Acts of Xanthippe and Polyxena,* and the *Acts of Andrew and Paul.*

[11] *Actes de l'apôtre Philippe* (Turnhout: Brepols, 1996) in *Apocrypha: Collection de livre de poche* 8. Another *livre de poche,* number 9, in the same series (Rémi Gounelle and

p. 246, is seen a plate from a miniature showing Philip's inverse crucifixion, possibly originally taken from a cycle.

Iconic additions to stories concerning Jesus' family may be seen in the Annunciation to Mary. Many an Annunciation scene has Mary indoors, either at work spinning the veil of the Temple or holding a book, or outside, gathering water. We see a fine example of the scene with Mary spinning in an icon at St. Catherine's, Mount Sinai and on a burial cloth now at the Victoria and Albert Museum. The Benedictional of St. Aethelwold (British Library Additional MS. 49598) has a good example (fol. 5 verso) of Mary with a book, it being a common Western tradition to emphasize Mary's learning. The scene of Mary at the well is to be found in a fourth-century sarcophagus lid in Syracuse and on a fifth-century ivory book-cover in the cathedral treasury, Milan. Such details may seem to be merely theatrical props added by an artist to give the incident a convincing domesticity and to dramatize the momentous announcement amid a scene of ordinariness, but it should not go unnoticed that these props may have been chosen consciously from stories known to the artists that go back to earlier written or to oral apocryphal traditions. The Annunciation at the well certainly parallels the written account in the *Protevangelium* 11. It is not clear if any written parallels to the other scenes exist and it may be that these iconic representations are unique to that medium, although we must always allow for the fact that some apocryphal traditions survive now in iconic form and that the rhetorical forms of them have been lost. We also need to bear in mind that not every apocryphal detail found in iconic form *must* have been written down at one time: the iconic artists must be permitted to have had access to oral sources and church traditions which did not reach or ever inspire writers. Authors of texts did not have the monopoly of inspiration and creativity. Our fixation with the written word must not blind us to the fact that some stories may have survived in iconic form because that was the only form in which they ever occurred; in some other cases, of course, the sheer chance of survival may have resulted in the complete loss of a written form and the existence today of only an iconic parallel. As far as manuscripts are concerned, a more rigorous investigation into the manuscript holdings of certain libraries may reveal some hitherto unknown treasures. Bovon himself was responsible for recovering a manuscript of the *Acts of Philip* (Xenophontos 32) and making it available to the scholarly world.[12] Other manuscripts, some doubtless containing illustrations, await the keen eye of a cataloguer or researcher.

Turning to details in Jesus' ministry, we note that some illustrations of the Baptism of Jesus include elements absent from the canonical gospels' accounts,

---

Zbigniew Izydorczyk, *L'Évangile de Nicodème* [1997]) makes use of illustrations taken from a manuscript in Madrid (vitr 23–8 II fol. 162r–200v).

[12] Initially (with Bertrand Bouvier) in the Schneemelcher Festschrift (*Oecumenica et Patristica* [ed. D. Papandreou, W. A. Bienert, and K. Schäferdiek; Chambésy-Geneva: Metropolitan of Switzerland, 1989]), 367–94.

particularly (1) the personification of the Jordan by means of a figure in the stream (as in the famous mosaic in the Arian Baptistery in Ravenna and the comparable scene in the Baptistery of the Orthodox, also in Ravenna); (2) the swirling up of the water around the body of Jesus in a gravity-defying manner reminiscent of the description of the catalepsy of nature at Jesus' birth (in the *Protevangelium* 17 and *Arundel 404* ch. 72); and (3) the presence of angels, for example in a sixth-century ivory carving in Ravenna and in a tenth-century ivory book-cover in the John Rylands University Library, Manchester. Ephraim of Syria, *Paschal Chronicle* refers to such phenomena but there are, as far as I am aware, no known apocryphal writings proper that include these details. All that we can therefore conclude from this is either that iconic representations of the Baptism include elements not found in surviving rhetorical parallels or that artistic licence and creativity were responsible for the additions.

Where both iconic and written forms exist the commonly-held assumption that the written form came first is not necessarily correct: sometimes the existence of an iconic form may precede the surviving written parallel. Let us take as an example the ubiquitous depiction of an ox and an ass in scenes of Jesus' Nativity: this is not merely due to artists' attempts to add verisimilitude to the biblical account of Jesus' birth in an animal's manger but is specifically parallel to the written story available to us in the *Gospel of Pseudo-Matthew* 14[13] where the presence of an ox and an ass allegedly fulfils a prophecy in Isa 1:3. However, *Pseudo-Matthew* is an eighth-century composition (although based on earlier written sources). Our earliest artistic representation is much earlier: a carving of the birth of Jesus accompanied by these two animals is found on a sarcophagus lid, now reworked into the pulpit of St. Ambrose in Milan. That sarcophagus dates from the fourth century. Thus the iconic representation precedes the written account. Did that fourth-century sculptor know of a written source comparable to the one that was eventually included in *Pseudo-Matthew*? Or did the author of *Pseudo-Matthew* put in writing what he had seen in a carving or painting or mosaic or fresco? Or could one say that both are independent of each other but coincidentally dependent on a church tradition that developed the New Testament practice of seeking Old Testament prophecies to amplify or explain details in the Christian story?

In other cases a direct link of iconic and rhetorical parallels is dubious. I list four examples:

1) Scenes of Jesus' crucifixion illustrate Jesus clothed. This may be due to modesty and the unwillingness of artists to show Jesus naked,[14] despite the canonical account that implies that he was stripped (as was normal) prior to his being crucified (John 19:23–25). But the illustrators of crucifixions depicted

---

[13] Elliott, *ANT*, 94.

[14] On this see R. C. Trexler, "Gendering Jesus Crucified," in *Iconography at the Crossroads* (ed. B. Cassidy; Princeton, N.J.: Princeton University Press, 1993) (= *Index of Christian Art: Occasional Papers II*).

a clothed Jesus and may conceivably have been aware of that detail in the first part of the *Gospel of Nicodemus*, known as the *Acta Pilati*[15] (pre-fifth century) which states that Jesus was indeed clothed at his crucifixion ("girded with a linen cloth"). Or, again, we may merely wish to conclude that the iconic and rhetorical details evolved independently, possibly for similar motives, and that neither was the inspiration for the other.

2) There are numerous scenes in which Jesus' Triumphal Entry into Jerusalem astride an animal is accompanied by small, beardless figures waving palms of victory (e.g., Berlin, State Museum, Stiftung Preussischer Kulturbesitz inv. 1590). If that is merely an artistic convention that became commonplace then it does not precisely follow the canonical gospels' account of Palm Sunday in which crowds (of adults) welcome Jesus (Matt 21:8–9). But if the inclusion of children is based on a written source, that source could be the apocryphal *Gos. Nic.* 1.3 which has "... and the children of the Hebrews held branches in their hands ..."; "the children" being taken literally as "boys and girls." However, it could be that both traditions evolved independently or were both separately based on earlier (oral?) sources. In any case all we can do is to note the parallel.

3) Many artists depict the scene of the visitation of the Magi in which Jesus is often shown much larger than a neonate. He may be a tiny infant in scenes of the Nativity or even of the circumcision (a scene seldom depicted), but in many scenes of the Adoration the child could be a two-year-old. Is it fanciful to draw a parallel with an apocryphal written source here, namely *Pseudo-Matthew* 16, when the Magi arrive "after the second year" from the Nativity? Could it be that there were traditions in the early centuries that made this separation between the Nativity and the Adoration and that these manifested themselves separately in *Pseudo-Matthew* and in certain paintings? Again, these parallels may be independent of one another.

4) In the scene of the Presentation of Jesus in the Temple from Luke 2 the depiction in the triumphal arch in St. Maria Maggiore, Rome, has the priest look as if he is hurrying. We note that *Pseudo-Matthew* 15 says of Simeon "Et *festinans* adoravit eum." Again, we ask: Were these parallel details independent of each other or not?

Even if no direct connexion exists between the iconic and rhetorical parallel, other links such as oral tradition or theological argument may prove to be relevant lines of enquiry.

There are, of course, some episodes that have survived in only written form—even when the story is vivid and capable of illustration. As far as I am aware, there are no illustrations of the dramatic story of the conversion of the leopard and the kid in the *Acts of Philip* 8.[16] Paul's baptizing a lion in Judea is a story missing from the *Acts of Paul* although it is referred to retrospectively

---

[15] Elliott, *ANT*, 176.
[16] Elliott, *ANT*, 515f.

when Paul is in Ephesus.[17] Again, as far as I am aware artists ignored this photogenic scene (or it has not survived).

Sometimes the iconic form, be it canonical or apocryphal, disagrees with written forms. The overwhelming number of early pictures of the Ascension has Mary present, even though there is no written parallel to this. In the Bavarian National Museum in Munich there is a fourth/fifth-century ivory plaque that has two *male* figures as the only ones present at the Ascension.[18] In the *Acts of John* 102 John recalls that he was the sole witness to the Ascension "without any of the multitude having seen him." The Nag Hammadi *Apocryphon of James* speaks of only Peter and James present at this event. The canonical Gospel of Luke and Acts claim that the eleven disciples were present.

Illustrations may elucidate details that are obscure or unclear in the written parallel. A striking example is the enigmatic reference to the "royal headband" in the story of Anna, the Virgin's mother, and her maid, Judith, in the *Protevangelium of James* 2. The problem is how to translate the reference to the headband. I suggest that the headband "bears a royal cipher" but offer, as an alternative, "you have a royal appearance."[19] Albert Frey in *Écrits apocryphes chrétiens*, edited by François Bovon and Pierre Geoltrain,[20] translates "... il porte une marque royale" following the earlier French translation by É. de Strycker (Amann has "il a une allure royale"). Oriental versions of the *Protevangelium* (such as the Armenian and the Georgian) ignore this detail in the story. Nicole Thierry in an article (originally delivered at a colloquium held in the universities of Lausanne and Geneva co-organized by Bovon), now published among the papers of that conference,[21] has found several artifacts—illustrations of which she includes in ten plates in her article—which show that the headband was seen by artists as a diadem, folded like the crown-like cloth presented to conquerors and indeed with a cipher intended to mark royal status. No doubt the iconic and rhetorical reference is intended to show that the mother of the Queen of Heaven must also be accorded royal status. But in the story the gift by her maid is seen as a rebuke to the then barren Anna, and possibly that problematic reading caused its relative disappearance from both rhetorical and iconical depictions of the story of Anna and Joachim.

At other times an artist's illustration may complement the rhetorical, for example a way of illustrating the differing nature of Jesus may be an interpretation of what in written form turns into descriptions of the many-guised Jesus (e.g. *Acts of John* 88–90; *Acts of Peter* 21). Both forms independently are wrestling with a problematic theological issue; each uses differing conventions

---

[17] Ibid., 379, where I refer also to an unpublished Coptic fragment that relates Paul's exploits in Ephesus and the sermon in which Paul describes that conversion.

[18] Shown (as Plate 4.36) in Cartlidge and Elliott, *Art and the Christian Apocrypha*.

[19] Elliott, *ANT*, 57.

[20] Volume 1 published in 1997 (Paris: Gallimard = *Bibliothèque de la Pléiade*).

[21] Nicole Thierry, "Iconographie cappadocienne de l'affront fait à Anne d'après le *Protévangile de Jacques*," *Apocrypha* 7 (1996): 261–72.

to make the same point. For an artist it may be appropriate to show a young and vigorous, beardless Jesus performing miracles because this was one way to convey the new dynamic initiator of a world religion—one who has to bear comparison with classical saviour gods like Serapis, Apollo, or Dionysus, and other pagan precedents like the Sun God. [A mosaic of Christ as Helios in a chariot drawn by horses is to be seen in the pre-Constantinian mausoleum at St. Peter's, Vatican]. In other depictions he may appear as a seated philosopher to emphasize his rôle as the supreme teacher.[22] Some illustrations selected for Cartlidge and Elliott, *Art and the Christian Apocrypha*, show Jesus in these different rôles. For example, our Figure 3.8, a manuscript illumination in the Bibliothèque nationale, Paris (ms. gr. 74 fol. 167 recto) contains three medallions of Christ—as Pantocrator, as the Ancient of Days, and as Immanuel. Our figure 3.9, the diptych of St. Lupicin, which is a sixth-century ivory book cover, has in its left plaque Jesus; in the central panel, the Ancient of Days; in the surrounding panels he is shown as a miracle-worker, and there he is a beardless youth. In Sant' Apollinare Nuovo, Ravenna, the mosaics of those scenes preceding the Passion have a beardless Jesus, whereas for the scenes during and after the Passion Jesus is bearded. These two parallel approaches, in art and in writing, are probably independent workings-out of a theological debate about the person and nature of the incarnate Christ, which occupied early Christian thinkers, Fathers, and church councils as they debated issues underlying various subsequent credal statements.

One clear example where the iconic precedes the rhetoric is the description of Jesus' appearance in the *Letter of Lentulus*, which is a medieval concoction. There the writer seems to be putting into words what he sees before him.[23] Iconography was well established, as we may see in the depictions of the Mandylion (especially in the East) and of the Veronica story in the West. Both of the legends behind those portrayals (the *Doctrina Addai* in the East and *Vindicta Salvatoris* in the West) fix a stereotypical image of Jesus; the rhetorical form is later.

Another such example is the attempt to portray Peter as a new Moses. There are many early images of Peter striking a rock, such as that in the Catacomb of Comadilla. The written account of Peter's striking a rock in his gaol, from which water gushes forth and with which he baptizes the gaoler, comes later and is found in Pseudo-Linus, *Martyrium beati Petri* 5 of the fourth–sixth century.[24]

The popularity of apocryphal stories such as the *Protevangelium*, and *The Infancy Gospel of Thomas*, some of which were given a new lease on life in

---

[22] See R. M. Jensen, *Understanding Early Christian Art* (London and New York: Routledge, 2000), 44–46 with illustrations.

[23] M. R. James (*The Apocryphal New Testament* [Oxford: Clarendon, 1924]), 477) thinks the letter was written in the presence of a traditional portrait.

[24] For further examples see G. Stuhlfauth, *Die apocryphen Petrusgeschichten in der altchristlichen Kunst* (Berlin: de Gruyter, 1925).

Jacobus de Voragine's *Golden Legend*, written circa 1266, inevitably meant that these scenes were illustrated. We reserve judgement whether these written scenes always influenced illustrators directly. But we conclude this brief overview by citing one very clear case where there is no ambiguity that the iconic form follows and illustrates the early infancy gospels; it is in the Ambrosian Library in Milan. In a fifteenth-century manuscript (L58 sup) the illustrator seems to have had access to copies of the *Infancy Gospel of Thomas*, *Pseudo-Matthew*, the *Gospel of Nicodemus*, Jacobus of Voragine's *Golden Legend*, as well as the canonical Gospels before him. Fortunately this manuscript has actually been reproduced by photolithography and published, albeit with a tendentious title.[25] Its line drawings are delightful and simple and show how apocryphal tales blended with canonical and almost cried out for illustration.

More needs to be researched in this area, but we owe it to François Bovon for having stimulated us into taking seriously the importance, influence, and inspiration of the apocryphal texts. Their iconic counterparts are important for our understanding much in early and medieval Christianity. Older studies accepted that text influenced art. We now need to be more sceptical of that assumption. Barriers between the work of art historians and that of literary critics in this area are obstacles still to be removed. Bovon has initiated many a boundary crossing and a bridge building: his example should spur us on to further developments.

---

[25] Angelo della Croce, *Canonical Histories and Apocryphal Legends Relating to the New Testament* (Milan: Pogliani, 1873).

CHAPTER TWENTY-TWO

"TWO MEN IN WHITE":
OBSERVATIONS ON AN EARLY CHRISTIAN LAMP FROM
NORTH AFRICA WITH THE ASCENSION OF CHRIST

John Herrmann and Annewies van den Hoek

François Bovon is distinguished not only for his profound studies of Luke-Acts in their original context but also for his acute interest in the reception of these texts in later times—an interest that has extended to the realm of the visual arts. His studies of apocrypha also display his understanding of popular currents of Christian antiquity. The breadth of his scholarship and teaching makes us hope that this study of a work of late Antique popular art based on a Lukan substrate can give him some pleasure.

The Lamp

A ceramic oil lamp in an American private collection (fig. 1)[1] is one of a relatively small group of lamps that is distinguished from most such works of popular art in presenting an ambitious Christological composition—the Ascension. Five examples, were previously known, three of which came from Carthage or Sicily.[2] A mould of African provenance for producing lamps of this type

---

[1] Harlan J. Berk, Ltd., 1997, *94th Buy or Bid Sale*, lot 1020, Chicago; J. Herrmann and A. van den Hoek, *Light From the Age of Augustine: Late Antique Ceramics from North Africa (Tunisia)* (Cambridge: Harvard Divinity School, 2002), cat. no. 37.

[2] Collected with bibliography by Fathi Bejaoui, *Céramique et religion chrétienne: Le thèmes bibliques sur la sigillée africaine* (Tunis: Institut National du Patrimoine, 1997), 141.
  a. Syracuse, Museum (?): Paolo Orsi in *Notizie degli scavi di antichità* 1915, 208, fig. 18; Bejaoui, *Céramique*, fig. 77.
  b. Carthage (fragmentary): Henri Leclerq, art. "Lampes" in Fernand Cabrol and Henri Leclerq, *Dictionnaire d'archéologie chrétienne et de liturgie* (Paris: Letouzey et Ané, 1928), 8, 1086–1221, cols. 1171–74, no. 1085 (fig. 4); Abdelmajid Ennabli, *Lampes chrétiennes de Tunésie* (Musées du Bardo et de Carthage) (Paris: Éditions du CNRS, 1976), 52, cat. 75, pl. 3; Bejaoui, *Céramique*, fig. 77a.
  c. Viviane Hoff, 1986, in Christiane Lyon-Caen and Viviane Hoff, *Musée du Louvre: catalogue des lampes en terre cuite grecques et chrétiennes* (Paris: Réunion des musées nationaux, 1986), 102–1103, no. 50.
  d. Piazza Armerina: illustrated in Gino V. Gentili, "Lucerne cristiano-bizantine a croce romana della villa imperiale di Piazza Armerina," in *Nuovo Didaskaleion: Studi di letteratura e storia cristiana Antica* 5 (1952), 86, figs. 1, 4.

Figure 1. North African ceramic lamp with the Ascension of Christ, Tunisia, 440–490. American private collection (photo: authors)

is also known.³ Another example of the lamp has appeared on the international art market (fig. 2).⁴ All show the same scene with the same framing elements. Some appear to be made from relatively fresh, sharp moulds and may be relatively early (fig. 2); others, such as the American example, appear to be made of worn moulds and could be somewhat later (fig. 1).⁵ While the identity of the scene on these eight pieces is no longer in doubt,⁶ the com-

---

e. Private collection, Germany: illustrated in Jochen Garbsch and Bernard Overbeck, *Spätantike zwischen Heidentum und Christentum* (Munich: Prähistorische Staatsammlung München and Museum für Vor- und Frühgeschichte, 1989), 76 (color plate), 138.

³ Bejaoui, *Céramique*, fig. 77b. The material, which is not described, is probably plaster.

⁴ Andrew Spira, "Pottery," in R. Temple (ed.), *Early Christian and Byzantine Art* (Longmead & London: Element Books and Temple Gallery, 1990), 70–87, esp. 80, 83; cat. 34; Herrmann and van den Hoek, *Light*, 49, fig. H.

⁵ Indistinct detail can also be caused by later generation moulds; that is, moulds made from lamps rather than from freshly modeled patrices. In such cases, the indistinct lamps could be substantially later than the original design.

⁶ Bejaoui points out some previously unidentified or misidentified pieces: Bejaoui, *Céramique*, 141.

Figure 2. North African ceramic lamp with the Ascension, Tunisia, 440–470. Formerly Temple Gallery, London (photo: from Spira, 1990: cat. 34)

position has not been examined in its broader setting in Early Christian art and thought. The ambitious scope of the iconography merits such attention— in spite of the modest level of workmanship that the objects present.

In all the lamps, the figural composition appears in the central, keyhole-like field of the lamp: the field is composed of a central disc, which is perforated by two filler holes for oil, and a broad channel, which extends out to the spout, where a wick would have been placed. Christ is dressed in a long tunic, carries a staff or standard topped by a cross over his left shoulder, and raises his right hand. His head is circled by a halo, and he is enclosed in a slightly oval ring probably intended to represent radiant light. In some examples, the border of the ring was embellished with a row of dots or beads,[7] and in another, the border is hatched.[8] Beside his feet, two angels, whose wings and bodies are interrupted by the filler holes, carry Christ upwards toward heaven. Around the upper part of Christ's ring of radiance are the four symbols of the evangelists: from left to right, an eagle's head, a man's head, the forepart of a bull, and the forepart of a lion.

Below Christ and the angels, two men in long belted tunics face forward (or outwards), and the one on the right raises his hand. Some ambiguity

---

[7] Garbsch and Overbeck, *Spätantike*, 138; Spira, "Pottery," 80, cat. 34.
[8] Bejaoui, *Céramique*, fig. 77.

remains in the identification of these figures. As several writers have pointed out, the two figures could represent the "two men in white" who speak to the apostles and foretell the Second Coming in Acts 1:10–11.[9] Their positions, turned out as if to address the spectator, as well as their number, favor this latter interpretation. Alternatively, they could stand as an abbreviation for the eleven apostles present at the Ascension: Luke 24:50–53; Acts 1:9–12.[10] It has also been suggested that they reflect influence from the *Apocryphon of James*, in which Christ selected Peter and James to witness his ascension.[11] It remains questionable, however, whether this apocryphal text, which seems not to have left a trace in Early Christian literature,[12] could have had an influence in the realm of art.

Another problem is posed by Christ's raised right hand. Something appears to extend it beyond the border. Bejaoui has interpreted the detail as a scroll.[13] Christ, however, does not normally gesture in this way with a scroll, nor do scrolls have such long, funnel-shapes. When Christ is shown in majesty with a scroll, as in the doors of Santa Sabina, Rome (fig. 4) and the Rabbula Gospels (fig. 12), the scroll is held in the left hand and hangs down.[14] It seems more likely that the ill-defined detail represents the arm and hand of God clasping Christ by the hand and lifting him, as in some representations of the Ascension, particularly a famous ivory in the Bayerisches Nationalmuseum, Munich (fig. 3).[15]

The broad rim of the lamp is decorated with an alternation of square and round medallions in relief, and on each side of the spout is a triangular medallion. Some of the round medallions are filled with the chi-rho monogram of Christ, the others are enlivened with geometric figures.[16] The same series of medallions appears in all the lamps with the Ascension.

---

[9] L. Bernabo Brea, "Lucerne de età cristiana nel Museo di Siracusa," in *Nuovo Didaskaleion: Studi di letteratura e storia cristiana Antica* 1 (1947), 59; Spira, "Pottery," 83; Bejaoui, *Céramique*, 144.

[10] Bejaoui, *Céramique*, 142; Garbsch and Overbeck, *Spätantike*, 138.

[11] Cited by Herbert Kessler in Kurt Weitzmann, (ed.), *Age of Spirituality* (New York: Metropolitan Museum of Art and Princeton University Press, 1979), 454.

[12] Dankwart Kirchner, "The Apocryphon of James" in Wilhelm Schneemelcher (ed.), *New Testament Apocrypha* (Louisville, Ky.: Westminster/John Knox, 1991), 1, 285–99, esp. 286.

[13] Bejaoui, *Céramique*, 143. Leclerq thought that it was the key to the kingdom of heaven given to Peter: Leclerq, "Lampes," col. 1171.

[14] For these and other examples, see André Grabar, *Christian Iconography: A Study of its Origins* (Bollingen series xxxv, 10; Princeton: Princeton University, 1968), pl. I (p. 34), figs. 117, 195, 280, 328.

[15] Henri Leclerq, art. "Ascension (dans l'art)" in Fernand Cabrol and Henri Leclerq, *Dictionnaire d'archéologie chrétienne et de liturgie* (Paris: Letouzey et Ané, 1924), 1.2: 2926–2934, esp. 2928–2931, figs. 986–88; A. A. Schmid, "Himmelfahrt Christi" in Engelbert Kirschbaum et al. (eds.), *Lexikon der christlichen Ikonographie* (Rome: Herder, 1970), 2, 269–276, 273, fig. 1; Wolfgang F. Volbach, *Early Christan Art* (New York: Abrams, 1962), cat. 93; Garbsch and Overbeck, *Spätantike*, 138.

[16] Ennabli, *Lampes*, 1st foldout, motifs A4 (var.), D8, F3, F5.

Figure 3. Ivory panel with the Holy Women at the Tomb and the Ascension, Rome ca. 400. Munich, Bayerisches Nationalmuseum (photo: from Kitzinger, 1980: fig. 76)

It has long been known that the Ascension lamps were produced in the area of modern Tunisia. These and vast numbers of similar lamps with different figural decoration were exported from kilns in central Tunisia.[17] The Ascension lamps probably came from Sidi Marzouk Tounsi, near Maktar, where lamp molds and lamp fragments with the same medallions on the rim have been found.[17b] From the first through the seventh centuries enormous numbers of fine red-ware bowls, plates, and jugs, often with figure decoration, were also produced in Tunisia and exported around the Mediterranean.[18] The lamps are called "African lamps," and the other ceramics "African Red Slip Ware" or "terra sigillata chiara." Whether made from worn or fresh moulds, all the Ascension lamps belong to Hayes type IIA, which is characterized by an unperforated handle, a canal between the disc and the spout, a broad flat rim, and relatively crisp workmanship. Hayes, followed by Bejaoui, dates the type from 420 to 500+. Hayes' type IIB is coarser and ranges from some time in the second half of the fifth century through the seventh century.[19] An early chronological reference point is provided by impressions of a *solidus* of Theodosius II of 430 used as a shoulder ornament on some lamps of type IIA.[20]

The Ascension lamps, some of which are nicely made and finely detailed, find a comfortable location in the main period of type IIA (fifth century). Garbsch and Overbeck date an example in a private collection to the fifth century.[21] Further support for the chronology may be found in a medallion on the shoulder of the Ascension lamps. One kind of medallion used is a double circle enclosing arcs, which in turn enclose a small circle and a dot. A pair of these medallions flanks the handles on the African lamps (figs. 1–2).[22] This same form is also stamped into African Red Slip plates, and Hayes classifies the stamped roundel as type 87 and connects it with the early phase

---

[17] John W. Hayes, *Late Roman Pottery* (London: British School at Rome, 1972), 310–14; Bejaoui, *Céramique*, 17–18.

[17b] D. F. S. Peacock, F. Bejaoui, and N. Ben Lazreg, "Roman pottery production in central Tunisia," *Journal of Roman Archaeology* 3 (1990): 70, 73, 74, fig. 9c, h.

[18] Hayes, *Pottery*, 13–299; Andrea Carandini, Lucia Saguì, Stefano Tortorella, Edoardo Tortorici, 'Ceramica africana,' *Enciclopedia dell'arteclassica e orientale: Atlante delle forme ceramiche 1. Ceramica fine romana nel bacino Mediterraneo* (Rome: Istituto della Enciclopedia italiana, 1981), 9–227, pls. 13; for Christian images, see Bejaoui, *Céramique*; Annewies van den Hoek and John Herrmann, "Thecla the Beast-fighter: A Female Emblem of Deliverance in Early Christian popular Art," *In the Spirit of Faith: Studies on Philo and Early Christianity in Honor of David Hay* ed. (David T. Runia and Gregory E. Sterling; The Studia Philonica Annual XIII; Atlanta: Scholars Press, 2001), 212–249; Herrmann and van den Hoek, *Light*, 49.

[19] Hayes, *Pottery*, 313–314; Bejaoui, *Céramique*, 17–20; L. Anselmino and C. Pavolini in Carandini et al, *Atlante*, 207. Recent excavations in the Crypta Balbi at Rome have demonstrated the strong presenced of Hayes type IIB in the late seventh century: Lucia Sagui in M. S. Arena et al. (eds), *Roma dall'antichità al medioevo: archeologia e storia nel Museo Nazionale Romano Crypta Balbi* (Rome, Electa, 2001): 276–78.

[20] Hayes, *Pottery*, 313; Bejaoui, *Céramique*, cat. 82, 83, 83a.

[21] Garbsch and Overbeck, *Spätantike*, 138.

[22] For this type, see also Ennabli, *Lampes*, foldout, motif F5.

of his style D.[23] He dates style D to about 440–500.[24] A date relatively early in this span would place the stamp type around 440–460. If, as seems likely, the potters producing lamps were in close communication with the potters producing plates, and if, as again seems likely, the lampmakers picked up motifs from the dishmakers rather rapidly, then the creation of the Ascension lamp design would also date around the middle of the fifth century, perhaps 440–470. Once the design had been established, Ascension lamps could have remained in production for decades.

Changing Visions of the Ascension

The presentation of the Ascension on these lamps elaborates well beyond the textual basis provided by Luke-Acts and seems to mark a watershed in the history of artistic efforts to convey the departure of Christ from the earth. The biblical accounts are extremely brief in their descriptions. In Luke 24: 50–51, it is said that "[t]hen he led them (the apostles) out as far as Bethany, and lifting up his hands he blessed them. While he blessed them, he parted from them and was carried up into heaven." The most detailed biblical account is that offered in Acts 1:9; "And when he had said this, as they were looking on, he was lifted up, and a cloud took him out of their sight."[25] The immediate aftermath is provided by the following verses (Acts 1:10–11): "And while they were gazing into heaven as he went, behold, two men stood by them in white robes, and said, "Men of Galilee, why do you stand looking into heaven? This Jesus, who was taken up from you into heaven, will come in the same way as you saw him go into heaven." In Acts 1:12, the locus of the event is given as Mount Olivet.

The details of the account in Acts seem to have been the stimuli for the earliest representations of the Ascension (late fourth or early fifth century): the mountainous setting, the cloud, and the "taking up" reappear on two Gallic sarcophagi and in the ivory in Munich ascribed to Rome (fig. 3); Christ is shown in profile, stepping up vigorously in a mountainous terrain, and his hand is taken by the hand of God, reaching down from a cloud.[26] On the Munich ivory, two awestruck apostles crouch below Christ. While the visual retellings of the story are relatively close to the account in Acts, there are also

---

[23] Hayes, *Pottery*, 245, no. 87, fig. 44c.

[24] Hayes, *Pottery*, 221.

[25] The longer ending of Mark (16:19) is least specific about the means of transit; "So then the Lord Jesus, after he had spoken to them, was taken up into heaven, and sat at the right hand of God."

[26] Leclerq, "Ascension," 2928–31, figs. 986–88; Schmid, "Himmelfahrt," 270–73; Kessler in *Age of Spirituality*, 454, fig. 67; Ernst Kitzinger, *Byzantine Art in the Making: Main lines of stylistic development in Mediterranean Art, 3rd–7th Century* (Cambridge, Mass.: Harvard, 1980), 39–40, fig. 76.

non-textual elements. Christ's active pose, the agency of the divine hand, and the gestures of fear and awe of the apostles are elements apparently improvised by artists or derived from some other textual source. The animation of the apostles, for example, could have been borrowed from the account of the Transfiguration in Matthew (17:6).[27] The animation of the apostles was certainly assumed by contemporary sources; in his Sermon 265 on the Ascension, St. Augustine speaks of the astonishment and joy of the apostles in his interpretation of Acts 1:11.

In the famous wooden doors of Santa Sabina in Rome, datable between 422 and 440 (fig. 4), the Ascension is shown in similar terms to the Munich ivory, but with significant alterations, which to some degree move the image closer to the text of Acts. Although still shown in profile, Christ no longer climbs the mountain vigorously but is taken up passively to the cloud by a group of angels. The upper bodies of two winged angels emerge from the cloud, and one takes him by the hand, while another angel stands by. Four apostles now gesture with amazement and bewilderment on the mountainside below Christ.[28] Christ is made more passive, as in the text of Acts, but the angels are interpolated as the agents of his elevation. Two apocryphal texts have been cited as possible sources for their presence: *Gospel of Peter* 10 and *Epistula Apostolorum* 51.[29] The idea of angelic presence, however, was current in theological interpretations of the time, as shown again by Augustine's *Serm.* 265, where the "men in white" of Acts 1:11 are called angels.

Although originally created no more than a few decades later, the African lamps have profoundly altered this relatively direct translation of the biblical account of the Ascension (figs. 1, 2). Christ has turned frontally, stands tranquilly, carries a cross-standard, has a halo around his head, and has an ovoid ring of radiance around his entire body. A symmetrical pair of flying angels carries him upwards, supporting the ring below his feet. The four symbols of the evangelists appear above the ring. The image has become that of Christ in majesty, with a strong allusion to the Second Coming. The four evangelist symbols are clearly an abbreviated version of the four beasts that introduce the Second Coming (Rev 4:6–8); their wings must have been omitted because of the extremely small size of the images on the lamps. The biblical beasts appeared around the enthroned one, who was surrounded by a rainbow (Rev 4:2–3), which is evoked by the oval ring surrounding Christ. This ovoid ring of radiance might also be described as a "corona lucido globo," the term that Paulinus of Nola used for the element surrounding the cross in

---

[27] Gisela Jeremias, *Die Holztür der Basilika S. Sabina in Rom* (Tübingen: Wasmuth, 1980), 70–71.

[28] Elisabetta Lucchesi-Palli in Weitzmann, *Age of Spirituality*, 486–88, cat. 438; Jeremias, *Holztür*, pls. 60–65.

[29] Hennecke and Schneemelcher, *Apocrypha*, 1, 123, 155; cited in Jeremias, *Holztür*, 71, 144 n. 262.

Figure 4. Wooden door panel with the Ascension, 422–440. Rome, Santa Sabina (photo: Deutsches Archäologisches Institut, Rome, 61.2573)

an apse mosaic he commissioned.[30] The two men on the canal of the Ascension lamp, who seem to be the "two men in white," introduce an element specifically drawn from Acts. None of the other elements of the lamps' composition, however, adhere to the details of the biblical account of the Ascension, other than presenting Christ as passively taken up. The general concept, however, can be justified as a legitimate development of the implications of the passage of Acts (1:11) that says that Jesus will come again as he departed.[31] Revelation makes it clear that he will return in majesty, and the imagery of Revelation was used to enrich the imagery of Ascension. The imagery might almost be considered a Second Coming or Parousia,[32] but the hand of God helping Christ upwards and the two men (in white?) make it clear that the primary meaning of the scene is that of the Ascension.

A similar image of Christ in majesty had already appeared in the doors of Santa Sabina (422–440), but not in the context of the Ascension. In one panel entitled by Gisela Jeremias "Parousie," Christ stands blessing and holding a scroll inscribed IXYΘC (fig. 5).[33] He is haloed, and his entire body is enclosed in a circular laurel wreath. The letters Alpha and Omega in the field beside him make the allusion to Revelations clear (Rev. 1:8; 21:6; 22:13). The four beasts appear around the wreath. Below is a semicircle defining a starry field in which Saints Peter and Paul hold a ringed cross above the head of a woman (Mary or the Church). The sun and moon appear above the three figures. The composition on the African lamps (figs. 1, 2) can be understood essentially as a transposition of elements of this image of Christ in majesty from the Santa Sabina panel into the context of an Ascension. Angels remain necessary for the elevation of Christ, and the divine hand also remains from earlier tradition. Apparently this re-thinking of Ascension iconography took place approximately within the period of 430–440 (doors of Santa Sabina finished) and circa 440–470 (date of the lamp design). Needless to say, the radical reworking of artistic tradition was not due to the humble potters who produced the lamps; they must have been inspired by some major work of art in their North African homeland, whether in mosaic, painting, or illuminated manuscript.

Various other new elements in the lamp's composition come from other artistic traditions. The symmetrical pair of angels flying horizontally and carrying the ring of radiance could well have been influenced by busts or entire figures of Christ enclosed in a wreath carried by pairs of angels or cherubim. Examples are sculpted on the wooden doors from Saint Barbara, Cairo of the

---

[30] Paulinus of Nola, *Ep.* 32, 10: cited in Joseph Engmann, "Zu den Apsis-Tituli des Paulinus von Nola," *Jahrbuch für Antike und Christentum* 17 (1974), 21–46, esp. 21–22.

[31] André Grabar, *Ampoules de Terre Sainte (Monza-Bobbio)* (Paris: Klincksieck, 1958), 59; Engmann, "Apsis-Tituli," 40–41, also citing Beat Brenk and Henri Stern.

[32] Compare Engmann, "Apsis-Tituli," 39–42.

[33] Jeremias, *Holztür*, 80–88, pls. 68–69; Lucchesi-Palli in *Age of Spirituality*, cat. no. 438.

Figure 5. Wooden door panel with an appearance of Christ, 422–440. Rome, Santa Sabina (photo: Deutsches Archäologisches Institut, Rome, 61.2579)

late fifth or early sixth century,[34] on the limestone doorlintel of the Evangelists Basilica at Alahan in Cilicia (fig. 6), dated variously in the range of 450–540,[35] and on two fifth-century marble sarcophagi in Marseille (fig. 7).[36] The image might be understood as a generic image of Christian triumph or a *Parousia* as well as an Ascension.[37] The image is probably derived from a centuries-old Roman emblem of heroization or apotheosis; innumerable third-century sarcophagi in Italy show a portrait of the deceased in a roundel carried by a pair of horizontally flying Erotes; an example from the Gardner Museum in Boston can represent this numerous type (fig. 8).[38]

In the next step of the composition's development, the pair of angels carries not a wreath but an oval ring of radiance, which encloses a full figure of Christ enthroned. One example is on a wooden doorlintel from Cairo (fig. 9),[39] another on a limestone lintel from Bawit.[40] Both pieces, which are in the Coptic Museum in Cairo, are usually dated to the sixth century. As Grabar has pointed out, this kind of body halo, "aureole," or "mandorla" makes its first securely dated appearance in the nave mosaics of S. Maria Maggiore at Rome.[41] In one mosaic, the aureole appears around Aaron and his companions as a protection against the stones thrown by the people and seems to translate the "gloria domini" of the biblical text (Num. 14:10). The African lamps belong to this phase of development; Christ is enclosed in an oval ring

---

[34] *L'Art Copte* (Petit Palais Paris, 17 June–15 September 1964, Minstère d'État Affaires Culturelles), cat. no. 92. H.-G. Severin in B. Brenk, *Spätantike und frühes Christentum* (Propyläen 1977), cat. no. 286; G. Gabra with contributions by A. Alcock, *Cairo: The Coptic Museum and Old Churches* (Cairo 1993), cat. no. 45.

[35] Gerard Bakker in Mary Gough (ed.), *Alahan, An Early Christian Monastery in Southern Turkey* (Toronto: Pontifical Institute of Mediaeval Studies, 1985), 87–88, pl. 19. For a date of 450–470, see Martin Harrison in Gough, *Alahan*, 21–34; for a date of 530–540, see Christine Strube, "Die Kapitelle von Qasr ibn Wardan," *Jahrbuch für Antike und Christentum* 26 (1983), 59–106, esp. 103, 105.

[36] Paola Borraccino, *I sarcofagi paleocristiani di Marsiglia* (Bologna: Patron, 1973), 75–79, cat. nos. 22–23, figs. 29–31; Bejaoui, *Céramique*, 142.

[37] In Alahan, the tetramorph of the vision of Ezekiel is represented on the underside of the lintel: Gough, *Alahan*, pl. 20. If the images on the front and underside of the lintel are to be read together, they could form either the Second Coming or the Ascension.

[38] Cornelius Vermeule in Cornelius C. Vermeule, Walter Cahn, Rollin Hadley, *Sculpture in the Isabella Stewart Gardner Museum* (Boston: Isabella Stewart Gardner Museum, 1977), cat. 62.

[39] From Al-Mo'allaqa: Engmann, "Apsis-Tituli," 39, 41–42, pl. 3; Severin in Brenk, *Spätantike*, cat. no. 287b; H. Kessler in *Age of Spirituality*, cat. no. 451; Gabra, *Cairo*, cat. no. 41. Two of the four apocalyptic beasts appear beside Christ. From the context it is clear that the doorframe represents the Ascension—while alluding to a second coming.

[40] André Grabar, *Byzantium from the Death of Theodosius to the Rise of Islam* trans. Stuart Gilbert and James Emmons; (Thames and Hudson, 1966) 244, 403, fig. 278; Bejaoui, *Céramique*, 142.

[41] As a protective envelope around Moses and his companions (Num. 14, 10) and around the body of the central of the three angels at Mamre: Grabar, *Christian Iconography*, 117–18, figs. 276, 286. For the possible influence of a rabbinic text, see H. Kessler in *Age of Spirituality*, cat. no. 420.

Figure 6. Bust of Christ in wreath elevated by angels: Limestone doorframe of the Evangelist's basilica, 450–540. Alahan Monastery, Cilicia (photo: authors)

Figure 7: Stone sarcophagus with the enthroned Christ, angels, and Saints Peter and Paul, 450–500. Crypt of S. Victor, Marseille, drawing by A. De Ruffi (photo: from Borraccino, 1973: fig. 30)

Figure 8. Marble sarcophagus with the deceased transported above Earth and Sea by Cupids, ca. 230. Isabella Stewart Gardner Museum (photo: museum)

Figure 9. Wooden door lintel depicting the Ascension from the church of Al-Mo'allaqa, sixth century. Coptic Museum, Cairo, no. 753 (photo from Brenk, *Spätantike*, cat. no. 287b)

of radiance rather than a circular wreath. There is a further novelty; the angels have changed their position and support the mandorla from below. The upper circuit of the mandorla is occupied by the busts of the evangelist symbols. Two evangelist symbols also appear in the wooden lintel from Cairo—below the mandorla.

Images combining the Ascension and Christ in majesty went on to have a great popularity in the sixth century; the evidence is entirely from the East. Typically Christ is enthroned and holds a book. His aureole is supported by not one but two pairs of angels. The spectacle is viewed from below by the Virgin Mary and twelve apostles in a state of agitation. The scene is common on the lead ampullae from the Holy Land preserved in the cathedrals of Monza and Bobbio in Lombardy (fig. 10).[42] The scene is shown with particular animation on a gold medallion with Greek inscription on the art market (fig. 11).[43] Frescoes from the apses of churches at Bawit, Egypt, of about c.e. 550–650 follow a similar scheme, but the four beasts of the apocalypse replace the angels.[44] The Rabbula Gospels, illuminated in Syria in 586 show another variation on the theme (fig. 12).[45] Christ in majesty stands enclosed by an aureole and holding a scroll. The aureole is carried upwards from below by the tetramorph, rendered in terms that closely follow the description by Ezekiel. A pair of flying angels supports the aureole at the sides while another pair brings crowns. Two more angels flank the Virgin and instruct the apostles, developing the "two men in white" of Acts.

Eastern or Western?

In recent times, these sixth-century Ascensions with Christ in majesty have universally been considered to be a distinctly Eastern type.[46] Christ is characterized as passive, and the type is contrasted with the "active" Western type, where Christ steps upwards (fig. 3).[47] The two types are implicitly regarded as timeless creations inherent in two different cultural outlooks. However, the similar Ascension in majesty on the African lamps, stemming as it does from the Latin-speaking, western Roman provinces of Byzacena and Africa Proconsularis, presents a certain inconvenience for this scheme. The lamps reveal the presence of the "Eastern" type in the Latin West, and even more inconveniently they are apparently as early or even earlier in date than any of the preserved "Eastern" examples of the type. The problem posed by the Ascension lamps, however, has not been confronted, since they generally seem to be either unknown or ignored. Bejaoui himself dutifully accepts received wisdom and simply identifies the Ascension on the lamps as the Eastern type, resulting from Eastern influence.[48]

Eastern influence could, of course, reach fifth century Tunisia; the impressions of *solidi* of Theodosios II (the emperor in Constantinople) on the rims

---

[42] Grabar, *Ampoules*; Grabar, *Christian Iconography*, fig. 319 (considered "symbolic scenes").

[43] Unpublished. The Ascension is inscribed: ἡ χάρις τοῦ κ(υρίο)υ ἡμῶν Ἰ(ησο)ῦ Χ(ριστο)ῦ μετὰ πάντων ὑμῶν (cf. 2 Thess 3:18; Rom 16:20). The reverse shows the Annunciation and the Nativity, with the inscription: χαῖρε κεχαριτομένη ὁ κ(ύριο)ς μετὰ σοῦ (Luke 1, 28).

[44] Grabar, *Christian Iconography*, fig. 325; John Beckwith, *Early Christian and Byzantine Art* (Harmondsworth: Penguin, 1979), 71–72, fig. 55.

[45] Grabar, *Christian Iconography*, 35, pl. 1; Kessler in *Age of Spirituality*, 454–55, fig. 68.

[46] Schmid, "Himmelfahrt," 1970; Engmann, "Apsis-Tituli," 39–42: Jeremias, *Holztür*, 87; Kessler in *Age of Spirituality*, 454–55, fig. 68.; Robin M. Jensen, *Understanding Early Christian Art* (London and New York: Routledge, 2000), 166–67.

[47] Jeremias, *Holztür*, 70; Kessler in *Age of Spirituality*, 454, fig. 67.

[48] Bejaoui, *Céramique*, 142. He, however, gives a fifth-century date for the Bawit lintel rather than the sixth-century date advanced by Grabar, *Byzantium*, 403.

Figure 10. Lead ampulla with the Ascension, sixth or early seventh century. Treasury of S. Giovanni, Monza (photo: Marburg/Art Resource: NY)

Figure 11. Gold medallion with the Ascension, 550–620. International art market (photo: courtesy R. Hecht)

Figure 12. Ascension, Rabbula Gospels, from Zagba on the Euphrates, Syria, ca. 586. Biblioteca Medicea-Laurenziana, Florence, Ms. Plut. 1, 56 (photo: Scala/Art Resource, NY)

of some African lamps can in a sense be considered eastern influence, but there is no evidence that the composition of the Ascension lamps was known in the East at that time. It seems worth considering the possibility that the Ascension in majesty composition seen on the lamps was the result of an empire-wide development in which North Africa may have played a significant role. North Africa, after all, was a powerful artistic producer in late antiquity. Its ceramics dominated the Mediterranean market from the fourth through the sixth centuries,[49] and North African craftsmen traveled widely in the west during the fourth century to produce mosaic pavements, and North African pavements had a significant influence in the East as well.[50] The absence of wall mosaics or paintings has subtracted what must have been the most ambitious North African artistic compositions from our view. Although we cannot follow it directly, creativity in major realms of Christian iconography may well have accompanied the undeniable creativity of North African artists in the realms of popular and decorative art.

Not less significantly, theological activity, exemplified by the work of St. Augustine of Hippo in Numidia, located close to the border of Africa Proconsularis, provided an intellectual matrix to nuture such iconographic creativity. His writings, moreover, show that the importance of the Ascension as a feast had a historical development, and it is in this context that an evolving rather than a timeless conception of the artistic presentation should be understood.

Augustine and the Ascension

Though established by the beginning of the fifth century, the origins of the feast of the Ascension are far from clear.[51] Early sources had indicated that the Easter vigil was followed by a period of fifty days (Pentecost), in which various elements of Christ's resurrection were commemorated; this fifty-day period ended with a celebrative last day.[52] Available information does not suggest that individual events such as the Ascension were celebrated separately.[53]

---

[49] Hayes, *Pottery*, 13–299; Carandini et al., *Atlante*.

[50] Katherine Dunbabin, *The Mosaics of Roman North Africa: Studies in Iconography and Patronage* (Oxford: Clarendon, 1978), 196–233. A sharp decline in the quality of African mosaics has been linked to the Vandal conquest ca. 430: Dunbabin, *Mosaics*, 225. Pottery production, however, continued as if unafffected by political events.

[51] In *Serm.* 265F (Lambot 25) dated to around 405, Augustine claims that the celebration of the Ascension was well established throughout the Christian world just as the celebration of Pentecost was. He called the former the "holy day of Quadragesima" and termed the latter "Quintagesima," the Latin equivalent of the Greek πεντηκοστή.

[52] Ambrose, *Exp. Luc.* 8.25; Hansjörg auf der Maur, *Feiern im Rhythmus der Zeit I, Herrenfeste in Woche und Jahr* (Regensburg: Verlag Friedrich Pustet, 1983), 80.

[53] This is the general opinion among scholars of liturgy. Cantalamessa has a slightly different opinion and cautions against oversimplification in the reconstruction of the development, see Raniero Cantalamessa, *Easter in the Early Church: An Anthology of Jewish and Early Christian Texts* (Minnesota: Liturgical Press, 1993), 21–22.

In the course of the fourth century a more articulated situation emerges, in which commemorations of the Ascension and the descent of the Holy Spirit became increasingly separate elements. Several sources attest to this evolution: the *Doctrina Apostolorum*, a Syrian document, prescribes that at the completion of fifty days after the resurrection a commemoration of the Ascension should be held, a tradition to which Eusebius also attests.[54] Moreover, there are indications in Palestine of a two-fold commemoration on the fiftieth day: that of the coming of the Holy Spirit and the Ascension.[55]

Other traditions single out the fortieth day. In one of its canons the council of Elvira (held between 300–309) mentions the custom of having the period end on the fortieth day.[56] The council condemns this practice as heretical and wants to maintain a fifty-day period. The council of Nicea also mentions the fortieth day after Easter as an important point in time.[57] Neither of these canons spell out what the theological significance of this day was,[58] leaving open questions of why the period would end on the fortieth day and whether the Ascension or the descent of the Spirit were featured events. By the beginning of the 5th century, however, the celebration of the Ascension on the fortieth day was well established as was the coming of the Holy Spirit on the fiftieth day.

This development accentuates the individual elements of the post-Easter period and arranges them in a kind of chronological order. The Lukan account clearly offered the theological backbone for this evolution, since the numbers forty and fifty were embedded in the post-resurrection narratives of Acts.[59] The development as a whole—here sketched in a nutshell—meant that the original unity of the Easter celebrations from the passion, death and resurrection to the glorification of Christ was now divided into separate memorial days, a tendency that was not unique to the Easter cycle but extended to other parts of the ecclesiastical year as well from this time onward.[60] The emergence of the feast of the Ascension in liturgical terms seems to parallel the rather late appearance of Ascension iconography, since depictions of the Ascension are missing in the art of the catacombs and in Roman fourth-century sarcophagi.[61]

Augustine is one of the first theologians in the West known to have given Ascension sermons.[62] Since the North African lamps originated not long after his lifetime (354–430), his sermons provide us with material that forms a

---

[54] *Doctr. Apost.* canon 9; Eusebius, *De Solemn. Pasch.* 5; Auf der Maur, *Feiern*, 80.

[55] Egeria 42–43; Jerome, *Com. in Gal.* 2, 4, 10–11; *Com. in Eph. Prol.*; Auf der Maur, *Feiern*, 80–81.

[56] Mansi, *Concilia*, II, 13.

[57] Mansi, *Concilia*, II, 669.

[58] Auf der Maur, *Feiern*, 82.

[59] Acts 1 and 2.

[60] H. A. J. Wegman. "Hemelvaart," in *Grote Winkler Prins* (Amsterdam: Elsevier, 1979–1984).

[61] Schmid, "Himmelfahrt," 268, 270–71.

[62] In the East Chrysostom was one of the first to preach Ascension sermons. His *Hom. in Ascens.* (*PG* 50, 441–52) given in Antioch dates to around 386.

remarkable parallel to and preparation for these visual images. Just as the lamps were works of popular art, the sermons were addressed to a popular audience. They were not composed as exercises for a highly intellectual discourse but given as spontanuous and lively speeches, as it were, off the cuff. The main task of the bishop was to preach, and Augustine was a preacher par excellence. It has been calculated that he must have delivered between five to seven thousand sermons in the almost forty years of his service as a bishop. He addressed his people weekly on Saturday nights, Sunday mornings and sometimes evenings, with additional sermons on special occasions and festive days, such as the celebration of the Ascension.[63] About 550 authentic sermons have come down to our time, and occasionally new ones are discovered. Many more sermons have been transmitted under Augustine's however, that he did not write.

Augustine's popular style presumably reflects the taste of his audience. His sermons were often improvised, certainly at a later stage of his career.[64] They often reflect interaction with his audience. Some repetitions and summaries were a response to an influx of latecomers. At times he had to cut his sermon short when the people (who had to stand through these long discourses in the African heat) became restless and noisy.[65] Augustine's sermons frequently contain plays on words; given the acclamations that followed, the people greatly appreciated his puns.[66]

In a lively interaction on Ascension day, we see the bishop in full action: "Tell me now, choose what you want! What do you want to be, a human who is blind or an animal that can see? You all applauded, you made your choice. Where did you see what you chose? What did I show you to make you applaud like that?"[67] At another Ascension ceremony Augustine reminds his audience ironically about their behaviour: "For I know that particularly on these days the church is filled with such people who wish to depart more speedily than they came; they consider us a pain if we happen to talk a little longer. But if these people are held up at their dinner parties, to which they are in such a hurry, they do not suffer, nor do they refuse or are in any way

---

[63] For Augustine as a preacher, see Frits van der Meer, *Augustinus de zielzorger: Een studie over de praktijk van een kerkvader* (Utrecht: Spectrum, 1957), 2.122–79. Hans van Reisen, *Augustinus, bisschop van Hippo: Beknopt overzicht van zijn leven en werk* (Eindhoven: Augustijns Instituut, 1995), 10.

[64] Improvisation was almost required if the lector happened to read the wrong passage, other than what the bishop had intended; see Martijn Schrama, *Aurelius Augustinus: Als licht in het hart. Preken voor het liturgisch jaar* (Baarn: Ambo, 1996), 13–14.

[65] It has been calculated that the average duration of Augustine's sermons must have been between half an hour and an hour and a half—but sermons of over two hours were also within range.

[66] See Christine Mohrmann, *Sint Augustinus: Preken voor het volk handelende over de heilige schrift en het eigen van den tijd* (Utrecht: Spectrum, 1948), XLV.

[67] *Serm.* 265C; Mohrmann, *Sint Augustinus*, LXII.

ashamed and leave."[68] All of this gives the modern reader an idea of the contemporary reception of these sermons, and it was this ambiance that produced
the African lamps with their popular Christian symbols and biblical allusions.[69]

About fifteen of Augustine's Ascension sermons are known to us.[70] Since
there was no fixed lectionary at the time, it was up to the bishop to choose
the appropriate readings. As far as the Gospel readings go, they were never
taken from the Gospel of Mark but rather from Luke 24:36–53 or Matt
28:16–20, sometimes in combination with the Gospel of John, either John
14:23–28 (esp. 28) or occasionally John 20:11–18 (esp. 17).[71] The epistle reading was from the first chapter of Acts, just as the second chapter was read
on Whitsunday. Augustine cites the beginning of Acts (Acts 1:1–11) frequently
throughout his writings—he has more quotations from those verses than any
other Latin author of his time or earlier. *Serm.* 265, in particular, follows the
text closely and consistently; the other sermons cite the passage without much
further elaboration. Acts 1:11 often occurs in combination with Zech 12:10/John
19:37.[72]

There are a number of other favorites as well in this context: Augustine is
fond of citing Phil 2:6–11 as well as John 3:13.[73] When he quotes from the
Psalms, he tends to select verses that have a special "upward" resonance; they
contain verbs, such as to be "lifted up," to be "exalted," or to "rise up" (Ps
56:12; 67:19; 96:9; 107:6).[74] Along the same pattern he borrows words from
the eucharistic service, *sursum corda*, "lift up your hearts" and he combines
these words almost seamlessly with a quotation from Col 3:1–2.[75]

There is a great variety of themes in the Ascension sermons, supposedly
due to what was on the bishop's mind at the time. His emphasis changed,

---

[68] *Serm.* 264; van der Meer, *Augustinus*, 1.166. These incidents and reactions were
occasionally reported by the stenographers, the *notarii* who recorded Augustine's sermons.

[69] See Bejaoui, *Lampes*, 21–31; van den Hoek and Herrmann, "Thecla the Beastfighter,"
212–14.

[70] The numbers vary: compare J. G. Davies, *He Ascended into Heaven* (New York:
Association Press, 1958), 190–91; William H. Marrevee, *The Ascension of Christ in the
Works of St. Augustine* (Ottawa: Saint Paul University, 1967), 21–22. Martijn Schrama,
Aurelius Augustinus: Als licht in het hart. Preken voor het liturgisch jaar (Baarn: Ambo, 1996),
280–281.

[71] John 14:28: "vado ad patrem meum quia pater maior me est"; John 20:17: "ascen-
dam ad patrem meum et patrem vestrum"; see also G. G. Willis, *St. Augustine's Lectionary*
(London: S.P.C.K., 1962), 28.

[72] "videbunt in quem pupugerunt," see *Serm.* 127.10; 265.2; *Tract. in Ioh.* 21.13; 36,
12; *Enarr. in Ps.* 85.21.

[73] John 3:13 "nemo ascendit in caelum, nisi qui de caelo descendit."

[74] Ps. 56:12 (107, 6): "exaltare super caelos, deus, et super omnem terram gloria
tua" (*Serm.* 262; 263A; 265). Ps. 67, 19 (Ep. 4:8): "(qui) ascendit in altum" (*Serm.* 261).
Ps. 96:9: "tu es dominus altissimus super omnem terram. nimis exaltatus es super omnes
deos" (*Serm.* 265E).

[75] Col. 3:1–2: "si resurrexistis cum Christo quae sursum sunt quaerite ubi Christus
est in dextera dei sedens" (*Serm.* 263A).

but the themes were always embedded in an vast repertory of biblical texts. If Augustine was dealing with the number forty, he would track down all the famous examples in scripture where this number surfaced.[76] If the Arians were on his mind, he would focus on the divinity of Christ and the unity of Father and Son.[77] Other writings and other sermons of the liturgical year contain Ascension motifs as well; of particular interest are his expositions on the Symbolum, in which the bishop expounds on the formulation of the Creed.

Ascension and Second Coming

In Augustine's hermeneutics there is a close link between the Ascension and the Second Coming, a link which is firmly based in the text of Acts and the Symbolum. Augustine gives a good example of this in *Serm.* 265, in which he gives full weight to both parts of Acts 1:11: the Ascension and Christ's return. The bishop also brings out the implication that humans will participate in the Ascension[78] emphasizing the idea that God will come as a man in order for humans to become gods:

> *Serm.* 265.2. Tunc ergo posteaquam id quod videbant ascendere mirabantur, sursum tamen ire gaudebant; capitis enim praecessio, spes membrorum est; audierunt et angelicam vocem, *viri Galilaei, quid statis aspicientes in coelum?* Hic *Jesus sic veniet, quemadmodum vidistis eum euntem in coelum.*[79] Quid est, *sic veniet?* In ea forma veniet: ut impleatur quod scriptum est, *Videbunt in quem pupugerunt.*[80] *Sic veniet.* Ad homines veniet, homo veniet; sed Deus homo veniet. Veniet verus homo et Deus, ut faciat homines deos. Ascendit iudex coeli, sonuit praeco coeli.[81]
>
> (At that time then they were astonished at what they saw ascend but yet they rejoiced to see him go up. For the head that precedes is the hope for the members. They also heard an angelic voice: *men of Galilee, why do you stand looking into heaven? This Jesus will come in the same way as you saw him go into heaven.* What does it mean: *he will come in the same way?* He will come in the same form, in order that scripture may be fullfilled: *They will see the one whom*

---

[76] *Serm.* 264.

[77] *Serm.* 265A.

[78] The glorification of Christ supports the glorification of humans as a promise. In *Serm.* 261 on the Ascension, Augustine explains that the proper celebration of Christ's ascension would result in the human ascension.

[79] Acts 1:11.

[80] Zech 12:10; John 19:37.

[81] See also: *Serm.* 265.8. duae sunt glorificationes secundum suscepti hominis formam: una, qua surrexit a mortuis tertio die; alia, qua ascendit in coelum ante oculos discipulorum suorum. duae sunt istae, quae commendantur, glorificationes eius iam factae. Restat una et ipsa in conspectu hominum, cum se iudicio praesentabit . . . 12. Hoc resurrectione glorificatus. Quid ascensione glorificandus? quod audistis, *eritis mihi testes in Ierusalem, et in tota Iudaea et Samaria, et usque in fines terrae* (Acts 1:8).

they pierced. Thus he will come. He will come to men; he will come as a man, but God will come as a man. He will come as true man and God, in order to make men into gods. The judge of heaven has ascended, the herald of heaven has sounded.)

A major theme in Augustine's thoughts on the Ascension and Christ's return is the concept of glory and majesty,[82] since the full glory is particularly manifest in Christ's second coming. The textual substratum for his treatment goes well beyond the first chapter of Acts and has a broad biblical base, as the following passage from *Ep.* 199 shows. Describing the second coming of Christ in majesty and power, Augustine refers in a complex way to other gospel texts, such as Luke 21:27 (and par.) dealing with the parousia of the Son of man and Matt 26:64 (and par.) on Jesus before the Sanhedrin. According to Augustine, the Lukan text can be understood in two ways: either through Christ's presence in the church or through his glorified body:

> *Ep.* 199.41: *Et tunc videbunt Filium hominis venientem in nube cum potestate magna et majestate.*[83] quod video duobus modis accipi posse sive in ecclesia tanquam in nube venientem, sicut etiam nunc venire non cessat secundum id, quod ait: *amodo videbitis Filium hominis sedentem a dextris virtutis et venientem in nubibus coeli;*[84] sed ideo tunc cum potestate magna et maiestate,[85] quia maior potestas et maiestas illius apparebit sanctis, quibus magnam virtutem dabit, ne tanta persecutione vincantur, sive in corpore suo, in quo sedet ad dexteram Patris, in quo etiam mortuus est et resurrexit et ascendit in coelum, secundum quod scriptum est in Actibus Apostolorum, *His dictis nubes suscepit eum, et sublatus est ab eis.*[86] Et quia illic etiam dictum est ab angelis, *Sic veniet, quemadmodum vidistis eum euntem in coelum,*[87] merito credendus est non solum in eodem corpore verum etiam in nube venturus, quoniam sic veniet, sicut abiit et nubes eum suscepit abeuntem.

> (*and then they will see the Son of man coming in a cloud with great power and majesty;* this, as I see it, can be understood in two ways, either that he is coming in the church as it were in a cloud, since even now he does not stop coming, according to what he said: *hereafter you will see the Son of man sitting at the right hand of power and coming in the clouds of heaven*—but therefore then with great power and majesty, because his greater power and majesty will appear to the saints, to whom he will give great strength, so that they not be overcome by such a great persecution; or (that he is coming) in his own body, in which he sits at the right hand of the Father, in which he died, rose again, and ascended to heaven, according to what has been written in the Acts of the Apostles: *after these words a cloud supported him and he was taken up away from them;*

---

[82] The terminology in Latin varies but conveys the same idea: maiestas, potestas, gloria, claritas.
[83] Luke 21:27 (parousia of the son of man; cf. Matt 24:30; Mark 13:26 [nubibus]).
[84] Matt 26:64; Mark 14:62 (Jesus before the Sanhedrin).
[85] Cf. Luke 21:27; Matt 24:30; Mark 13:26.
[86] Acts 1:9.
[87] Acts 1:11.

and because there the angels even said: *he will come in the same way as you saw him going into heaven*, one should believe with good reason that he is not only going to come in the same body but also in a cloud, since he will come as he left, and a cloud supported him when he went away.)

Another prominent source for Augustine's characterization of the glory of Christ's reappearance and the last judgement is the text of Matt 25:31–46. In this pericope the Son of man comes in glory before all nations. They will be gathered, and he will separate them as a shepherd separates the sheep from the goats.[88] This text, however, has no specific link to the Ascension for Augustine.

The same constellation of thoughts (Ascension, second coming, glory) with a greater stress on the last judgement emerges in a section of the *Serm. de Symbolo*. This sermon, transmitted under Augustine's name, has been attributed to Quodvultdeus, a student, friend, and admirer of Augustine, who became the bishop of Carthage in 437.

De Symbolo 2.8.1–4 Inde enim venturus est iudicare vivos et mortuos. Adventum eius liber indicat Actuum Apostolorum. Postea enim quam a mortuis resurrexit, conversatus est cum discipulis suis quadraginta diebus et quadraginta noctibus, intrans et exiens, manducans et bibens, non quod haberet infirmitatem, sed ut doceret veritatem. Quadragesimo die, ipsis videntibus et quodam modo in coelum oculis deducentibus, astiterunt illis duo viri in veste alba, qui dixerunt eis: *Viri Galilaei, quid statis intuentes in coelum? Iste Jesus qui assumptus est in coelum a vobis, sic veniet quemadmodum vidistis eum euntem in coelum.*[89] Veniet ergo, fratres mei, veniet: ille qui prius venit occultus, veniet in potestate manifestus; ille qui iudicatus est, veniet iudicaturus; ille qui stetit ante hominem, iudicaturus est omnem hominem. *Deus manifestus veniet.*[90] Quid est, *Deus manifestus veniet?* Non sicut prius, homo humilis; sed sicut Deus homo, maiestate sublimis.

(For thereafter he is going to come to judge the living and the dead. The book of the Acts of the Apostles gives information about his coming. For after he had risen from the dead, he lived with his disciples for forty days and forty nights, going in and going out, eating and drinking, not because he was weak but in order to teach the truth. On the fortieth day while they were looking and while somehow their eyes turned away to heaven, two men in white clothing stood by them, who said to them: *men of Galilee, why do you stand looking into heaven? This Jesus who has been taken up from you into heaven, will come in the same way as you saw him go into heaven.* Therefore, he will come, my brothers, he will come. He who came before secretly, will come openly with power. He who has been judged, will come in order to judge. He who stood before a man is going to judge all man. *God will come openly.* What does this mean: *God will come openly?* Not as before as a lowly man, but as a God man, exalted in majesty.)

---

[88] See *Serm.* 18; 60; 137; 251; 351; 353; *Civ.* 20.5; *Trin.* 1.13; *Gest. Pelag.* 1.3.
[89] Acts 1:11.
[90] Ps 49:3.

While the text may be post-Augustinian, the content is a continuation and development of Augustine's interest in and treatment of the Ascension.[91] The same themes of second coming, glory, and judgement, moreover, are implicit in the iconography of the Ascension lamps, which, of course, present differences of treatment; in the compressed scenes on the lamps, majesty is reinforced through the imagery of the tetramorph/evangelist symbols of biblical visions. Augustine does not connect these images with the Ascension, although he does associate these apparitions with the last judgement, citing the texts of Rev 4:6–8, and Ezek 1:5–10.[92]

Augustine's retelling of the Ascension in *Serm.* 265 and *Ep.* 199, moreover, provides additional detail that parallels most visual representations of the Ascension. The apostles are said to react with astonishment and joy. He also makes angels present; they take the places of the mysterious men in white who interpret the event for the apostles. In the works of art the angels go on to become the agents of Christ's elevation to the skies.

Conclusion

The North African lamps present the Ascension in terms that differ greatly from earlier Ascensions. The principal distinguishing feature is that Christ is shown in majesty, enclosed in a oval of radiance and surrounded by the Evangelist symbols. In the latter respect the imagery draws on the visions of Ezekiel and Revelation. The only specifically Lukan feature remaining (or newly introduced) are the two men in white below the apparition.

The presentation of the Ascension in this way (as Christ in majesty) has long been considered a distinctly Eastern type. The North African lamps, however, show the limitations of this geographical perspective. Not only were the lamps produced in the Latin-speaking western part of the Empire (modern Tunisia), but they are also earlier than any of the (surviving) eastern examples of the imagery. It is clear, however, that the elements for this presentation of the Ascension were available in the artistic traditions of Rome and southern Gaul in the second quarter of the fifth century. There is ample reason to believe that the synthesis of iconograhic and textual elements could have been made in the Latin-speaking area.

From a literary and cultural point of view, the synthesis of Ascension narration and glory imagery on the North African lamps finds a supportive matrix not only in the Latin west but specifically in the area around modern Tunisia, where the lamps were produced. Theological writings of the first half of the fifth century—those of St. Augustine and his circle—gave much attention to the

---

[91] For the connection between Ascension and last judgment in Augustine, see *C. Faustum* 4; *Tract. In Ioh.* 21.13; 22.11; 36.12; *Serm.* 127.10; 214.9; 265.2; 277.17; 328.5. Augustine, of course, does not always link the last judgement to the Ascension.

[92] See his *Tract. in Ioh.* 36.

newly defined feast of the Ascension. Some details of earlier Ascension iconography that have been difficult to explain (the agitation of the apostles, the presence of angels) find good parallels in Augustine's writings. The North African texts, moreover, bring together the concepts of the Ascension and the majesty or glory of Christ. Much stress is laid on the idea that Christ's Second Coming is linked to his departure from the earth. The glory of his departure was like that of his return. The basis for this idea, of course, lies in the texts of Acts and the Symbolum. While Augustine did not cite the texts with the tetramorphs of Revelations and Ezekiel in connection with the Ascension, he did on occasion cite them as a way of visualizing the glory of Christ, the judge.

These fifth-century theological writings do not offer an exact description of the iconography of the fifth century North African Ascension lamps, but they virtually offer a prescription for it. Artists—presumably those creating wall mosaics for churches—could fill out the implied new program by recombining pre-existing visual sources, conveniently available in the Latin west. From there the designs could have passed to the humble local ceramists.

CHAPTER TWENTY-THREE

HEARING, SEEING, AND KNOWING GOD:
ALLOGENES AND THE *GOSPEL OF MARY*

KAREN L. KING

Introduction

In the midst of Job's ordeal, the Lord speaks to him out of the whirlwind. Where was Job, God asks, when the foundations of the earth were laid?[1] How dare he, a mortal, challenge God?[2] By the end, Job finally understands and acknowledges God, saying: "I had heard of You by the hearing of the ear, but now my eye sees You; therefore I despise myself, and repent in dust and ashes."[3]

How are we to understand this scene? God "appears" to Job as speech, a voice out of the whirlwind. But Job dismisses *hearing* and instead says that now he *sees* with his *eye*. "I had heard of You," he says, but "now my eye sees You." We might rather expect him to have said, "I had heard others talk about you, but now I have heard you speak with my own ears." Why privilege seeing over hearing even when God is present as speech? What is it Job sees? Why is it that although most of the book of Job is talk—dialogues between God and Satan, between Job and his friends, and finally God's epiphanic speech—*it is the visionary encounter with God in creation that brings wisdom and insight.* There God's power was manifest and there God could be encountered.

By the first centuries C.E., the confidence that God might be seen in the world, that ultimate meaning could be encountered in the created order, seems to have faltered, at least among some. To such people, revelation appeared not to be found in creation or even in history, but in the experience of the prophet, in vision, ecstasy, and ascent. The prophet no longer encountered God in the world, whether walking among mortals as the Greek Gods did or by intervening in history and politics as the God of Elijah, Jonah, and Amos had. Rather a perspective above or beyond the world of everyday sensory experience, beyond the mundane vision of the mortal eye, was needed in order to comprehend the nature of Reality and approach near to the Divine.

Not only among Jews, but Christians and so-called pagans all seem to be turning inward and going upward to seek the presence and power of the Divine. The *topos* of visionary ascent cuts across what otherwise appear to be

---

[1] See Job 38:1–4 and following.
[2] See Job 26–31.
[3] Job 42:5–6 (RSV).

the religious dividing lines of antiquity. Of course, not everyone feels this need to turn inward or upward. The Gods are still visible and accessible for many in the temples, among the stars, in the regularity and harmony of creation, and in divine(s) mingling among them. But the phenomenon is sufficiently widespread to be notable.

We cannot doubt that such visionary experiences were very real occurrences since they are widely attested cross-culturally in our own day. Such experiences are, however, interpreted differently within different social and cultural contexts. My own culture of American individualism tends to treat such experiences in terms of individual psychology or spirituality, but the expression and meaning of such "personal" experiences are socially constructed and often socially controlled.[4] Societies have a great deal to say about them and about the people who have such experiences, whether they are put up as culture heroes, put to work as practicing shamans, or put away as crazy people. The very content of the experience is culturally informed: Bengali Hindus have visions of Kali, Catholics have visions of the Virgin Mary.

This fact is demonstrated in part by the fact that accounts of such experiences were written down with the intent that they be read and used by others. If visionary experiences were solely for or about the individual, there would be no point in writing them down and passing them on. Written texts are directed in part *toward others*.[5]

In antiquity, many such writings were figured as archetypal narratives, a point illustrated by the fact that many are written in the name of culture heroes. They go far beyond a simple recording of individual experience by providing authority for the prophet and the text's teaching or to aid others in having similar experiences.

In the end, the question is not why the site for encountering God shifted in this period, but what difference it makes where and how one encounters God. To examine this question, we will look briefly at two visionary ascent narratives from antiquity: *Allogenes* and the *Gospel of Mary*.

Allogenes

The third-century philosopher Plotinus tells the seeker:

> "Not to be told; not to be written": in our writing and telling we are but urging towards (unity with the One): out of discussion we call to vision; to

---

[4] See Joan W. Scott, "'Experience,'" in *Feminists Theorize the Political* (ed. Judith Butler and Joan W. Scott; Routledge: New York and London, 1992), 22–40.

[5] *Allogenes* even contains a narrative of its own textual production. At the end of the work, Allogenes narrates a divine command to record and preserve the account of his revelation and ascent with magical power for those who would be worthy in ages to come. This self-conscious narrative of origins forces the reader to acknowledge that this "individual" experience was intentionally meant for others.

those desiring to see, we point the path; our teaching is of the road and the travelling; the seeing must be the very act of one that has made this choice.[6]

One account of such a journey is found in *Allogenes*, a pseudonymous third-century revelation dialogue,[7] in which the protagonist, named Allogenes, first prepares himself through auditory instruction, and then ascends to a vision of God. At the highest point of his ascent, he tells us:

> A stillness of silence existed in me. . . . And through primary revelation of the First . . . I saw the God that surpasses perfection. . . . I was seeking God, who is ineffable and unknowable, such that to know God at all is to be ignorant.[8]

When Plotinus or Allogenes say these things, they do not sound so very different from Job: they all agree that auditory instruction is but the beginning; the goal is vision. But Plotinus and Allogenes meant something very different from Job.

One key is in how they imagined creation. In Job, God acts as a work-man, taking measurements, laying out the plumb line, sinking bases, and laying the cornerstone.[9] For Plotinus, the multiplicity of existing things emanates from the One in a process of ontological and epistemological unfolding, resulting in hierarchical levels of existence. For the book of *Allogenes*, multiplicity also appears as the hierarchical unfolding of the Divine, but now through a complex order of divine beings who empower those beneath them.

In all three cases, an intellectual comprehension of the order of creation is necessary in order to be able to orient human life in the world. In the second and third centuries, this orientation was often articulated metaphorically in terms of verticality, for example, in understanding spiritual progress as the ascent through various levels of reality. That, of course, is not a surprise in societies that were consciously ordered in social and political hierarchies. For these societies, hierarchy defined the appropriate ordering of justice and good-ness, operative not only in constructions of proper social relations but imag-ined in the nature of the divine order as well. What is "higher" is better; to go up is to improve in spirit, mind, and being.

The revelation contained in *Allogenes* describes a model of Reality that pro-vides a framework within which identity and practice can be oriented and given meaning. *Allogenes* implies that those who accept the exalted teaching of the text as true are "worthy,"[10] raising their status above those who might reject the truth of the writing. Being *worthy* defines a minimal component of

---

[6] *Enn.* 6.9.4.

[7] See Karen L. King, *Revelation of the Unknowable God*: NHC XI,3: *Allogenes, Introduction, Critical Text, Translation and Notes* (California Classical Library 1; Santa Rosa, Calif.: Polebridge Press, 1996). All citations of *Allogenes* are from this work, occasionally modified.

[8] *Allogenes* 60.15; 61.8–10, 14–19.

[9] See Job 38:4–6 and following.

[10] See *Allogenes* 52.22–28.

the shared self-identity of those who read and used this work. To be worthy
was not merely a matter of accepting some given status. It required hard work,
both social and intellectual. The figure of Allogenes provides both a model of
the ideal prophet and a model for the kind of prophetic experience that is
potentially available to anyone.[11] Allogenes said that he prepared himself for
100 years (!) through philosophical study and moral labor. He had to overcome his fear, turn away from the distractions and misconceived loyalties and
opinions of the multitude, shape internal stability of character, and learn about
the nature of Reality from his spiritual guide, Iouel. The teaching from Iouel
no doubt also modeled practices of instruction by those who are more spiritually advanced to those who had proceeded less far along the path.[12] In addition, the inclusion of a list of magical names suggests complementary theurgic
practices were involved (54). These practices of intellectual and moral discipline, instruction, and theurgic practice would have shaped a certain group
identity and cohesion.

What kind of group might this be? The social theorist Mary Douglas has
suggested a model linking forms of belief, ritual practice, and social structure.
We have to be tentative about applying her model given the paucity of information, social and otherwise, we have about those who wrote and read
Allogenes—but having set this caveat, let us go on anyway. Hear how she
describes one type:

> If the social groups are weakly structured and their membership weak and
> fluctuating, then I would expect low value to be set on symbolic performance.
> Along this line of ritual variation appropriate doctrinal differences would
> appear. With weak social boundaries and weak ritualism, I would expect doc-
> trinal emphasis on internal, emotional states. Sin could be more a matter of
> affect than of transgression; sacraments and magic would give way to direct,
> unmediated communion, even to the sacralisation of states of trance and
> bodily dissociation.[13]

The main elements of this profile fit *Allogenes* well:

• The work certainly exemplifies doctrinal emphasis on internal states. For
  example, when Allogenes is disturbed by the revelation given him by Iouel,
  he writes: "I turned inward toward myself alone. I perceived the light that
  surrounds me and the good that is in me; I became divine" (52.9–13).
• The ascent of Allogenes emphasizes direct and unmediated communion by
  ensuring that he sees for himself what he has heard about from Iouel
  (58.27–37).

---

[11] For the notion of "a model of and a model for," see Clifford Geertz, *The Interpretation
of Cultures: Selected Essays* (New York: Basic Books, 1973).
[12] The text clearly warns against giving the teaching to those who are uninstructed
(*Allogenes* 52.25–28).
[13] Mary Douglas, *Natural Symbols: Explorations in Cosmology* (New York: Pantheon Books,
1970, 1973), 14.

- *Allogenes* says that sin derives from nature, presumably from the mixing of the spiritual self with the lower nature of the world (51.30–35). Thus sin is more a matter of nature than transgression of social law or mores.
- The ascent of Allogenes offers a clear case of bodily dissociation; the text tells us that he was "seized by an eternal light from out of the garment that clothed me" and "taken up to a place that is holy" (58.26–38). Comparison with related texts, especially *Three Steles of Seth* and *Zostrianos*, suggests that this practice of ascent was ritualized.[14]

These similarities to Douglas' model can lead us to posit a social location for *Allogenes* in a weakly structured social group, whose membership was weak and fluctuating, although without further corroborating evidence, that would need to remain an hypothesis. It is less important, however, whether this description is historically accurate than it is to emphasize that Douglas' model points toward a social group location for even the most internal states and unmediated communion with the Divine. Experience is always itself socially constructed and always, no matter how private, has social implications.[15]

What role would a text like *Allogenes* play in such a group? If the point is for the readers to obtain their own experience of the Divine, how do written texts figure in? One use was to instruct students. The genre of the text as revelation dialogue points toward one kind of instruction. As revelation, *Allogenes* bases its claims to truth not on the exercise of logic, reference to empirical data, or the invocation of traditional wisdom, custom, or law, but on archetypal auditory revelation and visionary experience. Although a preeminently written work, it claims to be dialogue. Writing here records both auditory revelation and visionary ascent, but the work itself is conceived of as a reenactment of speech, not of vision. The writing claims that the source of its teaching was revelatory speech. In Plotinus's terms, this recorded speech points the way but it is not the very act.[16] The book of *Allogenes* speaks in just this manner, pointing the way for those who are "worthy" students.

Yet in this dialogical pedagogy, seeing is still privileged epistemologically over hearing. Indeed the final vision of the Unknowable God is accompanied by silence. Speech apparently conveys too much division, confusion, and movement. The negative theology accompanying the ascent revelation expressly

---

[14] See Hans-Martin Schenke, "Das sethianische System nach Nag-Hammadi-Handschriften," in *Studia Coptica* (ed. Peter Nagel; Berlin: Akademie Verlag, 1974), 165–74; idem, "The Phenomenon and Significance of Gnostic Sethianism," in *The Rediscovery of Gnosticism: Proceedings of the International Conference on Gnosticism at Yale, New Haven, Connecticut, March 28–31, 1978* (SHR 41; Leiden: Brill, 1981), 2:588–616; and John Turner, "Ritual in Gnosticism," in *SBLSP* (ed. Eugene H. Lovering; Atlanta, Ga.: Scholar's Press, 1994), 136–81.

[15] See Scott, "Experience."

[16] The exception may be the magical invocation of names, which seems aimed at enacting the ascent ritually (see *Allogenes* 54). I set this consideration aside for the moment.

pushes the limits of linguistic expression; speech ultimately fails where only vision can succeed. Instruction only points the way; seeing is "the very act." There is, of course, no particular reason why this should be so. Vision, as we all know, is markedly limited in its capacity to distinguish reality. It is perspectival, and the eye is easily fooled. The ancients knew that as well as we and used the terminology of vision metaphorically to articulate a kind of unknowing knowing. In *Allogenes'* terminology, vision belongs to the "quiescent eye of the revelation." After his ascent vision, the great Power asks rhetorically whether it is possible to *say* about the Unknowable that it can be known (64.18–21). The answer is no. Anyone who made such a claim, they tell Allogenes, "would be impious towards (God) (and) would receive judgement on the charge of not knowing God," being blind and "outside of the quiescent eye of the revelation." (64.21–33).

This metaphorical privileging of sight over the other senses is a common trope of antiquity, one that appears already in Job. In this tradition, vision is clearly associated metaphorically with first-hand knowledge: "Seeing is knowing." You have to see for yourself in order to know; you cannot simply be told. In *Allogenes*, this narrative trope of seeing and knowing is figured as a journey. He must go in order to see for himself. Vision has become journey. Seeing has become ascent.

Yet there seems to be no real reason for Allogenes' ascent. In the middle of the text, long before his ascent, he tells us: "I perceived the light that surrounds me and the good that is in me; I became divine" (52.9–13). And just before the ascent itself he has a vision of everything (58.12–26). Surely that would be enough for most of us. Why is the ascent needed? It does not function to convey personal immortality; Allogenes has already achieved that. Nor does it provide knowledge he did not have before: his spiritual director Iouel had already given a very good description of the ascent experience, and it was confirmed in his vision. It is true that at the peak of the ascent he received an additional verbal revelation from the Powers, but this teaching was not part of the visionary experience per se. The verbal revelation was given largely in terms of negative theology, tending to confirm the superiority of vision over speech. The function of the vision can only be to confer the authority of firsthand experience on the text's teaching. Auditory revelation is insufficient. Only seeing will guarantee the truth. And in order to see truly, one must go where the object of the vision is.

Speech cannot lead the readers to the ultimate truth. For that, they need to imitate the authoritative model of the culture hero, Allogenes, by re-enacting his ascent. They not only have to understand the teaching of the work, but put it into practice by in some sense becoming an Allogenes. The purpose of the work is not to give a "historical" account of a particular individual, but to provide a model of spiritual attainment that is potentially accessible to everyone.

The Gospel of Mary

The *Gospel of Mary*[17] is framed as a set of dialogues. At the beginning, the Savior appears to his disciples after the resurrection and answers their questions. After he departs, the disciples talk among themselves. Peter asks Mary to recount any words the Savior may have told to her, and she describes a dialogue with him. He tells her about the ascent of the soul past the four Powers that seek to keep it entrapped in the material world. The soul is able to overcome these Powers by responding to their lies with truth. Hence the genre of the work effects dialogue within dialogue, effectively offering the writing itself as a record of various sorts of speech: the revelation of the Savior, the questions and anxieties of the disciples, the lies of the Powers, and the truth of the soul.

It is not at all clear that vision is superior to speech since the disciples both see and hear the Savior. The reader is able both to visualize the soul ascending past the Powers and also to hear the dialogue between them. Moreover, the culmination of the ascent is figured as silence, not vision. Both hearing and seeing are important aspects of revelation, but restful silence surpasses both. It is in silence that one ultimately encounters God.

Like the unknowing of Allogenes, silence expresses neither mere ignorance nor the mere absence of sound, but divine transcendence. The image belongs to the work's dualistic cosmology, which opposes material existence and divine Reality. The only nature that truly exists is transcendent Reality, which the Savior calls "the Good." According to the Savior, humanity has been deceived into believing that the body and the world are real, when in fact they are but false images. This opposition is figured in the contrast between the soul's state of agitation and suffering in the world below and the soul's true spiritual nature of rest and silence. The Savior warns his disciples that they get sick and die because they love what deceives them. They are tied to the passions of false material nature, and they need to reject this false nature in order to overcome sickness and death.

In order to understand its own true spiritual nature, the soul must recognize the false nature of the Powers and reject their rule. The ascent of the soul represents this process in the dialogue between the soul and the Powers of Darkness, Desire, Ignorance, and Death. By understanding its own nature and

---

[17] See Karen L. King, "The Gospel of Mary" in *The Complete Gospel: Annotated Scholars Version* (ed. Robert J. Miller, rev. and ex. ed.; Sonoma, Calif.: Polebridge Press, 1994), 357–66; "The Gospel of Mary Magdalene," in *A Feminist Commentary* (vol. 2 of *Searching the Scriptures*; ed. Elisabeth Schüssler Fiorenza; New York: Crossroad, 1994), 2:601–34; "Prophetic Power and Women's Authority: The Case of the Gospel of Mary Magdalene," in *Women Preachers and Prophets through Two Millenia of Christianity* (ed. Beverly Mayne Kienzle and Pamela J. Walker; Berkeley and Los Angeles: University of California Press, 1998), 21–41.

the nature of the world, the soul is first able to overcome its own desire and passionate nature. It then rejects the system of sin and judgment that binds people to false notions of the divine Nature. Finally, it understands that all violence and suffering are illusions, against which no struggle need be waged for they are already like dead things. The only truth that exists is the divine Goodness. Here the soul may rest in silence, beyond the constraints of time and mortality.

The whole dialogue between the soul and the Powers is characterized by a sharp contrast between the world above and the world below. The world above is the true kingdom of light, peace, knowledge, love, and life; the lower world is under the rule darkness, desire, arrogance, ignorance, jealousy, and the zeal for death. This contrast expresses more than either a simple belief in the immortality of the righteous souls, or the need to struggle against injustice and falsehood. The dialogue instructs the reader about the true nature of Reality by contrasting it with the deception that characterizes life in the world. The dialogue stresses, as no other ascent account does, the unjust nature of the Powers' illegitimate domination. In so doing, it presents a biting critique of the way power is exercised in the world.

What kind of group might have written and read the *Gospel of Mary*? Like *Allogenes*, this work fits Douglas's profile of a weakly structured group, with weak and fluctuating membership:

- The work emphasizes internal states. The Savior teaches his disciples to acquire peace within themselves and be content at heart (4.2; 3.13).[18] Mary, too, admonishes the disciples not to weep or be distressed, nor let their hearts be irresolute (5.5). She has achieved this inward state, and the Savior himself praises her for her stability of mind, saying: " 'Blessed are you for not wavering at the sight of me. For where the heart is, there also is the treasure' " (7.3–4).
- The work emphasizes direct and unmediated communion with the divine. The disciples are not to await a Savior from without but to seek the Son of Man within themselves (4.3–7). Mary receives a vision of the Lord and communes with him directly; her authority is based on this unmediated revelation, not on office or gender status (5–10).
- Sin is more a matter of affect than transgression. The Savior states quite directly that there is no such thing as sin (3.3). Since matter will eventually dissolve back into its constituent nature, the material world cannot be the basis for determining good and evil, right and wrong. Sin, therefore, does not really exist insofar as it is conceived as action in the material world. Rather the Savior defines sin in spiritual terms: improper (adulterous) attachment to material things (3.4–6). The disciples themselves produce

---

[18] All references use the numbering system from Miller, *The Complete Gospels*.

sin by acting "according to the nature of adultery."[19] The metaphor fits his point quite well. Like adultery, sin joins together what should not be mixed: in this case, material and spiritual natures. Moreover the Savior admonishes his disciples not to lay down any laws beyond what he has given them, lest they be enslaved by those very laws (4.9–10).

• The work also shows some evidence of a high valuation upon states of trance and bodily dissociation, first in Mary's dream vision of the Savior (7.1) and second in the portrayal of the soul's ascent (9). In the first case, the vision ensures that Mary has understood the true spiritual nature of the Savior by seeing him in a vision, not merely with the eyes of the flesh. In the second case, the whole point of the rise of the soul is dissociation from the body in order to achieve salvation.

It would appear again, then, that those who wrote and read the *Gospel of Mary* may have constituted at best a weak and ephemeral group. But we can say much more about the character of this group than we could with *Allogenes* because the work emphasizes discord within the group over issues that had strong social consequences. The main issue was authority and leadership. The Savior is the source of both, and Mary is portrayed as the model for ideal leadership by imitating him. She alone is not distressed when the Savior departs, but comforts the other disciples and turns their thoughts toward a discussion of the Savior's word. The Lord himself praises her for her stability of mind. In his absence, she becomes a teacher of the gospel. And again, when she finishes speaking to the other disciples, her bodily posture of silence reproduces the state of the soul that has escaped the Powers. By defending her, the work defends and authorizes the teaching of the Savior.

What makes this portrayal all the more striking is that it is attacked within the *Gospel of Mary* by some of the other disciples, notably Peter and Andrew. They challenge the strangeness of her teaching, that the Savior spoke only to her, and that the Savior chose to give such teaching to a woman rather than to themselves. As we know from other polemical Christian literature, the attack of Peter and Andrew on Mary raised issues that were current in second-century Christianity: the meaning of the teachings of Jesus, who was authorized to say what that teaching meant, and whether women could legitimately play public leadership roles. The *Gospel of Mary* argues that Jesus did give special teaching to some of his disciples who were more spiritually advanced. Having been a disciple of Jesus was in itself not sufficient for leadership. Only spiritually advanced disciples could properly preach the gospel, by reproducing Jesus' words and deeds in their own speech and actions. Finally, the *Gospel of Mary* strongly argues that gender is irrelevant for leadership, since sex and

---

[19] See Anne Pasquier, *L'Évangile selon Marie* (Bibliothèque copte de Nag Hammadi, Section "Textes" 10; Québec: Les Presses de Université Laval, 1983), 53.

gender are written on bodies that are destined to pass away. Only the spiritual state of the soul is ultimately important.

These controversies let us see the issues of social organization that were being debated within at least one early Christian group. The *Gospel of Mary* argues that hierarchies based on bodily differences or unjust exercise of power have to be rejected. It strongly criticizes any exercise of power bound to the laws of the material world, with its patterns of suffering and injustice. The only true authority is based on spiritual development and the capacity to meet the needs of others. Identity as a true disciple of the Savior is based on imitating him by appropriating his teaching within, achieving spiritual stability, and teaching others to do likewise. Here again, hearing—but also seeing—point the way to God. But the act itself of apprehending the Divine comes not with hearing or even seeing, but by seeking and clothing themselves with the Son of Man within, achieving rest in silence.

Comparison with Irenaeus

To test my thesis that there are social interests at stake in how one hears and sees God, it is instructive to turn to a theologian who takes a different approach to vision and spiritual development. The second-century theologian Irenaeus argued that humans are bodily creatures, made in the image and likeness of God (Gen 1:22). Although humanity always kept the image of God, humans lost their likeness to God through sin. Irenaeus argued that the incarnation of Jesus made God visible, so that by "becoming what we are, He might brings us to be even what He is Himself,"[20] and restore humanity's likeness to God. Irenaeus insists:

> We could have learned in no other way than by seeing our Teacher, and hearing His voice with our own ears, that, having become imitators of His works as well as doers of His words we may have communion with Him, receiving increase from the perfect One, and from Him who is prior to all creation. . . . [He] has poured out the Spirit of the Father for the union and communion of God and humanity, imparting indeed God to humans by means of the Spirit, and, on the other hand, attaching humanity to God by His own incarnation, and bestowing upon us at His coming immortality durably and truly, by means of communion with God.[21]

Here God has come down, so ascent is not necessary to hear or see God. Irenaeus's figuration of vision and knowledge of the Divine has no place for individual ascent experience. There is no reason to make the journey, for God is here. Nor does Irenaeus privilege vision over auditory revelation. Seeing and hearing are complementary experiences, as they are in the *Gospel of Mary*.

---

[20] *Against Heresies* 5, Preface (*ANF* 1:526). All translations are adapted from this edition.
[21] *Against Heresies* 5, 1 (*ANF* 1:526, 527), adapted.

Both what one saw of the Lord and what one heard from him are equally to be enacted. But Irenaeus has a very different understanding of creation and what it means to be human. He agrees with Job that God created the material universe, but unlike Job, God is not fully revealed in creation. Yet unlike *Allogenes* or the *Gospel of Mary*, neither does one have to leave the body in order to see God. The body is itself the site/sight of divine revelation and simultaneously the subject of divine salvation. It is in the body that humanity receives the Spirit and is restored to its likeness of God. The presence of Spirit is not a future event; it is "dwelling in us, rendering us spiritual even now, and the mortal is swallowed up by immortality." Irenaeus assures us that this "does not take place by a casting away of the flesh, but by the importation of the Spirit."[22]

Although Irenaeus does not press the point too strongly, it seems plausible that he regarded Christians as the bodily, visible presence of God in the world. With the ascent of Jesus, the Divine was not removed from the world or given over to the invisible operations of an invisible Spirit; the Divine continued to be manifest bodily by Christians as the image and likeness of God. It had become possible to see God by seeing God in one another. Irenaeus's position is quite radical, asking the reader to see the image of God in every human being, and calling everyone to be restored to likeness to God by imitating the divine man, Jesus.

Irenaeus's radical theology exerted enormous force within many strands of the Christian movement, but it nonetheless floundered on the realities of continued human imperfection. It is not that easy to see God in each other. In practice, it seems that some bodies manifested the image of God more than others: virgins, prophets, martyrs, and saints, for example. *Allogenes* and the *Gospel of Mary* avoided this problem by rejecting the body as the site of divine revelation altogether, even though both offered human models of and for spiritual development in the figures of Allogenes and Mary.

All these writings offer visions, if you will, of encountering God, whether in the exterior world (Job), in unmediated visionary experience in which the subject/object divide is for a moment fractured and crossed (*Allogenes*), by turning within and ascending beyond the reach of the world's Powers to encounter the Divine (*Gospel of Mary*), or finally in the belief that God may be encountered—at least potentially—in other people, insofar as they manifest the image and likeness of God (Irenaeus). Each of these visions carries with it quite different social possibilities and political implications.

Even though Job questioned the justice of God head-on, his vision ultimately could be used to support the *status quo* by fostering an acceptance that God has ordered the universe in ways we as humans may not question. Wisdom requires understanding the way things are, maintaining faith, friendship, and

---

[22] *Against Heresies* 5, 8 (*ANF* 1:533), adapted.

confidence in what is good, even in the presence of suffering and injustice.

If the application of Douglas's theory is at all correct, *Allogenes* fostered only an ephemeral group with a minimal organization of teacher and student, adept and initiate, however powerful or desirable their spiritual experiences may have been. So, too, does the *Gospel of Mary*, although it offers a significantly higher capacity for social critique of suffering due to injustice. By arguing that God is spiritual and that humanity was created in the spiritual likeness of God, humanity too had to be conceived as essentially spiritual in nature. The Savior came to recall humanity to that spiritual likeness. Following the Savior meant resisting the violence and injustice of the world, and preaching the gospel out of compassion to others. To say that people are non-bodily spiritual beings meant that one's sex, race, or other bodily characteristics are spiritually irrelevant; one's image in the eyes of God resides in the state of one's soul, not one's body.

As we all know, Irenaeus's theology became crucial in the development of nascent Christian orthodoxy, with its increasingly strong hierarchical leadership, doctrinal definition, and ordered ritual practices. But it seems to me that its radical possibilities were not exploited or even fully explored. Indeed it would seem that Irenaeus himself might have drawn back from the radical inference of his theology, that God is visible in direct and immediate form in human encounters with one another. The multiform phenomena of Christianity that absorbed his theology recognized that the human body is a potential site for the presence of God; that meant that whatever is inscribed on the human body could potentially be elided with the power and manifestation of God. Gender hierarchy, racial prejudice, social class, or any of the other multitude of messages that bodies are constructed to convey could be seen as God-given, not merely as the social construction of a particular time and place.

The challenge of Irenaeus's theology is to see in every human body the image of God and to conform to the likeness as well as the image. Such a theology gives ultimate value to the bodily well-being and moral life of human beings. But in my view, the enormous theological potential of this perspective fell short by reproducing the patriarchal values of Irenaeus's day: men's bodies had more value than women's bodies; men were said to conform more fully to the image of God because Jesus was male.

Insofar as our own twenty-first century societies give more value to bodies of certain sex and skin color, age, or form, we too fall short of the call of incarnational theology to see every human being created equally in the image of God. A true incarnational theology in my view would lead us to the extraordinarily difficult task of seeing the full image of God in every person, would ask us to look at where we have failed to live up to true compassion toward others, economically and politically, and seek in our hearts and minds to pursue God's justice and compassion. Spiritual theology, such as that offered by the *Gospel of Mary*, would help us recognize that we should have no fear, that evil can do no harm to our true immortal selves, that God calls upon us to risk suffering and death to fight evil by preaching and living the true gospel of God's compassion to all.

Where and how one encounters God—whether in creation, in speech and vision, or in other human beings—there are tremendous consequences not only for personal spiritual development, but for identity and social organization, ethics, and theology. Hearing, seeing, and knowing God are matters that reach to the core of who we think we are and how we live together before God.

CHAPTER TWENTY-FOUR

THE SPIRIT AS A DOVE AND HOMERIC BIRD SIMILES

Dennis R. MacDonald

The earliest evangelist wrote that when Jesus emerged from the waters of the Jordan where John baptized him, "he saw the heavens rent and the Spirit, like a dove, descending to him. A voice then came from heaven, 'You are my beloved son; in you I take delight'" (1:10–11). Q almost certainly told its own version of Jesus' baptism by John and identified him as God's son (Q 4:3 and 9: εἰ υἱὸς εἶ τοῦ θεοῦ), but it is impossible to know if Q contained any reference to "the Spirit, like a dove, descending to him."[1] Identifications of the Spirit of God with a dove do not appear in Jewish texts until several centuries later, and all Christian texts with this identification may well have been influenced by Mark.[2]

Scholars long have attempted to locate the origin and significance of Mark's simile of the Spirit as a dove; surveys of research may be found elsewhere.[3] Despite the impressive erudition devoted to this problem, no one has investigated the richest ancient repositories of bird similes: the *Iliad* and the *Odyssey*. Just as biblical scholars have investigated the origin and meaning of Mark's Spirit-dove simile, classicists have sought the origin and meaning of Homer's god-bird similes, but these two lines of research have never converged.[4] No

---

[1] To be sure, Q could account for the agreement of Matthew and Luke in using ἠνεῴχθησαν or ἀνεῳχθῆναι against Mark's σχιζομένους, but Matthew and Luke share nothing in common against Mark's καὶ τὸ πνεῦμα ὡς περιστερὰν καταβαῖνον εἰς αὐτόν except the substitution of ἐπ' αὐτόν for Mark's problematic εἰς αὐτόν.

[2] Insofar as the author of the Gospel of John probably knew Mark and Luke, the reference to the Spirit as a dove in John 1:32 cannot be taken to be independent. *Odes of Solomon* 24:1–3 speaks of the dove at Jesus' baptism, but it, too, probably is dependent on the Gospels.

[3] See especially Leander E. Keck, "The Spirit and the Dove," *NTS* 17 (1970–71): 40–56; Fritzleo Lentzen-Deis, *Die Taufe Jesu nach den Synoptikern: Literarkritische und gattungsgeschichtliche Untersuchungen* (Frankfurter theologische Studien 4; Frankfurt: Josef Knecht, 1970), 173–83; Stephen Gero, "The Spirit as a Dove at the Baptism of Jesus," *NovT* 18 (1976): 17–35, esp. 30–31, nn. 33 and 34; and Gerhard Sellen, "Das Leben des Gottessohnes," *Kairos* ns. 25 (1983): 249, nn. 24 and 25.

[4] For the most important discussion of the Homeric similes, see Martin P. Nilsson, *The Minoan-Mycenaean Religion* (2d ed.; Lund: Gleerup, 1950), 330–40; Franz Dirlmeier, *Die Vogelgestalt homerischer Götter*, Sitzungsberichte der Heidelberger Akademie der Wissenschaften. Philosophisch-historischen Klasse 2 (1967): 5–36; Wolfgang Fauth, "Zur Typologie mythischer Metamorphosen in der homerischen Dichtung," *Poetica* 7 (1975):

evidence exists that these venerable scholarly traditions were aware of each other, even though the solution to Mark's simile may well reside in a comparison with the Homeric epics.[5]

Most Homeric god-bird similes pertain to their movements, such as their rapid flights from Mount Olympus.

Iliad 5.778: Hera and Athena "went with steps *like those of timorous doves.*"

Iliad 13.62–65: "*Just as a hawk,* swift of flight, rises to fly, and poising himself aloft above a high sheer rock, darts over the plain to chase some bird; so from them sped Poseidon."

Iliad 15.237–38: Apollo "went down from the hills of Ida *like a fleet falcon,* the slayer of doves, which is the swiftest of winged things."

Iliad 19.352–54: Athena "*like a falcon,* wide of wing and shrill of voice, leapt down from heaven through the air."

Iliad 21.493–95: Artemis, weeping, fled from Hera "*like a dove* (ὥς τε πέλεια)."

Odyssey 5.50–54: Hermes "stepped down upon the sea, and then sped over the waves *like a bird, the cormorant.* . . . In such fashion did Hermes convey himself over the multitudinous waves."

Odyssey 5.337–38: The sea goddess Leukothea "rose up from the waters *like a sea mew* on the wing, and sat on the stoutly bound raft."

Odyssey 5.351–53: Leukothea "entered into the stormy sea *like a sea gull.*"

None of these examples requires one to assume that the god took the actual form of a bird; indeed, the epic poets used bird similes of mortals as well.[6]

Several interpreters have taken Mark's phrase ὡς περιστεράν to modify not τὸ πνεῦμα, which precedes it, but with the participle καταβαῖνον, which follows it, giving it adverbial force: "descending like a dove." In this case, the Homeric similes of gods moving like birds would be relevant. But elsewhere Mark invariably uses phrases introduced by ὡς to modify what comes before, not after. Furthermore, Mark's point seems to be that Jesus was able to "see" the Spirit because it manifested itself as a dove. The authors of Matthew and John changed the word order to make the phrase work adverbially with καταβαῖνον, presumably because Mark's word order failed to make this meaning clear. Luke, however, interpreted Mark to mean that the Spirit assumed

---

235–68; H. Bannert, "Zur Vogelgestalt der Götter bei Homer," *Wiener Studien* 91 ns. 12 (1978): 29–42; Harmut Erbse, "Homerische Götter in Vogelgestalt," *Hermes* 108 (1980): 259–74; Bernard C. Dietrich, "Divine Epiphanies in Homer," *Numen* 30 (1983): 53–79; and Jane B. Carter, "Ancestor Cult and the Occasion of Homeric Performance," in *The Ages of Homer: A Tribute to Emily Townsend Vermeule* (ed. Jane B. Carter and Sarah P. Morris; Austin: University of Texas Press, 1995), 285–312.

[5] On Mark's use of Homeric epic, see my book *The Homeric Epics and the Gospel of Mark* (New Haven: Yale University Press, 2000).

[6] *Iliad* 16.581–83 and *Odyssey* 12.418 (= 14.308) and 22.468–72. All translations of the epics are from the second Loeb edition (A. T. Murray and William F. Wyatt).

the "physical appearance" (σωματικῷ εἴδει) of a dove.[7] *The Gospel of the Ebionites*, Justin Martyr, and subsequent Christian art agreed with Luke in taking the Spirit-dove simile as a physical metamorphosis.[8]

Homer's deities, too, assumed the actual form of birds, sometimes to disguise their divinity.

Iliad 7.58–61: To avoid detection by soldiers, Athena and Apollo "sat down *like birds, vultures,* upon the high oak of father Zeus."

Iliad 14.286–91: To avoid detection by Zeus, Hypnos (Sleep) "sat, hidden by the pine branches, *like the clear-voiced bird* in the mountains that the gods call 'chalkis' but mortals the 'kymindis.'"

Odyssey 22.239–40: During the slaying of the suitors, Athena sat upon a joist, *"like a swallow* to look upon." From this perch the goddess observed the carnage undetected.

These similes have little to do with Mark's statement concerning the Spirit "like a dove" descending on Jesus insofar as they disguise the identities of the gods.

Two other Homeric similes, both near the beginning of the *Odyssey* and both related to Athena, are more relevant to Jesus' baptism. According to the first, Athena flew like a bird and by so doing revealed her divinity to Telemachus, Odysseus's son.

Odyssey 1.319–23: "So spoke the goddess, flashing-eyed (γλαυκῶπις) Athena, and departed, flying *like a bird* up the smoke-vent (ὄρνις δ᾽ ὣς ἀνοπαῖα διέπτατο), and in his heart she put strength and courage, and made him think of his father even more than before. And in his mind he marked what had happened and marveled, for he knew that she was a god."[9]

Homer uses the epithet γλαυκῶπις, translated here "flashing-eyed," of Athena eighty-seven times. Its derivation is disputed, but it most likely comes from γλαύξ, "little owl." This etymology accounts for the popular depiction of Athena as a γλαύξ in ancient art.

The second passage takes place at Nestor's palace at Pylos, where Athena performed a similar stunt.

Odyssey 3.371–78: "So spoke the goddess, flashing-eyed (γλαυκῶπις) Athena, and she departed in the likeness [εἰδομένη] of a sea eagle; and amazement fell upon everyone at the sight, and the old man [Nestor] marveled, when his eyes beheld (ἴδεν) it. And he grasped the hand of Telemachus, and spoke, and addressed him: 'Friend, I do not think you will prove a base man or a

---

[7] Matt 3:16, John 1:32, and Luke 3:22.

[8] Fragment 4 of *The Gospel of the Ebionites* appears in Epiphanius *Panarion* 30.13.7; cf. Justin Martyr *Dialogue with Trypho* 88.3 and 8.

[9] The verb for flying used here, διαπέτομαι, is applied to Hera and Iris in *Iliad* 15.83 and 172.

craven if truly when you are so young the gods follow you to be your guides. For truly this is no other of those who have their dwellings on Olympus but the daughter of Zeus.'"

Martin P. Nilsson and more recently Jane B. Carter have related the Homeric bird similes to bird epiphanies in Minoan-Mycenaean art.[10] Literary critics of Homer, on the other hand, have argued that the bird similes are poetic conventions with little or no connection to primitive religion.[11] The debate among classicists continues, but two conclusions seem safe. First, the density of bird similes in Homeric epic issues from an archaic identification of gods with birds, whether actual or metaphorical, that later was reduced to a trope. Second, Athena's transformations into a bird and her flights from Telemachus and Nestor were indeed epiphanies: Telemachus then "knew that she was a god"; Nestor recognized that "this is . . . the daughter of Zeus." Similarly in Mark, when Jesus saw the dove descending to him, he recognized it as God's Spirit. Coincidence? Perhaps, but the similarities between Mark and the opening books of the *Odyssey* do not end here and suggest literary imitation.

Athena's visitation to Telemachus in Book 1 began with Zeus sending her to Ithaca from Mount Olympus. She "bound beneath her feet her beautiful sandals, which were wont to bear her both over the waters of the sea and over the boundless land swift as the blasts of the wind. . . . Then she went darting down from the heights of Olympus."[12] Hermes, too, owned a pair of these magical sandals, the famous winged sandals that helped ancient artists identify him and Mercury, his Roman clone. When Homer speaks of the sandals of Hermes he uses precisely the same lines used to describe Athena's sandals but expands them with a bird simile: "He bound beneath his feet his beautiful sandals, which were wont to bear her both over the waters of the sea and over the boundless land swift as the blasts of the wind. . . . With this [wand] in his hand he flew. On to Pieria he stepped from the upper air and then sped over the waves *like a bird, the cormorant.*"[13] When describing Athena's descent the poet is less explicit, but the notion of flight may be implicit in the line "went darting down (βῆ δὲ κατ' . . . ἀΐξασα) from the heights of Olympus." Six times elsewhere the Homeric poets use precisely the same line to depict descending goddesses: five times again of Athena and once of Thetis.[14] The Greek verb lying behind the participle "darting" is ἀΐσσω, which the poets also used for the rapid movements of birds.[15]

---

[10] Nilsson, *Minoan-Mycenaean Religion*, 330–40, and Carter, "Ancestor Cult," 285–312.
[11] Especially Dirlmeier, *Vogelgestalt*, and with qualifications Fauth, "Metamorphosen," Bannert, "Vogelgestalt," Erbse, "Homerische Götter," and Dietrich, "Epiphanies."
[12] *Odyssey* 1.96–98 and 102.
[13] *Odyssey* 5.44–46 and 49–51. The sandals of Athena and Hermes both are adaptations of *Iliad* 24.340–45, where it is said that Hermes flew (πέτετο).
[14] Of Athena: *Iliad* 2.167, 4.74, 7.19, and 22.187, and *Odyssey* 24.488; of Thetis: *Iliad* 24.121. Hera, too, can fly according to *Iliad* 15.84.
[15] *Iliad* 23.868 and *Odyssey* 2.154 and 15.164.

More relevant to Mark is the poet's verb for her descent: βῆ δὲ κατ' is tmesis (the separation and inversion of preposition-verb compounds) for καταβαίνω, precisely the same verb for the Spirit's descent at Jesus' baptism: καταβαῖνον. Coincidence? Perhaps, but the parallels between the Gospel and the epic do not end here.

Athena disguised herself as Odysseus's old comrade Mentes and stood at the door of his home. Even though the house was overrun with more than one hundred suitors waited on by a staff of servants, only Telemachus saw her at first. "The godlike Telemachus was far the first to see (ἴδε) her."[16] "He saw (εἴσιδ') Athena."[17] Similarly, even though Jesus and John seem to have been in the presence of a crowd, only Jesus "saw (εἶδεν) the heavens rent and the Spirit, like a dove, descending to him." Here we find the same verb as in the *Odyssey*, and, like Telemachus, only Jesus saw the heavenly visitor. Coincidence? Perhaps, but the parallels between the Gospel and the epic do not end here.

Poor Telemachus was not sure who his father was. Odysseus had left for Troy when his son was but a babe, so the lad's only assurance of his paternity was the word of others. In the epic, when he first speaks of Odysseus he does not call him his father or even name him. It is Athena/Mentes who identifies Odysseus as the boy's father (σὸν πατέρ') and asks the lad to confirm the fact: "Tell me this and declare it truly whether, indeed . . . you are the son of Odysseus."[18] Telemachus responds that other people said so, though he would rather be "the son (υἱός) of some fortunate man," not the son of "the most ill-fated of mortal men."[19] The visitor tells him he/she will assist him in learning about his father, but in any case, he must assert himself against the suitors and reclaim his inheritance. The youth was grateful for the advice, given "as a father to his son."[20] It is at this point that the goddess left him, "flying like a bird up the smoke-vent, and in his heart she put strength and courage, and made him think of his father even more than before."[21]

According to Mark, the dove said nothing, but the voice from heaven told Jesus, "You are my beloved son; in you I take delight." Coincidence? Perhaps. The baptismal proclamation of Jesus as God's Son surely circulated among his followers prior to Mark, as one can see from Q 4:3 and 9, when the Devil, immediately following the baptism, challenges Jesus' identity as the Son of God. It is likely that already in Q the voice from heaven echoed Ps 2:7, though not verbatim. Psalm 2 does not contain a reference to the son as "beloved," though ἀγαπητός does appear in the Septuagint in contexts potentially

---

[16] *Odyssey* 1.113.
[17] *Odyssey* 1.118.
[18] *Odyssey* 1.195 and 206–7.
[19] *Odyssey* 1.217–20.
[20] *Odyssey* 1.308.
[21] *Odyssey* 1.320–22.

relevant to Jesus' baptism.²² Be that as it may, Mark twice elsewhere uses the word of Jesus, suggesting it is redactional (ὁ υἱός μου ὁ ἀγαπητός, 9:7; υἱὸν ἀγαπητόν, 12:6). One should note, however, that the *Odyssey* occasionally calls Telemachus Odysseus's παῖς ἀγαπητός, "beloved son."²³ The parallels between the Gospel and the epic do not end here.

When Telemachus saw Athena transformed into a bird and fly away, "he knew she was a god; and at once he went among the suitors a godlike (ἰσόθεος) man."²⁴ He then confronted the suitors. Even though he wanted to rule as king (βασιλευέμεν), he would give way to any of the "other kings (βασιλῆες) of the Achaeans" in Ithaca, if he could be lord (ἄναξ) of his father's house and slaves. A leader of the suitors ostensibly conceded, all the while intending to oust the youth from his home. "This matter surely lies on the knees of the gods, who of the Achaeans shall be king (βασιλεύσει) in seagirt Ithaca; but as for your possessions, keep them yourself, and be lord (ἀνάσσοις) in your own house."²⁵ By the end of the epic, the suitors lay dead and Odysseus is king (ὁ μὲν βασιλευέτω αἰεί), and Telemachus will rule after him.²⁶

Immediately after his baptism and temptation by Satan in the desert, Jesus set out to claim his kingdom, even though the temple, his home, was in the hands of murderous foes. He announced, "The time is fulfilled, the kingdom (βασιλεία) of God has arrived." Coincidence? I doubt it. The following parallels suggest literary mimesis.

Odyssey 1	Mark 1:1–15
• Near the beginning of the epic, Athena dons her magical sandals and descends from Olympus (βῆ δὲ κατ' Οὐλύμποιο), assuming the appearance of Mentes. [When she leaves, she flies "like a bird (ὄρνις δὲ ὥς)," and Telemachus then knows her to be a god.]	Near the beginning of the Gospel, the Spirit, like a dove (ὡς περιστεράν), descends (καταβαῖνον) to Jesus.
• At first, only Telemachus sees her (ἴδε and εἴσιδ').	Only Jesus sees (εἶδεν) heavens open and the Spirit, like a dove.
• Athena/Mentes reassures Telemachus he is indeed the son of Odysseus. Later he is called Odysseus's "beloved son (παῖς ἀγαπητός)."	A voice from heaven tells Jesus, "You are my beloved son (ὁ υἱός μου, ὁ ἀγαπητός)."

---

²² E.g., Gen 22:2 and Jer 38:20 (LXX).
²³ *Odyssey* 4.727 and 817 and 5.18; cf. 2.365.
²⁴ *Odyssey* 1.324.
²⁵ *Odyssey* 1.386–402.
²⁶ *Odyssey* 24.483.

• Reassured of his paternity and the help of a god, Telemachus goes among the suitors "like a god (ἰσόθεος)" and sets out to reclaim his estate and to rule (βασιλευέμεν), as his father had.

On learning of his divine paternity, Jesus sets out for Galilee, where he proclaims the kingdom (βασιλεία) of God has come.

• By the end of the epic, Telemachus and his father rule over their kingdom.

Someday Jesus will rule his kingdom.

If Mark had the beginning of the epic in mind in composing this scene, what does it imply about the dove simile? I propose that Mark used it as an intertextual flag to the reader to compare the baptism of Jesus with the visitation of Athena to Telemachus. But Mark's Jesus far outstrips Homer's Telemachus. Telemachus was the son of Odysseus; Jesus was the Son of God. Telemachus one day would rule as king of his father's estate; Jesus one day would rule over a cosmic kingdom.

Mark's selection of the dove instead of some other bird remains a mystery. Bird similes in the Hebrew Bible (and Septuagint) are predominantly negative. Doves symbolize fear, moaning, flight, hiding, and even ignorance.[27] In Homeric epic, too, gods tremble or flee like doves.[28] On the other hand, biblical authors considered no bird more pure, gentle, innocent, or loving than the dove, as in the frequent references to the beloved as a dove in the Song of Songs. Doves were the only birds sufficiently pure to be acceptable in Israelite sacrifices, and Philo allegorized this to mean that the dove (or turtledove) represented reason, mind, and wisdom.[29] Doves had noble reputations also in the Greek world. According to Plutarch, "The Greeks are correct in saying that the dove is sacred to Aphrodite."[30] So close was the association of the dove with love that it often functioned as an artistic symbol for love. Occasionally doves carry in their beaks gifts from the gods to humans. No bird would be a more fitting manifestation of God's love for his Son than the dove.

---

[27] E.g., Ps 55:6; Isa 38:14, 59:11, 60:8; Jer 48:28; Ezek 7:16; Hos 7:11 and 11:11; Nah 2:7; and Zech 3:1.

[28] *Iliad* 5.778 and 21.493–95.

[29] On doves as sacrifices see Lev 1:14, 5:7 and 11, 12:6 and 8, 14:30, 15:14 and 29, and Num 6:10. For Philonic references see *De mutatione nominum* 248, *Quis rerum divinarum heres sit* 126–27, and *De specialibus legibus* 4.117. See also *The Letter of Aristeas* 145–47.

[30] *On Isis* 71 (379D).

CHAPTER TWENTY-FIVE

LE MYTHE DE LA CHUTE DE SATAN ET LA QUESTION DU
MILIEU D'ORIGINE DE LA *VIE D'ADAM ET ÈVE*

Jean-Daniel Kaestli

L'étude de la littérature apocryphe chrétienne connaît aujourd'hui une renaissance qui doit beaucoup aux initiatives et aux travaux de François Bovon.
Nous avons été amenés, grâce à lui, à remettre en question des frontières bien
établies: entre le canonique et l'apocryphe bien sûr, mais aussi entre "pseudépigraphes de l'Ancien Testament" et "apocryphes du Nouveau Testament." C'est
dans cet espace nouveau que François a contribué à créer que je voudrais
inscrire l'étude qui suit sur l'origine du mythe de la chute de Satan et de la
Vie d'Adam et Ève (abr. *V.A.E.*).

Il existe deux grandes versions de ce mythe, qui attribuent une cause
différente à la chute de Satan. La première version, que l'on peut appeler le
"mythe de Lucifer," a pour thème central l'orgueil de l'Ange déchu, qui a eu
la prétention de devenir l'égal de Dieu. Elle a pour fondement scripturaire
Ésaïe 14: la lamentation satirique sur la chute du roi de Babylone a été
appliquée à la chute d'une figure angélique.[1]

La seconde version met la chute de Satan en rapport avec la création
d'Adam et peut être appelée le "mythe du refus." Lorsque Dieu a ordonné
aux anges de se prosterner devant l'homme nouvellement créé, Satan a refusé
d'obéir en affirmant jalousement sa supériorité sur Adam, et Dieu l'a châtié
en l'expulsant du ciel. Nous reviendrons sur la question des attaches scripturaires de ce mythe du refus, qui sont plus difficiles à cerner.[2]

---

[1] Voir surtout Ésa 14:12–14: "Comment es-tu tombé du ciel, Astre brillant, Fils de
l'Aurore? Comment as-tu été précipité à terre, toi qui réduisais les nations, toi qui
disais: 'Je monterai dans les cieux, je hausserai mon trône au-dessus des étoiles de Dieu,
je siégerai sur la montagne de l'assemblée divine, à l'extrême nord, je monterai au
sommet des nuages, je serai comme le Très-Haut.' "

[2] A propos du récit de la *Vie d'Adam et Ève*, Gary A. Anderson écrit: "No biblical
texts appear to be cited by this tradition; the story seems to float independently of the
Bible" ("Ezekiel 28, the Fall of Satan, and the Adam Books," in *Literature on Adam and
Eve: Collected Essays* [éd. Gary Anderson, M. Stone, et J. Tromp; SVTP 15; Leiden:
Brill, 2000], 141). En fait, l'ordre donné aux anges est à rapprocher de la formulation de Ps 97:7 et de Deut 32:43 dans la Bible grecque: Ps 96:7^LXX (MT 97:7): προσκυνήσατε
αὐτῷ, πάντες οἱ ἄγγελοι αὐτοῦ. Deut 32:43^LXX: εὐφράνθητε, οὐρανοί, ἅμα αὐτῷ, καὶ
προσκυνησάτωσαν αὐτῷ πάντες υἱοὶ θεοῦ (voir aussi Odes 2:43^LXX: εὐφράνθητε, οὐρανοί,
ἅμα αὐτῷ, καὶ προσκυνασάτωσαν αὐτῷ πάντες οἱ ἄγγελοι θεοῦ). De même, le thème de
la jalousie du diable est à mettre en rapport avec un passage de la Sagesse de Salomon:

Ces deux versions du mythe de la chute de Satan sont-elles d'origine juive? Dans leur grande majorité, les savants répondent par l'affirmative.[3] C'est notamment le cas de Jean-Marc Rosenstiehl. Dans une remarquable étude sur la chute de l'Ange, il a rassemblé et traduit un grand nombre de sources, en les regroupant en deux grandes catégories, l'une centrée autour du thème de l'orgueil de l'Ange qui prétend s'égaler à Dieu, l'autre autour du thème de la jalousie qui l'empêche d'adorer Adam.[4] Dans les deux cas, il se prononce en faveur d'une origine juive de la légende.

Cependant, il est frappant de constater que cette conclusion repose sur une base documentaire très étroite: la quasi-totalité des textes cités par le chercheur de Strasbourg appartiennent à la tradition chrétienne, alors que les documents d'origine juive se comptent sur les doigts d'une main. Ainsi, pour établir que la chute de l'ange par orgueil est "une légende juive fondée sur un *midrash* d'*Ésaïe* 14, passée dans le Christianisme,"[5] le seul texte allégué est un passage du *Livre des Secrets d'Hénoch* (*2 Hén.* 29.4‒5). Pour le thème de la chute par refus d'adorer Adam, la thèse de l'origine juive repose essentiellement sur le récit de la *Vie d'Adam et Ève*, sur lequel nous reviendrons. Deux autres témoignages cités par Rosenstiehl—mais qu'il n'exploite pas—ont aussi été invoqués par ailleurs en faveur d'une origine juive du mythe du refus: un passage d'un midrash médiéval, *Bereshit Rabbati*, attribué à Moïse Haddarshan; la mention répétée du thème dans le Coran, qui serait la reprise de sources juives.

Face à l'abondance des témoignages chrétiens, l'extrême rareté des sources

---

"Par la jalousie du diable la mort est entrée dans le monde" (Sag 2:24). Mais ces rapprochements ne portent que sur certains éléments du mythe du refus. Il faudra notamment se demander pourquoi les anges reçoivent l'ordre d'adorer Adam, alors que les textes scripturaires invoqués parlent d'une adoration de Dieu.

[3] Voir par exemple l'article récent d'Elaine H. Pagels, "The Social History of Satan, the 'Intimate Enemy': A Preliminary Sketch," *HTR* 84 (1991): 105‒28, spéc. 114‒15. Selon Pagels, certains auteurs juifs, durant les deux derniers siècles avant notre ère, ont cherché à répondre à la question: comment se fait-il que l'un des anges de Dieu ait pu s'égarer? Ils ont répondu en élaborant trois groupes de récits. Le premier, inspiré de Genèse 6 et de traditions reflétées dans *1 Hénoch* et *Jubilés*, raconte comment certains anges ou "Fils de Dieu" ont transgressé l'ordre divin en prenant des femmes parmi les humains. A côté de ce thème de la chute des Veilleurs, la savante américaine mentionne deux autres groupes de récits. L'un, fondé sur Ésa 14:12‒14, raconte que l'un des anges s'est révolté contre Dieu et a été jeté hors du ciel. L'autre, qu'elle présente comme "populaire dans les sources rabbiniques et plus tard dans les sources islamiques," met en cause une rivalité entre Satan et Adam; elle est illustrée par le récit juif de la *Vie d'Adam et Ève*. Mis à part cette référence, Pagels n'indique pas sur quels documents elle se fonde pour établir l'existence de ces deux "groups of stories" au deuxième et au premier siècle avant J.-C.; elle se contente de renvoyer en note au livre de Peter Schäfer, *Rivalität zwischen Engeln und Menschen: Untersuchungen zur rabbinischen Engelvorstellung* (Berlin: de Gruyter, 1975).

[4] Jean-Marc Rosenstiehl, "La chute de l'Ange: Origines et développement d'une légende. Ses attestations dans la littérature copte," dans *Écritures et traditions dans la littérature copte* (Cahiers de la Bibliothèque Copte 1; Louvain: Peeters, 1983), 37‒60.

[5] Ibid., 44.

attribuées à la tradition juive est étonnante.[6] Mais il y a plus: de sérieux doutes peuvent être émis au sujet de l'enracinement juif des sources invoquées: faut-il vraiment rattacher au judaïsme les textes allégués, à savoir *2 Hén.* 29.4–5 pour le mythe de Lucifer, la *Vie d'Adam et Eve*, le témoignage de *Bereshit Rabbati* et les sources du Coran pour le mythe du refus?

Le caractère interpolé de *2 Hén.* 29.4–5: L'application d'Ésaïe 14 à la chute de Satan est sans doute d'origine chrétienne.

2 Hénoch, qui n'est transmis qu'en slave, est conservé dans une recension longue et dans une recension brève. La question du rapport entre ces deux recensions est complexe. Aujourd'hui, on renonce à trancher globalement en faveur de l'antériorité de l'une ou de l'autre, et on admet que la recension longue contient à la fois des éléments primitifs et des amplifications secondaires.[7] Le passage sur la chute de Satan (29.4–5) ne figure que dans la recension longue. Il s'insère dans le récit du deuxième jour de la création, au cours duquel les armées angéliques ont été créées à partir du feu. Il est précédé d'une rubrique manifestement secondaire, propre au seul manuscrit P: "Ici Satanail fut précipité des hauteurs, en compagnie de ses anges." On lit ensuite le texte suivant:

> (29.4) "Mais un de l'ordre des archanges fit défection, en compagnie de la division qui était sous son autorité. Il conçut la pensée impossible d'établir son trône plus haut que les nuages qui sont au-dessus de la terre, et de devenir l'égal de ma puissance. (5) Et je le précipitai de la hauteur en compagnie de ses anges, et il était volant dans l'air sans cesse, au-dessus de (l'abîme) sans fond."

A mon avis, on ne peut pas invoquer le témoignage de *2 Hén.* 29.4–5 en faveur de l'origine juive du mythe de la chute de Satan par orgueil. De sérieuses raisons incitent en effet à penser que ce passage constitue une interpolation secondaire dans le texte slave:[8] (1) il est absent dans la recension brève; (2) la chute de Satanael et de ses anges est un motif populaire dans la littérature slave; (3) en dehors de *2 Hénoch*, l'association entre Ésaïe 14 et la chute de Satan n'est attestée que dans la tradition chrétienne.[9]

---

[6] Je ne vois pas ce qui permet à Marshall D. Johnson de dire que la légende de la chute de Satan est reflétée "in numerous rabbinic writings" (*OTP* 2:262 n. a). La rareté constatée pourrait certes s'expliquer par le fait que le mythe est né dans des milieux marginaux ou sectaires, dont la voix aurait été étouffée par le judaïsme rabbinique.

[7] Dans ce sens, voir l'introduction à *2 Hénoch* de Francis I. Andersen, dans *OTP* 1:93–94.

[8] Même si l'on admet que le passage remonte au texte primitif, on ne peut en tirer aucune conclusion sûre; voir Andersen dans ibid., 1:95–97, spéc. 97: "In every respect 2 Enoch remains an enigma. So long as the date and location remain unknown, no use can be made of it for historical purposes."

[9] La possibilité d'une interpolation chrétienne en *2 Hén.* 29.4–5 est aussi envisagée par Andersen: "Christian explanations of the origin of evil linked Lk 10:18 with Isa

Ce dernier point m'amène à formuler la conclusion suivante: l'utilisation d'Ésaïe 14 comme fondement scripturaire de la révolte et de la chute de Satan est un produit de l'exégèse chrétienne. La *Biblia Patristica*[10] permet de constater que la prophétie d'Ésaïe est rapportée au diable chez Tertullien[11] et à l'antéchrist chez Hippolyte.[12] Mais c'est surtout chez Origène qu'elle trouve place dans le dossier des textes scripturaires attestant la chute de Satan.[13] Par la suite, ce fondement scripturaire va assurer le succès du mythe de Lucifer dans la tradition chrétienne. Il va devenir la seule version doctrinalement autorisée de la chute de Satan, par opposition au mythe du refus qui se verra suspecté et rejeté du côté de l'hérésie.[14]

Le récit de la chute de Satan dans la Vie d'Adam et Ève

Parmi les arguments invoqués en faveur de l'origine juive du mythe du refus, la *Vie d'Adam et Ève* joue un rôle décisif. On y trouve en effet un récit circonstancié de la chute de Satan. Pendant longtemps, on n'a connu ce récit que dans la version latine éditée par Wilhelm Meyer.[15] Mais depuis quelque temps, il est également accessible dans une version arménienne et dans une version

---

14 and Ezech 28, eventually with Gen 3. So vs. 4 could be a Christian interpolation. . . . Jewish theology concentrated on Gen 6, and this is prominent in the Enoch cycle as in other apocalypses" (ibid., 1:149 n. i)

[10] Jean Allenbach et al., *Biblia Patristica: Index des citations et allusions bibliques dans la littérature patristique* (6 vols.; Paris: Éditions du Centre National de la Recherche Scientifique, 1975–1995).

[11] *Marc.* 5.11.11 (CCSL 1, p. 698.19); 5.17.8 (ibid. p. 714.1).

[12] *Antichr.* 17 et 53 (GCS 1.2, p. 12.23 et 35.19); *Comm. Dan.* 4.12 (GCS 1.1, p. 218.10).

[13] Voir en particulier *Princ.* 1.5.4–5; *Cels.* 6.43–44; *Hom. Num.* 12.3.

[14] Plusieurs textes attestent l'acceptation du premier mythe et le rejet polémique du second. Voir Rosenstiehl, "Chute de l'Ange," 51 (*Livre de la création du Ciel et de la Terre*, slave); 52 n. 93 (Jacques d'Édesse); 54 et n. 104 (*Martyre de saint Georges*, copte); 55 (Pierre d'Alexandrie; Jean de Parallos). Voir également les exemples cités par Rainer Stichel, "Die Verführung der Stammeltern durch Satanael nach der Kurzfassung der slavischen Baruch-Apokalypse," dans *Kulturelle Traditionen in Bulgarien: Bericht über das Kolloquium der Sudosteuropa-Kommission, 16.–18., Juni 1987* (éd. Reinhard Lauer et Peter Schreiner; Abhandlungen der Akademie der Wissenschaften in Göttingen, Philologisch-Historische Klasse³ 177; Göttingen: Vandenhoeck & Ruprecht, 1977), 119–20. Un texte des *Quaestiones ad Antiochenum ducem* du Pseudo-Athanase 10 (PG 28:604c) est particulièrement significatif: "Question: Quand et pourquoi le diable est-il tombé? Certains en effet font courir la fable qu'il a refusé d'adorer Adam et que c'est pour cette raison qu'il est tombé. Réponse: De tels discours sont le fait d'hommes insensés. Car le diable est tombé avant qu'Adam ait été créé. Il est évident que c'est à cause de son orgueil, comme le dit le prophète Ésaïe: Je placerai mon trône au-dessus des nuages et je serai semblable au Très-Haut (Ésa 14:14)."

[15] Wilhelm Meyer, *Vita Adae et Evae* (*Abhandlungen der philosophisch-philologischen Klasse der königlich Bayerischen Akademie der Wissenschaften* 14.3; Munich: Verlag der k. Akademie, 1878), 185–250.

géorgienne, grâce aux publications de Michael E. Stone et Jean-Pierre Mahé.[16] Autre progrès: les diverses formes "primaires" du Livre d'Adam et Ève (grec, latin, arménien, géorgien et slave) peuvent maintenant être aisément comparées grâce à la synopse publiée par Gary A. Anderson et Michael E. Stone.[17]

Commençons par donner une traduction du récit qui nous intéresse, tel qu'il figure dans la version latine. Le contexte est le suivant. Après leur expulsion du paradis, les premiers humains entament une période de pénitence. Adam doit rester plongé dans l'eau du Jourdain pendant 40 jours, et Ève dans celle du Tigre pendant 34 jours[18] (chs. 5–8). Mais Ève se laisse abuser une nouvelle fois par Satan, déguisé en ange de lumière, et elle sort du fleuve avant le terme qui lui était assigné. Satan la conduit alors auprès d'Adam (ch. 9). Celui-ci lui reproche cette nouvelle transgression, puis il demande[19] au diable la cause de son inimitié (chs. 10–11).

(13.1) Le diable répondit: "Adam que me dis-tu là? C'est à cause de toi que j'ai été précipité hors de ce lieu. (2) Lorsque tu fus créé, j'ai été rejeté loin de la présence de Dieu et banni de la communauté des anges. (3) Lorsque Dieu insuffla en toi le souffle de vie, et que ton aspect et ta ressemblance furent faits à l'image de Dieu, Michel t'amena et fit que l'on t'adorât en présence de Dieu."[20]

Et le Seigneur Dieu dit: "Voici Adam! Je l'ai fait à notre image et à notre ressemblance." (14.1) Et Michel partit et convoqua tous les anges en disant:

---

[16] Michael E. Stone, *The Penitence of Adam* (2 vols.; CSCO 429 texte arménien et CSCO 430 introduction et traduction anglaise; Louvain: Peeters, 1981); Jean-Pierre Mahé, "Le Livre d'Adam géorgien," dans *Studies in Gnosticism and Hellenistic Religions: Presented to Gilles Quispel on the Occasion of His 65th Birthday* (éd. Roelof van den Broek et Maarten J. Vermaseren; ÉPRO 91; Leiden: Brill, 1981), 227–60 (trad. française).

[17] *A Synopsis of the Books of Adam and Eve* (SBLEJL 17; Atlanta: Scholars Press, 1994; 2d rév. éd., 1999). Signalons ici l'importante découverte, par Jean-Pierre Pettorelli, d'un manuscrit latin de Paris qui contient une version de la *Vie d'Adam et Eve* beaucoup plus proche de l'arménien et du géorgien que du latin connu jusqu'ici (édition à paraître dans *Archivum Latinitatis Medii Aevi*). La synopse va ainsi s'enrichir d'une nouvelle colonne.

[18] Chiffre de l'arménien et du géorgien, préférable au 37 jours du latin.

[19] Nous suivons l'arménien et le géorgien, qui placent la question dans la bouche d'Adam, plutôt que le latin, qui fait parler Ève.

[20] "Adduxit te Michael et fecit te adorare in conspectu dei." On pourrait aussi traduire: "Michel t'amena et te fit te prosterner devant Dieu," en s'appuyant sur l'arménien ("Michael came and made you bow before God") et le géorgien ("And Michael came; he presented you and made you bow down before God"). Mais cette adoration de Dieu par Adam s'accorde mal avec le contexte: pourquoi Michel devrait-il conduire Adam devant Dieu, qui vient de lui faire don du souffle de vie? A mon avis, la phrase citée ne décrit pas une scène particulière, mais annonce sous une fome résumée le récit détaillé qui suit: Michel convoque les anges et leur intime l'ordre d'adorer "l'image de Dieu." Il n'était donc pas question d'un hommage rendu par la créature à son Créateur dans le texte primitif (l'arménien et le géorgien sont secondaires par rapport au latin). L'absence de cet élément remet en cause la parenté entre *2 Hénoch* 21–22 et *V.A.E.* 11–17 qu'établit Michael E. Stone dans "The Fall of Satan and Adam's Penance: Three Notes on *The Books of Adam and Eve*," *JTS* 44 (1993): 144–48.

'Adorez l'image de Dieu, comme le Seigneur Dieu l'a ordonné!' (2) Et Michel lui-même adora le premier, puis il m'appela et dit: 'Adore l'image de Dieu, le Seigneur!' (3) Et je répondis: 'Je n'ai pas à adorer Adam.' Et comme Michel continuait à me forcer à adorer, je lui dis: 'Pourquoi me forces-tu? Je n'adorerai pas un être inférieur et plus jeune que moi.[21] Je suis plus ancien que lui dans la création; avant qu'il eût été fait, j'avais déjà été fait. C'est lui qui devrait m'adorer.'

(15.1) Lorsqu'ils entendirent cela, d'autres anges qui m'étaient subordonnés refusèrent de l'adorer. (2) Et Michel dit: 'Adore l'image de Dieu. Mais si tu ne veux pas l'adorer, alors le Seigneur Dieu se mettra en colère contre toi.' (3) Et je dis: 'S'il se met en colère contre moi, je placerai mon trône au-dessus des étoiles du ciel et je serai semblable au Très-Haut.'[22]

(16.1) Et le Seigneur Dieu se mit en colère contre moi, et il me chassa, moi et mes anges, hors de notre gloire; et à cause de toi, nous fûmes expulsés de nos demeures vers ce monde et nous fûmes précipités sur la terre. (2) Et aussitôt, nous fûmes plongés dans la tristesse, puisque nous avions été dépouillés d'une si grande gloire. Et nous étions affligés de te voir dans de tels joie et délices. (3) Ainsi, par une tromperie, je m'attaquai à ta femme, et je fis en sorte que, par son intermédiaire, tu fusses jeté hors de tels joie et délices, comme moi-même j'avais été jeté hors de ma gloire.'"[23]

Le texte fournit un bon point de départ pour tenter de dégager les éléments constitutifs du mythe du refus. La comparaison avec les autres sources inventoriées par Rosenstiehl permet d'identifier ces éléments et de dégager certaines variantes caractéristiques.

(1) La chute de Satan se situe après la création d'Adam.[24]
(2) Dieu ordonne aux anges d'adorer Adam.[25]
(3) Satan refuse d'adorer Adam.[26]
(4) Satan justifie son refus d'adorer Adam. Les raisons qu'il invoque peuvent être de deux ordres: (a) son antériorité dans l'ordre de la création (il a été créé avant Adam); (b) la supériorité de sa nature par rapport à celui qui a été tiré de la terre.[27]

---

[21] "Deteriorem et posteriorem meum." Dans l'arménien et le géorgien, Satan mentionne seulement le fait qu'Adam a été créé après lui, et non sa nature inférieure. Ce dernier trait ne remonte sans doute pas au récit primitif.

[22] La répétition de l'ordre adressé par Michel à Satan (*V.A.E.* 15.2) et la réponse orgueilleuse de Satan inspirée d'Ésa 14:13 (*V.A.E.* 15:3) ne se trouvent ni dans l'arménien ni dans le géorgien. La référence à Ésaïe 14 est une addition secondaire, mais sans doute ancienne, comme l'a justement relevé Rosenstiehl, "Chute de l'Ange," 45.

[23] Traduction de l'édition de Meyer, *Vita Adae et Evae*, 225–27.

[24] Dans certaines sources, l'action créatrice de Dieu est évoquée, comme ici, à l'aide de motifs provenant du texte de la Genèse ou de traditions qui s'y rattachent. Elle peut aussi faire l'objet d'une simple mention ou être seulement présupposée.

[25] Dans *Vie d'Adam et Ève* et dans les *Questions de Barthélemy*, l'ordre est placé dans la bouche de Michel. Mais dans la plupart des autres sources, il est donné directement par Dieu lui-même.

[26] Son refus est presque toujours opposé à l'attitude d'autres anges qui obéissent à l'ordre divin.

[27] Plusieurs types de textes peuvent être distingués: antériorité seulement (e.g., *Vie*

(5) Satan entraîne d'autre anges dans sa chute.[28]

(6) La chute de Satan est à l'origine de son hostilité contre l'humanité. Elle sert de prélude à la faute d'Adam et Eve, et explique l'influence des forces mauvaises tout au long de l'histoire humaine.

Les différentes formes de la *Vie d'Adam et Ève* ont été transmises dans la tradition chrétienne et comportent des passages qui n'ont pu voir le jour qu'à l'intérieur du christianisme. Comme pour d'autres pseudépigraphes de l'Ancien Testament, cet état de fait n'empêche nullement de la faire remonter à un original juif. C'est la position adoptée par la grande majorité des savants: la *Vie d'Adam et Ève* est une oeuvre juive, qui a subi quelques retouches chrétiennes aisément identifiables.[29] Cette thèse s'appuie essentiellement sur le contenu et sur le style du récit: les idées et les traditions qu'il véhicule reflètent un point de vue juif; certaines particularités de langue suggèrent que le texte grec est la traduction d'un original hébreu.

Ces dernières années cependant, certains savants ont mis en doute le consensus traditionnel. Cette nouvelle approche est particulièrement sensible dans les travaux de Michael E. Stone. Son récent état de la recherche contient d'utiles mises au point.[30] Dans un excursus rédigé en collaboration avec Gideon Bohak, il passe en revue les arguments mis en avant par les tenants d'un original sémitique et il conclut qu'ils ne sont pas probants.[31] Par ailleurs, Stone formule un principe méthodologique très important: pour établir l'origine juive d'un texte comme la *Vie d'Adam et Eve*, il ne suffit pas, comme on l'a souvent fait, de dresser une liste d'idées ou de traditions qui ont des parallèles dans des écrits juifs, mais il faut s'appuyer sur des parallèles qui se rencontrent seulement dans des écrits juifs. En effet, on doit toujours compter avec la possibilité que des matériaux traditionnels juifs aient été intégrés dans une oeuvre d'origine chrétienne.[32]

---

d'Adam et Ève arméniene et géorgiene); supériorité seulement; association des deux raisons (e.g., *Vie d'Adam et Ève* latine et *Questions de Barthélemy*); absence de justification.

[28] Ces anges sont souvent présentés comme une troupe ou un ordre dont il est le chef. Quelques textes précisent qu'ils sont devenus des démons (Rosenstiehl, "Chute de l'Ange," 48, 56–57, 60). Mais d'autres sources (e.g., le Coran et *Bereshit Rabbati*) ne mentionnent pas les anges qui accompagnent Satan dans sa chute.

[29] Parmi les nombreux tenants de cette position, citons à titre d'exemple W. Meyer, éditeur de la *Vita* latine, C. Fuchs, traducteur de cette même *Vita* dans *Die Apokryphen und Pseudepigraphen des Alten Testaments* (éd. Emil Kautzsch; 2 vols.; Tübingen: Mohr, 1900), 2:506–28, et Marshall D. Johnson, qui l'a traduite dans *OTP* 2:249–95.

[30] Michael E. Stone, *A History of the Literature of Adam and Eve* (SBLEJL 3; Atlanta: Scholars Press, 1992), spéc. 58–61; dans *The Penitence of Adam*, il écrivait déjà: "It may be the case that in light of passages like this [*V.A.E.* 42 arménienne] the presumed Jewish character of the Adam books must be reconsidered and the possibility of a Christian sectarian origin entertained" (CSCO 430, 2:xvi).

[31] Ibid., 42–53. L'examen de Bohak ne prouve pas que le livre a été rédigé en grec, mais il établit avec certitude que les arguments en faveur d'un original hébreu ou araméen sont sans valeur démonstrative.

[32] Ibid., 58. En conclusion de son état de la recherche sur l'origine du texte, Stone cite la "position prudente" de Hedley Frederick Davis Sparks, qui correspond sans

Ces derniers temps, d'autres savants sont allés au-delà de la position dubitative de Stone et ont entrepris de montrer que la *Vie d'Adam et Ève* a été composée dans un milieu chrétien. Cette thèse est notamment défendue dans le récent ouvrage de Marinus de Jonge et Johannes Tromp.[33] Les arguments qu'ils avancent méritent une discussion approfondie qu'il n'est pas possible de mener ici. Je me propose seulement d'ajouter une pièce au débat en cours. Dans la ligne de la règle méthodologique formulée par Stone, il s'agit de vérifier si le récit de la chute de Satan peut vraiment être mis en parallèle avec des textes de la tradition juive. Si ce n'est pas le cas, il conviendra de prendre acte de la singularité du témoignage de la *Vie d'Adam et Ève* et de se demander si cette singularité ne plaide pas en faveur de l'hypothèse d'une origine chrétienne.

L'adoration d'Adam et le refus de Satan dans Bereshit Rabbati

A côté de la *Vie d'Adam et Ève*, il n'existe qu'un seul texte juif qui atteste conjointement l'ordre donné aux anges de se prosterner devant Adam et le refus de Satan. Il s'agit du midrash *Bereshit Rabbati*, attribué à un rabbin de la première moitié du onzième siècle, Moïse ha-Darshan de Narbonne.[34] Le passage qui nous intéresse est également cité par le dominicain Raimundo Martini (XIIIe siècle), dans son ouvrage polémique contre les Juifs, le *Pugio Fidei*.[35] C'est ce texte latin que je traduis.

---

doute à la sienne. Il existe de nombreuses légendes juives sur Adam et Ève et leurs enfants: "Yet there is no direct evidence for the existence of any pre-Christian written collection of these legends in either Hebrew or Aramaic" (*AOT* 141–142, cité par Stone, ibid., 61). La *Vie d'Adam et Ève* ne contient rien qui soit nécessairement chrétien, mais il ne s'ensuit pas qu'elle soit nécessairement juive.

[33] *The Life of Adam and Eve and Related Literature* (Guides to Apocrypha and Pseudepigrapha; Sheffield: Sheffield Academic Press, 1997); voir en particulier les arguments des pp. 65–77. Voir aussi Marinus de Jonge, "The Christian Origin of the *Greek Life of Adam and Eve*," dans Anderson et al., *Literature on Adam and Eve*, 347–63. On relèvera aussi les remarquables études de Gary A. Anderson sur les traditions exégétiques juives et chrétiennes qui sont à l'arrière-plan du récit de la *Vie d'Adam et Ève*. (dans l'ibid., 3–42, 57–81, et 215–31). En conclusion de la dernière étude citée, Anderson écrit: "We have seen that the tradition of bodily pain as the penalty for the fall and the punishment understood as penitential disciplines fits very tightly within the world of early Christian exegesis. This would explain why the text was so popular in Late Antiquity and early Medieval Christian world and lend significant support for its Christian origin" (ibid., 231).

[34] L'ouvrage a été édité par Chanoch Albeck, *Midrash Bereshit Rabbati ex libro R. Mosis Haddarshan collectus e codice Pragensi cum adnotationibus et introductione* (Jérusalem: Mekitse nirdamim, 1940; réimpr. 1967), voir 24–25 pour le texte qui nous intéresse. Cette édition m'étant restée inaccessible, je ne peux me référer qu'à la traduction allemande de Schäfer, *Rivalität zwischen Engeln und Menschen*, 83.

[35] Ramon Marti, *Raymundi Martini Ordinis Praedicatorum Pugio Fidei adversus Mauros et Judaeos, cum observationibus Josephi de Voisin, et introductione Jo. Benedictini Carpzovi* (Leipzig: Wittegau, 1687), 563–64. Marti commence par introduire son chapitre 5, qui va traiter

Voici ce qu'on lit dans Bereschit Rabba de R. Moïse haddarsan à propos du verset que voici: Et tous les jours de la vie d'Adam furent de neuf cent trente ans, et il mourut (Gn 5,5,): "Notre maître Josué fils de Noun dit: le jour où s'unit à lui la pensée du premier Adam(?), le Saint, béni soit-il dit, aux anges du service: 'Prosternez-vous devant lui'. Les anges du service suivirent la volonté du Saint, béni soit-il. Le Satan était plus grand que tous les anges des cieux; et il dit au Saint, béni soit-il: 'Maître du monde, tu nous as créés à partir de l'éclat de la Shekinah, et tu ordonnes que nous nous prosternions devant quelqu'un que tu as créé à partir de la poussière de la terre'. Le Saint, béni soit-il, lui répondit: 'Celui-ci, qui est tiré de la poussière de la terre, a en lui plus de sagesse et d'intelligence que toi.'[36] Et il arriva, comme il ne voulut pas se prosterner devant lui et n'obéit pas à la voix du Saint, béni soit-il, qu'on le chassa des cieux, et il devint Satan. Et c'est à son propos qu'Ésaïe dit: 'Comment es-tu tombé des cieux, Splendeur, Fils de l'Aurore?' " (Ésa 14:12). Voilà (ce qu'on lit) dans *Bereschit Rabba*.

Dans son étude sur le thème de la rivalité entre les anges et les hommes, Peter Schäfer associe ce midrash à deux autres; l'un figure dans l'*Alphabet de Rabbi Aqiba*[37] et l'autre dans les *Pirqé de Rabbi Eliézer* 11.[38] Selon Schäfer, ces trois textes conservent les restes d'une seule et même tradition, dont la forme la plus ancienne est conservée dans *Bereshit Rabbati*: Dieu a demandé aux anges d'adorer Adam; Satan a refusé; il a été expulsé du ciel (*Pugio Fidei*) ou a été vaincu par Adam lors de la nomination des animaux (*Bereshit Rabbati*). A la suite d'Altmann, Schäfer pense que ce motif de l'adoration d'Adam par les anges n'est pas né dans le judaïsme, mais qu'il est d'origine gnostique.[39] Il ne pouvait pas être repris tel quel dans la littérature rabbinique, et a donc été remanié dans un sens acceptable pour le judaïsme. Dieu a fait échec à la

---

du diable, du serpent, de la faute d'Adam et de ses conséquences; il note ensuite que les Juifs attribuent une "cause incroyable" au péché du premier Ange et à son orgueil.

[36] A partir de là, le texte de *Bereshit Rabbati* diverge de la citation du *Pugio Fidei*: la nomination des animaux permet à Adam de démontrer sa supériorité; bien que vaincu, Satan persiste dans son refus. Son expulsion du ciel n'est pas mentionnée.

[37] *Bet ha-Midrasch* (éd. Adolph Jellinek; 6 vols.; 2e éd.; Jerusalem: n.p., 1938), 3:59–60; trad. August Wünsche, *Aus Israels Lehrhallen* (5 vols.; Leipzig: Pfeiffer, 1907–1910; réimpr., Hildesheim: Olms, 1967), 4:189. Lorsque les anges du service ont vu Adam, dont la taille allait de la terre au firmament, ils ont pris peur devant lui et se sont adressés à Dieu: " 'Maître du monde, y a-t-il deux puissances dans le monde, l'une dans le ciel et l'autre sur la terre?' Que fit le Saint, béni soit-il? A cette heure, il posa la main sur lui (Ps 139,5) et réduisit (sa taille), à mille coudées."

[38] Trad. Marc-Alain Ouaknin et Éric Smilévitch, *Pirqé de Rabbi Eliézer* (Les Dix Paroles; Paris: Verdier, 1983), 73. A la vue d'Adam, qui était à la ressemblance de Dieu et dont la taille se déployait d'est en ouest (Ps 139:5), "toutes les créatures prirent peur, car elles crurent qu'il était leur créateur; elles allèrent donc se prosterner devant lui. Adam s'exclama: 'Quoi! Qu'avez-vous à vous prosterner ainsi devant moi? Venez, allons ensemble nous revêtir de majesté et de force, puis faisons régner sur nous Celui qui nous a créés.' "

[39] Schäfer, *Rivalität zwischen Engeln und Menschen*, 84–85; Alexander Altmann, "The Gnostic Background of the Rabbinic Adam Legends," *JQR* 35 (1945): 371–91.

fausse réaction des anges devant Adam en diminuant sa taille (*Alphabet de Rabbi Aqiba*); Adam lui-même a détourné les créatures de leur erreur et les a invitées à acclamer le Créateur seul (*Pirqé de Rabbi Eliézer*). Seule la source la plus récente, *Bereshit Rabbati*, a conservé ce mythe dans sa version primitive.

Plusieurs observations m'amènent à mettre en doute cette interprétation de Schäfer. En premier lieu, je relève que la question des sources utilisées par Moïse ha-Darshan est grevée d'incertitudes. Ainsi, pour le passage qui nous intéresse, certains auteurs sont d'avis que *Bereshit Rabbati* a puisé chez Eldad ha-Dani (fin du IXe siècle) et que l'histoire de la chute de Satan remonte à des sources musulmanes.[40] En outre, seul le motif de l'adoration d'Adam permet d'établir une parenté entre les trois textes. Mais Schäfer ne tient pas compte d'autres motifs, qui sont propres à *Bereshit Rabbati*: (1) l'ordre d'adorer donné par Dieu lui-même; (2) le refus de Satan et la motivation qu'il en donne; (3) sa désignation comme "le plus grand de tous les anges"; (4) son expulsion du ciel, interprétée à l'aide d'Ésaïe 14 (ce dernier élément n'est attesté que dans le *Pugio Fidei*). Or ces motifs sont précisément ceux qui n'ont pas de parallèle dans la littérature juive—si l'on fait exception de la *Vie d'Adam et Ève*.

Ma conclusion est donc la suivante: le passage de *Bereshit Rabbati* sur le refus de Satan d'adorer Adam ne conserve pas une tradition juive ancienne, mais représente une composition midrashique tardive, inspirée de sources non-juives.[41]

L'ordre d'adorer Adam et le refus d'Iblis dans le Coran

Le refus du diable (Iblis) d'adorer Adam figure en bonne place dans le Livre saint de l'islam. Il est mentionné dans sept sourates différentes.[42] Pour comprendre la fonction de ce thème et pour déterminer s'il est parvenu à Mahomet par le biais de sources juives ou chrétiennes, j'ai comparé entre elles les diverses mentions en les replaçant dans leur contexte.[43] Je cite ici celui des sept passages qui réunit le plus grand nombre d'éléments, soit la 7e Sourate, vv. 11–25.

---

[40] Voir Louis Ginzberg, *The Legends of the Jews* (7 vols.; Philadelphia: Jewish Publication Society of America, 1909–1938; réimpr., 1968), 5:84 (note 34 du vol. 1), qui renvoie à Abraham Epstein, *Eldad ha-Dani* (Pressburg: Alkalay, 1891), 66–68, et à Max Grünbaum, *Neue Beiträge zur Semitischen Sagenkunde* (Leiden: Brill, 1893), 57–59.

[41] Cette inspiration extérieure peut provenir de la tradition musulmane, puisque l'ordre divin d'adorer Adam et le refus d'Iblis sont mentionnés à sept reprises dans le Coran. Mais le motif de la supériorité de Satan par rapport aux autres anges est absent dans le Coran; je vois là un indice qui plaide plutôt en faveur d'un contact de *Bereshit Rabbati* avec la tradition chrétienne, où le motif en question est bien attesté. Sur Satan comme "premier créé" (interprétation de Job 40:19), voir *Ques. Bart.* 4.28–29; 4.54; *Apocalypse de Sedrach* 5.2, ainsi que les textes coptes qui désignent l'Ange déchu comme l'"Archiplasme" ou le "Protoplasme" (voir Rosenstiehl, "Chute de l'Ange," 56, 59, 60).

[42] Sourate 2:34; 7:11; 15:18–19; 17:61; 18:50; 20:116; 38:71–72.

[43] Dans ce but, j'ai établi une synopse qui met en évidence les parallèles entre les sept passages suivants: (a) Sourate 2:30–39; (b) Sourate 7:11–25; (c) Sourate 15:26–42; (d) Sourate 17:61–65; (e) Sourate 18:50–51; (f) Sourate 20:115–24; (g) Sourate 38:71–85.

(11) Oui, nous vous avons créés et nous vous avons modelés; puis nous avons dit aux Anges: "Prosternez-vous devant Adam." Ils se prosternèrent, à l'exception d'Iblis, car il n'a pas été de ceux qui se sont prosternés. (12) Dieu dit: "Qu'est-ce qui t'empêche de te prosterner, lorsque je te l'ordonne?" Il dit: "Je suis meilleur que lui. Tu m'as créé de feu et tu l'as créé d'argile." (13) Dieu dit: "Descends d'ici! Tu n'as pas à te montrer orgueilleux en ce lieu. Sors! Tu es au nombre de ceux qui sont méprisés!" (14) Il dit. "Accorde-moi un délai jusqu'au Jour où ils seront ressuscités." (15) Dieu dit: "Oui, ce délai t'est accordé." (16) Il dit: "A cause de l'aberration que tu as mise en moi, je les guetterai sur ta voie droite, (17) puis, je les harcèlerai, par-devant et par-derrière, sur leur gauche et sur leur droite. Tu ne trouveras, chez la plupart d'entre eux, aucune reconnaissance." (18) Dieu dit: "Sors d'ici, méprisé, rejeté! Je remplirai la Géhenne de vous tous et de tous ceux qui t'auront suivi."

(19) O Adam! Habite le jardin, toi et ton épouse. Mangez de ses fruits partout où vous voudrez; mais n'approchez pas de cet arbre que voici, sinon vous seriez au nombre des injustes." (20) Le Démon les tenta afin de leur montrer leur nudité qui leur était encore cachée. Il dit: "Votre Seigneur vous a interdit cet arbre pour vous empêcher de devenir des anges ou d'être immortels." (21) Il leur jura: "Je suis, pour vous, un conseiller digne de confiance" (22) et il les fit tomber par sa séduction. Lorsqu'ils eurent goûté aux fruits de l'arbre, leur nudité leur apparut; ils disposèrent alors sur eux des feuilles du jardin. Leur Seigneur les appela: "Ne vous avais-je pas interdit cet arbre? Ne vous avais-je pas dit que Satan est, pour vous, un ennemi déclaré?" (23) Ils dirent. "Notre Seigneur! Nous nous sommes lésés nous-mêmes. Si tu ne nous pardonnes pas, et si tu ne nous fais pas miséricorde, nous serons au nombre des perdants." (24) Dieu dit: "Descendez! Vous serez ennemis les uns des autres. Vous trouverez sur la terre un séjour et une jouissance pour un temps limité." (25) Il dit encore: "Vous y vivrez, vous y mourrez et on vous en fera sortir."[44]

Ce passage, et les textes parallèles avec lequel je l'ai comparé, montrent que le Coran ne s'intéresse pas à la révolte d'Iblis pour elle-même, mais en rapport avec la présence du mal dans l'histoire de l'humanité. L'ange qui a refusé d'adorer Adam a été maudit par Dieu, mais Dieu lui a accordé un délai qui lui permet d'égarer les hommes jusqu'à la fin des temps (7:12–18). Le Démon est devenu l'ennemi d'Adam, il a provoqué sa désobéissance et son expulsion du paradis (7:19–25).

Le thème coranique de l'adoration des anges et du refus de Satan provient-il de sources juives ou de sources chrétiennes? La première explication a les faveurs de ceux qui pensent que le motif de l'adoration d'Adam par les anges est juif.[45] La thèse opposée a été défendue par Heinrich Speyer, pour qui "la

---

[44] Traduction de Denise Masson, *Le Coran* (Bibliothèque de la Pléiade; Paris: Gallimard, 1967), 180–82.

[45] Récemment, David J. Halperin (*The Faces of the Chariot: Early Jewish Responses to Ezekiel's Vision* [TSAJ 16; Tübingen: Mohr, 1988], 102 n. 41) s'est prononcé dans ce sens: Mahomet dépendrait sur ce point "from a non-rabbinic variety of Judaism, to

légende coranique est indubitablement d'origine chrétienne."[46] Mon propre examen m'amène à donner raison à Speyer. L'argument décisif me semble être l'opposition qui structure la justification du refus de Satan: "Je suis meilleur que lui. Tu m'as créé de feu, et tu l'as créé d'argile" (7:12; 38:76). Cette opposition entre le feu et l'argile n'est attestée que dans des sources chrétiennes;[47] elle ne se trouve pas dans la *Vie d'Adam et Ève* (comme nous l'avons vu, sa présence dans *Bereshit Rabbati* explique sans doute par un emprunt à une source non-juive).

Le Coran, lorsqu'il parle du refus d'Iblis d'adorer Adam, dépend de la tradition chrétienne. Son témoignage ne peut donc pas être invoqué en faveur de l'origine juive du mythe de la chute de Satan.

Héb 1:6 et le récit de la chute de Satan dans la *Vie d'Adam et Ève*: Dans quel sens va la dépendance?

Il me reste à examiner un dernier argument invoqué en faveur de l'origine juive de la tradition attestée dans *V.A.E.* 12–16. Il s'agit d'Héb 1:6, "Lorsqu'à nouveau il introduit le premier-né dans le monde, il dit: 'Et que se prosternent devant lui tous les anges de Dieu.' "[48] L'argument a été développé par Rosenstiehl. Selon lui, Héb 1:6 fournit un *terminus ante quem* pour la tradition midrashique reflétée dans le récit de la *Vie d'Adam et Ève*. Cette tradition juive a situé l'ordre donné aux anges au moment de la création d'Adam et l'a placé dans la bouche de Dieu ("Vous, tous les anges, révérez Adam!"). Pour Rosenstiehl, "cette légende est déjà largement répandue à la fin du premier siècle de notre ère et c'est elle que cite *Hébreux* 1,6. . . . Or, à cette époque, le seul texte connu qui comporte cette légende est justement la *Vie d'Adam et Ève*. On peut donc imaginer que l'auteur de l'*Épître aux Hébreux* a pu connaître ce texte."[49] En

---

which we owe some at least of the material in the 'Vita Adae,' and which survived in one form or another in seventh-century Arabia."

[46] Heinrich Speyer, *Die biblischen Erzählungen im Qoran* (Gräfenheinischen o.J.: n.p., 1931; réimpr., Darmstadt: Wissenschaftliche Buchgesellschaft, 1961), 54–58. Speyer avance trois argument: le nom donné à l'ange rebelle, Iblis, qui provient de διάβολος, avec disparition du δι initial, identifié à tort avec la particule araméenne du génitif; Iblis justifie son refus en invoquant la supériorité du feu dont il est issu; le midrash juif ne parle jamais d'une adoration d'Adam ordonnée par Dieu.

[47] Voir notamment *Ques. Bart.* 4.54; *Didascalie grecque* 23; *Caverne des Trésors* 3.2 (Rosenstiehl, "Chute de l'Ange," 47, 48, 51).

[48] Le début de l'Épître aux Hébreux cite une série de témoignages scripturaires qui servent à établir la supériorité du Fils de Dieu sur les anges. Le troisième de ces témoignages figure au verset 6: ὅταν δὲ πάλιν εἰσαγάγῃ τὸν πρωτότοκον εἰς τὴν οἰκουμένην, λέγει, καὶ προσκυνησάτωσαν αὐτῷ πάντες ἄγγελοι θεοῦ. Le texte scripturaire cité (Deut 32:43 ou Ps 97:7 selon la LXX; voir plus haut n. 2) signifie que les anges reçoivent l'ordre d'adorer le Christ—le premier-né.

[49] Rosenstiehl, "Chute de l'Ange," 46. Dans le même sens, voir Louis Ginzberg, *The Legends of the Jews* (7 vols.; Philadelphia: Jewish Publication Society of America, 1909–1938; réimpr., 1968), 5?:85 (note 35 du vol. 1): il est "très probable qu'Hébr 1,6 remonte à la *Vita Adae*" et attribue au second Adam (Jésus) ce que la *Vie d'Adam et Ève* attribuait au premier Adam; cf. Marshall D. Johnson (*OTP* 2:262 n. 14a): "Heb 1:6 may be an allusion to an early form of this legend."

note, Rosenstiehl relève également qu'Héb 1:6 "gêne les commentateurs. Il ne peut s'agir d'une citation directe de l'Ancien Testament. Seul un intermédiaire midrashique peut y expliquer l'utilisation de *Psaumes* LXX 96,7 et de *Deutéronome* LXX 32,43."[50]

A mon avis, l'argumentation de Rosenstiehl n'est pas convaincante. Les commentaires de l'*Épître aux Hébreux* que j'ai consultés ne témoignent d'aucune "gêne" à propos du texte scripturaire cité en 1:6; ils ne disent rien d'une possible dépendance par rapport à la *Vie d'Adam et Ève* ou à une tradition midrashique. Ce silence me semble justifié. En effet, la citation du verset 6 fait partie d'une chaîne de témoignages scripturaires parfaitement identifiés et tous empruntés aux Psaumes.[51] Il me semble donc exclu de faire dépendre Héb 1:6—ou l'interprétation christologique du Ps 97:7 qui y est reprise—de la *Vie d'Adam et Ève* ou d'une tradition midrashique préexistante.

Ne faut-il inverser le rapport de dépendance? Ne serait-ce pas l'interprétation christologique du texte scripturaire cité en Héb 1:6 qui a donné naissance au motif de l'adoration d'Adam par les anges dans *V.A.E.* 12–17? L'hypothèse mérite d'être sérieusement envisagée. Elle peut être précisée de la manière suivante. L'exégèse chrétienne n'a pas transféré sur le "second Adam" une tradition midrashique selon laquelle les anges auraient reçu l'ordre d'adorer Adam, mais elle a interprété l'ordre d'adorer du Ps 97:7 en rapportant le pronom αὐτῷ au Christ. Cette interprétation christologique a ensuite été reportée sur le premier Adam, sous l'influence de la typologie Christ-Adam qu'on trouve dans Rom 5:12–14. Le Christ, objet de l'adoration des anges, serait ainsi venu rétablir le statut glorieux d'Adam avant sa chute, qui le rendait digne à l'origine d'être adoré lui aussi par les anges.

Un point reste à expliquer: pourquoi, dans le récit de la *Vie d'Adam et Ève*, ce thème de l'adoration d'Adam par les anges a-t-il été associé à celui de la jalousie et du refus de Satan? Je pense que ce motif de la jalousie provient d'une exégèse chrétienne de Sag 2:24: "Par la jalousie du diable la mort est entrée dans le monde" (φθόνῳ δὲ διαβόλου θάνατος εἰσῆλθεν εἰς τὸν κόσμον). Il y a en effet une parenté frappante entre la formulation de ce passage et celle de Rom 5:12, où Paul affirme que "par un seul homme le péché est entré dans le monde, et par le péché, la mort" (Διὰ τοῦτο ὥσπερ δι' ἑνὸς ἀνθρώπου ἡ ἁμαρτία εἰς τὸν κόσμον εἰσῆλθεν καὶ διὰ τῆς ἁμαρτίας ὁ θάνατος). Mon hypothèse est que le récit de la chute de Satan en *V.A.E.* 12–16 est influencé par le rapprochement de ces deux passages scripturaire. Le péché et la mort sont certes entrés dans le monde par l'intermédiaire d'Adam (Rom 5:12), mais ils ont

---

[50] Ibid., 46, n. 54.
[51] En Héb 1:5–13 sont successivement cités: Ps 2:7; 32:43; 97:7 (ou Odes 2:4); 104:4; 45:7–8; 102:26–28; 110:1. La citation du Ps 97:7 ne constitue donc pas un cas à part et ne suppose nullement l'existence d'un "intermédiaire midrashique." Comme les autres citations, elle repose sur une relecture christologique de l'Écriture. L'emploi du terme πρωτότοκος dans la phrase introductive est typique de cette interprétation messianique des Psaumes.

pour cause première la jalousie du diable (Sag 2:24). Cette jalousie s'est manifestée dans son refus de reconnaître le statut éminent d'Adam, créé à l'image de Dieu. Le Ps 97:7, interprété christologiquement (cf. Héb 1:6), a également influencé le récit de la *Vie d'Adam et Ève*: par le biais de la typologie Christ-Adam, l'ordre d'adorer donné aux anges a été reporté sur le premier homme.

Je propose donc de voir dans le récit de la chute de Satan de la *Vie d'Adam et Ève* une composition chrétienne.[52] L'absence de références spécifiquement chrétiennes dans le récit ne suffit pas à invalider cette hypothèse. Le parallèle des *Questions de Barthélemy* (4.52–59) apporte en effet la preuve qu'un auteur chrétien pouvait raconter la chute de Satan sans faire la moindre allusion au salut futur accompli par le Christ. Le rapprochement est d'autant plus intéressant que les *Questions de Barthélemy* reprennent aussi à leur compte d'autres traditions exégétiques d'origine juive.[53] Nous avons affaire à un écrit qui présente des parallèles frappants avec des sources midrashiques, mais qui a été composé par un auteur chrétien. La *Vie d'Adam et Ève* pourrait très bien constituer un cas semblable.

---

[52] Anderson ("Ezekiel 28," 146–47) parvient à la même conclusion, mais en rattachant le récit à une tradition spécifiquement chrétienne qui rapportait Ézéchiel 28 à la chute de Satan. Cependant, son argumentation ne me convainc pas: je considère comme secondaires les allusions à Ézéchiel 28, propres à l'arménien et au géorgien de *V.A.E.* 12.1 (tout comme la référence à Ésa 14:13 dans le latin de *V.A.E.* 15.3). De plus, je pense que le passage sur la chute de Satan n'a pas été ajouté après coup au récit de la pénitence d'Adam, mais qu'il en fait partie dès l'origine.

[53] Voir Jean-Daniel Kaestli et Pierre Cherix, *L'Évangile de Barthélemy d'après deux récits apocryphes* (Apocryphes: Collection de poche de l'AELAC [1]; Turnhout: Brepols, 1993), 84–93.

CHAPTER TWENTY-SIX

THE ANCIENT CHRISTIAN TEACHER IN
THE *PSEUDO-CLEMENTINES*

F. STANLEY JONES

The early Christian teacher has been the subject of recent significant advances in the historical knowledge of ancient Christianity.[1] In particular, the independence of the teacher from the rising church bureaucracy has proven food for thought,[2] especially in view of the teachers' interface and dialogue with the Greco-Roman intellectual tradition.[3]

The *Pseudo-Clementines* contain a considerable amount of raw data on the early Christian teacher. This data warrants its own critical review in part because the broader investigator of the ancient Christian teacher can hardly be expected to unfurl completely the involved tradition history of the Pseudo-Clementine materials and thus usually ends up relying on brief indications in the general secondary literature on the *Pseudo-Clementines*. Furthermore, the *Pseudo-Clementines* seem to call into question an emerging basic theory on the

---

[1] See the complementary monographs by Alfred F. Zimmermann, *Die urchristlichen Lehrer: Studien zum Tradentenkreis der διδάσκαλοι im frühen Urchristentum* (WUNT 2.12; Tübingen: Mohr Siebeck, 1984), and Ulrich Neymeyr, *Die christlichen Lehrer im zweiten Jahrhundert: Ihre Lehrtätigkeit, ihr Selbstverständnis und ihre Geschichte* (VCSup 4; Leiden: Brill, 1989). The history of recent research is reviewed in Neymeyr, *Die christlichen Lehrer im zweiten Jahrhundert*, 3–6; for older literature, see Hermann Robert Nelz, *Die theologischen Schulen der morgenländischen Kirchen während der sieben ersten christlichen Jahrhunderte in ihrer Bedeutung für die Ausbildung des Klerus* (Bonn: Rhenania-Druckerei, 1916), 2–4. Some other recent contributions are found in Jan Willem Drijvers and Alasdair A. MacDonald, eds., *Centres of Learning: Learning and Location in Pre-Modern Europe and the Near East* (Brill's Studies in Intellectual History 61; Leiden: Brill, 1995) and in the literature referred to below in n. 3.

[2] A collection of references to the ancient Christian teacher was made by Adolf Harnack, *Die Lehre der zwölf Apostel nebst Untersuchungen zur ältesten Geschichte der Kirchenverfassung und des Kirchenrechts* (TU 2.1–2; Leipzig: J. C. Hinrichs, 1884), 131–37, and was repeated and expanded in his *Die Mission und Ausbreitung des Christentums in den ersten drei Jahrhunderten* (4th rev. and enl. ed.; Leipzig: J. C. Hinrichs, 1924), 365–77. Gustave Bardy developed the appreciation of the independence of the teachers in "Les écoles romaines au second siècle," *RHE* 28 (1932): 501–32: "Nous sommes aujourd'hui frappés de la liberté avec laquelle enseignaient alors les docteurs privés, dans leurs écoles ouvertes à tous les vents" (p. 521).

[3] Discussion of this interface and dialogue in two particular cases is the main contribution of Katharina Greschat, *Apelles und Hermogenes: Zwei theologische Lehrer des zweiten Jahrhunderts* (VCSup 48; Leiden: Brill, 2000). See the overview of recent literature on the general topic here, pp. 39–44.

evolution of the teacher that has been expressed in the following words: "Die christlichen Lehrer des zweiten Jahrhunderts standen also nicht in historischer Kontinuität mit den urchristlichen Lehrern, sondern mit ihnen begann eine neue Phase in der Geschichte des christlichen Lehrertums."[4]

One body of traditions in the *Pseudo-Clementines* that pertains to the office of the teacher is quite apparently related to the *Book of Elchasai.*[5] The Pseudo-Clementine *Adjuration*, found prefaced to the *Homilies*, consists of an oath to be taken by prospective teachers. This oath contains a list of seven witnesses that runs quite parallel to the lists of seven witnesses documented for the *Book of Elchasai* by Hippolytus and Epiphanius:

Pseudo-Clementine *Adjuration*	Epiphanius, *Pan.*	Epiphanius, *Pan.*	Hippolytus, *Haer.*
(1.1) Therefore, after James read the letter, he summoned the presbyters, read it to them, and said, "Our Peter has necessarily and fittingly reminded to be careful with regard to the truth in order that we pass on the books of his preachings that have been sent to us to no one at random other than to one who is good and pious, to one who chooses also to teach and is a faithful circumcised person. And not all these together so that if he be discovered as thoughtless in the first matters, he not be entrusted with the			(9.15.1) "when he hears this book, let him be baptized a second time in the name of the great and highest God and in the name of his Son, the great king. (2) Let him cleanse, let him be pure, and let him adjure for him-

---

[4] Neymeyr, *Die christlichen Lehrer im zweiten Jahrhundert*, 237. On p. 5, Neymeyr states that he adopted this theory from Zimmermann, *Die urchristlichen Lehrer*, 209, 218. Zimmermann, however, probably had an insufficient database for this broad conclusion since he limited his investigations to the New Testament and the Apostolic Fathers. An earlier expression of this theory is found in K. H. Rengstorf, "διδάσκαλω κτλ," *TDNT* 2:135–65, esp. 159; this article, similar to Zimmermann's study and many other articles in the *TDNT*, makes apodictic statements about the early Christian evidence outside the canon without thoroughly reviewing it.

[5] For general orientation on the Book of Elchasai (116–17 c.e.), see the two fairly recent monographs: Gerard P. Luttikhuizen, *The Revelation of Elchasai: Investigations into the Evidence for a Mesopotamian Jewish Apocalypse of the Second Century and Its Reception by Judeo-Christian Propagandists* (TSAJ 8; Tübingen: Mohr Siebeck, 1985), and Luigi Cirillo, *Elchasai e gli Elchasaiti: Un contributo alla storia delle comunità giudeo-cristiane* (Studi e ricerche 1; Cosenza: Marra, 1984), as well as Luigi Cirillo, "Livre de la révélation d'Elkasaï," in *Écrits apocryphes chrétiens* (ed. François Bovon and Pierre Geoltrain; vol. 1; Bibliothèque de la Pléiade 442; Paris: Gallimard, 1997), 827–72, and Johannes Irmscher, "The Book of Elchasai," in *New Testament Apocrypha* (ed. Wilhelm Schneemelcher; trans. R. McL. Wilson; 2 vols.; rev. ed.; Louisville: Westminster/John Knox Press, 1991–92), 2:685–90.

Pseudo-Clementine *Adjuration*	Epiphanius, *Pan.*	Epiphanius, *Pan.*	Hippolytus, *Haer.*

Pseudo-Clementine *Adjuration* second. (2) Therefore, let him be tested for not less than six years. Then, thus according to the discipline of Moses, lead him to a river or a spring, which is living water in which the regeneration of the righteous occurs, not to swear, for it is not allowed, but to stand by it to bid the water and to call to witness, as also we, when we were regenerated and having been commanded, did for the sake of not sinning.

(2.1) "Now let him say, 'May I have as witnesses **heaven, earth, water**, in which everything is contained, and in addition to all these the *air* that pervades all, apart from which I do not breathe, that I will eternally be obedient to the one who gives me the books of the preachings and that whichever of the books he might give me I will not pass on to anyone in any manner . . .'

(4.1) " 'That I will act in this manner I again call to witness a second time **heaven, earth, water**, in which everything is contained, and in addition to all these the *air* that pervades all, apart from which I do not breathe, that I will eternally be obedient to the one who gives me the books of the preachings and that I will guard them in every way that I have testified or even more. (2) There will therefore be a share for me with the holy ones when I keep the agreements, but should I act against what I have agreed to, then may the universe be hostile to me and also the all pervading **ether** and the God who is above all things, for whom no one is superior, no one greater. (3)

Epiphanius, *Pan.*

(19.1.6a) . . . [sc. Elxai] having appointed **salt, water, earth, bread, heaven, ether,** and *wind* as an oath for them unto service, (19.6.4) . . . the one having spoken in [the Book of] "Elxai," who compelled swearing not only by God but also by **salt**, by **water**, by **ether**, by *wind*, by the **earth**, and by **heaven**.

Epiphanius, *Pan.*

(19.1.6b) . . . [sc. Elxai] having appointed seven other witnesses, I mean, the **heaven**, the **water, holy spirits**, he says, the **angels of prayer**, the **oil**, the **salt**, and the **earth**.

Hippolytus, *Haer.*

self the seven witnesses recorded in this book: the **heaven**, the **water**, the **holy spirits**, the **angels of prayer**, the **oil**, the **salt**, and the **earth**." (9.15.5) "let him baptize himself with all his apparel and let him pray to the great and highest God in faith of the heart. And then let him adjure the seven witnesses recorded in this book: 'Behold, I call to witness the **heaven**, the **water**, the **holy spirits**, the **angels of prayer**, the **oil**, the **salt**, and the **earth**.' "

Pseudo-Clementine *Adjuration*	Epiphanius, *Pan.*	Epiphanius, *Pan.*	Hippolytus, *Haer.*
Yet even if I should come to the supposition of another god, I now swear also by that one that I will not do otherwise, whether he be or not. Beyond all these things, if I commit perjury I will be accursed while alive and after death and I will be punished with eternal punishment.' After this let him partake of **bread** and **salt** with the one who is handing over."			

Scholarship has not settled on an explanation for why Epiphanius has two different lists of witnesses (19.1.6a and 19.6.4, on the one hand, and 19.1.6b, on the other hand). The second list (*Pan.* 19.1.6b) agrees exactly with the list recorded twice by Hippolytus (*Haer.* 9.15.2, 9.15.5). The presence of yet a third list in Epiphanius (*Pan.* 30.17.4) has perhaps discouraged scholars from seeking the root of Epiphanius's presentation:

> For whenever one of them [sc. the Ebionites] either suffers an illness or has been bitten by a snake, he goes down into water and calls upon the names in [the Book of] "Elxai" of the heaven, the earth, the salt, the water, the winds, angels of righteousness, they say, the bread, and the oil and begins to say, "Rescue me and take the suffering away from me." (Epiphanius, *Pan.* 30.17.4)

This third list occurs much later in the *Panarion*—no longer in the nineteenth book, which is dedicated to the sect of the Ossaeans and in which Epiphanius has his main treatment of Elchasai, but in the midst of his thirtieth book, which is dedicated to the Ebionites. The distinctive differences in the list here are thus best ascribed to citation from memory.

The exact correspondence between Epiphanius's second list and the list in Hippolytus has led many researchers from A. Ritschl[6] to G. P. Luttikhuizen[7] to view it as the original one. A. Hilgenfeld similarly seems implicitly to ascribe the first list in Epiphanius to his own confusion.[8]

The problem with the ascription of the first list to Epiphanius's confusion, however, is that it corresponds noticeably with the list in the *Pseudo-Clementines*.[9]

---

[6] Albrecht Ritschl, "Über die Secte der Elkesaiten," *ZHT* 23 (1853): 573–94, esp. 586.
[7] Luttikhuizen, *The Revelation of Elchasai*, 118.
[8] Adolf Hilgenfeld, "Das Urchristentum und seine neuesten Bearbeitungen von Lechler und Ritschl," *ZWT* 1 (1858): 54–140, 377–440, 565–602, esp. 422 n. 2.
[9] Hans Joachim Schoeps, *Theologie und Geschichte des Judenchristentums* (Tübingen: Mohr Siebeck, 1949), 291 n. 4, in contrast, went so far as to deny all Elchasaite influence on the list in the *Pseudo-Clementines*; he attributes the similarities just to a general reli-

Lipsius saw this correspondence and appropriately noted that the first list in Epiphanius must have been a different list. Noticing the qualification of this first list as an "oath unto service," Lipsius stated that this list was used for the ordination of those people called to higher service (i.e., church officers), as also found in the Pseudo-Clementine *Adjuration*, which uses this list for precisely the purpose of ordaining people who are entrusted with the possession of the books.[10] The evidence allows little doubt that Lipsius's neglected insight is right. This insight also shows up a weakness in the two recent monographs on the *Book of Elchasai*: neither treats the *Pseudo-Clementines* as an independent witness to the *Book of Elchasai* despite the fact that there is an acknowledged dearth of independent sources (usually thought to be three or four) for this apocryphon. In this particular case, evidence pertinent to the generally misunderstood genre of the *Book of Elchasai* has been overlooked: the *Book of Elchasai* contained a detailed oath for prospective teachers, which again accords to a much greater degree with an understanding of the *Book* as a church order (one of the earliest!) rather than as an apocalypse as generally thought.[11] The reality of the reference of this material on teachers in the *Pseudo-Clementines* is disputed. While some scholars have assumed (on the basis of the *Epistula Petri* and the *Adjuration*) that the Jewish Christians must have had a college of seventy teachers who stood under the authority of a bishop in the Jerusalem succession of James,[12] U. Neymeyr dismisses this material as idealistic and not

---

gious phenomenon. See also John Chapman, "On the Date of the Clementines," *ZNW* 9 (1908): 21–34, 147–59, esp. 152: "There is indeed some likeness. The dissimilarity is more striking." Eduard Schwartz, "Unzeitgemäße Beobachtungen zu den Clementinen," *ZNW* 31 (1932): 151–99, esp. 196, agreed.

[10] Richard Adelbert Lipsius, *Zur Quellenkritik des Epiphanios* (Vienna: Wilhelm Braumüller, 1865), 146 n. This qualification of the oath had been dismissed by Hilgenfeld ("Das Urchristentum und seine neuesten Bearbeitungen," 422 n. 2), as a misunderstanding by Epiphanius ("Epiphanius, welcher das Gelübde fälschlich als einen Dienst-Eid auffasst . . .").

[11] For a discussion of the genre of the *Book of Elchasai* including a history of research, see my article "The Genre of the Book of Elchasai: A Primitive Church Order, Not an Apocalypse," in *Historische Wahrheit und theologische Wissenschaft: Gerd Lüdemann zum 50. Geburtstag* (ed. Alf Özen; Frankfurt: Peter Lang, 1996), 87–104, and the response by Gerard P. Luttikhuizen, "The Book of Elchasai: A Jewish Apocalyptic Writing, Not a Christian Church Order," *SBL Seminar Papers, 1999* (SBLSP 38; Atlanta: Society of Biblical Literature, 1999), 405–25. It was first in preparation for my response to Luttikhuizen's paper that I recognized the significance of the correspondences between the list in the *Adjuration* and the first list in Epiphanius and discovered that Lipsius had already seen it. Consequently, my article "The Genre of the Book of Elchasai" does not yet contain this significant evidence as a further argument. Impetus to account for the various lists of witnesses was received at my 1990 Paris seminar on Jewish Christianity in the form of a question from Professor Pierre Geoltrain, whom I would like to take the occasion to thank.

[12] Carl Schmidt, *Studien zu den Pseudo-Clementinen nebst einem Anhange: Die älteste römische Bischofsliste und die Pseudo-Clementinen* (TU 46.1; Leipzig: J. C. Hinrichs, 1929), 316–27; Schoeps, *Theologie und Geschichte des Judenchristentums*, 289–92; Jung-Sik Cha, "Diamartyria and the Ordination of Jewish Christian Teachers," *AJT* 13 (1999): 124–58.

employable for evaluation of the other Pseudo-Clementine references to cat-echists.[13] Neymeyr's perspective rests on the tradition of scholarship that views the use of the Elchasaite material in the *Pseudo-Clementines* as merely a literary farce.[14] Neither of these options seems to be fully adequate. Though the lit-erary capabilities of the Pseudo-Clementine Basic Writer should not be under-estimated, the farcical elements in the *Pseudo-Clementines* (e.g., the ruse of Clement in H 5.2–3 along with the accompanying erotic epistle and its fictitious reply in H 5.10–26) seem to be, by and large, contributions by the Homilist. Furthermore, the contacts of the *Epistula Petri* and the *Adjuration* with the *Book of Elchasai* are truly significant.[15] Though the *Book of Elchasai* has often been considered a strange aberration in early Christianity, the fairly recent discov-ery that Mani grew up in an Elchasaite Christian community has demon-strated that Elchasai is actually a religious figure of world-historical significance. The contacts of the *Pseudo-Clementines* with the *Book of Elchasai* are thus best understood as an indication that the Pseudo-Clementine Basic Writer stood in the tradition of the variety of Christianity associated with the *Book of Elchasai*.

The office of "teacher" seems to have been particularly alive in this Elchasaite tradition. Beyond the oath for teachers in the *Book of Elchasai* that was just discussed, there is Hippolytus's detailed account of the arrival of an Elchasaite named Alcibiades from Apamaea in Rome in circa 220 C.E. Since Hippolytus describes Alcibiades' activity as "teaching" (*Haer.* 9.16.1), it seems likely that Alcibiades was an Elchasaite teacher who lived at the time of the Pseudo-Clementine Basic Writing and also close to its home in Syria.[16] More of the legacy of the Elchasaite teachers is found doubtlessly in the "teachers" men-tioned among Mani's Babylonian baptists[17] as well as probably in the twelve "teachers" at the top of the Manichaean church hierarchy.[18]

---

[13] Neymeyr, *Die christlichen Lehrer im zweiten Jahrhundert*, 157; Hans von Campenhausen, *Ecclesiastical Authority and Spiritual Power in the Church of the First Three Centuries* (trans. J. A. Baker; Stanford: Stanford University Press, 1969), 180–81, whom Neymeyr cites, is actually closer to the position of Schmidt and Schoeps.

[14] Cf. Wilhelm Brandt, *Elchasai, ein Religionsstifter und sein Werk: Beiträge zur jüdischen, christlichen und allgemeinen Religionsgeschichte* (Leipzig: J. C. Hinrichs, 1912), 20, who main-tained "daß der Verfasser von elchasäischen (oder elchasäisch beeinflußten ebionäis-chen) Bräuchen gewußt und sie bei diesem schriftstellerischen Scherze sich zum Muster genommen hat." Chapman, "On the Date of the Clementines," 148, stated regarding the *Epistula Petri* and the *Adjuration*: "the writer is romancing." Cf. Georg Strecker, *Das Judenchristentum in den Pseudoklementinen* (2d ed., rev.; TU 70; Berlin: Akademie, 1981), 144.

[15] These contacts extend well beyond the list of witnesses and include such phrases as μέρος μετὰ τῶν δικαίων plus a dative of person in the quotation from the *Book* in Hippolytus, *Haer.* 9.15.3, and μέρος ἔσται μετὰ τῶν ὁσίων plus a dative of person in *Adjuration* 4.2.

[16] "Teacher" also may well have been a title borne by Elchasai himself: the *Book* addresses its readers as "pupils": μαθηταί in Hippolytus, *Haer.* 9.16.2; μαθηταί is also used in the stories about Elchasai in the so-called *Cologne Mani Codex* (P. Colon. 4780) 95.17, 22; 97.12.

[17] *Cologne Mani Codex* 88.6; 143.4–5.

[18] For a useful chart of the Manichaean hierarchy, see Michel Tardieu, *Le manichéisme*

There is thus every reason to believe that the Pseudo-Clementine Basic Writer is positively appropriating Elchasaite traditions regarding the "teachers." That this author later mentions "catechists" seems to be prima facie evidence that these catechists are to be interpreted as heirs of the Elchasaite teachers, as least in the tradition and perspective of the Basic Writer.[19] Without further historical corroboration of the various other details in the *Adjuration*, however, one should be cautious about using it alone to construct a comprehensive picture of the Ebionite hierarchy in the first and second centuries.

The references to the "cathechists" in the body of the *Pseudo-Clementines* have, in turn, posed an independent set of problems for historical research. The nub of these problems is found in the fact that while the *Epistula Clementis* 13–15 lists the catechists among what are apparently ecclesial offices (bishop, presbyters, deacons, catechists), there is no mention of catechists in the account of the ordination of Zacchaeus as bishop at Caesarea in R 3.66 par. H 3.66–67, although presbyters and deacons are explicitly discussed. To account for this difference, it has been suggested that *Epistula Clementis* 13–15 derives from an older source and that at the time of the Basic Writer (who is given responsibility for R 3.66 par. H 3.66–67), the catechist was no longer known.[20] H 3.71.5, however, reads τιμᾶτε πρεσβυτέρους, κατηχητάς, διακόνους χρησίμους, χήρας εὖ βεβιωκυίας, ὀρφανοὺς ὡς ἐκκλησίας τέκνα in the context of a discussion of the necessity of financially supporting the bishop. Nevertheless, this statement has often been considered too problematic for clarification of the standing of the teacher/catechist according to the Basic Writing. On the one hand,

---

(Que sais-je? 1940; Paris: Presses universitaires de France, 1981), 78; see also Samuel N. C. Lieu, *Manichaeism in the Later Roman Empire and Medieval China* (2d ed., rev. and exp.; WUNT 63; Tübingen: Mohr Siebeck, 1992), 27, where, however, the most important language (Syriac) is omitted. Various explanations have been given for the genesis of Mani's hierarchical system: Tardieu, *Le manichéisme*, 76–77, seems to see the hierarchy as an adoption from the evolving Great Church in Mesopotamia; F. C. Burkitt, *The Religion of the Manichees: Donnellan Lectures for 1924* (Cambridge: Cambridge University Press, 1925), 83, attributes the Manichean organization to Marcionite influence; John C. Reeves, "The 'Elchasaite' Sanhedrin of the Cologne Mani Codex in Light of Second Temple Jewish Sectarian Sources," *JJS* 42 (1991): 68–91, attributes the impulse to a nexus of heterodox Jewish thought also found in the Qumran writings; F. C. Baur, *Das manichäische Religionssystem nach den Quellen neu untersucht und entwickelt* (Tübingen: C. F. Osiander, 1831), 449–51, saw Jain and Buddhist influence. Surprisingly, no one has looked to the most likely source, the Elchasaites, for a similar pattern of church organization.

[19] See, similarly, Roger Gryson, "The Authority of the Teacher in the Ancient and Medieval Church," *JES* 19, no. 2 (1982): 176–87, esp. 182; Alexandre Faivre, "Les fonctions ecclésiales dans les écrits pseudo-clémentins," *RevScRel* 50 (1976): 97–111, esp. 107–11; idem, *Naissance d'une hiérarchie: Les premières étapes du cursus clérical* (ThH 40; Paris: Beauchesne, 1977), 168–69; idem, *Ordonner la fraternité: Pouvoir d'innover et retour à l'ordre dans l'église ancienne* (Histoire; Paris: Cerf, 1992), 264–67. Cf. also Allen Brent, *Hippolytus and the Roman Church in the Third Century: Communities in Tension before the Emergence of a Monarch-Bishop* (VCSup 31; Leiden: Brill, 1995), 491 n. 52. Even Strecker, *Das Judenchristentum in den Pseudoklementinen*, 111, states that the catechist here is "der Nachfolger des charismatischen Lehrers."

[20] Strecker, *Das Judenchristentum in den Pseudoklementinen*, 105–6.

it has been stated that in H 3.71.5 the catechists are out of their proper order (as found in the *Epistula Clementis* where they follow the deacons) and that this disorder is only a further sign (beyond H 3.66–67) that the Homilist did not know this office[21] and/or that the Basic Writer did not know the office.[22] On the other hand, it has been suggested that there should not be a comma after πρεσβυτέρους so that the text actually speaks of presbyter-teachers, not separately of catechists at all.[23]

This last opinion would seem to be refuted by the two Greek manuscripts of the *Homilies* because both of them apparently have a mark of punctuation indicating a pause after πρεσβυτέρους.[24] Furthermore, since the Basic Writer shows an interest in the "teacher," as has been seen in the exposition of the *Adjuration* (cf. also R 4.35.1 par. H 11.35.4), there seems to be no a priori reason to assume that this author did not know the office of "catechist." Indeed, a growing edge of historical research is revealing precisely the mounting evidence for the survival of the "teacher" alongside the rising bureaucratic hierarchy of bishops, presbyters, and deacons much longer than has been thought.[25] The "teacher" is a counterbalancing pendant to the bureaucratic hierarchy in the same way that the prophet and martyr/confessor remained independent counterbalancing pendants. While the history of the subordination of the prophet and martyr to the hierarchy is fairly well known,[26] the history of the "teacher" and the taming of this office are still open to debate.

Despite the critical positions developed in previous literature, there are reasons to take the text of the *Pseudo-Clementines* as it stands[27] and to accept and

---

[21] Schmidt, *Studien zu den Pseudo-Clementinen*, 59 n. 1, 122.

[22] Strecker, *Das Judenchristentum in den Pseudoklementinen*, 105–6.

[23] Harnack, *Die Mission und Ausbreitung des Christentums*, 369 n. 3; idem, *Geschichte der altchristlichen Literatur bis Eusebius* (2d ed., exp.; 2 vols. in 4; Leipzig: J. C. Hinrichs, 1958), 2.2:530–31 n. 2, followed by Faivre, "Les fonctions ecclésiales dans les écrits pseudo-clémentins," 103, who combines this suggestion with Strecker's source-critical hypothesis (p. 99, also *Ordonner la fraternité*, 257, 261); Faivre is followed by John Kevin Coyle, "The Exercise of Teaching in the Postapostolic Church," *EgT* 15 (1984): 23–43, esp. 26–27. Omission of the comma is advocated also by Josep Rius-Camps, "Sucesión y ministerios en las Pseudoclementinas," in Mons. Capmany et al., *La potestad de orden en los primeros siglos* (TeSa 9; Burgos: Ediciones Aldecoa, 1977), 163–215, esp. 211–12.

[24] This is clearly the case for Paris gr. 930 and appears to be the case for Vatican Ottobonianus gr. 443, as evidenced by microfilms of the manuscripts.

[25] There is doubtless even more to be learned about the ancient Christian teacher in the oriental traditions. For example, the full-scale survival of the teacher in the Syrian realm is documented in *The Statutes of the School of Nisibis* (Arthur Vööbus, ed. and trans., *The Statutes of the School of Nisibis* [Papers of the Estonian Theological Society in Exile 12; Stockholm: Estonian Theological Society in Exile, n.d. (1961)], 83 [canon 20], 95 (canon 7)]). See the attempt to trace the early history of the Edessan school in E. R. Hayes, *L'école d'Édesse* (Paris: Les presses modernes, 1930).

[26] The topics are dealt with largely in the literature on the Montanist controversy (prophet) and on the Decian persecution and its aftermath (martyr/confessor).

[27] Scepticism towards the theories summarized above is expressed also by Georg Schöllgen, *Die Anfänge der Professionalisierung des Klerus und das kirchliche Amt in der syrischen Didaskalie* (JAC.E 26; Münster: Aschendorffsche Verlagsbuchhandlung, 1998), 77 n. 297: "entschieden zu hypothetisch."

unfold its witness to the office of "teacher." First, that the "catechists" are not mentioned in R 3.66 par. H 3.66–67 may well be due to the fact that, as followers of the teachers, they were not yet ordained members of the clergy, while R 3.66 par. H 3.66–67 is either a report about ordination (so R; see similarly R 3.74.1–2 and R 6.15.4–5 par. H 11.36.2) or an account of the church hierarchy (H 3.67). Second, that the "catechists" should be mentioned, in contrast, in H 3.71.5, which discusses groups that deserve the support of the church, is not very remarkable because this passage also lists widows and orphans as deserving of support, too; widows and orphans are not listed in R 3.66 par. H 3.66–67 either. Third, the placement of the "catechists" in the list in H 3.71.5 after the presbyters and before the deacons is not as extraordinary as has been thought. It is, instead, understandable that their place in this list posed a difficulty: they did not belong with the widows and orphans. Their placement after the presbyters seems even less remarkable when one considers that the *Apostolic Church Order* similarly deals with the "lectors" (also apparently heirs of the "teachers") after the bishop and presbyters but before the deacons and widows (so in chapter 19).[28] Another order is found in the *Apostolic Tradition* of Hippolytus, which treats the reader after bishops, presbyters, deacons, confessors, and widows but before virgins and subdeacons.[29] Tertullian, too, lists the teacher after the bishop, deacon, and widow but between the virgin and the martyr (*Praescr.* 3.5).[30]

An interesting question arises from this scenario: How did these "catechists" or teachers achieve and maintain their authority in the church? In view of the texts that were just reviewed, the witness of the *Pseudo-Clementines* would seem to stand in accord with Hippolytus's *Apostolic Tradition* 11 that the teachers were not ordained.[31] The catechists' authority seems to have rested, instead, on their knowledge—as recognized by their students—in line with earlier independent Christian teachers such as Justin.[32] In sum, the witness of the *Pseudo-Clementines* to the ancient Christian teacher is not as complex as has often been thought.[33] On the one hand, the Pseudo-Clementine Basic Writing, through

---

[28] Theodor Schermann, ed., *Die allgemeine Kirchenordnung, frühchristliche Liturgien und kirchliche Überlieferung*, pt. 1: *Die allgemeine Kirchenordnung des zweiten Jahrhunderts* (SGKA.E 3.1; Paderborn: Ferdinand Schöningh, 1914), 27.

[29] Bernard Botte, ed. and trans., *Hippolyte de Rome: La tradition apostolique d'après les anciennes versions* (2d ed; SC 11; Paris: Cerf, 1968), ch. 11, p. 67.

[30] Cf. Harnack, *Die Mission und Ausbreitung des Christentums*, 369–70, for further such passages.

[31] Contra the implication of Neymeyr's statement, *Die christlichen Lehrer im zweiten Jahrhundert*, 156: "Vielleicht waren sie die Nachfolger der in der Didache genannten Lehrer. Allerdings hatten sie ein Gemeindeamt inne und gehörten wahrscheinlich zum Klerus." It is historically revealing that *Did.* 13.2 also prescribes support for the teacher.

[32] Cf. Gryson, "The Authority of the Teacher," 179: "They owed their authority to their knowledge and to the reputation it gave them within and without the circle of their disciples."

[33] As a consequence of the interpretation above, it does not seem to be necessary to postulate a special source for the Basic Writer's material on the church hierarchy (contra Strecker, *Das Judenchristentum in den Pseudoklementinen*, 97–116, who based his argu-

its employment of an Elchasaite oath for prospective teachers, seems to show that, at least in this tradition, the later Christian teacher or catechist was indeed the heir to the early Christian teacher (contra the thesis of Neymeyr).[34] On the other hand, the Basic Writer, from about 220 C.E., turns out to be a valuable witness to the time when the "catechists" were not yet ordained members of the clergy but still maintained some of their independent authority. The basis for this authority apparently still lay in their recognition as persons of Christian learning by the congregation generally.

---

ment squarely on the statements about the catechists: "Es [sc. das Schiffsgleichnis] hat dem G-Autor in einer fixierten Quelle vorgelegen, wie aus den Aussagen über das Katechetenamt zu erschließen ist," p. 105); here I am in agreement with Rius-Camps, "Sucesión y ministerios en las Pseudoclementinas," 172.

[34] Neymeyr's thesis owes its origin, in my opinion, to the rapid transformations that were occurring virtually across the board in the earliest Christian movement; the early Christian teacher was transformed in various ways, and the philosophical teacher, for example, was merely one transformation and not an absolutely new phenomenon. Neymeyr's own demonstration that Justin, for example, understood "seine Lehrbefähigung als Frucht einer charismatischen Begabung" (Die christlichen Lehrer im zweiten Jahrhundert, 35) actually points in this direction.

CHAPTER TWENTY-SEVEN

LES REPRÉSENTATIONS THÉOLOGIQUES DE LA CROIX DANS LA PLUS ANCIENNE LITTÉRATURE CHRÉTIENNE DU DEUXIÈME SIÈCLE

JEAN-MARC PRIEUR

Le fait que Jésus a été crucifié appartient aux éléments fondamentaux de la tradition et de la prédication du christianisme, non seulement parce qu'il concerne la biographie du Seigneur des chrétiens, mais surtout parce que ceux-ci y reconnaissent, dans la foi, une des causes essentielles, souvent même la cause principale, de leur salut. La place conférée à cette cause dans la réflexion théologique comme l'interprétation qui en est donnée sont pourtant loin de faire l'objet d'un consensus. Sans d'ailleurs qu'il y ait nécessairement débat, on peut observer que la signification accordée à cet aspect de la foi et le souci même d'y réfléchir varient assez considérablement d'un auteur ou d'un texte à l'autre. Par ailleurs, l'importance traditionnelle de ce fait a conduit certains auteurs à ne pas s'intéresser seulement, voire pas du tout, à la mort de Jésus sur une croix, mais à l'instrument lui-même, qui devient alors l'objet de symbolisations ou de spéculations.[1]

Dans la littérature chrétienne du deuxième siècle, on peut repérer des auteurs et des textes pour lesquels la croix est le lieu du supplice et de la mort de Jésus et d'autres qui y voient autre chose. Non qu'ils contestent nécessairement la réalité de cette mort et doivent, de ce fait, être rangés parmi les docètes et les hétérodoxes. Certains le font effectivement, mais les autres, du moins en l'état des documents qui nous sont parvenus, préfèrent valoriser une forme ou une autre de symbolisation ou de spiritualisation de la croix, plutôt que la réalité de la mort du Christ sur cet instrument de supplice.

C'est à la première catégorie d'auteurs ou de textes, parmi les plus anciens du deuxième siècle, qu'est consacrée cette étude, ceux chez lesquels la croix est le lieu de la mort du Christ.[2] Sans reprendre tous les détails d'analyses

---

[1] Voir, par exemple, Jean-Marc Prieur, "La dimension cosmique de la crucifixion du Christ et de la croix dans la littérature chrétienne ancienne," *RHPR* 78 (1998): 39–56; et idem, "La croix vivante dans la littérature chrétienne du IIe siècle," *RHPR* 79 (1999): 435–44.

[2] Nous ne prenons pas en compte ici la littérature de Nag Hammadi que nous avons étudiée de ce point de vue dans "La croix et la crucifixion dans les écrits de Nag Hammadi," dans *Anthropos laïkos: Mélanges Alexandre Faivre à l'occasion de ses 30 ans d'enseignement* (éd. Marie-Anne Vannier, Otto Wermelinger, et Gregor Wurst; Paradosis 44; Fribourg, Suisse: Éditions universitaires, 2000), 251–66.

textuelles effectuées par d'autres auteurs ou par nous-même, nous nous efforcerons de présenter les principales orientations attestées par ces documents, pour les confronter les unes aux autres et faire apparaître des dominantes. Précisons que cette recherche porte sur la croix, non sur toutes les allusions à la mort du Christ, même si les deux réalités ne sauraient être dissociées.[3]

I. *La* Lettre du Pseudo-Barnabé

Si l'on situe les lettres d'Ignace d'Antioche à une date tardive assez généralement admise, la *Lettre du Pseudo-Barnabé*, qui est d'ailleurs plutôt une sorte de catéchèse, est le premier document après le Nouveau Testament qui propose des développements sur la croix. Il en traite dans le cadre de collections de citations empruntées à la Bible juive, ces Écritures ayant chez lui pour seule fonction d'annoncer le Christ.[4]

Les réflexions sur la croix s'inscrivent sur le fond d'une conception de la souffrance du Christ clairement élaborée et plusieurs fois affirmée (*Barn.* 5.1–14; 6.1–7; 7.2) selon laquelle le Seigneur a accepté de livrer sa chair à la corruption "pour que nous soyons purifiés par le pardon des péchés, c'est-à-dire par l'aspersion de son sang" (5.1–2). Cette souffrance revêt une dimension sacrificielle affirmée dans les chapitres 7 et 8, et un lien est établi entre elle et le baptême (6.11). Elle a pour effet d'anéantir la mort (5.5) et de donner la vie (7.2). Quatre préfigurations vétérotestamentaires de la croix sont repérables.

La première figure au chapitre 8 et s'inspire de Nmbr 19:1–10, qui concerne l'immolation et l'holocauste d'une génisse rousse et stipule que l'on recueille le sang de cet animal pour en faire sept aspersions, puis que le prêtre prenne du bois, de l'hysope et de l'écarlate et qu'il les jette au milieu du brasier où se consume la génisse. Cette lettre est, à notre connaissance, le seul écrit qui exploite ce récit des Nombres, au prix d'une fusion des rites dont on peut se demander si elle est le fait de l'auteur ou si elle figurait déjà dans une source qu'il utilise:[5] "Que des enfants prennent alors les cendres et les mettent dans des vases, qu'ils enroulent sur un bois la laine écarlate—vous retrouvez ici la préfiguration de la croix et la laine écarlate—et l'hysope, et qu'ainsi les enfants aspergent individuellement tous les membres du peuple afin qu'ils soient purifiés de leurs péchés." Comme le précise lui-même l'auteur, le bois représente la

---

[3] Signalons les études de Gerardus Q. Reijners, *The Terminology of the Holy Cross in the Early Christian Literature as Based upon Old Testament Typology* (Graecitas Christianorum primaeva 2; Nijmegen: Dekker & Van de Vegt, 1965); et de Heinz-Wolfgang Kuhn, "Jesus als Gekreuzigter in der frühchristlichen Verkündigung bis zur Mitte des 2. Jahrhunderts," *ZTK* 72 (1975): 1–46.

[4] Nous citons les traductions de Pierre Prigent, *Épître de Barnabé* (SC 172; Paris: Cerf, 1971).

[5] Selon Prigent (ibid., 137–38), il s'agit d'un midrasch chrétien. Voir aussi idem, *Les testimonia dans le christianisme primitif: L'Épître de Barnabé I–XVI et ses sources* (EBib; Paris: Gabalda, 1961).

croix, et la laine rappelle celle qui, selon le chapitre 7 de la lettre et en contradiction avec le récit de Lév 16:20–22 auquel il se réfère pourtant, est posée sur la tête du bouc chassé au désert. Bien que placée sur le bois, elle ne saurait être identifiée au Christ, mais le rapprochement avec le chapitre 7 suggère d'y voir plutôt une couronne, attribut de sa souffrance et de sa puissance.[6]

La seconde préfiguration concerne un chiffre et se trouve au chapitre 9. Comme au chapitre 8, l'auteur ou sa source fusionne deux passages bibliques; ici Gen 17:23–27, qui rapporte la circoncision de la maison d'Abraham, et Gen 11:14, où le patriarche va reprendre Loth à ses ennemis accompagné de trois cent dix-huit hommes. Ce qui donne dans la lettre: "Et Abraham circoncit parmi les gens de sa maison dix-huit et trois cents hommes" (Barn. 9.8). Or, remarque l'auteur, dix-huit s'écrit en grec *I* (dix) et *H* (huit), ce qui correspond aux deux premières lettres du nom de Jésus; et trois cents s'écrit *T*, ce qui désigne la croix. Cette symbolique montre que la véritable circoncision est celle de l'oreille, afin de croire, et que si Abraham subit la circoncision de la chair c'était parce que l'Esprit dirigeait prophétiquement ses regards vers la connaissance de Jésus et de la croix qui devait apporter la grâce.

La troisième préfiguration appartient à un ensemble (Barn. 11.1–11 et 12.1–7) qui examine si le Seigneur a révélé à l'avance ce qui concerne l'eau, en d'autres termes le baptême, et la croix. Il s'agit du Ps 1:3–6, qui évoque un arbre planté près d'un ruisseau et permet d'affirmer que le salut consiste à espérer en la croix et à recevoir le baptême. Puis de deux extraits (Barn. 11.9–10) introduits par ces mots "un autre prophète," mais non identifiables dans les Écritures: "Et la terre de Jacob était célébrée plus que toute autre" et "Il y avait un fleuve qui coulait, venant de la droite, et des arbres splendides en tiraient leur croissance. Quiconque en mangera vivra éternellement." Cette seconde citation, qui renvoie à Gen 3:22, associe également l'eau et le bois et montre que l'arbre de vie de la Genèse est perçu comme une préfiguration de la croix. Après quoi l'auteur passe à la croix (Barn. 12.1–7) par la citation des "paroles d'un autre prophète" toujours impossibles à identifier, mais connues par ailleurs:[7] "Quand viendra l'achèvement de ces choses? Le Seigneur dit: Quand un bois aura été couché et se sera relevé, et quand du sang gouttera du bois." L'auteur indique clairement qu'il convient d'y voir la croix et celui qui devait être crucifié, et le sang qui jaillit du bois est une préfiguration

---

[6] Ce que confirment ces mots: "Elle (la laine sur le bois) signifie que le règne de Jésus est sur le bois" (8.5). Le Pseudo-Barnabé propose ici la première attestation de l'adjonction "depuis le bois" au Ps 95:10. Voir Jean-Marc Prieur: "Le Seigneur a régné depuis le bois. L'adjonction chrétienne au Ps 95:10 et son interprétation," dans *Rois et reines de la Bible au miroir des Pères* (Cahiers de Biblia Patristica 6; Strasbourg: Université Marc Bloch, Centre d'Analyse et de Documentation Patristiques, 1999), 127–40. Sur cette adjonction, voir aussi: J. Duncan M. Derrett, "Ο ΚΥΡΙΟΣ ΕΒΑΣΙΛΕΥΣΕΝ ΑΠΟ ΤΟΥ ΞΥΛΟΥ," *VC* 43 (1989): 378–92.

[7] Pseudo-Grégoire de Nysse dans PG 46:213d et Pseudo-Jérôme dans PL 30:639c. Voir Jean Daniélou, "Un testimonium sur la vigne dans Barnabé XII, 1," *RSR* 50 (1962): 389–99.

de celui qui s'écoulera du corps du Christ, si bien qu'on observe une sorte d'identification entre le bois et le Seigneur qu'il portera.

La suite du chapitre 12 concerne des préfigurations suggérées par deux épisodes de la vie de Moïse: le combat entre Israël et Amaleq (Exod 17:8–13) résumé de manière assez libre et où l'attitude de Moïse est perçue comme une préfiguration de la croix et de celui qui devait souffrir, rappelant aux Israélites qu'ils ne peuvent être sauvés à moins d'espérer en Jésus (*Barn.* 12.3).[8] Puis le récit du serpent d'airain (Nmbr 21:6–9), également reproduit assez librement et auquel est conféré un sens exclusivement christologique, en sorte que le serpent préfigure Jésus, et l'objet sur lequel il est placé la croix, qui se nomme comme dans la Septante un signe. L'auteur relève qu'il existe une contradiction entre cette initiative de Moïse et l'interdiction formulée par lui-même d'avoir des images pour en faire un Dieu. Le serpent est une exception qui se justifie par le fait qu'il représente le Christ. L'association de ces deux textes se retrouvera chez d'autres auteurs.

II. *Justin*

Les références de Justin à la croix et à la crucifixion sont nombreuses, et, tant dans la *Première Apologie* que dans le *Dialogue avec Tryphon*, interviennent essentiellement en rapport avec des références scripturaires. Certaines figurent dans les deux ouvrages, de sorte que nous les aborderons conjointement, dans la partie consacrée au *Dialogue*.[9]

La Première Apologie

Au chapitre 55 de sa *Première Apologie*, Justin montre que rien dans le monde ne peut exister sans la croix, et que tout ce qui est efficace ou symbolise l'autorité revêt cette forme. Il existe une sorte de préfiguration naturelle de la croix qui est envisagée ici comme instrument de force et de victoire. La symbolique développée relève de trois types: des objets performants tout d'abord, comme la voilure d'un navire, nommée trophée, et la charrue; l'anatomie humaine ensuite, avec la station debout, la faculté d'étendre les mains[10] et le nez, organe de la respiration; des attributs de pouvoir enfin, comme les étendards, à quoi Justin ajoute subtilement: "quand vos empereurs viennent de

---

[8] Le Pseudo-Barnabé insère ici une citation d'Ésa 12:4.

[9] Sur Justin, voir l'étude de Michel Fédou, "La vision de la Croix dans l'œuvre de saint Justin philosophe et martyr," *Recherches Augustiniennes* 19 (1984): 29–110; Oskar Skarsaune, *The Proof from Prophecy. A Study in Justin Martyr's Proof-Text Tradition: Text-Type, Provenance, Theological Profile* (NovTSup 56; Leiden: Brill, 1987). Les traductions sont celles de Charles Munier en *Saint Justin Apologie pour les chrétiens* (Paradosis 39; Fribourg, Suisse: Éditions Universitaires, 1995) pour l'*Apologie*, et de *Justin Martyr: Œuvres complètes* (Bibliothèque; Paris: Migne, 1994) pour le *Dialogue avec Tryphon*.

[10] Allusion à Ésa 65:2 et Exod 17:8–13.

mourir, vous consacrez leurs images sous cette forme," suggérant que les autorités emploient les mêmes insignes que ce qui a assuré la victoire du Christ qu'elles persécutent.

La chapitre 60 affirme que le philosophe Platon emprunta des théories aux prophètes juifs tout en ne saisissant qu'imparfaitement ce qu'ils disaient. C'est la personne du Fils de Dieu qu'il envisageait quand il écrivit dans le *Timée*: "Il l'a imprimé en chi dans l'univers."[11] Selon Justin, Platon aurait emprunté cette idée à l'épisode du serpent d'airain de Nombres 21, mais sans le comprendre vraiment, et s'il vit bien qu'il était question du fils de Dieu, il ne saisit pas que le récit évoquait une croix et crut qu'il s'agissait d'un chiasme.

Justin reconnaît par conséquent dans le serpent d'airain une préfiguration de la croix du Christ. De plus, il admet que Platon en eut une vision partielle. Mais pense-t-il que le philosophe eut raison de voir le Fils de Dieu imprimé dans l'univers, et reprend-t-il cette idée à son compte? En d'autres termes, la vérité perçue par Platon concerne-t-elle la reconnaissance du Fils de Dieu seulement ou également sa possible impression en chi dans l'univers? Et puisque Justin admet une part d'erreur chez Platon, sur quoi porte-t-elle? Assurément sur la confusion entre la croix préfigurée par le serpent d'airain et le chi. Également sur le fait que le Fils de Dieu a été imprimé dans l'univers? Cela est problématique, et il nous semble difficile de déterminer ce qu'a effectivement voulu dire Justin.[12] En tout cas, il nous paraît qu'il ne faut pas tenir pour assuré que, pour Justin, le Fils de Dieu est imprimé en chi dans l'univers ni voir trop rapidement dans ses propos l'expression d'une vision cosmique de la croix.

Quoi qu'il en soit de l'intention profonde de Justin, la chose a été écrite. Elle sera répétée et influencera la pensée d'autres auteurs. Deux idées importantes ont été lancées: le Fils de Dieu s'étend corporellement aux dimensions de l'univers et cela se fait selon un mode qui évoque la crucifixion; cette extension est mise en rapport avec la crucifixion historique de Jésus, celle que préfigure l'érection du serpent d'airain.

Le Dialogue avec Tryphon

Trois ensembles doivent être pris en considération du *Dialogue avec Tryphon*.

Le chapitre 40

Le chapitre 40 du *Dialogue avec Tryphon* voit dans l'agneau pascal d'Exode 12 un symbole de la souffrance de la croix du fait qu'il est disposé comme un crucifié, une des broches le traversant de bas en haut tandis que l'autre lui maintient les pattes écartées. Ce registre d'idée rappelle les comparaisons de la *Première Apologie* 55 où le mot "forme" est utilisé, comme ici.

---

[11] Il s'agit d'une allusion au *Tim.* 34a–37c, où il est question de l'âme du monde. Le passage ne se trouve pas tel quel dans cette œuvre.

[12] Voir notre étude de ce passage dans Prieur, "La croix vivante," 40–44.

Les chapitres 71 à 74

Aux chapitres 71 à 74 de son *Dialogue* Justin donne des exemples de passages de la Septante que, selon lui, les docteurs juifs ont modifié dans leurs nouvelles traductions prétendues plus fidèles à l'hébreu afin de supprimer ce qui attestait que le crucifié était Dieu, homme et ressuscité. Le premier est censé figurer chez Esdras, une citation qui n'est pourtant nullement repérable dans cet écrit:

> Esdras dit au peuple: "Cette Pâque est notre Sauveur et notre refuge. Si vous réfléchissez et que vous monte au cœur cette pensée que nous devons l'humilier sur un signe, que nous espérerons ensuite en lui, ce lieu ne sera point désert à jamais, dit le Seigneur des Puissances; mais si vous ne croyez pas en lui, si vous n'écoutez pas son message, vous serez la risée des nations!" [Justin, *Dial.* 72.1].[13]

Le second exemple est clairement repérable en Jér 11:19, avec la formule "jetons du bois sur son pain" qui caractérise la Septante. Le rapprochement avec Ésa 53:7 permet à Justin de reconnaître la crucifixion dans cette formule, le bois représentant naturellement la croix. A vrai dire, c'est peut-être cette seule formule qui manque dans les traductions juives de la Bible en question, et non pas tout le verset cité, car à cet endroit, notre auteur ne paraît pas très sûr de son fait et concède que ce passage figure dans quelques exemplaires présents dans les synagogues juives.

Le troisième exemple est emprunté au Ps 95:10^{LXX} où, selon Justin, les mots "le Seigneur a régné" étaient suivis de "depuis le bois." En réalité, cette forme longue du passage est absente de la Septante et manque curieusement également dans la citation très littérale que fait ensuite Justin de la totalité du Psaume. Il a dû la connaître dans le recueil de *Testimonia* qu'il utilise ici et qui incluait la citation modifiée de Jér 11:19 et le texte attribué à Esdras. Il la connaissait en tout cas par une harmonie du Ps 95:1–10^{LXX} et de 1 Chr 16:23–31 qu'il cite dans la *Première Apologie* 41 et qui contient l'ajout "depuis le bois."

Les chapitres 86 à 105

Les chapitres 86 à 105 du *Dialogue avec Tryphon* débutent par cette phrase "Les Écritures nous montrent donc qu'après avoir été crucifié, il doit revenir à nouveau dans la gloire" et sont principalement consacrés à la crucifixion et à la mort de Jésus.

Le chapitre 86 introduit un long catalogue de références bibliques par ces mots: "écoutez comment ce Jésus a eu pour symbole l'arbre de vie." On croise tout d'abord la figure de Moïse porteur d'un bâton pour libérer le peuple. Il sépare les eaux de la mer, fait jaillir de l'eau d'un rocher, rend douce l'eau de Mara. Vient ensuite Jacob qui jette des bâtons dans les auges des brebis

---

[13] On la trouve chez Lactance, *Inst.* 4.18.22.

et qui, grâce à son bâton, traverse un fleuve. Il voit une échelle sur laquelle Dieu est appuyé, et Justin de préciser que celui-ci n'est pas le Père, ce qui laisse penser que pour lui cette échelle est une représentation de la croix sur laquelle se trouve le Christ. L'auteur évoque ensuite la floraison du bâton d'Aaron, le bâton de la racine de Jessé, l'arbre planté près d'un cours d'eau du Ps 1:3, le palmier du Ps 91:13^{LXX}, le chêne de Mambré, les soixante-dix saules et les douze sources trouvées par le peuple après sa traversée du Jourdain, le bâton et la baguette par lesquels Dieu console selon le Ps 22:4^{LXX}, le bois grâce auquel Élisée repêche un fer de hache, seule de ces préfigurations, il faut le préciser, explicitement rapportée à la croix par Justin.

Six des textes cités associent le bois et l'eau, ce qui permet à Justin d'affirmer que lors du baptême le Christ a racheté les croyants par la crucifixion sur le bois et la purification de l'eau. Ce qui doit être rapproché du *Dialogue* 138 où le salut de Noé par le bois de l'arche est présenté comme un symbole du salut en Christ par l'eau, la foi et le bois. Pour finir, le chapitre 86 se réfère encore au bâton qui désigna Juda comme père des enfants de Thamar.

Il est très vraisemblable que l'ensemble de ce chapitre doive être compris comme énonçant une série de préfigurations de la croix comme arbre de vie, et, mis à part le Psaume 1, ces textes sont mis pour la première fois en rapport avec la croix, et beaucoup ne le seront pas par un autre auteur.

Les chapitres 89 à 99 du *Dialogue* s'attachent pour leur part à montrer que le Christ devait être crucifié en dépit de la malédiction prononcée en Deut 21:23 sur ceux dont le corps a été pendu.[14] Justin pose tout d'abord que les prophètes ont fait des révélations par le biais de figures (ch. 90), après quoi son argumentation consiste essentiellement à montrer que Moïse, qui proféra la malédiction, est aussi celui qui annonça la croix par des figures. La démonstration s'organise autour des deux textes déjà rencontrés dans la *Lettre du Pseudo-Barnabé*, auxquels Justin fait plusieurs allusions.

Dans le combat contre Amaleq (ch. 90), ce sont les bras étendus de Moïse réalisant le signe de la croix, non pas sa prière, et la présence de Josué homonyme de Jésus à la tête du combat, qui permit aux Israélites de vaincre.[15] Étroitement liée à ce récit est la préfiguration suggérée par le Deut 33:13–17, dont Justin reproduit notamment le verset 17: "sa beauté est celle du taureau, ses cornes sont des cornes d'unicorne: par elle il frappe de sa corne les nations ensemble jusqu'au bout de la terre" (*Dial.* 91.1). Et l'auteur de se livrer à une comparaison très réaliste de la croix à une ou à des cornes et d'expliquer que les nations ont reçu les coups de corne du Christ, soit que les hommes, pénétrés de douleur, se soient convertis, soit que, pour ne s'être

---

[14] Voir l'étude de W. C. van Unnik, "Der Fluch der Gekreuzigten: Deuteronium 21, 23 in der Deutung Justinus des Märtyrers," dans *Theologia crucis—Signum crucis: Festschrift für Erich Dinkler zum 70. Geburtstag* (éd. Carl Andresen et Gunter Klein; Tübingen: Mohr, 1979), 483–99.

[15] Le récit est également évoqué aux chapitres 97, 111, 112, et 131.

pas convertis, ils aient couru à leur ruine. Il comparera encore la croix à une corne au chapitre 105, à partir du Ps 21:22^{LXX}: "Sauve-moi de la gueule du lion, et sauve mon humilité des cornes des unicornes."

Justin en vient ensuite au serpent d'airain (*Dial.* 91.3–4), qui sera évoqué encore plusieurs fois en compagnie de celui de la victoire sur Amaleq (chs. 111–112 et 131). C'est avec force qu'il souligne que ce récit ne doit pas être compris comme s'il fallait mettre sa confiance en un serpent, mais qu'il signifie deux choses: par Jésus crucifié, la mort atteindra le serpent, à savoir le diable; et ce même crucifié sera cause de salut pour ceux qui se réfugieront en lui. Plus bas (ch. 94), il lève à son tour la contradiction avec l'ordre de ne pas faire d'image en déclarant que l'intention de Moïse en érigeant le serpent était de proclamer le salut en Christ. Si bien que deux contradictions avec des préceptes de la loi sont levées: l'interdiction de se faire des images, la malédiction du pendu au bois.

Comme la *Première Apologie* 35, le chapitre 98 du *Dialogue* mentionne enfin la préfiguration d'Ésa 65:2, "J'ai étendu mes mains sur un peuple incrédule et contradicteur," suivie d'une citation complète du Psaume 21.

La réflexion de Justin sur la croix et la crucifixion se développe en contexte polémique. Dans un tel contexte, la référence aux Écritures est décisive, en direction des païens pour montrer que Jésus est l'accomplissement de prophéties anciennes, en direction des Juifs pour établir qu'il est bien le Messie annoncé par leurs Écritures.

Il se montre attentif à la notion de symbole. Selon la *Première Apologie* 55, tout ce qui a été dit au sujet de Jésus dans l'Ancien Testament l'a été de manière symbolique, et la crucifixion est le symbole de la force et de l'autorité du Christ. Une symbolique que ne comprennent ni les démons qui ont essayé de travestir la révélation (*Première Apologie* 54), ni les Juifs qui ne reconnaissent pas les symboles là où ils figurent dans les Écritures (*Dialogue* 112). Justin reconnaît également des formes de la croix dans la nature ou des objets de force et de pouvoir.

La réflexion de Justin porte davantage sur le discernement de ces symboles et de ces formes que sur le sens même de la croix pour le salut. Cette signification est pourtant clairement indiquée: la croix est un instrument de force et de victoire sur tous les ennemis, tant démoniaque qu'humains. Elle est également un instrument de pouvoir et de règne sur l'ensemble de la race humaine. Selon la manière dont on comprend le développement de la *Première Apologie* 60, on peut aussi reconnaître à la crucifixion, non pas à la croix, une fonction cosmique du Christ imprimé en chi dans l'univers.[16]

---

[16] En *Dial.* 131.2 et 134.5, Justin utilise l'expression "mystère de la croix."

III. *Ignace et Polycarpe*[17]

Ignace

La crucifixion est au cœur de la sotériologie d'Ignace, et, comme Paul dont il est tributaire, il parle de la croix du Christ ou de la croix de manière absolue; ainsi dans sa *Lettre aux Éphésiens* (18:1) qui se réfère à 1 Corinthiens (1:18–25) de l'apôtre. S'il ne précise pas de quelle manière la croix et la crucifixion du Christ apportent le salut, Ignace affirme la réalité des souffrances et de cette crucifixion en polémique avec ceux qui les nient (*Aux Tralliens* 9–11; *Aux Smyrniotes*).

En revanche, il emploie un langage imagé qui concerne la vie chrétienne et exprime l'union au Christ et par le Christ. En *Éph.* 9.1, il indique que les chrétiens de cette Église ont su résister aux porteurs de mauvaises doctrines parce qu'ils sont "élevés jusqu'en haut par la machine (μηχανή) de Jésus-Christ, qui est la croix."[18] En *Trall.* 11.2, toujours en polémique contre les négateurs des souffrances du Christ, il compare la croix à un arbre dont les croyants sont les rameaux et, de ce fait, portent du fruit. Elle unit les membres du Christ qui est leur tête.[19] En *Smyrniotes* (1:1) enfin, encore en polémique, Ignace énonce une confession de foi précédée d'une action de grâce où est affirmé que les chrétiens de Smyrne "sont achevés dans une foi inébranlable, comme s'ils étaient cloués de chair et d'esprit à la croix du Christ." Dans ces trois passages, la croix est un agent unificateur des croyants, cette union s'effectuant en Christ; en même temps qu'elle distingue les croyants des porteurs de mauvaises doctrines.

Selon Ignace, l'attachement spirituel à la croix, qui présuppose la reconnaissance des souffrances de Jésus, fonde et justifie le martyre des chrétiens en général et le sien en particulier. Tel est vraisemblablement ce que signifient ces mots difficiles à interpréter d'*Éph.* 18.1: "Mon esprit est la victime (περίψημα)[20] de la croix." C'est ce que confirme *Tralliens* 9–11, car si le Christ n'a souffert qu'en apparence, le martyre n'a pas de sens et il faut y voir un mensonge contre le Seigneur.

---

[17] Les traductions sont celles de Pierre-Thomas Camelot, *Ignace d'Antioche; Polycarpe de Smyrne, Lettres; Martyre de Polycarpe* (4ᵉ éd., rev. et corr.; SC 10 bis; Paris: Cerf, 1969; réimpr., 1998).

[18] William R. Schoedel (*Ignatius of Antioch: A Commentary on the Letters of Ignatius of Antioch* [Hermeneia; Philadelphia: Fortress, 1985], 65–67) récuse l'interprétation gnostique de μηχανή proposée par Heinrich Schlier (*Religionsgeschichtliche Untersuchungen zu den Ignatiusbriefen* [BZNW 8; Giessen: Topelmann, 1929], 110–24) à partir de la roue des Manichéens.

[19] Cf. 1 Cor 6:15 et 12:12–27; Col 1:18.

[20] Sur ce mot, qui figure dans 1 Cor 4:13, voir la note de Camelot, *Ignace d'Antioche*, 64–65.

Dans la *Lettre aux Philadelphiens* (8:2), apparemment en polémique contre des judaïsants cette fois, Ignace s'oppose enfin à ceux qui ne veulent croire que ce qui se trouve dans les "archives" (ἀρχεῖα), c'est-à-dire l'Ancien Testament. Quant à lui, ses archives sont vivantes, et c'est par elles qu'il veut être justifié. Ce sont le Christ, "sa croix, sa mort, sa résurrection et la foi qui vient de lui." La croix en fait partie.

La Lettre aux Philippiens *de Polycarpe de Smyrne*

Dans les chapitres 7 et 8 de sa *Lettre aux Philippiens*, Polycarpe de Smyrne reproche à des faux frères de ne pas confesser que Jésus-Christ est venu dans la chair, ni non plus le "témoignage de la croix." Cette polémique rejoint celle d'Ignace, mais vise plus généralement les négateurs de l'incarnation, tandis que la précédente, vraisemblablement du fait de son contexte de martyre, se concentrait sur les contestataires de la réalité de la souffrance de Jésus. Polycarpe parle également de la croix de manière absolue et la situe au cœur de l'enseignement chrétien. En conclusion de ce passage, il exhorte ses lecteurs à rester attachés au Christ qui, selon une citation légèrement modifiée de 1 Pier 2:24, "a porté nos fautes en son propre corps sur le bois."

La croix figure encore au chapitre 12 de la lettre, où Polycarpe demande de prier "pour ceux qui vous persécutent et vous haïssent, et pour les ennemis de la croix," une formule qui doit être rapprochée de Phil 3:18, mais où les ennemis sont des persécuteurs extérieurs plutôt qu'une catégorie de chrétiens.

IV. *Méliton de Sardes*[21]

Deux textes de cet évêque mettent en rapport la crucifixion et l'œuvre créationnelle du Christ. Son écrit *Sur la Pâque*, vraisemblablement une homélie, tout d'abord, qui contient une envolée rhétorique sur le paradoxe inouï et scandaleux de la crucifixion: "Celui qui suspendit la terre est suspendu, celui qui fixa les cieux est fixé, celui qui est le Maître est outragé, celui qui est le roi d'Israël est écarté par une main israëlite." La Fragment XIV ensuite, qui conserve une suite d'affirmations antithétiques sur la double condition du Fils de Dieu et s'achève par ces mots: "Il se tenait devant Pilate et il était assis avec son Père; il était fixé au bois et soutenait l'univers."[22] Ces deux textes portent davantage sur la crucifixion que sur la croix elle-même, mais ils ont de l'intérêt car ils sont les premiers témoins d'une mise en rapport de la crucifixion et du soutien de l'univers, qui sera exploité plus tard sous la forme d'un soutien par la crucifixion ou par la croix elle-même. Chez Méliton, ce

---

[21] Les traductions sont celles d'Othmar Perler, *Méliton de Sardes, Sur la Pâque et fragments* (SC 123; Paris: Cerf, 1966). Voir l'étude de Raniero Cantalamessa, "Méliton de Sardes: Une christologie antignostique du IIᵉ siècle," *RevScRel* 37 (1963): 1–26.

[22] Le même genre de paradoxe est exprimé dans le Fragment XIII.

n'est pas par sa crucifixion que le Christ soutient le monde, et l'homélie évoque plutôt le caractère passé de l'œuvre de création, afin de formuler le scandale de la crucifixion. Dans le Fragment, la dimension paradoxale n'est pas absente, quoique l'objectif ne soit pas de mettre en évidence le scandale; crucifixion et soutien de l'univers sont simultanés.

Parmi les influences vétérotestamentaires, citons pour finir le sacrifice d'Isaac dans les Fragments IX, XI et XII, qui combinent la représentation du Christ comme agneau et les éléments du sacrifice du fils d'Abraham, voyant dans le bélier pris dans un buisson une image de Jésus crucifié et dans le buisson la croix elle-même.

Conclusions

Les documents que nous avons examinés sont les plus anciens après ceux du Nouveau Testament et couvrent une période d'environ trente ou quarante ans.

On peut relever le vocabulaire employé pour désigner la croix, souvent métaphorique et tributaire de préfigurations vétérotestamentaires. Il y a tout d'abord le bois, influencé par Deut 21:23, et l'arbre. Le mot signe, qui figure chez le Pseudo-Barnabé et Justin, vient de Nmbr 21:8, tandis que l'extension des mains est inspirée d'Ésa 65:2 et Exod 17:8–13.[23] Nous avons aussi rencontré le mot corne, à partir du Ps 21:22 et de Deut 33:17. Deux images d'origine profane sont également apparues: le trophée et la machine.

La réflexion sur la croix est largement tributaire du besoin de trouver dans les Écritures juives des préfigurations de cet événement.[24] Cela est particulièrement vrai des auteurs les plus anciens qui ont en commun plusieurs citations: les Ps 1:3 et 95:10, la combinaison d'Exod 17:8–13 (combat de Moïse conte Amaleq) et de Nmbr 21:6–9 (serpent d'airain), avec l'allusion à la contradiction apparente avec l'interdiction de se faire des images. A quoi il faut ajouter Ésa 65:2. Le Pseudo-Barnabé et Justin sont manifestement tributaires d'un recueil de testimonia sur la mort et la crucifixion du Christ.

La croix a également inspiré à Justin des rapprochements avec la nature ou des objets: la voilure, la charrue, les étendards.

Nos auteurs ne poussent pas très loin la réflexion sur la portée sotériologique de la croix. Son importance est certes affirmée, mais les raisons n'en sont guère

---

[23] Cf. la *Did.* 16.6: "Et alors les signes de la vérité apparaîtront: premièrement le signe de l'extension dans le ciel." Traduction de Willy Rordorf, *La doctrine des Douze Apotres* = *Didaché: Introduction, texte critique, traduction, notes, appendice, annexe et index* (2ᵉ éd., rev. et augm.; SC 248 bis; Paris: Cerf, 1998), qui y reconnaît la croix (pp. 198–99). L'extension des mains et le signe du Seigneur sont également associés dans l'*Ode de Salomon* 27.

[24] C'est ce qu'indique la *Prédication de Pierre*: "Nous y (les livres que nous tenons des prophètes) avons trouvé sa venue, sa mort, sa croix . . ." (cité par Clément d'Alexandrie, *Strom.* 6.15 §128.1).

développées. On ne reconnaît pas ce que l'on pourrait appeler une théologie de la croix,[25] de plus, les significations reconnues à la croix diffèrent d'un texte à l'autre. Naturellement, la réalité de la crucifixion est affirmée chez les auteurs que nous avons retenus. Mais un examen de documents contemporains aurait révélé que d'autres auteurs contestent cette réalité ou, sans le faire, développent d'autres représentations de la croix.

Le Pseudo-Barnabé est celui qui développe le plus le sens de cette mort à laquelle il confère, grâce aux préfigurations vétérotestamentaires, une portée sacrificielle. Justin et Méliton lui reconnaissent également une telle signification, en référence à l'agneau pascal. Sans en tirer les mêmes conséquences, le Pseudo-Barnabé et Ignace connaissent une identification entre la croix et le Christ, et chez le second, celle-ci fonde une exhortation à s'unir à la croix et, par ce moyen, au Christ, ce qui se réalise par le martyre. Dans un contexte apologétique Justin développe l'idée de la croix comme instrument de victoire et de domination par le biais d'images empruntées à l'Ancien Testament ou à la vie concrète, et par le recours à l'adjonction de "depuis le bois" au Ps 95:10. C'est ainsi que la croix, lieu de souffrance et d'humiliation est para-doxalement devenue un instrument de force. Une évolution qui est déjà en germe dans la vision cosmique de la croix suggérée, chacun à leur manière, par Justin et Méliton. Il n'y a pas jusqu'au baptême qui ne figure aussi dans la réflexion sur la croix de certains de nos auteurs, par le biais des textes asso-ciant l'eau et un arbre.[26]

---

[25] Kuhn ("Jesus als Gekreuzigter," 1–46) aboutit à la même conclusion, sauf pour les lettres d'Ignace.

[26] L'*Ascension d'Ésaïe* parle de croire au Seigneur et à sa croix pour être sauvé (3.18), et de mettre sa confiance en lui et dans sa croix (9.26).

CHAPTER TWENTY-EIGHT

"ONE BREAD GATHERED FROM MANY PIECES" (*DID.* 9:4): THE CAREER OF AN EARLY CHRISTIAN ALLEGORY

PETER VOGT

Early Christian texts are texts with a history. This is obviously true in the sense that any given text has a history of how it came into being under specific historical circumstances. Much of New Testament scholarship is occupied with investigating this sort of "history of origin" (*Entstehungsgeschichte*). Yet, early Christian texts also have a history in the sense that once they came into being they began to circulate, were proclaimed and interpreted, were passed on from one generation to the next and in this process exerted their influence on the formation of the Christian tradition. This kind of history, sometimes referred to as "history of effects" (*Wirkungsgeschichte*), describes their ongoing transmission, reception, and interpretation throughout the history of the church. Like a valuable object of art that has been handed down from antiquity to the present through various circumstances and events, so each early Christian text possesses its particular history, which is the history of its *traditio* through the changing scenes of time and space.

One example of a modern biblical commentary that is attentive to this kind of history is the series *Evangelisch-Katholischer Kommentar zum Neuen Testament*, for which François Bovon has been writing the commentary on the Gospel of Luke.[1] Here the discussion of each pericope includes besides its historical critical exegesis also a review of several passages from patristic, medieval, or modern sources that illustrate the text's *Wirkungsgeschichte*. For the parable of the Good Samaritan, to cite an example from François Bovon's commentary, the discussion of the *Wirkungsgeschichte* includes references to Irenaeus, Origen, Ambrose, Augustine, Luther, and Calvin with widely different interpretations.[2] Looking at an early Christian text in this way clearly opens up new dimensions of understanding. Still, as François Bovon has noted in the introduction to his commentary, very little scholarly work has been done in this area so far, and it seems that the available studies focus on scriptural passages rather than apocryphal or extra-canonical texts.

The following discussion will present the case of the extraordinary *Wirkungsgeschichte* of an early Christian motif: the allegory of the bread gathered from

---

[1] François Bovon, *Das Evangelium nach Lukas* (EKKNT 3; Zürich: Benziger Verlag, 1989–).

[2] Ibid., 2:93–98.

many pieces in *Did.* 9:4.[3] One of the earliest extra-canonical Christian texts, the *Didache* had some circulation during the patristic period but was subsequently lost and remained unknown to modern scholarship until its rediscovery in 1873. Its ninth and tenth chapters contain the oldest known liturgical prayer for the consecration of the Eucharist. Here, we find the allegorical comparison of the church with the Eucharistic bread attested for the first time:

ὥσπερ ἦν τοῦτο [τὸ] κλάσμα διεσκορπισμένον ἐπάνω τῶν ὀρέων καὶ συναχθὲν ἐγένετο ἕν, οὕτω συναχθήτω σου ἡ ἐκκλησία ἀπὸ τῶν περάτων τῆς γῆς εἰς τὴν σὴν βασιλείαν.[4]	Just as this broken bread was scattered upon the mountains and then was gathered together and became one, so may your church be gathered together from the ends of the earth into your kingdom.[5]

Decisive for the power of this image is the ecclesiological interpretation of the Eucharistic bread. Its physical property of being composed of many pieces is linked to a particular theological connotation (cf. 1 Cor 10:16–17) against an eschatological horizon (cf. *Did.* 10:5). The unity of the bread symbolizes the unity of the church and stands as a sign of hope for the final gathering and unification of its scattered members.

The studies of Luigi Clerici and Kurt Niederwimmer have identified several parallels to the allegory of the bread in ancient Greek and Coptic liturgies.[6] Although it is impossible to say whether these parallels are directly dependent on the *Didache*, the similarities between the *Did.* 9:4 and other instances are striking and suggest the presence of a common tradition. It appears that from very early on the image of the bread gathered from many pieces must have enjoyed a wide-ranging circulation. Yet while Clerici and Niederwimmer see this tradition as a liturgical tradition limited essentially to early North-African Christianity, this essay will show that the allegory of the bread has a much broader *Wirkungsgeschichte*, involving a wide variety of liter-

---

[3] During my research on the idea of the church as a community of love, François Bovon first brought the image of the bread in *Did.* 9:4 to my attention. Once alerted, I repeatedly noticed it elsewhere, and I am pleased to present here as a tribute to him its *Wirkungsgeschichte* all the way to Jean Calvin.

[4] Andreas Lindemann and Henning Paulsen, eds., *Die Apostolischen Väter, Griechisch-deutsche Parallelausgabe auf der Grundlage der Ausgaben von Franz Xaver Funk/Karl Bihlmeyer und Molly Whittaker* (Tübingen: Mohr, 1992), 14. I gratefully acknowledge the assistance of Dr. Iain Maclean, James Madison University, and Dr. Beverly Kienzle, Harvard Divinity School, in the translation of the Greek and Latin texts.

[5] Michael W. Holmes, ed., *The Apostolic Fathers* (trans. J. B. Lightfoot and J. R. Harmer; 2d ed.; Grand Rapids: Baker, 1989), 154.

[6] See Luigi Clerici, *Einsammlung der Zerstreuten: Liturgiegeschichtliche Untersuchung zur Vor- und Nachgeschichte der Fürbitte für die Kirche in Didache 9,4 und 10,5* (Liturgiewissenschaftliche Quellen und Forschungen 44; Münster: Aschendorff, 1966), 104–12, and Kurt Niederwimmer, *Die Didache* (Kommentar zu den Apostolischen Vätern 1; Göttingen: Vandenhoeck & Ruprecht, 1989), 185–91.

ary forms and extending beyond the patristic period and through the Middle Ages to the time of the Reformation.

Patristic texts

We begin our survey with the seven liturgical texts mentioned by Clerici and Niederwimmer. The earliest witness is probably the following passage from the *Apostolic Constitutions* (VII, 25.3), a collection of ecclesiastical law and liturgy of Syrian origin (ca. 350), which quotes *Did.* 9:4 almost verbatim:

Σὺ δέσποτα παντοκράτορ, Θεὲ αἰώνιε, ὥσπερ ἦν τοῦτο διεσκορπισμένον καὶ συναχθὲν ἐγένετο εἰς ἄρτος, οὕτως συνάγαγέ σου τὴν ἐκκλησίαν ἀπὸ τῶν περάτων τῆς γῆς εἰς τὴν σὴν βασιλείαν.[7]	Do you, O Lord almighty, eternal God, so gather together your church from the ends of the earth into your kingdom, as this [corn] was once scattered, and is now gathered together and become one loaf.[8]

The second text comes from the treatise *De virginitate*, attributed to Athanasius, bishop of Alexandria (ca. 296–373). Here, the allegory of the bread is taken out of the Eucharistic context and is used within a blessing for a regular meal:

καθὼς ὁ ἄρτος οὗτος ἐσκορπι- σμένος ὑπάρχει ὁ ἐπάνω ταύτης τῆς τραπέζης καὶ συναχθεὶς ἐγένετω ἕν, οὕτως ἐπισυναχθήτο σου ἡ ἐκκλησία ἀπὸ τῶν περάτων τῆς γῆς εἰς τὴν βασιλείαν σου.[9]	Just as this bread, having been scattered, is upon this table, and having been gathered, has become one, so also may your church be gathered together from the ends of the earth into your kingdom.

A third text is the Eucharistic rite of St. Serapion, who served in the middle of the fourth century as Bishop of Thmuis (Egypt). The allegory of the bread occurs between the words of institution as a prayer for the unity of the church.

καὶ ὥσπερ ὁ ἄρτος οὗτος ἐσκορ- πισμένος ἦν ἐπάνω τῶν ὀρέων καὶ συναχθεὶς ἐγένετο εἰς ἕν, οὕτω καὶ τὴν ἁγίαν σου	And as this bread was scattered over the mountains and was gathered together and became one loaf, so also gather together your holy Church

---

[7] Marcel Metzger, *Les Constitutions Apostoliques* (vol. 3; SC 336; Paris: Cerf, 1987), 54.

[8] W. Jardine Grisbrooke, ed., *The Liturgical Portions of the Apostolic Constitutions: A Text for Students* (Alcuin/GROW liturgical study 13–14; Bramcote, Nottingham: Grove Books, 1990), 18.

[9] *Virg.*, 13, in Eduard Freiherr von der Goltz, ed., *ΛΟΓΟΣ ΣΩΤΗΡΙΑΣ ΠΡΟΣ ΤΗΝ ΠΑΡΘΕΝΟΝ (De virginitate): Eine echte Schrift des Athanasius XIII* (TUGAL 29; Leipzig: J. C. Hinrich, 1905), 47.

ἐκκλησίαν σύναξον ἐκ παντὸς
ἔθνους καὶ πάσης χώρας καὶ
πάσης πόλεως καὶ κώμης καὶ
οἴκου καὶ ποίησον μίαν ζῶσαν
καθολικὴν ἐκκλησίαν.[10]

from every nation and every region
and every city and village and house
and make one living catholic Church.[11]

The fourth text comes from the *Dêr Balizeh* papyrus, a Greek codex (ca. 6th century) from Egypt. Here, the allegory of the bread occurs directly before the words of institution. While the phrasing of this passage shows some interesting similarities to Serapion's text, the scope of the allegory has been extended to include also the wine.

[και ον τρο]πον ο[υτος ο αρ]τος
εσκορπισμενος ην [ε]πανω [των ορεων]
και βο[υ]νων και αρουρων κα[ι
συμμ]ιγεις ε[γεν]ετο εν σωμα . . . οσω
[. . . καθ]ως ο οινος ο[υτος] ο εξελθων
εκ τη[ς αγιας α]μπελου Δ[αυειδ] και
το υδωρ εξ αμ[νου αμω]μου και συμ-
[μικτα] .ειο εγενετο εν [μυ]στηριον
Ουτ[ως] επ[ισυνα]ξον τη[ν]
καθολικην [εκ]κλη[σιαν του
Ι(ησο)υ Χ(ριστο)υ].[12]

In the same manner in which this
bread was scattered upon the
mountains and hills and farms, and
having been mixed together, became
one body [. . .] so this wine, which
came forth from the holy vine of
David, and the water from the
undefiled lamb and mixed together
became one mystery. Thus gather
together the catholic church of
Jesus Christ.

The remaining texts mentioned by Clerici and Niederwimmer are three ancient Ethiopian liturgies of uncertain date. The Anaphora of Jacob of Sarug presents the allegory of the bread in the context of an intercessory prayer for the members of the church:

> [Priest:] I pray for your people and your heirs [. . .] and if there is someone among the laity whose mind has strayed from you, then grant that he may enter into your will, just as you have gathered this bread, even though it was scattered on the mountains and on the plain country and in the valleys, and in being gathered it became one single loaf of sacrifice.[13]

The Anaphora of St. John places the allegory immediately after the words of the institution, alluding to its closing sentence "do this in memory of me as often as you gather together":

---

[10] *Euchologii Serapionis* 13.13, in Johannes Quasten, *Monumenta eucharistica et liturgica vetustissima*, pars I (Florilegium Patristicum 8; Bonn: Peter Hanstein, 1935), 62.

[11] R. J. S. Barrett-Lennard, ed., *The Sacramentary of Sarapion of Thmuis: A Text for Students with Introduction, Translation, and Commentary* (Alcuin/GROW Liturgical Study 25; Bramcote, Nottingham: Grove Books, 1993), 26.

[12] *Dêr Balizeh*, fol. 2, 3–11, in C. H. Roberts and B. Capelle, eds., *An Early Euchologium: The Dêr-Balizeh Papyrus Enlarged and Reedited* (Bibliothèque du Muséon 23; Louvain: Bureaux du Muséon, 1949), 26.

[13] Sebastian Euringer, "Die athiopischen Anaphoren des Hl. Evangelisten Johannes des Donnersohnes und des Hl. Jacobus von Sarug," *OCP* 33 (1934): 97.

O Lord, even we, who have gathered to commemorate your suffering and to participate with you in your resurrection from the dead, are praying to you, O Lord, our God: as this bread was gathered, although it was scattered between the mountains and hills and on the plain country and in the valleys, and in being gathered became one single and perfect bread, so gather us away from any evil thought of sin to your perfect faith.[14]

The Anaphora of St. Gregorius, finally, places the allegory of the bread just before the words of the institution in a diptychon, where Christ is invoked as the one who rectifies the sinners and gathers those who are scattered:

As you have gathered this bread, although it was scattered upon the mountains and hills, and as it became through the gathering one perfect loaf, so gather also us through your divinity from every evil thought to your perfect faith.[15]

It is noteworthy that these three Ethiopian liturgies have preserved and expanded the ancient notion that the bread was scattered upon the mountains. Yet, there is an interesting shift in emphasis: the prayer for the eschatological gathering of the church has been replaced by a plea for spiritual and moral perfection.

Beyond the scope of texts listed by Clerici and Niederwimmer, we find the allegory of the bread in three other patristic writers: Cyprian of Carthage (d. 258), John Chrysostom (347–407), and Augustine (356–430).

Cyprian employs the allegory twice in his corpus of letters. In Letter 63 he discusses the spiritual meaning of the Eucharist and argues that the Eucharistic bread symbolizes the bond between Christ and the church, as well as the communion of believers within the church. The first is shown in the union of water and flour in the one loaf of bread, latter in the unity of the bread itself:

And under this same sacred image our people are represented as having been made one, for just as numerous grains are gathered, ground, and mixed all together to make into one loaf of bread, so in Christ, who is the bread of heaven, we know there is but one body and that every one of us has been fused together and made one with it.[16]

In Letter 69, discussing the danger of the Novatianist schism, Cyprian expands the allegory of the bread to include also the element of the wine.

And what is more, the very sacrifices offered by our Lord demonstrate how in Christianity men are of one mind, linked together by the bonds of a powerful and unbreakable charity. For when the Lord calls bread his own body—and bread is a conglomerate of many individual grains, made into one—He signifies that we, the people whom He bore, are united into one. Similarly,

---

[14] Ibid., 45.

[15] Oscar Löfgren and Sebastian Euringer, "Die beiden gewöhnlichen äthiopischen Gregorius-Anaphoren," *OCP* 30 (1933): 45.

[16] *Ep.* 63, 13.4, in *The Letters of St. Cyprian of Carthage* (trans. G. W. Clarke; 4 vols.; New York: Newman Press, 1984–89), 3:105 (= CCSL, 3c:408–9).

when He calls wine His own blood—and wine is pressed from a great many clusters of individual grapes, squeezed into one juice—He again indicates that we, His flock, being a multitude gathered together, are mingled and joined into one.[17]

Cyprian's version of the allegory differs in one important point from the form attested to in the *Didache* and the North African tradition: instead of describing the bread as having been scattered upon the mountains, it uses the more natural image of the bread being made out of many grains.

John Chrysostom uses the image of the grain and the bread in a homily to illustrate the meaning of 1 Cor 10:17 ("For we, who are many, are one body"):

> What is the bread? The Body of Christ. And what do they become who partake of it? The Body of Christ: not many bodies, but one body. For as the bread consisting of many grains is made one, so that the grains nowhere appear; they exist indeed, but their difference is not seen by reason of their conjunction; so are we conjoined both with each other and with Christ: there not being one body for thee, and another for thy neighbor to be nourished by, but the very same for all.[18]

Augustine, finally, refers to the allegory of the bread at least four times. The first instance occurs in his treatise on Baptism against the Donatists (ca. 404) and is a direct quote from Cyprian's Letter 69 cited above.[19] The second passage, with indirect allusion to Cyprian, can be found in his "Tractates on the Gospel of John" (ca. 406–420) in explanation of John 6:55 ("my flesh is food indeed, and my blood is drink indeed"):

> For although by food and drink men strive for this, that they hunger not and thirst not, only this food and drink truly offer this; for it makes those by whom it is taken immortal and incorruptible, that is, the very society of saints, where there will be peace and full and perfect unity. For this reason, indeed, even as men of God knew this before us, our Lord, Jesus Christ, manifested his body and blood in those things which are reduced from many to some one thing. For the one is made into one thing from many grains, the other flows together into one thing from many grapes.[20]

Augustine's Sermon 272 (ca. 408) addresses newly baptized Christians about the spiritual meaning of the Lord's Supper. Here, the image of the bread is applied not only to the unity of the church, but also to the process by which new members are received into the Christian community:

---

[17] *Ep.* 69, 5.2, in *Letters* 4:36 (= CCSL, 3c:476–77).
[18] *Hom.* 24, in *NPNF*[1] 12:140 (= PG 61:200).
[19] *De Baptismo* VII, 50,98, in *NPNF*[1] 4:511 (= PL 43:240).
[20] *Tract. Ev. Jo.* 26.17, Augustine of Hippo, *Tractates on the Gospel of John* (trans. John W. Rettig; 5 vols.; Washington: Catholic University of America Press, 1988–1995), 2:274 (= PL 35:1614).

One bread; what is this one bread? The one body which we, being many, are. Remember that bread is not made from one grain, but from many. When you were being exorcised, it's as though you were being ground. When you were baptized it's as though you were mixed into dough. When you received the fire of the Holy Spirit, it's as though you were baked. [. . .] Just as many grains are mixed into one loaf in order to produce the visible appearance of the bread, as though what holy scripture says about the faithful were happening: *They had one soul and one heart in God* (Acts 4:32); so too with the wine. Brothers and sisters, just remind yourselves what wine is made from; many grapes hang in the bunch, but the juice of the grapes is poured together in one vessel. That too is how the Lord Christ signified us, how he wished us to belong to him, how he consecrated the sacrament of our peace and unity on his table.[21]

In Sermon 227 (ca. 414–15), Augustine describes the initiation of new believers in a similar way:

In this loaf of bread you are given clearly to understand how much you should love unity. I mean, was that loaf made from one grain? Weren't there many grains of wheat? But before they came into the loaf they were all separate; they were joined together by means of water after a certain amount of pounding and crushing. Unless wheat is ground, after all, and moistened with water, it can't possibly get into this shape which is called bread. In the same way you too were being ground and pounded, as it were, by the humiliation of fasting and the sacrament of exorcism. Then came baptism, and you were, in a manner of speaking, moistened with water in order to be shaped into bread. But it's not yet bread without fire to bake it. So what does fire represent? That's the chrism, the anointing. Oil, the fire-feeder, you see, is the sacrament of the Holy Spirit.[22]

These last two texts show how creatively Augustine used the tradition that he had received from Cyprian. Through him, in turn, the allegory was passed on to the scholastics.

Medieval texts

In contrast to the varied and creative interpretations of the allegory of the bread in the patristic material, the medieval sources present us with a development that might best be described as the respectful appropriation of an established tradition. Especially passages from Cyprian and Augustine are frequently cited by medieval theologians to lend graceful and authoritative support to their arguments. Paschasius Radbertus (ca. 790–ca. 860), for example,

---

[21] John E. Rotelle, ed., *The Works of St. Augustine: Sermons* (trans. Edmund Hill; vol. 7; New Rochelle, N.Y.: New City Press, 1993), 301 (= PL 38:1247).

[22] Ibid., 6:254 (= PL 38:1100).

refers to Augustine's "Tractates on the Gospel of John" in his "Letter to Fredugard."[23] Berengar of Tours (ca. 1010–1088) explicitly cites both Cyprian's letter 69 and Augustine's "Tractates" in his "Reply to Lanfranc" during the eleventh century controversy over the Eucharist.[24] And an unknown medieval commentator of the works of Paulinus of Nola quotes passages from Cyprian, John Chrysostom, and Augustine alike to show that Christ instituted the Eucharistic elements as symbols of unity.[25]

In the medieval sources, the allegory of the bread occurs frequently in the context of scriptural interpretation. Many medieval commentaries of the Bible use the allegory in their explanation of 1 Cor 10:17 and John 6:55.[26] Here, the image of the bread serves to illumine the ideal of ecclesial unity and its inherent connection to the Eucharist. Haymo of Halberstadt (d. 853), for example, writes about the body and blood of Christ:

Sicut enim panis, qui sacratus fit corpus Christi, ex multis granis fit unus panis, et potus ille qui sanctificatus efficitur sanguis Christi, ex multis acinis fit unus potus: sic omnes digne sumentes hoc sacramentum ex multis unum corpus in Christo efficiuntur.[27]	For just as the bread, which once consecrated becomes the Body of Christ, is made one bread from many grains, and the drink, which once sanctified becomes the blood of Christ, is made one drink from many grapes, so all worthily receiving this sacrament are out of many made one body in Christ.

And Hugh of Saint Victor (d. 1142) states in a discussion of the sacraments:

Quia sicut panis ex multis granis efficitur unus, vinum ex multis racemis in vinum confluit; ita ex plurimis membris Ecclesia, quae est corpus Christi, adunatur.[28]	Because just as the bread is made one from many grains and the wine flows into wine from many clusters of grapes; thus the Church, which is the body of Christ, is made one from many members.

---

[23] *Ep. ad Fredugardum*, III/3, in *Corpus Christianorum, Continuatio Mediaevalis* (vol. 16; Turnhout: Brepols, 1961), 165.

[24] *Rescriptum contra Lanfrannum*, in *Corpus Christianorum, Continuatio Mediaevalis* (vol. 84; Turnhout: Brepols, 1988), 76–77.

[25] PL 61:841–42. There are frequent references to Augustine's exposition of John 6:55 (*Tract. Ev. Ioan.* 26.17), see, for example, PL 74:929, 92:719, 96:938–39, 100:835, 149:1460, and 186:255.

[26] For 1 Cor 10:17 see PL 103:148, 175:530, 181:917, and 191:1624. For John 6:55 see PL 114:384, 118:349, and 196:469.

[27] *De Corpore et Sanguine Domini*, in PL 118:817.

[28] *Summa Sententiarum Septem Tractatibus Distincta*, in PL 176:140. Similar passages abound: PL 103:1398, 106:68, 114:936, 162:544, 170:208, 172:554, 172:1129, 180:823, 204:717, and 217:879.

Particularly significant for the medieval period was that the allegory of the bread came to circulate widely in the following pithy formulation, often attributed to Augustine:

Sicut unus panis ex multis granis, et unum corpus ex multus membris componitur, sic Ecclesia ex multis fidelibus charitate copulante connectitur.[29]	As the one loaf of bread is formed out of many kernels of grain and one body out of many members, so the Church is joined together out of many believers through the bond of love.

This text, which neatly summarizes the allegory's significance for the scholastic view of the church, occurs both in Peter Lombard's *Sententiarum* (1158) and in the *Glossa Ordinaria* (12th century) as a marginal gloss on 1 Cor 10:17.[30]

It is not surprising that through Peter Lombard's *Sententiarum* and the *Glossa* this version of the allegory passed into the works of the later scholastics. Thus, Thomas Aquinas (ca. 1225–1274) uses the allegory of the bread twice in his *Summa Theologiae*, attributing it once to the *Glossa* and once directly to Augustine: "The Church is the gathering together of all the different baptized faithful; in the same way *bread is made of different grains of wheat and wine flows together from different grapes*, as the Gloss on 1 Corinthians 10, 17 puts it."[31] And, presenting an argument for the proposition that the sacrament of the Eucharist bestows grace:

> Consider the species under which the sacrament is given. Augustine says, *Our Lord entrusted his body and blood to those things where a single whole is rendered from many particles, for out of many grains is one thing made*, namely bread, *and from many grapes flows one thing*, namely wine. And so he cries, O sacrament of piety, O sign of unity, O bond of charity.[32]

Thomas also refers to the allegory in his commentary on Peter Lombard's *Sentences*.[33] Similar references can be found in the commentaries of Albertus Magnus, St. Bonaventure, and Richard of Mediavilla.[34]

---

[29] Peter Lombard, *Sentences*, IV, 8.4, in PL 192:857–58; cf. his commentary on 1 Cor 10:17 (PL 191:1624). The attribution to Augustine is erroneous, but a similar passage can be found in the pseudo-Augustinian *Sermones ad Fratres in Eremo* 28 (PL 40:1283): "Sicut enim multa grana unum panem conficiunt, et ex multis racemis unum vinum extrahitur; sic ex multis hominibus Christi corpus conficitur."

[30] See PL 192:857–58; and Karlfried Froehlich and Margaret T. Gibson, eds., *Biblia Latina cum Glossa Ordinaria* (Facsimile Reprint of the Editio Princeps by Adolph Rusch of Strassburg 1480/81; Turnhout: Brepols, 1992), vol. 4, left marginal note on 1 Cor 10:17 (no pagination).

[31] *Summa Theologiae* 3a 74,1, Thomas Aquinas, *Summa Theologiae: Latin Text and English Translation* (64 vols.; New York: McGraw-Hill, 1964–), 58:27.

[32] *Summa Theologiae* 3a 79,1; ibid., 59:5.

[33] Roberto Busa, ed., *S. Thomae Aquinatis Opera Omnia* (vol. 1; Stuttgart: Frommann-holzboog, 1980), 461, 474, and 479.

[34] Albertus Magnus, *Opera Omnia* (vol. 29; Paris: Ludovium Vives, 1894), 204;

Reformation texts

We turn now to the material of the Protestant Reformation, where the allegory of the bread occurs both among representatives of the magisterial Reformation and among representatives of the radical Reformation.

Martin Luther (1483–1546) was most likely familiar with the allegory of the bread through his knowledge of Peter Lombard's *Sententiarum* and the writings of Augustine and Cyprian. Perhaps the earliest reference occurs in a Latin sermon on the spiritual preparation for the Eucharist from 1518. Here Luther says about the sacrament:

> The name is Communion, the matter is the union of hearts, just as there is one faith, one baptism, one Lord, one hope, that all is mutual and common. That is also figuratively expressed in the form of the sacrament, where many grains in losing their individual difference are transformed into one bread, and likewise many berries, also in losing their difference, into one wine.[35]

Luther's distinct interpretation of the traditional image becomes more apparent in his famous "Sermon on the Blessed Sacrament of the Holy and True Body of Christ" of 1519, where he sets forth his view of the Eucharist. The central idea is the dynamic of mutual participation, which he describes elsewhere as a "joyful interchange" (*fröhlicher Wechsel und Streit*).[36] Between the believers and Christ sin is exchanged for righteousness, and among the believers themselves joy and sorrow, strength and weakness, assets and needs are held in common. The allegory of the bread serves Luther to describe this twofold process of mutual participation more closely.

> For just as the bread is made out of many grains ground and mixed together, and out of the bodies of many grains there comes the body of one bread, in which each grain loses its form and body and takes upon itself the common body of the bread; and just as the drops of wine, in losing their own form, become the body of the common wine and drink— so it is and should be with us, if we use this sacrament properly. Christ with all saints, by his love, takes upon himself our form [Phil 2:7], fights with us against sin, death, and all evil. This enkindles in us such love that we take on his form, rely upon his righteousness, life, and blessedness. And through the interchange of his blessings and our misfortunes, we become one loaf, one bread, one body, one drink, and have all things in common. O this is a great sacrament, says St. Paul, that Christ and the church are one flesh and bone [Eph 5:32]. Again through this same love, we are to be changed and to make the infirmities of all other

Bonaventura, *Opera Omnia* (vol. 4; Florence, 1889), 255; Richard of Mediavilla, *Super Quatuor Libros Sententiarum* (vol. 4; Brixiae, 1591; repr. Frankfurt: Minerva, 1963), 95 and 106–7.

[35] "*Sermo de digna praeparatione cordis pro suscipiendo sacramento Eucharistie*" (1518), in *D. Martin Luthers gesammelte Werke: Kritische Gesamtausgabe* (58 vols.; Weimar: Böhlau, 1883–), 1:329; hereafter abbreviated *WA*.

[36] *Von der Freiheit eines Christenmenschen* (1520), in *WA* 7:25.

Christians our own; we are to take upon ourselves their form and their necessity, and all the good that is within our power we are to make theirs, that they may profit from it.[37]

For Luther, the crucial feature of the allegory is that the individual grains and grapes lose their form in order to take on the common form of the bread and the wine. However, as the reference to Phil 2:7 makes clear, the point of the argument is not the complete loss of individual distinction in some sort of mystical union but rather the depth of mutual participation where each truly gives him- or herself to the other in love.

Luther frequently repeats this emphasis in his writings throughout the 1520s and 1530s. In his treatise "On the Adoration of the Sacrament" (1523), for example, he states that through the Lord's Supper the believers are united into one loaf and become, as it were, each other's food and drink.

> The fact that we consume one bread and drink makes us to be one bread and drink. And just as one member serves another in such an integrated body, so each one also eats and drinks the other; that is, each consumes the other in everything, and each one is food and drink for the other, so that we are simply food and drink to one another, just as Christ is simply food and drink to us. With words such as these, St. Paul portrayed the riches and the nature of faith and of love, using the very terms appropriate to natural bread and wine [1 Cor 10:17]. For the many grains that are ground together become a single loaf; each grain loses its own form and becomes the flour of another. Likewise, many grapes become one wine; each grape too loses its own form and becomes the juice of the others. Likewise, Christ has become all things to us; and we, if we are Christians, have become all things among ourselves, each to the other. What one has belongs to the other, and what one lacks is a matter of concern to each of the others as if he were lacking it himself.[38]

Elsewhere, Luther combines the allegory of the bread with the striking image of the Christian community becoming "one cake" (*eyn kuche*).[39] In his "Sermon on the Sacrament—Against the Fanatics" (1526), finally, Luther uses the image of the bread to emphasize the church's unity and concord in face of sectarian dissent:

> Just as each grain loses its form and takes on a common form with the others, so that you cannot see or distinguish it from the other, and all of them are identical, yet separately present; so too should Christendom be one, without sects, that all may be one, of one heart, mind, and will, just as faith, the gospel, and baptism are one.[40]

---

[37] Helmut T. Lehmann, ed., *Luther's Works* (55 vols.; St. Louis: Concordia Publishing House, 1955–86), 35:58 (= *WA* 2:748).

[38] *Luther's Works* 36:287 (= *WA* 11:441).

[39] See *WA* 12:489 (sermon Maundy Thursday, 1523), cf. 37:376 (sermon April 8, 1534) and 52:209 (*Hauspostille* 1544).

[40] *Luther's Works* 36:352–53 (= *WA* 19:511). Other references to the allegory of the

Luther's last text was directed "against the fanatics," that is, representatives of the radical Reformation, who tended to separate from the larger church to form exclusive believers' churches. Interestingly, these groups themselves appropriated the allegory of the bread—probably directly from Luther—in support of their dissenting views. The sixteenth century documents of the radical Reformation contain numerous references to the allegory. Perhaps the earliest trace of it occurs in Balthasar Hubmaier's treatise on the Lord's Supper from 1525:

> We all are one bread and one drink—we all, who have fellowship in one bread and one drink. As one little kernel does not keep its own flower, but shares it with the others, and a single grape does not keep its juice for itself, but shares it with the others, so should we Christians also act—or we eat and drink unworthily from the table of Christ.[41]

The next text, a report by Hans Nadler from 1529, connects the allegory of the bread with the characteristic Anabaptist emphasis on following the example of Christ's suffering:

> Then we celebrated the Lord's Supper at Augsburg in 1527, the Lord's wine and bread. With the bread the unity among brethren is symbolized. Where there are many small kernels of grain to be combined into one loaf there is need first to grind them and to make them into one flour, [. . .] which can be achieved only through suffering. Just as Christ, our dear Lord, went before us, so we too want to follow him in like manner.[42]

Peter Riedemann's "Gmunden Confession" (1530) expresses a similar thought:

> Christ's love and our love are shown to us in the bread and wine. Just as there are many grains of corn, which are ground by the millstones and become flour, then baked and become bread—and in the bread we no longer distinguish one particle of flour from another—the same thing is true of us human beings, many as we are. When we are ground by the millstone of divine power, believe his word and submit to the cross of Christ, we are brought together, bound with the bond of love to one body of which Christ is the head. [. . .] And just as each grain of corn gives the others all it has in order that there may be one loaf of bread, Christ our captain has given himself to us as an example that each should love the other as he has loved us, no longer living for himself, but giving his members to live for the whole body and serving the others with the gift he has received, so that the body may grow and build itself up.[43]

---

bread in Luther's work are *WA* 4:706 (sermon 1519), 15:503 (sermon Maundy Thursday, 1524); 30¹:26 (sermon Sept. 14, 1528), and 30¹:56 (sermon Sept. 25, 1528).

[41] H. Wayne Pipkin and John H. Yoder, eds., *Balthasar Hubmaier: Theologian of Anabaptism* (Scottdale, Pa.: Herald Press, 1989), 75.

[42] Cited in Robert Friedmann, *The Theology of Anabaptism: An Interpretation* (Scottdale, Pa.: Herald Press, 1973), 140.

[43] Peter Riedemann, *Love is Like Fire: The Confessions of an Anabaptist Prisoner Written at Gmunden, Upper Austria, between 1529 and 1532* (Farmington, Pa.: Plough Publishing House, 1993), 51–52.

Menno Simons, in his exposition of Christian doctrine from 1539, uses the allegory of the bread to emphasize the process of spiritual formation.

> Just as natural bread is made of many grains, pulverized by the mill, kneaded with water, and baked by the heat of the fire, so is the church of Christ made up of true believers, broken in their hearts with the mill of the divine Word, baptized with the water of the Holy Ghost, and with the fire of pure unfeigned love made into one body.[44]

Finally, the "Great Article Book" (1577) of the Hutterite bishop Peter Walpot presents the allegory of the bread with an interesting addition concerning the rejection of those pieces of grain that have remained whole:

> No matter how many grains of corn there may be, each is a separate body; but when ground, they give their whole property, and when each has lost what is his, a loaf results. Any grain, however, that remains whole in the bread is picked out and cast away. Thus, although each believer is a separate person and a special creation, yet, ground by the Word of God, they must be made one cake, and present all that they have to the true community of the body of Christ, that is, to His church.[45]

Throughout these texts, to which others could be added,[46] the allegory of the bread is marked by a two-fold emphasis on the importance of community among the believers and on the importance of self-surrender and suffering for the sake of this community.

The last figure of relevance to our discussion is the leader of the Reformation at Geneva, Jean Calvin (1509–1564). He uses the allegory of the bread in his *Institutes* when he discusses the benefits of the Lord's Supper (IV, 17.38). According to this passage, Christ intended the bread of the sacrament to be an example by which the believers would be moved to holiness of life and concord among themselves:

Car nostre Seigneur ainsi nous communique là son corps, qu'il est entierement fait un avec nous, et nous avec luy. Or puis qu'il n'a qu'un corps, duquel il nous fait tous	For the Lord so communicates his body to us there that he is made completely one with us and we with him. Now, since he has only one body, of which he makes us

---

[44] John Christian Wenger, ed., *The Complete Writings of Menno Simons, c. 1496–1561* (Scottdale, Pa.: Herald Press, 1956), 145; see also his treatise "Confession of the distressed Christians" (1552), ibid., 515.

[45] Robert Friedmann, ed., "A Notable Hutterite Document Concerning True Surrender and Christian Community of Goods," *Mennonite Quarterly Review* 32 (1958): 22–62, here 45–46 (spelling modernized).

[46] See William Klassen and Walter Klaassen, eds., *The Writings of Pilgram Marpeck* (Scottdale, Pa.: Herald Press, 1978), 267; Walter Klaassen, ed., *Anabaptism in Outline: Selected Primary Sources* (Scottdale, Pa.: Herald Press, 1981), 202–3 and 207–8; and Robert Friedmann, ed., *Brotherly Community—The Highest Command of Love: Two Anabaptist Documents of 1650 and 1560 by Andreas Ehrenpreis and Claus Felbinger* (Rifton, N.Y.: Plough Publishing House, 1978), 22–23 and 113.

participans, il faut necessairement que par ceste participation nous soyons faits aussi tous ensemble un corps, laquelle unité nous est representée par le pain qui nous est offert au Sacrement. Car comme il est fait de plusieurs grains de blé, qui y sont tellement meslez et confuz ensemble, qu'on ne pourroit discerner ne separer l'un de l'autre: en ceste maniere nous devons aussi estre par accord de volonté tellement conioincts et assemblez entre nous, qu'il n'y ait aucune noise ne division.[47]

all partakers, it is necessary that all of us also be made one body by such participation. The bread shown in the Sacrament represents this unity. As it is made of many grains so mixed together that one cannot be distinguished from another, so it is fitting that in the same way we should be joined and bound together by such great agreement of minds that no sort of disagreement or division may intrude.[48]

The result of such union, according to Calvin, is an ethos of mutual care where the believers share in each other's sufferings and attend to each other's needs.

Conclusion

The history of the allegory of the bread gathered from many pieces is a striking example of how an early Christian motif has been passed down through the ages. What makes the *Wirkungsgeschichte* of this allegory so remarkable is the fact that it is a tradition whose origin and textual basis lie outside of the New Testament canon. Nothing other than the persuasiveness and charm of the image itself accounts for the scope of its long career from the second century to the time of the Reformation.

The evidence presented in this essay allows us to conclude with three general observations. First, the allegory of the bread gathered from many pieces circulated in two basic versions. The earlier version, attested in the Greek and Coptic liturgical texts, describes the bread as having been "scattered upon the mountains" (*Did.* 9:4). The emphasis lies on the landscape and on the idea that the bread has been gathered together from "scattered" pieces, although it is unclear whether these pieces are crumbs or simply the bread's ingredients. The later version speaks about the bread as being "a conglomerate of many individual grains made into one" (Cyprian, Letter 69) without any reference to the landscape. Instead, the imagery of the bread is sometimes

---

[47] Jean Calvin, *Opera* (vol. 4; Corpus Reformatorum 32; Braunschweig: Schwetschke, 1866), 1014.

[48] John Calvin, *Institutes of the Christian Religion* (vol. 2; trans. Ford Lewis Battles, Library of Christian Classics 21; Philadelphia: Westminster Press, 1961), 1414–15.

expanded to include various details of the baking process (pounding, mixing, moistening, etc.), as well as the parallel image of the wine squeezed from many grapes. This version belongs to the tradition that runs from Cyprian to the Reformation.

Second, there is a wide variety of settings and interpretations. The first version is used liturgically, mostly in close conjunction with the institution of the Eucharist. The second version does not occur in liturgical settings but rather in the context of theological arguments related to the topics of Church and Eucharist. While the first version serves to express an eschatological hope (the church's unity and perfection at the end of time), the second serves to explain some aspect in the nature of ecclesial communion. Within each of these two traditions we find divergent nuanes in interpretation and usage. There are, for example, interesting variations among the texts of the first version in the allegory's place and function within the liturgy. Even more pronounced are the differences among the texts of the second version. In some cases the allegory of the bread serves to underscore the church's unity, in others it explains the meaning of the sacrament or illustrates the process of spiritual formation. And, of course, the theological perspectives differ considerably between the Catholic, the magisterial Protestant, and the Anabaptist sources.

The third observation, finally, concerns the question of constancy and change in the transmission, reception, and interpretation of the allegory of the bread. The common denominator throughout the allegory's history is the image of a loaf of bread being composed of many pieces and its figurative application to the church. The wide variety of different versions and interpretations indicates that the allegory's circulation was not bound to one particular text. Although *Did.* 9:4 represents the earliest witness, it was not normative for the subsequent tradition. Strictly speaking, the *Wirkungsgeschichte* of *Did.* 9:4 is not the *Wirkungsgeschichte* of the written text but of the image attested to in this text. The image itself circulated—in textual form, of course, but not fixed by a codified formulation. The allegory's wide-ranging reception quite likely suggests that its form and content proved to be open and adaptable enough to be appropriated by very diverse traditions in widely different historical circumstances.

In sum, the process of the allegory's transmission and reception presents itself as a process of constant re-interpretation and modification. While the medieval appropriation emphasized continuity with the patristic tradition and thus showed some degree of codification, the Reformation brought a new round of fresh interpretations. This resulted in the paradoxical situation that the allegory of the bread was claimed by each of the antagonistic parties during the Reformation in support of their conflicting views of the Eucharist and the nature of ecclesial communion. In retrospect, however, all these diverse and divergent interpretations still belong together as parts of one overarching story, namely the *Wirkungsgeschichte* of the allegory of the bread, which presents itself to us as a long and colorful career stretching from *Did.* 9:4 to the *Institutes* of Jean Calvin.

PART SIX

EARLY CHRISTIAN VOICES AND ANCIENT MANUSCRIPTS

CHAPTER TWENTY-NINE

LE MIRACLE DE L'ARCHANGE MICHEL À CHONAI: INTRODUCTION, TRADUCTION, ET NOTES

Bertrand Bouvier et Frédéric Amsler

Avec ses phénomènes telluriques surprenants, la vallée du Lycos en Phrygie a excité les imaginations des mythographes chrétiens. Non seulement Hiérapolis avec ses sources chaudes et ses falaises calcaires est le théâtre grandiose des *Actes de Philippe*, mais encore Colosses et son torrent capricieux, le Cadmos, est le paysage naturel du miracle de l'archange Michel. La parenté entre les deux textes ne s'arrête pas à la géographie. L'auteur du *Miracle de l'archange Michel* connaît les *Actes de Philippe*, tout au moins le *Martyre*, et ces deux textes partagent le triste privilège d'avoir été délaissés pendant près d'un siècle avant de regagner, grâce à François Bovon, l'intérêt de la recherche, à laquelle nous espérons contribuer en offrant une première traduction française du *Miracle*.

Le récit du *Miracle de l'archange Michel à Chonai* (ou Colosses sous son appellation classique et néotestamentaire) est transmis dans trois rédactions grecques: une rédaction anonyme, éditée d'abord par Max Bonnet en 1889,[1] puis rééditée par François Nau sur la base du texte inférieur en onciale du VIIIe siècle d'un palimpseste du XIe–XIIe siècle conservé à Paris;[2] une relation attribuée à Sisinnius, archévêque de Constantinople au Xe siècle,[3] éditée par les Bollandistes,[4] et enfin une forme métaphrastique qui figure dans tous les Ménées grecs, éditée également par Bonnet.[5]

Comme l'a démontré cet auteur, la plus ancienne des trois recensions est la rédaction anonyme. Bien que l'édition de Nau soit plus récente que celle de Bonnet et intègre un témoin de première valeur mais lacuneux (Paris, B.N.

---

[1] Max Bonnet, "Narratio de miraculo a Michele archangelo Chonis patrato adjecto Symeonis Metaphrastae de eadem re libello," *AnBoll* 8 (1889): 289–307 et 317–22 pour la traduction latine. Texte grec seul avec une étude préliminaire dans Max Bonnet, *Narratio de miraculo a Michele archangelo Chonis patrato adjecto Symeonis Metaphrastae de eadem re libello* (Paris: Hachette, 1890).

[2] François Nau, *Le miracle de saint Michel à Colosses: Texte grec publié avec l'ancienne version latine* (PO 4.5 n° 19; Paris: Firmin-Didot, 1907; réimpr., Turnhout: Brepols, 1981), 542–62. Sur le *Paris. suppl. gr. 480*, voir idem, *Analyse des mss. grecs palimpsestes Paris, suppl. 480 et Chartres, n°s 1753 et 1754* (PO 4.5; Paris: Firmin-Didot, 1907; réimpr., Turnhout: Brepols, 1981), 515–20.

[3] A ne pas confondre avec son homonyme, prédécesseur de Nestorius sur le siège constantinopolitain en 426–427, voir Bonnet, *Narratio*, p. x.

[4] *ASS* sept. VIII, pp. 38–49, cf. PG 114, p. 93.

[5] Bonnet, "Narratio," 308–316 et 323–328 pour la traduction latine.

suppl. grec 480), nous avons pris pour base, pour une raison que l'on devinera, l'excellente édition du philologue vaudois à laquelle François Nau rend d'ailleurs hommage.[6]

En suivant les indications temporelles qui pourraient bien trahir le caractère composite du texte, le récit se laisse diviser en trois parties:[7] le rappel initial des hauts faits des apôtres Philippe et Jean à Hiérapolis (1), puis l'annonce par eux d'un signe de l'archange Michel, qui se réalise peu après leur départ sous la forme du jaillissement d'une source, inscrit la légende dans l'héritage des apôtres, tout en évitant soigneusement de les impliquer directement (2).[8] Forte de cette caution apostolique, la deuxième partie, située "après la dormition des saints apôtres" et de "longues années" après la découverte de la source, relate la conversion d'un païen de Laodicée qui, en signe de reconnaissance pour la guérison de sa fille muette par l'eau de la source miraculeuse, édifie à cet endroit un petit oratoire dédié à Michel, chef des armées (3). La troisième partie, de beaucoup la plus importante, qui se déroule "quatre-vingt-dix ans après la construction de l'oratoire," peut être subdivisée en deux sections. La première relate la vie ascétique d'Archippe,[9] venu d'Hiérapolis encore enfant et qui devient le premier desservant dudit oratoire (4).[10] La seconde section retrace l'ultime épisode du conflit entre païens et chrétiens pour le contrôle de la source et la victoire d'Archippe grâce à l'intervention miraculeuse de l'archange Michel (5–12).

Les études consacrées à ce Miracle ont été relativement abondantes au XIXe siècle.[11] Ensuite, la réédition du texte par François Nau n'a pas suscité de regain d'intérêt, si bien que ce récit hagiographique est pratiquement tombé

---

[6] "On constatera, vu leur petit nombre, avec quelle sagacité le savant éditeur a su reconstruire le texte primitif à l'aide de manuscrits du XIe au XIVe siècle qui différaient au point que les variantes occupent, dans son édition, plus de place que le texte" (Nau, *Miracle de saint Michel*, 546).

[7] Cf. Bonnet, "Narratio," p. i.

[8] Johannes Peter Rohland a finement discerné une concurrence entre les deux lieux de culte aux vertus curatives, celui de Philippe à Hiérapolis où se pratiquait l'incubation et celui de Michel à Colosses où les guérisons étaient opérées surtout par les vertus de l'eau; voir Johannes Peter Rohland, *Der Erzengel Michael: Arzt und Feldherr. Zwei Aspekte des vor- und frühbyzantinischen Michaelskultes* (Beihefte der Zeitschrift für Religions- und Geistesgeschichte 19; Leiden: Brill, 1977), 72 n. 60 et p. 96.

[9] Le desservant du sanctuaire de saint Michel doit sans doute son nom au chrétien de Colosses (Col 4:17), que l'apôtre Paul qualifie de compagnon d'armes en Phlm 2.

[10] Dans la ligne tracée par Rohland, nous ajoutons que notre *Miracle* veut rendre le culte de Michel rigoureusement orthodoxe, alors que celui de Philippe était sans doute de tendance encratite, ce qui rend tout son poids théologique au transfert d'Archippe d'Hiérapolis à Colosses-Chonai.

[11] William Mitchell Ramsay, *The Church in the Roman Empire before A. D. 170* (Londres: Hodder and Stoughton, 1892; 9e éd., 1907), 465–80; idem, *The Cities and Bishoprics of Phrygia being an Essay of the Local History of Phrygia from the Earliest Times to the Turkish Conquest*, vol. 1: *The Lycos Valley and South-Western Phrygia* (Oxford: Clarendon, 1895; réimpr., New York: Arno, 1975), 214–16; Wilhelm Lueken, *Michael: Eine Darstellung und Vergleichung der jüdischen und der morgenländisch-christlichen Tradition vom Erzengel Michael* (Göttingen: Vandenhoeck und Ruprecht, 1898).

dans l'oubli jusqu'aux travaux de von Rintelen et de Rohland.[12] Selon l'orientation critique de cette époque, c'est le problème des *realia* qui a surtout retenu l'attention de la recherche. Un certain consensus s'est créé autour de l'idée que ce texte était directement inspiré par le cours en partie souterrain du Lycos vers Colosses et les tremblements de terre fréquents dans la région.

Chonai (Χῶναι, aujourd'hui Honaz), qui signifie "ravins," "gorges," "entonnoirs," est le nom d'un village situé à trois kilomètres au sud de Colosses au pied du mont Cadmos (aujourd'hui Honaz Dag, orthographié aussi Chonas Dagi). A la fin du VIIIe siècle, sans doute en conséquence de la conquête arabe, le siège épiscopal va se déplacer de Colosses à Chonai. Curieusement, Chonai n'apparaît que dans le titre de notre récit, lequel situe la source et les miracles qui lui sont rattachés à Chairetopa (2). Cette ville est de localisation incertaine.[13] Ramsay situe Chairetopa ou Keretapa en Lycie (7) et estime que la légende résulte de la collision de deux traditions, l'une "lycienne," attestée par les Ménologes au 6 septembre, l'autre phrygienne.[14] Mais les noms d'Hiérapolis (1 et 4) et de Laodicée (3–7), de Lycocapros, qui combine le nom de deux cours d'eau connus, le Lycos et le Capros, voire les noms du Chrysès et du Couphos, orientent nettement vers la Phrygie.

Concernant le miracle des eaux, les principaux auteurs anciens invoqués sont Hérodote (*Hist.* 7.30),[15] Pline l'Ancien (*Nat.* 31.2 [20] 29)[16] et Strabon (*Géogr.* 12.8, 16).[17] Ces témoignages ne concordant pas, toutes sortes d'hypothèses ont été avancées pour les harmoniser entre eux, avec les observations qu'il est possible de faire sur le terrain et avec notre récit. Il n'y a pas

---

[12] Wolfgang von Rintelen, *Kultgeographische Studien in der Italia byzantina: Untersuchungen über die Kulte des Erzengels Michael und der Madonna di Constatinopoli in Süditalien* (Munich, 1967; thèse qui nous est restée inaccessible); idem, "Kult- und Legendenwanderung von Ost nach West in frühen Mittelalter," *Saeculum* 22 (1971): 71–100; Rohland, *Der Erzengel Michael.*

[13] Klaus Belke et Norbert Mersich, *Tabula Imperii Byzantini,* vol. 7: *Phrygien und Pisidien* (Österreichische Akademie der Wissenschaften, Philosophisch-historische Klasse 211; Vienne: Verlag der Österreichischen Akademie der Wissenschaften 1990), 221.

[14] Ramsay, *Church,* 468.

[15] "[Xerxès] parvint à Colosses, grande ville de Phrygie; là, le fleuve Lycos se précipite dans un gouffre où il disparaît; il reparaît à cinq stades environ de distance et se jette lui aussi dans le Méandre" (Hérodote, *Hist.* 7 [Polymnie]). Texte établi et traduit par Philippe-Ernest Legrand (Paris: Les Belles-Lettres, 1951), 76.

[16] "A Colossae, il y a un fleuve d'où l'on retire pétrifiées les briques qu'on y a jetées" (Pline l'Ancien, *Nat.* 31). Texte établi, traduit et commenté par Guy Serbat (Paris: Les Belles-Lettres, 1972), 37.

[17] "A Laodicée aussi, le Capros se jette dans le Méandre, de même que le Lycos, grande rivière à laquelle Laodicée doit son nom de Laodicée sur le Lycos. Au-dessus de la ville s'élève le Mont Cadmos, duquel descend non seulement le Lycos, mais aussi un autre cours d'eau portant le même nom que la montagne. Ce dernier coule sous terre sur la plus grande partie de son cours et ne resurgit ensuite qu'à l'endroit de son confluent avec les autres rivières, ce qui démontre à la fois la nature caverneuse de cette région et sa propension aux séismes" (Strabon, *Géogr.* 9 [Livre 12]). Texte établi et traduit par François Lasserre (Paris: Les Belles-Lettres, 1981), 144–45.

lieu de retracer ici l'histoire de la recherche qui, à certains égards, n'a pas abouti à une solution précise.

Cette solution pourrait bien ressortir d'une meilleure compréhension du texte de Strabon, auteur du seul récit remontant à l'Antiquité qu'on puisse tenir pour un témoignage oculaire. Serrant de près le texte de Strabon, François Lasserre, le regretté helléniste de l'Université de Lausanne, estime que le géographe attribue au Cadmos et non au Lycos un cours souterrain. Du coup, la réapparition à l'air libre du Cadmos, ce qui fait penser à l'invention de la source de notre texte, n'est autre chose que "la forte résurgence jaillissant au pied du rocher du Chonas Dagi, à 3 km à l'est de Denizli, qu'on pouvait croire dérivée de quelque torrent."[18] Notons que selon Ramsay,[19] le Lycos, à l'instar du Chrysès de notre récit (6), a la particularité de se diviser en deux bras qui se rejoignent quelques kilomètres en aval de Colosses et entre lesquels se trouveraient les ruines d'une église, mais qui n'a pas été identifiée.

Concernant le miracle lui-même accompli par l'archange Michel, il pourrait avoir pour substrat la gorge très encaissée au fond laquelle coule le Lycos en aval de Colosses.[20] Il est facile d'imaginer que si cette gorge venait à être obstruée, cela provoquerait un lac qui viendrait inonder les environs immédiats de Colosses et l'église, si c'en est une, un peu plus en amont.

Pour la composition du *Miracle*, Ramsay[21] proposait le IXe siècle au plus tôt, mais la découverte du Paris. suppl. 480, dont l'écriture inférieure remonte au VIIIe siècle, oblige à avancer la date. La référence aux *Actes de Philippe* et l'absence d'allusion à la conquête arabe militent pour une rédaction de notre texte entre la fin du IVe et la fin du VIIIe siècle. Sur la base d'une étude du titre d'archistratège, Rohland propose le VIe siècle.[22] Quant à la légende elle-même du miracle, de caractère étiologique, elle pourrait être plus ancienne encore, du IVe ou Ve siècle.[23]

La dévotion aux anges à Colosses est ancienne et solidement implantée, puisque les témoignages systématiquement cités et couvrant plusieurs siècles ne se lassent pas de la condamner: ainsi l'épître de Paul aux Col 2:18, le canon 35 du concile de Laodicée, daté généralement entre 341 et 363,[24] et Théodoret de Cyr dans son commentaire de Col 2:18[25] qui remonte aux

---

[18] Ibid., 145 n. 1.

[19] Ramsay, *Church*, 471.

[20] Ibid., 473–76.

[21] Ibid., 468.

[22] Rohland, *Der Erzengel Michael*, 3 et 95.

[23] Ibid., 95.

[24] "Que les chrétiens ne doivent pas abandonner l'Église de Dieu et s'en détourner, et vénérer les anges, et introduire un culte (des anges). . . ." (Karl Joseph von Hefele et Henri Leclercq, *Histoire des conciles d'après les documents originaux* [12 vols.; Paris: Letouzey et Ané, 1907], 1.2:1017).

[25] "Ceux qui défendaient la Loi les engageaient à vénérer également les anges, en disant que la Loi avait été donnée par eux. Cette manière vicieuse de penser a longtemps subsisté en Phrygie et en Pisidie. C'est pourquoi un concile réuni à Laocidée de Phrygie a interdit par un canon d'adresser des prières aux anges; et jusqu'à nos jours, il est

années 420–450. En soulignant l'orthodoxie des fidèles de Michel, notre *Miracle* témoigne d'un net changement de stratégie.[26]

Ce culte des anges, et sans doute de l'archange Michel en particulier, trouve probablement son origine à l'époque hellénistique et dans l'implantation forcée d'une colonie juive vers 210 av. J.-C. par Antiochus III, comme l'indique avec une grande précision une lettre du souverain séleucide au satrape de Phrygie et de Lydie, Zeuxis, citée par Flavius Josèphe:

> Le roi Antiochus à Zeuxis son père, salut. Si tu es en bonne santé, c'est bien; moi-même, je me porte bien. Ayant appris que les habitants de Lydie et de Phrygie se livraient à des mouvements séditieux, j'ai pensé que le fait méritait une grande attention de ma part; j'ai pris conseil de mes amis sur ce qu'il convient de faire, et j'ai décidé de tirer de Mésopotamie et de Babylonie, pour les envoyer dans les garnisons et les places les plus importantes, deux mille familles juives avec leur équipement.
>
> Je suis persuadé, en effet, qu'ils seront de bons gardiens de nos intérêts à cause de leur piété envers Dieu, et je sais que mes ancêtres ont éprouvé leur fidélité et leur prompte obéissance aux ordres reçus. Je veux donc, bien que la chose soit difficile, qu'on les transporte, avec la promesse de les laisser vivre suivant leurs propres lois.
>
> Quand tu les auras amenés dans les lieux indiqués, tu donneras à chaque famille un emplacement pour bâtir une maison, un champ pour labourer et planter des vignes, et tu les laisseras pendant dix ans exempts de tout impôt sur les produits de la terre. Et jusqu'à ce qu'ils récoltent les produits de la terre, qu'on leur distribue du blé pour la nourriture de leurs esclaves. Que l'on donne aussi tout ce qui est nécessaire à ceux qui ont en charge le service du culte afin qu'en reconnaissance de notre bonté ils montrent plus de zèle pour nos intérêts. Veille aussi avec tout le soin possible sur ce peuple, afin qu'il ne soit molesté par personne.[27]

A en croire André Paul, "il est certain qu'une partie au moins de la population rurale d'Asie Mineure, de Syrie et des provinces de l'est de l'Euphrate, était composée de militaires fermiers avec leurs familles, soit de ressortissants, juifs parfois, qui jouissaient des privilèges correspondant à leur statut ponctuel."[28] Des implantations juives au sein de colonies de militaires ont constitué un terreau idéal pour le développement du culte de saint Michel, l'archistratège et protecteur des armées.[29] Dans les années 60 de notre ère, il a été possible

---

possible de voir chez eux et chez leurs voisins des oratoires de saint Michel. Ils conseillaient d'en construire, mus soi-disant par l'humilité, en déclarant que le Dieu de l'univers est invisible, inaccessible et inintelligible, et qu'il convient de se ménager la bienveillance divine par l'intermédiaire des anges" (PG 82:613b).

[26] Cf. Rintelen, "Kult- und Legendenwanderung," 87.

[27] Flavius Josèphe, *Ant.* 12.147–53, extrait de André Paul, *Le monde des Juifs à l'heure de Jésus. Histoire politique* (Petite bibliothèque des sciences bibliques: Nouveau Testament 1; Paris: Desclée, 1981), 115–16.

[28] Paul, *Le monde des Juifs*, 116; voir aussi Lueken, *Michael*, 80.

[29] Rohland, *Der Erzengel Michael*, 71–72.

d'estimer à 11000 le nombre d'hommes libres juifs versant l'impôt du Temple sur le territoire de Laodicée.[30] Au IVe siècle, l'influence du judaïsme était encore très forte en Phrygie, comme en témoignent les canons 29 (interdiction de pratiquer le sabbat), 37 (interdiction de célébration avec des juifs) et 38 (interdiction d'accepter des azymes des juifs) du concile de Laodicée.[31]

A Byzance, saint Michel était vénéré comme le patron des armées impériales; il figurait sur les enseignes et jouissait d'une grande dévotion, comme l'indique, par exemple, la croix-reliquaire de Genève,[32] dédiée dans la seconde moitié du Xe siècle par un haut personnage militaire "au divin Michel, chef des armées, apparu à Chonai sous l'apparence d'un jeune homme." De l'empire byzantin, le culte de saint Michel[33] a rayonné dans tout le monde chrétien, aussi bien en Orient qu'en Occident[34] donnant lieu à une riche iconographie.[35] Nous nous contenterons d'en signaler un spécimen remarquable que François Bovon a pu admirer au monastère de Saint-Catherine du Sinaï.[36]

---

[30] Lueken, *Michael*, 80; Rohland, *Der Erzengel Michael*, 70, n. 52.

[31] Lueken, *Michael*, 80.

[32] Musée d'art et d'histoire, inv. AD 3062. Voir Alice Bank, Bertrand Bouvier, Ivan Djuric, et Laskarina Bouras, "Études sur les croix byzantines du Musée d'art et d'histoire de Genève," extrait de *Genava* 28 n.s. (1980): 97–124.

[33] Ugo Zanetti, "Fêtes des anges dans les calendriers et synaxaires orientaux," dans *Culto e insediamenti micaelici nell'Italia meridionale fra tarda antichità e medioevo: Atti del Convegno Internazionale. Monte Sant'Angelo 18–21 novembre 1992* (éd. Carlo Carletti et Giorgio Otranto; Scavi e ricerche 7; Bari: Edipuglia, 1994), 323–49.

[34] Dans l'abondante littérature relative à Michel, nous nous limiterons à quelques travaux synthétiques récents. On trouvera un bon aperçu de la diffusion de ce culte dans Victor Saxer, "Jalons pour servir à l'histoire du culte de l'archange saint Michel en Orient jusqu'à l'iconoclasme," dans *Noscere sancta: Miscellanea in memoria di Agostino Amore OFM († 1982)*, vol. 1: *Storia della Chiesa, archeologia, arte* (éd. Isaac Vázquez Janeiro OFM; 2 vols.; Bibliotheca Pontificii Athenaei Antoniani 24–25; Rome: Pontificium Athenaeum Antonianum, 1985), 357–426; Bernadette Martin-Hisard, "Le culte de l'archange Michel dans l'empire byzantin (VIIIe–XIe siècles)," dans *Culto e insediamenti micaelici* (éd. Carletti et Otranto), 351–73; Antonio Enrico Felle, "Culte et pèlerinages à saint Michel en Occident: Les trois Monts dédiés à l'archange" (Colloque international, Centre Culturel de Cerisy-la-Salle Abbaye de Mont-Saint-Michel, 27–30 septembre 2000)," *Vetera christianorum* 38 (2000): 185–92; G. Merel, "A la découverte de réseaux de sanctuaires dédiés à saint Michel," *Bulletin de la Société de mythologie française* 199 (2000): 35–43.

[35] Smiljka Gabelić, "The Iconography of the Miracle at Chonae: An Unusual Example from Cyprus," *Zograf* 20 (1989): 95–103; Glenn Peers, "Holy Man, Supplicant, and Donor: On Representations of the Miracle of the Archangel Michael at Chonae," *Mediaeval Studies* 59 (1997): 173–82.

[36] Sortie sans doute d'un atelier de Constantinople, dans la seconde moitié du XIIe siècle, l'icône est représentative de l'art raffiné de l'époque des Comnènes, caractérisé par l'allongement des figures et les savants accords de couleurs (voir Kurt Weitzmann, "The Classical in Byzantine Art, as a Mode of Individual Expression," dans *Byzantine Art, An European Art: Lectures* (Athens: [Office of the Minister to the Prime Minister of the Greek Government, Dept. of Antiquities and Archaeological Restoration], 1966), 166–67. Cette icône est reproduite dans l'ouvrage Σινᾶ· οἱ θησαυροὶ τῆς Ἱ. Μονῆς Ἁγίας Αἰκατερίνης (éd. Constantin A. Manaphis; Athènes: Ἐκδοτικὴ Ἀθηνῶν, 1990), pl. 23.

Le miracle de l'archange Michel à Chonaï: Traduction et notes

Récit de saint Archippos le desservant
au sujet du miracle opéré par Michel le grand chef des armées à Chonaï

1. Le commencement des guérisons, des dons et gratifications que Dieu nous a prodigués par la grâce et l'intercession du chef des armées Michel, fut proclamé dès l'origine par les saints apôtres Philippe et Jean le théologien. En effet, saint Jean, après avoir chassé d'Éphèse l'impure Artémis, monta à Hiérapolis auprès de saint Philippe; celui-ci, de son côté, était en lutte avec la Vipère. S'étant embrassés l'un l'autre, saint Philippe dit à Jean: "Que faire, mon frère Jean? Je ne parviens pas à extirper l'impure et scélérate Vipère de cette ville." La scélérate et pernicieuse Vipère était en effet, de tous les reptiles et animaux impurs, la première. Tout son corps était ceint de serpents, un dragon encerclait sa tête, un autre encerclait son cou; elle se tenait au-dessus de deux dragons, entourée de toutes sortes de reptiles immondes et, en un mot, elle était comme une reine dans toute sa parure. Et les païens la considéraient comme une grande déesse, tous se prosternaient devant elle et lui offraient des sacrifices. Souvent, tandis que saint Philippe était assis et les enseignait, elle incitait les serpents à l'assaillir pour le tuer. Elle lui disait: "Sors de cette ville, Philippe, avant que je te fasse périr de male mort!" Cependant, saint Philippe restait à prêcher la parole de la vérité et de la foi. Puis ayant fait une prière, les apôtres la chassèrent, elle aussi, d'Hiérapolis.

2. Après quoi s'étant mis en chemin, les vénérables hérauts de la vérité s'arrêtèrent en un lieu dit Chairetopa, où la grâce et le don et les miracles du saint et glorieux chef des armées Michel allaient se manifester. Ayant fait une prière, ils signifièrent au peuple que le grand commandeur et chef des armées de la puissance du Seigneur allait descendre en ce lieu pour y accomplir des miracles extraordinaires. Puis les apôtres partirent pour aller prêcher dans les villes alentour. Et aussitôt une source jaillit en ce lieu, opérant des guérisons.

3. Après la dormition des saints apôtres, les païens se remirent à rugir et à se déchaîner contre les chrétiens. De longues années s'étant écoulées depuis sa découverte, la source sainte était devenue célèbre sur toute la terre. En effet, ceux qui se réfugiaient en ce lieu y étaient guéris, quel que fût le mal qui les accablait. Si bien que de nombreux païens, arrivant sur place et constatant les guérisons, croyaient en le Seigneur Jésus-Christ et se faisaient baptiser.

Or, il y avait dans la cité de Laodicée un homme impie qui sacrifiait aux idoles. Cet homme avait une fille unique qui était muette depuis le ventre de sa mère. Son père, à plusieurs reprises, avait voulu, en compagnie d'autres gens de sa secte, aller détruire la source sainte, où accouraient une foule de païens, y trouvaient la guérison de leurs maux et croyaient en notre Seigneur Jésus-Christ. Un beau jour, comme dans une vision de la nuit, le commandeur du Seigneur, Michel, le chef des armées, lui apparaît et lui dit: "Rends-toi avec ton enfant à l'endroit où la source sainte a surgi, et par mon nom, si tu viens à croire, tu ne t'en retourneras point chagriné." L'homme se leva et partit avec son enfant. Et lorsqu'il eut vu le bienfait de Dieu, il crut et il demanda à ceux qui venaient chercher guérison: "Qui invoquez-vous en répandant cette eau sur vos corps?" Ils lui répondirent: "Nous, nous invoquons le Père, le Fils et le Saint-Esprit et Michel, le chef des armées." Alors, levant les yeux et les mains vers le ciel, l'homme dit: "Père, Fils et Saint-Esprit, Dieu, par l'intercession de Michel, le chef des armées, viens en aide au pécheur que je suis!" Et prenant de l'eau, il la versa dans la bouche de son enfant, qui aussitôt poussa un cri et s'exclama: "O Dieu des chrétiens, viens à mon aide, en vérité ta puissance est grande, Michel, chef des armées!" L'homme reçut le baptême et toute sa maison. Puis il édifia là un petit oratoire au nom de Michel, le chef des armées, et abrita d'un couvert la source sainte. Après quoi il s'en retourna avec sa fille, glorifiant Dieu. Quant aux païens, ils rugissaient contre les chrétiens et contre la source sainte, cherchant à la détruire et à la faire disparaître de cette terre.

4. Et quatre-vingt-dix ans après la construction de l'oratoire au-dessus de la source, un enfant arriva d'Hiérapolis, âgé d'environ dix ans, nommé d'Archippos, d'une famille de fidèles chrétiens. Il s'y établit et en devint le premier desservant.

Voici quelle fut sa vie: il vécut soixante-dix ans, à savoir soixante ans dès l'instant où il se mit au service de l'oratoire de Dieu, sans jamais goûter de pain, de viande ni de vin, et sans jamais se baigner. Voici quelle était sa nourriture: il faisait bouillir des herbes sauvages et les mangeait sans sel, et cela, le bienheureux le pratiquait une fois par semaine; son âme précieuse, il l'humectait trois fois par jour de trois onces d'eau, et cela, le bienheureux le pratiquait pour rafraîchir son corps. Pour tout vêtement, il avait deux sacs rugueux. Le bienheureux portait l'un sans jamais l'enlever de sa chair, jusqu'à ce qu'il ait fait son temps et alors, il revêtait l'autre sac. Sa couche était jonchée de cailloux pointus, recouverts d'une étoffe grossière, pour que les visiteurs ne les voient pas. Sous sa tête vénérable, il mettait un sac rempli de ronces. C'est là-dessus que le bienheureux s'étendait à l'heure de prendre son repos, et couché chaque nuit sur les pierres et les ronces, c'est ainsi que le serviteur de Dieu prenait le très amer sommeil de la veille. Jamais en effet le serviteur de Dieu ne trouvait de répit, exerçant son corps, conservant son âme sans tache, à l'abri des pièges de l'Étranger.[37] Progressant dans la voie étroite et douloureuse, il disait: "Ne permets pas, Seigneur, que le pécheur que je suis, jouisse sur cette terre. Ne laisse pas les biens de ce monde entrer et paraître à mes yeux. Que je ne connaisse pas, Seigneur, ne serait-ce qu'une seule bonne journée par an. Que mes regards ne s'exaltent point de la vanité de ce siècle. Remplis plutôt mes yeux, Seigneur, de larmes spirituelles, et illumine mon coeur de la connaissance de tes commandements. Et fais-moi don de la grâce dont tu as gratifié ceux qui, de tous les temps, se sont rendus agréables à toi. Mon corps

---

[37] C'est-à-dire le diable.

d'argile, qu'est-il en effet? Un bourbier de puanteur: l'embellir serait dénuder l'âme incorruptible. Le vêtement de l'âme, c'est la foi droite en Dieu; le dénuement et le mépris de la chair, ce sont la faim et la soif et l'ascèse angélique, la couche dure et la veille, la prière et les larmes, les soupirs et les pénitences, la méditation silencieuse et les aumônes, et tout ce qui est agréable à Dieu. Voilà les embellissements auxquels l'âme se plaît. Que demande l'âme au corps? Rien, si ce n'est toute justice et piété. Quant au corps, voici ce qu'il demande: la gloutonnerie et la débauche dévorantes, l'avarice et toute forme d'impureté, les fantasmes et les perversités, les viles convoitises et tout ce qui déplaît à Dieu. Voilà les envies dont se délecte le corps et qui assujettissent l'âme infortunée. Quant à moi, pécheur et misérable, que puis-je faire? Viens à mon aide, Seigneur mon Dieu, et réduis mon corps comme le grain de moutarde, broie mon cœur et humilie-le, afin que je ne sois pas rejeté par toi. Car à l'aube, Seigneur mon Dieu, j'ai fleuri comme l'herbe, mais le soir je déchois et je passe. Néanmoins, je n'aurai de cesse de mortifier mes membres, pour leur enlever tout mauvais désir."

5. Voilà ce que méditait Archippos, le serviteur de Dieu. Et pratiquant l'ascèse angélique, il glorifiait chaque jour le Dieu qui lui accordait une pareille patience. Et la multitude des chrétiens et des païens accouraient en ce lieu. Tous ceux qui, dans la crainte et la foi, confessaient la Trinité, disaient: "Père, Fils et Saint-Esprit, Dieu, par l'intercession de Michel, le chef des armées, aie pitié de nous!" Et ce disant, ils répandaient de l'eau sur leurs membres malades et étaient guéris. Mais les infidèles et les ennemis de la vérité ne voulaient pas contempler la gloire de Dieu et rugissaient à toute heure comme des lions, voulant détruire la source sainte et du même coup mettre à mort le serviteur de Dieu. Souvent les impies venaient le fouetter, d'autres s'emparaient des croix de l'oratoire et les brisaient sur la tête du saint, d'autres encore le saisissaient par les cheveux et le traînaient à l'extérieur, d'autres lui arrachaient les poils de la barbe et le jetaient à terre. Ils s'attaquaient à la source sainte pour la détruire, mais aussitôt leur mains étaient retenues; d'autres en s'approchant voyaient une flamme de feu jaillir de l'eau contre leurs visages, si bien que les impies revenaient sur leur pas couverts de honte. Ils se disaient entre eux: "Si nous ne détruisons pas cette source et si nous ne tuons pas cet homme qui vit dans une cabane, tous nos dieux seront réduits à néant par ceux qui sont guéris en ce lieu." Ils restaient donc à tourmenter quotidiennement le serviteur de Dieu, de sorte que le bienheureux endura mille maux de la part des païens qui sacrifiaient aux idoles. Mais en endurant tout cela, il ne cessait de glorifier Dieu, de jour et de nuit.

6. Il y avait en ce lieu une rivière qui descendait par la gauche, appelée Chrysès; elle longeait le sanctuaire de Dieu, depuis l'origine du monde. A de nombreuses reprises, les ennemis de la vérité avaient tenté de mêler les eaux de cette rivière à la source sainte sans y parvenir. Malgré leurs efforts, l'eau de la rivière s'écartait et, se divisant en deux bras, s'écoulait également du côté droit du sanctuaire: c'est le cours qu'elle suit jusqu'à ce jour.

7. En ces temps-là, deux autres fleuves descendaient de l'orient, s'approchant du lieu saint d'environ trois milles. On appelait l'un Lycocapros, l'autre Couphos.[38] Ils faisaient jonction au sommet de la haute montagne et, tournant à droite, s'écoulaient vers les régions de la Lycie. Or le diable, le calomniateur depuis les origines, le maudit, le planteur des idées perverses au cœur des hommes, le défenseur et l'avocat du mal, le négateur de Dieu et l'ennemi juré des anges, le meurtrier des saints et le persécuteur des saintes églises, la ruine des guérisons et la tentation des malades, celui qui a suborné le monde et ne s'en est jamais rassasié, qui a pris en horreur le ciel et la terre et s'est épris des ténèbres éternelles, qui pousse à la défection ceux qui veulent être sauvés et l'adversaire de ceux qui luttent pour leur salut, l'ennemi du bien et du Christ, enténébré et plongé dans l'erreur, ne cessa de harceler ceux qui sacrifiaient aux idoles pour qu'ils foulent aux pieds la source sainte de Dieu. Il suggère à leur cœur de détourner les fleuves contre la source sainte de Dieu, afin de l'engloutir; le terrain se prêtait en effet au déferlement des eaux. Les impies arrivent donc de toutes les cités alentour, environ cinq mille hommes, et se rassemblent à Laodicée. Le peuple de l'injustice[39] tint conseil avec eux et ils complotèrent contre Michel l'incorporel, le chef des armées.

Les premiers parmi les impies disaient à la foule: "Le terrain se prête à l'engloutissement de la source; les fleuves en effet dévalent d'une grande hauteur. Et nous allons dériver leur cours contre celui qui a jeté un sort à nos dieux et brisé leurs divines puissances par les guérisons qu'il opère en ce lieu. Du moment que nous-mêmes sommes incapables de tuer cet homme et d'éliminer cette fange, il se pourrait que par l'audace des fleuves et la masse de l'eau et avec le secours de nos dieux, ce lieu soit anéanti."

8. Il y a tout près du sanctuaire un rocher solide d'une grande largeur et longueur, et dont la profondeur est immense. Ce rocher faisait devant le temple une saillie d'environ soixante-dix coudées et de même à l'arrière.[40] Arrivent alors les impies et les ennemis de la vérité qui entreprennent, entre le sommet du rocher et le sommet de la haute montagne où coulaient les fleuves Couphos et Lycocapros, de creuser la terre, pour frayer une voie aux eaux, de manière à détourner le cours des fleuves et à leur faire submerger la source sainte de Dieu. En effet, le diable homicide les harcelait à le faire. Ayant achevé le canal, ils barrèrent les fleuves pour une durée de dix jours, afin qu'une quantité d'eau s'accumule pour submerger ce saint lieu. Et voici que les fleuves se gonflèrent d'eaux abondantes par le déversement des torrents des montagnes.

9. Archippos, le serviteur de Dieu et desservant du sanctuaire, voyant les machinations du diable et les desseins impurs de ceux qui sacrifiaient aux idoles, se jeta à terre et y resta comme mort, suppliant Dieu et saint Michel,

---

[38] Le loup-sanglier et le léger.
[39] Nous adoptons le texte de Bonnet qui fait le jeu de mots sur les deux composants de Laodicée, qui signifie "la justice du peuple."
[40] L'oratoire est donc situé dans une sorte de fer à cheval rocheux.

le chef des armées, de préserver le lieu saint du déferlement des eaux. Il passa dix jours, sans manger, ni boire, ni se relever du sol, mais glorifiant Dieu, il disait ces mots: "Dieu soit béni, non, je ne sortirai pas de cet oratoire, ni ne prendrai la fuite, mais je périrai avec lui dans les flots, car je crois en mon Dieu qui me sauve de la défaillance et de l'assaut des éléments, par l'intercession de Michel l'incorporel, le chef des armées, sûr qu'il n'abandonnera point sa sainte demeure, ni cette terre, jusqu'à la consommation des temps."

10. Les dix jours passés, arrivent les impies pour lancer les fleuves contre le chef des armées. Ils se disaient les uns aux autres: "Lâchons les fleuves et partons en courant, pour nous arrêter en face et observer l'envahissement des lieux." S'étant concertés de la sorte, ils libérèrent les fleuves à la première heure de la nuit et s'enfuirent aussitôt pour ne pas être devancés par les eaux; puis, comme ils l'avaient dit: "Courons, et allons nous placer en face pour observer l'envahissement des lieux," ils s'arrêtèrent sur la gauche et avaient les yeux fixés au midi, se montrant les uns aux autres l'eau qui dévalait des hauteurs des montagnes avec un formidable mugissement. Ils en étaient tout effrayés.

11. Cependant Archippos, le serviteur de Dieu et desservant du sanctuaire, était couché dans l'oratoire la face contre terre, mouillant le sol de ses larmes et sans relâche invoquant Dieu. Soudain, mû par le Saint-Esprit, il se releva et entonna le psaume que voici: "Les fleuves ont élevé, Seigneur, les fleuves ont élevé leurs voix. Les fleuves ont soulevé des flots destructeurs dans le fracas des eaux. Admirables sont les enflements de la mer, admirable le Seigneur dans les lieux élevés. Tes témoignages se sont attestés avec force. La sanctification sied à ta demeure, ô Seigneur, pour toute la longueur des jours." Quand il eut achevé le psaume, le tonnerre gronda puissamment et le saint chef des armées, descendu en ce lieu, se dressa au sommet du solide rocher, puis, d'une voix forte, dit au serviteur de Dieu: "Sors de ton oratoire, desservant, avant que l'eau ne t'engloutisse!" Lorsque le bienheureux sortit et aperçut la vision fulgurante de sa gloire, il tomba sur le sol comme mort. A nouveau, Michel, le chef des armées, l'apostropha pour la seconde fois disant: "Relève-toi, âme juste, et viens à moi." En réponse, Archippos, le serviteur de Dieu, dit: "Seigneur, je ne suis pas digne de venir à toi, car je tremble à ta vue." Alors Michel, le grand commandeur du Seigneur, dit: "Ne te trouble point et n'aie pas peur, mais lève-toi!" Le bienheureux se releva, se réfugia dans l'oratoire et pénétra sous la table sainte, tremblant et désespérant de survivre. Mais saint Michel, le chef des armées, lui dit: "Prends courage et viens à moi, car les fleuves arrivent en mugissant droit contre toi." Archippos, le serviteur de Dieu, lui dit: "Pour moi, je crois, mon Seigneur, que grande est la puissance de notre Dieu et de Michel, le chef des armées, lesquels ne permettront pas que ce saint lieu soit détruit, jusqu'à la consommation des temps." A ces mots, il sortit de l'oratoire. Et le chef des armées lui dit: "Si tu crois, bienheureux, que le Seigneur peut préserver des eaux cette terre, approche, afin de contempler sa puissance." Alors le serviteur de Dieu sortit et se plaça à sa gauche. Il entendait sa voix et apercevait la grandeur de sa gloire, une colonne de feu qui de la

terre s'élevait jusqu'au ciel. Michel, le chef des armées, lui dit alors: "Sais-tu qui je suis, pour trembler ainsi à ma vue?" L'autre répondit: "Non, mon Seigneur, je ne te connais pas." Le grand commandeur lui dit: "Je suis Michel, le chef des armées de la puissance du Seigneur; c'est moi qui me tiens à la face de Dieu. Et la terrible gloire de la divinité, dont on ne peut suivre la trace, et l'insoutenable flamme de la puissance infinie que dégage sa vue, je suis incapable de les contempler. Mais toi, tu ne peux supporter ma vue et tu frissonnes devant la figure et la force du serviteur. Comment alors les mortels pourront-ils regarder en face ce Dieu que moi-même j'assiste avec crainte?"[41]

Le chef des armées lui dit encore: "Vois-tu l'eau qui dévale des hauteurs des montagnes?" L'autre répondit: "Non, mon Seigneur, mais j'entends de mes oreilles l'énorme fracas des eaux." Le chef des armées lui dit alors: "N'aie crainte, mais tiens ferme."

12. Tandis qu'ils parlaient encore, voici que l'eau dévalant des hauteurs des montagnes allait toucher leurs personnes. Élevant la voix, le chef des armées dit aux fleuves: "Contre qui vous ruez-vous, Couphos et Lycocarpos? Qui vous a subornés et fait quitter votre lit, pour déferler en ce lieu?" A ces mots, il fit le signe de la croix à la face des eaux en disant: "Arrête-toi!" Et aussitôt les fleuves s'immobilisèrent, le front des eaux s'élevant à dix tailles d'homme. Le chef des armées dit à Archippos, le serviteur de Dieu: "Vois-tu, bienheureux, la puissance de Dieu?" L'autre répondit: "Oui, mon Seigneur." Le chef des armées reprit: "Ne crains pas, bienheureux, la menace des eaux."

Et de même que Moïse, dans la mer Rouge, en étendant son bras avait divisé les flots au moyen de son bâton, de même Michel, le grand commandeur et chef des armées, étendant sa droite et tenant <sa lance> à la manière d'un bâton,[42] en frappa le sommet du solide rocher: et aussitôt le solide rocher se fendit d'une extrémité à l'autre, de haut en bas, tandis que le bruit de la pierre fendue retentissait comme un coup de tonnerre et que toute la terre tremblait à l'entour. Le chef des armées dit encore au serviteur de Dieu: "Vois-tu, bienheureux, la puissance de Dieu?" L'autre répondit: "Oui, mon Seigneur, je vois les miracles et la puissance du Dieu qui agit avec toi."

Alors étendant sa droite, il fit à nouveau le signe de la croix sur la faille qui s'était ouverte à ses pieds et la bénit en ces termes: "En ce lieu sera terrassée toute maladie et toute mollesse, tout sortilège et toute incantation et influence du Malin; ici, les entravés et les harcelés par des esprits impurs seront délivrés, les malades seront guéris et quiconque se réfugiera en ce lieu invoquant dans la foi et la crainte le Père, le Fils et le Saint-Esprit et Michel, le chef des armées. Par le nom de Dieu et par mon nom, personne ne s'en reviendra chagriné. La grâce de Dieu et ma puissance étendront ici leur ombre et sanctifieront ce lieu, au nom du Père et du Fils et du Saint-Esprit. Quant

---

[41] P "pourrez-vous regarder en face" ce passage surprenant à la deuxième du pluriel nous a conduit à suivre le texte de Bonnet.
[42] Litt. "à la manière, dit-on, tenant un bâton."

à nos ennemis qui se tiennent là et nous regardent, qu'ils restent pétrifiés sur place, jusqu'à ce que les fleuves engloutissent ma source sainte." Puis il dit à Archippos, le serviteur de Dieu: "Viens à ma droite, bienheureux." Et aussitôt il se plaça à sa droite. Alors, élevant la voix, le chef des armées dit aux fleuves: "Quant à vous, restez frappés de ma lance[43] au fond de cet entonnoir, entonnés dans cette faille et mugissant jusqu'à la fin des temps pour avoir attenté contre moi."

Et la gloire de ce saint lieu durera éternellement, par Jésus-Christ notre Seigneur, à qui la gloire et la puissance, maintenant et à jamais, aux siècles des siècles. Amen.[44]

---

[43] P "Donnez un coup de lance."
[44] La formule "aux siècles des siècles. Amen" ne figure pas dans P.

CHAPTER THIRTY

REVELATIONS AND NOTES ON A BYZANTINE
MANUSCRIPT AT HARVARD

JOHN DUFFY

François Bovon is a frequent and devoted visitor to the Greek manuscripts kept in the Houghton Library at Harvard University. I hope, therefore, that this small contribution on a Byzantine book in the collection, which has not yet received his attention, will be accepted as an appropriate token of friendship and esteem.

What is it?

Since the present case is a good illustration of how slowly sometimes an old book will reveal its true nature, particularly to eyes focused only on certain aspects of the object, it will be best to start from the beginning of a minor odyssey of identification.

Ms. Typ 243H carries on the inside of its front cover the *Ex Libris* of Philip Hofer (1898–1984), the distinguished collector and long-time curator of the College Library's Department of Printing and Graphic Arts.[1] The flyleaf has a note in his hand stating that the book was "bought of Raphael Stora NYC November 1947."[2] Inside the back cover we are informed by a printed sticker that the manuscript was "bequeathed to Harvard College 1984," meaning that it passed at that time from the private collection to the College, as part of the Hofer bequest to the Department of Printing and Graphic Arts. A much older note, handwritten by pen in French, is glued to the inside front cover, identifying the book as a twelfth-century Byzantine parchment manuscript containing homilies of Gregory of Nazianzus accompanied by six illustrations.[3] So much for the information available from notes inscribed on or attached to the volume.

---

[1] I am very grateful to the current curators and staff of the Houghton Library, especially Susan Halpert, for easy access to and help with this manuscript. For a biographical essay on Philip Hofer, see William Bentinck-Smith, "Prince of the Eye: Philip Hofer and the Harvard Library," *Harvard Library Bulletin* 32 [no. 4] (1984): 317–47.

[2] At end of the note Mr. Hofer added his personal code for the price paid.

[3] This may be an indication that the book spent some time in France or passed through the hands of a French book dealer, but in truth we know nothing at the present time about its movements after it left its Greek milieu.

The first official description appeared in print in 1955 on the occasion of a brief exhibition of illuminated and calligraphic manuscripts. The catalog put together for that event announces the content as "Gregorius Nazianzenus: *Homeliarum Liber*" and goes on to list in a little over two lines some of the essential codicological features.[4] The next stage in the story takes place three years later and marks a step forward. The "Internal File" on the volume kept by the library includes a typed set of notes made by the Byzantine and Armenian specialist Sirapie Der Nersessian and is dated January of 1958. Here we find, among other details, three crisp statements that are worth quoting: (1) "*Not* Gregorius Nazianzenus as catalogued"; (2) "This is a collection of notices of saints, known as a *Synaxarium*"; (3) "At the end there is a long text, not identified."

The intervention of Der Nesessian soon bore some fruit, because in the second official description published in 1962 the misidentification of the "Harvard Catalogue" is acknowledged and the contents are now described as "Greek Church: Synaxarion, 14 Nov. to end of Feb., in Greek; followed by an unidentified text."[5]

There the matter has rested for forty years and, as far as the world is concerned, Typ 243H still consists of a partial *synaxarion* and a document of unknown nature. The puzzle presented by that document would surely have been solved some twenty years ago, when the Belgian scholar Justin Mossay was examining the American manuscripts preserving the *Orations* of Gregory of Nazianzus. Though granted access to another Harvard manuscript in the Houghton collection, he was unable to examine our codex, which was at that time still in the private hands of Mr. Hofer. In the circumstances the *Repertorium* could only repeat the information of the Exhibition catalog and the corrected version of Bond and Faye.[6]

Today for the first time in the book's Harvard history we can unlock the mystery of the hitherto unidentified text, but not before underscoring this remarkable fact: not only is the beginning of the work in question distinguished by a handsomely decorated miniature headpiece, but the title, written in gold letters, is intact and fully legible with just a little extra attention. That title is:

Τοῦ ἀγί(ου) γρηγ(ο)ρ(ίου) ἐπισκόπ(ου) νύσσ(ης)·
π(ερ)ὶ θεότητο(ς) υἱοῦ καὶ πν(εύματο)ς καὶ εἰς τὸν ἀβραάμ.

---

[4] William H. Bond and Philip Hofer, *Harvard College Library. Illuminated and Calligraphic Manuscripts: An Exhibition Held at the Fogg Art Museum and Houghton Library. Febr. 14–Apr. 1, 1955* (Cambridge, Mass., 1955), 12 and figure 3.

[5] William H. Bond and Christopher U. Faye, *Supplement to the Census of Medieval and Renaissance Manuscripts in the United States and Canada* (New York: Bibliographical Society of America, 1962), 273–74.

[6] Justin Mossay (with Xavier Lequeux), *Repertorium Nazianzenum. Orationes. Textus Graecus. 2. Codices Americae, Angliae, Austriae* (Paderborn: Ferdinand Schöningh, 1987), 26.

In other words, it is Gregory of Nyssa's treatise *De deitate Filii et Spiritus Sancti*, of which our manuscript—unfortunately having lost several leaves of its final quire—preserves only somewhat less than half of the complete text.

Where did it come from?

Having settled the question of the book's precise contents, we will now go on to consider briefly a chapter in its earlier history—before it reached North America. For it goes without saying that all Greek manuscripts currently in American collections had already lived long lives, inside or sometimes outside the former Byzantine empire. And while it is very difficult to trace the actual steps by which a given manuscript, having left its previous home, made its way to these shores, it is sometimes possible to be very definite about a particular phase of its history. It has recently been shown, for instance, that another Greek book in the Harvard collections once belonged to the Orthodox community at Berat in Albania and left there most likely at the beginning of the last century.[7]

In the case of Typ 243H we will be able to determine for the first time and with surprising speed where exactly it was housed in the Greek world before its migration. The clue is provided by Gregory's treatise and courtesy of the recent critical edition that gives a listing of no less than seventy-nine witnesses for the *De deitate*.[8] A careful perusal of the short descriptions provided for those witnesses turns up a likely match, a manuscript from the island of Lesbos which the editor was not able to examine but came to know from the 1884 catalog description of Athanasius Papadopoulos-Kerameus. At that time it was ms. 1 in the monastery of St. John the Theologian and was succinctly characterized by Papadopoulos-Kerameus as a parchment volume in

---

[7] See John Duffy and Dimiter G. Angelov, "Observations on a Byzantine Manuscript in Harvard College Library," *HSCP* 100 (2000): 501–14.

[8] *Gregorii Nysseni Sermones*, Pars III (ed. Ernst Rhein et al.; Leiden: Brill, 1996). In this composite volume Rhein is the editor of *De deitate*, and his manuscript survey is considerably augmented in an appendix by Friedhelm Mann.

Since they are limited in number, we take the opportunity to list the peculiar readings of Typ 243H collated against the Rhein edition.

120, 2 τελειοτέροις Rhein] πλειοτέροις Typ 243H
124, 18 ἀπαυγάζον] ἀπαυγαζόμενον
125, 4 ante δυνατόν add. δυνατῆς
125, 10 ἀναπεφ.] ἐναπεφήνασιν
127, 1 ὑμῖν] post προκειμένων trsp.
127, 11 τὸν υἱὸν εἰ μὴ ὁ πατήρ] τὸν πατέρα εἰ μὴ ὁ υἱὸς
127, 12 καὶ¹] ὁμοίως καὶ
127, 17 ἀφ᾽ ἑαυτοῦ τι ποιεῖν] αὐτοῦ ποιεῖν τί ἀφ᾽ ἑαυτοῦ
127, 18 post λαλήσω add. καὶ
128, 9 πῶς om.
The copy runs out at 128, 17 τὸ πᾶν.

quarto, consisting of 88 leaves, written in two columns probably at the beginning of the twelfth century, and having a considerable number of its leaves missing at the beginning and end.[9] The contents, laid out with equal brevity, are given as: 1) a six-month truncated *synaxarion* beginning at November 11 and ending in February (folios 1ʳ–86ᵛ) and 2) Gregory of Nyssa's *De deitate*, with incipit οἶόν τι πάσχουσι (86ᵛ). The reason why a photocopy could not be obtained from Lesbos by the new editor is now clear: that manuscript has been residing under another name in Cambridge, Massachusetts, for the past fifty-five years.

What more can be said about it?

A lot of things, of course, since like any antique book this one contains a small world within its covers and presents a number of issues that would be worth pursuing, such as the particular mixture of the contents, the place of this exemplar in the category of *synaxaria*, the illustrations and other decorative elements, the covers themselves, and other aspects of the volume's history between the twelfth and twentieth centuries. On this occasion, however, it will only be possible to contribute some preliminary notes on a limited number of points, but it is to be hoped that they will lead to further work on Typ 243H in the future.

Throughout the manuscript, and particularly in the major document, the *synaxarion*, there are frequent examples of illuminated initial letters, gold lettering in titles, and decorative borders marking off main sections of the text. Also in the main text there have survived six miniatures, of good quality, which undoubtedly played no small role in the book's fate in the marketplace. In any case they, rather than the texts, caught a more attentive eye in this part of the world. The Der Nesessian notes, referred to earlier, already record a list of the miniatures with identification of figures and feasts. Since that information has not been published and because it needs correction in a couple of places, I will present here a revised accounting, noting that each of the six folia exhibiting a miniature is marked by a small protruding (and now well worn) piece of leather of unknown date.

1. fol. 1ʳ [Nov. 11]   St. Menas and companions Victor and Vicentius
2. fol. 13ʳ [Nov. 25 (sic)]   St. Clement of Rome
3. fol. 22ʳ [Dec. 6]   St. Nicholas of Myra

---

[9] Κατάλογος τῶν ἐν ταῖς βιβλιοθήκαις τῆς νήσου Λέσβου ἑλληνικῶν χειρογράφων, in Ὁ ἐν Κωνσταντινουπόλει Ἑλληνικὸς Φιλολογικὸς Σύλλογος. Μαυρογορδάτειος Βιβλιοθήκη. Παράρτημα τοῦ ΙΕ΄ τόμου (Constantinople, 1884). Since it is very difficult nowadays to get one's hands on the original, I have used the P.-K. catalog for this monastery as reproduced by Iakobos Kleombrotos in *Mytilena sacra*, vol. I: Ἡ ἱερὰ Μονὴ Ὑψηλοῦ. Ἱστορία, τέχνη (Athens: [Hiera Monē Hypsēlou Lesbou], 1970), 133.

4. fol. 47ᵛ [Dec. 25]   The Nativity
5. fol. 54ᵛ [Jan. 1]   The Circumcision
6. fol. 58ᵛ [Jan. 6]   The Theophany (Epiphany)

With regard to the text of the *synaxarion* it is worth citing a descriptive definition by the noted Bollandiste, François Halkin: "Le synaxaire est un livre liturgique contenant pour chaque jour de l'année, du 1ᵉʳ septembre au 31 août, de brèves notices biographiques sur les saints vénérés ce jour-là. Les manuscrits du synaxaire grec sont nombreux, mais ils diffèrent plus ou moins profondément les uns des autres d'après les usages locaux et les remaniements introduits au cour des âges."[10] The Harvard copy is an example of the type that covers half the liturgical year, in this case the "winter" half (from September to February). Unfortunately Typ 243H had lost, sometime before the late nineteenth century, its first eleven quires containing all the material for September 1 to November 10. The first extant folium opens with the commemorations for November 11, beginning with the martyrdom of St. Menas and his companions, and here already we find evidence for the point made by Halkin, namely that *synaxaria* can differ considerably from one to the other. The Harvard copy has two noteworthy elements in the Menas section. First, the biography is preceded by two lines of 12-syllable iambic verse and one old-style hexameter, highlighting the saint's martyrdom:

Αἴγυπτος ὄντως εἰ τέκη τίκτει μέγαν,
Τμηθεὶς ἀληθὲς τοῦτο Μηνᾶς δεικνύει.
Μηνᾶς ἑνδεκάτη ξίφος ἔτλη γηθόσυνος κῆρ (sic).

This feature, which is repeated more or less consistently for other saints and feast days, may be one of the new elements introduced in *synaxaria* of the twelfth century. Secondly, the biography of Menas is followed immediately by a set of five miracles associated with the saint, a fact of some significance for the history and transmission of those stories.[11] A thorough study of the rest of the text would probably lead to some other interesting and useful discoveries.

At first sight it might appear to be anomalous for the single homily of Gregory of Nyssa to show up as the only other occupant of the book. The

---

[10] In the Avant-Propos to Hippolyte Delehaye, *Synaxaires byzantins, ménologes, typica* (London: Variorum Reprints, 1977), i.

[11] There has only ever been one edition of a set of thirteen miracles of Menas, attributed to the Patriarch Theophilus of Alexandria. It was published just over a hundred years ago on the basis of a manuscript in Moscow by I. Pomjalovskij in his monograph *Zhitie prepodobnago Paisija velikago i Timotheja patriarkha Aleksandrijskago poviestvovanie o chudesakh Sv. velikomuchenika Miny* (St. Petersburg, 1900), 62–89. Karl Krumbacher gave it a quite critical review in *BZ* 10 (1901): 344. A glance at the entries on Menas in the *Bibliotheca hagiographica graeca* shows how rare the witnesses for this miracle collection are, and there appears to be just one other with the selection of the same five. The present writer and Emmanuel Bourbouhakis are preparing a study of the five stories in Typ 243H for an upcoming publication.

manuscript itself, however, has preserved an explanation in the form of a later marginal note inserted alongside the beginning of Gregory's text. It is written in what appears to be a fourteenth-century hand in dark brown ink, with two or three letters lost at the start of most of the lines. The note can be tentatively reconstructed as follows:

τοῦ τυπι(κοῦ)
<δι>άταξις· ὁ
<πα>ρὼν λόγο(ς),
<κυ>(ρια)κ(ῇ) μετα τὴν
<χ(ριστο)ῦ γ>έννησιν
<ἀνα>γινώσκεται
<ὁ> γὰρ ἐντυχὼν
<. . .>. . . .[12]

Regardless of the exact wording the main point for present purposes is found in the core section which clearly tells us that this homily of Gregory was read on the <Sunday> following the feast of the Nativity. And while the precise construction of the abbreviation for the day of the week in question may be problematic, we have good supporting evidence for the likelihood of its being a Sunday.[13]

On the other hand, even if the marginal note provides a good reason for Gregory's presence in a church book that covers the month of December, there is still the noteworthy fact that not a single one of the many other copies transmitting the *De deitate* is a *synaxarion*. Quite a few of them represent other kinds of special liturgical books, to a great extent *panegyrika* and *menologia*; only Typ 243H among them is a *synaxarion*.

At some future date, when the huge mass of *synaxaria* is subjected to systematic research, the Harvard copy—a twelfth-century version and illustrated— may turn out to be a book of some special interest in the history of the genre's development.

---

[12] The last line, whose end is marked in typical fashion by a small cross, is difficult to restore and the use of an ultraviolet lamp did not produce results. The first couple of letters are completely lost, and then there follow traces of others that could be, for example, τις or σεις, neither of which as fragments would seem likely to contribute to a satisfactory ending.

[13] For the restoration of κυριακῆ (i.e. κυριακῇ) we can point to the fact that in another twelfth-century witness for the *De deitate*, Istanbul Patriarchal Library ms. Panagia Kamariotissa 10, the oration is specifically labeled with the words: Κυριακῇ μετὰ τὴν χριστοῦ γέννησιν. See Aimilianos Tsakapoulos, Περιγραφικὸς κατάλογος τῶν χειρογράφων τῆς Βιβλιοθήκης τοῦ Οἰκουμενικοῦ Πατριαρχείου. Τόμος Α΄. Τμῆμα χειρογράφων Παναγίας Καμαριωτίσσης (Istanbul: Patriarchal Printing House, <1953>), 30. Two later manuscripts give the same information, as reported by Albert Ehrhard, *Überlieferung und Bestand der hagiographischen und homiletischen Literatur der griechischen Kirche von den Anfängen bis zum Ende des 16. Jahrhunderts* (3 vols.; Leipzig: J. C. Hinrichs, 1937–1939), 2:503 (= Athos Dionysiou 173, 17th century) and 3:195 (= Athos Gregoriou 9, 16th–17th century). See also the remarks of F. Mann in Rhein *De deitate* 81.

Appendix

Ms. Typ 243H has not only suffered losses at the beginning and end, but is missing two internal quires as well and, as presently bound, has some leaves out of their proper places. Fortunately most of the quire marks remain in the surviving parts, the first (partly erased) one appearing on the current fol. 1ʳ and indicating quire XII in Greek letters. Using these as guides it is possible to sketch an approximate reconstruction of the original manuscript. In the scheme below we indicate in separate columns: 1) the quire numbers; 2) the folio numbers for the extant parts (including the correct and restored order of leaves within quires XII and XXI); and 3) the contents. Angled brackets indicate lost material. In the two damaged quires the letters W X Y Z Z¹ Y¹ X¹ W¹ represent the normal order of quire leaves.

Quires	Folia	Contents
<I–XI>	< >	<Sept. 1–Nov. 10>
XII	1	Nov. 11
	3	Nov. 11
	<Y>	<End of Nov. 11,
	<Z>	all of Nov. 12, 13
	<Z¹>	and beginning
	<Y¹>	of Nov. 14>
	4	Rest of Nov. 14
	2	Nov. 15, part of Nov. 16
XIII	5–12	Nov. 16 cont. to Nov. 23
XIV	<W>	<Rest of Nov. 23, most of Nov. 24>
	13–18	Last part of Nov. 24 to first part of Dec. 2
	<W¹>	<Rest of Dec. 2 and first part of Dec. 3>
XV–XX	19–66	Rest of Dec. 3 to Jan. 18
XXI	67	Rest of Jan. 18, beg. of Jan. 19
	<X>	<End of Jan. 19, beg. of Jan. 20>
	69	Rest of Jan. 20, beg. of Jan. 21
	70	Jan. 21 continued
	71	End of Jan. 21, beg. of Jan. 22
	72	End of Jan. 22, first part of Jan. 23
	68	Rest of Jan. 23, first part of Jan. 24
	<W¹>	Last part of Jan. 24 to ?Jan. 25
<XXII–XXIII>	< >	<Jan. 25? to almost the end of Feb. 14>
XXIV	73–80	End of Feb. 14 to first part of Feb. 25
XXV	81–88	Rest of Feb. 25 to Feb. 28 (i.e. end of the month), plus Gregory of Nyssa *De deitate filii* pp. 117, 1–128, 17 (ed. Rhein)
<XXVI>	< >	<The rest of Gregory's treatise would have occupied approximately 4 folios>

CHAPTER THIRTY-ONE

HOMÉLIE COPTE SUR LES APÔTRES AU JUGEMENT DERNIER

FRANÇOISE MORARD

Homélie copte Zoega 265: Introduction[1]

L'auteur

L'"humble moine Bachios," ainsi se nomme lui-même l'auteur de l'Homélie sur les apôtres au Jugement dernier dont nous présentons ici les huit feuillets du texte conservés par la Collection Borgia de Naples.[2] Un fragment en provenance de la Bibliothèque universitaire d'Oslo[3] nous en donne vraisemblablement l'*incipit* et nous renseigne sur l'identité de cet "humble moine": il était "évêque de Maiouma de Gaza dans les frontières de Jérusalem" et il "prononça ce discours pour l'honneur et la gloire de nos pères les saints apôtres du Christ Jésus." Le même fragment nous dit de plus "qu'il enseigna Isaac le Samaritain." On a là une allusion à un épisode de la vie de Bachios raconté par une homélie "A la louange de la Croix" attribuée à Cyrille de Jérusalem.[4] Dans cet épisode, "un pieux prêtre orthodoxe du nom de Bachios" convertit à la foi chrétienne un Samaritain qui doutait de l'efficacité de la Croix de Jésus en rendant douce une eau amère dans laquelle il avait plongé la croix. Cette même homélie nous apprend un peu plus loin que "ce prêtre vivait dans un petit monastère, non loin d'Ascalon, et que, comme archimandrite, il était à la tête des moines qui l'habitaient." Enfin dans une autre homélie en l'honneur des Trois jeunes gens de Babylone,[5] Bachios nous apprend qu'il a, lui,

---

[1] Je tiens, en commençant, à remercier très chaleureusement le professeur Jean-Daniel Kaestli qui n'a ménagé ni sa peine ni son temps pour me conseiller et me venir en aide dans l'établissement de ce texte et de sa traduction souvent problématiques.

[2] Ces 8 feuillets sont répertoriés par Georg Zoega dans son *Catalogus Codicum Copticorum manuscriptorum*, sous le numéro 265 (Rome: Sacra Congregatio de Propaganda Fide, 1810; rééd. Joseph-Marie Sauget; Hildesheim: Olms, 1973), 619.

[3] Ce fragment d'Oslo 46 (et non 217) est signalé par Tito Orlandi dans "Bacheus," *The Coptic Encyclopedia* (éd. Aziz S. Atiya; 8 vols.; New York: Macmillan, 1991), 2:324.

[4] *Ps. Cirillo di Gerusalemme: Omelie copte sulla Passione, sulla Croce e sulla Vergine* (éd. Antonella Campagnano; Testi e Documenti per lo studio dell'Antichita 65, Serie copta 9; Milano: Cisalpino-Goliardica, 1980), 85–99.

[5] Répertoriée dans le Catalogue de Zoega sous le numéro 264.

"le très humble Bachios," "l'espoir d'aller en Égypte, auprès de mon Seigneur et père Jacques, afin de voir la contrée de son corps et de son saint martyrion" (p. 12, col. 1). Or ce Jacques, appelé en raison de son martyre, "Jacques l'Intercis," fut dépecé, membre après membre, en Perse, au troisième siècle et ses restes transportés en Égypte par les soins de Pierre l'Ibérien, moine et évêque de Maiouma près de Gaza. Celui-ci lui fit construire un sanctuaire dans les environs d'Oxyrhynque dans le courant du cinquième siècle.[6] Cette précision historique nous permet donc de situer notre homélie après le cinquième siècle, sans doute au sixième, à l'époque où, d'après Orlandi,[7] on peut placer la formation des Cycles homilétiques et hagiographiques dans la littérature copte et donc, vraisemblablement, le cycle attribué à Bachios.

Le texte

Le sermon est adressé "au peuple qui aime le Christ" et il s'attache à montrer la gloire des apôtres, rendus dignes par le Seigneur de l'assister au jour du jugement en siégeant avec lui sur douze trônes, dans la vallée de Josaphat. La description de cette scène du jugement emprunte des éléments à l'Apocalypse johannique avec ses énumérations d'anges, d'archanges, de prophètes, de justes, de martyrs, et ses quatre animaux. Le texte présente cependant des traits particuliers comme la personnification des péchés et des bonnes actions qui "se tiennent debout" de part et d'autre des pécheurs (p. 83) et que le Seigneur emporte loin de ceux auxquels il a pardonné (p. 94). De plus le texte suppose un état intermédiaire où les pécheurs ont déjà souffert en se trouvant au pouvoir de la mort dans l'Amenté, c'est-à-dire les Enfers dans la littérature copte, et dont ils sont supposés sortir pour le dernier jugement. Les apôtres, quant à eux, sont déjà glorifiés, portant des couronnes et des vêtements de gloire, assistés des anges, "ils sont dans la paix avec leur Seigneur," alors que le monde des pécheurs tremble et se lamente. Mais le trait le plus frappant de cette homélie réside dans l'insistance qu'elle met sur la miséricorde, celle du Père dont le Fils est revêtu (p. 84), mais surtout celle que Jésus demande à ses apôtres dans l'exercice de leur jugement sur les pécheurs. Chaque interpellation que le Sauveur adresse aux apôtres individuellement est marquée par cette nécessité d'user de miséricorde à l'égard des humains et des pécheurs qui se présentent au jugement: "Considère mes miséricordes, ô Pierre. Toutes celles que j'ai accomplies pour toi sur la terre, accomplis-les, toi aussi, pour ma créature" (p. 88). A chaque apôtre, Jésus rappelle la bienveillance et l'indulgence qu'il a eues pour lui sur la terre: "Souviens-toi de mon amitié pour toi, au jour de ton incrédulité" dit le Seigneur à Thomas: "C'est moi qui vous ai accordé la miséricorde depuis le commencement, je veux que vous per-

---

[6] Voir l'article "James Intercisus," dans *Coptic Encyclopedia*, 4:1321.
[7] Dans l'article "Bacheus," *Coptic Encyclopedia*, 2:324.

sévériez en elle aujourd'hui envers ma créature" (p. 91). Et Jésus rappelle aux apôtres que c'est parce qu'ils ont été atteints eux-mêmes par la miséricorde et l'amour du Christ qu'ils ont été faits dignes de rendre le jugement avec lui (p. 94). En conclusion le Christ proclame que c'est en raison de ses miséricordes envers les pécheurs qu'il va leur pardonner tous leurs péchés (p. 95). "Alors quand le diable verra ce qui est arrivé, il pleurera en disant: 'Tout mon effort a été anéanti aujourd'hui.'" C'est sur ce constat d'échec du démon que notre texte s'arrête, laissant l'auditeur, quelle que soit la fin du sermon, dans le réconfort d'une espérance sans faille en la miséricorde de Dieu pour tous les pécheurs. Il est difficile de ne pas penser qu'en Occident, à la même époque, un autre moine, saint Benoît de Nursie, recommandait dans sa *Règle* à ses fils de "ne jamais désespérer de la miséricorde de Dieu: "Et de Dei misericordia numquam desperare."[8]

Le manuscrit

C'est Oskar von Lemm qui, le premier, attira l'attention sur les huit feuillets que nous éditons ici.[9] Il avait remarqué qu'un fragment copte de la Bibliothèque Nationale de Paris, le P 129[18]126 que Pierre Lacau ne savait où placer dans la reconstitution de ce qu'il appelait avec hésitation un "*Évangile (?) apocryphe,*"[10] recouvrait exactement un passage de l'homélie contenue dans ces huit feuillets. En réalité, le texte publié par Lacau était une homélie sur "L'amour de Jésus pour ses apôtres"[11] qui se présentait en trois manuscrits différents: A, B, et C. Lacau attribuait le fragment de Paris P129[18] 126 au manuscrit A; les huit feuillets de l'homélie sur "Les Apôtres au Jugement Dernier" signalés par von Lemm devaient donc appartenir au manuscrit B. Ainsi, il y aurait eu deux homélies différentes sur les apôtres dans un même codex. La chose semble possible du fait que l'homélie éditée par Lacau s'étend de la page 19 à la page 62; celle du moine Bachios, couvrant les pages 81 à 96. Le fragment d'Oslo 46[12] contenant le début de l'homélie de Bachios appartiendrait, lui aussi, au manuscrit A. C'est ce que pense Enzo Lucchesi dans la reconstitution

---

[8] S. Benoît, *Reg.* 4.90.

[9] Voir le *Bulletin de l'Académie Impériale des Sciences de St. Pétersbourg* III, N° 5, LXIV, pp. 348–54 = réédition par Peter Nagel, *Koptische Miscellen* 1–148 (Subsidia byzantina lucis ope iterata 11; Leipzig: Zentralantiquariat der Deutschen Demokratischen Republik, 1972), 146–52.

[10] Voir Pierre Lacau, "Évangile (?) apocryphe," *Fragments d'Apocryphes coptes* (Mémoires publiés par les membres de l'Institut Français d'Archéologie Orientale du Caire 9; Le Caire: Imprimerie de l'Institut Français d'Archéologie Orientale, 1904), 79–108.

[11] Signalée dans la *Clavis Apocryphorum Novi Testamenti* sous le no. 81, pp. 58–59 (Narratio evangelica apocrypha cum homilia contexta in qua Jesum regem creare volunt). Traduction française de Françoise Morard dans *Les Écrits apocryphes chrétiens*, vol. 2 (Bibliothèque de la Pléiade; Paris: Gallimard, prêt à paraître).

[12] Voir plus haut n. 3.

qu'il a proposée[13] de nos deux homélies, tout en faisant remarquer avec raison qu'il existe bon nombre de codices copiés par le même scribe et auxquels nos deux textes seraient susceptibles d'appartenir.

Homélie sur les apôtres au Jugement dernier—Borgianus 265, Naples, BN, Cassetta I.B.13, fascicolo 442 (Zoega 265)[14]

(81a) ⲚⲎⲦⲚ ⲉⲃⲟⲗ ϩⲚⲦⲠⲉ · ⲉϯϩⲁⲡ ⲙ̅ⲡⲕⲟⲥⲙⲟⲥ ⲦⲎⲣϥ ÷[5] ›Ⲛⲁⲓ̈ⲁⲦϥ ⲙ̅ⲡⲉⲦ-
Ⲛⲁⲉⲓ [ϩⲚ]ⲟⲩⲙⲚⲦⲚⲁ ϩ̅ⲙⲡⲣⲁⲛ ⲚⲚⲉⲓ̈ⲁⲡⲟⲥⲧⲟⲗⲟⲥ·[10]ⲉⲧⲟⲩⲁⲁⲃ· ⲍⲉ[ϥ]Ⲛⲁⲍ̈ⲓ
ⲙ̅ⲡ[ⲥⲟⲗ]ⲥⲗ ⲙ̅ⲡⲙⲁ[ⲛ̅ⲙ̅ⲧⲟⲛ] [- - -] ⲡⲉⲧ[15][- - -][- - -][- - -][- - -][- - -][20][- - -]
[- - -][- - -][- -]ⲥⲙ[- - -][. . .]ⲉⲡⲍ[. .][25][. . .]ⲉⲙⲡ [. .][. ⲛ̅]ϣⲁⲉⲛⲉϩ
[ⲡⲉⲧ]ⲁϥϥⲓⲡⲣⲟⲟⲩϣ ⲙ̅ⲡⲉⲧⲚ̅ⲣ̅ⲡⲙⲉⲉⲩⲉ ϩⲓ̈ⲍ̅ⲙ̅ⲡⲕⲁϩ · ϥⲚⲁϣⲱⲡⲉ ⲚⲎ(81b)ⲦⲚ̅
ⲚϣⲎⲣⲉ ϩⲚ̅ⲦⲁⲙⲚⲦⲉⲣⲟ Ⲛϣⲁⲉⲛⲉϩ ÷

÷ϯⲍ̅ⲱ ⲙ̅ⲙⲟⲥ ⲚⲎ[5]ⲦⲚ ⲱ ⲡⲗⲁⲟⲥ ⲙ̅ⲙⲁⲓ̈ⲡⲉⲭ̅ⲥ̅ ⲁⲚⲟⲕ ⲡⲉⲓ̈ⲉⲗⲁⲭⲓⲥⲧⲟⲥ ⲃⲁⲭⲉⲟⲥ·
ⲍⲉⲡⲉⲧ[10]Ⲛⲁⲣ̅ⲡⲙⲉⲉⲩⲉ ⲚⲚⲉⲓ̈ⲁⲡⲟⲥⲧⲟⲗⲟⲥ ⲉⲧ[ⲟⲩ][ⲁⲁⲃ . . .]Ⲛ[. .][. . .]ⲗⲁⲁⲩ.
ϩⲟ[15][. . .] ⲙ̅ⲙⲚⲦ[Ⲛⲁ ϩ]ⲙ̅ⲡⲉⲩⲣⲁⲛ [ⲙ]Ⲛ ϩⲚⲟⲩⲡⲣⲟⲥⲫⲟⲣⲁ · ⲁ[. .]
ϩⲚⲟⲩⲚⲁ[20]ⲕⲁⲚⲟⲩⲍ[. .]ⲙ̅ⲙ[. .] Ⲛ̅ϥϥ[ⲓ] ⲙ̅ⲡⲣⲟⲟⲩϣ Ⲛ̅ϥⲥϩⲁⲓ̈
ⲙ̅ⲡⲉⲩⲣ̅ⲡⲙⲉⲉⲩⲉ· ⲙ̅Ⲛ̅[25]Ⲛⲉϩⲓⲥⲉ Ⲛ̅ⲧⲁⲩϣⲟⲡⲟⲩ ϩⲁⲡⲁⲣⲁⲛ ÷ ÷ⲕⲁⲚ ⲟⲩϣⲟⲡⲥ
[ⲉϥ]Ⲛⲁⲁⲁⲥ ⲉⲛⲉ[30][ϩ]ⲏ]ⲕⲉ · ⲥⲉⲛⲁ[ⲣ̅]ⲕⲗⲏⲣⲟⲛⲟ(82a)ⲙⲉⲓ̈ ϩⲙ̅ⲡⲙⲁ ⲙ̅ⲡⲥⲟⲗⲥ̅
ⲗ̅ⲙⲡⲉϩⲟⲟⲩ̄ ⲙ̅ⲡϩⲁⲡ ⲙ̅ⲙⲉ ÷ ›[5]ⲉⲣⲉⲡⲉⲓ̈ⲙ̅Ⲛ̅ⲧⲥⲛⲟⲟⲩⲥ Ⲛⲁⲡⲟⲧⲟⲗⲟⲥ
ϩⲓ̈ⲍ̅ⲙⲡⲉⲩⲙ̅Ⲛ̅ⲧⲥⲛⲟⲟⲩⲥ Ⲛ̅ⲑⲣⲟⲛⲟⲥ [10]ϩⲙ̅ⲡⲕⲱⲧⲉ ⲙ̅ⲡⲉⲩⲍⲟⲉⲓ̈ⲥ ÷ ›[ⲉⲩϯ]ϩⲙⲟⲧ
ⲙ̅ⲡⲍⲟⲩⲧⲁϥⲧ[ⲉ] ⲙ̅ⲡⲣⲉⲥⲃⲩ[ⲧⲉ][15]ⲣⲟⲥ ⲉⲩϩⲙ̅ⲡⲕⲱⲧⲉ ⲙ̅ⲡⲉⲩⲍⲟⲉⲓ̈ⲥ ϩⲚⲛⲙ̅ⲡⲏⲩⲉ
ϩⲓ̈ⲍⲛⲛⲉⲩⲑⲣⲟ[20]Ⲛⲟⲥ ÷

›ⲧⲁⲓ̈ⲧⲉ ⲑⲉ Ⲛ̅Ⲛⲉⲓ̈ⲁⲡⲟⲥⲧⲟⲗⲟⲥ ⲉ[ⲩ]ϩⲙⲟⲟⲥ ϩⲓⲍ̅Ⲛ̅Ⲛⲉⲩⲑⲣⲟⲛⲟⲥ ϩⲙ̅ⲡⲉⲓ̈ⲁ
[25]Ⲛ̅ⲓ̈ⲱⲥⲁⲫⲁⲧ ϩⲙ̅ⲡⲕⲱⲧⲉ ⲙ̅ⲡⲣⲣⲟ ⲡⲉⲭ̅ⲥ̅ ⲉⲩϯϩⲁⲡ ⲉⲡⲕⲟⲥⲙⲟⲥ ⲦⲎⲣ[ϥ ÷][30] ›ⲱ
ⲧⲉⲓ̈ ⲚⲟϬ [Ⲛ̅Ⲧⲓ̈ⲙ](82b)ⲱⲣⲓⲁ Ⲛ̅ϣⲏⲣⲉ ⲙ̅ⲡⲉϩⲟⲟⲩ ⲙ̅ⲡϩⲁⲡ ⲙ̅ⲙⲉ ÷ ÷ⲉⲣⲉ ϩⲚϣⲟ·
Ⲛ̅[5]ϣⲟ · ⲙ̅Ⲛ̅ϩⲚⲧⲃⲁ Ⲛ̅[ⲧ]ⲃⲁ ⲥⲟⲟⲩϩ ⲉⲛⲉⲩⲉⲣⲏⲩ ÷ ÷ⲉⲣⲉⲟⲩϣⲧⲟⲣⲧⲣ̅
ⲙ̅Ⲛ̅ⲟⲩⲚⲟϬ[10]Ⲛ̅ⲥⲧⲱⲧ ⲡⲟⲣϣ ⲉⲃⲟⲗ ϩ[ⲙ̅]ⲡⲉⲓ̈ⲁ Ⲛ̅ⲓ̈ⲱ[ⲥⲁ]ⲫ[ⲁⲧ . . . .][- - -]
[15][- - -][- - -][- - -][- - -][- - -] [20][- - -][- - -][- - -][. . . . . .]ⲟ[. . .]
[- - - ÷] [25] ÷ⲟ[.] ⲙ̅ⲡⲕⲁ[ϩⲉ]ⲣⲁⲧⲟⲩ ϩ[ⲓⲍ̅ⲙⲡ]ⲙⲁⲛ̅ϯϩⲁⲡ ϣⲁⲁⲧ Ⲛ̅Ⲛⲉⲩ[Ϭ]ⲣⲏⲡⲉ
÷[30] ÷Ⲛ̅ⲁⲡⲟⲥⲧⲟⲗⲟⲥ ϩⲱⲟⲩ ⲫⲱ(83a)ⲣⲉⲓ̈ Ⲛ̅ϩⲚ̅ⲕⲗⲟⲙ Ⲛⲉⲟⲟⲩ ÷ ›Ⲛ̅ⲣⲣⲱⲟⲩ
ⲙ̅ⲡⲕⲁϩ ϣⲁⲁⲧ Ⲛ̅[5]Ⲛⲉⲩⲥⲧⲟⲗⲏ ϩⲙ̅ⲡⲉ[ⲓ̈]ⲁ Ⲛ̅ⲓ̈ⲱⲥⲁⲫⲁⲧ ÷ ›Ⲛ̅ⲁⲡⲟⲥⲧⲟⲗⲟⲥ
ϩⲱⲟⲩ ⲫⲟ[10]ⲣⲉⲓ̈ ⲚⲚⲉⲩⲥⲧⲟ[ⲗⲏ] Ⲛⲉⲟⲟⲩ ⲙ̅[ⲡ]ⲙ̅ⲧⲟ ⲉⲃⲟⲗ ⲙ̅ⲡⲉⲩⲍⲟⲉⲓ̈ⲥ ÷
[. . . . .]ⲩⲗⲗ[15][. . .] ϣⲁⲁⲧ Ⲛ̅Ⲛⲉⲩⲥⲛϥⲉ ϩ[ⲙ̅][ⲡ]ⲉⲓ̈ⲁ Ⲛ̅ⲓ̈ⲱ[ⲥⲁ][ϥⲁⲧ] ·
[. . . . .]ⲟⲩⲚ[. . . . ⲁⲡ]ⲟⲥⲧ[ⲟ][20][ⲗⲟⲥ . . . .]ⲧⲉ ϩⲙ
[. . . . .]ⲉ[. . . . . . .]ⲡ[- - -][. . . . .]ⲁⲧ [25][. . . . .]
[- - -][- - -][- - -][- - -] [30][- - -][- - -][- - -]

---

[13] Enzo Lucchesi, "Un évangile apocryphe imaginaire," *OLP* 28 (1997): 176 nn. 11 et 12.

[14] Le signe > précédant une majuscule reproduit le chevron placé au-dessous des grandes majuscules en marge des colonnes de gauche dans le manuscrit. Le signe ÷ précédant une majuscule reproduit le trait entre deux points placé au-dessus, ou parfois à côté, des grandes majuscules en marge des colonnes de droite dans le manuscrit.

(83b) саппїром ∻ ∻тмѝтршме тнрс̄ аѕератс̄ ѕїх̄ѝнеуоуе⁵рнте
ѕм̄пеїа ѝїшсафат м̄пеѕооу м̄пѕап мме ∻ ∻ѝапостолос ѕш¹⁰оу
ѕм̄оос ѕїх̄ѝнеуоромос ѕм̄пкште м̄пеух̄оеїс ∻ ∻сарѯ̄ мїм кнк
а¹⁵ѕну м̄пеѕооу м̄пѕап ѕм̄пеїа ѝїшсафат ∻ ∻ѝапостолос ²⁰ѕшоу
форєї м̄пеооу м̄пмоуте ∻ ∻лас мїм ѝ̄ршме матшм м²⁵пеѕооу
м̄пѕап мме ∻ ∻плас ѝ̄неїапостолос ѕшоу †ѕап м̄ѝпеу³⁰х̄оеїс ∻
[∻]ѝ̄мобе м̄поуа [п]оуа аѕератоу (84a) еусооѕе ероч ѕм̄пмам†ѕап ·
∻мас‹ѕелос ѕшоῦ ѕї⁵тоушоу ѝ̄напостолос · еусолса м̄мооу ∻
‹пкосмос тнрч̄ рїме м̄пе¹⁰ѕооу м̄пѕап ∻ ‹мапостолос ѕшоу раще
х̄ееуѕмоо[с] еу†ѕап мѝ̄¹⁵пеух̄оеїс ∻ ‹пкосмос тнрч̄ щ̄тр̄тшр
м̄пеѕооу м̄пѕап · ма²⁰‹постолос ѕшоу ѕѝ̄†рнмн м̄пеух̄оеїс ∻
‹ке малїста пето ммоб ²⁵ емаї тнроу ерепщнре м̄пмоуте ѕм̄оос
м̄пеум̄то евол еч†ѕап мм̄³⁰мау етоїк[оу]менн тнр[с ∻] (84b)
∻ѕотамѕе ершампщнре м̄мерїт бооλеч м̄тмѝт⁵мѕнт м̄пеїшт[·]
ечѕмоос м̄пмто евол ѝ̄неїапостолос ѕм̄пеїа ¹⁰ѝїшсафат ∻
∻мм̄пнуе масш еуоу[шм] м̄ѕїсе мо[.]мо[. . .]ере ¹⁵ш[. .]ч[. . .]
песмт х̄[. . .]м]ечщнре [ѕ]моос [ѕ]їх̄ѝ[е]ором[ос ѝ̄м]²⁰апо[столос]
[- - -][- - -][- - -] ∻є [- - -] ²⁵о [. . . . . .]а [- - -][- - -][- - -][- - -]
³⁰[- - -][- - -]

(85a) ‹оуλаѯ̄їс ѝ̄тумамїс ѝ̄саоутасма ∻ ‹оутаѯ̄їс мар⁵хаѕѕелос
ѝ̄саоуеї ∻ ‹оутаѯ̄їс меѯоусїа ѝ̄саоуеї ∻ ¹⁰ ‹оутаѯ̄їс маѕѕелос
ѝ̄саоуеї ∻ ‹маїѕе тнроу еумма епе¹⁵сн[т] евол ѕѝ̄тпе · ѕїтм̄пеїшт
ѝ̄моуое[ї]м · [. . . . .] епеч²⁰[. . . .] ∻ [. п]щнре ѕш[оч . . .] ѕе
[. .] о [. .] мечапостолос е²⁵тоулаав ∻ ‹ѕ̄ммобме метаеїо̄ еткште
емемеїоте мапосто³⁰лос · ереоуом мїм етсооуѕ (85b) ѳешреї
м̄мооу еуѕмоос ѕїх̄ѝнеуоромос ∻ еу†еооу мау ⁵ ѕїтѝ̄небом
тнроу ѝ̄мм̄пнуе ∻

∻тоте пеїшт матѝ̄ммоу е¹⁰вол ѕѝ̄тпе ѝ̄ѕѝ̄кетаѯ̄їс ѝ̄самеуєрну ·
еуѕаеооу мате · оуѕрн¹⁵∻пе ѝ̄рро ѝ̄саоуеї ∻ ∻ѕѝ̄клом меоу
ѝ̄саѕѝ̄клом меоу ∻ ²⁰ ѕѝ̄столн етсотѝ̄ ѝ̄саѕѝ̄столн ∻ ∻ѕм̄моус
ѝ̄саппїром· ѝ̄са²⁵ѕѝ̄моус ѝ̄саппїром ∻ ∻ѕѝ̄ѳромос меоу ·
ѝ̄саѕѝ̄ѳромос мео³⁰оу ∻ ∻ѕѝ̄аѕаѳом мса(86a)ѕѝ̄аѕаѳом ∻ ‹оупусн
м̄мооу ѝ̄саоупусн м̄мооу ∻ ⁵‹оупараѕїсос ѝ̄саоупараѕїсос ∻
‹маїѕе тнроу ч̄х̄ооу ммеч¹⁰апостолос евол ѕїтм̄пеїшт ѝ̄меоубеїм ∻

‹ачкотч̄ ѝ̄бї ¹⁵ї̄с̄ · пех̄ач м̄петрос · х̄епамерїт петрос · еїспеѕооу
еїмаеїме е²⁰мекмѝ̄тщѝ̄ѕтнч ѝ̄ѕнтч̄ · мѝ̄мекс̄мну мапостолос
еѕоум епата²⁵мїо̄ · ѝ̄ѕоуоѕе ѝ̄ток ш петрос ∻ ‹евол х̄ееремещ̄шщ̄т
ѝ̄ма³⁰ѕ̄шшр ѝ̄мм̄пнуе ѝ̄тоотк̄ ∻ (86b)∻бшщ̄т ш петрос ѕїоумам
ѝ̄меречр̄мове · ѝ̄с̄⁵мау емеукоуї м̄петмамоуч̄ · ѝ̄тоуѕ ѕїх̄шоу
∻ ∻м̄пр̄бшщ̄т ш ¹⁰ петрос · ѕїѕвоур м̄мооу ѝ̄мау етащн ѝ̄меумове
[м̄пр̄]р̄¹⁵оуаѕї[н]т еѕоум ерооу ѝ̄с̄крїме [м̄]мооу ∻ ∻крїм[е . . . .]
²⁰ ш пе[трос] м̄мої
мѝ̄ме[с̄му] м̄моїѝ̄[метѕїоу]мам м̄моѝ̄ [∻] ∻щаїкрїме ѕш
²⁵ѝ̄метѕ̄ѕвоур х̄епаоушщ̄ м̄пштѝ̄ оуалє ∻

[30] ÷ⲙ̅ⲡⲉⲧⲛ̅ⲟⲩⲍⲁⲓ̈ ⲱ̄ ⲡⲉⲧⲣⲟⲥ (87a) ⲛ̅ϣⲁⲕⲃⲁⲃⲱ ⲛⲉⲣⲉϥⲣ̅ⲛⲟⲃⲉ · ⲙ̅ⲙⲟⲛ
ⲁⲩϩ̅ⲓⲥⲉ ⲉⲩⲍⲡⲓ̈ⲟ̅ [5]ⲙ̅ⲙⲟⲟⲩ ⲛ̅ⲧⲟⲟⲧⲟⲩ ⲛ̅ⲛⲉⲧⲟⲩⲁⲁⲃ ÷ ‹ⲙ̅ⲡⲉⲧⲛⲟⲩⲍⲁⲓ̈ ⲱ̄
ⲛⲁⲥⲛⲏⲩ · [10]ⲛ̅ϣⲁⲧⲉⲧⲛ̅ⲛⲁⲩ ⲉ̅ⲛⲁⲅⲅⲉⲗⲟⲥ ⲉⲩⲙⲟⲥⲧⲉ ⲙ̅ⲙⲟⲟⲩ ·
ⲛ̅ⲛⲉⲧⲛ̅ⲙⲉⲥⲧⲱ[15]ⲟⲩ ϩⲱⲧⲧⲏⲩⲧⲛ̅ ÷ [‹ⲙ̅]ⲡⲉⲧⲛⲟⲩⲍⲁⲓ̈ ⲱ̄ ⲛⲁⲥ[ⲛⲏⲩ]
ⲛ̅ϣⲁ[20][ⲧⲉⲧ]ⲛ̅ϯ̅ⲙ̅ⲕⲁϩ [ⲛⲁⲩ ·] ⲙ̅ⲙⲟⲛ [ⲁⲩϩ̅ⲓⲥ]ⲉ ϩⲛ̅ⲧⲁⲩⲡⲉⲓ̈ ⲙ̅ⲡⲉⲓ̈ⲛⲟϭ
ⲛⲟⲩⲟ̅ⲉⲓϣ ÷ [25]‹ⲙ̅ⲡⲉⲧⲛ̅ⲟⲩⲍⲁⲓ̈ ⲱ̄ ⲛⲁⲥⲛⲏⲩ · ⲛ̅ϣⲁⲧⲉⲧⲛ̅ⲍⲟⲟⲩⲥⲟⲩ ⲉ̅ⲃⲟⲗ
ⲉⲩϩⲕⲁⲉⲓ̈ⲧ · [30]ⲙ̅ⲙⲟⲛ ⲁⲩϩ̅ⲓⲥⲉ ϩⲙ̅ⲡⲉϩⲕⲟ ϩⲛ̅ (87b)ⲛⲉⲕⲟⲗⲁⲥⲓ̈ⲥ ÷
÷ⲙ̅ⲡⲉⲧⲛ̅ⲟⲩⲍⲁⲓ̈ ⲱ̄ ⲛⲁⲥⲛⲏⲩ · ⲛ̅ϣⲁⲧⲉⲧⲛ̅[5]ⲍⲟⲟⲩⲥⲟⲩ ⲉⲃⲟⲗ ⲉⲩⲟⲃⲉ · ⲁⲩⲱ
ⲉⲩⲥⲁ̅ϣⲙ̅ · ⲙ̅ⲙⲟⲛ ⲁⲩϩ̅ⲓⲥⲉ ϩⲙ̅ⲡⲥⲱ̅ϣⲙ̅ [10]ⲙ̅ⲡⲕⲱϩⲧ̅ ⲛⲁⲙⲡⲧⲉ ÷
÷ⲙ̅ⲡⲉⲧⲛ̅ⲟⲩⲍⲁⲓ̈ ⲱ̄ ⲛⲁⲥⲛⲏⲩ ⲛ̅ϣⲁⲧⲉⲧⲛ̅[15]ⲕⲱⲧⲉ ⲙ̅ⲡⲉⲧⲛ̅ϩⲣⲟ ⲛ̅ⲥⲁⲃⲟⲗ ⲙ̅ⲙⲟⲟⲩ·
ⲙ̅ⲙⲟⲛ ⲁⲩⲱⲕⲙ ϩⲓ̈ⲧⲛ̅ⲧⲁⲩⲡⲉⲓ̈ ⲙⲛ̅[20]ⲡ̅ⲙ̅ⲕⲁϩ ⲛ̅ϩⲏⲧ [÷] ÷ⲁⲩϩ̅ⲓⲥⲉ ⲱ̄ ⲛⲁⲥⲛⲏⲩ·
ⲉⲩϭⲱϣⲧ̅ ⲧⲏⲣⲟⲩ ⲛ̅ⲥⲁⲡⲟⲟⲩ [25]ⲍⲉⲉⲩⲉⲍⲓ̈ ⲛⲟⲩⲕⲟⲩⲓ̈ ⲛ̅ⲥⲟⲗⲥ̅ⲗ̅ ⲛ̅ϩⲏⲧϥ̅ ÷
÷ⲉⲓ̈ⲙⲉ ⲛⲏⲧⲛ̅ ⲱ̄ ⲛⲁⲥⲛⲏⲩ ⲍⲉ[30]ⲡⲉⲧⲉⲣⲉⲧⲉϥϩⲉⲗⲡⲓ̈ⲥ ⲛⲁⲱⲍⲛ̅ ⲙ̅ⲡⲟⲟⲩ ·(88a)
ⲁ̅ⲥⲱⲍⲛ̅ ⲛ̅ϣⲁⲉⲛⲉϩ ÷ ‹ⲉⲣϣⲁⲛϩ̅ⲧⲏϥ ⲉϩⲟⲩⲛ ⲉⲣⲟⲟϥ ⲙ̅[5]ⲡⲟⲟⲩ ⲱ̄ ⲛⲁⲥⲛⲏⲩ ·
ⲙ̅ⲙⲟⲛ ⲁⲩϩ̅ⲓⲥⲉ ⲉⲩⲛ̅ⲧⲟⲟⲧϥ̅ ⲙ̅ⲡⲙⲟⲩ ÷ ‹ⲟⲩⲱⲛ ⲛⲁⲩ ϩⲛ̅[10]ⲛⲉⲕϣⲁϣⲧ̅ ⲱ̄
ⲡⲉⲧⲣⲟⲥ· ⲧⲟⲩⲛⲁⲩ ⲉⲡⲣⲁϣⲉ ⲛ̅ⲛⲉⲕⲁⲩⲁⲛ · ⲃⲱⲗ [15]ⲉ̅ⲃⲟⲗ ϩⲙ̅ⲡⲉⲧⲛ̅ⲗⲁⲥ ⲱ̄
ⲛⲁⲥⲛⲏⲩ · ⲙ̅ⲙⲟⲛ ⲁⲓ̈ⲕⲱ ⲉ̅ⲃⲟⲗ ϩⲱⲱⲧ [20]ⲙ̅ⲡⲣⲱⲙⲉ ⲛ̅ⲧⲁϥⲡⲁⲣⲁⲃⲁ ⲛ̅ⲧⲁⲉⲛⲧⲟⲗⲏ ·
ϭⲱϣⲧ̅ ‹ⲉⲛⲁⲙⲛ̅ⲧϣⲉ[25]ⲛ̅ϩ̅ⲧⲏϥ ⲱ̄ ⲡⲉⲧⲣⲟⲥ · ⲛⲁⲓ̈ ⲧⲏⲣⲟⲩ ⲛ̅ⲧⲁⲓ̈ⲁⲁⲩ ⲛ̅ⲙ̅ⲙⲁⲕ
ϩⲓ̈ⲍ̅ⲙ̅ⲡⲕⲁϩ · [30] ⲁ̅ⲣⲓ̈ⲥⲟⲩ ϩⲱⲱⲕ ⲙ̅ⲛ̅ⲡⲁⲡⲗⲁⲥⲙⲁ ÷ (88b) ÷ϭⲱϣⲧ̅ ⲉⲡⲉⲕⲣⲓ̈ⲙⲉ
ϩⲱⲱⲕ ϩⲛ̅ⲧⲁⲩⲁⲛ ⲙ̅ⲡⲁⲣⲭⲓ̈ⲉⲣⲉⲩⲥ [5]ⲛ̅ⲑⲉ ⲛ̅ⲧⲁⲓ̈ⲛⲁ ⲛⲁⲕ · ⲕⲱ ⲉ̅ⲃⲟⲗ ϩⲱⲱⲕ
ⲛ̅ⲛⲉⲧⲣⲓ̈ⲙⲉ ⲉ̅ⲣⲟⲕ ÷ ÷ⲙⲉϩⲛⲉⲕⲙⲁⲛ[10]ϣⲱⲡⲉ ϩⲛ̅ⲛⲉⲣⲉϥⲣ̅ⲛⲟⲃⲉ ⲁⲛⲟⲕ
ⲡⲉⲧⲛⲁⲇⲓ̈ⲁⲕⲟⲛⲉⲓ̈ ⲉ̅ⲣⲟⲟⲩ ÷ [15]÷ⲛⲱⲕⲛⲉ ⲛⲉϣⲟϣⲧ̅ ⲱ̄ ⲡⲉⲧⲣⲟⲥ · ⲛ̅ⲱⲓ̈
ϩ[ⲱ][ⲱⲧ]ⲛⲉ ⲛⲁⲅ[ⲁ]ⲑⲟⲛ ÷ [20] ÷ⲁⲛⲟⲕⲡⲉ [ⲡⲍⲟ]ⲉⲓ̈ⲥ · ⲛ̅[ⲧⲟⲕ]ⲡⲉ ⲡ[ϩⲙϩⲁⲗ]
ⲉⲧϯⲃⲉⲕⲉ ⲛ̅ⲛⲉⲣⲅⲁⲧⲏⲥ ⲛ̅[25]ⲥⲁⲑⲛ ÷ ÷ⲁⲓ̈ⲕⲱ ⲛⲁⲩ ⲉ̅ⲃⲟⲗ ⲱ̄ ⲡⲉⲧⲣⲟⲥ
·ⲥⲙⲉⲛⲡⲉⲩⲃⲉⲕⲏ ⲛⲁⲩ ⲕⲁ[30]ⲗⲱⲥ · ⲍⲉⲁⲓ̈ⲣ̅ⲡⲱⲃϣ̅ ⲛ̅ⲛⲁⲡⲁϩⲟⲩ ÷

(89a) ‹ⲁⲛⲇⲣⲉⲁⲥ ⲡⲁⲙⲉⲣⲓ̈ⲧ · ⲁ̅ⲣⲓ̈ⲡⲙⲉⲉⲩⲉ ⲛ̅ⲧⲉⲩϣⲏ ⲛ̅ⲧⲁⲕ[5]ⲡⲱⲧ ⲁⲕⲗⲟ
ϩⲁⲣⲟⲓ̈ · ϣⲁⲛⲧⲟⲩⲥ̅ⲣ̅ⲟ̅ⲩ ⲙ̅ⲙⲟⲓ̈ · ⲁⲩⲱ̄ ⲙ̅ⲙⲟⲓ̈ · ⲁⲩⲱ̄ ⲙ̅ⲡⲓ̈ⲃⲁϣⲕ̅
ⲛ̅[10]ⲧⲉⲕⲙⲛ̅ⲧⲁⲡⲟⲥⲧⲟⲗⲟⲥ · ⲉⲧⲃⲉⲧⲁⲙⲛ̅ⲧϣⲉⲛϩ̅ⲧⲏϥ · ⲉⲣϣⲁⲛϩ̅ⲧⲏϥ ϩⲱ[15]ⲱⲕ ⲛ̅ⲧⲁϩⲉ
ⲱ̄ ⲡⲁⲙⲉⲣⲓ̈ⲧ ⲉⲧⲃⲉⲡⲁⲡⲗⲁⲥⲙⲁ · ⲉϥⲣⲓ̈ⲙⲉ ⲉⲣⲟⲛ ÷

[20] ‹ⲓ̈ⲱϩⲁⲛⲛⲏⲥ ⲡⲉⲧⲟ ⲛϣ̅ⲙⲛ̅ⲧ[ⲏϥ] ⲛ̅ⲛⲁⲩ ⲛⲓ̈ⲙ · ⲁ̅ⲣⲓ̈ⲡⲙⲉⲉⲩⲉ ⲙ̅[25]ⲡⲉϩⲙⲉ
ⲛ̅ϩⲟⲟⲩ ⲉⲕϣⲉⲉⲓ̈ ⲙ̅ⲛⲉⲙⲟⲟⲩ ⲛ̅ⲑⲁⲗⲁⲥⲥⲁ · ⲉⲓ̈ⲣⲟⲉⲓ̈ⲥ ⲉ̅ⲡⲉⲕⲥⲱ[30]ⲙⲁ ·
ⲉⲓ̈ⲥⲕⲉⲡⲁⲍⲉ ⲙ̅ⲙⲟⲕ ⲙ̅ⲛⲧⲉⲕⲯⲩⲭⲏ · (89b) ⲕⲁⲗⲱⲥ · ⲉⲣϣⲁⲛϩ̅ⲧⲏϥ ⲙ̅ⲡⲁⲗⲁⲟⲥ
ⲙ̅ⲡⲟⲟⲩ · ⲕⲥⲟⲟⲩⲛ [5]÷ⲱ̄ ⲡⲁⲙⲉⲣⲓ̈ⲧ ⲓ̈ⲱϩⲁⲛⲛⲏⲥ · ⲍⲉⲡⲉⲕⲁⲓ̈ⲧⲉⲓ̈ ⲙ̅ⲙⲟⲓ̈
ⲛⲟⲩϩⲱⲃ ⲉ̅ⲛⲉϩ · ⲧⲁⲧⲥ̅[10]ⲧⲟⲕ ⲉ̅ⲃⲟⲗ ϩⲙ̅ⲡⲉⲕⲁⲓ̈ⲧⲏⲙⲁ ÷ ÷ⲉⲓ̈ⲟⲩⲱϣ ⲧⲉⲕⲁⲓ̈ⲧⲉⲓ̈
ⲙ̅ⲙⲟⲓ̈ ⲙ̅ⲡⲟⲟⲩ ⲛ̅ⲧ[15]ⲡⲁϣⲉ ⲛ̅ⲛⲉⲣⲉϥⲣ̅ⲛⲟⲃⲉ ⲧⲁⲭⲁⲣⲓ̈ⲍⲉ ⲙ̅ⲙⲟⲟⲩ ⲛⲁⲕ ⲛ̅ⲧⲁⲉⲓ̈ⲟ
ⲛⲁⲧϩ̅ⲓⲥⲉ ÷

[20]÷ⲁⲍⲓ̈ⲥ ⲛⲓ̈ⲁⲕⲱⲃⲟⲥ ⲡⲉⲕⲥⲟⲛ ⲍⲉⲛ̅ⲑⲉ ⲉ̅ⲧⲙⲡⲉⲓ̈ⲁⲩⲡⲉⲓ̈ ⲙ̅ⲡⲉⲕⲉⲓ̈ⲱⲧ
[25]ⲙ̅ⲛ̅ⲧⲉⲕⲙⲁⲁⲩ ϩⲙ̅ⲡⲉⲩⲁⲓ̈ⲧⲏⲙⲁ · ⲉⲧⲣⲉⲧⲉⲧⲛ̅ϩⲙⲟⲟⲥ ϩⲓ̈ⲟⲩⲛⲁⲙ ⲙ̅[30]ⲙⲟⲓ̈ ·
ⲁ̅ⲣⲓ̈ⲙⲛ̅ⲧϣⲛ̅ϩ̅ⲧⲏϥ ⲉϩⲟⲩⲛ ⲉ̅(90a)ⲡⲁⲡⲗⲁⲥⲙⲁ ⲙ̅ⲡⲟⲟⲩ ÷

‹ⲫⲓ̈ⲗⲓⲡⲡⲟⲥ ⲡⲁⲇⲓ̈ⲁⲕⲟⲛⲓ̈[5]ⲧⲏⲥ ⲙ̅ⲡⲁⲧⲉϥⲣ̅ⲁⲡⲟⲥⲧⲟⲗⲟⲥ ϩⲟⲗⲱⲥ · ϯⲥⲟⲟⲩⲛ
ⲉ̅ⲧⲉⲕⲙⲛ̅ⲧϣⲛ̅ϩ̅ⲧⲏϥ [10]ⲉϩⲟⲩⲛ ⲉⲛⲉϩⲛⲕⲉ ⲧⲏⲣⲟⲩ · ⲍⲓ̈ⲛⲉⲕϣⲟⲟⲡ ϩⲓ̈ⲍ̅ⲙ̅ⲡⲕⲁϩ·
ⲉⲓ̈ⲟⲩⲱϣ ⲉⲧ[15]ⲣⲉⲕⲟⲩⲱϩ ϩⲓ̈ⲍⲱⲟⲩ ⲙ̅ⲡⲟⲟⲩ ⲛ̅ϩⲟⲩⲟ ÷ ‹ⲕⲱ ⲉ̅ⲃⲟⲗ ⲙ̅ⲡⲁⲗⲁⲟⲥ
ⲛ̅ⲛⲉⲩ[20]ⲛⲟⲃⲉ · ⲍⲉⲛ̅ⲧⲕ̅ⲟⲩⲇⲓ̈ⲁⲕⲟⲛⲓ̈ⲧⲏⲥ ⲛ̅ϣⲉⲛϩ̅ⲧⲏϥ ÷

‹ⲃⲁⲣⲑⲟⲗⲟⲙⲁⲓ̈ⲟⲥ [25] ⲡⲁⲙⲉⲣⲓ̈ⲧ ⲁ̅ⲣⲓ̈ⲡⲙⲉⲉⲩⲉ ⲛ̅ⲧⲁⲙⲛ̅ⲧϣⲃⲏⲣ ⲛ̅ⲙ̅ⲙⲁⲕ

ⲙ̄ⲡⲛⲁⲩ ⲉⲕ̅ⲣ̅ⲛ̅ⲛⲉ³⁰ⲧⲁⲣⲧⲁⲣⲟⲥ ⲙ̄ⲡⲛⲟⲩⲛ · ⲉⲓ̈ⲟ ⲛ(90b)ⲥⲁⲃⲉⲧ ⲉ̄ⲣⲟⲕ ⲉⲡⲡⲉⲑⲟⲟⲩ
ⲙ̄ⲡⲥⲁⲇⲁⲛⲁⲥ · ⲙ̄ⲡⲓⲕⲁⲁϥ ⲉ̄ⲣ⁵ⲡⲉⲑⲟⲟⲩ ⲛⲁⲕ · ÷ ÷ⲙ̄ⲡⲉⲕⲣⲟⲩⲁ̄ϩⲓ̈ϩⲏⲧ ϩⲱⲱⲕ
ⲉ̄ϩⲟⲩⲛ ⲉⲡⲁⲡⲗⲁⲥⲙⲁ ⲙ̄ⲡⲟ¹⁰ⲟⲩ · ⲁⲗⲗⲁ ÷ⲁⲣⲓ̈ⲥⲟⲛ ϩⲓ̈ϣⲃⲏⲣ ⲉ̄ⲣⲟⲟⲩ ⲉ̄ⲃⲟⲗ
ⲍⲉⲉ̄ⲣⲉⲛⲉⲩⲙⲁⲁⲍⲉ ⲣⲁⲕⲉ ⲛ̄¹⁵ⲥⲁⲡⲥⲁⲗⲥⲁ̄ ⲙ̄ⲡⲉⲕϣⲁⲍⲉ ·÷

÷ⲑⲱⲙⲁⲥ ⲡⲁⲙ[ⲉ]ⲣⲓ̈ⲧ · ⲁⲣⲓ̈ϣ[ⲉ]ⲛϩ̅ⲧⲏ[ϥ] ⲉ̄²⁰ϩⲟⲩⲛ ⲉⲡⲁⲗⲁⲟⲥ ⲙ̄ⲡⲟⲟⲩ ·
ⲉ̄ⲣⲉⲛⲉⲩⲃⲁⲗ [ⲑⲉ]ⲱⲣⲉⲓ̈ ⲛ̄ⲥⲱⲕ · ϩⲱⲥ ⲉ̄ⲣⲉⲧⲁ²⁵ⲛⲁⲥⲧⲁⲥⲓ̈ⲥ ⲛ̄ⲧⲟⲟⲧⲕ̄ ·÷
÷ⲁⲣⲓ̈ⲡⲙⲉⲉⲩⲉ̄ ⲛ̄ⲧⲁⲙⲛ̄ⲧϣⲃⲏⲣ ⲛⲙ̄ⲙⲁⲕ ³⁰ⲙ̄ⲡⲉϩⲟⲟⲩ ⲛ̄ⲧⲉⲕⲙⲛ̄ⲧⲁⲧⲛⲁϩⲧⲉ ·÷
(91a) ⲛ̄ⲑⲉ ⲛ̄ⲧⲁⲕⲍⲟⲟⲥ ⲍⲉⲛ̄ϯⲛⲁⲡⲓ̈ⲥⲧⲉⲩⲉ ⲁⲛ · ⲍⲉⲁⲡ⁵ⲍⲟⲉⲓ̈ⲥ ⲧⲱⲟⲩⲛ ⲉⲓ̈ⲉ
ⲙ̄ⲡⲓ̈ⲛⲁⲩ ⲉ̄ⲣⲟϥ ·÷ ›ⲁⲩⲱ ⲁⲓ̈ⲑⲉⲡⲏ ⲁⲓ̈ⲟⲩⲟⲛϩ̄ⲧ ⲉ̄¹⁰ⲣⲟⲕ ⲙ̄ⲛ̄ⲛⲉⲕⲥ̄ⲛⲏⲩ ⲱ̄
ⲑⲱⲙⲁⲥ · ⲁⲩⲱ ›ⲙ̄ⲡⲓ̈ⲁ̄ⲡⲟ ⲫⲁ ⲛⲉ ⲉ̄ⲍⲱⲕ ¹⁵ⲉⲧⲃⲉⲧⲉⲕⲙⲛ̄ⲧⲁⲧⲛⲁϩⲧⲉ · ⲁⲗⲗⲁ
ⲁⲓ̈ⲥ̄ⲁ̄ⲥⲱ ⲕ̄ ⲉⲓ̈ⲍⲱ ⲙ̄ⲙⲟⲥ ²⁰ⲛⲁⲕ · ⲍⲉⲁⲙⲟⲩ ⲱ̄ ⲑⲱⲙⲁⲥ ⲕⲱ ⲛ̄ⲧⲉⲕϭⲓ̈ⲍ
ϩⲓ̈ⲍⲙ̄ⲡⲁⲥⲡⲓ̈ⲣ ·÷ ²⁵›ⲁⲙⲟⲩ ⲱ̄ ⲑⲱⲙⲁⲥ ⲕⲱ ⲙ̄ⲡⲉⲕⲧⲏⲏⲃⲉ ϩⲓ̈ⲍⲛ̄ⲛⲁϭⲓ̈ⲍ ·÷
›ⲉⲓ̈ⲙⲉ ⲛⲁⲕ ⲱ̄ ³⁰ⲡⲁⲙⲉⲣⲓ̈ⲧ ⲑⲱⲙⲁⲥ · ⲍⲉⲁⲛⲟⲕ ⲟⲩⲍⲟⲉⲓ̈ⲥ ⲛ̄ϣⲉ(91b)ⲛϩ̄ⲧⲏⲩ·
ⲁⲩⲱ̄ ⲛ̄ⲛⲁⲏⲧ ·÷ ÷ⲁⲛⲟⲕ ⲡⲉⲛⲧⲁⲓ̈ⲕⲱ ⲛ̄ⲧⲙⲛ̄ⲧ⁵ϣ̄ⲛϩ̄ⲧⲏⲩ ⲛⲏⲧⲛ̄ ⲉϩⲣⲁⲓ̈
ⲛ̄ⲍⲓ̈ⲛⲛ̄ϣⲟⲣⲡ̄ ·÷ ÷ⲉⲓ̈ⲟⲩⲱϣ ⲛ̄ⲧⲉⲧⲛ̄ⲟⲩⲱϩ ϩⲓ̈¹⁰ⲍⲱⲥ ⲙ̄ⲡⲟⲟⲩ ⲉ̄ϩⲟⲩⲛ
ⲉ̄ⲡⲁⲡⲗⲁⲥⲙⲁ ⲙ̄ⲡⲟⲟⲩ ·÷

÷ϩⲁⲡⲁⲍ · ϩⲁⲡⲗⲱⲥ · ⲡⲟⲩⲁ̄ ¹⁵ⲡⲟⲩⲁ̄ ⲛ̄ⲛⲉⲓ̈ⲁⲡⲟⲥⲧⲟⲗⲟⲥ ⲁ̄ⲡⲉⲛⲍⲟⲉⲓ̈ⲥ ⲓ̅ⲥ̅
ⲥⲉⲥⲱⲗⲟⲩ ϩ̄ⲛⲛⲉϥⲙⲛ̄ⲧ²⁰ϣ̄ⲛϩ̄ⲧⲏⲩ ⲉ̄ϩⲟⲩⲛ ⲉ̄ⲡⲉϥⲡⲗⲁⲥⲙⲁ ·÷ ÷ⲉⲛⲉϥⲍⲱ ⲙ̄ⲙⲟⲥ
ⲛⲁⲩ ÷ ⲍⲉ²⁵ϭⲱϣⲧ ⲉⲡⲉⲟⲟⲩ ⲛ̄ⲧⲁⲓ̈ⲭⲁⲓ̈ⲍⲉ ⲙ̄ⲙⲟϥ ⲛⲏⲧⲛ̄ · ⲉ ⲣϣ̄ⲛϩ̄ⲧⲏϥ ⲉ̄³⁰ϩⲟⲩⲛ
ⲉ̄ⲡⲁⲡⲗⲁⲥⲙⲁ ⲙ̄ⲡⲟⲟⲩ ·÷ (92a) ›ⲟⲩ ϩⲙⲟⲧⲡⲉ ⲡⲁⲓ̈ ⲙ̄ⲛⲟⲩⲥⲟⲁⲥ̄ⲁ̄ · ⲙ̄ⲛⲟⲩⲉⲣⲏⲧ
ⲛ̄ⲧⲁⲓ̈⁵ⲭⲁⲣⲓ̈ⲍⲉ ⲙ̄ⲙⲟⲟⲩ ⲛⲏⲧⲛ̄ · ⲉ̄ⲧⲣⲉⲧⲉⲧⲛ̄ϣⲱⲡⲉ ⲛ̄ϣⲉⲛϩ̄ⲧⲏϥ ⲉ̄ϩⲟⲩⲛ
¹⁰ⲉ̄ⲡⲁⲡⲗⲁⲥⲙⲁ ⲙ̄ⲡⲟⲟⲩ ·÷ ›ⲧⲁⲣⲉⲟⲩⲟⲛ ⲛⲓ̈ⲙ ⲉⲓ̈ⲙⲉ ⲉⲡ ⲛⲟϭ ⲛ̄ⲧⲁⲉⲓ̈ⲟ
ⲛ̄¹⁵ⲧⲁⲓ̈ⲭⲁⲣⲓ̈ⲍⲉ ⲙ̄ⲙⲟϥ ⲛⲏⲧⲛ̄ ⲱ̄ ⲛⲁⲁⲡⲟⲥⲧⲟⲗⲟⲥ ⲉⲧⲟⲩⲁⲁⲃ · ⲛⲁϣ²⁰ⲃⲏⲣⲙⲉ-
ⲗⲟⲥ ⲉⲧⲧⲁⲉⲓ̈ⲏⲩ · ⲉⲧϩ̄ⲙⲟⲟⲥ ⲛⲙ̄ⲙⲁⲓ̈ ϩⲙ̄ⲡⲉⲓ̈ⲁ̄ ⲛ̄ⲓ̈ⲱⲥⲁⲫⲁⲧ · ²⁵ⲉⲧϯϩⲁⲡ ·÷
›ⲙ̄ⲙⲟⲛ ⲁ̄ⲛⲟⲕⲡⲉ ⲡⲍⲟⲉⲓ̈ⲥ ⲛⲟⲩⲟⲛ ⲛⲓ̈ⲙ · ⲁⲩⲱ ⲁ̄ⲛⲟⲕ ³⁰ⲡⲉⲛⲧⲁⲓ̈ⲧⲁⲙⲓ̈ⲟⲟⲩ
ⲧⲏⲣⲟⲩ ·(92b) ÷ⲁ̄ⲛⲟⲕ ⲟⲛ ⲡⲉⲛⲧⲁⲓ̈ⲙⲟⲩ ϩⲁⲣⲟⲟⲩ · ⲙⲏ ÷ⲙ̄ⲛ̄ϭⲟⲙ ⲙ̄ⲙⲟⲓ̈
⁵ⲉ̄ⲧⲣⲁⲕⲣⲓ̈ⲛⲉ ⲙ̄ⲙⲟⲟⲩ · ⲕⲁⲧⲁⲧⲉⲍⲟⲩⲥⲓ̈ⲁ ⲛ̄ⲧⲁⲡⲁⲉⲓ̈ⲱⲧ ⲧⲁⲁⲥ ⲛⲁⲓ̈ ⲉⲥ ⲛⲏⲩ
¹⁰ⲛⲁⲓ̈ ⲉ̄ⲃⲟⲗ ϩⲛ̄ⲧⲡⲉ ·÷

÷ⲁⲣⲓ̈ⲡⲙⲉⲉⲩⲉ̄ ⲱ̄ ⲛⲁⲥⲛⲏⲩ ⲍⲉⲁⲓ̈ⲍⲟⲟⲥ ϩ̄ⲛⲧⲁ¹⁵ⲧⲁⲡⲣⲟ ⲙ̄ⲙⲉ
ⲍⲉⲙ̄ⲡⲉϥⲧⲱⲟⲩⲛ ϩⲙ̄ⲡⲉⲍⲡⲟ ⲛ̄ⲛⲉϩⲓ̈ⲟⲙⲉ ⲛ̄ϭⲓ̈ⲡⲉ²⁰ⲧⲟ ⲛⲛⲟϭ ⲉⲓ̈ϩⲱⲁⲛⲛⲏⲥ
ⲡⲃⲁⲡⲧⲓ̈ⲥⲧⲏⲥ ⲛ̄ⲥⲁⲃⲉⲗⲗⲁⲓ̈ ⲙⲁⲩⲁⲁⲧ ·÷ ²⁵ ÷ⲁⲩⲱ ⲟⲛ ⲡⲉⲓ̈ⲕⲉⲧ ⲙ̄ⲡⲉⲓ̈ⲉⲣⲏⲧ
ⲛⲁϥ ⲙ̄ⲡⲙⲁⲛϯϩⲁⲡ ⲛ̄ⲧⲉⲧⲛ̄ϩⲉ ⲱ̄ ⲛⲁⲁ̄³⁰ⲡⲟⲥⲧⲟⲗⲟⲥ ⲉⲧⲟⲩⲁⲁⲃ ·
ⲍⲉⲙ̄(93a)ⲡⲉϥⲍⲓ̈ ⲉ̄ⲃⲟⲗ ϩⲙ̄ⲡⲁⲥⲱⲙⲁ ⲙ̄ⲡⲁⲥⲛⲟϥ ·÷ ›ⲛ̄ϯⲟⲩⲱϣ ⲁⲛ
⁵ϩⲱⲧⲧⲏⲩⲧⲛ̄ ⲉⲧⲣⲉⲧⲉⲧⲛ̄ⲕⲱ ⲉ̄ⲃⲟⲗ ⲛ̄ⲗⲁⲁⲩ · ⲉⲓ̈ⲙⲏⲧⲉⲓ̈ ⲛⲉⲛⲧⲁⲩ¹⁰ⲍⲓ̈ ⲉ̄ⲃⲟⲗ
ϩⲙ̄ⲡⲁⲥⲱⲙⲁ · ⲙ̄ⲡⲁⲥⲛⲟϥ ·÷

›ϯⲍⲱ ⲅⲁⲣ ⲙ̄ⲙⲟⲥ ⲛⲏⲧⲛ̄¹⁵ⲱ̄ ⲛⲁⲁⲡⲟⲥⲧⲟⲗⲟⲥ ⲉⲧⲟⲩⲁⲁⲃ ·
ⲍⲉⲡⲉⲧⲉϣⲁⲩϭⲛ̄ⲟⲩⲃⲁ̄ⲃⲓ̈ⲗⲉ ϩⲙ̄²⁰ⲡⲉϥⲉ̄ⲗⲟⲟⲗⲉ ϣⲁⲩⲙⲁϩ̄ϥ ⲙ̄ⲡⲉⲥⲙⲁϩ ⲧⲏⲣϥ·
ⲙⲏ ›ⲟⲩ ϩⲓ̈ⲥⲉⲡⲉ ⲉ ⲡ²⁵ⲙⲁ ⲛⲟⲩⲛⲁⲡⲣⲉ ⲛ̄ⲧⲉⲡⲉⲥⲙⲁϩ · ⲛ̄ⲥⲉϯ ⲛⲁⲩ ⲛⲟⲩⲇⲓ̈ⲡⲛⲟⲛ
·÷ ³⁰›ⲉⲡⲙⲁ ⲛⲟⲩⲫⲓ̈ⲁ̄ⲗⲏ ⲛⲏⲣⲡ̄ (93b) ϯⲛⲁⲩ ⲛ̄ⲟⲩⲁⲡⲟⲑⲏⲕⲉ ⲛ̄ⲱⲛϩ̄ ϣⲁⲉⲛⲉϩ
·÷ ÷ⲉⲡⲙⲁ ⲛⲟⲩⲟ̄⁵ⲉⲓ̈ⲕ ϯⲛⲁⲩ ⲛⲟⲩϩⲣⲉ ⲛ̄ⲱⲛϩ̄ ϣⲁⲉ̄ⲛⲉϩ · ⲛⲁⲧⲟⲩⲱ
ϩ̄ⲛⲛⲉⲡⲟⲩⲣⲁⲛⲓ̈¹⁰ⲟⲛ ·÷ ÷ⲉⲡⲙⲁ ⲛⲟⲩⲡⲉⲗϭⲉ · ⲙ̄ⲛⲟⲩⲡⲣⲏϣ ϯⲛⲁⲩ
ⲛⲟⲩⲙⲁⲛϣ¹⁵ⲗⲉⲉⲧ ϣⲁⲉ̄ⲛⲉϩ ·÷ ÷ⲉⲡⲙⲁ ⲛⲟⲩⲙⲛ̄ⲧⲙⲁⲓ̈ϣⲙ̄ⲙⲟ ϯⲛⲁⲩ
ⲛⲟⲩⲉⲓ̈ⲣⲏⲛⲉ ·÷ ²⁰÷ⲉⲡⲙⲁ ⲛⲟⲩⲙⲛ̄ⲧⲙⲁⲓ̈ⲥⲟⲛ ϯⲛⲁⲩ ⲛⲟⲩⲕⲁⲗⲱⲥ ·÷ ÷ⲉⲡⲙⲁ
ⲛⲟⲩⲭⲁⲓ̈²⁵ⲣⲉ ⲛ̄ⲥⲟⲗⲥⲗ̄ ·ϯⲛⲁⲩ ⲛⲟⲩⲡⲩⲗⲏ ⲛⲟⲩⲟ̄ⲉⲓ̈ⲛ ·÷ ÷ⲉⲡⲙⲁ

ΝΟΥϩΥΠΟΜΟΝΗ ³⁰ϩΝΟΥΠΪΡΑСΜΟС · ϯΝΑΥ ΝΟΥΜΕΡΟС (94a) ΕΒΟΛ
ϩΜΠϢΗΝ ΜΠⲰΝϨ ∻ ›ΕΠΜΑ ΝΟΥΑΓΑ⁵ΠΗ ϩΑΠΑΡΑΝ ΜΠΕΤΝΡΑΝ ·
ΜΠΠΡΑΝ ΝΝΕΤΟΥΑΑΒ ΤΗΡΟΥ · ¹⁰ ϯΝΑΥ ΝΤΑΠΥГΗ ΜΜΟΟΥ ΝⲰΝϨ
ϢΑΕΝΕϨ ∻ ›ΕΠΜΑ ΝΟΥϩΝΑΑΥ ΜΜΟΟΥ · ϯ¹⁵ΝΑΥ ΝθΑΪΒΕС ΝΝΑΠΥΛΗ
ΝΟΥΟΕΪΝ ∻ ›ΝΑΪΔΕ ΤΗΡΟΥ Ⲱ ΝΑСΝΗΥ ²⁰ϩΝΕΝΤΟΛΗΝΕ ΝΤΕΠΑΕΪⲰΤ ·
ΕΪϪⲰ ΜΜΟΟΥ ∻

›ϯСΟΟΥΝ Ⲱ ΝΑС²⁵ΝΗΥ ϪΕϨΝΡΕϤΡΝΟΒΕΝΕ ΑΛΛΑ ΑΠϨⲰΒ ΡⲰϢΕ
ΕΥϨΑΤΕϨΟΥСΪΑ ΜΠ³⁰ΜΟΥ ∻ ›ϯСΟΟΥΝ ϪΕΑΥΡ(94b)ϢΑΒΤΕ ΕΡΟΪ · ΑΥⲰ
ΑΥΜΕСΤⲰΪ ΕΠϪΪΝϪΗ · ΑΛΛΑ ⁵ΝΑΝΟΚΟΥΑϨΪϨΗΤ ΑΝ ∻ ∻ΕΪΜΕ ΝΗΤΝ
ΕΠΑΪ Ⲱ ΝΑСΝΗΥ ϪΕΟΥΑΓΑΠΗ ¹⁰ΜΝΟΥΜΝΤϢΝϨΤΗϤ ΤΝΤΑСΤΑϨΕΤΗΥΤΝ ·
ϢΑΝΤΕΤΝ ΜΠϢΑ Μ¹⁵ΠΕΪϨΜΟΤ ΝΤΕΤΝϯϨΑΠ ΝΜΜΑΪ ∻

∻ΤΟΤΕ СΕΝΑϪΟΟС ΝΑΥ ϨⲰ²⁰ⲰϤ ΝϬΪΝΑΠΟСΤΟΛΟС · ϪΕΠϪΟΕΪС
ΤΕΚΜΝΤϢΝϨΤΗϤ · ΑСΕΝΤΟΥ ²⁵ΕϨΡΑΪ ϨΝΝΕΚΟΛΑСΪС ∻ ∻ΑΝΝΑΥ
ΕΝΕΪϢΠΗΡΕ · ϪΕΑΚΕΪΝΕ ΝΝΕΥΝΟ³⁰ΒΕ ΝΜΜΑΥ · ΕΥСΟΟϨΕ ΕΡΟΟΥ ∻

(95a) ›ΤΟΤΕ ϤΝΑΟΥⲰϢΒ ΝϤϪΟΟС ΝΑΥ · ϪΕΕΤΒΕΝΑΜΝΤ⁵ϢΝϨΤΗϤ
ΝΤΑΪΕΝΤΟΥ ΕΠΕΪΜΑ · ΤΑΡΟΥΕΪΜΕ ϪΕΜΠΛΑΑΥ ϨΝ¹⁰ΝΕΥΝΟΒΕ ΝΑϨⲰΠ
ΕΡΟΪ · ΑΥⲰ ΕΤΒΕΝΑΜΝΤϢΝϨΤΗϤ ϯΝΑΚΑΑΥ ΝΑΥ ¹⁵ΕΒΟΛ ∻ ›ΤΕΝΟΥϬΕ
Ⲱ ΠΕΤΡΟС ΤⲰΟΥΝ ΝСΜΕΤΑϤⲰΒΟΥ ²⁰ΝΤΕΚΑΝΑϤΟΡΑ · ΝССΥΝΑГΕ ΜΜΑΥ
∻ ›ϪΕΑΠΕϨΡΟΟΥ ²⁵ΜΠΕΥΑГГΕΛΪΟΝ ΝΪⲰϨΑΝΝΗС ΠΟΡϪΟΥ ΕΒΟΛ ΝΤΑГΜΑ ·
ΤΑГ³⁰ΜΑ ϨΝΤΜΗΤΕ ΝΝΕϨΕθΝΟС (95b) ΤΗΡΟΥ ∻

∻ΤΟΤΕ ΟΥΕΝΟΥΝΟϬ ΝΡΪΜΕ ΝΑΑΜΑϨΤΕ ΕϨΡΑΪ ⁵ΕϪΝΝΕϨΕθΝΟС ΤΗΡΟΥ ·
ΝΑΪ ΕΤΜΠΟΥΠΪСΤΕΥΕ ΕΠϢΗΡΕ ΜΠΝΟΥ¹⁰ΤΕ ΕΥϪⲰ ΜΜΟС ·
ϪΕΕΪСΝΕΧΡΗСΤΪΑΝΟС ΑΥϯΟΥⲰ ΜΜΟΟΥ ϨΝΝΕ¹⁵ΚΟΛΑСΪС ΑΥⲰ ΑΥСΥΝΑГΕ
ΜΜΟΟΥ · ΑΝΕΥϨΟ ΕΡΟΥΟΕΪΝ · ∻ΑΝΑГГΕΛΟС ϯ²⁰ΠΕΪ ΕΤΕΥΤΑΠΡΟ · ΑΥⲰ
∻ΑΝΑΠΟСΤΟΛΟС ϯ ΝϯΡΗΝΗ ΝΑΥ · ΑΥϯ²⁵ϨΑΠ ΕΡΟΟΥ ϨΝΟΥΜΝΤϢΝϨΤΗϤ
∻ ∻ΑΥⲰ ΑΝΕΥΑГГΕΛΟС ΤΑΡΠΟΥ ΤΑГΜΑ · ΤΑГ³⁰ΜΑ · ΑΥⲰ∻ΑΝΑΠΟСΤΟ-
ΛΟС (96a) СⲰΚ ΝΜΜΑΥ ΕΠСΑΝΝΕΥθΡΟΝΟС ϢΑΝΤΟΥΝΑΥ ΕΝΕΥ⁵СΚΥΝΗ
∻ ›ΕΡΕΜΙΧΑΗΛ ϪΪ ΝϨΝϢΟ ΝϢΟ ΜΝϨΝΤΒΑ ΝΤΒΑ ∻ ¹⁰ ›ΕΡΕГΑΒΡΙΗΛ ϪΪ
ΝϨΝϢΟ ΝϢΟ · ΜΝϨΝΤΒΑ ΝΤΒΑ ∻ ›ΑΥⲰ ΟΝ ϨΡΑϤΑ¹⁵ΗΛ ϨΝΤΕΪΑГΑΠΗ
ΝΟΥⲰΤ ΝΜΜΑΥ ∻ ›ΝΕΠΡΟϤΗΤΗС ΕΥСⲰΚ ΝΝΟΥ²⁰ΟΥ ∻ ›ΝΕΔΪΚΑΙΟС
ϨⲰΟΥ ϨΝΝΟΥΟΥ ∻ ›ΝΕΜΑΡΤΥΡΟС ²⁵ΕΥСⲰΚ ΝΝΟΥΟΥ ∻ ›ΝϨΟΥΟΔΕ
ΝϨΟΥΟ ΤΠΑΡθΕΝΟС ΕΤΟΥΑΑΒ ΜΑ³⁰ΡΪΑ ΝΑΡϢΟΡΠ ΕϪΪ ΝΝΟΥС · (96b)
ΕϨΟΥΝ ΕΝΕΜΑΝΜΤΟΝ ΕϨΟΥΟ ΕΝΑΪ ΤΗΡΟΥ ∻ ∻ΝΑΠΟСΤΟΛΟС ⁵ΝΑϪΪ
ΝΝΟΥΟΥ ∻ ›ΠΕϤΤΟΟΥ ΝϪⲰΟΝ ΝΑϪΪ ΝΝΟΥΟΥ ∻ ¹⁰ ›ΝΕΤΟΥΑΑΒ ΤΗΡΟΥ
ΝΑϪΪ ΝΝΕΝΤΑΥΡΠΕΥΜΕΕΥΕ ϨΪϪΜΠΚΑϨ · ΑΥϯ ¹⁵ΝΟΥΚΟΥΪ ΜΜΝΤΝΑ
ϨΜΠΟΥΡΑΝ ∻ ∻ΠΚΕϢⲰϪΠ ϨⲰⲰϤ ΝΑΠΡ²⁰ΡΟ ΠΕΧСΝΕ ∻

∻ΤΟΤΕ ΕΡϢΑΝΠΔΪΑΒΟΛΟС ΝΑΥ ΕΠΕΝΤΑϤϢⲰΠΕ · ϤΝΑ²⁵ΡΪΜΕ · ΝϤϪΟΟС
ϪΕΑΠΑϨΪСΕ ΤΗΡϤ ΒⲰΚ ΕΠΤΑΚΟ ΜΠΟΟΥ ∻ ³⁰ ∻ΝΤΕΥΝΟΥ ϢΑΡΕΠΕΧС ΟΥΕϨ

Homélie sur les apôtres au jugement dernier traduction

81a pour vous à partir du ciel pour juger le monde entier. Bienheureux celui qui fera un acte de charité au nom de ces apôtres saints, car il recevra la consolation dans le lieu du repos [. . .]

lignes 14 à 22 manquent complètement

[. . .] pour l'éternité [. . .] Celui qui a pris soin de votre souvenir sur la terre[15] deviendra pour vous 81b un fils dans mon royaume éternel.

Je vous le dis à vous, ô peuple qui aime le Christ, moi, le très humble Bachios: celui qui fera mémoire de ces apôtres saints [. . .] un acte de charité en leurs noms, dans une offrande. [. . .] dans un(e) [. . .] il prend soin d'écrire leur souvenir et les souffrances qu'ils ont endurées à cause de mon nom. S'ils offrent un festin aux pauvres, ils deviendront héritiers 82a dans le lieu de la consolation, au jour du jugement de vérité, alors que les douze apôtres sont sur leurs douze trônes autour de leur Seigneur, rendant grâce aux vingt-quatre vieillards qui sont autour de leur Seigneur, dans les cieux, sur leurs trônes.

C'est ainsi que ces apôtres sont assis sur leurs trônes dans la vallée de Josaphat, autour du roi, le Christ, en train de juger le monde entier. O ce grand châtiment[16] 82b étonnant, au jour du jugement de vérité, quand des milliers de milliers et des myriades de myriades sont rassemblés, les uns avec les autres, et quand un trouble et un grand tremblement se produisent dans la vallée de Josaphat!

lignes 14 à 21 manquent complètement

[. . .] de la terre, debout, dans le lieu du jugement, privés de leurs couronnes. Mais les apôtres portent 83a des couronnes de gloire. Les rois de la terre sont privés de leurs vêtements dans la vallée de Josaphat. Mais les apôtres portent leurs vêtements de gloire en présence de leur Seigneur. [. . .] sont privés de leurs épées dans la vallée de Josaphat [. . .] les apôtres [. . .]

dernières lignes, 26 à 32, manquent complètement

83b de saphir. L'humanité entière se tient debout, sur ses jambes, dans la vallée de Josaphat au jour du jugement de vérité. Mais les apôtres sont assis sur leurs trônes autour de leur Seigneur. Toute chair est nue au jour du jugement, dans la vallée de Josaphat. Mais les apôtres, portent la gloire de Dieu.

---

[15] Comprendre: celui qui a veillé à ce qu'on se souvienne de vous.

[16] On pourrait lire aussi ⲑⲉⲱⲣⲓⲁ au lieu de ⲧⲓⲙⲱⲣⲓⲁ: ce grand spectacle étonnant. . . .

Toute langue humaine sera muette au jour du jugement de vérité, mais la langue de ces apôtres rend le jugement avec leur Seigneur. Les péchés de chacun se tiennent debout[17] 84a pour le réprimander, dans le lieu du jugement. Mais les anges se tiennent à côté des apôtres pour les encourager. Le monde entier pleure au jour du jugement. Mais les apôtres se réjouissent d'être assis en train de juger avec leur Seigneur. Le monde entier est bouleversé au jour du jugement. Mais les apôtres sont dans la paix avec leur Seigneur.

Et surtout, celui qui est le plus grand de tous, le Fils de Dieu, est assis en leur présence, rendant le jugement avec eux pour la terre entière.

84b Quand le Fils bien-aimé se revêt de la miséricorde du Père, tandis qu'il est assis en présence de ces apôtres dans la vallée de Josaphat, les cieux vont continuer à s'ouvrir; les neuf [. . .] en bas [. . .] ses fils assis sur les trônes des apôtres [. . .]

lignes 21 à 31 manquent complètement sauf la capitale de la ligne 24: Є

85a Une troupe de puissances, selon un ordre, une troupe d'archanges, l'une après l'autre, une troupe d'autorités, l'une après l'autre, une troupe d'anges, l'une après l'autre. Et tous ceux-là, descendant du ciel de la part du Père des lumières [. . .] le Fils [. . .] ses apôtres saints. Grands sont les honneurs qui entourent nos pères les apôtres. Chacun de ceux qui sont rassemblés 85b les contemple assis sur leurs trônes et ils leur rendent gloire par l'intermédiaire de toutes les puissances des cieux.

Alors le Père enverra du ciel d'autres troupes les unes après les autres, qui sont très glorieuses. Un sceptre de roi après l'autre, des couronnes de gloire après des couronnes de gloire, des vêtements choisis après des vêtements, des diadèmes de saphir après des diadèmes de saphir, des trônes de gloire après des trônes de gloire, des richesses après des richesses, 86a une source d'eau après une source d'eau, un paradis après un paradis. Toutes ces choses, il les envoie[18] à ses apôtres de la part du Père des lumières.

Jésus se retourna et dit à Pierre: "Mon bien-aimé Pierre, voici le jour où je vais connaître tes miséricordes, avec tes frères les apôtres, envers ma créature. Particulièrement toi, ô Pierre, car c'est dans ta main que sont les clés de mes trésors célestes. 86b Regarde, ô Pierre, à la droite des pécheurs pour voir leur peu de bonnes actions et augmente-les.[19] Ne regarde pas, ô Pierre, à leur gauche pour voir la multitude de leurs péchés, ne sois pas impitoyable envers eux et ne les juge pas. Juge [. . .] ô Pierre, avec [les frères], ceux qui sont [à ma droite]. Je juge moi-même ceux qui sont à ma gauche, car ma volonté et la vôtre ne font qu'un.

---

[17] Ici, comme à la fin de la page 94, les péchés sont personnifiés; à la page 86, les péchés et les bonnes actions se tiennent respectivement à gauche et à droite des pécheurs.

[18] Corriger ϥⲁ̅ⲟⲟⲩ (il les dit) en ϥⲁ̅ⲟⲟⲩⲥⲟⲩ (il les envoie).

[19] Littéralement: ajoute sur elles.

Vous n'avez pas été intègres, ô Pierre, 87a quand tu as méprisé les pécheurs. Assurément, ils ont souffert d'être réprimandés par les saints. Vous n'avez pas été intègres, ô mes frères, quand vous avez vu les anges les haïr.[20] Ne les haïssez pas vous aussi. Vous n'avez pas été intègres, ô mes frères, quand vous les avez affligés. Assurément, ils ont souffert dans le chagrin de ce grand moment. Vous n'avez pas été intègres, ô mes frères, quand vous les avez renvoyés alors qu'ils étaient affamés. Assurément, ils ont souffert dans la faim, dans 87b les châtiments. Vous n'avez pas été intègres, ô mes frères, quand vous les avez renvoyés alors qu'ils étaient assoiffés et brûlants. Assurément, ils ont souffert dans la chaleur du feu de l'Amenté.[21] Vous n'avez pas été intègres, ô mes frères, quand vous avez détourné votre visage d'eux. Assurément, ils ont été attristés par le chagrin et l'affliction. Ils ont souffert, ô mes frères, en regardant tous vers ce jour,[22] afin de recevoir en lui un peu de consolation.

Sachez donc, ô mes frères, que pour celui dont l'espérance va prendre fin aujourd'hui, 88a elle a pris fin pour l'éternité. Soyez miséricordieux envers eux aujourd'hui, ô mes frères. Assurément, ils ont souffert en étant au pouvoir de la mort.[23] Ouvre-leur avec tes clés, ô Pierre, et qu'ils voient[24] la joie de tes palais. Absolvez avec votre langue, ô mes frères. Assurément, j'ai absous moi aussi l'homme qui a transgressé mon commandement.

Considère mes miséricordes, ô Pierre, toutes celles que j'ai accomplies pour toi sur la terre, accomplis-les toi aussi pour ma créature.

88b Considère tes propres pleurs dans la cour du Grand Prêtre; de même que j'ai eu pitié de toi, pardonne toi aussi à ceux qui t'implorent.[25] Remplis tes demeures de pécheurs, et c'est moi qui les servirai. À toi sont les clés, ô Pierre, à moi sont les bienfaits. Je suis le Seigneur, tu es le serviteur qui rétribue les ouvriers à la fin. Je leur ai pardonné, ô Pierre; fixe donc leur salaire correctement, car j'ai effacé ce qui appartient à leur passé.

89a André, mon bien-aimé, souviens-toi de la nuit où tu as fui et m'as abandonné tandis qu'ils me crucifiaient. Et moi, je ne t'ai pas privé de ton apostolat à cause de ma miséricorde. Sois miséricordieux toi aussi, comme moi, ô mon bien-aimé, envers ma créature qui nous implore.

Jean, toi qui es miséricordieux en tout temps, souviens-toi des quarante jours où tu as été ballotté par les flots de la mer tandis que je veillais sur ton corps

---

[20] Sens obscur: les anges haïssent les pécheurs qui sont dans l'Amenté?

[21] Tout ce passage semble supposer un état intermédiaire, avant le jugement dernier, où les pécheurs sont soumis à des châtiments dans l'Amenté. Voir aussi à la page 88 qui rappelle que les pécheurs ont déjà souffert au pouvoir de la mort; de même page 94, note 16.

[22] C'est-à-dire: dans l'attente de ce jour (du jugement final).

[23] Littéralement: dans la main de la mort.

[24] D'après O. von Lemm (Koptische Miscellen, I–CXLVIII, rééd. P. Nagel, Zentral Antiquariat der Deutschen Demokratischen Republik, Leipzig, 1972, p. 349), la forme ⲦⲞⲨⲚⲀⲨ qu'on a ici, correspond à ⲚⲦⲞⲨⲚⲀⲨ qui équivaut au conjonctif sahidique ⲚⲤⲈⲚⲀⲨ: qu'ils voient.

[25] Littéralement: ceux qui pleurent vers toi.

et que je te protégeais soigneusement, toi et ton âme. 89b Sois miséricordieux avec mon peuple aujourd'hui. Tu sais, ô mon bien-aimé Jean, que tu ne m'as jamais demandé une chose pour qu'ensuite[26] je t'aie repoussé dans ta demande. Je veux que tu me demandes aujourd'hui la moitié des pécheurs, afin que je te les accorde comme un honneur acquis sans peine.

Dis à Jacques, ton frère: "De même que je n'ai pas chagriné ton père et ta mère dans leur requête pour que je vous fasse asseoir à ma droite, de même, sois miséricordieux envers 90a ma créature aujourd'hui."

Philippe, mon diacre avant d'être pleinement apôtre, je connais ta miséricorde envers tous les pauvres depuis que tu es sur la terre. Je veux que tu demeures d'autant plus avec eux aujourd'hui. Pardonne à mon peuple ses péchés car tu es un diacre miséricordieux.

Barthélemy, mon bien-aimé, souviens-toi de mon amitié avec toi au temps où tu étais dans les Tartares de l'abîme et que j'étais 90b pour toi un mur contre la malignité de Satan. Je ne l'ai pas laissé te faire de mal. Ne sois[27] pas toi-même dur de cœur envers ma créature en ce jour. Mais sois un frère et un ami pour eux, car leurs oreilles sont inclinées vers la consolation de ta parole.

Thomas, mon aimé, sois compatissant envers mon peuple aujourd'hui. Leurs yeux regardent vers toi, comme si la résurrection était en ton pouvoir. Souviens-toi de mon amitié pour toi au jour de ton incrédulité, 91a comment tu as dit: "Je ne croirai pas que le Seigneur est ressuscité alors que je ne l'ai pas vu." Et moi, je me suis hâté et je me suis montré, à toi et à tes frères, ô Thomas. Je ne t'ai pas fait de reproches au sujet de ton incrédulité, mais je t'ai consolé en te disant:[28] "Viens, ô Thomas, et mets ta main sur mon côté; viens, ô Thomas, et mets ton doigt sur ma main. Sache donc, ô mon bien-aimé Thomas, que je suis un Seigneur miséricordieux et 91b compatissant. C'est moi qui vous ai accordé la miséricorde depuis le commencement. Je veux que vous persévériez en elle aujourd'hui envers ma créature."

En un mot, les apôtres un à un, notre Seigneur Jésus les encouragea dans ses miséricordes envers sa créature. Et il leur disait: "Considérez la gloire que je vous ai donnée et soyez miséricordieux envers ma créature aujourd'hui. 92a C'est une grâce, une consolation et une promesse que je vous ai données, pour que vous deveniez miséricordieux envers ma créature aujourd'hui. Que chacun connaisse le grand honneur que je vous ai accordé, ô mes apôtres saints, mes amis, mes membres, qui êtes honorés et qui êtes assis avec moi dans la vallée de Josaphat pour rendre le jugement. Assurément, c'est moi qui suis le Seigneur de chacun, c'est moi qui les ai tous créés; 92b c'est moi aussi qui suis mort pour eux. N'ai-je pas le pouvoir de les juger selon l'autorité que mon Père m'a donnée et qui me vient du ciel?

---

[26] Ici commence le fragment de Paris 129[18] 126 qui a gardé un récit parallèle extrait d'un autre manuscrit (voir l'Introduction).

[27] Corriger le ⲘⲠⲈⲔⲢ̄, tu n'as pas été, en ⲘⲠⲈⲢⲢ̄, impératif négatif: ne sois pas.

[28] Ici prend fin le fragment de Paris 129[18] 126.

Souvenez-vous, ô mes frères: j'ai dit par ma bouche véridique qu'il ne s'est pas levé parmi les fils des femmes de plus grand que Jean le Baptiste, à l'exception de moi seul. Et encore cette autre chose: je ne lui ai pas promis le lieu du jugement comme à vous, ô mes saints apôtres, car 93a il n'a pas participé à mon corps et à mon sang. Je ne veux pas que vous-mêmes pardonniez à quelqu'un en dehors de ceux qui ont participé à mon corps et à mon sang.

Car je vous le dis, ô mes apôtres saints, celui dans la vigne duquel un grain est trouvé est rempli par la grappe entière. Est-ce une souffrance? Au lieu d'un grain de la grappe un festin leur est donné.[29] Au lieu d'une coupe de vin, 93b donnez-leur une réserve de vie pour l'éternité. Au lieu de pain, donnez-leur une nourriture vivante pour l'éternité, impérissable dans les lieux célestes. Au lieu d'un haillon et d'une couverture, donnez-leur une chambre nuptiale pour l'éternité. Au lieu d'un acte d'hospitalité, donnez-leur la paix. Au lieu d'un acte de fraternité, donnez-leur un bienfait. Au lieu d'une salutation consolatrice, donnez-leur une porte de la lumière. Au lieu de patience dans la tentation, donnez-leur une part 94a de l'arbre de la vie. Au lieu d'un acte de charité en mon nom, en votre nom et au nom de tous les saints, donnez-leur une source d'eau vive pour l'éternité. Au lieu d'une cruche d'eau, donnez-leur l'ombre de mes portes de lumière. Toutes ces choses, ô mes frères, ce sont les commandements de mon Père et je les dis.

Je sais ô mes frères, que ce sont des pécheurs, mais le fait qu'ils ont été sous l'autorité de la mort a suffi.[30] Je sais qu'ils ont péché 94b contre moi, qu'ils m'ont haï en vain, mais je ne suis pas impitoyable. Sachez donc ceci, ô mes frères, c'est un amour et une miséricorde qui vous ont atteints au point de vous rendre dignes de cette grâce de rendre le jugement avec moi."

Alors les apôtres lui diront à lui-même: "Seigneur ta miséricorde les a fait échapper aux châtiments. Nous avons vu ces merveilles: tu as enlevé leurs péchés qui, se tenant avec eux, les réprimandaient."[31]

95a Alors il leur répondra en disant: "À cause de mes miséricordes que j'ai apportées en ce lieu, qu'ils sachent qu'aucun de leurs péchés ne me restera caché; et à cause de mes miséricordes, je vais les leur pardonner. Maintenant, ô Pierre, lève-toi, apporte ton offrande[32] et rassemble (les) ici. Car la voix de l'évangile de Jean s'est répandue, ordre par ordre, parmi tous les peuples."

95b Alors une grande lamentation saisira toutes les nations, celles qui n'ont pas cru au Fils de Dieu et elles diront: "Voici les chrétiens: ils ont été délivrés des châtiments et ils ont été rassemblés; leurs visages ont resplendi. Les anges

---

[29] Sens incertain. Il faut sans doute comprendre, par analogie avec ce qui suit: est-ce une souffrance de recevoir un festin à la place d'un seul grain de la grappe?

[30] A rapprocher des pp. 87 et 88, note 7: l'idée semble bien être que les pécheurs méritent d'être traités avec miséricorde au jour du jugement parce qu'ils ont déjà souffert et expié leurs péchés pendant le temps où ils sont demeurés au pouvoir de la mort.

[31] Là encore les péchés sont personnifiés, voir la note 17.

[32] Le ⲘⲈⲦⲀϤⲱⲂⲞⲨ du texte doit sans doute être lu comme ⲘⲈⲦⲀϤⲱⲢⲞⲨ: transporter, apporter.

ont baisé leurs bouches. Les apôtres leur ont donné la paix, ils les ont jugés avec miséricorde. Leurs anges les ont saisis ordre par ordre et les apôtres 96a se sont avancés avec eux vers leurs trônes jusqu'à ce qu'ils voient leurs tentes. Michel reçoit des milliers de milliers et des myriades de myriades. Gabriel reçoit des milliers de milliers et des myriades de myriades. Raphaël aussi (se trouve) dans cet amour unique avec eux. Les prophètes rassemblent les leurs. Les justes aussi avec les leurs. Les martyrs rassemblent les leurs; surtout, surtout, la Vierge sainte Marie sera la première à recevoir les siens, 96b dans les lieux du repos, davantage que tous ceux-là. Les apôtres recevront les leurs. Les quatre animaux recevront les leurs. Tous les saints recevront ceux qui ont fait mémoire d'eux sur la terre et qui ont manifesté un peu de compassion en leurs noms. Quant au reste, il appartient au roi, le Christ.

Alors quand le diable verra ce qui est arrivé, il pleurera en disant: "Tout mon effort a été anéanti aujourd'hui." Sur l'heure, le Christ ordonne. . . .

CHAPTER THIRTY-TWO

UNE LETTRE MANICHÉENNE DE KELLIS (P. KELL. COPT. 18)

Jean-Daniel Dubois

Depuis quelques années, l'étude du manichéisme est entrée dans une phase nouvelle. L'affluence massive de documents provenant d'Asie centrale au début du XXe siècle, puis la découverte de documents coptes manichéens, depuis les années trente ont considérablement fait progresser les connaissances sur la religion manichéenne. Mais par delà les textes issus des communautés manichéennes et la documentation indirecte conservée dans les manuels d'hérésiologie depuis l'Antiquité, l'approche contemporaine du manichéisme passe maintenant par l'examen d'une documentation issue d'un chantier archéologique en Égypte, situé dans l'oasis de Dahklah, le site de l'antique Kellis.[1] Autrement dit, l'étude des doctrines et des pratiques rituelles des manichéens peut être confrontée aujourd'hui à l'examen d'une documentation très originale, évoquant la vie quotidienne de manichéens historiques ayant vécu en Haute Égypte au cours du IVe siècle, à quelque deux cent kilomètres du Nil, dans le désert lybique.[2] Dans le cadre d'un complexe architectural, on peut reconstruire petit à petit ce que fut la vie de manichéens ayant occupé l'espace de trois ou quatre maisons, pendant plusieurs générations, tout au long du IVe siècle, vraisemblablement depuis la période de persécution contre le manichéisme inaugurée en 302,[3] et jusque vers la fin du IVe siècle quand la persécution contre le manichéisme redouble avec les efforts répétés de la législation de Théodose, après 381.[4] Le site de ces maisons a été conservé par le sable qui a tout recouvert en laissant en place les restes de mobilier, de vaisselle, et quelques traces littéraires et documentaires. En effet, les occupants de ces maisons ont sans doute quitté les lieux avec leurs textes, mais ils ont laissé sur place quelques lambeaux de pages abîmées, en copte, grec et syriaque,[5] et surtout une

---

[1] *Dakhleh Oasis Project: Preliminary Reports on the 1992–1993 and 1993–1994 Field Seasons* (ed. Colin A. Hope and Anthony J. Mills; Dakhleh Oasis Project Monograph 8; Oxford – Oakville: Oxbow, 2000).

[2] Nous avons présenté l'intérêt de cette documentation dans "La redécouverte actuelle du manichéisme," *Connaissance des Pères de l'Église* 83 (septembre 2001): 3–15.

[3] Pour la fixation de la date, voir maintenant Samuel N. C. Lieu, *Manichaeism in the Later Roman Empire and Medieval China* (WUNT 63; Tübingen: Mohr, 1992).

[4] Per Beskow, "The Theodosian Laws against Manichaeism," *Manichaean Studies* (ed. Peter Bryder; Lund: Plus Ultra, 1988), 1–11.

[5] *Greek Papyri from Kellis* (vol. 1; *P. Kell. G. 1–90;* ed. K. A. Worp; Dakhleh Oasis Project Monograph 3; Oxford: Oxbow, 1995); *Kellis Literary Texts* (vol. 1; ed. Iain Gardner; Dakhleh Oasis Project Monograph 4; Oxford: Oxbow, 1996).

documentation à peine exploitée à l'heure actuelle, un lot considérable de lettres privées dont la publication vient de commencer.[6] Parmi les lettres actuellement publiées, nous avons choisi un exemple d'archives documentaires concernant des préoccupations courantes au sein de la communauté manichéenne. Nous en proposerons une traduction française en l'accompagnant de quelques remarques de commentaire. Nous aimerions offrir à notre ami, François Bovon, l'occasion de se plonger brièvement dans le monde manichéen antique. Alors qu'il a passé tant d'années à exhumer des textes anciens, apocryphes ou canoniques, célèbres ou oubliés, en vue de contribuer à l'histoire du christianisme primitif, nous pensons que le manichéisme constitue aussi un réservoir de questions nouvelles pour une meilleure compréhension des conflits situés au cœur de l'histoire du christianisme ancien.

La lettre privée que nous avons choisie, le P. Kell. Copt. 18, provient de la Maison n° 3, chambre 10 (3e dépôt), et des archives d'un certain manichéen, Horion. Partiellement conservée, elle mesure 177mm sur 90mm, avec des marges de 7–8mm. Elle est éditée dans le premier volume des textes documentaires coptes de Kellis, avec une planche de reproduction photographique.[7] On connaît du même Horion trois autres lettres dont le caractère manichéen est incontestable: P. Kell. Copt. 15, 16 et 17. La lettre n° 15 commence, par exemple, par une adresse caractérisée: "Au Seigneur, mon frère, le bien-aimé de mon âme et de mon esprit; fils de la justice, et membre excellent de l'Intellect-Lumière, dont le nom est doux dans ma bouche, mon frère bien-aimé, C'est moi, Horion, dans le Seigneur Dieu—Salut!". Ce genre de qualificatifs désignant le destinataire de la Lettre n° 15 renvoie très simplement à l'une des titres officiels de la communauté manichéenne, "la justice", dont les membres constituent un corps spirituel articulé au corps de l'Intellect-Lumière, l'une des figures christologiques du panthéon manichéen, l'Intellect manifesté sous forme de lumière pure, dans le cadre du macrocosme de l'univers ou du microcosme humain.

Horion ne semble pas résider à Kellis, mais dans les environs; la mention de moissons "au sud de la cuvette" (P. Kell. Copt. 15, 27), c'est-à-dire la dépression que représente l'oasis de Dakhlah, peut laisser croire qu'il n'est pas loin de Kellis. Comme il est aussi question d'un Horion dans un autre document (P. Kell. Copt. 50, 36)—à condition qu'il s'agisse du même personnage—il apparaît que Horion traite de questions relatives à l'organisation de "l'*agapè*" de la communauté, et de l'achat de certains produits de nécessité vitale. Tous les échanges de produits et d'argent mentionnés dans ces lettres illustrent à souhait le principe de base de l'organisation de la communauté manichéenne, les auditeurs ou catéchumènes.[8] Dans la Lettre 18, Horion

---

[6] *Coptic Documentary Texts from Kellis* (vol. 1; ed. Iain Gardner, Anthony Alcock, and Wolf-Peter Funk; Dakhleh Oasis Project Monograph 9; Oxford: Oxbow, 1999).

[7] Ibid., 152–54 et planche 11.

[8] On se rappellera que Saint Augustin a été catéchumène manichéen pendant 9 ans, avant sa conversion.

s'adresse aux artisans d'un atelier de confection, et donne des ordres à propos de quelques habits. On pourrait croire qu'il s'agit d'un petit commerce
local comme le laissent entendre les éditeurs du volume.[9] Cependant, le reste
des lettres écrites par Horion montre qu'il occupe un rang particulier au sein
de la communauté. Il fait saluer les élus et les catéchumènes (P. Kell. Copt.
15, 28–29; 16, 40–41; 17, 51–52). Il est donc vraisemblable qu'il soit un des
élus, donc un membre de la hiérarchie manichéenne. Cela expliquerait aussi
le ton d'autorité qu'il prend dans la Lettre 18. Les éditeurs du volume pensent
qu'il occupe une fonction de gestion administrative pour la communauté. Dans
ce cas, ce type de fonction confiée à un élu correspondrait au grade de *presbyteros* ou *oikodespotès* dans les sources grecques.[10] Il nous paraît normal de voir
en lui un élu qui commande des habits pour les besoins de la vie religieuse
et liturgique de la communauté.

Quant à la datation des lettres attribuées à Horion, le milieu du IVe siècle
semble le plus vraisemblable, étant donné les recoupements entre les diverses
générations de personnages mentionnés dans le corpus des lettres, et surtout
les références chiffrées à des prix de denrées alimentaires; en 15, 17–18, par
exemple, le prix du blé pourrait correspondre à la période de 352/353 à 385.

La Lettre n° 18 est adressée (en grec) au verso de la manière suivante:

A ma sœur bien-aimée, Tehat. (De la part de) Horion.

Tehat apparaît plusieurs fois dans le corpus des lettres de Kellis (18, 1; 43,
1; 51, 2; et peut-être implicitement en 50, 26). Elle est l'auteur de la Lettre
43 adressée à son fils (et peut-être de la Lettre 50); elle est destinataire des
lettres 18 et 51. Le début de la lettre elle-même (18, 1) la place à côté de
Hatrè, comme dans la lettre 50, 26–27 où les deux travaillent ensemble. Hatrè
apparaît trois fois dans les lettres attribuées à Horion (17, 41; 18, 1; 50, 26–27);
une autre figure de Hatrè, travaillant dans la vallée du Nil, intervient dans le
groupe des lettres de Makarios, l'un des occupants de la Maison n° 3. Pour
l'instant, on ne peut pas dire s'il s'agit de la même personne. Il vaut mieux donc
traiter ces deux figures indépendamment. La figure de Hatrè en 18, 1 correspond soit au mari de Tehat, soit plus vraisemblablement à son fils. En effet,
l'adresse grecque de la lettre au verso ne mentionne que Tehat, alors que le
début de la lettre indique les véritables destinataires, Tehat et Hatrè. L'étymologie
égyptienne de Hatrè pourrait faire croire qu'il s'agit d'un fils jumeau.

Le contenu de la Lettre 18 au recto peut-être traduit ainsi:

1. "A mes frères bien-aimés, Tehat et Hatrè. Moi, c'est
2. Horion dans le Seigneur. Salut!
3. A propos de la pièce d'étoffe que j'ai envoyée par l'intermédiaire de Lautine,

---

[9] Ibid., 26. La même opinion est reprise p. 152 dans la description du contenu de
la lettre: "Personal letter with business content."

[10] Michel Tardieu, *Le manichéisme*, *Que sais-je 1948* (Paris: Presses universitaires de
France, 1981), 77.

4. je vous ai écrit: "Faites-en un *kolobion*."
   Maintenant, il n'est pas besoin d'en faire un *sticharion*.
5. Du tissu bigarré, confectionnez une
6. coiffe, et filez une chaîne pour elle. Voici j'ai trouvé un autre *kolobion*.
7. Prenez-le et voyez s'il est possible de le
8. teindre.......................et ....
9. ....deux
10. ....et vous.....................Prenez aussi ce petit morceau
11. de laine blanche....................cinq[11] statères-là
12. et confectionnez-moi une trame pour...
13. un manteau[12]... Prenez soin (de lui?) et
14. confectionnez-le. S'il existe (?)[13] aussi un petit morceau
15. de laine de............................
16. à moi son prix, et la trame du petit morceau.
17. Je vous adresse, en vérité, la demande expresse
18. que vous trouviez 2500... (talents?)...
19. ...pour la valeur de[14] ....
20. que vous l'envoyiez et que vous filiez une coiffe
21. à deux franges pour notre frère Sa...ren, le presbytre.
22. Pierre, le. . . ., les a envoyés
23. lui-même. Ambroise dit, quant à lui,
24. ....et.........."

Comme le montre la dernière partie conservée de cette lettre, il devait y avoir encore quelques lignes de texte avant une salutation finale. Toutefois, on peut quand même tirer quelques renseignements précis de ce type d'échange épistolaire.

Répétant le nom de la personne destinataire explicitée au verso, la lettre s'ouvre par une adresse plus personnalisée. L'expression "Mes frères bien-aimés" regroupe le nom féminin de Tehat et le nom masculin de Hatrè, son fils vraisemblablement. La qualité de "frères" doit être prise au sens fort de membres de la communauté manichéenne, comme c'est le cas des autres adresses des lettres de Horion. La salutation "dans le Seigneur" correspond à celle que l'on connaît en milieu chrétien avec la mention paulinienne "en

---

[11] Le chiffre cinq termine un adjectif numéral dont les premières lettres ont disparu dans une lacune.

[12] Nous comprenons la fin de la ligne 13 avec un substantif suivi à la ligne 14 du terme qui désigne le manteau; le pronom personnel masculin suivant le terme de manteau pourrait renvoyer à la trame (au masculin en copte).

[13] Les quelques traces de lettres lisibles au milieu de cette ligne permettent d'envisager un début de phrase conditionnelle; mais il s'agit vraiment d'une conjecture.

[14] Les éditeurs voient ici le début d'un substantif accompagné du pronom personnel de la deuxième personne du singulier ("la valeur de ton . . ."); étant donné les traces de lettres qui suivent, il s'agit plutôt du début du mot "coiffe" (*tkleft*) employé plus haut ligne 7 et plus bas, ligne 21.

Christ". Même s'il peut s'agir d'une allusion à une référence biblique éventuelle, il faut l'entendre avec son contenu manichéen: le Seigneur représente aussi bien la figure christologique de l'Intellect-Lumière que la figure de Mani, sceau de la prophétie.

Dès la première phrase de la lettre, on comprend que l'échange épistolaire accompagne un échange de pièces de tissu, grâce à un intermédiaire, ici Lautine. On entre dans le monde de la confection et des techniques de manu-facture textile. La fin conservée de la lettre évoque d'ailleurs d'autres échanges de lettres et d'envois de marchandises. Apparemment, le premier envoi men-tionné avait pour but de faire confectionner un *kolobion*, soit une tunique fine à manches courtes ou sans manches, portée dans les milieux monastiques.[15] Même si Horion avait fait précéder son envoi d'une commande d'un *kolobion*, il revient sur cette commande et précise qu'il n'est pas besoin d'en faire un *sticharion*, soit une tunique aussi ou une sorte de chemise; le terme revient plusieurs fois à Kellis (26, 15; 34, 16; 44, 24); elle peut être noire (37, 31) ou tissée (28, 37). Le fait que Horion revienne sur sa commande laisse entendre qu'un *kolobion* est plus simple à faire qu'un *sticharion*. La proximité du manichéisme avec le monachisme chrétien au IVe siècle ne doit pas impliquer qu'il faille interpréter ces termes à partir des pratiques vestimentaires du monachisme chrétien. Méthodologiquement, il faut éviter d'interpréter le monachisme manichéen à partir du monachisme chrétien.[16]

En effet, le nouveau terme technique "la coiffe" (ligne 6) permet d'éviter la confusion des pratiques vestimentaires, chrétiennes et manichéennes. Ce terme "coiffe" désigne aussi un couvre-chef que l'on trouve en milieu monastique chrétien. Mais, nous avons choisi de le traduire par coiffe, étant donné ce que l'on sait par ailleurs des pratiques vestimentaires des manichéens. En effet, les manichéens portaient des coiffes s'ils étaient élus. On se souviendra des représen-tations iconographiques célèbres de la fête du Bêma, avec des élus habillés de blanc et leurs coiffes assorties; ces représentations provenant de manuscrits enluminés sont maintenant largement accessibles dans les reproductions en couleur du catalogue des collections berlinoises, de Z. Gulasci:[17] fig. 29, 2 p. 64 = MIK III 6265 et III 4966c recto (portait d'un élu); fig. 32, 1 p. 71 = MIK III 4979a,b verso (fête du bêma); fig. 82, 1 p. 183 = MIK III, 4815 a–d (représentation d'élues manichéennes avec coiffes sur un support textile); fig. 84 p. 187 = MIK III 141a (tête d'élue avec coiffe, sur un support textile).

---

[15] R. Coquin, "A propos des vêtements des moines égyptiens," *Bulletin de la Société d'archéologie copte* 31 (1992): 23.

[16] *Contra* Iain Gardner, " 'He has gone to the monastery . . .'," *Studia manichaica* (ed. Ronald E. Emmerick, Werner Sundermann, and Peter Zieme; Berliner Akademie der Wissenschaften, Berichte und Abhandlungen, Sonderband 4; Berlin, Akademie Verlag: 2000), 247–57.

[17] Zsuzsanna Gulácsi, *Manichaean Art in Berlin Collections* (vol. 1 of Corpus fontium manichaeorum, Series archaeologica et iconographica 1; Turnhout, Brepols: 2001).

Le papyrus copte donne trois détails supplémentaires à propos de ces coiffes: du premier tissu pour la coiffe, il est dit qu'il est bigarré (ligne 5). C'est la preuve qu'il ne s'agit sans doute pas d'une coiffe pour un(e) élu(e), car il serait de couleur blanche dans ce cas. On le rapprochera de coiffes colorées de dignitaires laïcs, socialement haut placés, tels qu'ils apparaissent dans la scène dite de la "Main droite", dans le catalogue de Z. Gulasci, fig. 32, 2 = MIK 4979a,b recto (cf. aussi fig. 28, 4 p. 60 = MIK 8259 fol. 1 (?) recto (scène du Sermon). Cette coiffe colorée est, de plus, dotée d'une chaîne filée; le terme de chaîne s'oppose à celui de trame utilisé plus loin, à la ligne 16. Il s'agit peut-être des décorations qui accompagnent la coiffe, mais plus vraisemblablement, de la structure interne de la coiffe qui assure la rigidité du bonnet. Enfin, à la ligne 22, le filage d'une autre coiffe implique la confection d'une coiffe plus élaborée puisqu'il y aurait "deux franges". Le terme technique que nous traduisons pas "frange" demeure malheureusement ambigu, car il renvoie en copte à plusieurs sortes de référents: boucle, frange, garniture, repli, rebord, paquet, touffe, faisceau, houppe, anneau. Les éditeurs ont choisi "double-fringed gown(?)",[18] en marquant leur incertitude sur la valeur exacte de ce terme. Le terme de "frange" permet de renvoyer d'une manière générale à une décoration particulière qui pourrait indiquer une fonction élevée dans une hiérarchie. Avec le dossier iconographique auquel nous avons accès maintenant par le catalogue de Z. Gulasci, nous nous demandons s'il ne s'agit pas d'une référence technique à une coiffe manichéenne particulière à double bonnet comme celles que les manichéens employaient pour des hauts dignitaires de la hiérarchie ecclésiastique. Le catalogue de Z. Gulasci en offre un bel exemple sur une bannière textile, à la figure 80 p. 177 (= MIK III 6283).

Si l'on voit que cette lettre manichéenne traite de la confection de vêtements concernant les élus manichéens, étant donné la référence à la laine blanche, et à la coiffe à "deux franges" ou "deux bonnets," la mention de membres de la hiérarchie à la fin de la lettre confirme la préoccupation du rédacteur de la lettre. Il s'agit bien de fournir certains vêtements aux élus. Et plus généralement, les familles manichéennes qui vivent à Kellis se préoccupent de couper ou faire couper des vêtements pour les besoins des auditeurs et des élus, comme l'attestent aussi les lettres n° 12, 9;[19] 19;[20] 20, 33;[21] 46, 3;[22] 52, 13.[23] Dans la lettre n° 18, la coiffe "à deux franges" doit être confectionnée pour le presbytre Sa[. . .]ren. Malheureusement une lacune au milieu du nom propre empêche de proposer une conjecture vraisemblable; s'agirait-il d'un certain Sabès, comme dans la Lettre n° 17?[24] Dans la Lettre n° 15 du

---

[18] Ibid., 153.
[19] Ibid., 132.
[20] Ibid., 157–58, particulièrement aux lignes 23, 29, 33, 36, 45.
[21] Ibid., 167.
[22] Ibid., 261.
[23] Ibid., 279.
[24] Ibid., 148–51, particulièrement à la ligne 21 du texte.

même Horion, on connaît un nom d'origine iranienne, Raz;[25] s'agirait-il ici aussi d'un prénom d'origine iranienne? Une forme de Sapores? Les noms de Pierre et Ambroise[26] renvoient plutôt au monde méditerranéen parlant grec. La qualification de Pierre commence par "pr . . .", mais le nombre de lettres à reconstruire ne permet pas la lecture "(p)presbyteros"; s'agirait-il alors du président de l'assemblée cultuelle, *pr[oestôs]*? Le terme de *presbyteros* pour Sa[. . .]ren est bien attesté dans les sources manichéennes pour renvoyer à la catégorie d'élus occupant des charges pastorales et des fonctions de gestion de la vie communautaire.

Parmi les indications vestimentaires, remarquons encore que la mention de la trame à la ligne 12 annonce la confection d'un manteau qui peut être bien utile dans le cas de déplacements des prédicateurs itinérants. Par ailleurs, le deuxième *kolobion* doit être teint; l'échange de teinture est attesté dans les lettres de Kellis, soit en relation avec la laine (en 47, 2 et 19),[27] soit en relation avec un coussin pour un livre (en 21, 24),[28] soit sans destination précisée (en 19,40).[29] Les éditeurs du volume ont récapitulé quelques informations socioéconomiques concernant les teintures dans les textes coptes et dans les documents de Kellis;[30] on y ajoutera que la mention de la teinture dans la lettre 18 désigne un vêtement destiné à un auditeur, sinon il serait blanc.

Enfin, l'évocation du prix (ligne 16), de la valeur (ligne 20), le chiffre 2500 (il faut sans doute compléter par talents), et peut-être la mention de cinq statères[31] renvoient aux échanges financiers des partenaires de la lettre. Si Horion, l'auteur de la Lettre 18, est bien un gestionnaire des biens de la communauté, ces échanges d'argent correspondent à des compensations financières, une sorte de salaire, pour le temps passé à ces travaux de confection et pour la valeur des bien achetés pour les besoins de la confection. L'ensemble de ces travaux de confection s'inscrivent aussi dans un jeu d'échanges entre auditeurs et élus, puisque les élus reçoivent la nourriture et les moyens de subsistance de la part des auditeurs. S'il s'agit, comme ici, de la confection de coiffes pour des dignitaires hiérarchiques, ou de manteaux comme pour les prédicateurs itinérants, ce genre de dépenses devaient être assurées sur les fonds de la communauté. On aperçoit donc par cette lettre n° 18 un type de relations socio-économiques, avec en toile de fond les activités d'un atelier familial de confection, à mettre en parallèle avec d'autres activités économiques de la communauté manichéenne, aussi attestées par le même corpus de lettres, les

---

[25] Ibid., 141–44, particulièrement à la ligne 15 du texte.

[26] Ibid., 153, ligne 23–24 du texte; littéralement: Petre (pour Petros) et Ambrosios.

[27] Ibid., 263–64.

[28] Ibid., 173.

[29] Ibid., 158.

[30] Ibid., 65–67.

[31] *Ouvrage cité* à la note 6: les éditeurs pensent (p. 59 et 154) qu'il faut y voir une référence à une sorte de poids étant donné le caractère obsolète des statères comme pièces de monnaies, au IVe siècle.

activités liées à la copie de livres, activités peut-être rentables de copies de livres ou de textes (comme dans les lettres 35 et 36 de Oualès),[32] et les activités agricoles dont on peut se faire une idée par le livre de comptes d'une ferme de Kellis.[33] Même si la lettre n° 18 est conservée de manière fragmentaire—on ne connaît pas la fin, et de nombreuses lacunes parsèment le texte— ces quelques lignes illustrent les demandes d'un élu manichéen à Tehat et Hatrè en vue de la confection d'habits nécessaires à la vie des membres de l'Église manichéenne. Il faut encore exploiter la masse d'informations techniques, à partir du lexique copte utilisé, mais aussi à partir du lexique grec manié par les habitants de Kellis. Cette nouvelle documentation de Kellis, datée du IVe siècle, conserve un lot d'informations pouvant intéresser des spécialistes de disciplines diverses. La lettre n° 18 représente une tranche de vie, au cœur d'un groupe de manichéens historiques, maintenant incontournables dans les études sur le manichéisme.

---

[32] Ibid., 223–31, et déjà l'étude antérieure de Paul Mirecki, Iain Gardner et Anthony Alcock, "Magical Spell, Manichaean Letter," *Emerging from Darkness* (ed. Paul Mirecki et James BeDuhn; NHMS 43; Leiden, Brill: 1997), 9–32.

[33] Roger S. Bagnall, *The Kellis Agricultural Account Book: P. Kell. IV Gr. 96* (Dakhleh Oasis Project Monograph 7; Oxford, Oxbow: 1997).

INDEX OF ANCIENT SOURCES

An "n" after a page number indicates that the reference appears only in the footnotes at the bottom of the page. A passage enclosed with parentheses indicates an allusion without explicit citation or a passage that is cited differently in the Septuagint (= LXX).

New Testament/Christian Scriptures

CHRISTIAN LITERATURE

OTHER WRITINGS

INDEX OF MODERN AUTHORS

An "n" after a page number indicates that the reference appears only in the footnotes at the bottom of the page.